The Complete Guide to
Microsoft Outlook 2010
Microsoft Office Specialist Exam 77-884 Study Guide

another
**Computer
Mama
Guide**

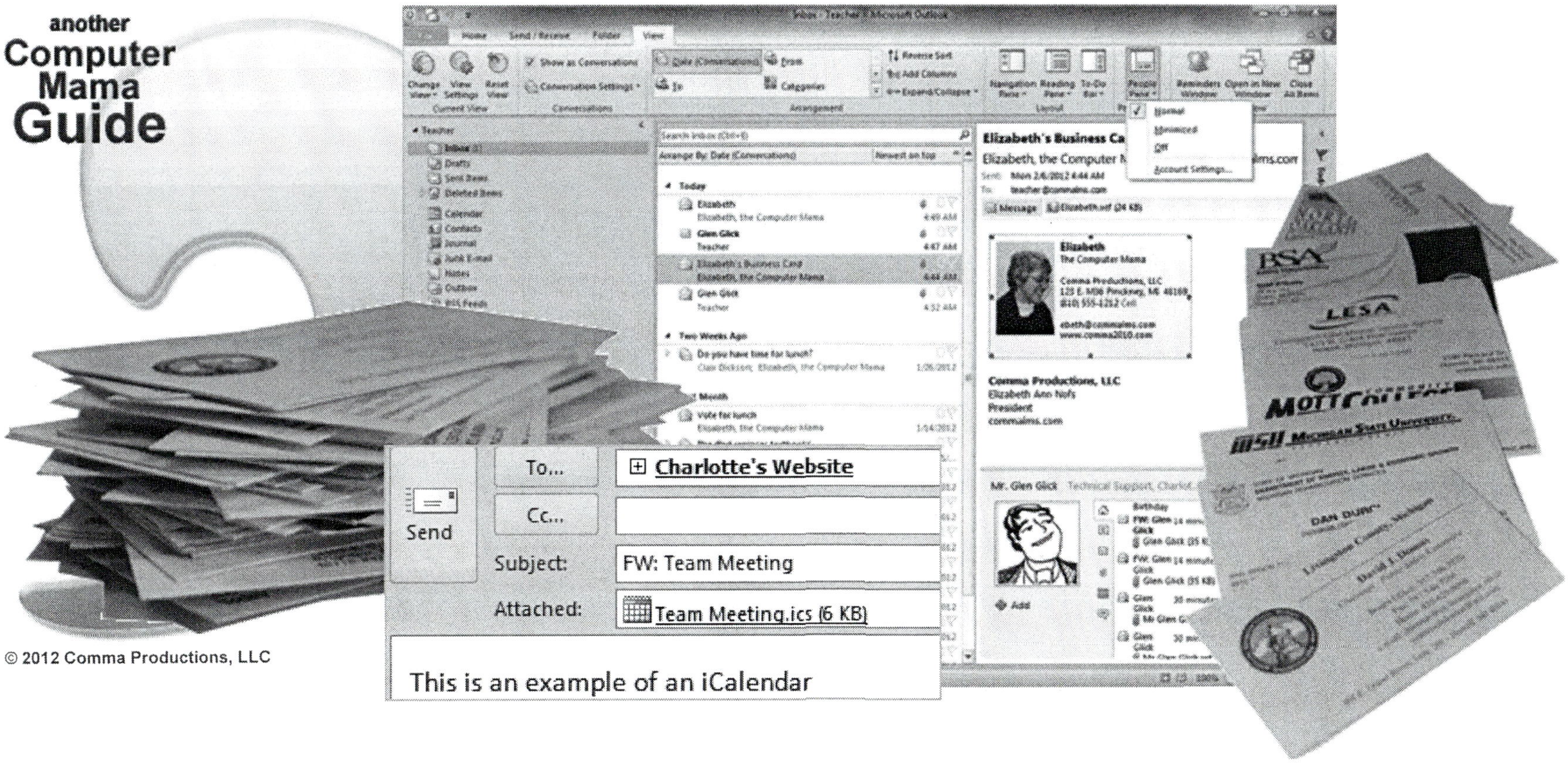

This is an example of an iCalendar

To...   ⊞ **Charlotte's Website**

Cc...

Send

Subject: FW: Team Meeting

Attached: Team Meeting.ics (6 KB)

another
**Computer
Mama**
Guide

The Complete Guide to Microsoft Outlook 2010

© 2012 Comma Productions, LLC
9090 Chilson Road
Brighton, MI 48116
978-0-9838917-7-2

Trademark and Copyright

Limit of Liability/Disclaimer of Warranty:

The Complete Guide to Microsoft Outlook 2010

Chapter 1: Getting Started
Take 1: Getting Started, page 11
Welcome, page 12
Take an online quiz, page 17
Submit your work, page 18

Take 2: Hello, Outlook, page 25
Objectives and Menu Map, page 26
Test Yourself, page 52

Chapter 2: Working with E-mail
Take 1: Messages and Messengers, page 53
Objectives and Menu Map, page 54
Test Yourself, page 82

Take 2: From Me to You, page 83
Objectives and Menu Map, page 84
Test Yourself, page 112

Chapter 3: Managing E-mail
Take 1: Signed, Sealed & Delivered, page 113
Objectives and Menu Map, page 114
Test Yourself, page 148

Take 2: Contacts and Connections, page 149
Objectives and Menu Map, page 150
Test Yourself, page 182

Chapter 4: Working with the Calendar
Take 1: Eight Days a Week, page 183
Objectives and Menu Map, page 194
Test Yourself, page 216

Take 2: Tasks and Management, page 217
Objectives and Menu Map, page 218
Test Yourself, page 250

Chapter 5: Outlook and the Internet
Take 1: Outlook: Online, page 251
Objectives and Menu Map, page 252
Test Yourself, page 290

Take 2: Outlook: In Print, page 291
Objectives and Menu Map, page 292
Test Yourself, page 316

Chapter 6: Managing Outlook
Take 1: Advanced Options, page 317
Objectives and Menu Map, page 318
Test Yourself, page 340

Take 2: Outlook Accounts, page 341
Objectives and Menu Map, page 342
Test Yourself, page 361

Outlook Skill Test, page 363

Microsoft Outlook 2010 Study Guide, page 7
Index, page 365

Microsoft Office Specialist Certification

What is the Microsoft Office Specialist Certification?

The Microsoft Office Specialist certification validates through the use of exams that you have obtained specific skill sets within the applicable Microsoft Office programs and other Microsoft programs included in the Microsoft Office Specialist Program. The candidate can choose which exam(s) they want to take according to which skills they want to validate.

CertiPort is the premier provider for validating technology skills.

The **Microsoft Office Specialist** tests are offered at authorized testing centers.

For more information on the MOS exam topics or to find a testing center near you please contact: **www.certiport.com**

What is the Microsoft Office Specialist Certification Program?

The **Microsoft Office Specialist (MOS) Certification Program** enables candidates to show that they have something exceptional to offer – proven expertise in Microsoft Office programs. Recognized by businesses and schools around the world, millions of certifications have been obtained in over 100 different countries. The **Microsoft Office Specialist (MOS) Certification Program** is the only Microsoft-approved certification program of its kind.

The Microsoft Office Specialist Certification Series

Core Certification: Pass any 1 test:
Word 2010 Core: Exam 77-881
Excel® 2010 Core: Exam 77-882
PowerPoint® 2010: Exam 77-883
Access® 2010: Exam 77-885
Outlook® 2010: Exam 77-884

Expert Certification: Pass either test:
Word 2010 Expert: Exam 77-887
Excel® 2010 Expert: Exam 77-888

Master: Pass 3 required and 1 elective test:
Required
Word 2010 Expert: Exam 77-887
Excel® 2010 Expert: Exam 77-888
PowerPoint® 2010: Exam 77-883

Elective
Access® 2010: Exam 77-885 or
Outlook® 2010: Exam 77-884

The Benefits of Certification

Why Get Certified?

For employers, the certification provides skill-verification tools that not only help assess a person's skills in using Microsoft Office programs but also the ability to quickly complete on-the-job tasks across multiple programs in the Microsoft Office system. (http://www.microsoft.com/learning/en/us/certification/mos.aspx). Certification proves a certain level of advanced competency with the programs in question. Employers don't have to wonder if the skills stated on the resume are honest and without exaggeration. This can lead to further employment opportunities and increased pay.

A person holding Microsoft Office Certification shows not just a level of skill, but an ability to quickly complete tasks, due to familiarity with the program and it's many time-saving features. The hard work that goes into learning Microsoft Office programs to the level of proficiency necessary for successful completion of the Certification Exams also indicates a desire on behalf of the student to learn and succeed.

The Benefits: Earn More, Find Jobs Quicker

Research indicates that employees with Microsoft Certification earn more and find jobs quicker than those employees without certification. Furthermore, employees with certification report a greater feeling of confidence. These things translate into greater job satisfaction. (http://www.microsoft.com/learning/en/us/certification/mos.aspx)

Research also shows that individuals with certification make up to 12% more than those without certification. In addition, 82% of Microsoft Office Specialists report a salary increase after receiving certification. Managers like the skills proven and the ability demonstrated by those with Microsoft Office Certifications.
http://www.certiport.com/Portal/desktopdefault.aspx?page=common/pagelibrary/mos2003.html

For More Information:
www.certiport.com
www.microsoft.com

⑨ About Our Certification Program

Books in this Series:
Complete Guide to
Microsoft® Outlook 2010

Microsoft Office Specialist (MOS) Certification for Outlook 2010

Overview: Our Microsoft Office Specialist certification program for Outlook 2010 covers all of the exam objectives for the Outlook certification exam.

Our Approach: In designing these Guides, we found that it made more sense to write the lessons based on the Ribbons and Tasks. The beginning of each lesson provides an overview of the Ribbons and Tasks covered.

The Complete Guide to Outlook 2010 demonstrates the following Ribbons as they are used in E-mail, Calendar, Contact, Task, Notes, and Journal applications: Home, Send/ Receive, Folder, View, Task, Contact, Insert, Format Text, and Review. Also, the Picture Tools, SmartArt Tools, and Search Tools Ribbons as well as Backstage commands and options were covered. The lessons focused on creating and working with emails, calendars, tasks, notes, contacts, and journal entries individually and in groups.

Course Prerequisites: Students who enroll in Microsoft Office Specialist (MOS) program should have basic computer skills including how to turn on the computer, how to use an Internet browser and how to select commands from a menu. Students should know how to save files and send attachments by email as well.

Microsoft Outlook 2010 Study Guide
Microsoft Office Specialist (MOS): Exam 77-884 for Outlook 2010

1. Managing the Outlook Environment
1.1 Apply and Edit Outlook Options
Backstage: General Options, 256
Backstage: Mail Options, 257
Backstage: Calendar Options, 271
Backstage: Task Options, 274
Backstage: Notes and Journal Options, 275
Backstage: Advanced Options, 355
Backstage: Language Options, 277

1.2 Tag Items
Tag Items: Categories, 226
Tag Items: Set Flags, 65
Tag Items: Sensitivity Level, 80
Tag Items: Mark as Read/Unread, 130
Tag Items: View Message Properties, 80

1.3 Arrange the Content Pane
Content: Show or Hide Fields in a View, 308
Content: Reading Views, 33
Content: Reminders Window, 12
Content: View People Pane, 173

1.4 Apply Search and Filter Tools
Search and Filter, 321

1.5 Print Outlook Items
Print Attachments, 298
Print: Calendars, 300
Print Multiple Messages, 299
Print Contact Records, 310
Print Tasks, 308
Print Notes, 312

2. Create and Format Content
2.1 Create and Send E-mail Messages
Format: Theme, 59
Message Format, 49
Message Format: Plain Text, 35
Message Format: Rich Text, 40
Message Format: HTML (web), 258
E-Mail: Show Cc and Bcc fields, 64
E-mail: Reminder for Recipient, 66
E-Mail: Specify Sending Account, 359
E-Mail: Specify Sent Item Folder, 147
E-Mail: Delivery Options, 76
E-Mail: Voting Options, 70
E-Mail: Tracking Options, 67
E-Mail: Contact Groups, 209

2.1 Create and Manage Quick Steps
Quick Steps, 129
Quick Steps: Create Steps, 130
Quick Steps: Edit Steps, 131
Quick Steps: Delete Steps, 132
Quick Steps: Duplicate, 133
Quick Steps: Reset Back to Default, 134

2.3 Create and Manage Quick Steps
Graphics, 61
Hyperlinks, 199

2.4 Format Item Content
Format Content, 41
Styles: Apply Styles, 42
Styles: Create Styles, 48
Format: Paste Special, 50
Format Graphics, 94

2.5 Attach Content
Attach: Outlook Item (Business Card), 164
Attach: External Files, 88

3. Managing E-mail Messages
3.1 Clean up the Inbox
Clean Up Mailbox: View Mailbox Size, 137
Save Attachment, 104
Save Message, 107
Clean Up Mailbox: Conversations, 140
Clean Up Mailbox: Cleanup Tools, 138

3.2 Create and Manage Rules
Rules: Create Rules, 121
Rules: Modify Rules, 127
Rules: Delete Rules, 125

3.3 Manage Junk Mail
Junk Mail: Allow a Message, 144
Junk Mail: Filter Junk Mail, 145
Junk Mail: Never Block Sender, 142
Junk Mail: Block Sender's Domain, 143
Junk Mail: Never Block Group or List, 141
Junk Mail: Block Sender, 141

Microsoft Outlook 2010 Study Guide
Microsoft Office Specialist (MOS): Exam 77-884 for Outlook 2010

3. Managing E-mail Messages
3.4 Managing Automatic Messages
Automatic: Signatures, 260
Automatic: Specify Fonts, 261
Automatic: Specify HTML Format, 258
Automatic: Specify Plain Text Format, 258
Automatic: Specify Reply Options, 266
Automatic: Specify Forward Options, 266
Automatic: Specify Default Theme, 263
Automatic: Message Options, 297
Automatic: Specify Stationery, 262
Automatic: Specify Fonts, 264

4. Managing Contacts
4.1 Create and Manage Contacts
Contacts: Modify Business Card, 162
Contacts: Forward a Contact, 164
Contacts: Update Business Card, 169

4.2 Create and Manage Contact Groups
Contacts: Contact Groups, 166
Contacts: Contact Group Membership, 167
Contacts: Show Notes, 170
Contacts: Forward Contact Group, 171
Contacts: Delete Contact Group, 170
Contacts: Send a Meeting to a Group, 209

5. Managing the Calendar
5.1 Create and Edit Appointments
Appointments: Options, 190
Print Appointment Details, 307
Appointments: Forward, 209
Appointments: Meeting with E-mail Sender, 211

5.2 Create and Edit Meeting Requests
Appointments: Set Response Options, 208
Appointments: Update a Meeting Request, 207
Appointment: Cancel Meeting Request, 213
Appointment: Propose New Time, 205

5.3 Manipulate the Calendar Pane
Calendar: Arrange Calendar View, 187
Calendar: Change Calendar Color, 273
Calendar: Hide or Display Calendars, 286
Calendar: Calendar Groups, 287

6. Tasks, Notes and Journal Entries
6.1 Create and Edit Tasks
Tasks: Create Tasks, 222
Tasks: Manage Task Details, 224
Tasks: Send Status Report, 235
Tasks: Mark Task Complete, 229
Tasks: Move Tasks, 240
Tasks: Assign Tasks, 233
Tasks: Accept or Decline Tasks, 234
Tasks: Update Assigned Tasks, 235

6.2 Create and Edit Notes
Note: View, 221
Notes: Create, 242
Notes: Arrange View, 244
Notes: Use Categories, 243

6.3 Create and Edit Journal Entries
Journal: Record Outlook Items, 245
Journal: Record Office Items, 247
Journal: Edit Journal Entry, 246

About the Authors

Microsoft Office Specialist (MOS): Exam 77-884 for Outlook 2010

Elizabeth Ann Nofs
Elizabeth is the Computer Mama. She developed the teaching methodology in the Complete Computer Guide series using breakthrough research in gender balanced training. Elizabeth has taught several thousand men and women from government, manufacturing, small business, and education in both online and hands-on classrooms.

She is the author of the Complete Computer Guides as well as a Microsoft Certified Office Specialist. She earned a BA in Biology from the University of Michigan.

Alex Sergay, Senior Instructional Designer
For more than 20 years, Alex has made complex technology easy to understand. Alex has developed instructional multimedia software for educational websites including the Sounds of English, a linguistics-training tool that earned a ComputerWorld/Smithsonian Laureate.

Alex earned his Masters of Educational Technology from the University of Michigan, Ann Arbor.

Clair Dickson, Student Services
Clair works with adult learners in online, face-to-face and hybrid classroom settings. She is considered "highly qualified" to teach introductory computers, including Microsoft Office.

Clair has a Graduate Certificate in Educational Media and Technology, an program that explored ways to infuse technology into the learning experience so that learning is interactive. She has earned Microsoft Office 2007 Master Certification. She also holds a BS in Secondary English Education from Eastern Michigan University.

Leo Michael Nofs, Technical Writing and Quality Control
Leo is a Microsoft Certified Professional and an Access database designer. He uses his exemplary attention to detail for copy editing the computer instructions for accuracy and clarity.

Traci Nofs, Photography and Photo Editing
Traci has been photographing children and nature since 2000. She works freelance out of her home, including weddings, engagements, and particularly children's photography. She has further enhanced her photos by use of image manipulation, focusing on light and color.

M. Jeanette McCrickard, Office Manager
Jeanette has years of experience as an office manager, including the increasing use of computer-related tasks. Her excellent attention to detail has lead her to work as an Access database administrator and a copy editor.

All of my books

are dedicated to

Fr. Paul Cummings

who taught me

computers.

Love, eBeth

How To Use This Guide
Microsoft Office Specialist Certification Training

The Comma Method

Observation is a perceptual strategy that asks: why am I doing this and which tools would be most effective? Each lesson begins with a discussion of the purpose and the objectives.

Orientation helps students start at the right place. The screen shots in the *Complete Compute Guides* show the entire window as well as a close up of the particular button or command.

Notation There are "breadcrumbs" above each screen image. Like Hansel and Gretel, the breadcrumbs show the pathway to a button or option. Our notation uses the following convention:
Ribbon->Group->Button->Options

Menu Maps

The Comma Method recognizes that there is a difference in how men and women navigate the menus. Men typically have the ability to see the map first. This method of acquiring knowledge is called *Breadth-first.* [1] Women tend to work with the details first. They learn several commands, such as copy, cut, and paste, then they put those concepts under the label, "edit." This method of learning is called *Depth-first.*

The Comma Method uses menu mapping to assist men and women to see both the Breadth and the Depth. An example of the menu map is can be seen here.

[1] Ford, Nigel, Sherry Chen, Matching/mismatching revisited: An Empirical Study of Learning and Teaching Styles. British Journal of Educational Technology v.32 no1 (Jan. 2001)

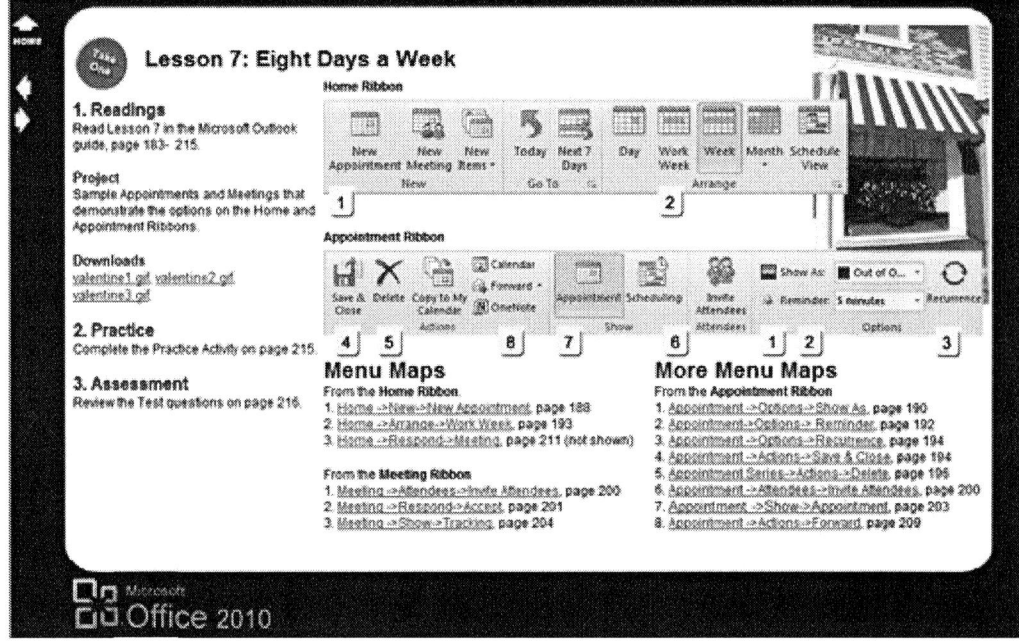

Attachments Ribbon

Outlook 2010: Getting Started

Welcome!

Course Objectives
Students will be able to:

1. Log in to the online course
2. Navigate the outline and lessons
3. Take quizzes online
4. Submit assignments online
5. Participate in the Forums and Chat

Welcome

This course presents a practical, hands-on approach to computers. The lessons are based on what you see on the screen, what you can do with the options, and what works on the job. The goal is to enable you to use Microsoft Windows and Office 2010 effectively, even creatively.

Use this *Guide* as part of your professional development plan to prepare for the Microsoft Business Certification exams, Microsoft Office Specialist (MOS) or as a reference book to solve problems as they come up.

This introduction provides information on:
• Navigation
• Practice
• Sample Documents
• Assessments

Log into the course

This online course requires a User Name and Password. You probably received an email with your username and password when you enrolled.

How to Login
Go to the website for your course.
1. Click on the (Login) link.
2. You will be prompted for your Username and Password.

What If This Doesn't Work?
First, look at the keyboard and make sure the Caps Lock is off (no light.) Passwords may include both upper and lower case letters.

Second, check the spelling. Your user name may not be exactly the same as your email address.

Third, you can click on the Live Chat and get immediate assistance.

Memo to Self: It's OK if your computer does not match exactly. The logon screen may show a logo or it may be a different color.

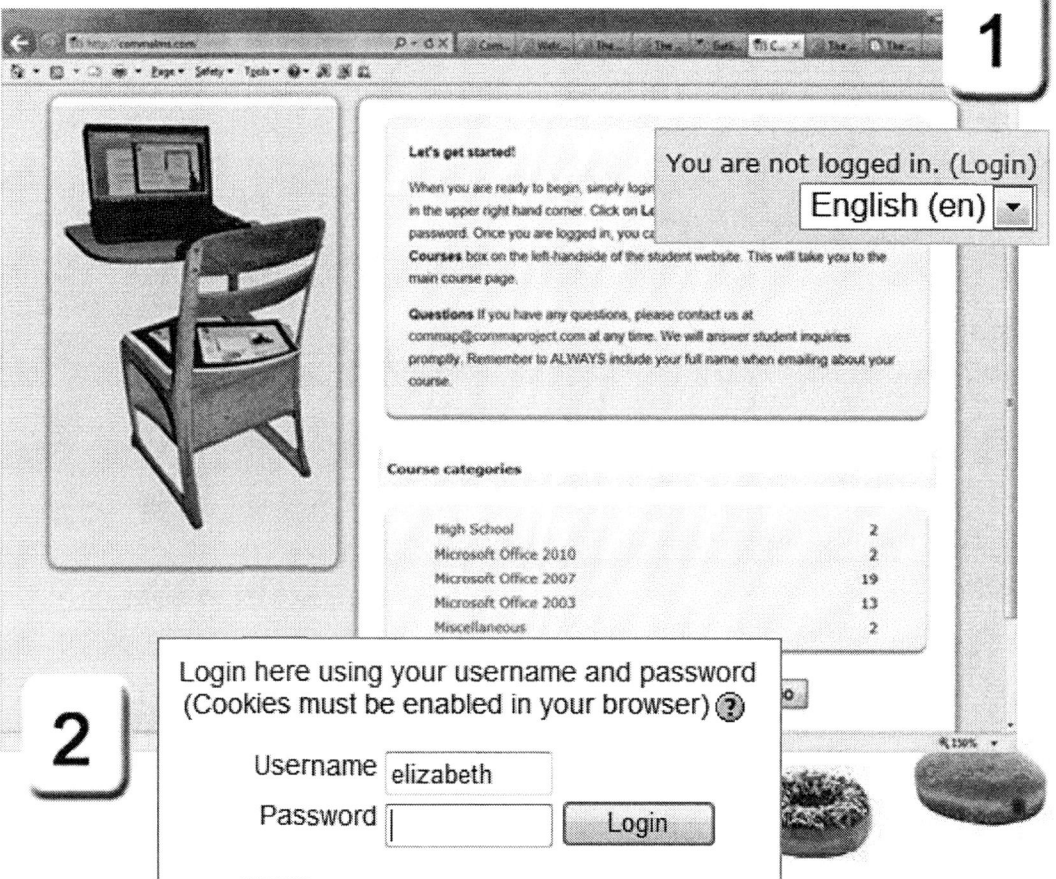

Let's get started!

When you are ready to begin, simply login in the upper right hand corner. Click on Login password. Once you are logged in, you can Courses box on the left-handside of the student website. This will take you to the main course page.

Questions If you have any questions, please contact us at commap@commaproject.com at any time. We will answer student inquiries promptly. Remember to ALWAYS include your full name when emailing about your course.

Course categories

High School	2
Microsoft Office 2010	2
Microsoft Office 2007	19
Microsoft Office 2003	13
Miscellaneous	2

You are not logged in. (Login)
English (en)

Login here using your username and password (Cookies must be enabled in your browser) ⑦

Username elizabeth
Password [   ] Login

The Topic Outline

When you log into your course, you should see the **Topic Outline**. The Topic Outline is a course syllabus: it lists your lessons, practice and quizzes.

Each Level has Lessons and Assessments. The lesson links are short discussions that demonstrate the options on a particular Ribbon. The lessons links may also list the page number where these pages can be found in the print version of the computer guides.

Many students prefer to read the lessons on a second monitor or in print, rather than switch from the lesson screens to Microsoft Office to practice the options.

Memo to Self: It's OK if your computer does not match exactly. The important part is learning the steps. Please contact your facilitator if you have any questions

My Course ->Topic Outline

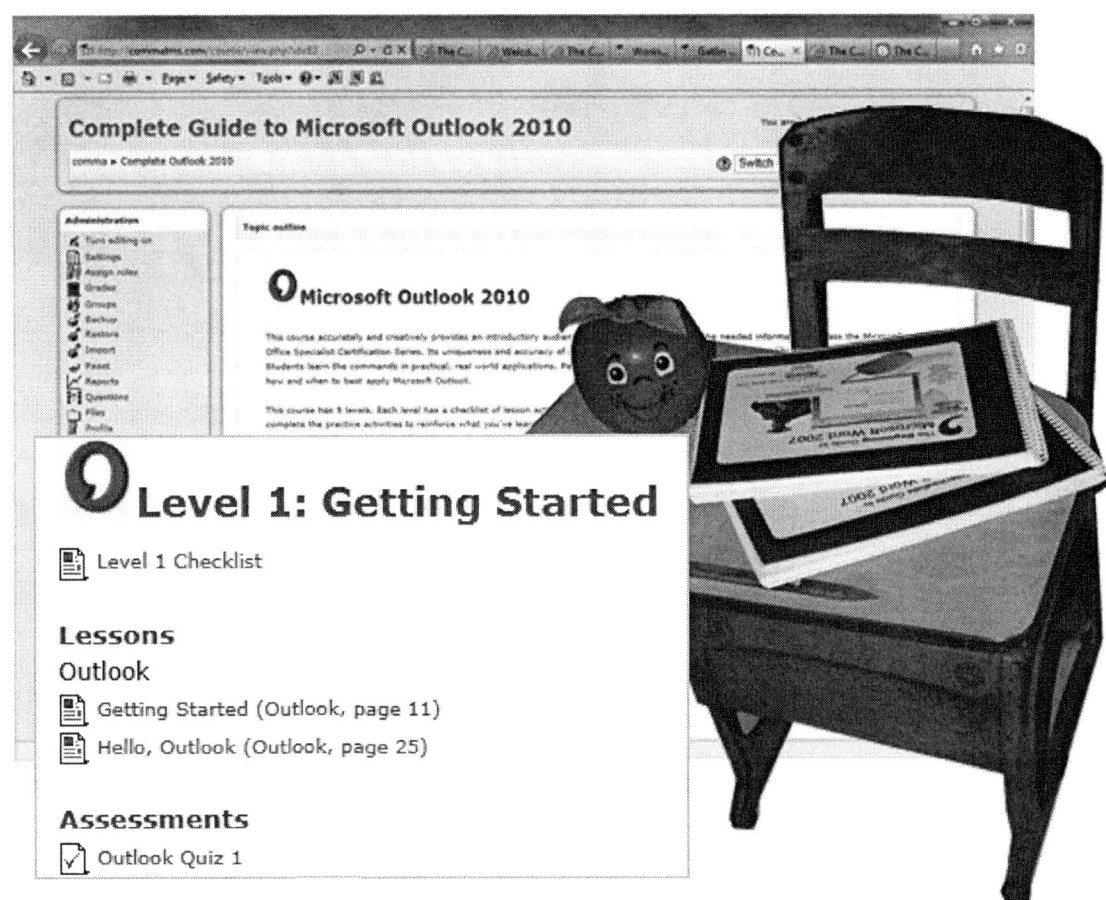

Lesson Links

When you click on a hyperlink to read a lesson, a new window will open.

What Do You See? On the left side of each screen you should see the white navigation arrows: Next, Previous, and Home

What Else Do You See? When you are done with a lesson, you can close the browser window. Go to the upper right corner of the lesson window and click on the X to Exit.

The Topic Outline should be there, the window was left open behind the lesson screen.

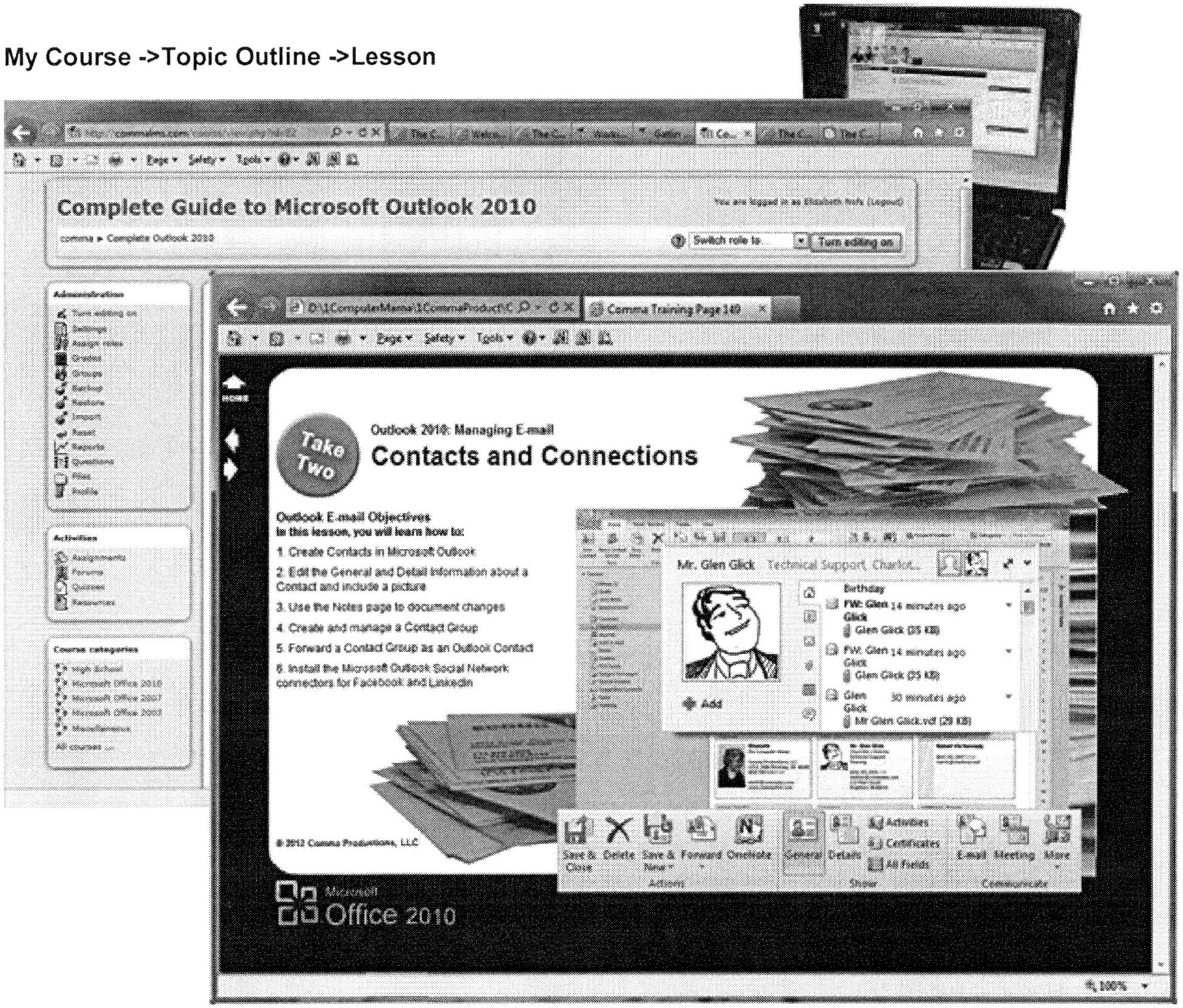

My Course ->Topic Outline ->Lesson

Level Checklists

Each Level has many lessons, sample files and practice sheets, depending on which course you are in. The **Level Checklists** offer a complete list of the lessons, download, practice and quizzes.

Downloads

When you click on a link to a Download, you will be prompted to **Open** or **Save** this file.

Click on **Save.**

Browse to your Documents folder. This will save a copy of the file on your computer.

Memo to Self: It's OK if your Checklist does not match exactly. Please contact your facilitator if you have any questions

My Course ->Topic Outline -> Level Checklist

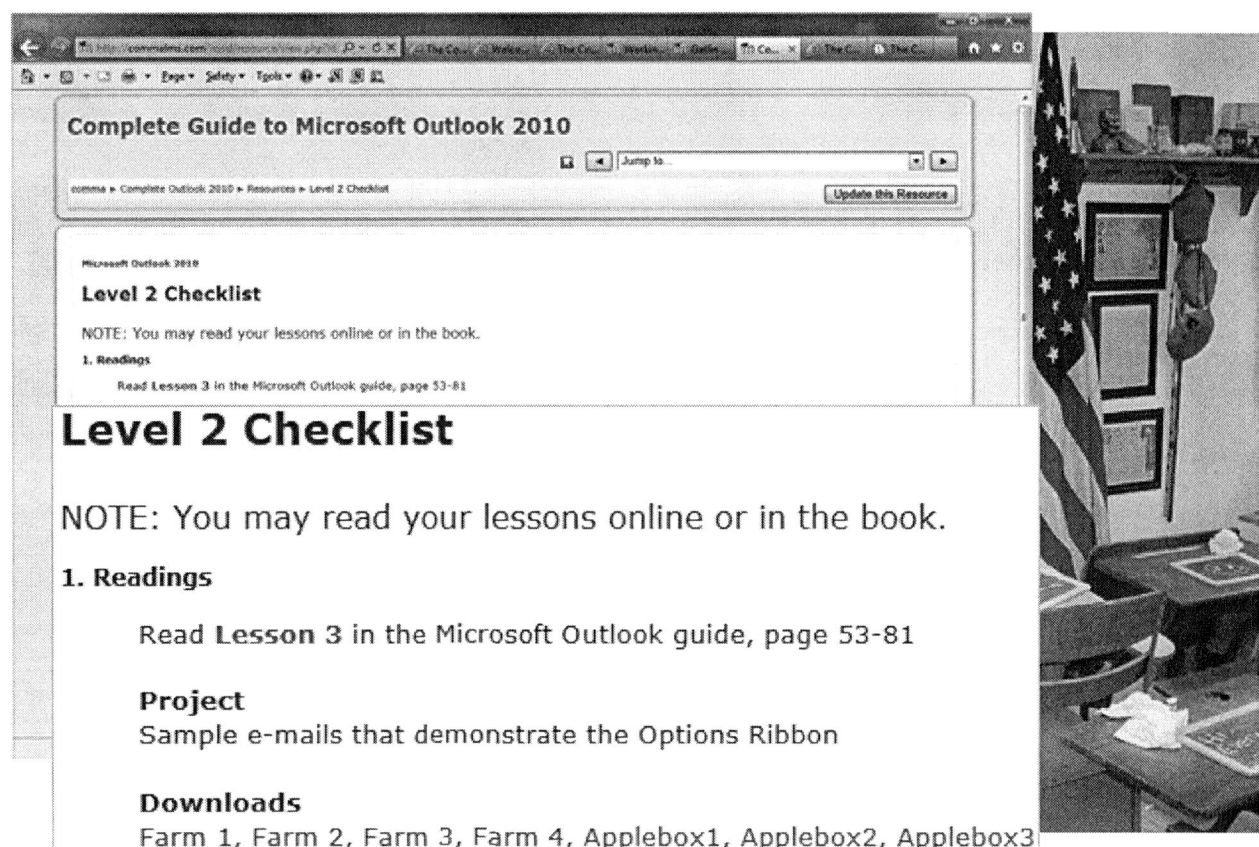

Level 2 Checklist

NOTE: You may read your lessons online or in the book.

1. Readings

Read **Lesson 3** in the Microsoft Outlook guide, page 53-81

Project
Sample e-mails that demonstrate the Options Ribbon

Downloads
Farm 1, Farm 2, Farm 3, Farm 4, Applebox1, Applebox2, Applebox3

2. Practice

Take a Quiz Online

After you review the materials online or with the *Guides*, you can log into the course online and take a **Quiz**. This is an open book quiz. You are allowed to look up the answers in your notes, online, or in the computer *Guides*.

Review the Quiz Buttons
Submit: This button posts your answer for the current question.

Save without submitting: This button saves your answers. You can leave the quiz and finish it later.

> Save without submitting

Submit page: This button sends your answers to all questions on the page.

Submit all and finish: Use this button to finish the quiz and submit your quiz online. When you Submit all and finish, you cannot go back and print your answers. So, print first!

> Submit all and finish

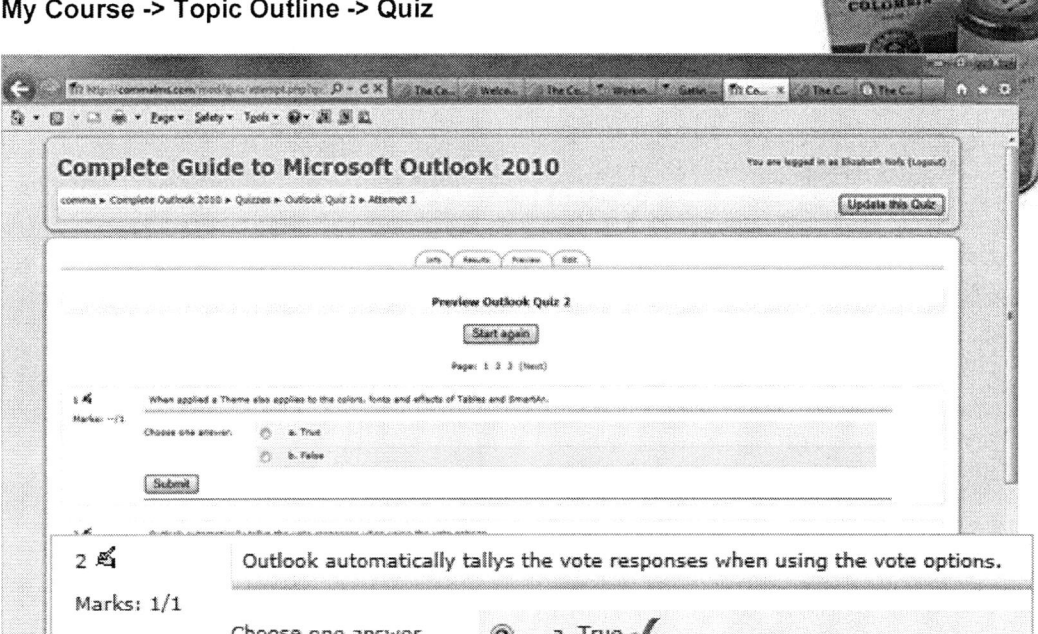

Submit Your Application Question

Most of our online courses also have Application Questions that test your knowledge of the software. These assessments ask you to type your answer and submit it online. Here are the steps.

Review This: Upload a file
1. Go to the **Topic Outline**.
Click on **Outlook Application 1**.

What Do You See? You will be taken to the Edit screen. The instructions should be available.

2. Click in the **Text Box** to type and format your answer. Please use complete sentences and check the spelling.

3. Click **Save Changes** to submit your Application Question. Your instructor will be notified automatically.

My Course -> Topic Outline -> Application Question

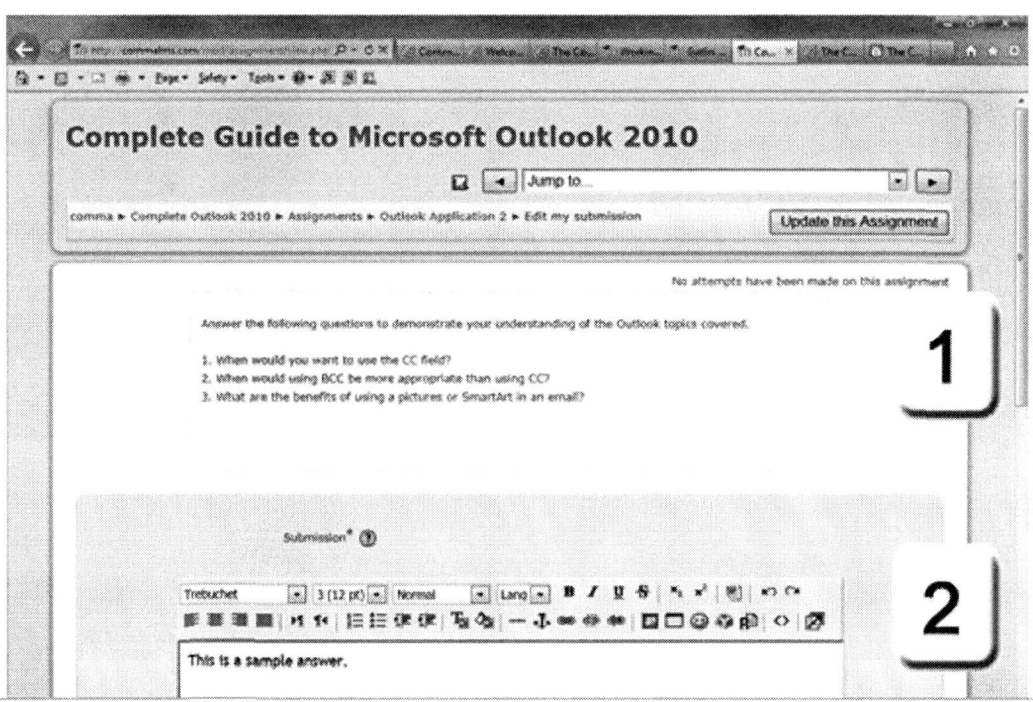

Answer the following questions to demonstrate your understanding of the Outlook topics

1. When would you want to use the CC field?
2. When would using BCC be more appropriate than using CC?
3. What are the benefits of using a pictures or SmartArt in an email?

Use the Forums

In an online class, a **Forum** is similar to raising your hand and asking a question. When you post a question to a Forum anyone can reply with a suggestion or comment. Some of the answers are very creative and useful.

Your instructor may also post an explanation or offer additional links.

Edit | Delete | Reply

Live Chats

Many instructors keep Office Hours. Chat allows you to type questions online and get an answer immediately from your instructor when your instructor is in the office.

Don't Explain and Don't Complain:
Please keep your posts professional and on topic!

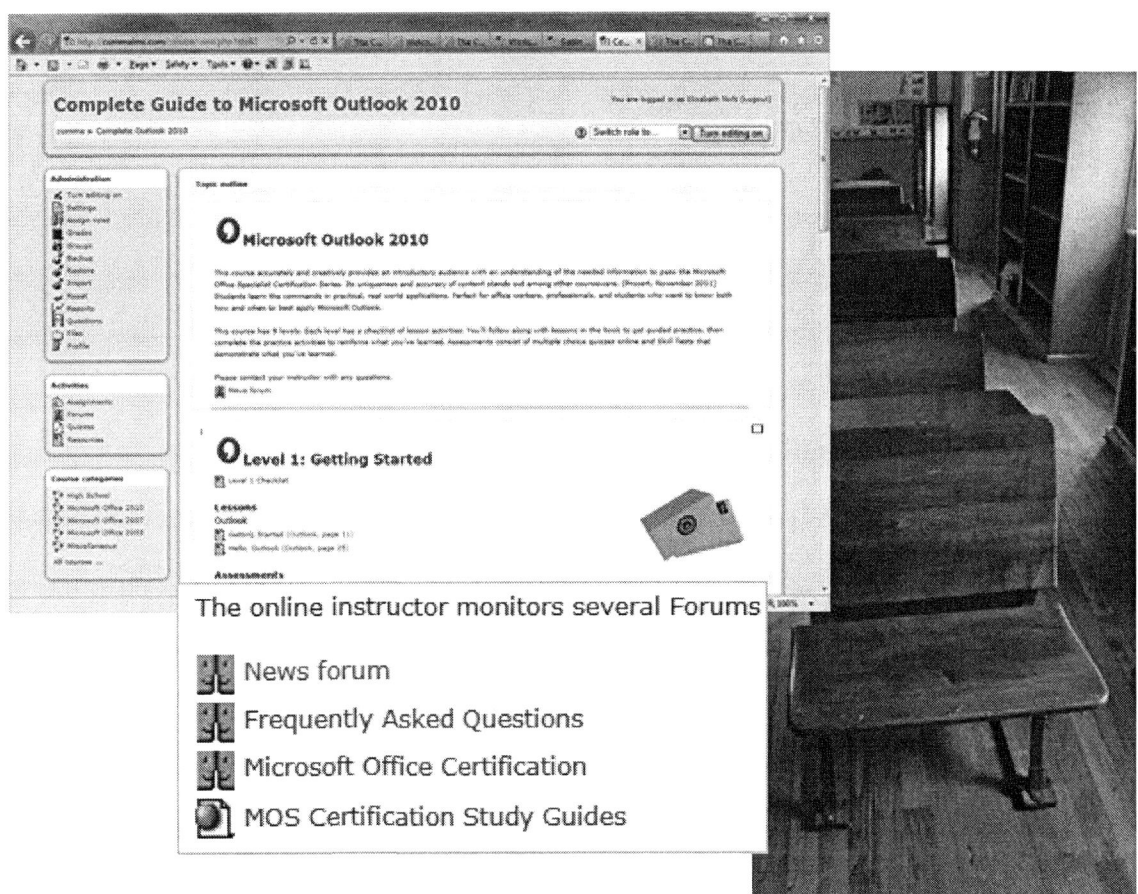

The online instructor monitors several Forums

News forum

Frequently Asked Questions

Microsoft Office Certification

MOS Certification Study Guides

Practice

This *Guide* offers additional reference materials and practice certification tests. You can use the multiple choice quizzes and skill tests to practice if you wish. When you are ready, please log into the course and do the assessments online.

The Microsoft certification tests are timed: you have to perform the process steps very quickly and efficiently in order to pass.
That takes practice!

More practice

If you have a question about a document or file you are working on you are always welcome to email a copy of your work to your instructor as an attachment.

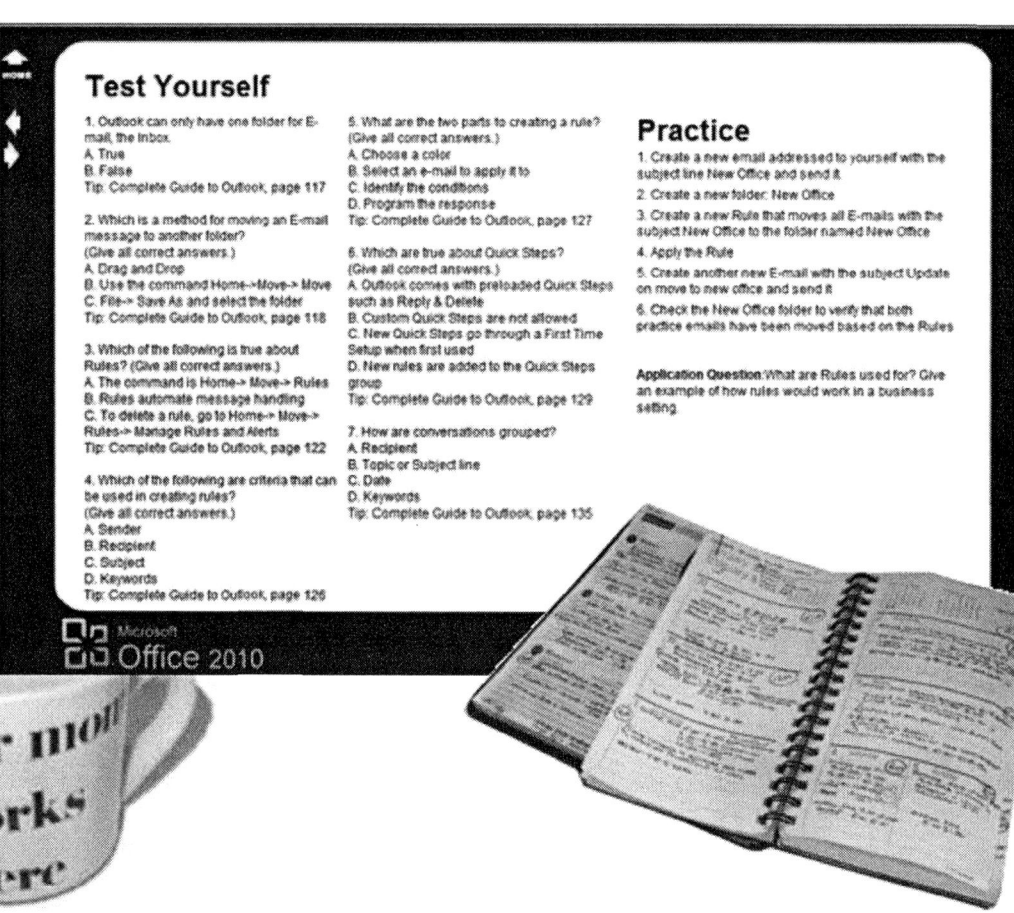

Test Yourself

1. Outlook can only have one folder for E-mail, the Inbox.
A. True
B. False
Tip: Complete Guide to Outlook, page 117

2. Which is a method for moving an E-mail message to another folder?
(Give all correct answers.)
A. Drag and Drop
B. Use the command Home->Move-> Move
C. File-> Save As and select the folder
Tip: Complete Guide to Outlook, page 118

3. Which of the following is true about Rules? (Give all correct answers.)
A. The command is Home-> Move-> Rules
B. Rules automate message handling
C. To delete a rule, go to Home-> Move-> Rules-> Manage Rules and Alerts
Tip: Complete Guide to Outlook, page 122

4. Which of the following are criteria that can be used in creating rules?
(Give all correct answers.)
A. Sender
B. Recipient
C. Subject
D. Keywords
Tip: Complete Guide to Outlook, page 126

5. What are the two parts to creating a rule?
(Give all correct answers.)
A. Choose a color
B. Select an e-mail to apply it to
C. Identify the conditions
D. Program the response
Tip: Complete Guide to Outlook, page 127

6. Which are true about Quick Steps?
(Give all correct answers.)
A. Outlook comes with preloaded Quick Steps such as Reply & Delete
B. Custom Quick Steps are not allowed
C. New Quick Steps go through a First Time Setup when first used
D. New rules are added to the Quick Steps group
Tip: Complete Guide to Outlook, page 129

7. How are conversations grouped?
A. Recipient
B. Topic or Subject line
C. Date
D. Keywords
Tip: Complete Guide to Outlook, page 135

Practice

1. Create a new email addressed to yourself with the subject line New Office and send it.
2. Create a new folder: New Office
3. Create a new Rule that moves all E-mails with the subject New Office to the folder named New Office
4. Apply the Rule
5. Create another new E-mail with the subject Update on move to new office and send it
6. Check the New Office folder to verify that both practice emails have been moved based on the Rules

Application Question: What are Rules used for? Give an example of how rules would work in a business setting.

Microsoft Business Certification

The course prepares you to pass the **Microsoft Office Specialist (MOS)** exams. This credential recognizes the business skills needed to get the most out of Microsoft Office 2010.

Microsoft Certification Exams are available through authorized testing centers. They are not included as part of the certification training program in the same way that taking the Bar Exam is not included with getting a degree in Law from a college or university.

More Information Online.
Certiport provides the official Microsoft certification tests. You can download the Microsoft certification topics and study guides. Here is their address: www.certiport.com

Please Note: *Comma Productions, LLC. is independent from Microsoft Corporation, and not affiliated with Microsoft in any manner. While the Complete Computer Guides may be used in assisting individuals to prepare for a Microsoft Business Certification exam, Microsoft, its designated program administrator, and Comma Productions, LLC. do not warrant that use of these Complete Computer Guides will ensure passing a Microsoft Business Certification exam.*

Can Microsoft Outlook Express be used?

Microsoft Outlook 2010 is a rich software program that includes E-mail, Calendar, Contacts, Tasks and Journal. The Ribbons use many of the same options as Microsoft Word for formatting Text and Pictures.

Microsoft Outlook Express is a free application that comes with many versions of Microsoft Windows. It does not have many of the features that are found in Microsoft Outlook 20102. So, students would not be able to practice most of the steps.

Memo to Self: If this is your first time you are going to use Microsoft Outlook 2010, please go to the last lesson in this book to find the instructions for creating an E-mail account.

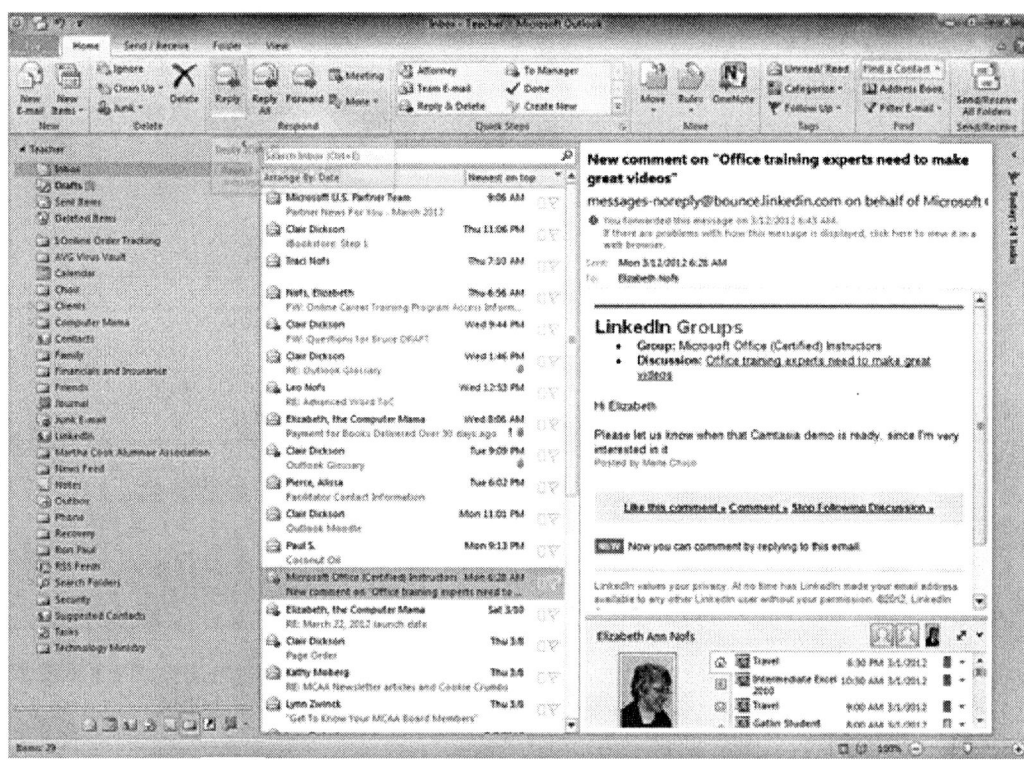

Self-Assessment

Skill Level-Outlook E-mail	Mastered	Needs Work	Required for my job
Create, address and send Plain Text E-mail			
Format E-mail content and apply Styles			
Use Message Flags to follow up			
Insert graphics and hyperlinks in an E-mail			
Attach content to E-mail messages			
Clean up the Mailbox and save attachments			
Filter Junk Mail and Block Sender or Group			
Create and manager Rules			

Beginning Excel is recommended if you selected "needs work" on three or more skills.

Skill Level-Outlook Calendar	Mastered	Needs Work	Required for my job
Create appointments and set the options			
Schedule meetings and track responses			
Create and use Contacts			
Create and manage Contact Groups			
Create, assign and track Tasks			
Use the Journal			

Intermediate Excel is recommended if you selected "needs work" on three or more skills.

Skill Level-Advanced	Mastered	Needs Work	Required for my job
Setup E-mail Accounts			
Backup the Personal Folders			
Export Outlook Data			
Use Categories			
Search and filter Outlook data			
Set a default theme for Messages			

Advanced Excel is recommended if you selected "needs work" on three or more skills.

Using an eReader

Now you can download our Microsoft Office certification training books to your eReader. In addition to being available online as a webpage we have included the materials , within the course as **Adobe PDF files** for download to your computer, eReader or Tablet of choice!

eReaders provide full color pages, zoom control, search, bookmarking and other great features. You can prop the eReader beside your mighty desktop or laptop computer as you read the lessons and practice the steps.

This is a simple, easy to use process. Our books work best on the **iPad** or other similarly sized tablets because of the large format of the pages. When a PDF is accessed online, such as in our courses, the iPad automatically offers to put that PDF file into the iBooks app.

Any **Kindle** with a web browser should be able to download the PDF to the Kindle, then open it with either a PDF app or in the Kindle App. Another option with the Kindle is to download the files to a desktop, email them to your Kindle account, then send them to the Kindle.

How Do You Practice?

80.6% I have the book beside my computer so I can look at both.

16.7% I read the lessons online on the the same computer I am working on, switching between screens.

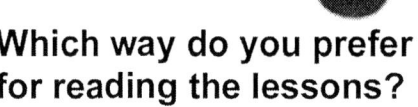

Which way do you prefer for reading the lessons?

54.1% In print (books)

37.8% Online (web pages)

8.1% eReader/Tablet (PDF pages)

If your course did not include books you can buy them on Amazon.com if you wish

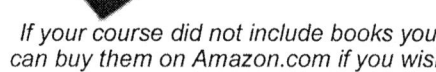

Outlook 2010: Getting Started
Hello, Microsoft Outlook!

Beginning Outlook Objectives
In this lesson, you will learn how to:

1. Use the Microsoft Outlook Home Ribbon to create and respond to E-mail messages

2. Use the Message Ribbon to format Basic (Plain Text) E-mail messages

3. Create Rich Text messages

4. Apply Quick Styles and use the formatting tools to create a custom Quick Style

© 2012 Comma Productions, LLC

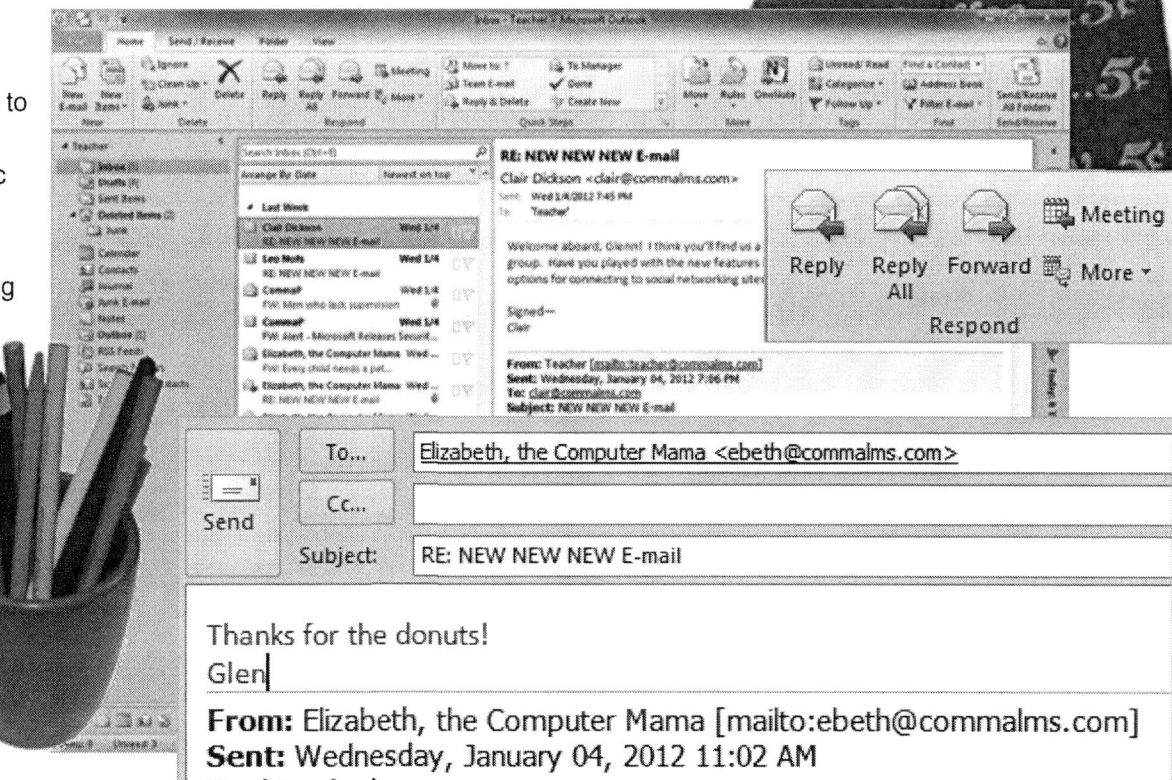

 **Lesson 2 : Introduction to E-mail**

1. Readings
Read Lesson 2 in the Microsoft Outlook guide, page 25-51.

Project
Create Plain Text and Rich Text E-mails.

Downloads
There are no downloads for this lesson.

2. Practice
There is no Practice Activity for this lesson.

3. Assessment
Review the Test questions on page 52.

Outlook View Ribbon

Outlook Home Ribbon

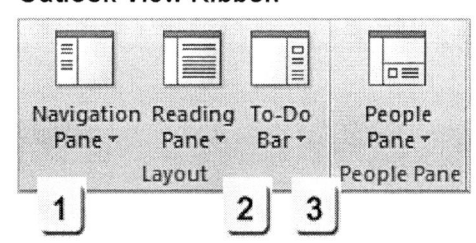

Format Text Ribbon

Outlook Menu Maps

From the **Outlook View Ribbon**
1. View->Layout->Navigation Pane, page 32
2. View->Layout->Reading Pane, page 33
3. View->Layout->To-Do Bar, page 34

From the **Outlook Home Ribbon**.
4. Home-> New->New E-Mail, page 35
5. Home ->Respond->Reply, page 36
6. Home ->Respond->Forward, page 37

E-mail Menu Maps

From the **Format Text Ribbon**
1. Format Text ->Font, page 40
2. Format Text ->Paragraph->Multilevel List, page 41
3. Format Text ->Styles, page 42
4. Format Text ->Styles->Change Styles, page 43
5. Format Text ->Styles->Options, page 45

Working with E-mail

Businesses share documents. A simple sale may include sending a price sheet, determining the costs, and confirming the payment. E-mail has replaced the US Postal service and even fax machines. E-mail is quick, portable, and available anywhere on a computer or even a Smartphone. Microsoft Outlook does E-mail. It is a rich application that powers most of the businesses and government offices around the world.

Microsoft Outlook also does Calendars, Contacts, Tasks and Journals. There's a lot to like, here.

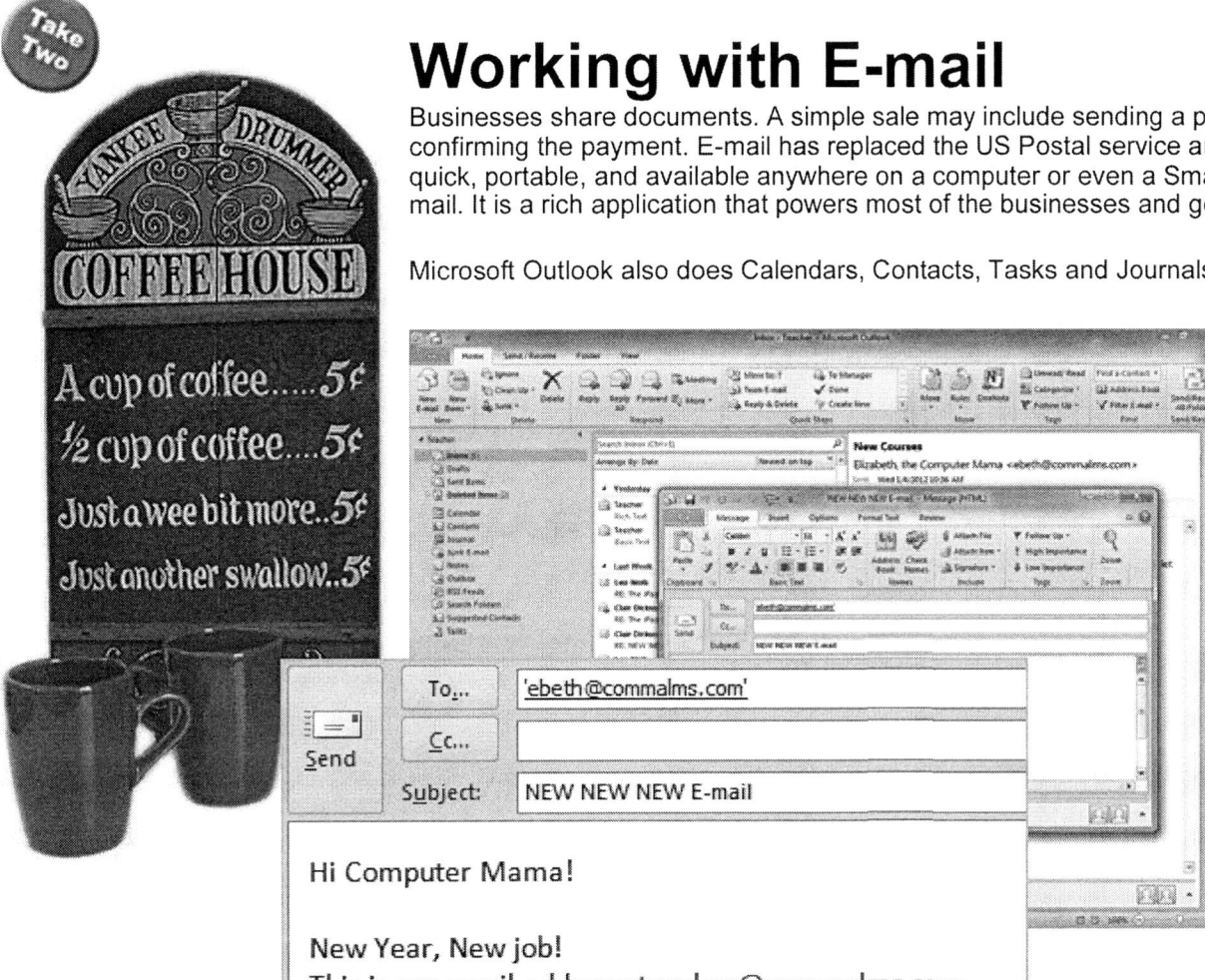

IMPORTANT: Business E-mail is NOT the same as personal E-mail or social network chatter.

Business communications, including E-mail, are PUBLIC.

E-mail in a government or military department is subject to FOIA-the Freedom of Information Act.

Please be very, very careful about office communication. Don't E-mail anything you wouldn't state publically in a meeting.

Before You Begin
Getting Started with Outlook
There are three different versions of Microsoft Outlook. From big to little in terms of functionality the different Outlook programs are:
Outlook Enterprise
Outlook Office
Outlook Web Access (Webmail)

Outlook Enterprise uses a corporate Exchange Server. The Exchange Server offers each user a personal mailbox as well as shared public folders.

Outlook Web Access is a simple way to access your corporate Exchange Server E-mail from any web browser.

Many government agencies and businesses use Outlook Web Access with an Exchange Server. For example, the County first responders use Outlook Web Access on their Smart Phones and laptops. Outlook Web Access is light and mobile.

Keep going...

Example of Microsoft Outlook Web Access

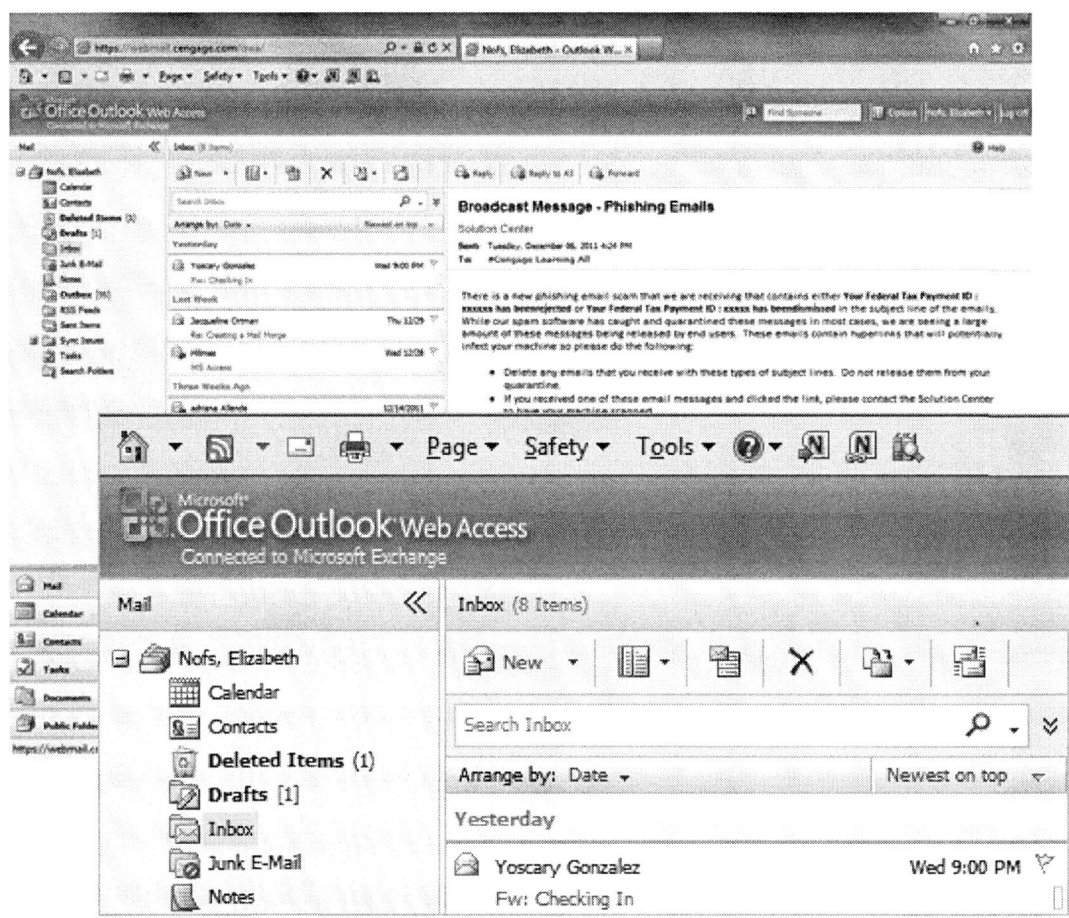

Hello, Microsoft Outlook

The desktop version of Microsoft Outlook is a very robust application in the Office 2010 software suite. Outlook is just as rich as Word and Excel. In fact, Outlook shares many of the same Ribbons and options.

1. Try it: Say, Hello Outlook!
Go to **Start -> All Programs ->Microsoft Office.**
Select: **Microsoft Office Outlook 2010**.

What Do You See? There are four Ribbons:
Home
Send/Receive
Folder
View
Keep going...

Memo to Self: If you have never installed Microsoft Outlook on your computer, please skip ahead to the Appendix at the end of this computer guide for the steps to set up Microsoft Outlook and configure an E-mail account.

Example of Microsoft Outlook 2010

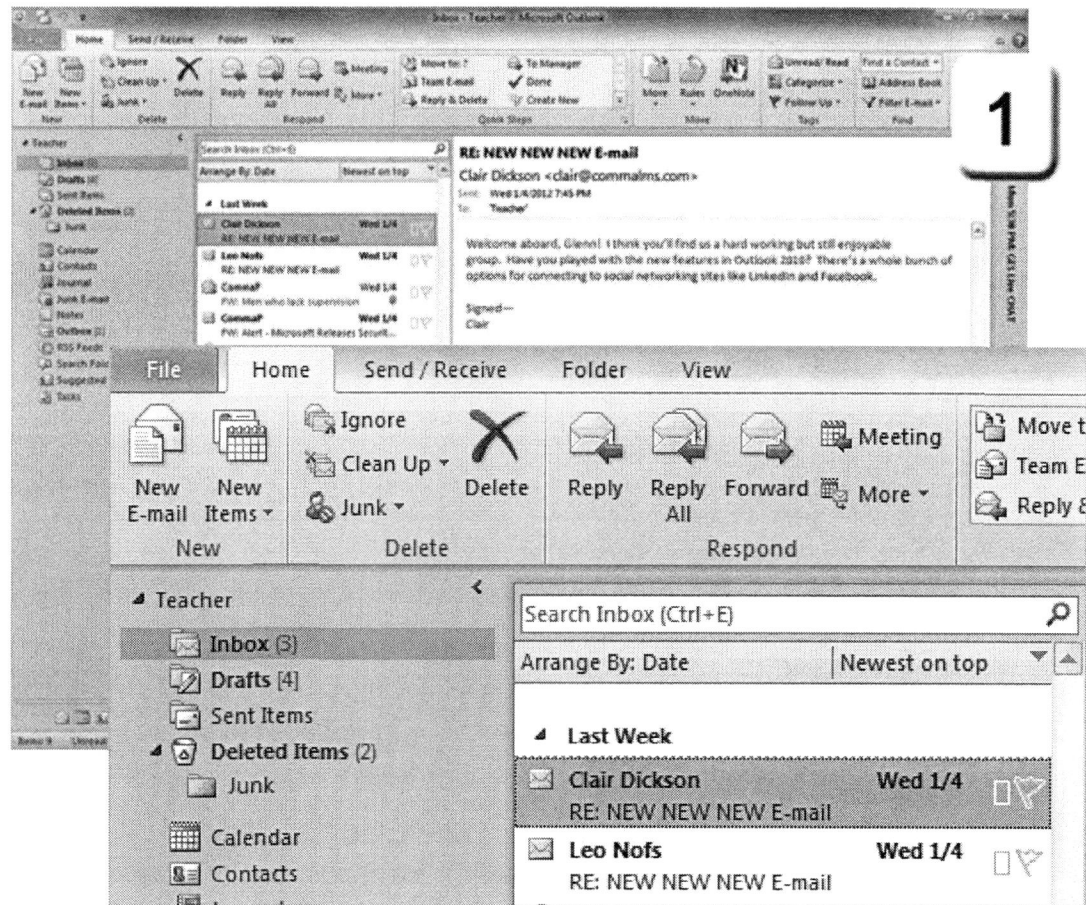

Start with the Inbox
2. Review a Sample Inbox
The Inbox is your mailbox. By default the **Inbox** is arranged by Date, the newest E-mail may be on top.

New E-mail that is unread is Bold and the envelope is closed. E-mail that you have is not Bold and the envelope is open.

What Else Do You See? E-mail that has an **Attachment**, say a picture, has a little paper clip. You can **Preview** the Message (the E-mail letter) or the Attachment (the Truck picture in this example).

These are the same clues in most email programs. Keep going...

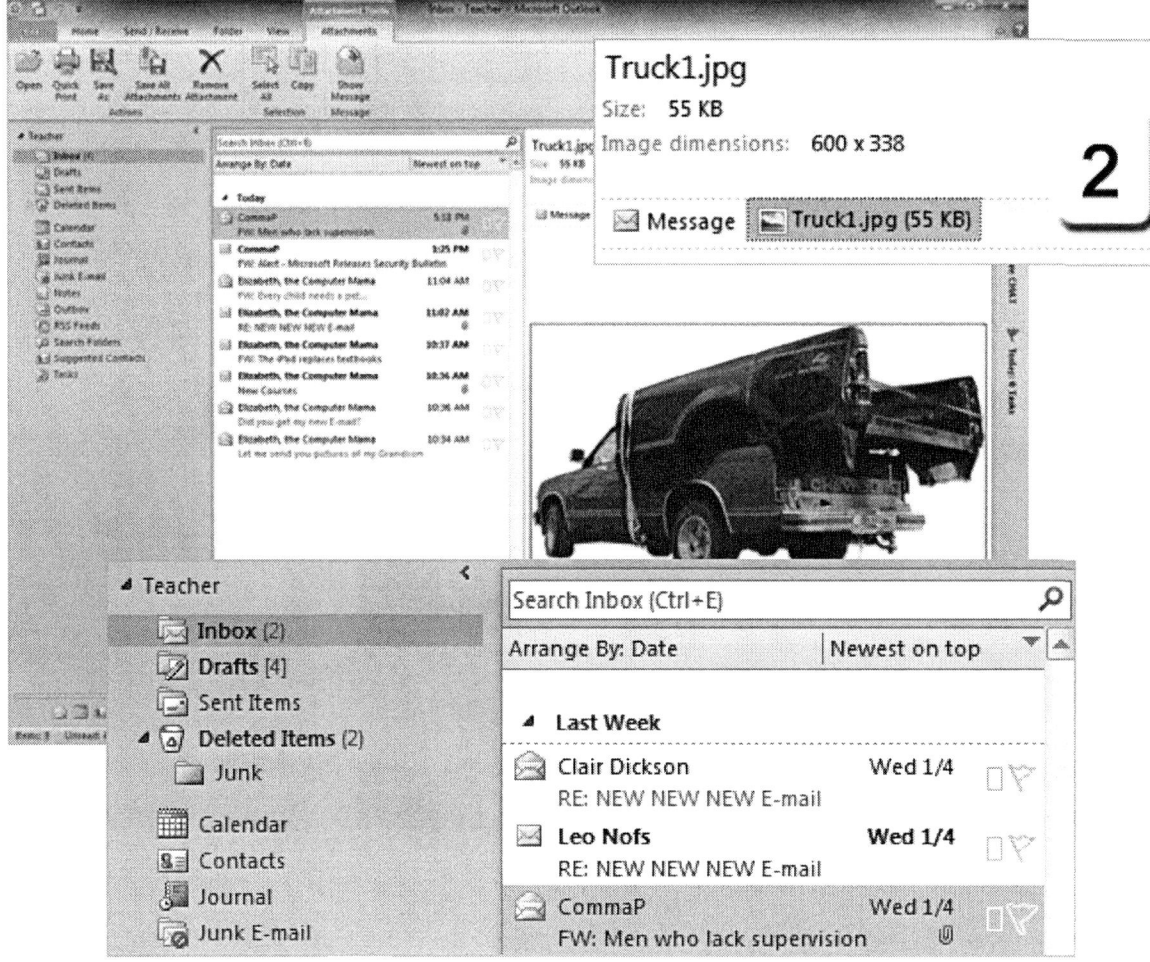

Exam 77-884: Microsoft Outlook 2010
1. Managing the Outlook Environment
1.3. Arrange the Content Pane: Navigation Pane

Manage the View

When you start Microsoft Outlook, your screen may or may not match the images in this computer guide. You can change the **Layout** if you wish.

3. Try it: Change the Layout
Go to **View ->Layout.**

What Do You See? The options include:
Navigation Pane
Reading Pane
To-Do Bar

What Else Do You See? There is also a People Pane that displays all of your activities, say meetings, E-mails and Notes, with this person. We will set up the People Pane and social network connectors later.

Keep going...

View ->Layout

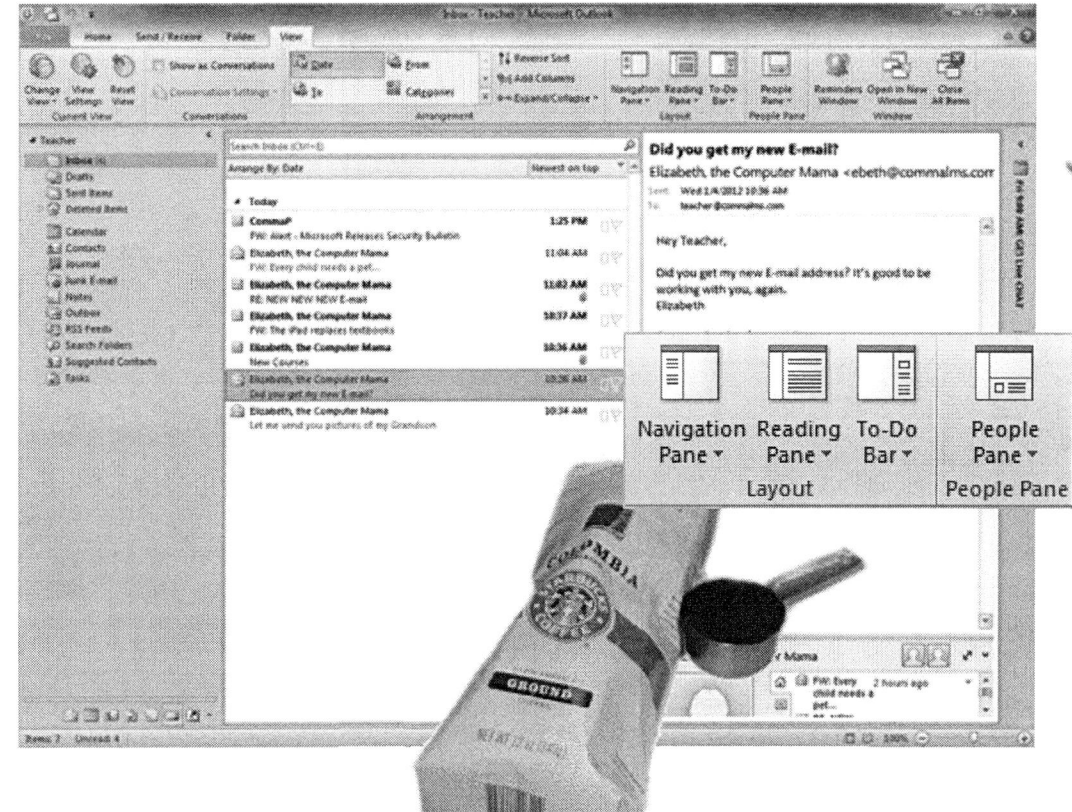

Exam 77-884: Microsoft Outlook 2010
1. Managing the Outlook Environment
1.3. Arrange the Content Pane: Navigation Pane

Layout: Navigation Pane

The **Navigation Pane** lets you choose a folder, say the Inbox, Calendar, or Journal.

4. Try it: Show the Navigation Pane
Go to **View ->Layout->Navigation Pane.**
Select: **Normal**.

What Do You See? The Navigation Pane should be available on the left side of Outlook. At the top is the name of the Mailbox. The one on this page belongs to Teacher. The folders are:
Inbox
Drafts
Sent Items
Deleted Items
Calendar
Contacts
Journal
Notes
Outbox
Tasks

Keep going...

View ->Layout->Navigation Pane

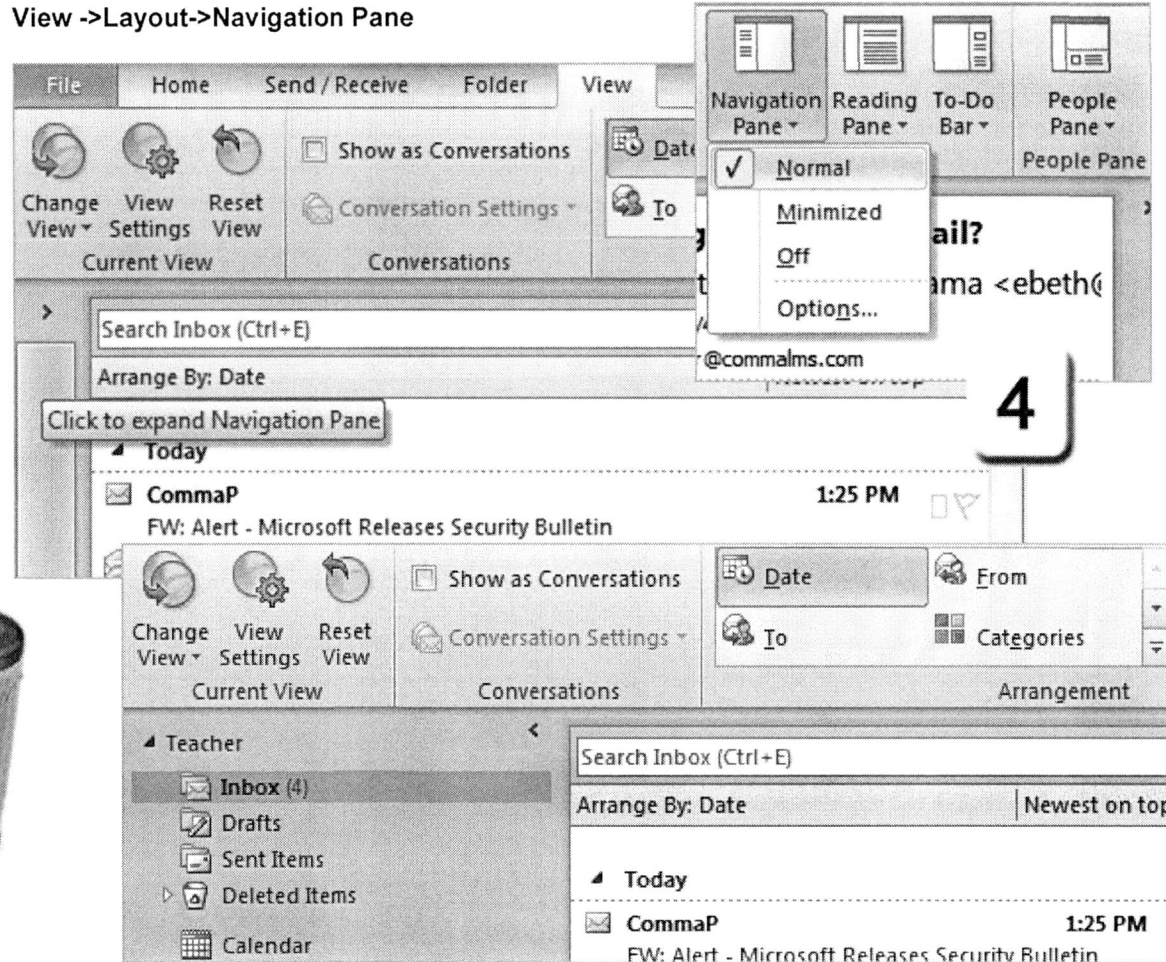

Exam 77-884: Microsoft Outlook 2010
1. Managing the Outlook Environment
1.3. Arrange the Content Pane: Navigation Pane

View ->Layout->Reading Pane

Layout: Reading Pane

The **Reading Pane** displays your E-mail messages. You can choose where you would like to see the Reading Pane: Right, Bottom or Off (hidden.)

5. Try it: Change the Reading Pane
Go to **View ->Layout->Reading Pane.**
Select **Bottom**.

What Do You See? The E-mail message will be displayed on the bottom.

Keep going...!

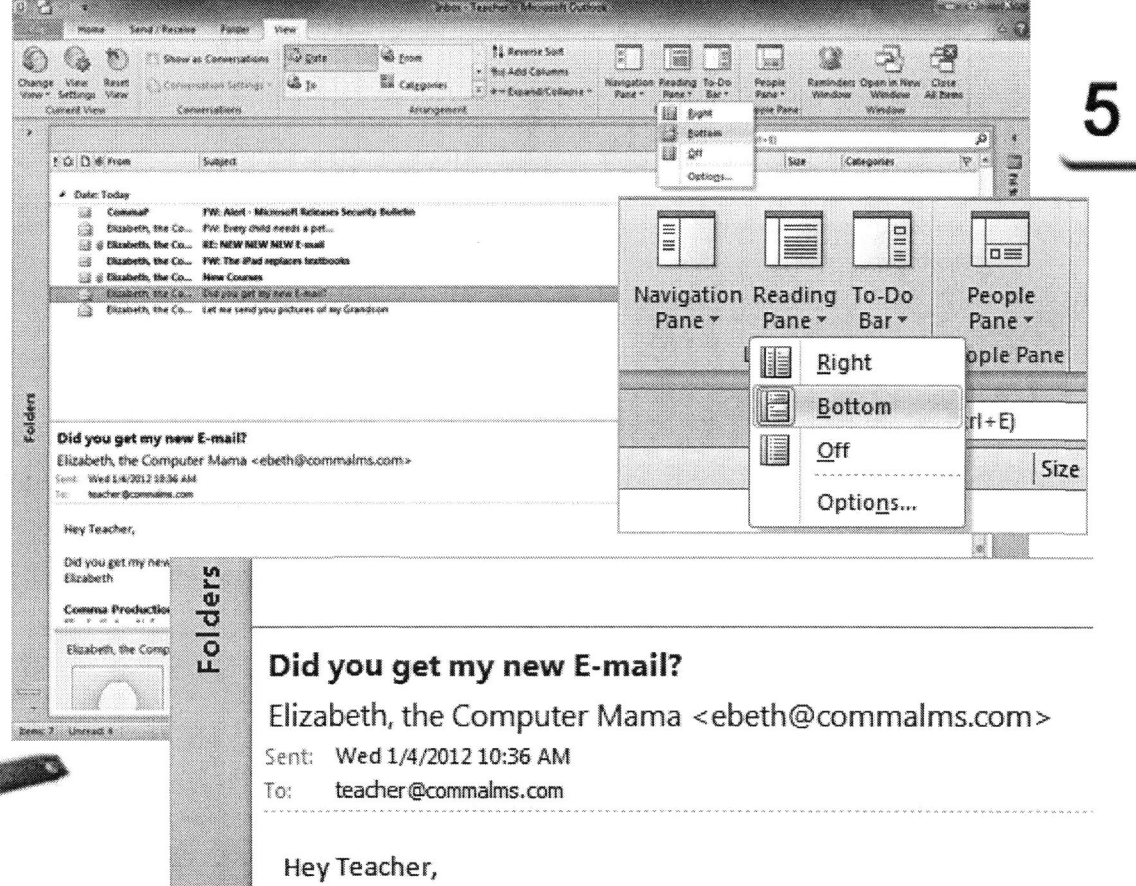

Exam 77-884: Microsoft Outlook 2010
1. Managing the Outlook Environment
1.3. Arrange the Content Pane: Reading Pane

5

Layout: To-Do Bar

The **To-Do Bar** is a list of Appointments and Tasks. The To-Do Bar rides on the right side of Outlook. This pane can be shown as Normal (expanded), Minimized (collapsed) or Off (hidden).

6. Try it: Change the To-Do Bar Layout
Go to **View ->Layout->To-Do Bar**.
Select **Normal**.

What Do You See? The To-Do Bar should be available on the right side of Outlook.

What Else Do You See? You can show the Date Navigator, Appointments and Task List if you wish. We will work with the Appointments and Tasks in the lessons on scheduling and Calendars. You can make the To-Do Bar **Minimized** if you wish.

View ->Layout->To-Do Bar

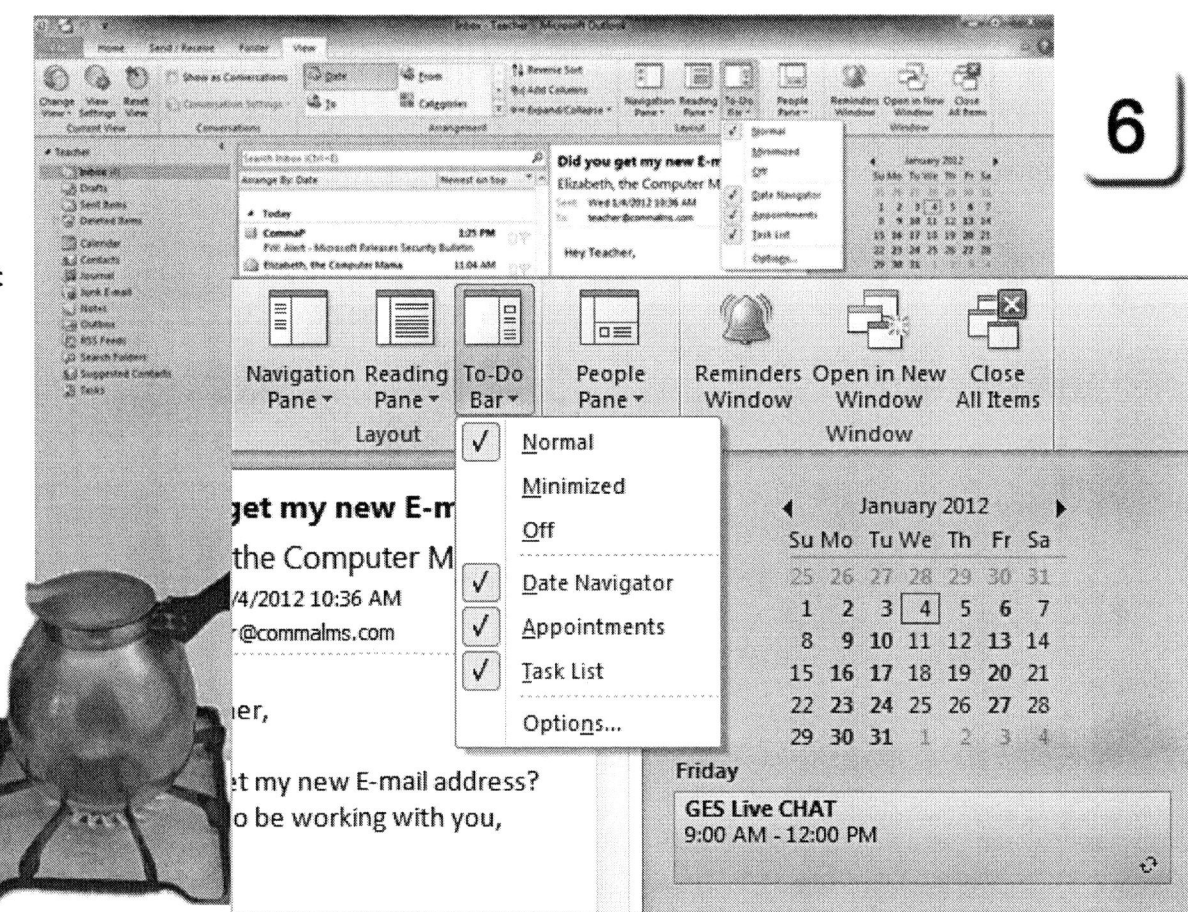

Exam 77-884: Microsoft Outlook 2010
1. Managing the Outlook Environment
1.3. Arrange the Content Pane: To-Do Bar

Create a New E-Mail

The next pages will walk through the steps to create a new E-mail. These lessons work best if you have someone who can respond to your E-mails and share in your practice.

If you do not have a partner, please follow the lessons and address the E-mail to yourself.

Try it: Create a New E-mail Message
Microsoft Outlook is open.
The Inbox is selected.

1. Go to **Home-> New->New E-Mail.**

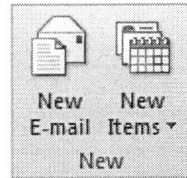

2. Enter an E-mail Address
3. Type the Subject: NEW NEW NEW E-mail
4. Enter your E-mail address.
5. Click on the **Send** button
Your message should arrive in the Inbox.
Keep going.

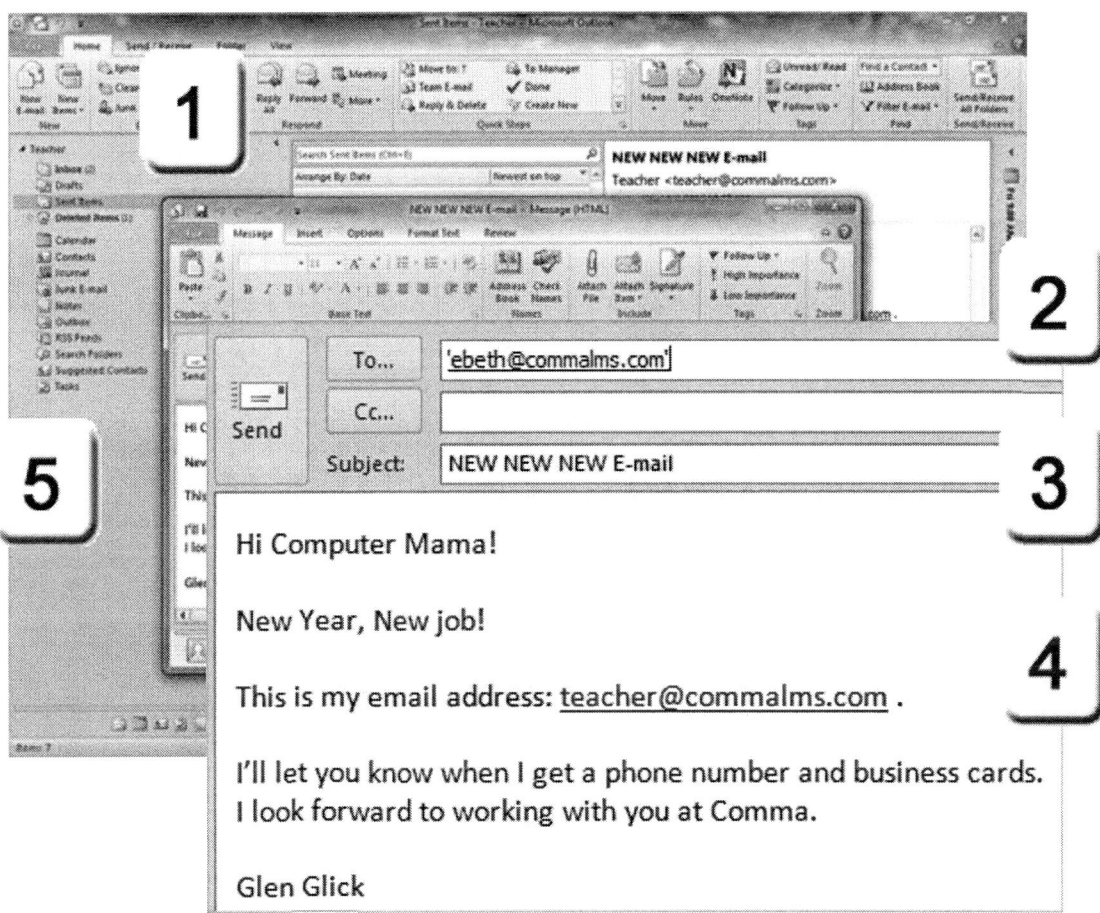

Hi Computer Mama!

New Year, New job!

This is my email address: teacher@commalms.com .

I'll let you know when I get a phone number and business cards.
I look forward to working with you at Comma.

Glen Glick

Exam 77-884: Microsoft Outlook 2010
2. Creating and Formatting Item Content
2.1. Create and send email messages: Plain Text

Return to Sender

What are the steps you can take to **Reply** to a message in your Inbox?

Try it: Reply to an E-mail
In this example, the "New New New E-mail" message is selected.
Go to **Home ->Respond->Reply.**

What Do You See? When you click on Reply, Outlook will create a new E-mail message and address it to the Sender.

The Subject begins with "RE:" which means it is "regarding" your message.

Type a response and click **Send.**
Your reply should arrive in the Inbox.

Keep going...

Home ->Respond->Reply

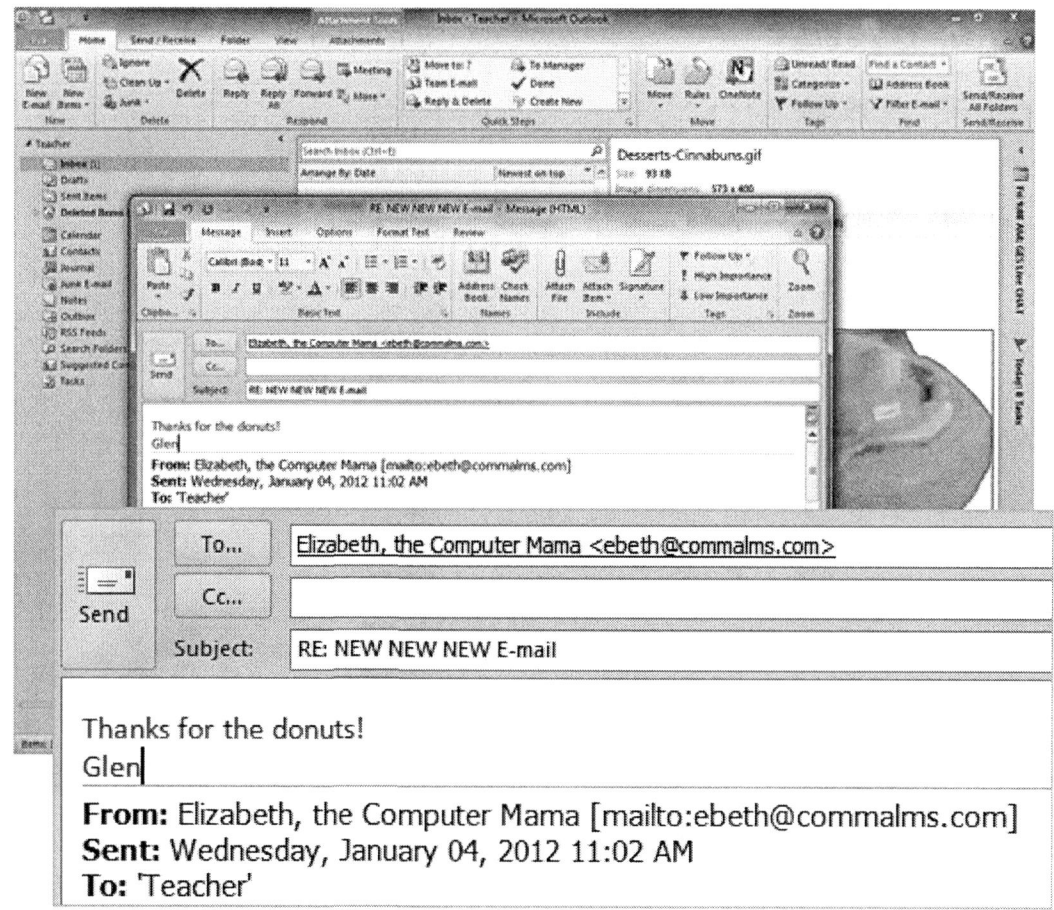

Exam 77-884: Microsoft Outlook 2010
2. Creating and Formatting Item Content
2.1. Create and send email messages: Reply to a Message

From Me to You

There are several ways you can respond to an E-mail: Reply, Reply to All and **Forward**.

Reply and Reply to All sends a message back. Forward sends it on to someone else. Here are the steps.

Try it: Forward a Message
Select a message in the Inbox.
Go to **Home ->Respond->Forward.**
Enter a different E-mail address.

What Do You See? In the example on this page, the E-mail from Clair was forwarded to Leo. The Subject line begins with "FW:" which indicates the message was forwarded.

Keep going...

Memo to Self: Please do NOT use the sample E-mail addresses shown in these screen shots.

Home ->Respond->Forward

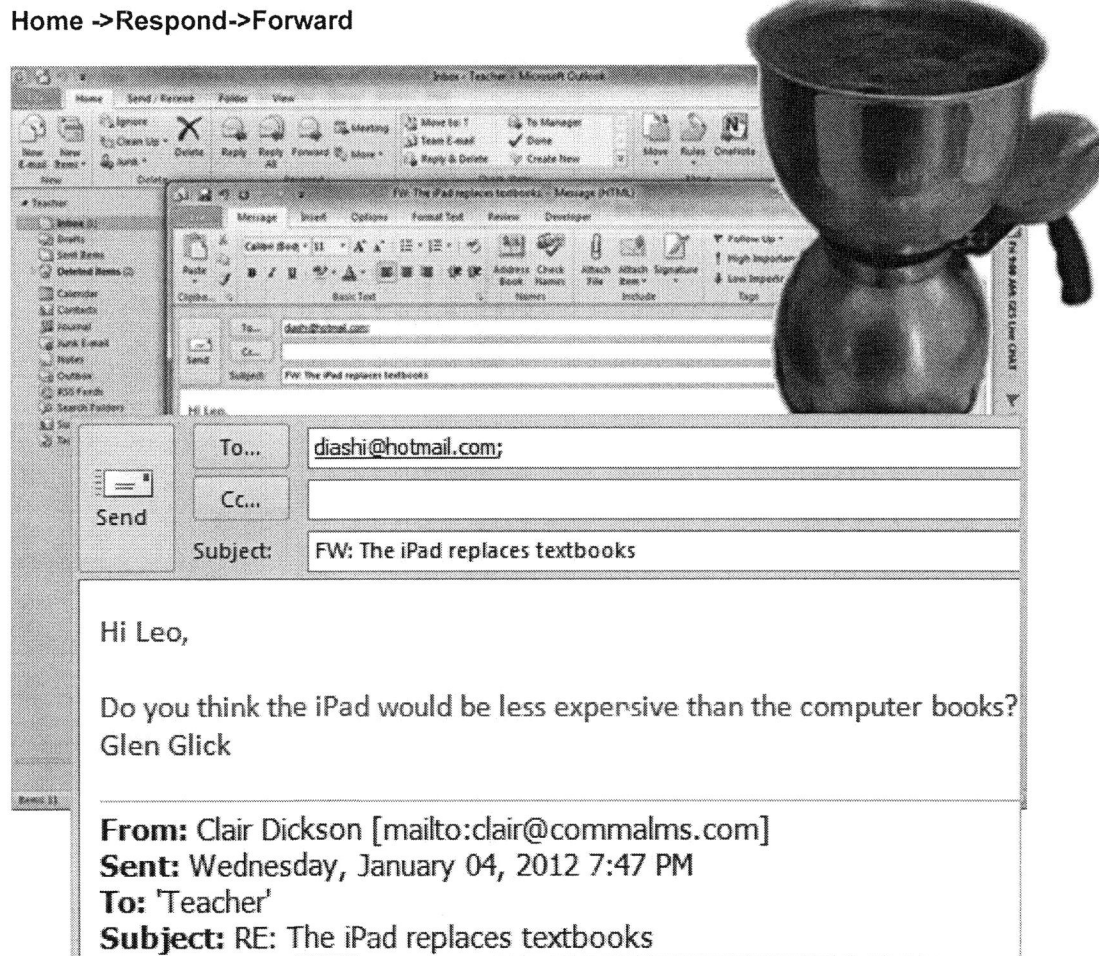

To...	diashi@hotmail.com;
Cc...	
Subject:	FW: The iPad replaces textbooks

Hi Leo,

Do you think the iPad would be less expensive than the computer books?
Glen Glick

From: Clair Dickson [mailto:clair@commalms.com]
Sent: Wednesday, January 04, 2012 7:47 PM
To: 'Teacher'
Subject: RE: The iPad replaces textbooks

Exam 77-884: Microsoft Outlook 2010
2. Creating and Formatting Item Content
2.1. Create and send email messages: Forward a Message

The E-mail Ribbons

Button, button whose got the button? There are two sets of Ribbons in these examples: Outlook and the Message both have Ribbons. The Home Ribbon in Outlook manages the Inbox. The Home Ribbon includes New and Respond. The E-mail Message also has a set of Ribbons for formatting content.

1. Try it: Format with Basic Text
Go to **Home ->New->New E-Mail.**
A new E-mail message should open.

What Do You See? The Untitled Message has the following Ribbons:
File
Message
Insert
Options
Format Text
Review

Keep going...

Home ->New->New E-Mail

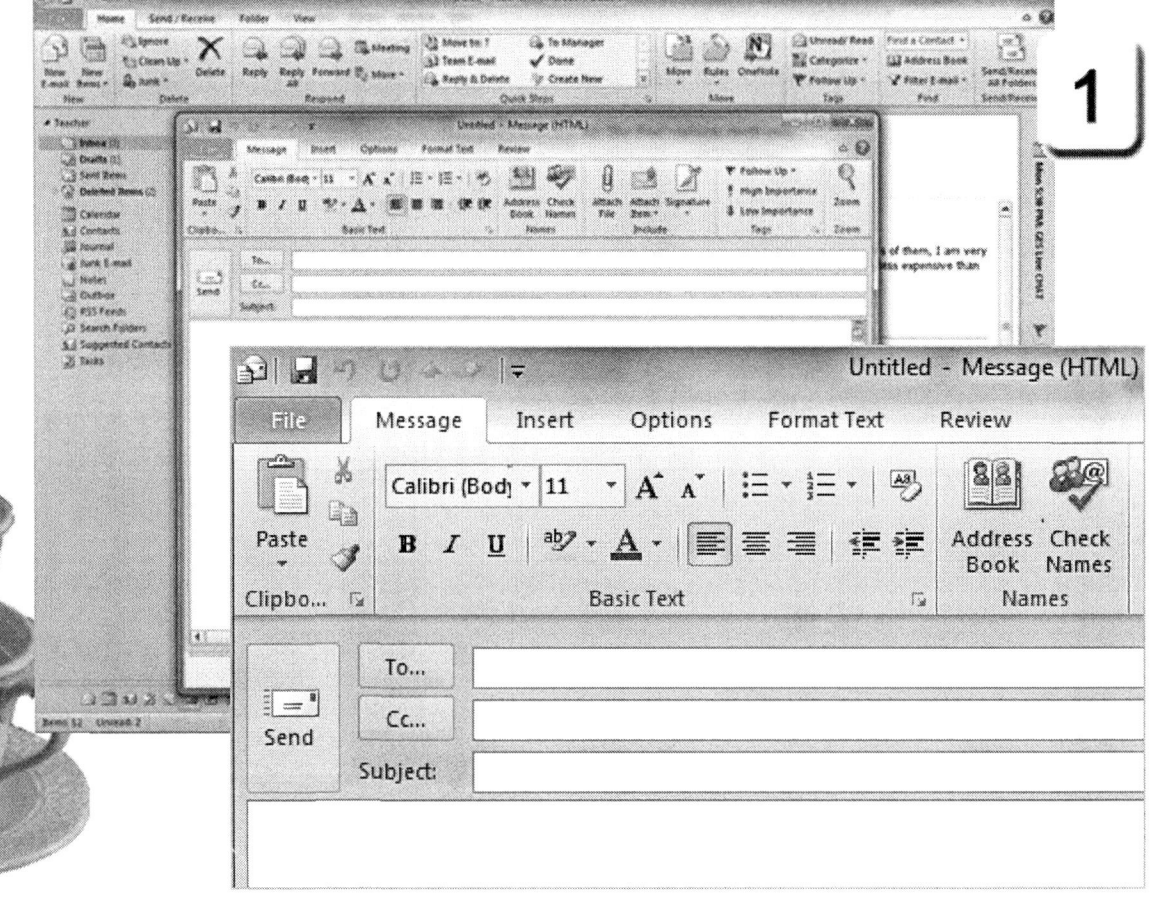

Exam 77-884: Microsoft Outlook 2010
2. Creating and Formatting Item Content
2.1. Create and send email messages: Plain Text

Basic Text Formatting

Basic, or Plain Text, formatting is compatible with most E-mail programs, including Gmail (Google) and Hotmail (Microsoft). Basic Text makes key words big, bold and colorful.

2. Try it: Format with Basic Text

A new, untitled Message is open.
Enter the following text in the Message Box:
Basic Text can be formatted:
Charlotte's Website

Select the text: Charlotte's Website.
Go to **Message ->Basic Text->Font.**
Select a Font: **Tahoma**

Go to **Message ->Basic Text->Size.**
Select a Size: **48**

Go to **Message ->Basic Text->Color.**
Select a Color: **Blue**

Enter your E-mail Address.
Enter the Subject: Basic Text.
Click **Send**. An E-mail with Basic Formatting should arrive in your Inbox. Keep going...

Message ->Basic Text

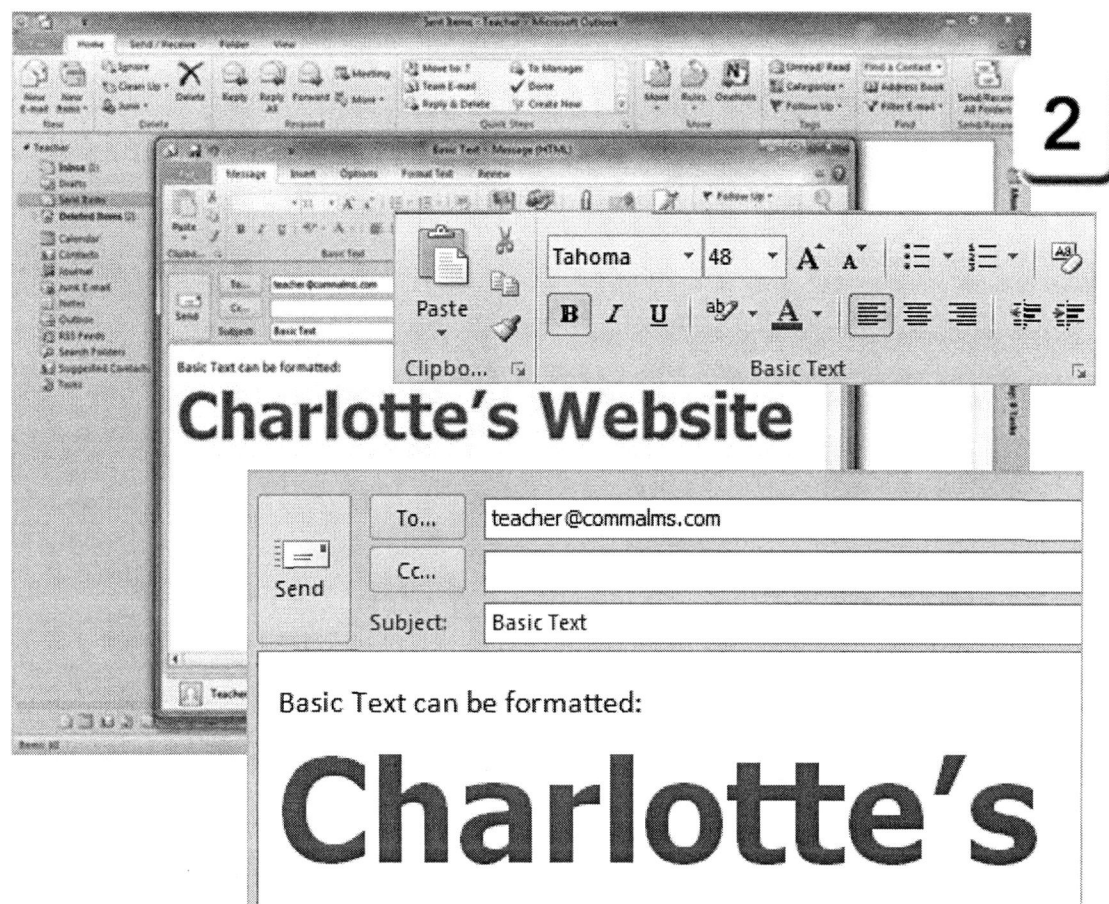

Exam 77-884: Microsoft Outlook 2010
2. Creating and Formatting Item Content
2.1. Create and send email messages: Plain Text

Rich Text Formatting

Microsoft Word is the word processor for Outlook. The Rich Text options that you use in Word can be found on the **Format Text** Ribbon.

3. Try it: Format the Font
Go to **Home ->New->New E-Mail.**
Enter your own E-mail Address.
Enter the Subject: Rich Text

Enter the following:
Charlotte's Website
Farm Fresh Food

Select: Charlotte's
Go to **Format Text->Font->Font.**
Select a Font: **Tahoma**
Go to **Format Text->Font->Size.**
Select a Size: **24**
Go to **Format Text->Font->Color.**
Select a Color: **Dark Blue.**

Select: Charlotte's, again.
Go to **Clipboard->Format Painter.**
Use the little yellow paintbrush to format the word Website: Tahoma, 24 pt. Dark Blue. Keep going...

Format Text ->Font

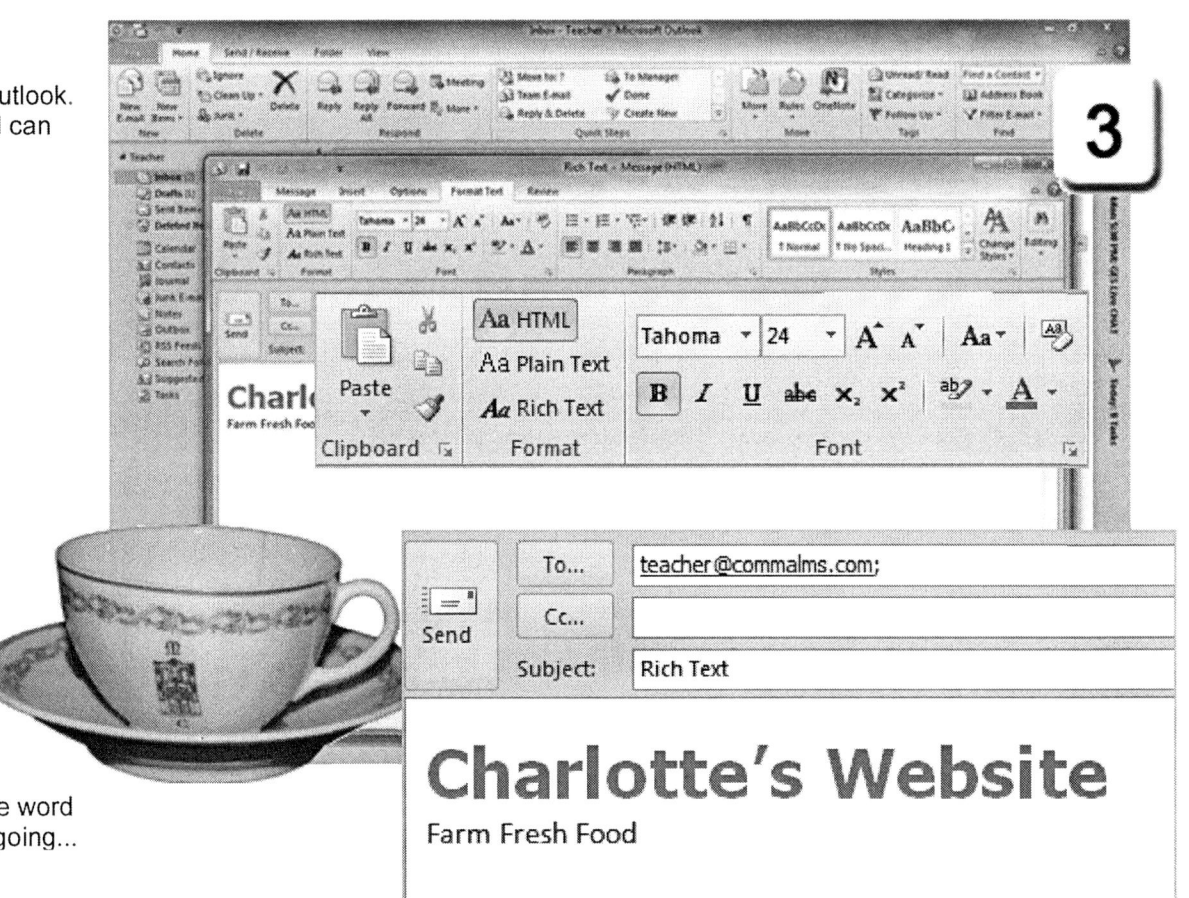

Exam 77-884: Microsoft Outlook 2010
2. Creating and Formatting Item Content
2.1. Create and send email messages: Use the Format Painter

Format Text: Paragraph

The Paragraph Group has options for Bullets and Numbering.

4. Try it: Create a Bulleted List
Add the following text:
Fruits
Veggies
Sweets

Select the new text.
Go to **Format Text ->Paragraph.**
Click on **Multilevel List.**
Choose a format from the List Library.

Place your cursor after Sweets.
Type ENTER to create a new item.
Type TAB to indent the new item.

Add the following text:
Apple Cider Crisp
Kiwi Lime Pie
Banana Fana Fo

Looks good. Keep going...

Format Text ->Paragraph->Multilevel List

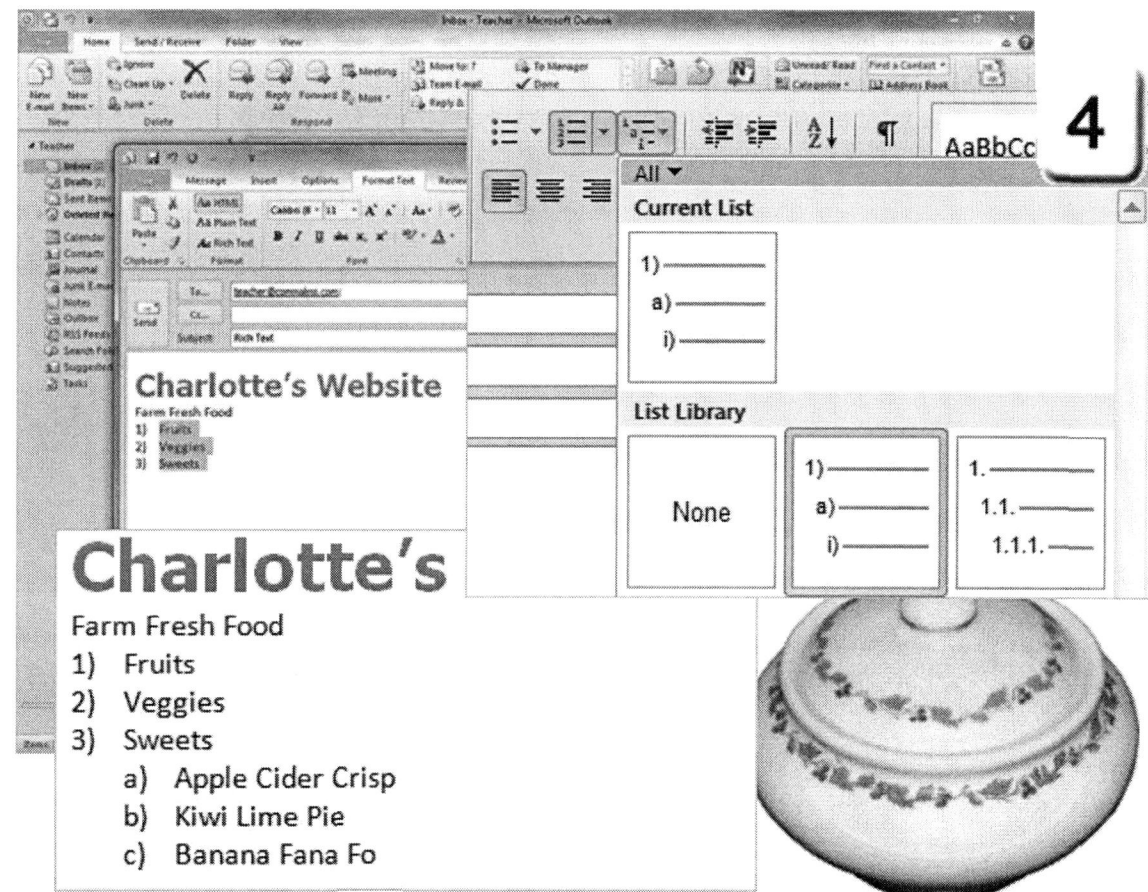

Exam 77-884: Microsoft Outlook 2010
2. Creating and Formatting Item Content
2.4. Format item content: Use Formatting Tools

Apply Quick Styles

Quick Styles format text consistently. The Quick Style formatting is based on use: Headlines, Text, Titles and Quotes.

5. Try it: Apply the Text Styles
The sample E-mail is still open.

Select the text: Charlotte's Website
Go to **Format Text ->Styles**.
Select a Style: **Heading1**.

Select the text: Farm Fresh Food
Go to **Format Text ->Styles**.
Select a Style: **Heading2**.

What Do You See? Heading1 has a larger Font Size than Heading2. Headings 1 and 2 have different Font Colors as well.

Keep going...

Format Text ->Styles

Exam 77-884: Microsoft Outlook 2010
2. Creating and Formatting Item Content
2.4. Format item content: Apply Styles

Change the Style

Microsoft Outlook has several templates in the **Quick Styles gallery**. These Styles are similar to the ones in Microsoft Word, Excel and PowerPoint.

6. Try it: Choose a Different Style

The sample E-mail is open and formatted with two Styles: Heading1 and Heading2.

Go to **Format Text ->Styles.**
Go **Change Styles->Style Sets.**
Select a Style Set: **Modern.**

What Do You See? The Style Sets include Elegant, Fancy, Formal and others. As you run your mouse over the Style Set, you should see a Live Preview of the Style.

Keep going...

Format Text ->Styles->Change Styles-> Style Set

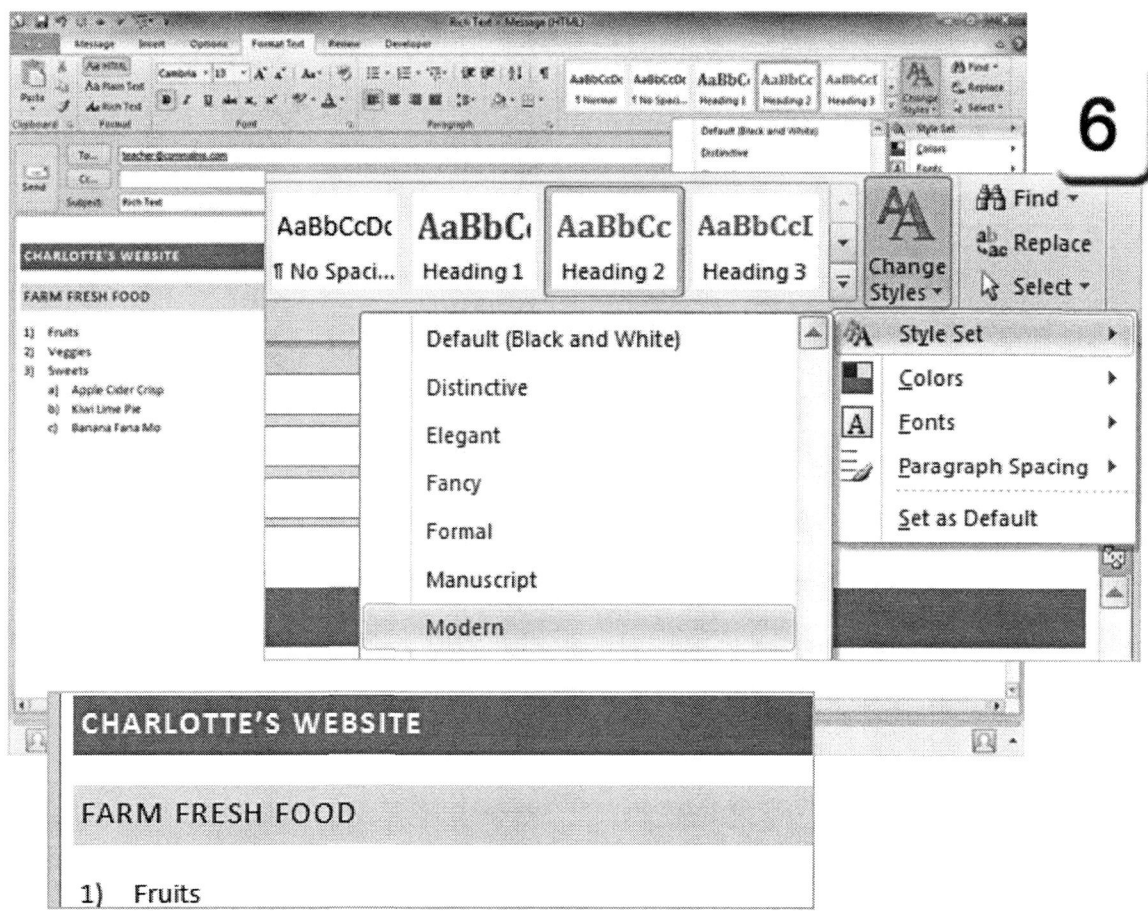

Exam 77-884: Microsoft Outlook 2010
2. Creating and Formatting Item Content
2.4. Format item content: Change Styles

Change the Style Color

Each Style Set edits the Font (type, size, color) as well as the Paragraph (alignment, indentation and line spacing). You can format the Color, Fonts and Paragraph Spacing separately if you wish.

7. Try it: Change The Style Colors
The sample E-mail is open and formatted with two Styles: Heading1 and Heading2.

Go to **Format Text ->Styles**.
Go to **Change Styles->Colors**.
Select a Style Color: **Metro**.

What Do You See? Headings 1 and 2 in the message have been formatted in the new Style Colors.

Keep going...

Format Text ->Styles->Change Styles-> Color

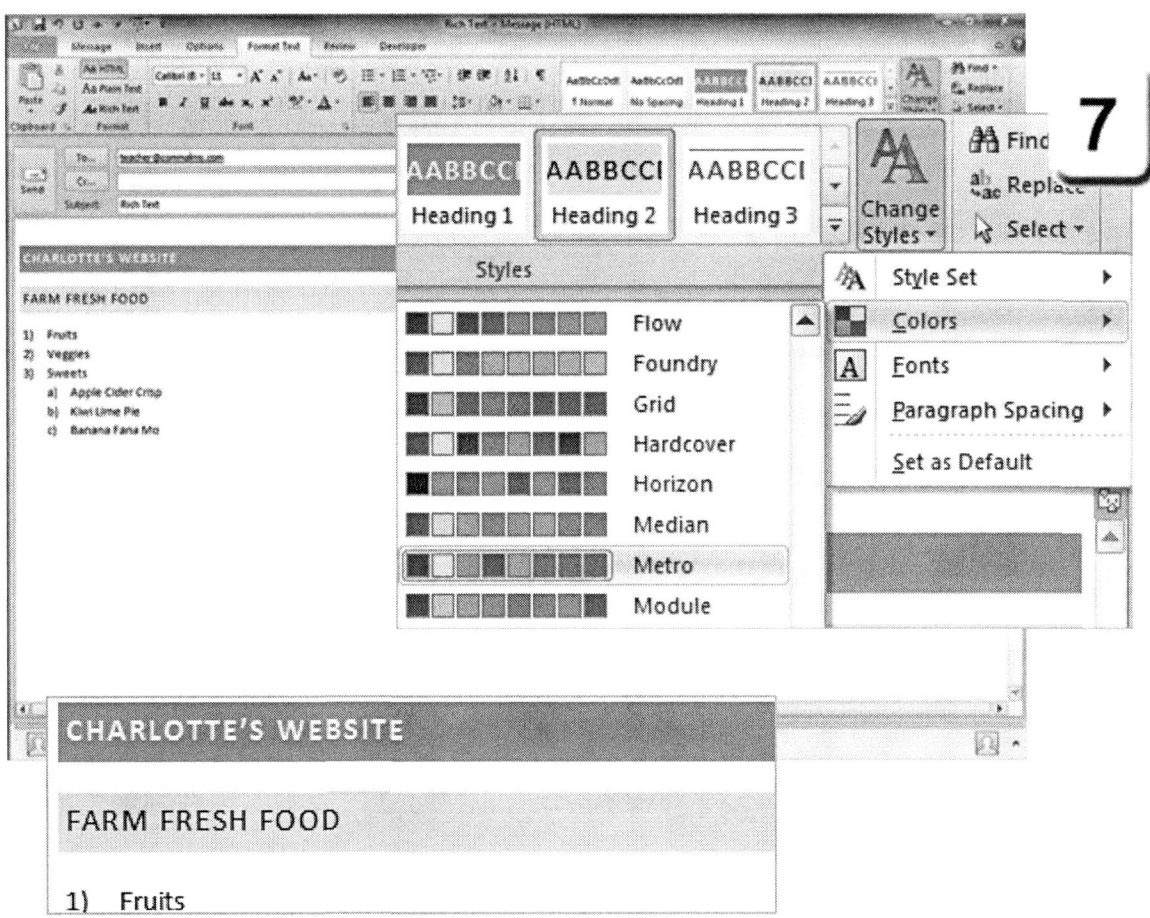

Exam 77-884: Microsoft Outlook 2010
2. Creating and Formatting Item Content
2.4. Format item content: Modify the Styles

Find More Style Options

Microsoft Outlook has several Quick Styles that you can use to format your E-mail message. You can also modify one of the Styles to create your own Quick Style.

You can edit the Quick Styles in the **Style Pane**. Here are the steps to open the Styles Pane.

1. Try it: Find More Style Options
Select the text: Charlotte's Website
Go to **Format Text ->Styles.**
Click on the **Options** arrow in the bottom right-hand corner.

What Do You See? The **Styles** Pane should open. Heading1, the formatting we applied to the text, should be highlighted.

Keep going...

Format Text ->Styles->Options

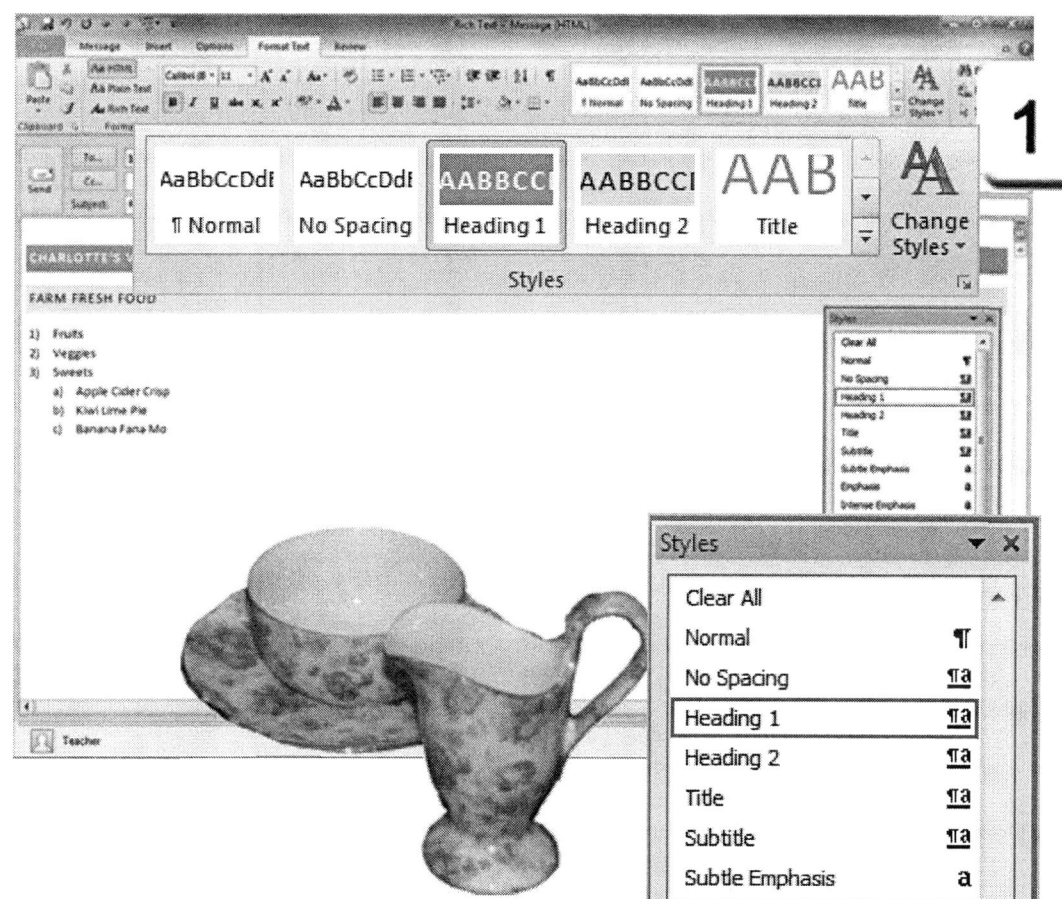

Exam 77-884: Microsoft Outlook 2010
2. Creating and Formatting Item Content
2.4. Format item content: Modify Styles

Modify a Style
2. Try it: Modify a Style
Select **Heading1**.

What Do You See? When you click on Heading1 in the Styles Pane you should see:
Update Heading1 to Match Selection
Modify...
Select All
Remove All
Delete Heading1...
Remove from Quick Style Gallery

Click on **Modify**...
Keep going, please.

Memo to Self: Say you had a long message with a lot of text that has been formatted with Heading1. You can Select All of the text that has been formatted as Heading1 and update them at the same time.

Format Text ->Styles->Options->Modify

Exam 77-884: Microsoft Outlook 2010
2. Creating and Formatting Item Content
2.4. Format item content: Modify Styles

Modify the Formatting

When you click **Modify** you will be prompted to review the Style Formatting. You can edit the Font and Paragraph settings if you wish.

3. Try it: Format the Font
Edit Heading1 as follows:
Font: Tahoma
Size: 18

What Do You See? There should be a Live Preview of the new formatting.

What Else Do You See? The Paragraph options include Alignment, Line Spacing and Indentation.

Keep going...

Format Text ->Styles->Options->Modify

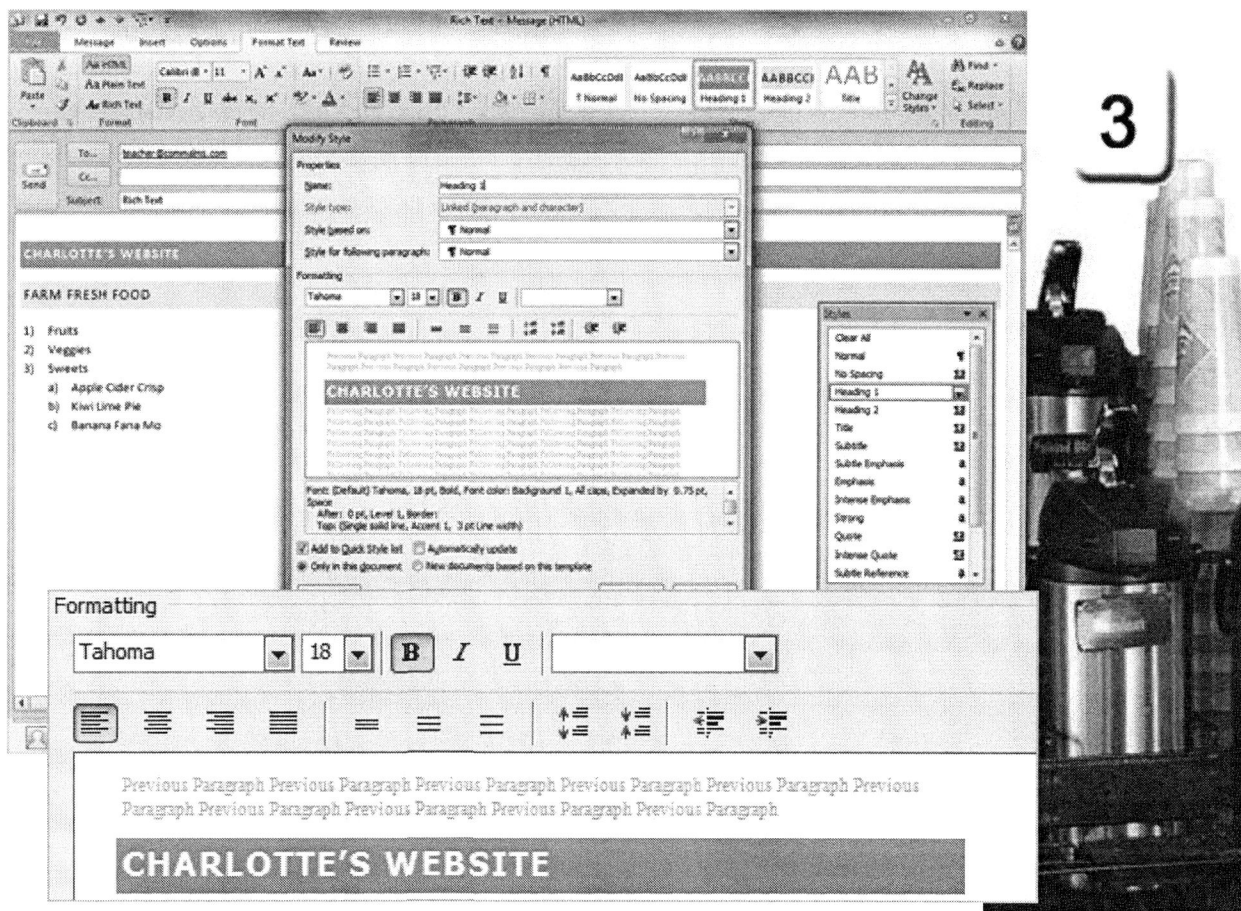

Exam 77-884: Microsoft Outlook 2010
2. Creating and Formatting Item Content
2.4. Format item content: Create Themes

Add to Quick Style List
4. Try it: Review the Options
The Style formatting is summarized at the bottom of the dialogue box. Look again at the settings just above the OK button.

Add to Quick Style List will display this Style in the Quick Styles on the Format Text Ribbon.

Only in this document adds this Style to this E-mail, only. It will not be available in the next new E-mail.

Automatically update is not selected. This option can be problematic.

When you select **New documents based on this template** all new E-mails will use this Style by default.

Click **OK** to close the Modify Style options.
Please close the Styles Pane as well.

Format Text ->Styles->Options->Modify

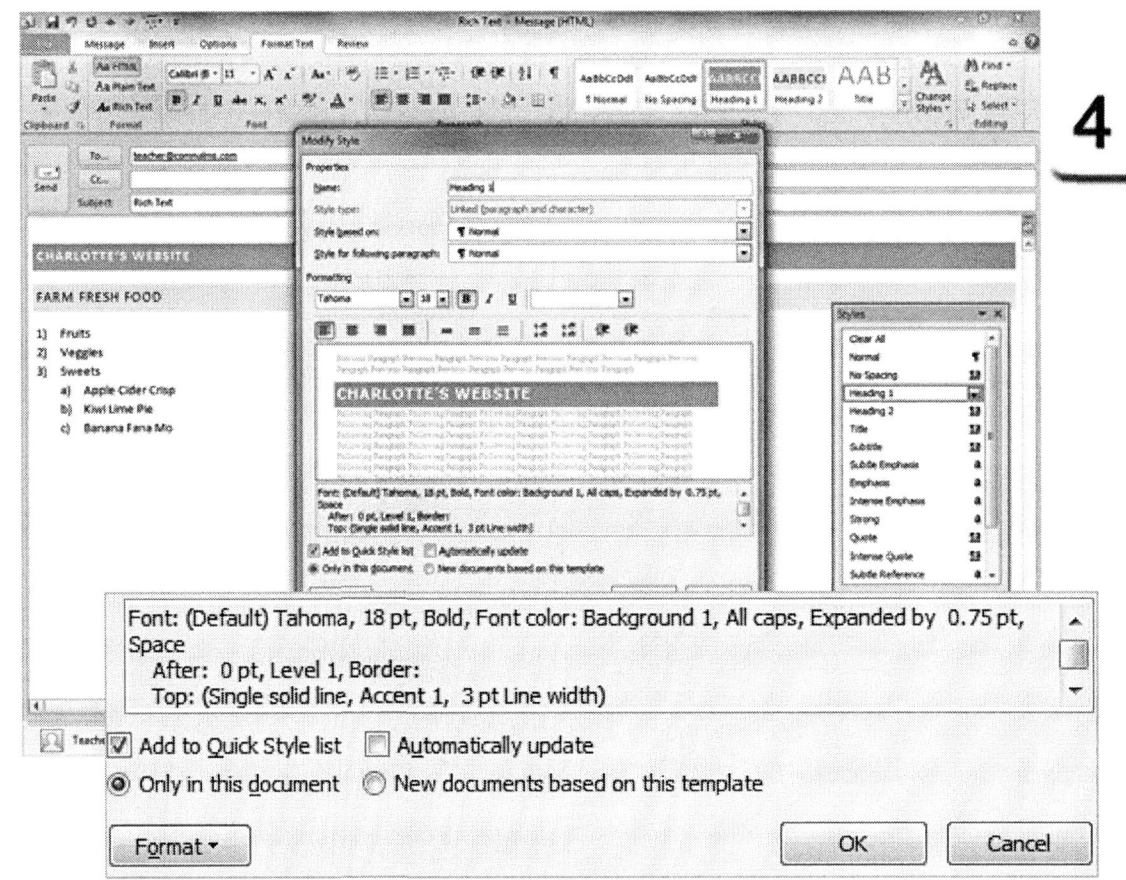

4

Exam 77-884: Microsoft Outlook 2010
2. Creating and Formatting Item Content
2.4. Format item content: Create Styles

Save as Default

Say you took some time to create a custom Style that used your company Font and Color. You can Set as Default

5. Try it: Set as Default Style
Select the text: Charlotte's Website
Go to **Format Text ->Styles.**
Go to **Change Styles-> Set as Default.**

Do This, Too: Send the E-mail
Click **Send.** An E-mail with Rich Text Formatting should arrive in your Inbox.

Very good.

Format Text ->Styles->Change Styles-> Set as Default

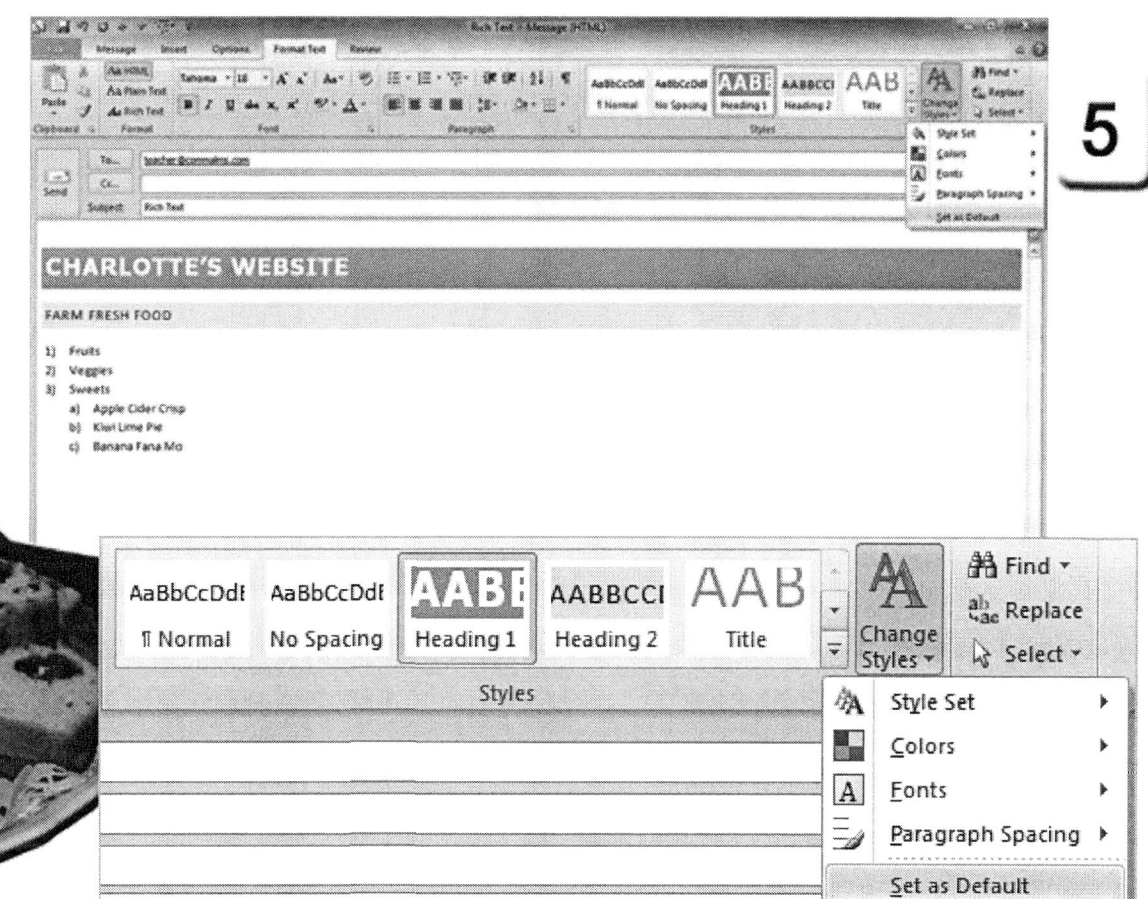

Exam 77-884: Microsoft Outlook 2010
2. Creating and Formatting Item Content
2.4. Format item content: Specify Message Content Format

Working with Rich Text

If you addressed this message to yourself, it should arrive in the Inbox. Say you received an E-mail with rich text formatting and you wanted to copy that information into another E-mail.

You can use **Paste Special** to copy and paste text without formatting if you wish.

6. Try it: Copy and Paste the Text
Go to the Inbox and select the Rich Text E-mail.
Go to **Home->Respond->Reply**.
The **Message** Ribbon should be available.

Copy the text: Charlotte's Website
Go to **Message->Clipboard->Paste Special.**

What Do You See? The Paste Special options include Rich Formatted Text (RFT), Picture, HTML (Web) and Unformatted Unicode.

Select: Unformatted Text.
Click **OK.**
The text will be pasted without formatting.

Keep going...

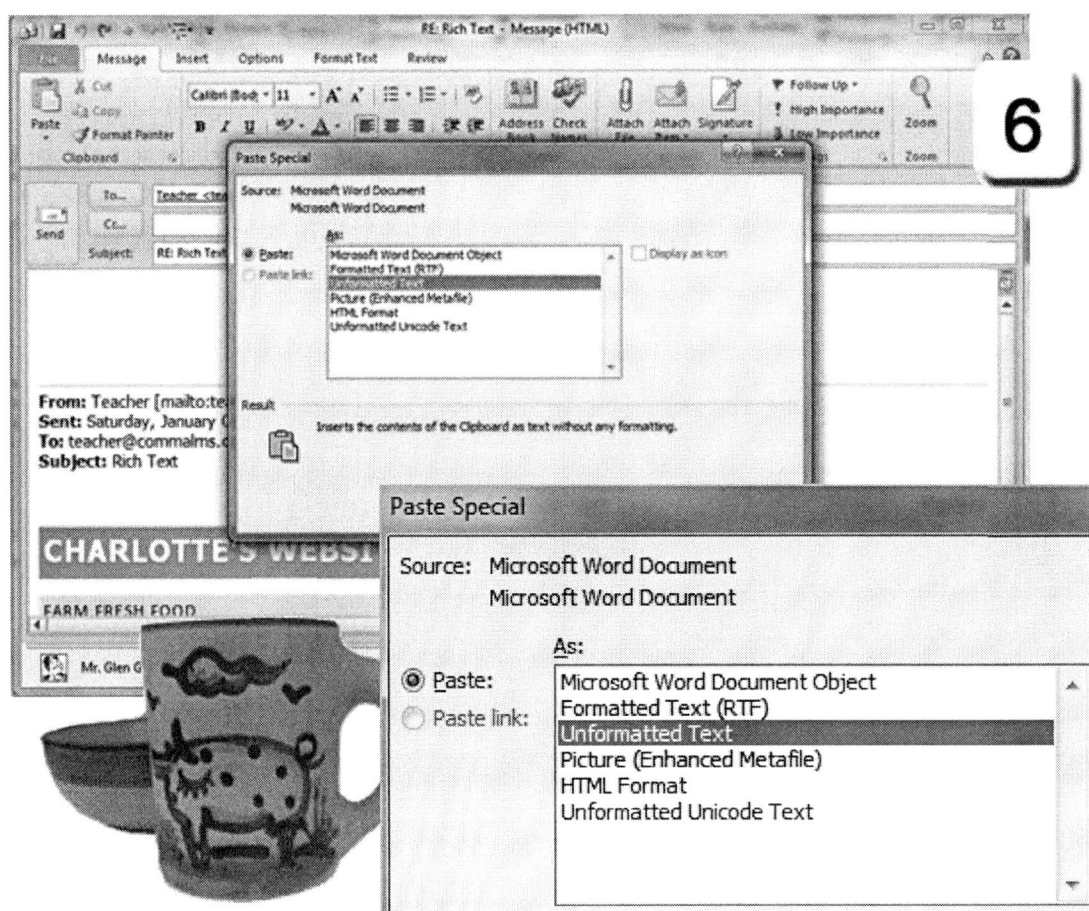

Exam 77-884: Microsoft Outlook 2010
2. Creating and Formatting Item Content
2.4. Format item content: Use Paste Special

Summary

So, Hello Microsoft Outlook. Our lesson began by changing the View: finding the Navigation Pane and the Reading Pane.

We looked at the two E-mail Ribbons as well: Message and Format Text. That was a start. Let's go a little further and see what a really good E-mail program can do.

Well, you done good. You get two cookies.

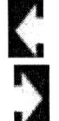

Test Yourself

1. Which of the following are Ribbons in Outlook's Mail view?
A. Home
B. Send/ Receive
C. Folder
D. View
E. Insert
Tip: Complete Guide to Outlook, page 29

2. Which is true about the Inbox?
(Select all correct answers.)
A. Unread e-mail is bold
B. By default, E-mail is sorted by recipient, in alphabetical order
C. The paper clip icon indicates that e-mail has an attachment
Tip: Complete Guide to Outlook, page 30

3. Which of the following is an option for the Reading Pane? (Give all correct answers.)
A. Reading Pane on the right, with inbox to the left
B. Reading Pane on the top, with inbox on the bottom
C. Reading pane off
Tip: Complete Guide to Outlook, page 33

4. Collapsing the To-Do Bar is the same as Hiding it.
a. True
b. False
Tip: Complete Guide to Outlook, page 34

5. In e-mail, what does the abbreviation RE stand for?
A. Reply
B. Regarding
C. Repeat
Tip: Complete Guide to Outlook, page 36

6. Which of the following are true?
(Give all correct answers.)
A. Reply sends a message back to the sender
B. Reply all sends a message to the sender and to all other original recipients
C. Forward sends a message to someone else

7. Which of the following is NOT an option for formatting an Outlook e-mail?
(Give all correct answers.)
A. Plain or Basic Text
B. Rich Text
C. Word document
Tip: Complete Guide to Outlook, page 39-40

8. Styles apply to which of the following?
(Give all correct answers.)
A. Font type
B. Font size
C. Font Color
D. Paragraph alignment
E. Indentation and Line Spacing
Tip: Complete Guide to Outlook, page 42

Application Question: When would Rich Text options in e-mail be inappropriate? When would Rich Text options be appropriate?

Messages and Messengers

Outlook E-mail Objectives

In this lesson, you will learn how to:

1. Create rich E-mail messages and specify a Theme

2. Show or Hide the From and Bcc Fields

3. Set Follow Up Flags on a Message

4. Configure the Delivery Options

5. Use the Options Ribbon to program the Message Tacking and Voting Buttons

6. View and edit the Message Properties

© 2011 Comma Productions, LLC

Lesson 3: Messages and Messengers

1. Readings
Read Lesson 3 in the Microsoft Outlook guide, page 53-81.

Project
Sample E-mails that demonstrate the Options Ribbon.

Downloads
Farm1.gif, Farm2.gif, Farm3.gif, Farm4.gif, Appplebox1.gif, Appplebox2.gif, Appplebox3.gif,

2. Practice
Complete the Practice Activity on page 82.

3. Assessment
Review the Test questions on page 82.

Message Options Ribbon

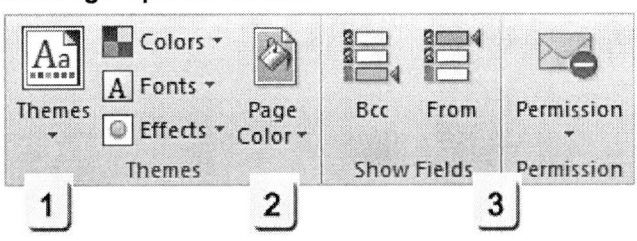

Message Options Ribbon (continued)

Menu Maps
From the **Message Options Ribbon**.
1. Options ->Themes->Themes, page 59
2. Options ->Themes-> Page Color, page 60
3. Options ->Show Fields, page 64
4. Options ->Tracking->Request a Delivery Receipt, page 67
5. Options ->Tracking-> Request a Read Receipt, page 68
6. Options ->Tracking-> Use Voting Buttons, page 70
7. Options ->More Options->Delay Delivery, page 76
8. Options ->More Options->Direct Replies To, page 79
9. Options ->More Options->More, page 80

More Menu Maps
From the **Outlook and Message Ribbons**
1. Home-> New-> New E-Mail, page 56
2. Message->Tags->Follow Up, page 65
3. Message-> Respond->Vote, page 71
4. Message ->Show->Tracking, page 73

Messages and Messengers

Messages have images and actions. The **image** draws attention to your company, your products and your brand. As we saw in the previous lesson, **Styles** can be used to format the message Text. In this lesson, we'll use **Themes** to format the E-mail message. Messages also have actions. The **actions** include Tracking, Delivery and Voting. Each E-mail can be loaded with follow up flags, receipts and even more options. If you are ready, please start Microsoft Outlook and go to the Inbox.

Start -> All Programs ->Microsoft Office-> Microsoft Office Outlook 2010

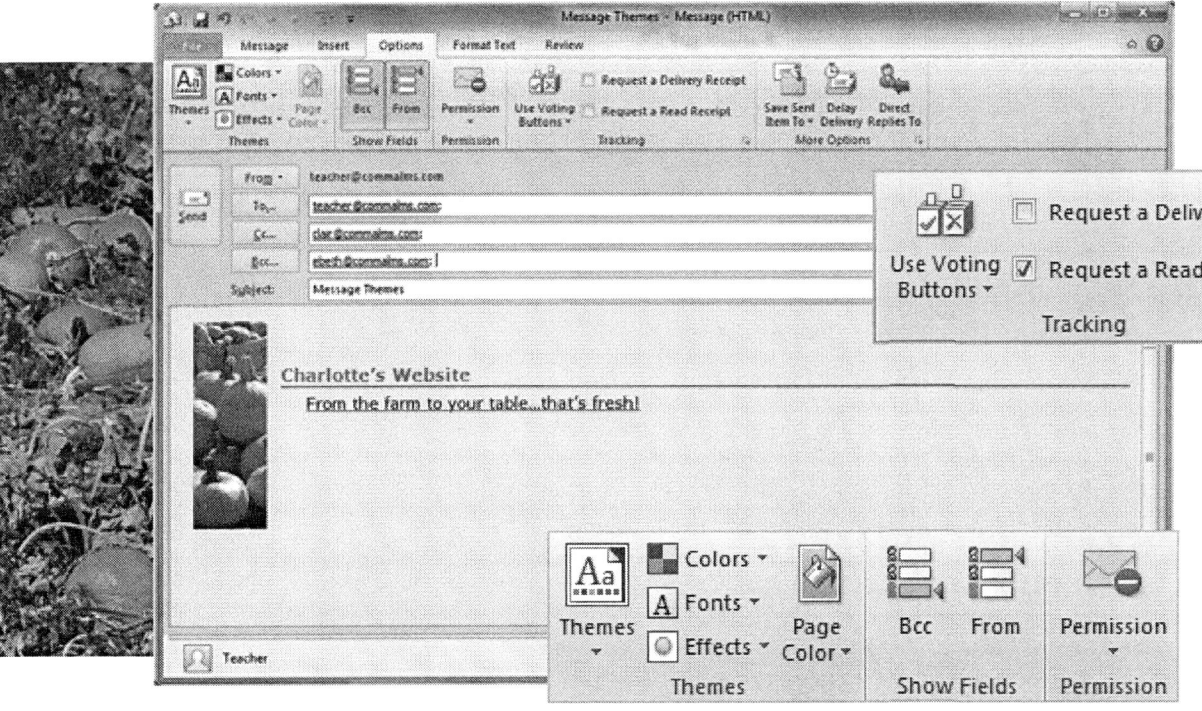

The theme for this lesson is Messages and Messengers.
The words that I say or email or text are messengers. The question is: Am I sending out angels or devils?

Many of the angels shown on these pages are from the collection of Herm and Connie Walters.

Create a New E-Mail

1. Try it: Create a New E-Mail
Go to **Home-> New-> New E-Mail.**
Enter your E-mail Address.
Enter the Subject: Message Themes.
Type the message text:

Charlotte's Website
From the farm to your table...that's fresh!

Keep going, please...

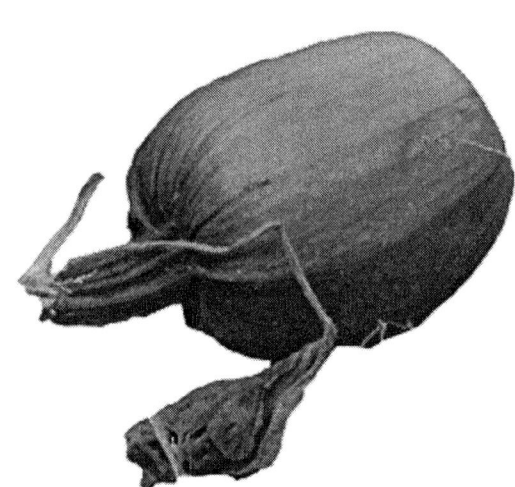

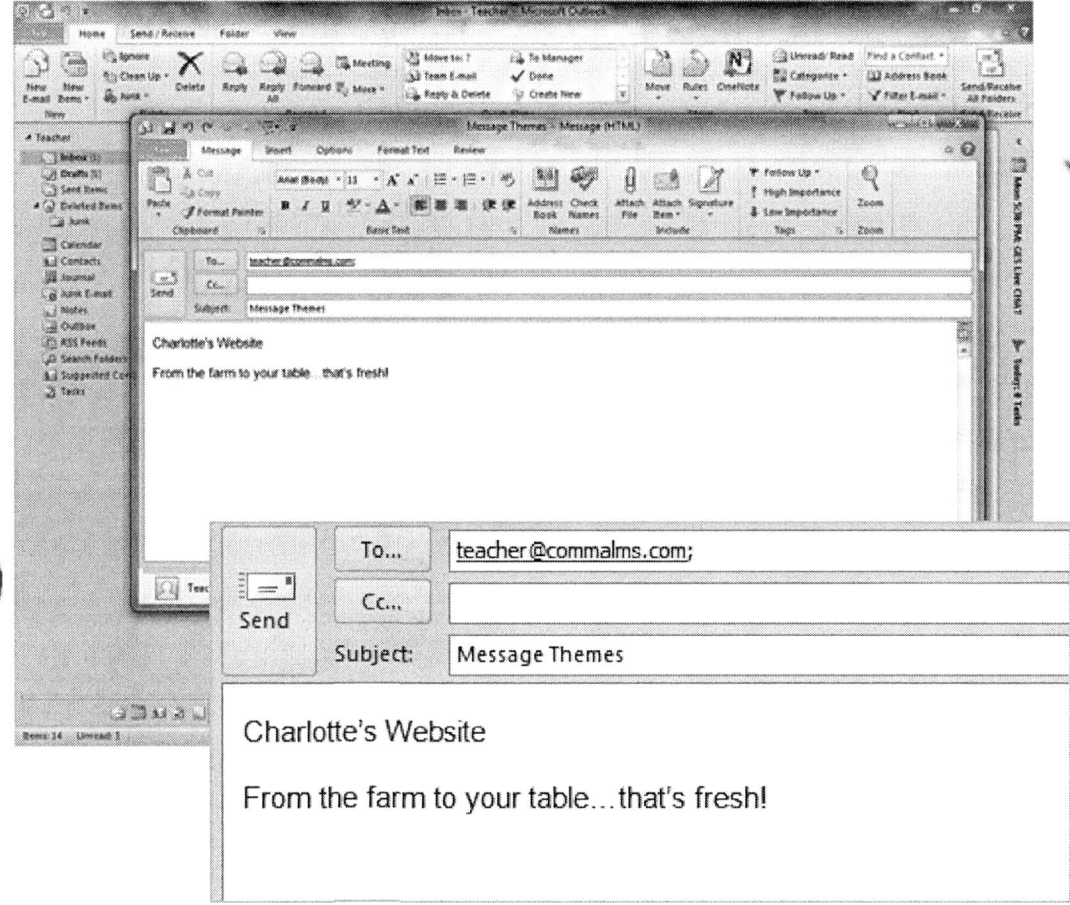

Exam 77-884: Microsoft Outlook 2010
2. Creating and Formatting Item Content
2.1. Create and send email messages: Plain Text

Use Quick Styles

2. Try it: Format the Text with Quick Styles
Select the Message Text:
Charlotte's Website.
Go to **Format Text->Styles.**
Choose a **Style**: Heading 1.

Select the Message Text:
From the farm to your table....That's fresh!.
Go to **Format Text->Styles.**
Choose a **Style**: Subtle Reference.

Keep going...

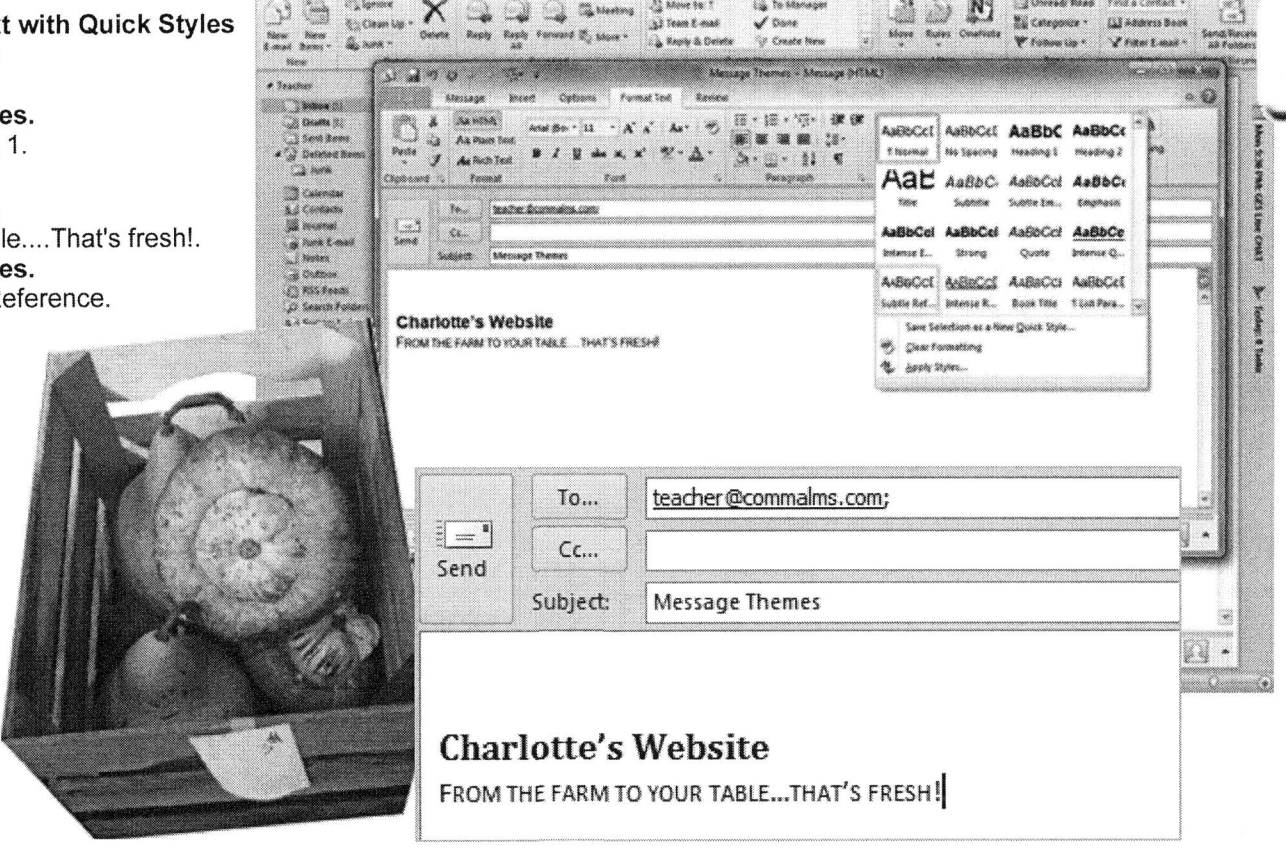

Exam 77-884: Microsoft Outlook 2010
2. Creating and Formatting Item Content
2.4. Format item content: Apply Styles

Modify the Style

Now that the text is formatted with Styles, you can use the **Style Set** to change the Font, Font Side, Alignment and Color.

3. Try it: Choose a Different Style
Go to **Format Text ->Styles**
Click on **Change Styles.**
Select a **Style**: Traditional.

Keep going...

Format Text ->Styles->Change Styles

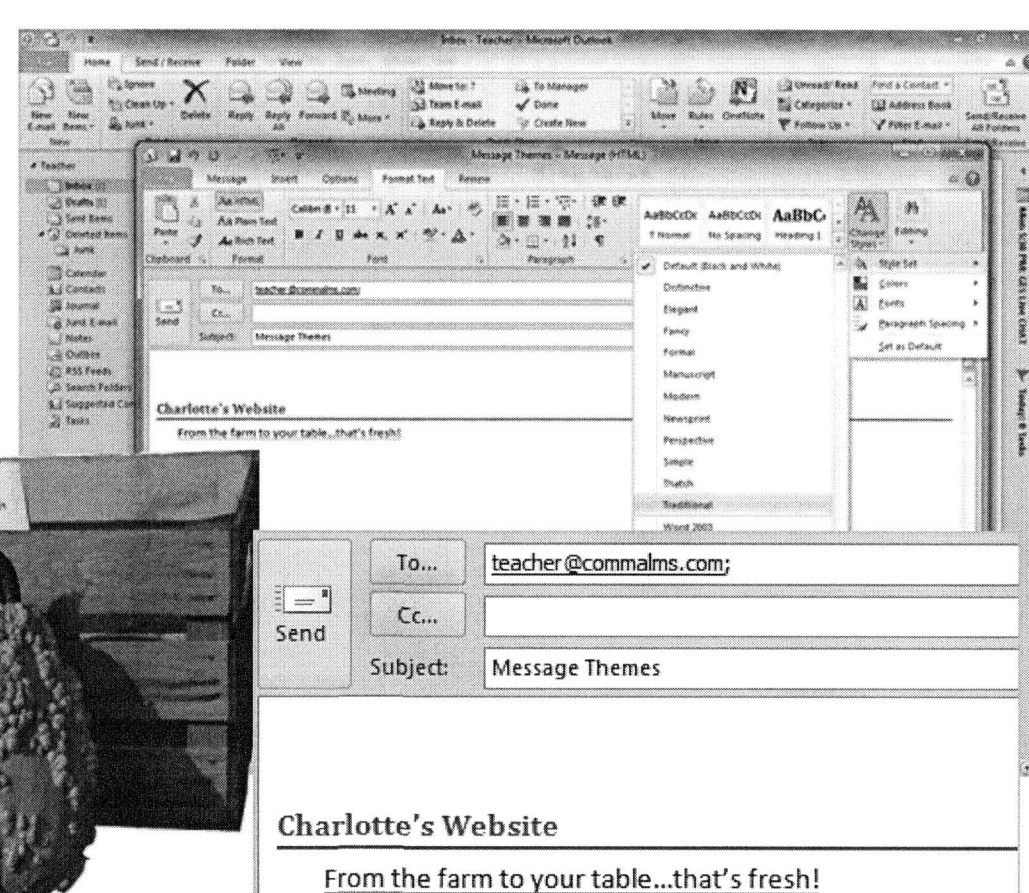

Exam 77-884: Microsoft Outlook 2010
2. Creating and Formatting Item Content
2.4. Format item content: Apply Styles

Apply a Theme

Styles format text. **Themes** are applied to everything in an E-mail message including the text, pictures, shapes and graphics.

The **Themes** are on the **Options Ribbon**.

4. Try it: Modify the Theme
The sample E-mail is open.
Go to **Options ->Themes->Themes**.
Choose a **Theme:** Grid.

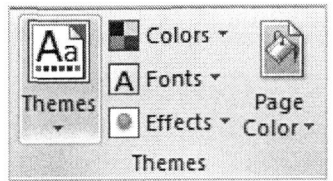

What Do You See? The Theme modified the Font, Font Color, Alignment and Size.

Keep going...

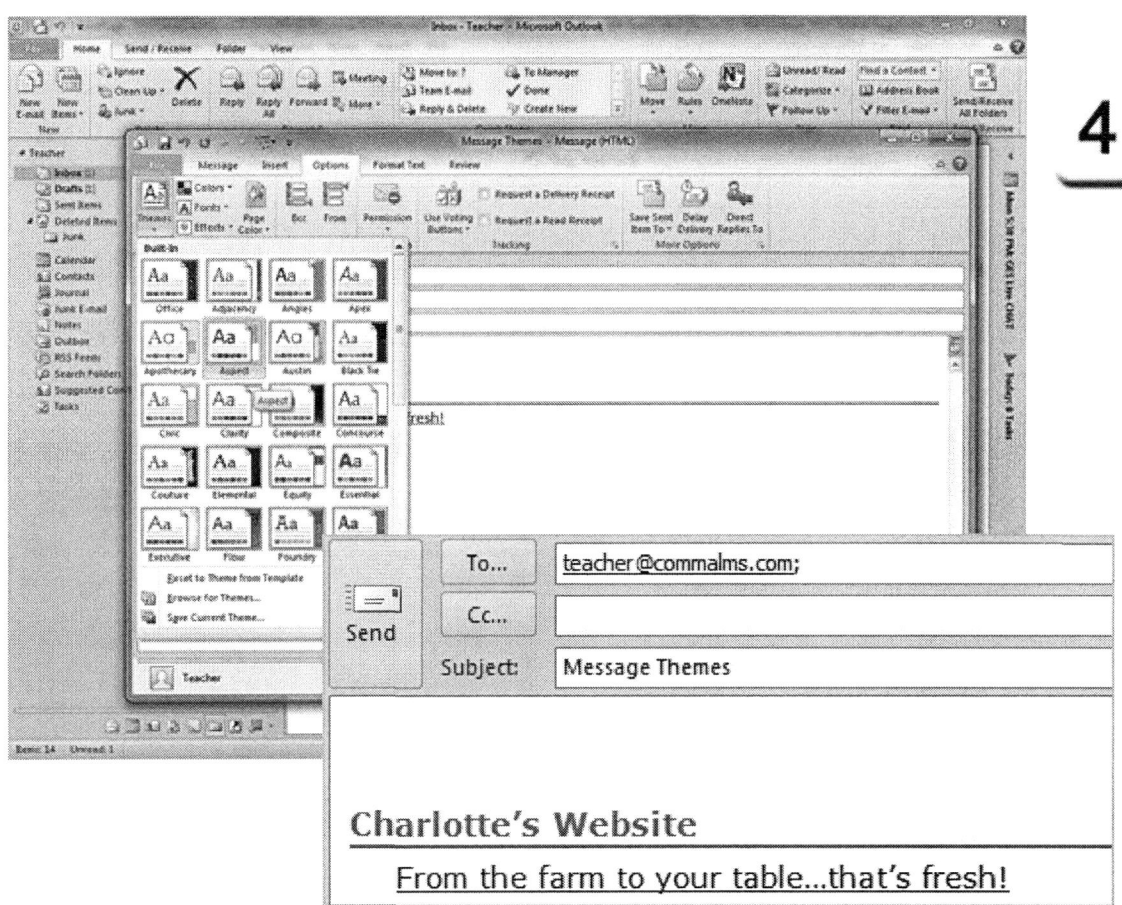

Exam 77-884: Microsoft Outlook 2010
2. Creating and Formatting Item Content
2.4. Format item content: Modify the Themes

Modify the Theme

You can modify the Theme Colors, Fonts and Effects. You can also change the Page Color for your E-mail if you wish.

5. Try it: Modify the Theme
The sample E-mail is still open.
Go to **Options ->Themes-> Page Color.**
Select a **Color**: Tan, Accent 6, Lighter 80%

What Do You See? The message should have a light tan Page Color.

Please keep going...

Memo to Self: It is very difficult to read messages with bright page colors such as screaming yellow zonkers or lime green Jell-O.

You do not have to MATCH the Page color in this lesson. Choose something light and easy to read, please.

Options ->Themes-> Page Color

Exam 77-884: Microsoft Outlook 2010
2. Creating and Formatting Item Content
2.4. Format item content: Modify the Themes

Message: Insert a Picture

You can add illustrations to your message, just as you would in Microsoft Word. The steps to insert a picture are the same in both programs.

Review the Insert Ribbon
The Insert Ribbon includes the following:
Include
Tables
Illustrations
Links
Text
Symbols

6. Try it: Insert a Picture
The sample E-mail is open. The cursor is placed in at the top of the message box.

Go to **Insert ->Illustrations-> Picture.**
Browse to your Documents folder.
Insert a sample picture: Farm1

Keep going...

Insert ->Illustrations-> Picture

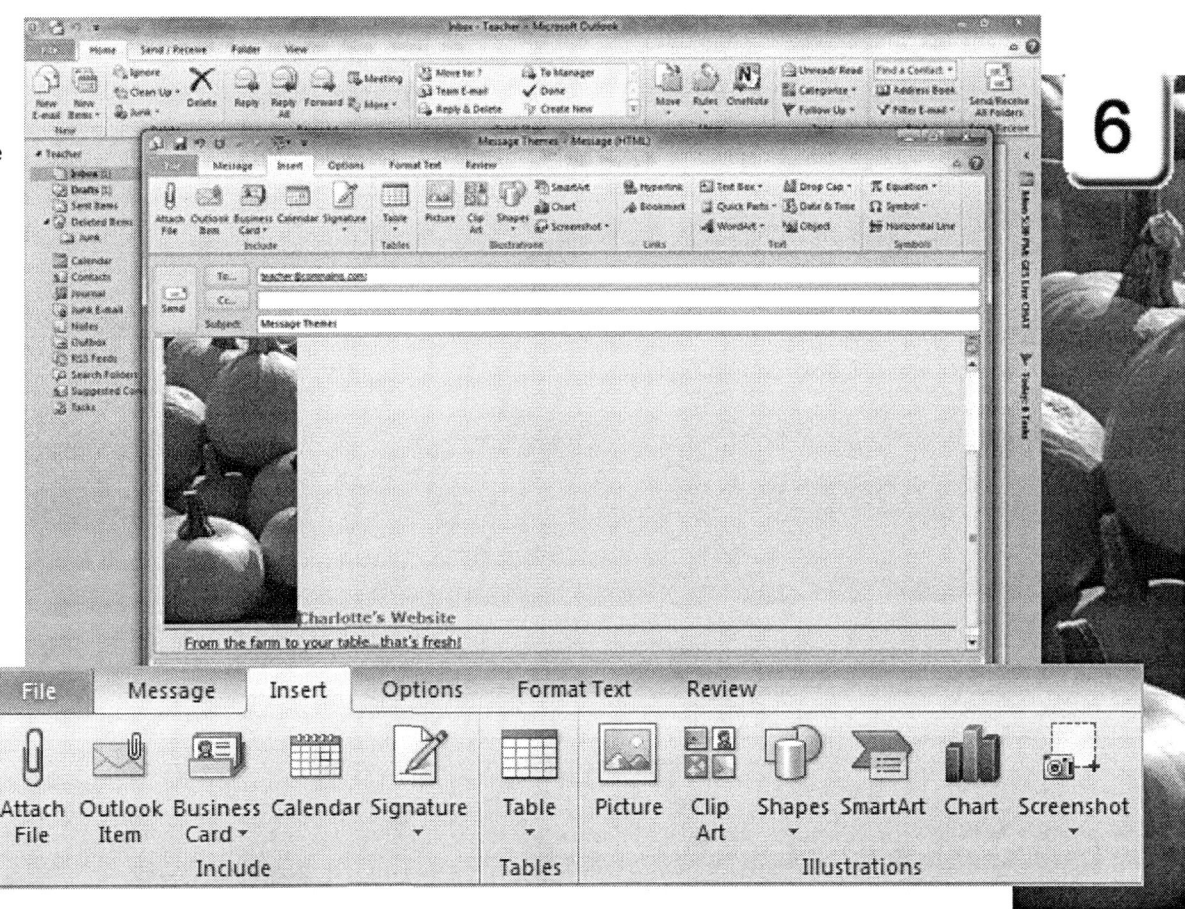

Exam 77-884: Microsoft Outlook 2010
2. Creating and Formatting Item Content
2.3. Create item content: Insert Graphical Elements

Picture Tools: Size

7. Try it: Resize the Picture
Select the new picture.
The Picture Tools should be available.

Go to **Picture Tools ->Size.**
Enter the Height: 2

You can type the number or use the arrows to change the size if you wish.

Keep going...

Memo to Self: These are the very same Picture Tools that are found in Microsoft Word. Please refer to the Beginning Guide to Word 2010 for a complete explanation of the Picture Tool options.

Picture Tools ->Size

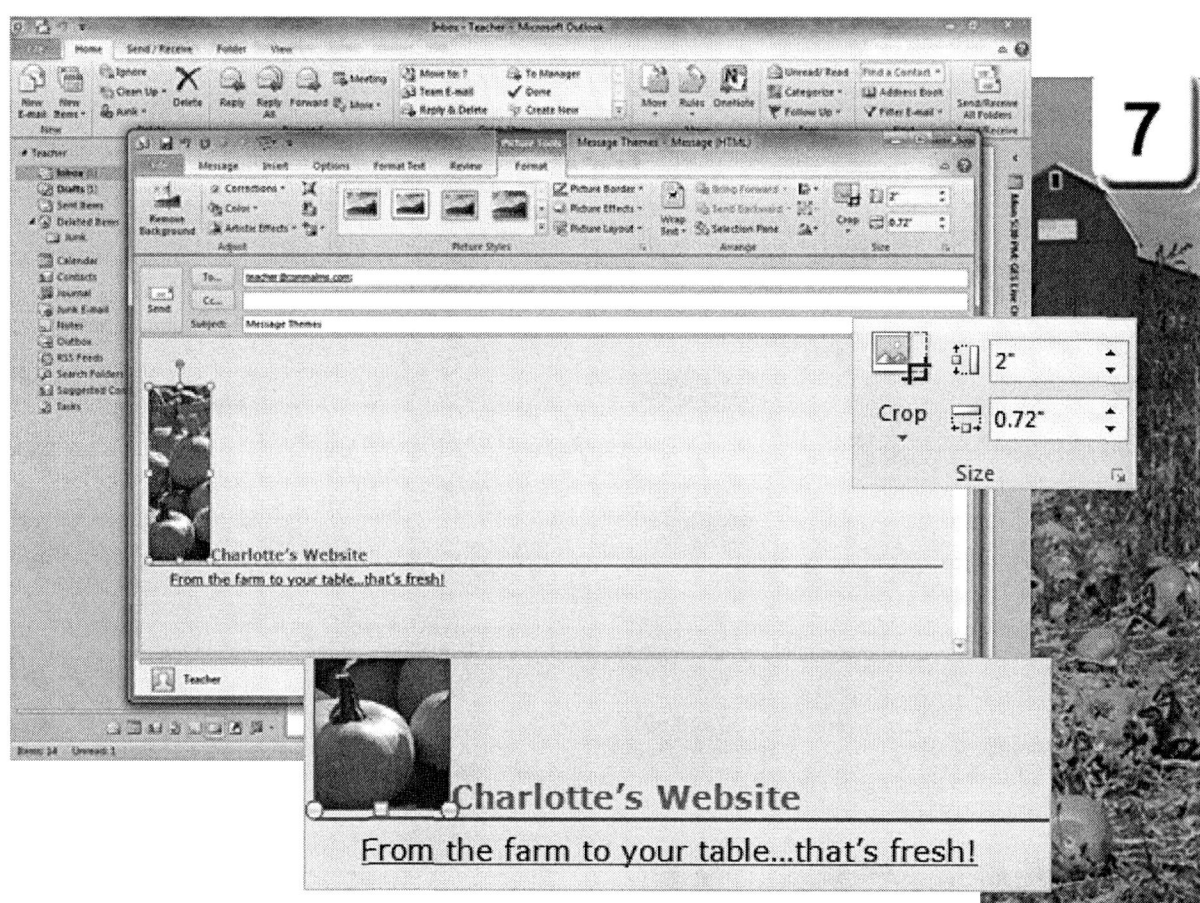

Exam 77-884: Microsoft Outlook 2010
2. Creating and Formatting Item Content
2.3. Create item content: Format Graphical Elements

Picture Tools: Wrap Text

8. Try it: Format the Text Wrapping
The picture is still selected.
The **Picture Tools** should be available.
Go to **Picture Tools ->Arrange->Wrap Text.**

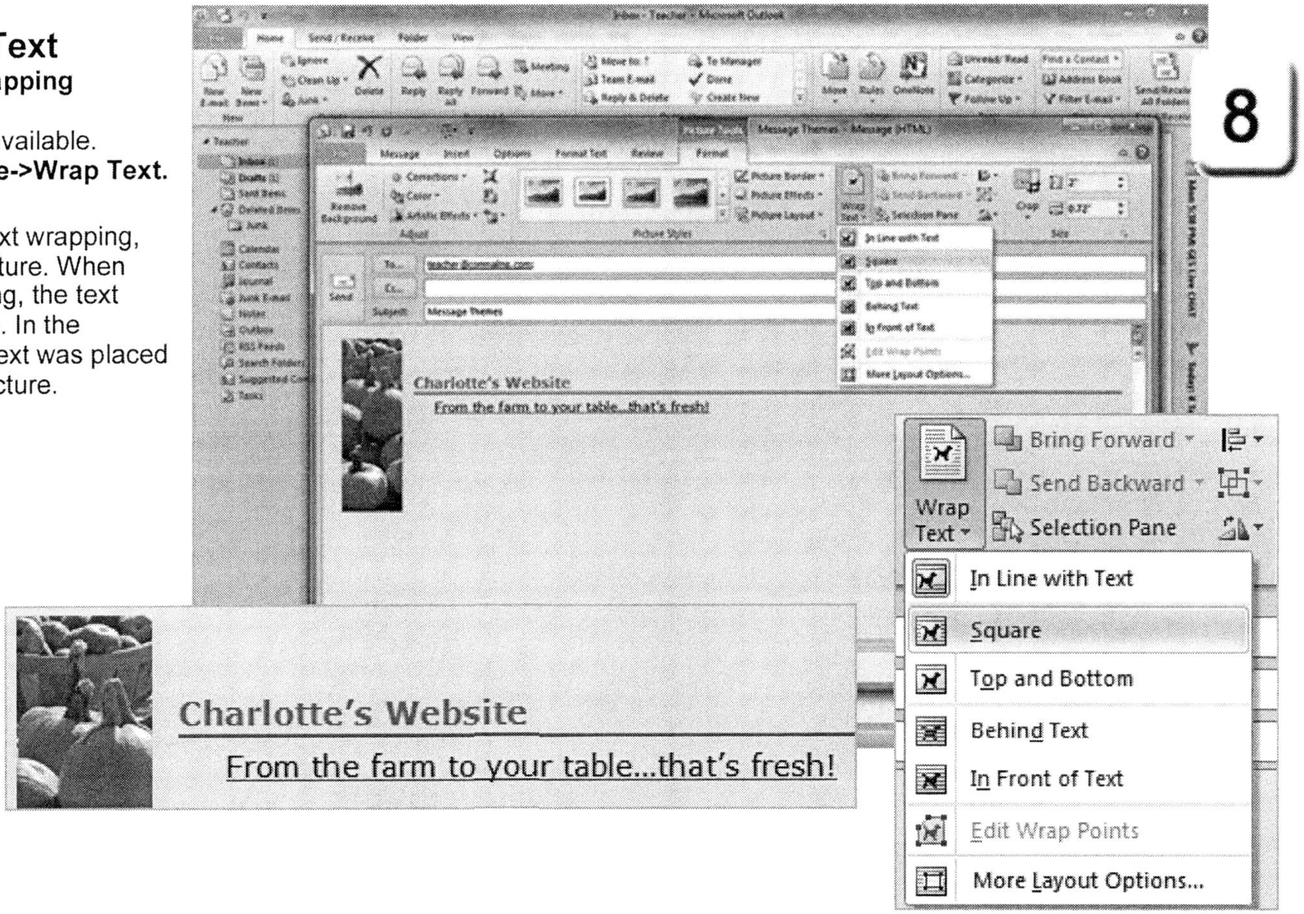

What Do You See? Without text wrapping, the text is placed below the picture. When you select **Square** text wrapping, the text should wrap around the picture. In the example in this message, the text was placed on the right hand side of the picture.

Keep going...it's looking good.

8

Exam 77-884: Microsoft Outlook 2010
2. Creating and Formatting Item Content
2.3. Create item content: Format Graphical Elements

More Message Options

By default, the message displays the recipient (To) and the carbon copy (Cc). You can also Show or Hide the Bcc and From Fields.

The **From Field** shows who sent the message. **Bcc** means Blind Carbon Copy. Names which are added to the Bcc field cannot be seen by the recipient. Bcc is usually used in adversarial relationships. Bcc is not commonly used and does not need to be displayed.

9. Try it: Show or Hide the Fields
The sample E-mail remains open.
Go to **Options ->Show Field->Bcc.**
The Bcc Field should be available.
Enter your E-mail address.

Try This as Well: Send the E-mail
Click **Send**. A well formatted E-mail with Themes should arrive in your Inbox.

Options ->Show Fields

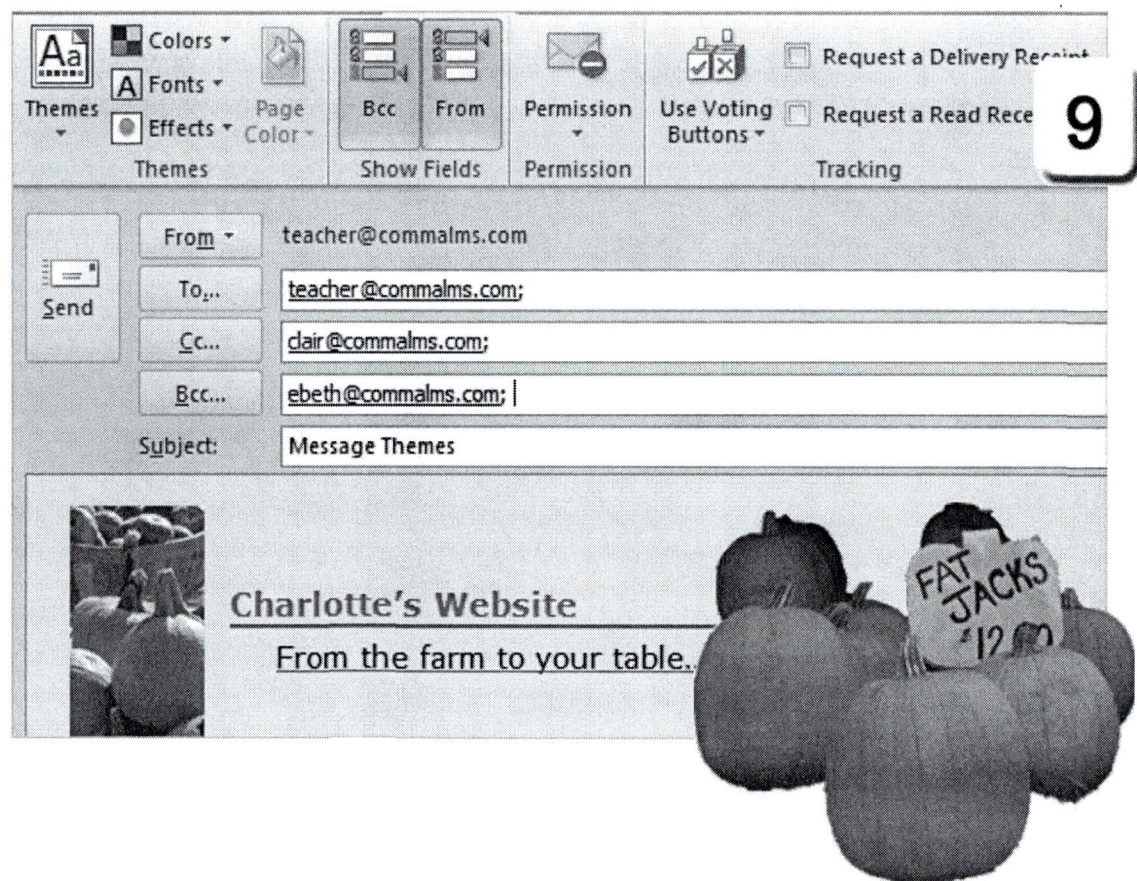

Exam 77-884: Microsoft Outlook 2010
2. Creating and Formatting Item Content
2.5. Attach content to email messages: Show or Hide the Bcc and From Fields

Create a New E-Mail
1. Try it: Format and Tag a Message
Go to **Home-> New-> New E-Mail.**
Enter your E-mail Address.
Enter the Subject: Tag, You're It.
Type the message: This message is tagged for follow up.

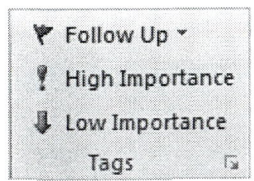

Try This, Too: Tag the Message
Go to **Message->Tags->Follow Up**
Select: **Tomorrow.**

Go to **Message ->Tags**
Select **High Importance.**

Click **Send.** An E-mail with Tags should arrive in your Inbox. Keep going...

Message->Tags->Follow Up

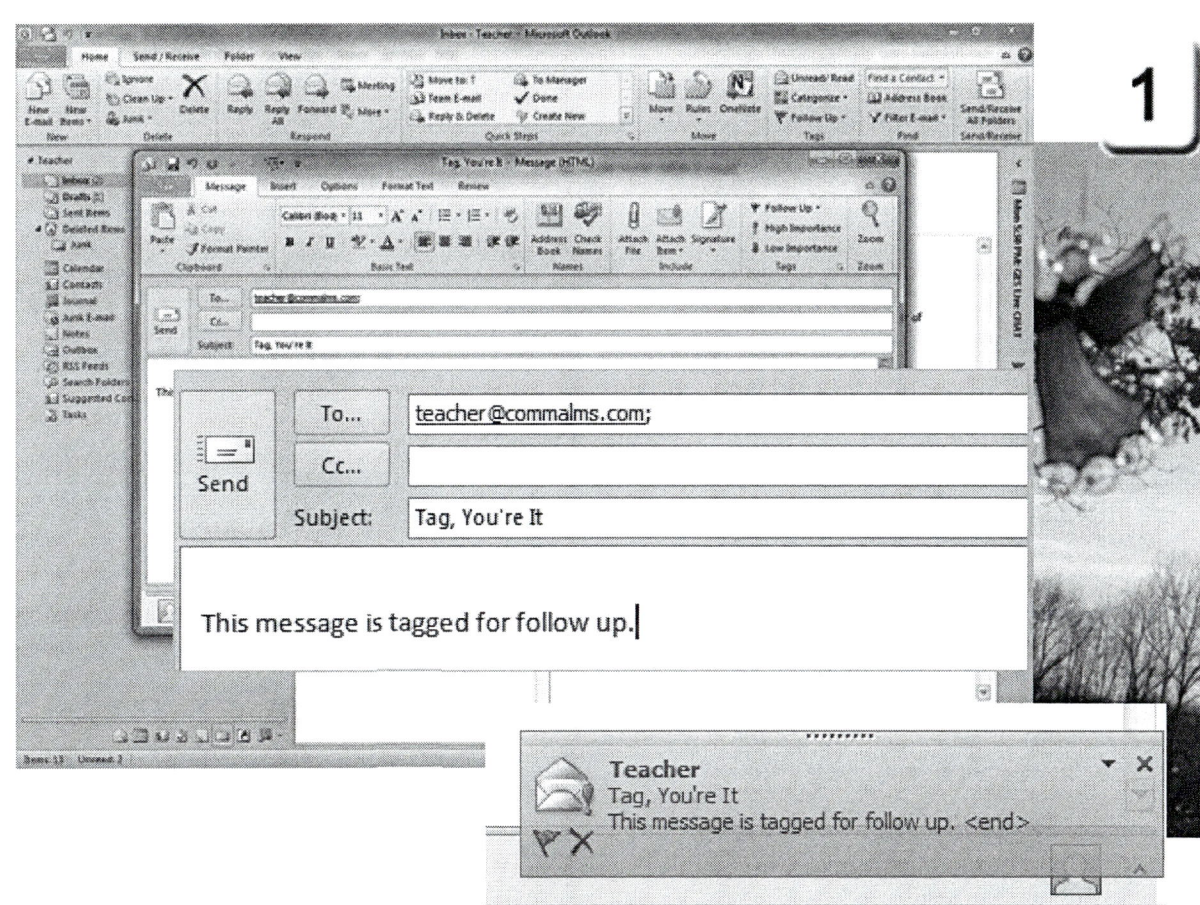

Exam 77-884: Microsoft Outlook 2010
1. Managing the Outlook Environment
1.2. Manipulate item tags: Set Flags

Tagged for Follow up

The Follow up Tags were added to the message you sent. So, you would go to the **Sent Items Folder** to find your message and review the options. Say this action is done. Here are the steps to **Mark it Complete**.

2. Try it: Mark the Follow Up Complete
Go to **Outlook ->Sent Items**.
Select the Tagged Message.

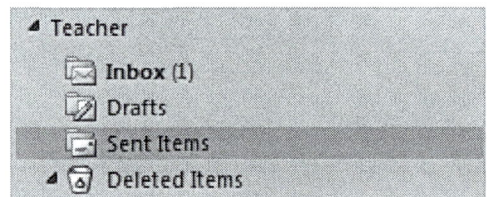

What Do You See? The Tagged E-mail has an Exclamation Point (!) for High Importance. There is a Follow Up Flag on the right side.

Try This, Too: Mark it Complete
Right Click the **Follow Up Flag**.
Select: **Mark Complete**.
The E-mail should have a check mark.

Outlook ->Sent Items

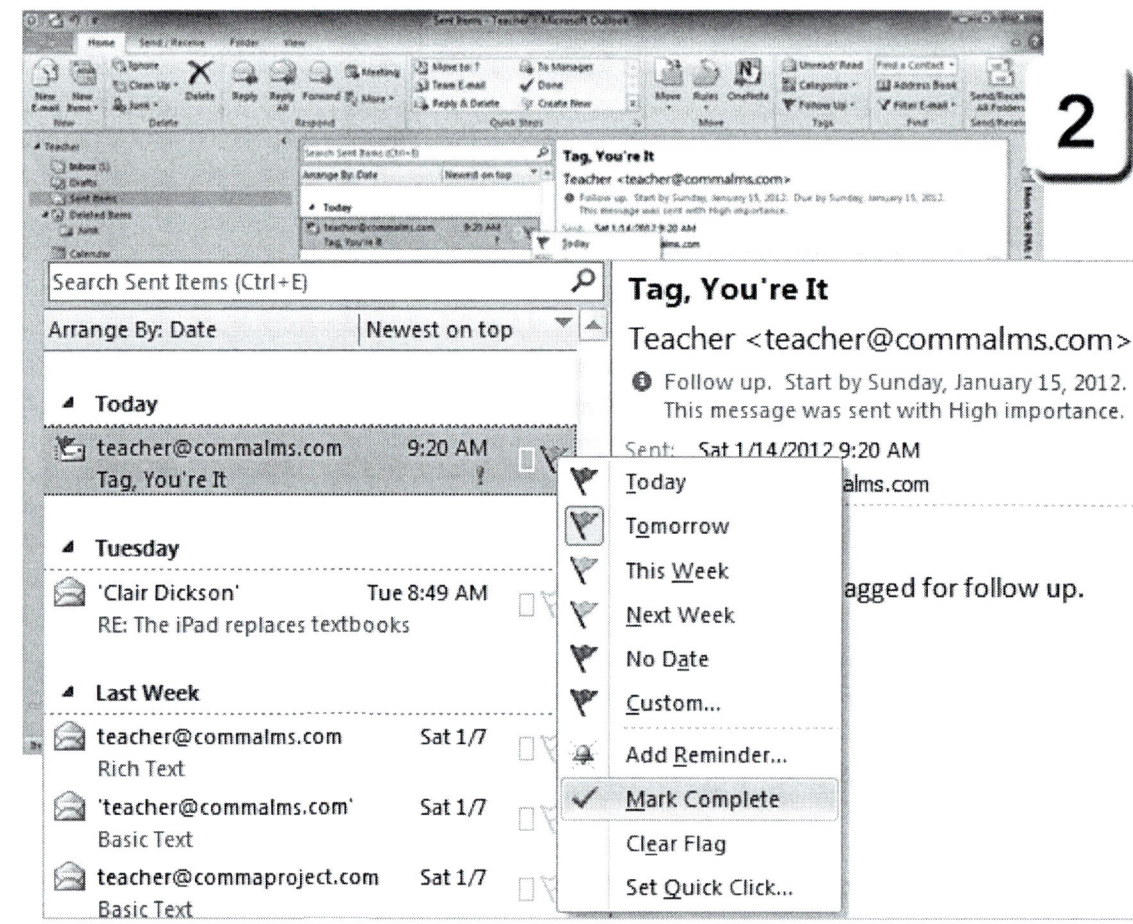

Exam 77-884: Microsoft Outlook 2010
2. Creating and Formatting Item Content
2.4. Format item content: Set a Message Reminder

Message Tracking

Microsoft Outlook can track your messages. For example, you can request confirmation that the message was delivered. You can also ask for confirmation that the E-mail was read.

1. Try it: Request a Delivery Receipt
Go to **Home-> New-> New E-Mail.**
Enter your E-mail Address.
Enter the Subject: Speedy Delivery.
Type the message: This message is a test of the Delivery Receipt.

Try This, Too: Set the Tracking Option
Go to Options ->Tracking.
Click on: **Request a Delivery Receipt.**
Click **Send.**

Try This, Too: Review the Delivery Receipt
A new E-mail may arrive in your Inbox.
Keep going.

Memo to Self: You may or may not receive a Delivery Receipt depending on which E-mail server you have.

Options ->Tracking->Request a Delivery Receipt

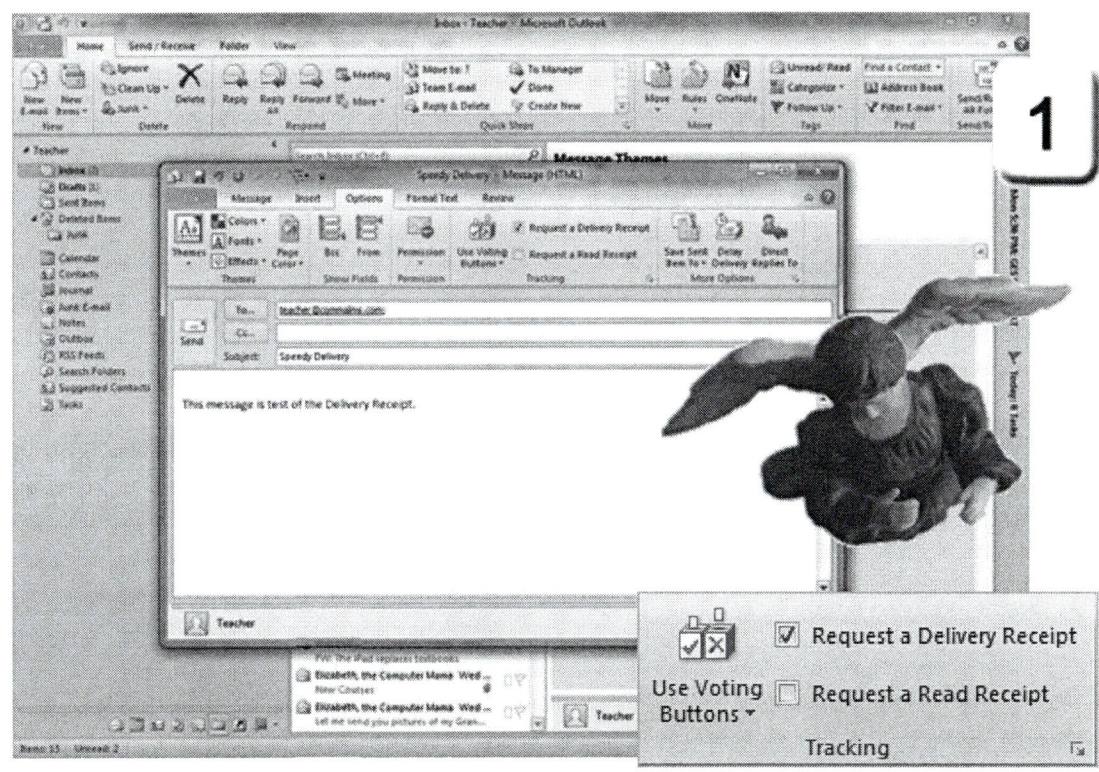

"The reason angels can fly is because they take themselves lightly."
G.K. Chesterton, "Orthodoxy"

Exam 77-884: Microsoft Outlook 2010
2. Creating and Formatting Item Content
2.1. Create and send email messages: Configure Tracking Options for Delivery Receipt

Take One

Options ->Tracking-> Request a Read Receipt

Tracking Options

2. Try it: Request a Read Receipt
Go to **Home-> New-> New E-Mail**.
Enter your E-mail Address.
Enter the Subject: Read All About It.
Type the message: This message is a test
of the Read Receipt.

Try This, Too: Set the Tracking Option
Go to **Options ->Tracking**.
Click on: **Request a Read Receipt**.

Click **Send**.

So, what does it look like to the person
who receives a message with a Read
Receipt? Keep going...

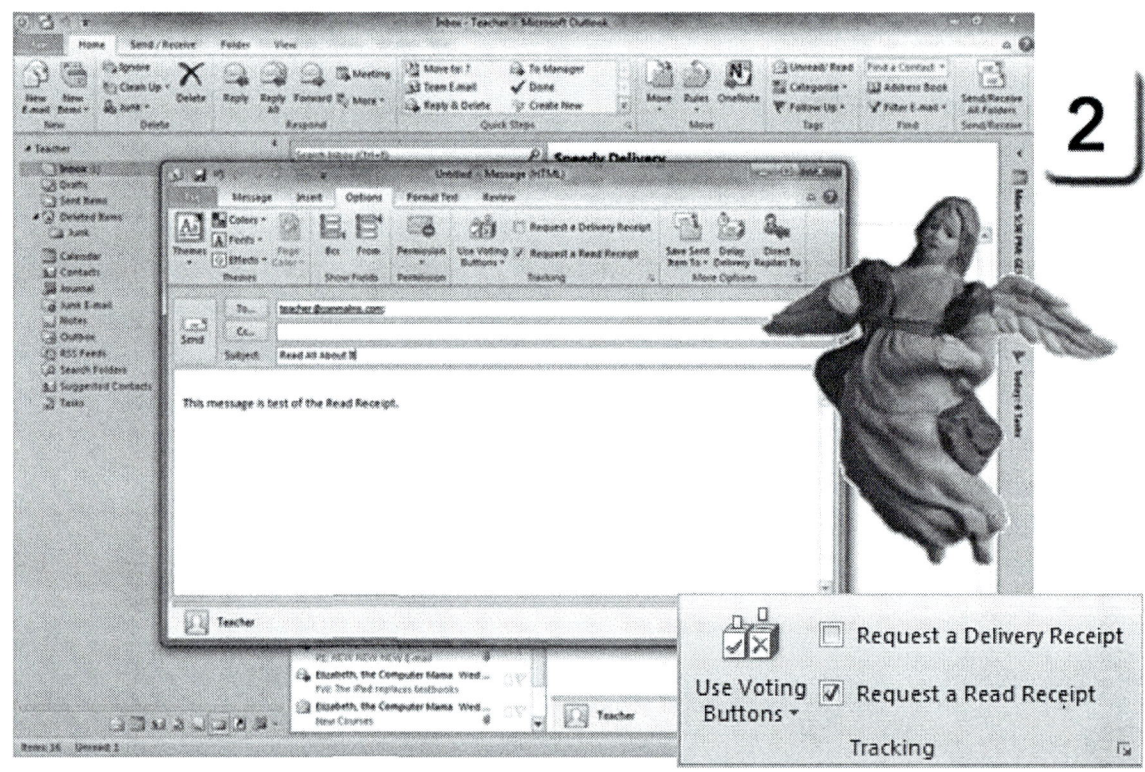

"I'm no angel, but I've spread my wings a bit."
Mae West

Exam 77-884: Microsoft Outlook 2010
2. Creating and Formatting Item Content
2.1. Create and send email messages: Configure Tracking Options for Read Receipts

Respond to a Read Receipt

3. Try This: Respond the Read Receipt
In our example, there should be a new E-mail with the subject, "Read All About It" in your Inbox. Double-Click to open that E-mail.

What Do You See? Microsoft Outlook will prompt you about sending a Read Receipt. You can choose Yes or No. You also have the option to turn off this prompt if you wish.

Try This, Too: Send the Read Receipt
Click **Yes**. Outlook will automatically send a Read Receipt. A Read Receipt has a small icon with a green check mark.

Memo to Self: Unlike the Delivery Receipt, people can decide whether or not to notify you when they read your E-mail. For some, it is an issue of privacy. For others, receipts are required for work.

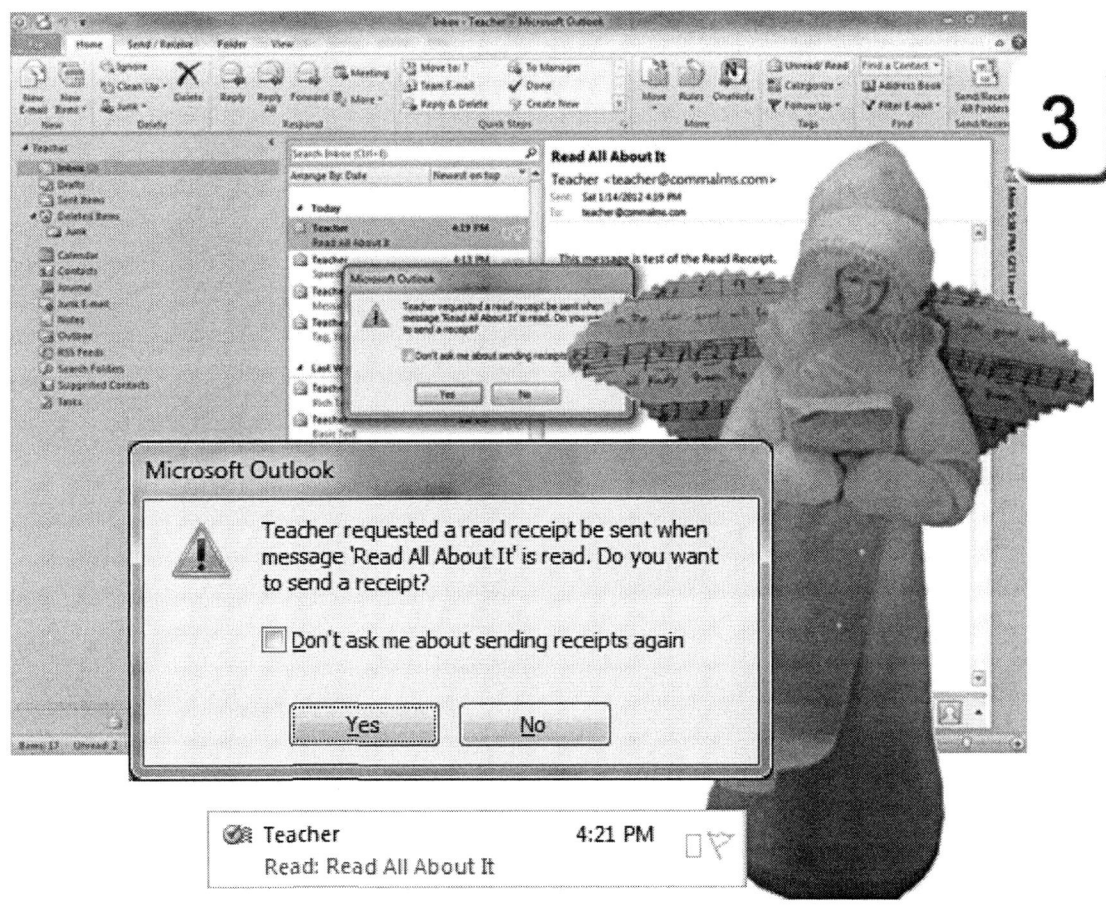

Exam 77-884: Microsoft Outlook 2010
2. Creating and Formatting Item Content
2.1. Create and send email messages: Configure Tracking Options for Read Receipts

More Tracking Options

You can use **Voting Buttons** to track people's responses to a question. This example works best if you can E-mail to a partner.

1. Try it: Use Voting Buttons
Go to **Home-> New-> New E-Mail**.
Enter your E-mail Address as well as one or two partners, if possible.
Enter the Subject: Do You Have Time for Lunch?
Type the message: This message is a test of the Voting Buttons.

Try This, Too: Set the Tracking Option
Go to **Options ->Tracking.**
Click on: **Use Voting Buttons**.
Select: Yes;No;Maybe

Click **Send** to E-mail the message.

Keep going...

Options ->Tracking-> Use Voting Buttons

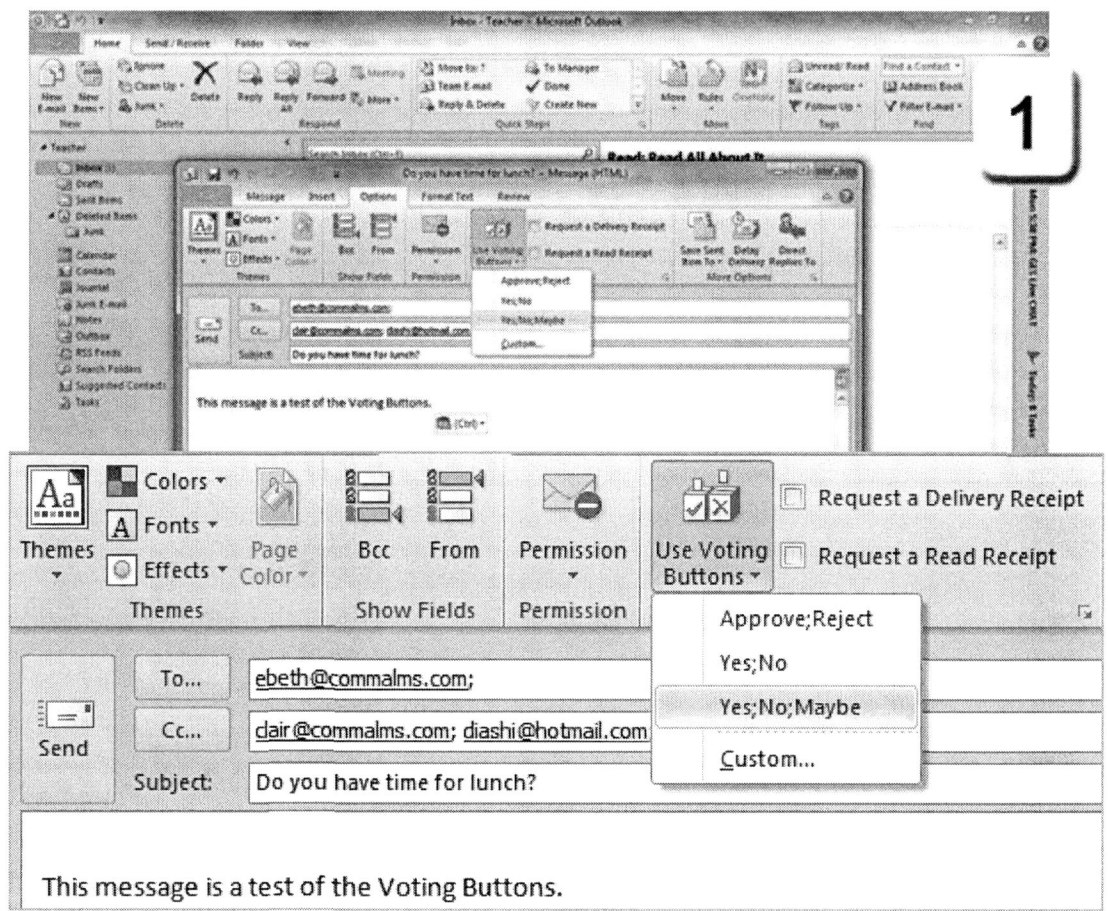

Exam 77-884: Microsoft Outlook 2010
2. Creating and Formatting Item Content
2.1. Create and send email messages: Configure Voting Options

Respond to the Vote
The Recipient's Response
The Recipient should receive a new E-mail with the subject, "Do you have..."

If you addressed the Vote to your self in the previous step, that E-mail should arrive in your Inbox. The message should have a new option in the Respond group: **Vote**.

2. Try This: Select an Answer
Go to **Message-> Respond->Vote**
Select: **Yes**.

When you select a Vote, you will be prompted to Edit or just Send your response. Click **Send**.

Keep going...!

Message-> Respond->Vote

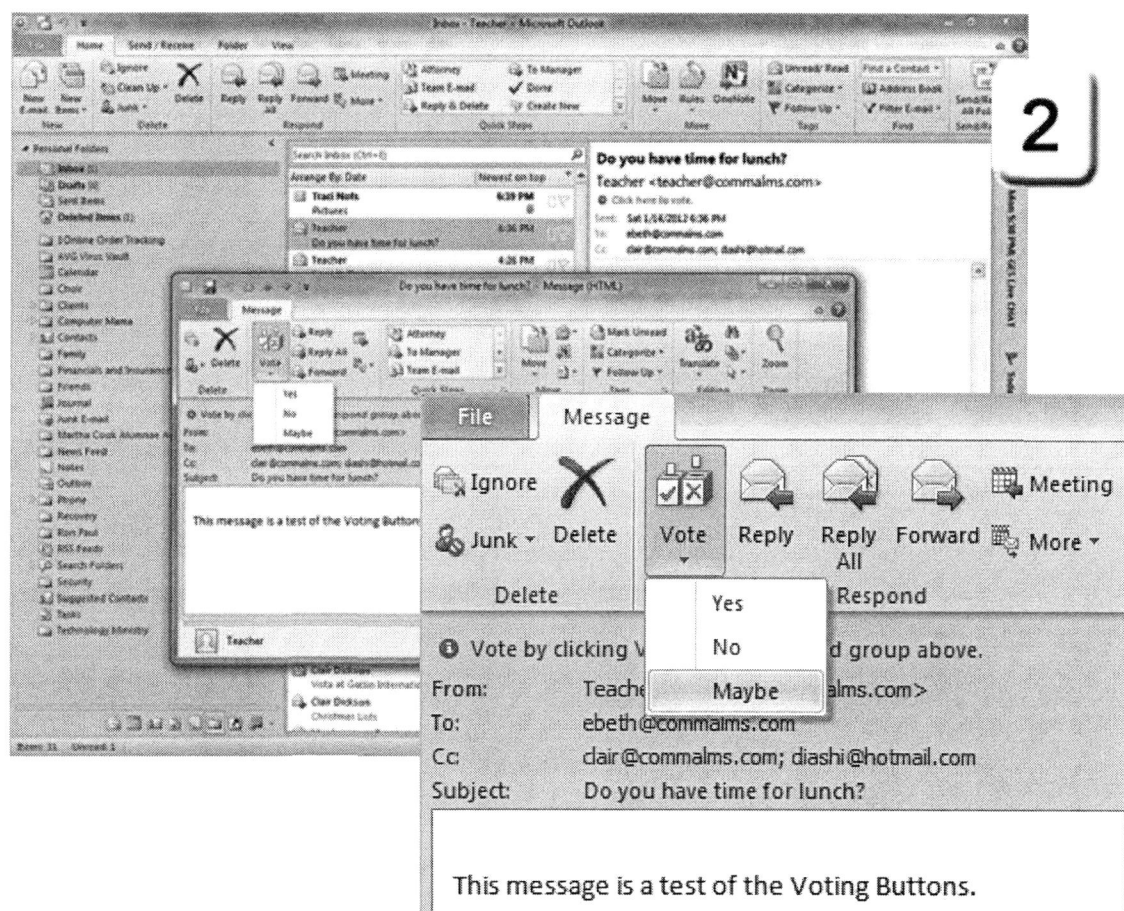

Exam 77-884: Microsoft Outlook 2010
2. Creating and Formatting Item Content
2.1. Create and send email messages: Configure Voting Options

The Votes Come In

The Votes Return to the Sender's Inbox
The message was E-mailed, the Responses have come back. Now, let's count the votes.

Each Recipient who responds to the Vote will E-mail an answer. The Subject is appended with the Vote: Yes, No, Maybe. Microsoft Outlook keeps a tally of all the responses.

3. Try This: View the Voting Reponses
Select one of the E-mail Vote responses
Click on the **Information Banner** that says, "The sender responded.."
Then click on **View Voting Reponses**.

Keep going, there's another step to finish the sequence...

The sender responded->View voting responses

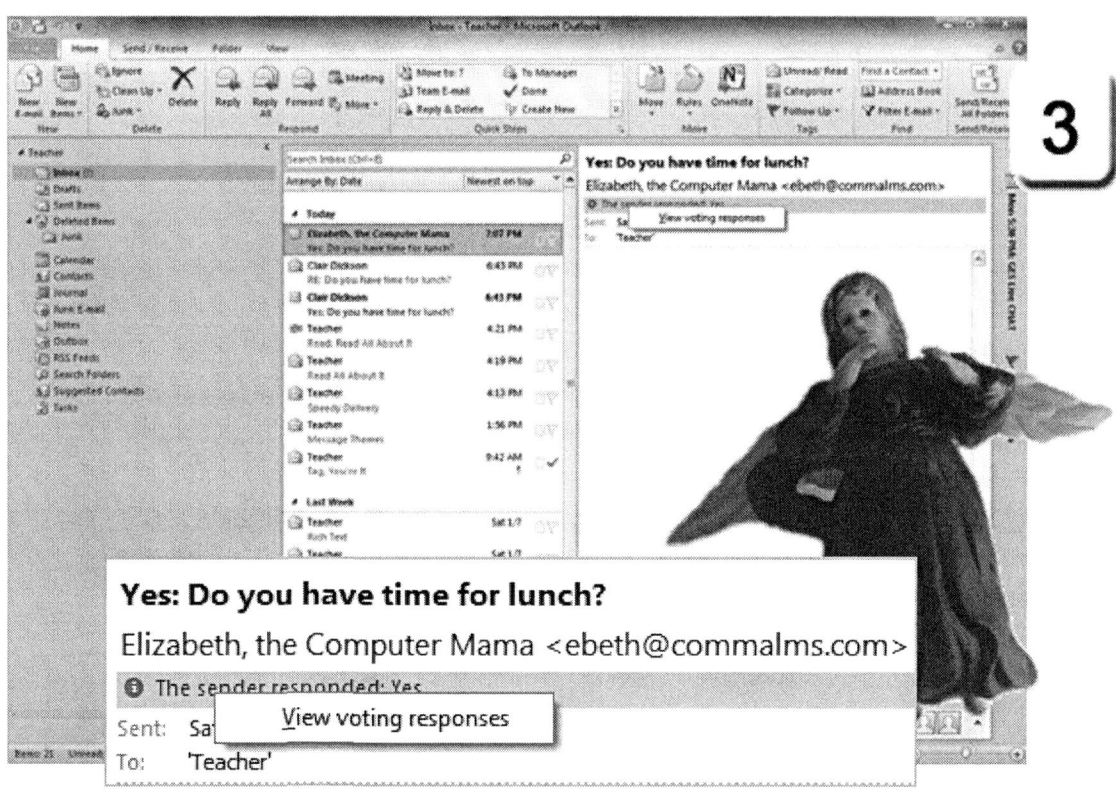

3

"Every man contemplates an angel in his future self."
Ralph Waldo Emerson

Exam 77-884: Microsoft Outlook 2010
2. Creating and Formatting Item Content
2.1. Create and send email messages: Configure Voting Options

Count the Vote

4. Try it: Track the Responses
When you click on **View Voting Reponses** you will see the **Reply Totals**. The Information Banner displays a summary of the replies. Each recipient's response is listed as well.

Try This, Too: Change the Show
The technical term for counting the results is called **Tracking**. Messages, Meetings and Tasks can be tracked. Tracking is written on the "backside" of the message. You can switch from the Tracking page back to the Message with the buttons in the **Show** Group.

Go to **Message->Show->Message.**
You should return to the E-mail.

Go to **Message ->Show->Tracking.**
And you will see the Reply Totals.

Message ->Show->Tracking

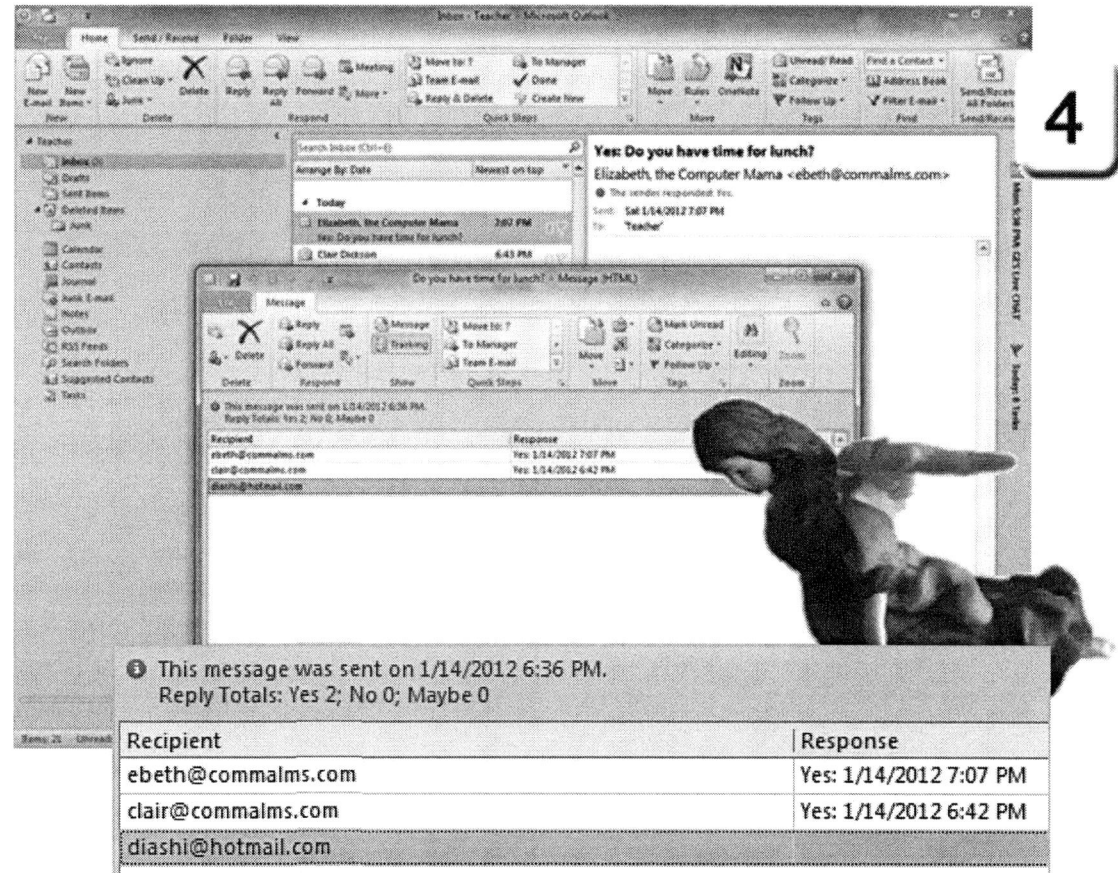

Recipient	Response
ebeth@commalms.com	Yes: 1/14/2012 7:07 PM
clair@commalms.com	Yes: 1/14/2012 6:42 PM
diashi@hotmail.com	

This message was sent on 1/14/2012 6:36 PM.
Reply Totals: Yes 2; No 0; Maybe 0

Exam 77-884: Microsoft Outlook 2010
2. Creating and Formatting Item Content
2.1. Create and send email messages: Configure Voting Options

Custom Voting Buttons

Computer legend sez that Voting Buttons were invented so that the dozen or so folks who worked at Microsoft could decide on lunch. Way cool use of technology. Here are the steps to create your own options.

5. Try It: Create Custom Voting Buttons
Go to **Home-> New-> New E-Mail**.
Enter your E-mail Address as well as one or two partners, if possible.
Enter the Subject: Vote for Lunch

Try This, Too: Set the Tracking Option
Go to **Options ->Tracking->Custom**.
Click on: **Use Voting Buttons**.
Type: Tomato Bros;Sushi Zen;Big Boys

Click **Close** to return to the message.
Click **Send** to E-mail the message.

Keep going...

Memo to Self: Look at the punctuation between the list items. It is a semi colon ;

Options ->Tracking->Use Voting Buttons->Custom

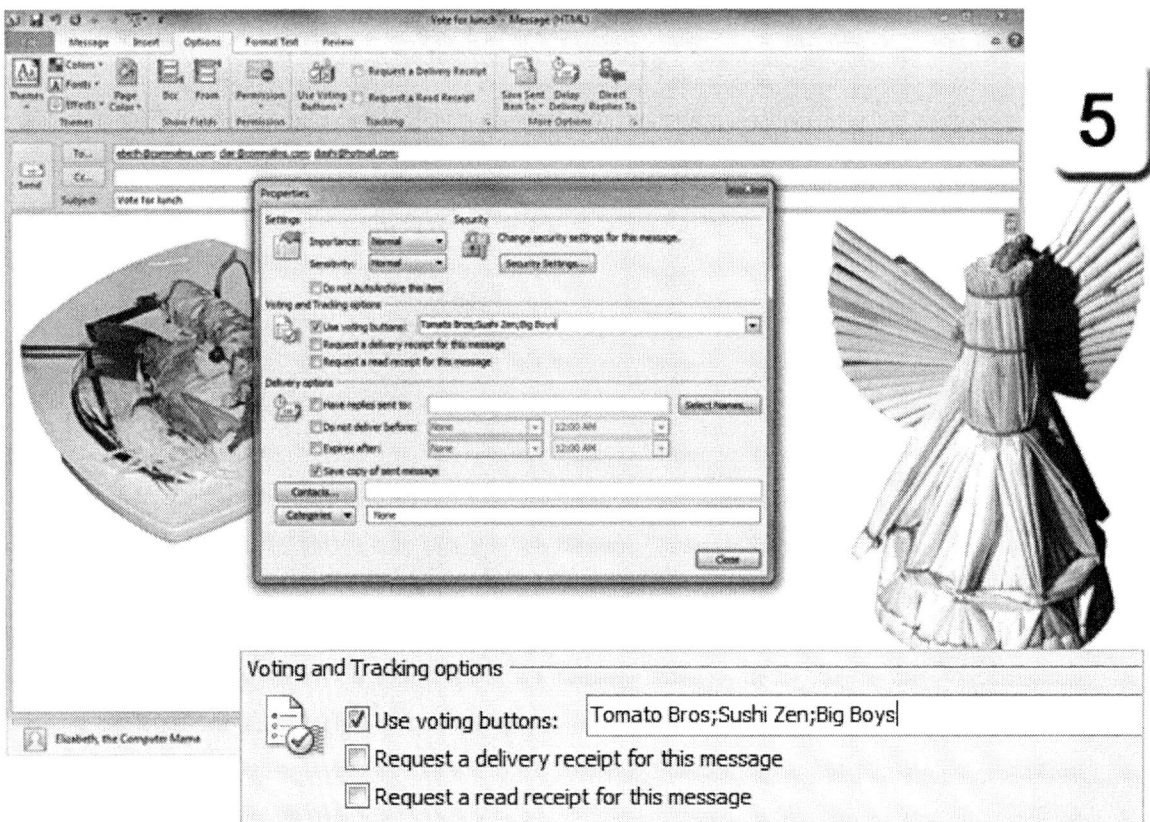

5

Voting and Tracking options
- ☑ Use voting buttons: Tomato Bros;Sushi Zen;Big Boys
- ☐ Request a delivery receipt for this message
- ☐ Request a read receipt for this message

Exam 77-884: Microsoft Outlook 2010
2. Creating and Formatting Item Content
2.1. Create and send email messages: Configure Voting Options

The Results Are In

6. Try it: View the Reponses

The Recipient's should receive an E-mail asking them to vote for lunch. The E-mail will have Voting buttons with your custom choices.

After the Recipients select a Vote, the Reponses will gather in the Sender's Inbox. If you click on any Vote you can **View voting responses.**

That's a good discussion on Voting Buttons. Now, let's look at some of the other Message Options.

" ... Be not forgetful to entertain strangers: for thereby some have entertained angels unawares..."
Hebrews 13:2

The sender responded->View voting responses

Exam 77-884: Microsoft Outlook 2010
2. Creating and Formatting Item Content
2.1. Create and send email messages: Configure Voting Options

Take One

More Options: Delay Delivery

There are a couple more **Message Options** that you should consider. The following pages will look at Delayed Delivery and using a different E-mail address for the reply.

1. Try This: Delay Delivery of an E-mail
Go to **Home-> New-> New E-Mail.**
Enter your E-mail Address.
Enter the Subject: Do Not Deliver Before...
You can add a picture or sample text if you wish.

Try This, Too: Set More Options
Go to **Options ->More Options.**
Click on: **Delay Delivery** and keep going...

Options ->More Options->Delay Delivery

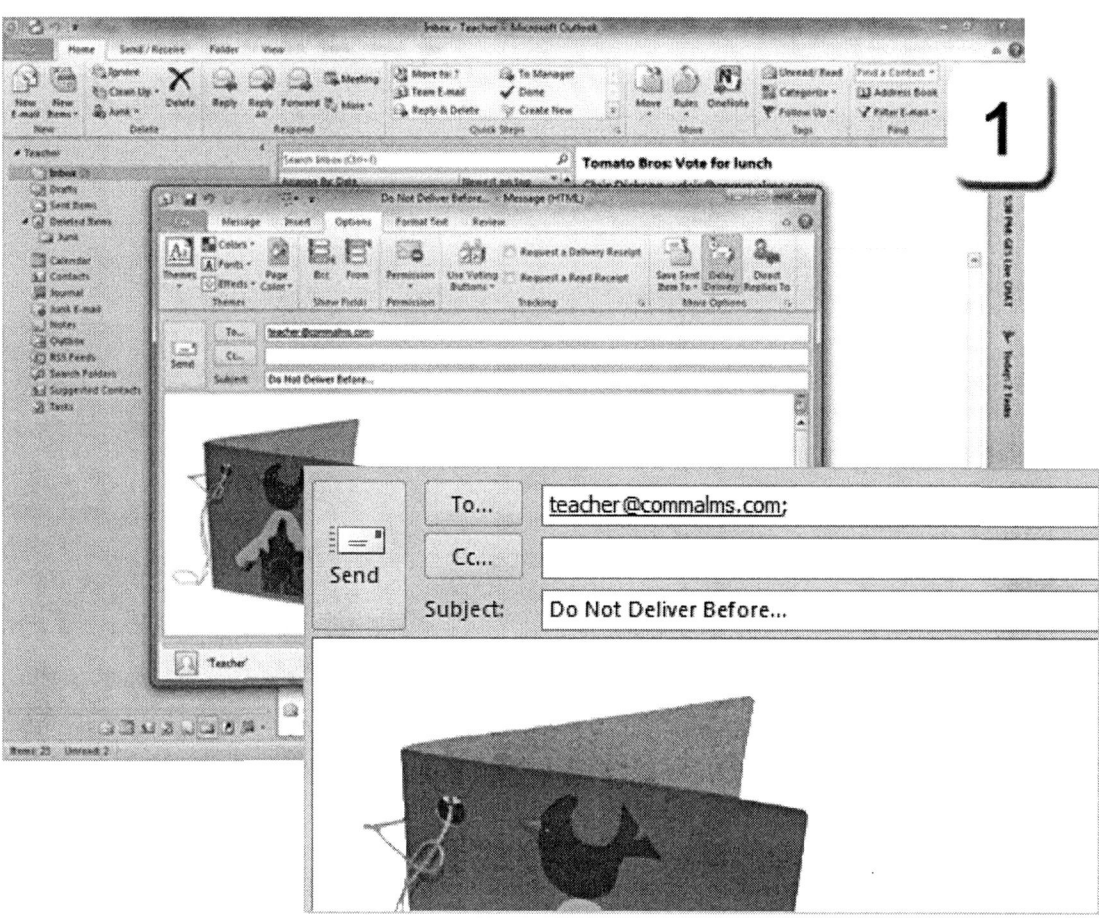

Exam 77-884: Microsoft Outlook 2010
2. Creating and Formatting Item Content
2.1. Create and send email messages: Configure Delivery Options

Delay Delivery Options

You can set the date and time that you want an E-mail to be sent. It is one of the Message Options and it works rather well. The message will wait in the Outbox until it is time to go.

2. Try This: Set the Delivery Options
How did we get here? The E-mail is open.
Go to **Options ->More Options.**
Click on: **Delay Delivery.**

Try This, Too: Edit the Message Properties
There is a section for **Delivery Options.**
Click on **Do not deliver before:**
Enter today's date at 5:00 PM

Click **Close** to return to the E-mail.
Click **Send** to E-mail this message.

Setting a Tomb Stone: You can also program your E-mail to **Expire** (go to data heaven in the Deleted Items Folder) after a certain date and time.

Options ->More Options->Delay Delivery

Exam 77-884: Microsoft Outlook 2010
2. Creating and Formatting Item Content
2.1. Create and send email messages: Configure Delivery Options

Take One

Delayed E-mail
3. Try it: Find the Delayed E-mail
Go to the **Outbox**

Notes
Outbox [1]
RSS Feeds
Search Folders
Suggested Contacts

What Do You See? The Outbox has one E-mail in the folder (1). The outbound E-mail is waiting for the right time to be sent.

Very good, keep going...

Options ->More Options->Delay Delivery

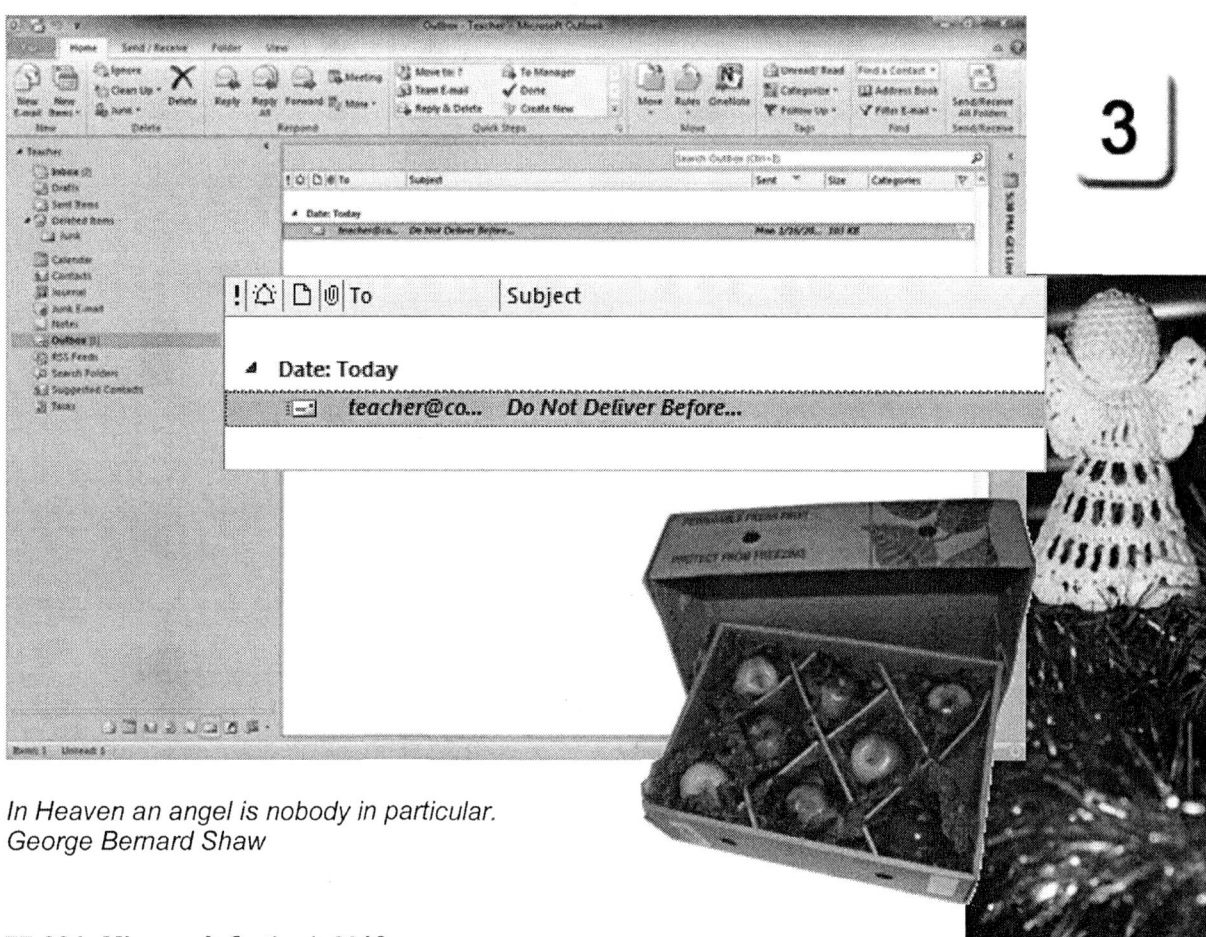

!	⌂	🗋	🔘	To	Subject
◢ Date: Today					
				teacher@co...	Do Not Deliver Before...

In Heaven an angel is nobody in particular.
George Bernard Shaw

3

Exam 77-884: Microsoft Outlook 2010
2. Creating and Formatting Item Content
2.1. Create and send email messages: Configure Delivery Options

Take One

More Message Options:
Direct Replies To

The person who designs and sends a marketing message may not be the same person who needs to follow up on the responses. You can have the replies go to a different E-mail, say your sales team. Here are the steps.

Try it: Direct Replies To
Go to **Home-> New-> New E-Mail.**
Enter your E-mail Address.
Enter the Subject: More Message Options.
You can add a picture or sample text if you wish.

Try This, Too: Edit the Message Properties
Go to **Options ->More Options.**
Click on **Direct Replies To.**

The **Message Properties** should open.
Go to the **Delivery Options.**
Click on **Direct Replies To:**
Enter your partner's E-mail address.

Click **Close** to return to the E-mail.
Click **Send** to E-mail this message.

Options ->More Options->Direct Replies To

Exam 77-884: Microsoft Outlook 2010
2. Creating and Formatting Item Content
2.1. Create and send email messages: Configure Delivery Options

Message Options: Settings

The Message Options are summarized in the **Properties.** The Message Properties includes all of the groups on the Options Ribbon:
Settings
Voting and Tracking
Delivery Options

Try it: View the Message Properties
Go to **Home-> New-> New E-Mail.**
Enter your E-mail Address.
Enter the Subject: Even More Options
You can add a picture or sample text if you wish.

Try This, Too: Set More Options
Go to **Options ->More Options->More.**
(More is the arrow in the bottom right corner.)
There is a section for **Settings**.
Edit the **Sensitivity**: Private

Click **Close** to return to the E-mail.
Click **Send** to E-mail this message.

An E-mail message with the subject Even More Options should arrive in your Inbox. It should be marked Private.

Options ->More Options->More

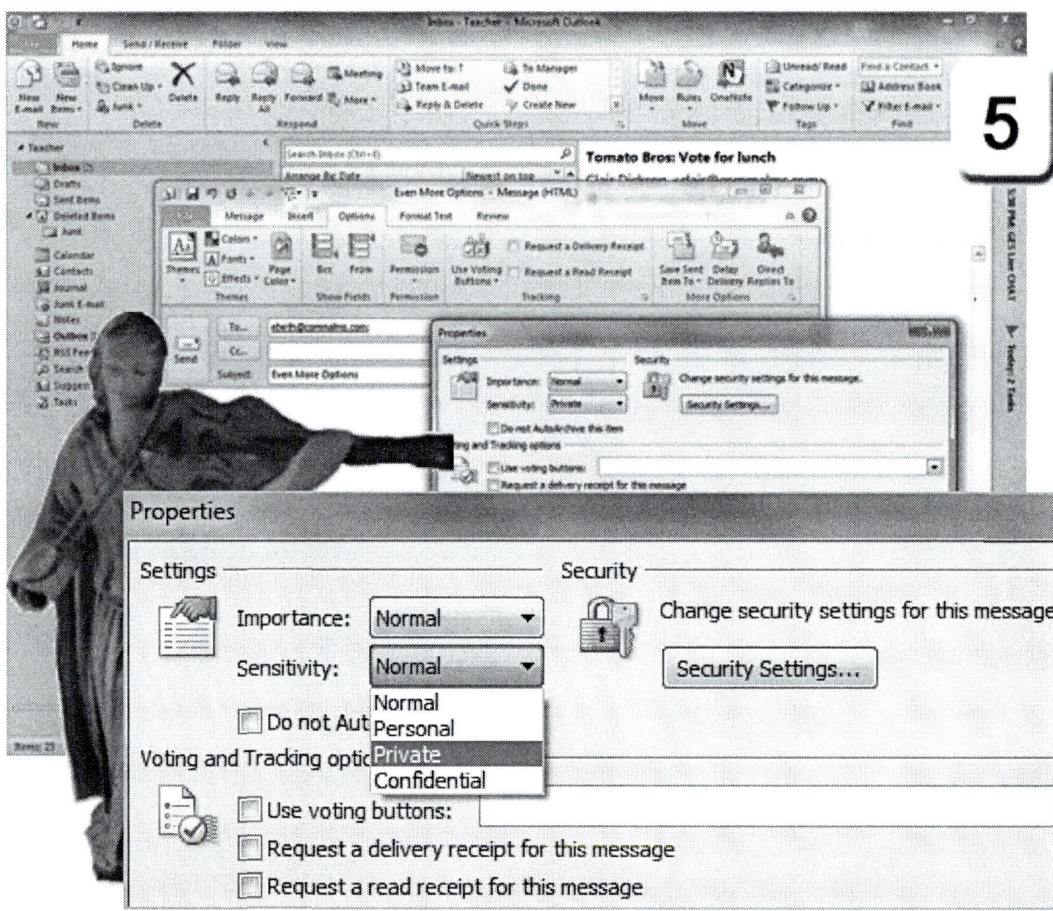

Exam 77-884: Microsoft Outlook 2010
1. Managing the Outlook Environment
1.2. Manipulate item tags: View Message Properties

Messages and Messengers

This lesson introduced the Message Options. The **Options Ribbon** lets you format the image with Themes, Color, Fonts and Effects. You can program the message action as well: Receipts, Tracking, Voting and Delivery.

Well, you done good.
You get the cookie.

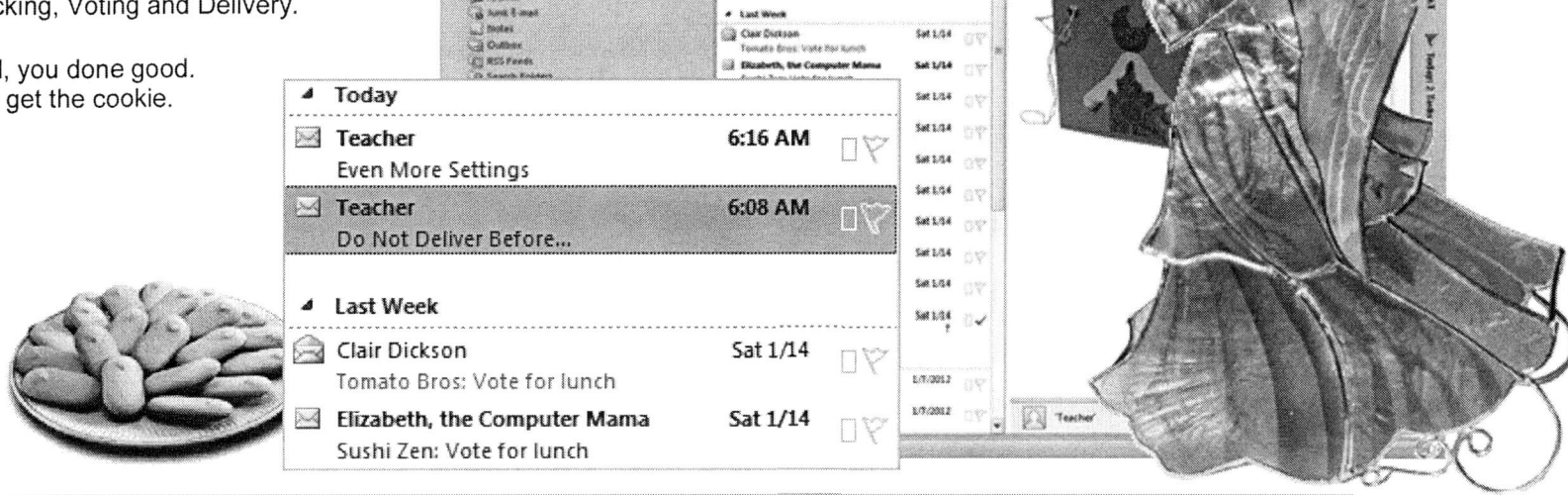

Exam 77-884: Microsoft Outlook 2010
1. Managing the Outlook Environment
1.2. Manipulate item tags: Mark as Read or Unread

Test Yourself

1. Themes are applied to which of the following? (Give all correct answers.)
A. Text
B. Pictures
C. Shapes
D. Graphics
Tip: Complete Guide to Outlook, page 59

2. Which Ribbon has the command for Themes?
a. Design
b. Insert
C. Options
Tip: Complete Guide to Outlook, page 59

3. Which Ribbon has the command to put a picture in an e-mail, NOT as an attachment?
A. Options
B. Insert
C. Home
Tip: Complete Guide to Outlook, page 61

4. Outlook automatically tallys the vote responses when using the vote options.
a. True
b. False
Tip: Complete Guide to Outlook, page 72

Practice

1. Open a new Email. Address the email to yourself.

2. Add the following Text:

Open House
Saturday 1-4pm
1234 Oak Wood Lane

3. Apply the Theme Austin

4. Format Font Green, 14 pt, Italic.

5. Change the font to Verdana

6. Add voting options for Yes, No, and Maybe

7. Add a BCC recipient of your choice

8. Tag this email as Low Importance

9. Send the E-mail to yourself.

10. Go to the Inbox and confirm.

Application Question: When would using BCC be more appropriate than using CC? When would you use the CC field?

An angel can illuminate the thought and mind of man by strengthening the power of vision.
St Thomas Aquinas

Outlook 2010: Working with E-mail
From Me to You

Beginning Outlook Objectives
In this lesson, you will learn how to:

1. Create an E-mail message that includes graphics and SmartArt

2. Format the E-mail message as a Table and use the Table Tools to modify the layout and design

3. Attach content to an E-mail message and work with the Attachments Ribbon

4. Forward an attachment, Save the attachments and save an E-mail message in an external format

© 2011 Comma Productions, LLC

Lesson 4 : From Me to You

1. Readings

Read Lesson 4 in the Microsoft Outlook guide, page 83-111.

Project

An E-mail message that uses a Table for the HTML design and includes pictures and SmartArt.

Downloads

Phone.gif
Laptop.gif
Keep It Clean.gif
Sign6Small.gif

2. Practice

Complete the Practice Activity on page 112.

3. Assessment

Review the Test questions on page 112.

Insert Ribbon

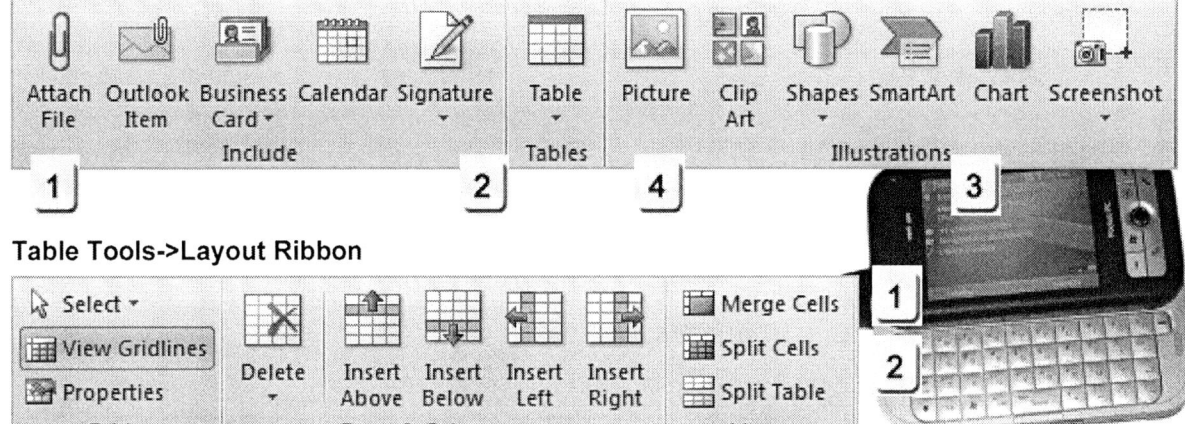

Table Tools->Layout Ribbon

Menu Maps

From the **Insert Ribbon**.
1. Insert ->Include->Attach File, page 88
2. Insert ->Tables->Table, page 91
3. Insert ->Illustrations->SmartArt, page 93

From the **Home Ribbon**
1. Home ->Respond->Forward, page 105
2. Home ->Respond->More, page 106

More Menu Maps

From the **Table Tools**
1. Table Tools ->Layout->Merge->Merge Cells, page 92
2. Table Tools ->Design->Table Styles->Borders, page 100

From the **Attachment Tools**
1. Attachment Tools ->Attachments, page 103
1. Attachment Tools->Attachments->Save As, page 104

From Me to You

Exciting E-mail campaigns can generate more business. The design tools in Microsoft Outlook can generate effective messages. For example, your marketing may include pictures of the products and Word documents that explain the features and benefits. However, infected attachments have brought many corporations and departments down. This lesson looks at the types of attachments you can use with Microsoft Outlook. We will also consider the security issues and what clues are available to insure that your message is well received.

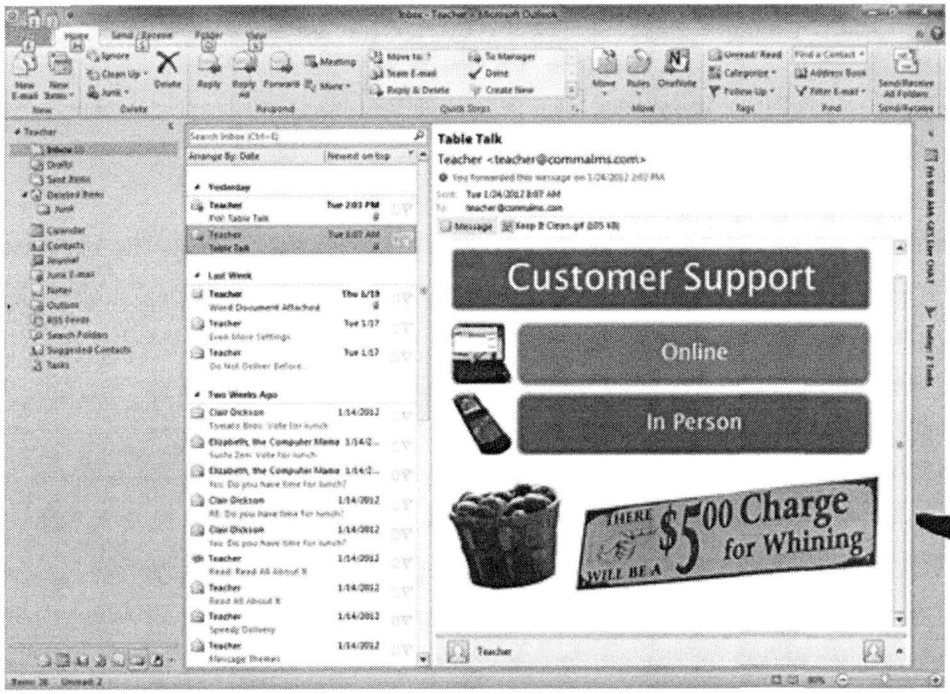

Before You Begin

An **attachment** is something which is added to a message and sent to all of the recipients. An attachment can be a Word document, an Excel spreadsheet, a presentation, or pictures from a digital camera.

The following pages will walk through the steps for adding a simple Word document as well as a picture to an Email message.

Before You Begin: Create a Document
Start Microsoft Word.
Type your name at the top of the document.

Go to **File->Save**.
Browse to the Documents Folder.
Enter the File Name: Small Word Attachment.
Click on **Save**.

Keep going...

Memo to Self: You do NOT have to match the pictures and samples in this lesson. It is more important that you walk through the steps and practice the options.

Microsoft Word 2010

File ->Save

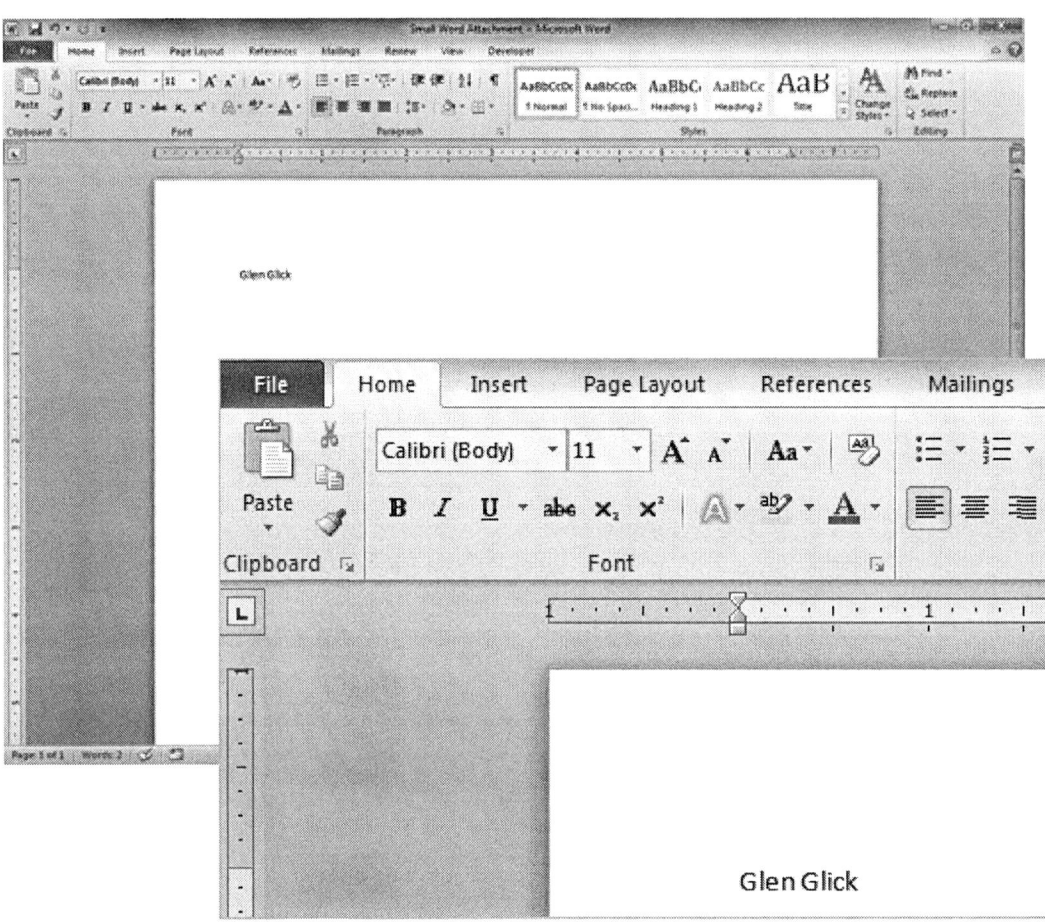

Create a New E-mail

Here are the steps to create a new E-mail and attach the Word document we just saved.

1. Try it: Create a New Email
Go to **Home-> New-> New E--Mail.**
Enter your E-mail Address.
Enter the Subject: Word Document Attached.
Enter the sample text: This message has a Word document attached.

Try This, Too: Review the Insert Ribbon
The **Insert** Ribbon has the following groups:
Include
Tables
Illustrations
Links
Text
Symbol

Keep going...

Exam 77-884: Microsoft Outlook 2010
2. Creating and Formatting Item Content
2.5. Attach content to email messages

Attach a File to a Message

Almost all E-mail programs use the paper clip icon to add an attachment.

2. Try it: Attach a File
Go to **Insert ->Include->Attach File.**
Browse to the Documents Folder.
Select: Small Word Attachment.docx
Click **Insert** to attach the file and return to the message.

What Do You See? There is a new field under the Subject called Attached.

The attachment has the little icon for Microsoft Word. The size of the file is shown in parenthesis (12 KB).

Click **Send**. Keep going...

Made You Look: You can also add an attachment by going to **Message->Include-> Attach File.**

Insert ->Include->Attach File

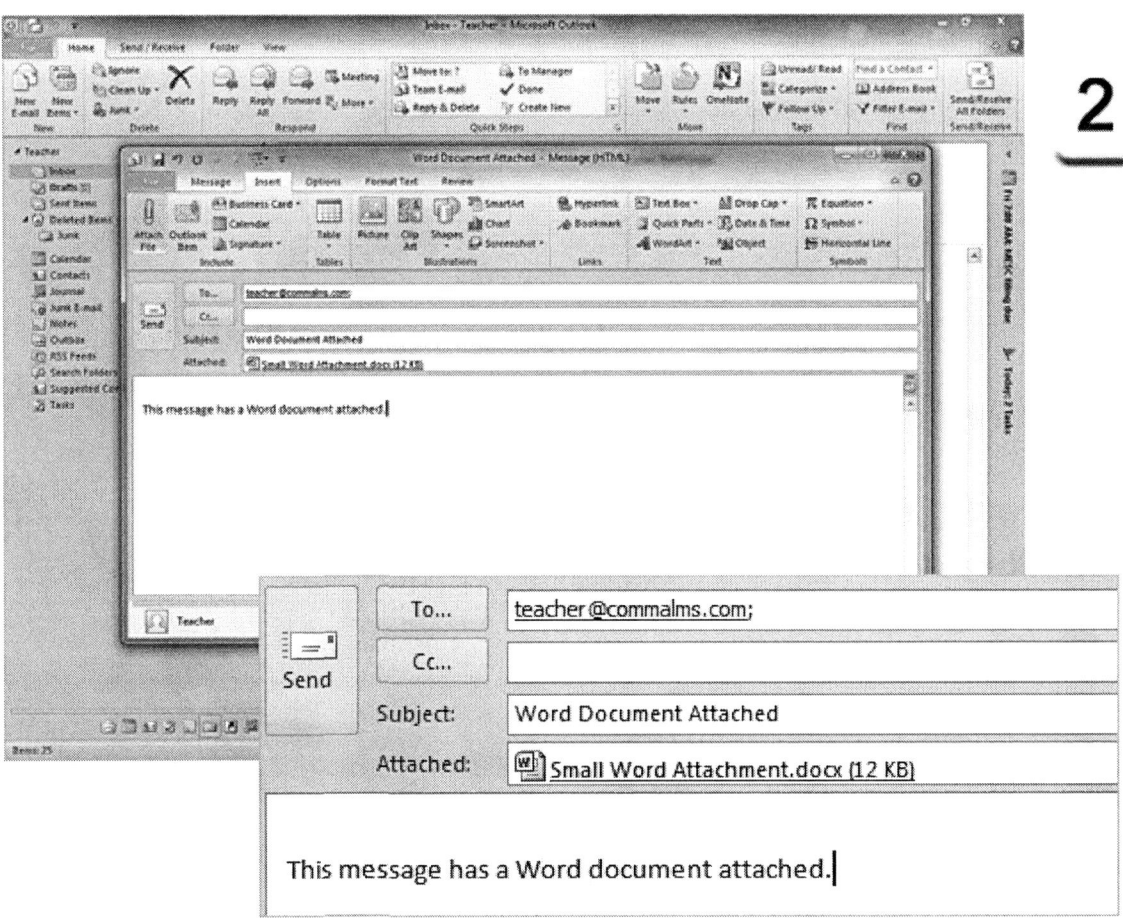

To... teacher@commalms.com;

Cc...

Subject: Word Document Attached

Attached: Small Word Attachment.docx (12 KB)

This message has a Word document attached.|

Exam 77-884: Microsoft Outlook 2010
2. Creating and Formatting Item Content
2.5. Attach content to email messages: Attach External Files

Receive Attachments

3. Try This: Review the Attachment

In our example, there should be a new E-mail with the subject, "Word Document Attached" in your Inbox. The paperclip indicates that this message has an attachment.

Select that E-mail.

What Do You See? In the Reading Pane on the right side of the screen capture has two views: Message and the Small Word Attachment. You can **Preview** the attached Word document by selecting it if you wish. You should see your name.

Keep going...

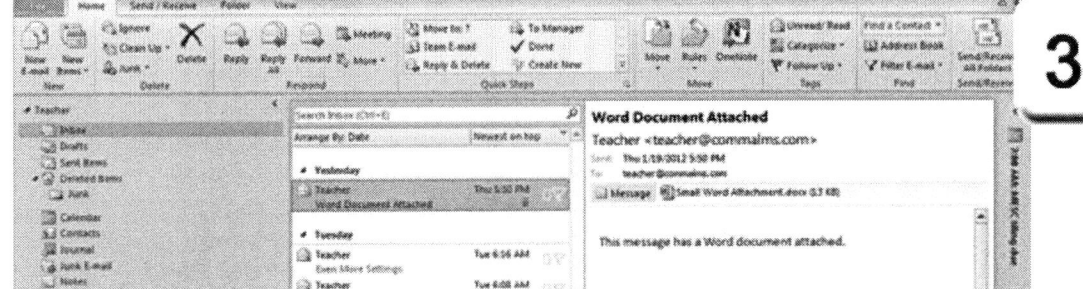

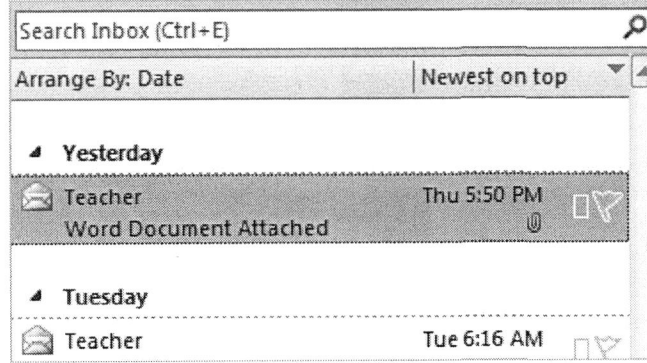

Search Inbox (Ctrl+E)	🔍
Arrange By: Date	Newest on top ▼

◢ Yesterday

✉ Teacher	Thu 5:50 PM
Word Document Attached 📎	

◢ Tuesday

✉ Teacher	Tue 6:16 AM

Word Document Attached

Teacher <teacher@commalms.com>

Sent: Thu 1/19/2012 5:50 PM

To: teacher@commalms.com

✉ Message 📄 Small Word Attachment.docx (13 KB)

This message has a Word document attached.

Exam 77-884: Microsoft Outlook 2010
2. Creating and Formatting Item Content
2.5. Attach content to email messages

Format Text ->Format->HTML

Create an E-mail Blast

An E-mail Blast is a marketing message that is sent to a mailing list. An E-mail Blast can be a customer support message or sales information, such as a price list.

You can use Microsoft Word and Microsoft Outlook to create an E-mail Merge. There are also commercial Microsoft Exchange Server systems available online. The Mail Merge lesson is shown in our Microsoft Word guide. This lesson focuses on the message options.

So far, we've made many messages with Plain or Rich Text. E-mail can be formatted in HTML like little web pages as well. Let's look at the authoring tools in Outlook.

1. Try it: Create a New E-mail
Go to **Home-> New-> New E-Mail.**
Enter your E-mail Address.
Enter the Subject: Table Talk.

Try This, Too: Confirm the Format
Go to **Format Text ->Format->HTML.**
Keep going...

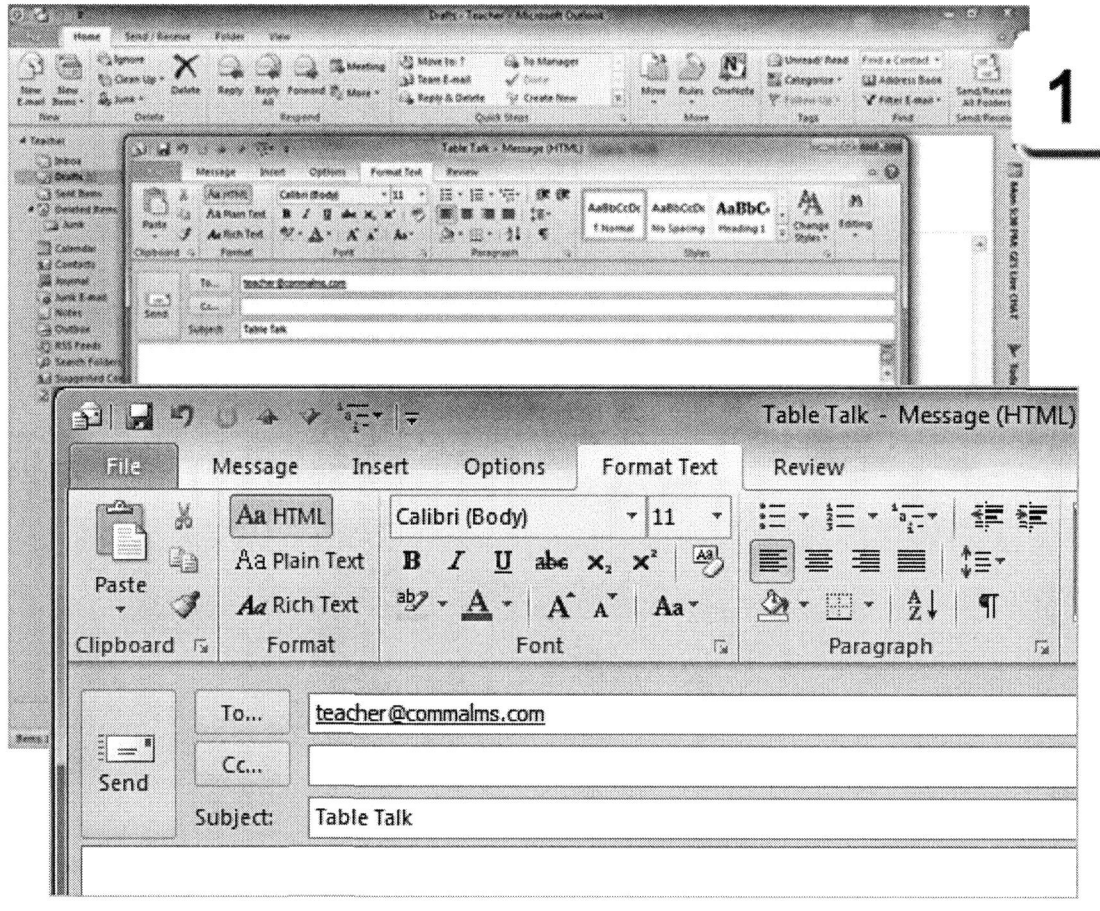

Exam 77-884: Microsoft Outlook 2010
2. Creating and Formatting Item Content
2.1. Create and send email messages: HTML Format

Insert a Table

Tables are used to organize web page layout and content. It is a basic design concept. In Microsoft Word we have several lessons that demonstrate how to insert and format tables.

You can use the same Table Tools to create an E-mail in Outlook. Here is a good example.

2. Try it: Insert a Table
The Table Talk Message is open.
Go to **Insert ->Tables->Table.**
Select the Cells: 3 Columns by 2 Rows.

Keep going...

Insert ->Tables->Table

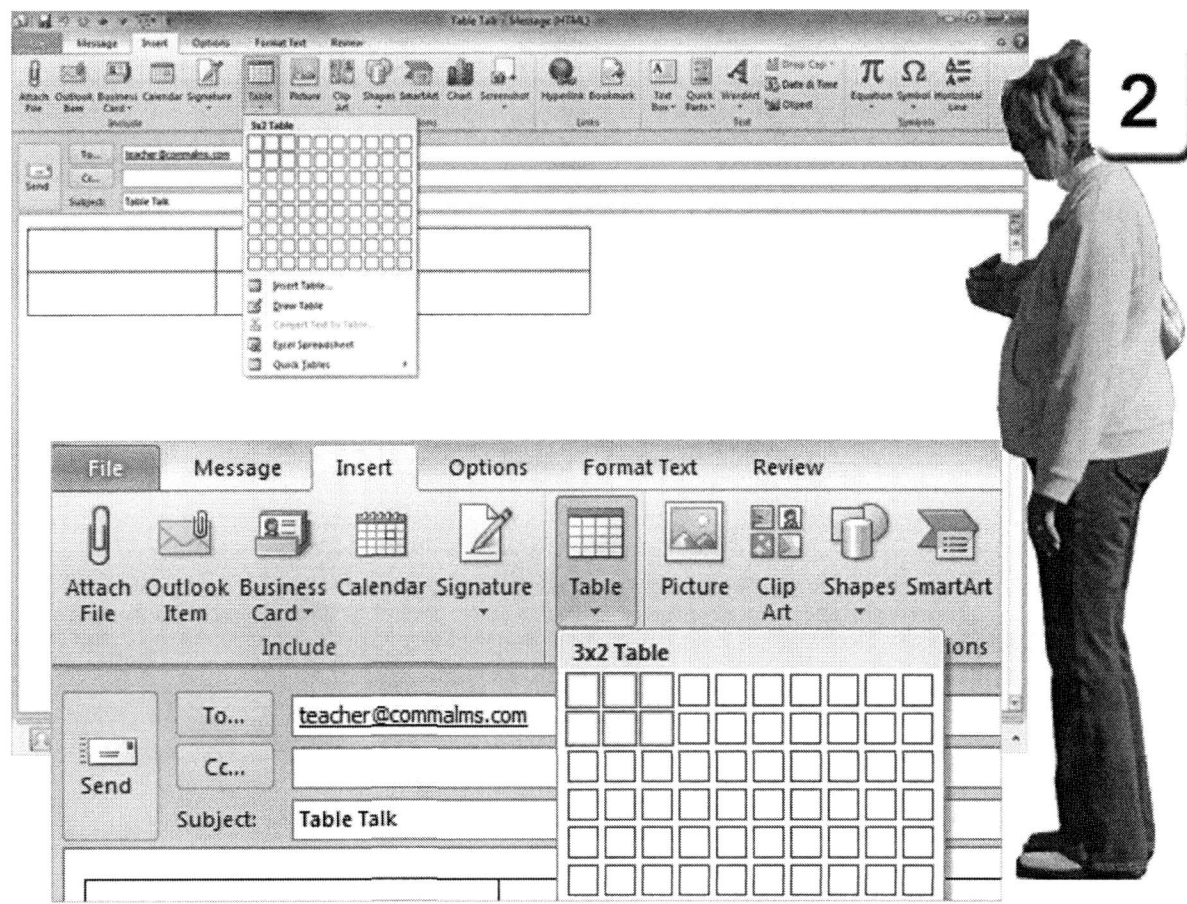

Exam 77-884: Microsoft Outlook 2010
2. Creating and Formatting Item Content
2.3. Create item content: Insert and Format Tables

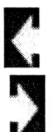

Hello, Table Tools

Tables are used to organize web page layout and content. It is a basic design concept. Microsoft Word has a good set of web page design tools. You can use the same **Table Tools** in Outlook. Here is a simple example.

3. Try it: Edit the Table Layout
Select the first row of the Table.
Go to **Table Tools ->Layout->Merge.**
Click on **Merge Cells.**

What Do You See? Cells A1:A3 were merged (combined) into one cell.

Keep going...

Table Tools ->Layout->Merge->Merge Cells

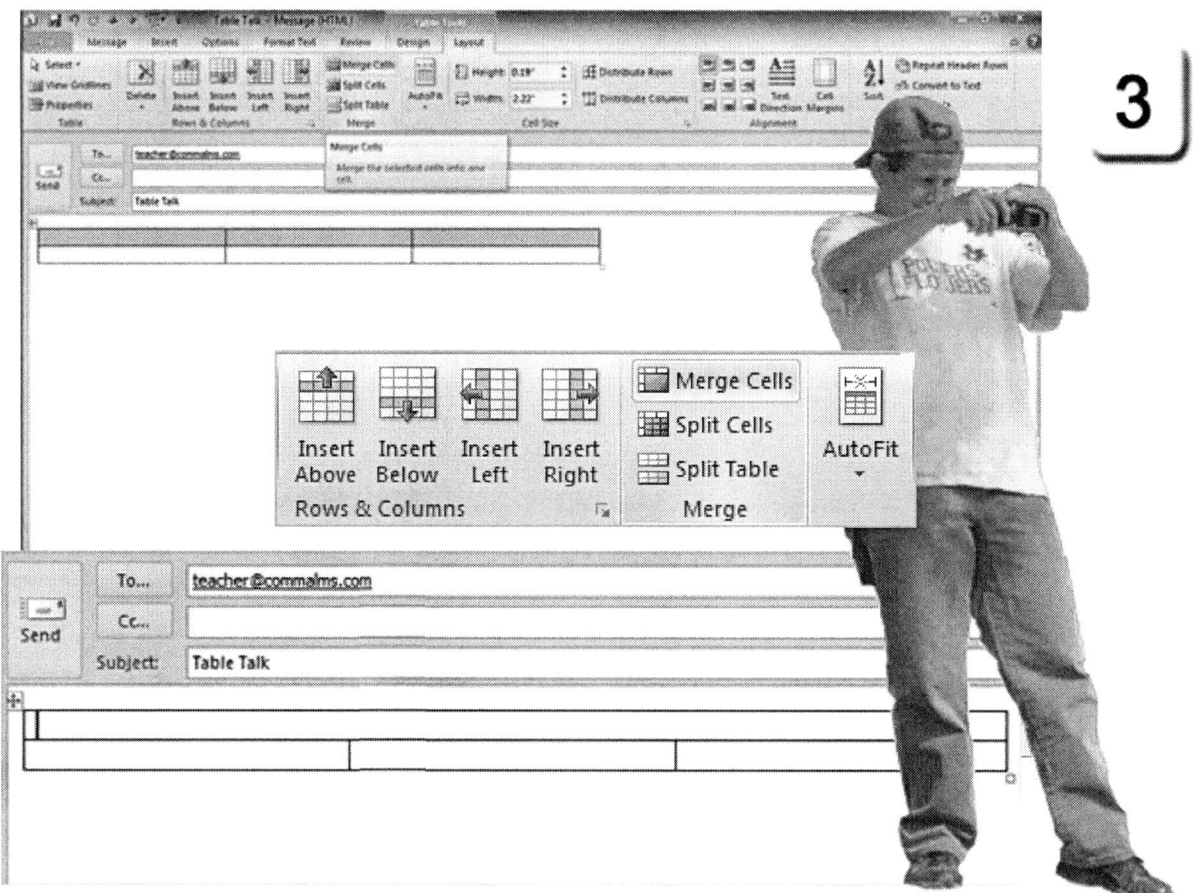

Exam 77-884: Microsoft Outlook 2010
2. Creating and Formatting Item Content
2.3. Create item content: Insert and Format Tables

Insert SmartArt

The Table can hold illustrations, text and links. This example will use SmartArt.

4. Try it: Insert SmartArt
The cursor is in Cell A1 of the table.
Go to **Insert ->Illustrations->SmartArt**.

What Do You See? You will be prompted to choose a SmartArt Graphic. On the left side is a list of categories.
Go to the **Picture** category.
Select **Titled Picture Accent List**.

Click **OK**. Keep going...

Insert ->Illustrations->SmartArt

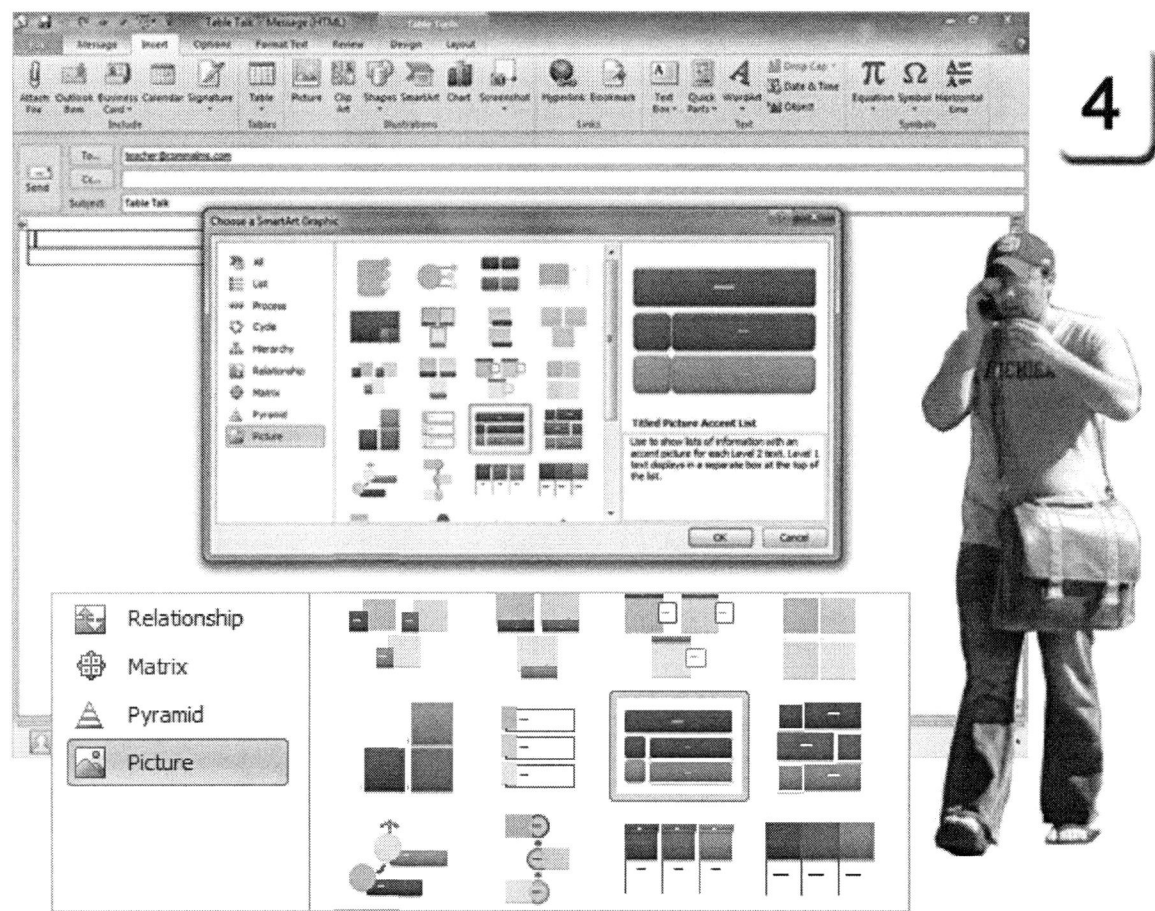

Exam 77-884: Microsoft Outlook 2010
2. Creating and Formatting Item Content
2.3. Create item content: Insert SmartArt

Hello, SmartArt
The SmartArt Graphic will be placed in Cell A1 of the table. There are two **SmartArt Tools**: Design and Format. There are also two **Table Tools**: Design and Layout.

5. Try it: Edit the SmartArt
Enter the following text in the SmartArt:
Shape 1: Customer Support
Shape 2: Online
Shape 3: In Person

Keep going...

SmartArt Tools

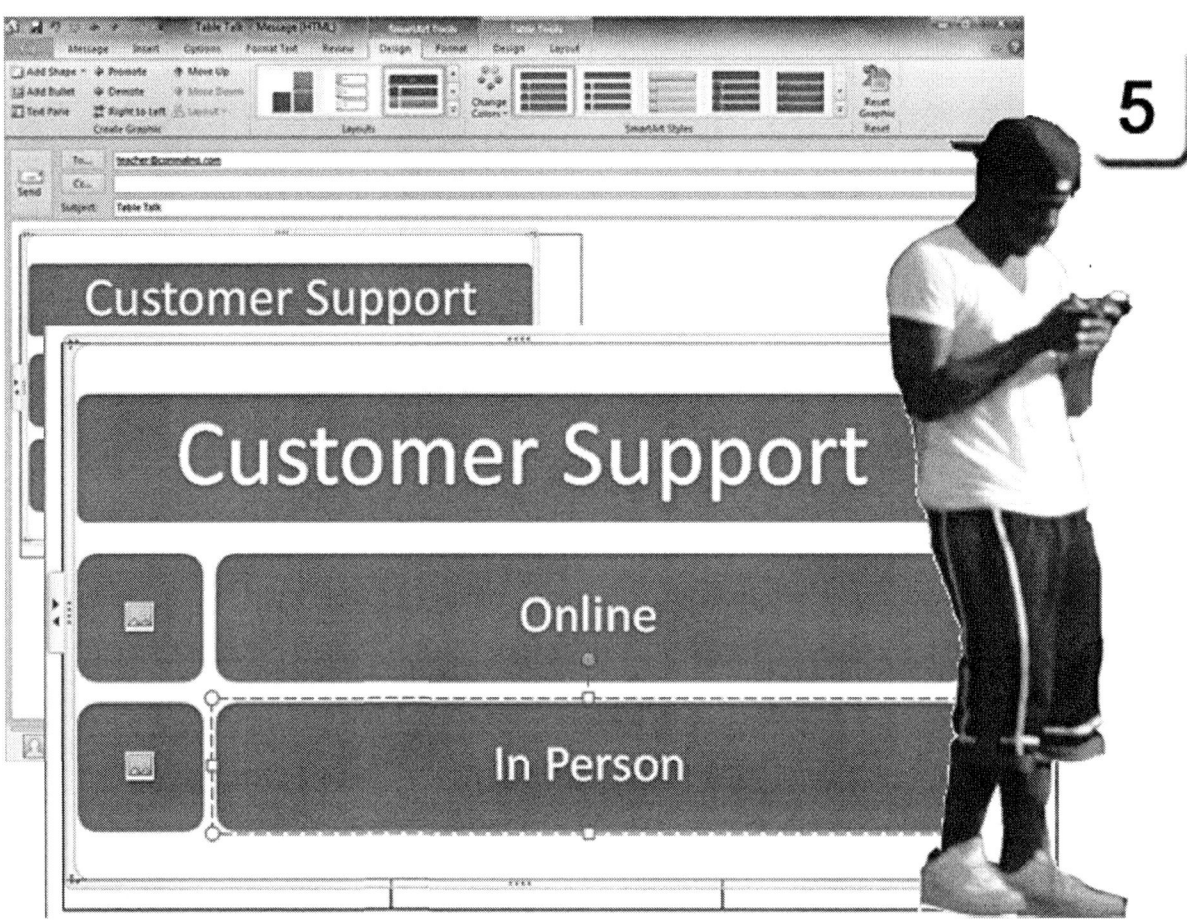

Exam 77-884: Microsoft Outlook 2010
2. Creating and Formatting Item Content
2.3. Create item content: Format SmartArt

Add a Picture to the SmartArt

6. Try it: Add a Picture to the SmartArt
Click on **Picture Placeholder 1**.
Browse to the Documents folder.
Select a picture: laptop
Click **Insert**.
The picture should fill the Shape.

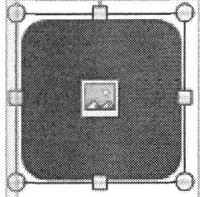

Click on **Picture Placeholder 2**.
Browse to the Documents folder.
Select a picture: phone
Click **Insert**.
The picture should fill the second Shape.

This is getting interesting. Keep going...

Insert ->Include

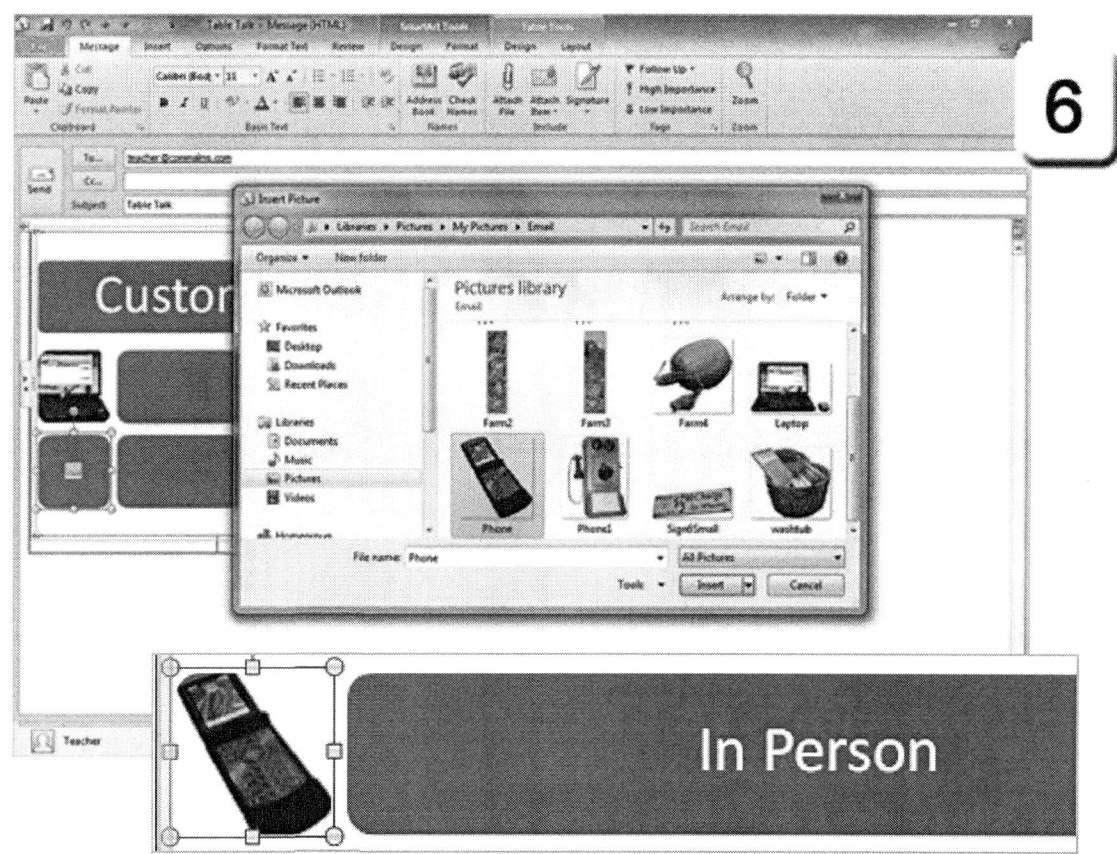

Exam 77-884: Microsoft Outlook 2010
2. Creating and Formatting Item Content
2.3. Create item content: Format SmartArt

Choose a Message Theme

7. Try it: Choose a Message Theme
Go to **Options ->Themes.**
Select a **Theme**: Concourse.

What Do You See? The Theme formatted everything in the message including the colors, fonts and Effects of the Table and the SmartArt.

Not done, yet. Keep going...

Options ->Themes->Theme

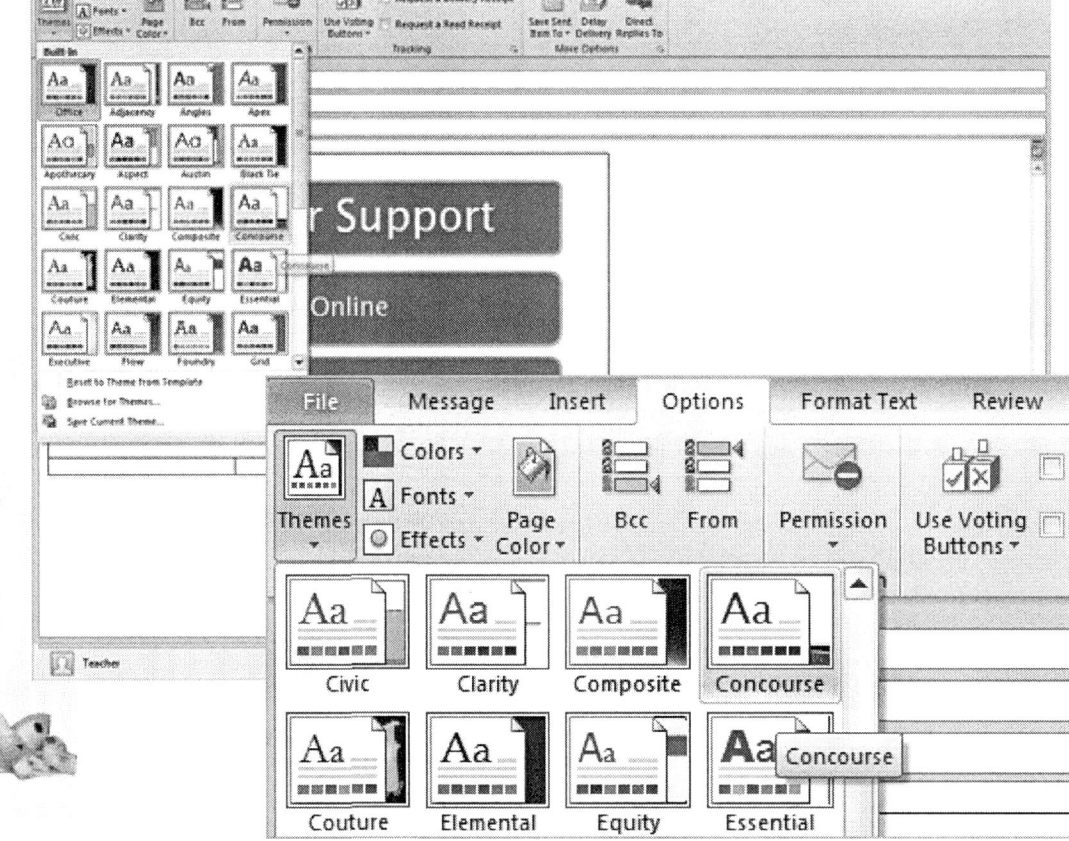

Exam 77-884: Microsoft Outlook 2010
2. Creating and Formatting Item Content
2.1. Create and send email messages: Specify a Message Theme

Change the SmartArt Colors
In addition to the message Theme Colors, you can edit the SmartArt Colors as well.

Before You Begin: Find the SmartArt Tools
Select the SmartArt. The **SmartArt Tools** should be available. The **Design Ribbon** has:
Create Graphic
Layouts
SmartArt Styles
Reset

8. Try it: Edit the SmartArt Design
Go to **SmartArt Tools ->Design**.
Go to **SmartArt Styles->Change Colors**.
Select: Colorful Range-Accent Colors 3-4

Keep going...

SmartArt Tools ->Design->SmartArt Styles->Change Colors

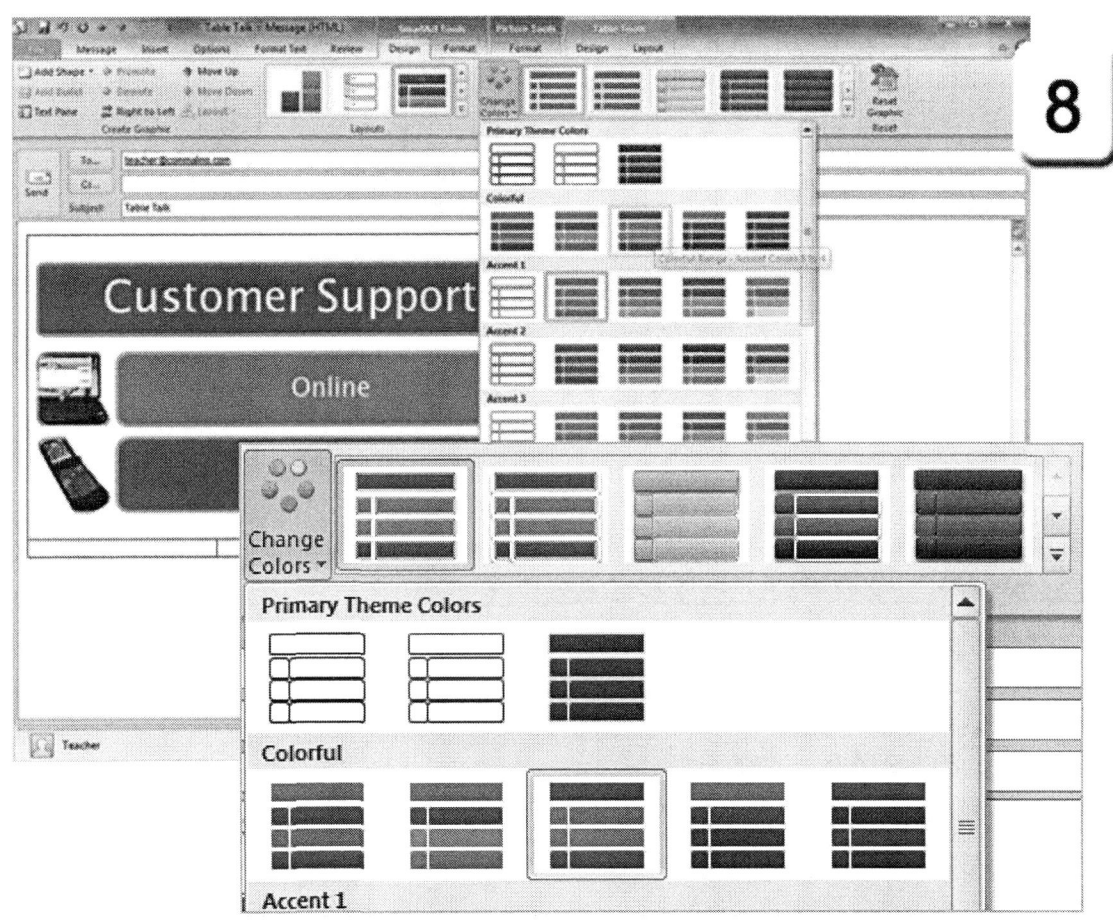

Exam 77-884: Microsoft Outlook 2010
2. Creating and Formatting Item Content
2.3. Create item content: Format SmartArt

Edit the Table Layout

The following pages will edit the Table layout and add a picture to complete the E-mail Blast.

9. Try it: Merge Table Cells
Select Cells B2:C2
Go to **Table Tools ->Layout->Merge.**
Click on **Merge Cells.**

What Do You See? The two cells were merged. This "super cell" will hold a picture.

Keep going...

Table Tools ->Layout->Merge->Merge Cells

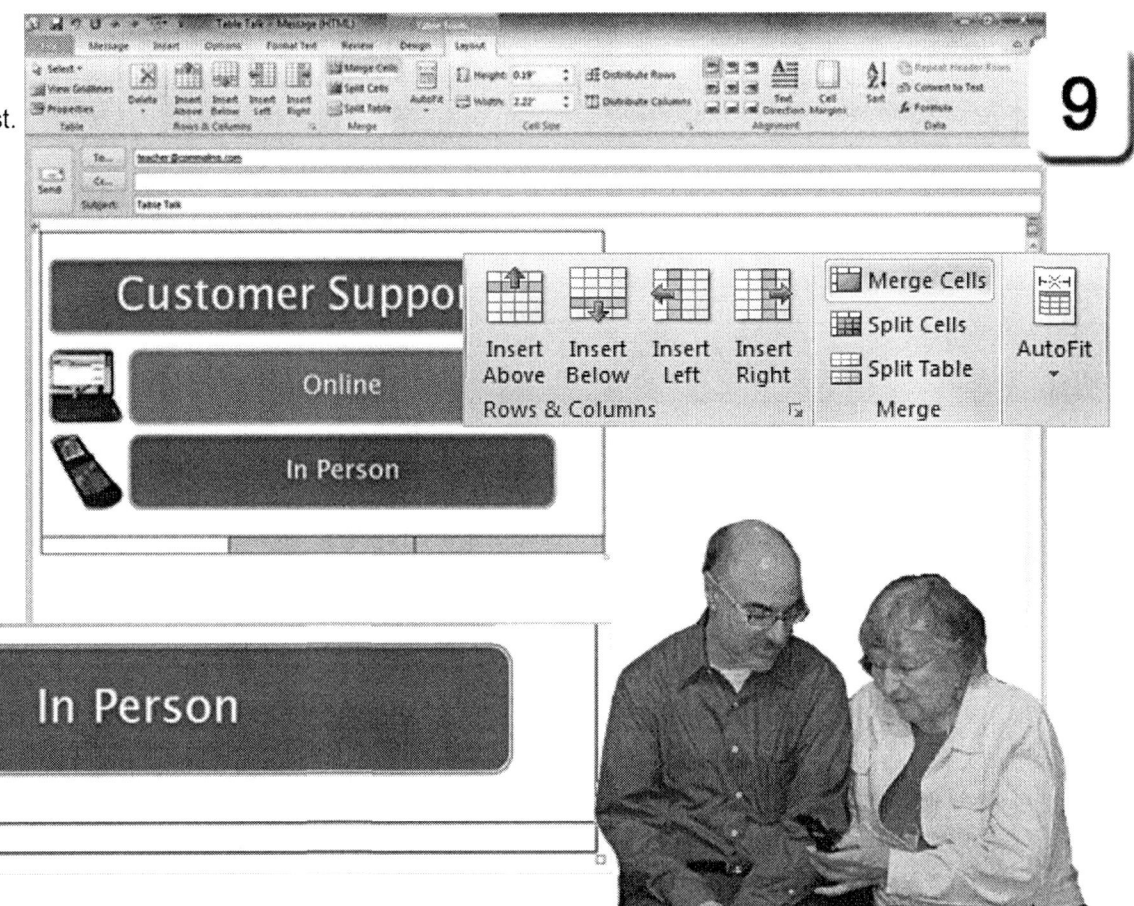

Exam 77-884: Microsoft Outlook 2010
2. Creating and Formatting Item Content
2.3. Create item content: Format Table Layout

Insert a Picture

Try it: Insert a Picture
Select Cell B1.
Go to **Insert ->Illustrations->Picture.**
Browse to the Documents folder.
Select: Applebox2.jpg

Select Cell B2.
Go to **Insert ->Illustrations->Picture.**
Browse to the Documents folder.
Select: Sign6Small.jpg

Keep going...

Insert ->Illustrations->Picture

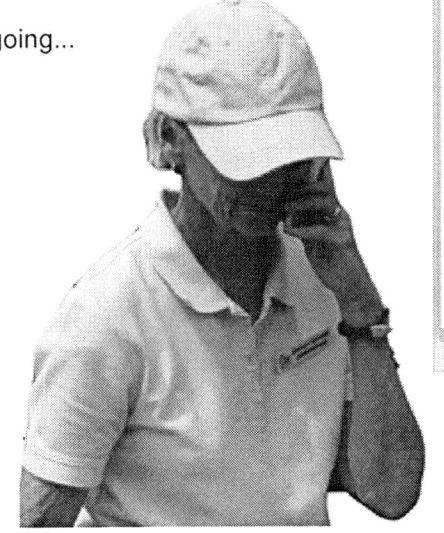

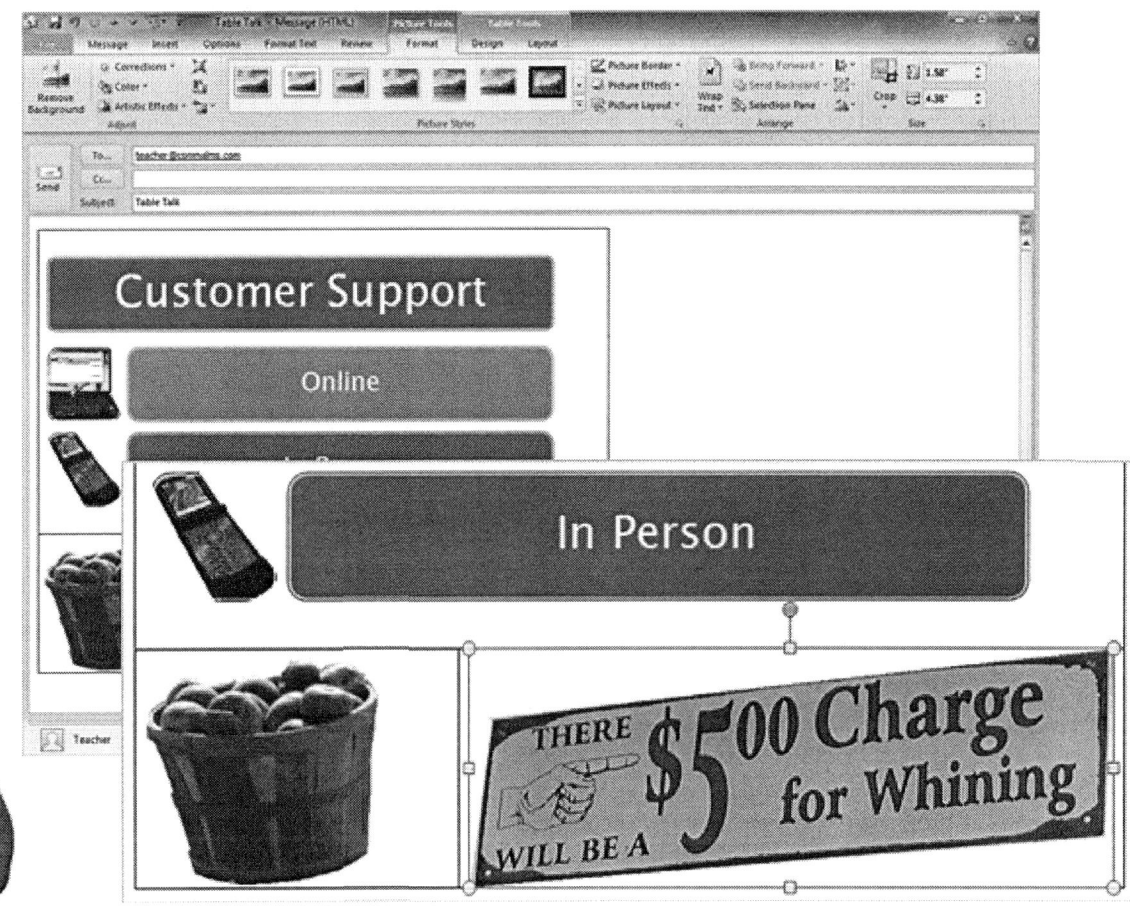

Exam 77-884: Microsoft Outlook 2010
2. Creating and Formatting Item Content
2.3. Create item content: Insert Pictures

Edit the Table Design
Try it: Format the Borders
Select the Table.
Go to **Table Tools ->Design->Table Styles.**
Go to **Borders->No Border.**

What Do You See? The Table is still there--
holding the pictures, text and graphics--
however the Table is hidden.

That was cool.

Table Tools ->Design->Table Styles->Borders

Exam 77-884: Microsoft Outlook 2010
2. Creating and Formatting Item Content
2.3. Create item content: Format Table Layout

Attach a Picture to a Message

There are three different ways to add pictures to a message: as part of a graphic or shape, such as SmartArt, as a picture in the message, and as an attachment.

Let's add an attachment to our mighty E-mail Blast and send it on it's way.

1. Try it: Include a Picture
The Sample E-mail is still open.
Go to **Insert ->Include-> Attach File.**
Browse to the Documents Folder.
Select: Keep It Clean.gif.
Click **Insert** to attach the file and return to the message.

What Do You See? There is an attachment in the Attached field under the Subject. The attachment has the little icon for picture. The size of the file is shown in parenthesis (105 KB).

Click **Send**. Keep going...

Insert ->Include-> Attach File

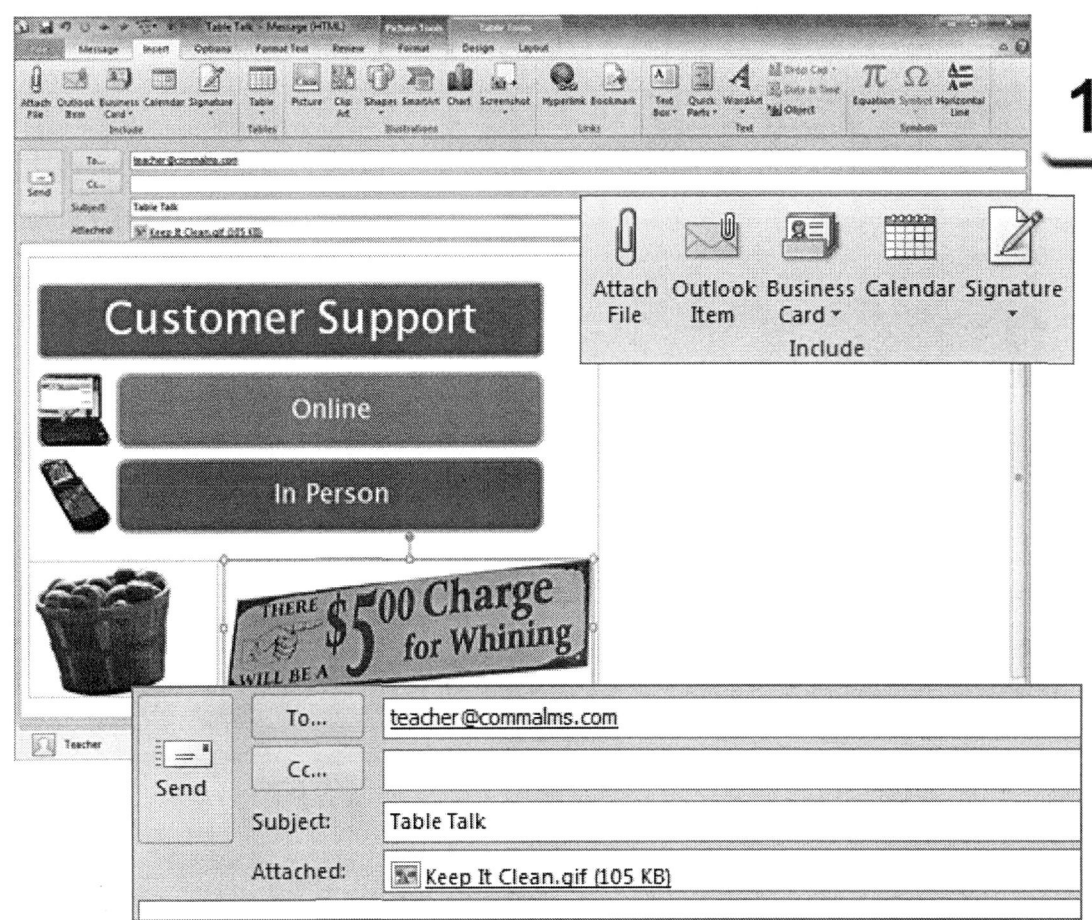

HOME

Review the E-Mail Blast
2. Try it: Review the Message
The E-mail Blast has arrived. A new message is in the Inbox with the Subject: Table Talk. The message has a paperclip which means there is an attachment.

What Do You See? The SmartArt and pictures look great. The Table keeps these graphics in place if the Preview pane is resized.

What Else Do You See? Look at the top of the message in the **Header.** This message has an attachment. The icon indicates that it is a picture. The size is shown in parenthesis (105 KB).

Keep going...

Outlook ->Inbox

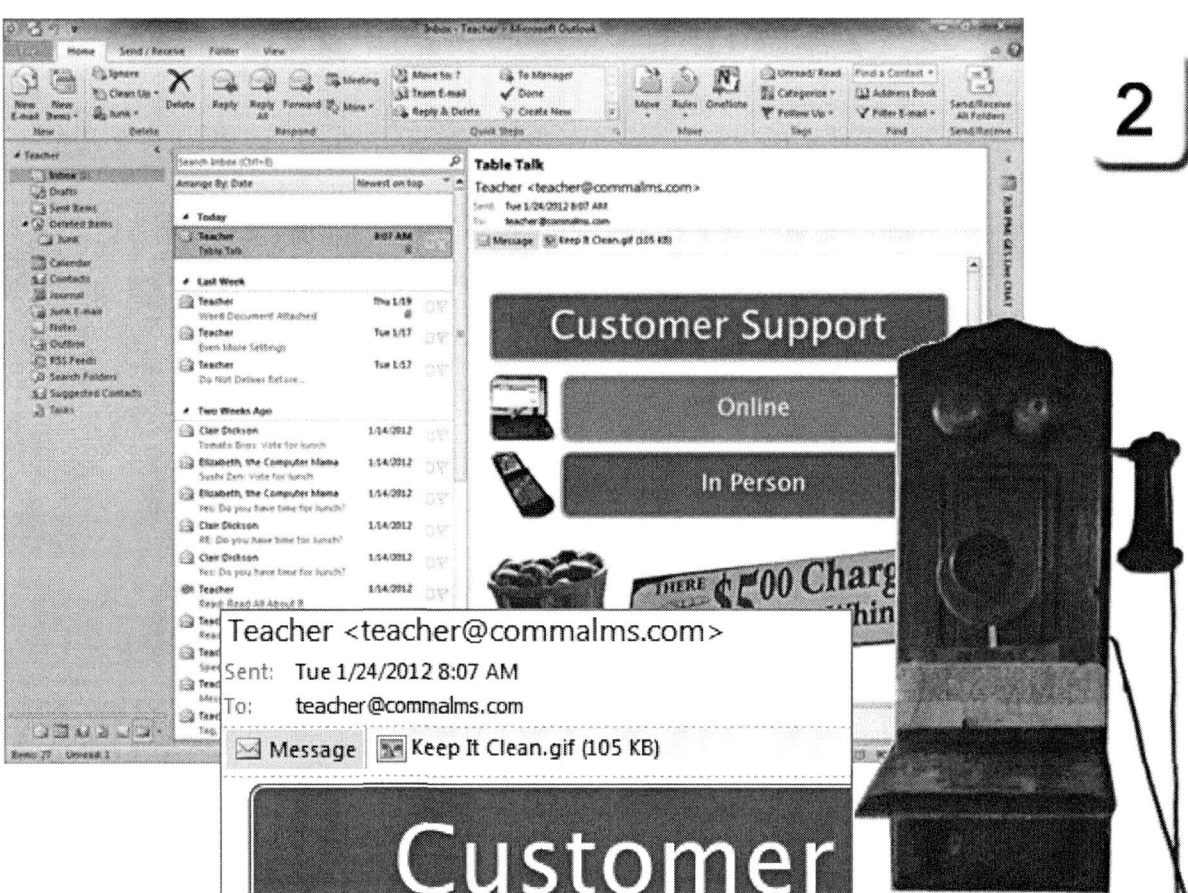

2

Hello, Attachment Tools

When you click on the attachment you can see the picture in the Preview pane. The **Attachment Tools** will be available, too.

3. Try it: Review the Attachment Tools
Select the attachment.
Go to **Attachment Tools->Attachments**.

What Do You See? The Attachment Tools include Action, Selection and Message.

Keep going...

Attachment Tools->Attachments

Keep It Clean.gif

Size: 105 KB

Image dimensions: 482 x 420

3

Exam 77-884: Microsoft Outlook 2010
2. Creating and Formatting Item Content
2.5. Attach content to email messages: The Attachment Tools

Save an Attachment

E-mail transfers millions of business files everyday. You should know how to **Save** the attachments to your drive.

Before You Begin: Select the Attachment
Go to the sample Table Talk E-mail.
Click on the attachment in the message.
The **Attachment Tools** should be available.

4. Try This: Save the Attachment
Go to **Attachment Tools->Attachments**.
Click on **Save As.**
Browse to your Documents Folder.
Click **Save.** You will return to the Inbox.

There's more on this subject. Keep going...

Memo to Self: Most of the Attachment Tools are available when you right-click an attachment as well.

Something to Remember: Save All Attachments can save a lot of time!

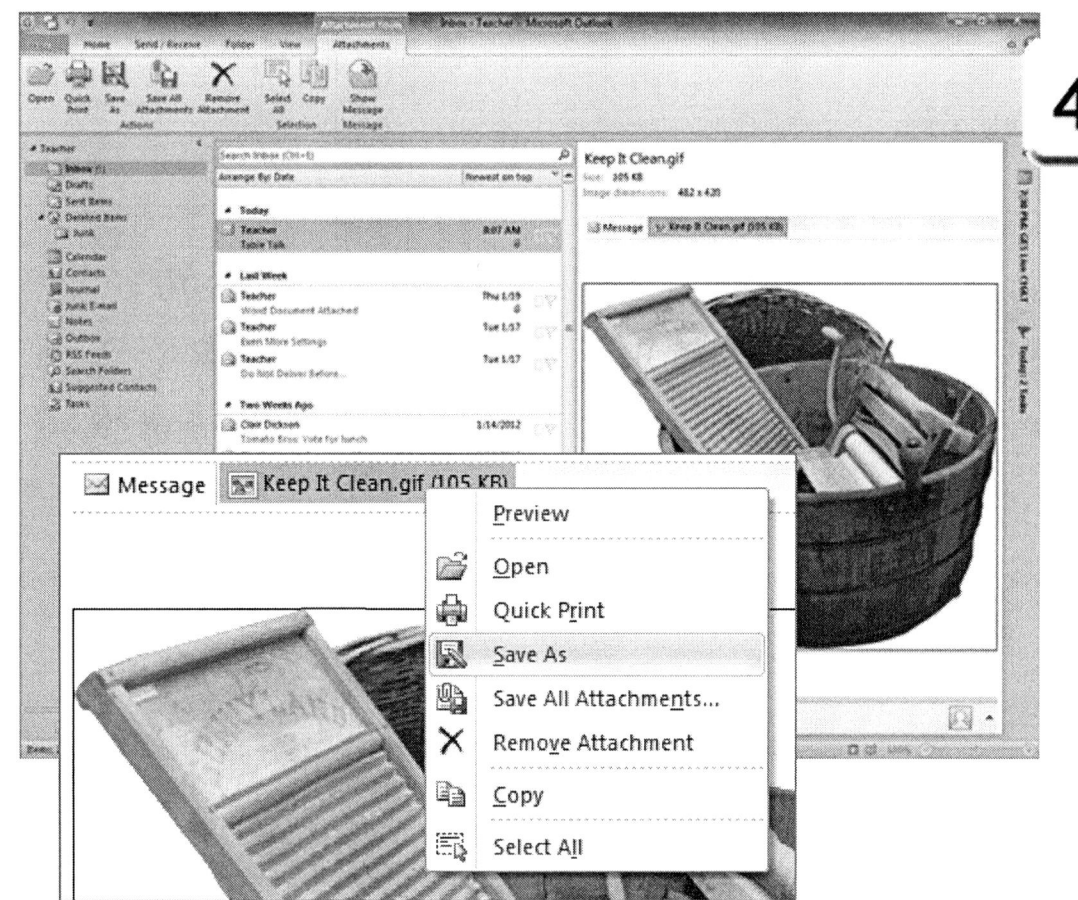

Exam 77-884: Microsoft Outlook 2010
3. Managing Email Messages
3.1. Clean up the mailbox: Save Message Attachments

Forward an E-mail Attachment

When you Reply to a message that has an attachment, the attachment is not included in the Reply. When you Forward a message, the attachment will be included.

5. Try it: Forward an E-mail Attachment
Select the sample Table Talk E-mail.
Go to **Home ->Respond->Forward.**

What Do You See? There should be a new message. The Subject has been appended as FW: Table Talk.

There is an attachment in the Attached field under the Subject. The attachment has the little icon for picture. The size of the file is shown in parenthesis (105 KB).

Do This, Too: Send the E-mail
Address the e-mail to yourself.
Click **Send**. Keep going...

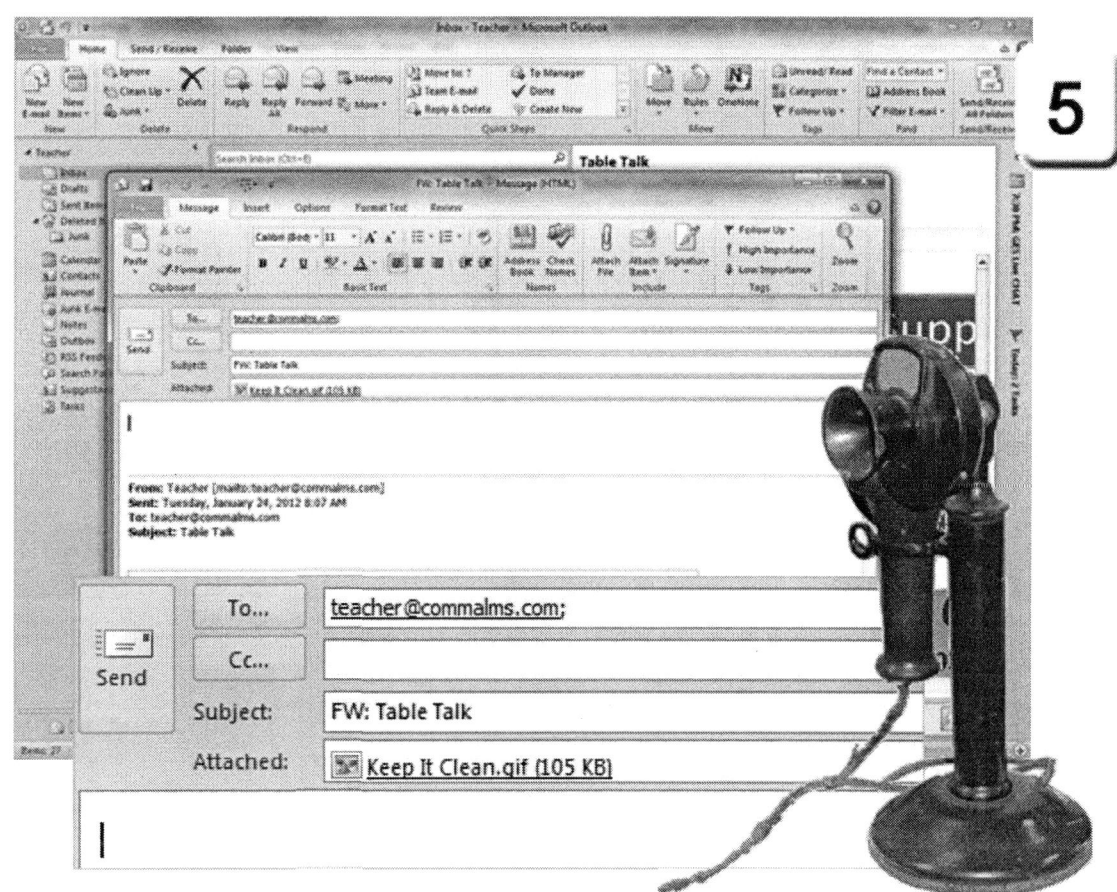

Exam 77-884: Microsoft Outlook 2010
2. Creating and Formatting Item Content
2.1. Create and send email messages: Forward an Attachment

Forward as an Attachment

You can also forward the E-mail message--including all of the pictures, SmartArt and attachments--as an attachment.

6. Try it: Forward as an Attachment
Select the sample Table Talk E-mail.
Go to **Home ->Respond->More**.
Select **Forward as Attachment**.

What Do You See? There should be a new message. The Subject has been appended as FW: Table Talk.

There is an attachment in the Attached field under the Subject. The attachment has the little message icon. The size of the file is shown in parenthesis (272 KB).

Do This, Too: Send the E-mail
Address the e-mail to yourself.
Click **Send**. Keep going.

Home ->Respond->More->Forward as Attachment

Exam 77-884: Microsoft Outlook 2010
2. Creating and Formatting Item Content
2.1. Create and send email messages: Forward as an Attachment

Save an E-mail Message

The default file type is the Outlook Message Format, which requires Outlook to read.

It is also possible to save the whole message in an external format so that you can read it without having to open it in Outlook.

7. Try it: Save an E-mail Message
Select the sample Table Talk E-mail.
Go to **File->Save As**.
Select a **Save as Type**: HTML.
Browse to your Documents Folder.
Click **Save**. You will return to the Inbox.

The message has been saved as an HTML document. So, what does that look like? Keep going...

File->Save As

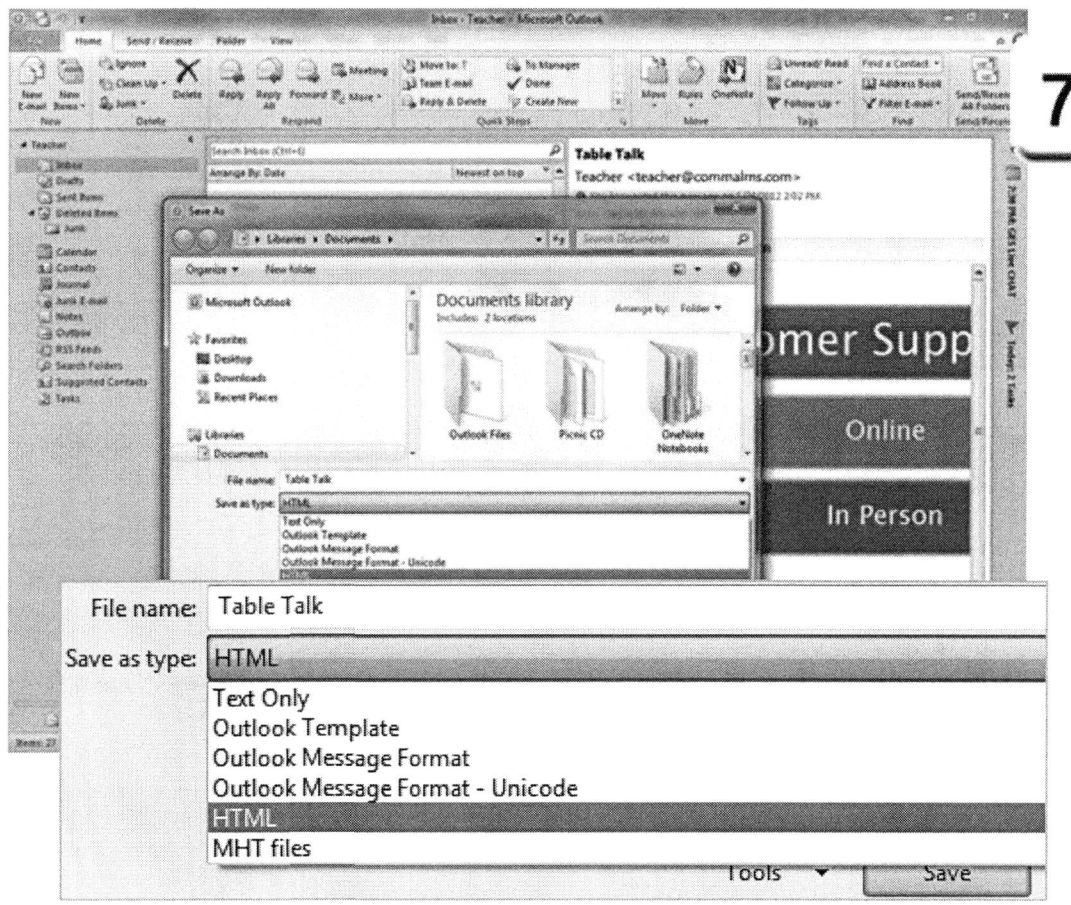

File name:	Table Talk
Save as type:	HTML
	Text Only
	Outlook Template
	Outlook Message Format
	Outlook Message Format - Unicode
	HTML
	MHT files

Exam 77-884: Microsoft Outlook 2010
3. Managing Email Messages
3.1. Clean up the mailbox: Save a Message in an External Format

Review the HTML file

In this example, the E-mail was saved to the Documents folder. Here are the steps to open and review the HTML file.

8. Try it: Open the HTML File

Go to the Documents Folder.
Double-click the Table Talk file.

Table Talk

What Do You See? The HTML file should open your Internet Browser. At the top of the page is the information from the message Header. The images and pictures are still organized in a Table. However, the attachment is not included. OK, that's a good lesson on how to add content to your E-mail.

The HTML file opened in a Web Browser

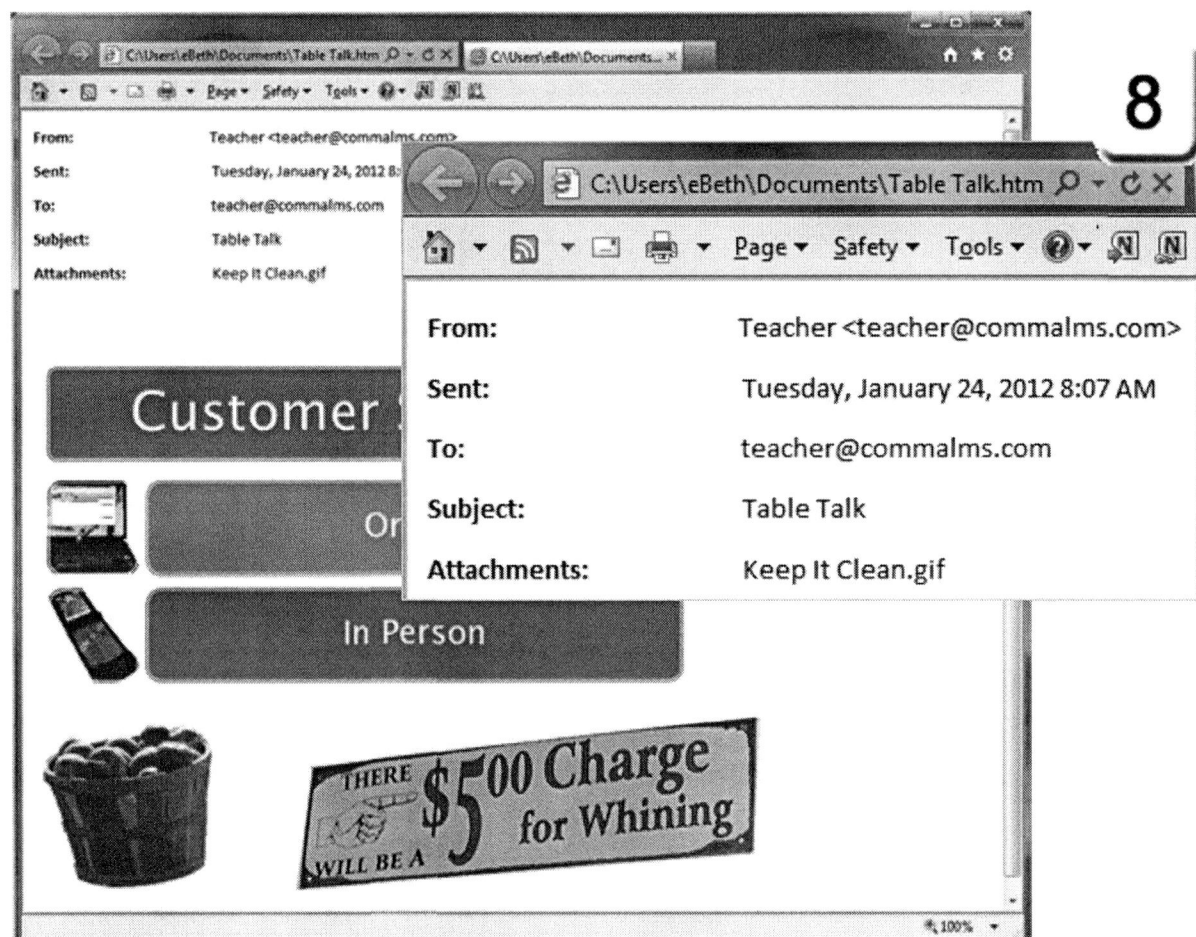

Inbox Caution Signs

Any discussion on E-mail attachments has to include some cautionary tales. E-mail attachments can be infected or worse.

Review a Sample Security Banner

The image on this page has a warning banner above the message Header. The banner indicates that Microsoft Outlook blocked the pictures and hyperlinks in this message to protect your privacy.

If you trust the sender you can click on the security banner and download the pictures.

Memo to Self: How can a picture invade your privacy? Pictures, and other files, can be infected with Spyware, software that monitors every keystroke and sends that information back to the source.

Microsoft Outlook->Inbox

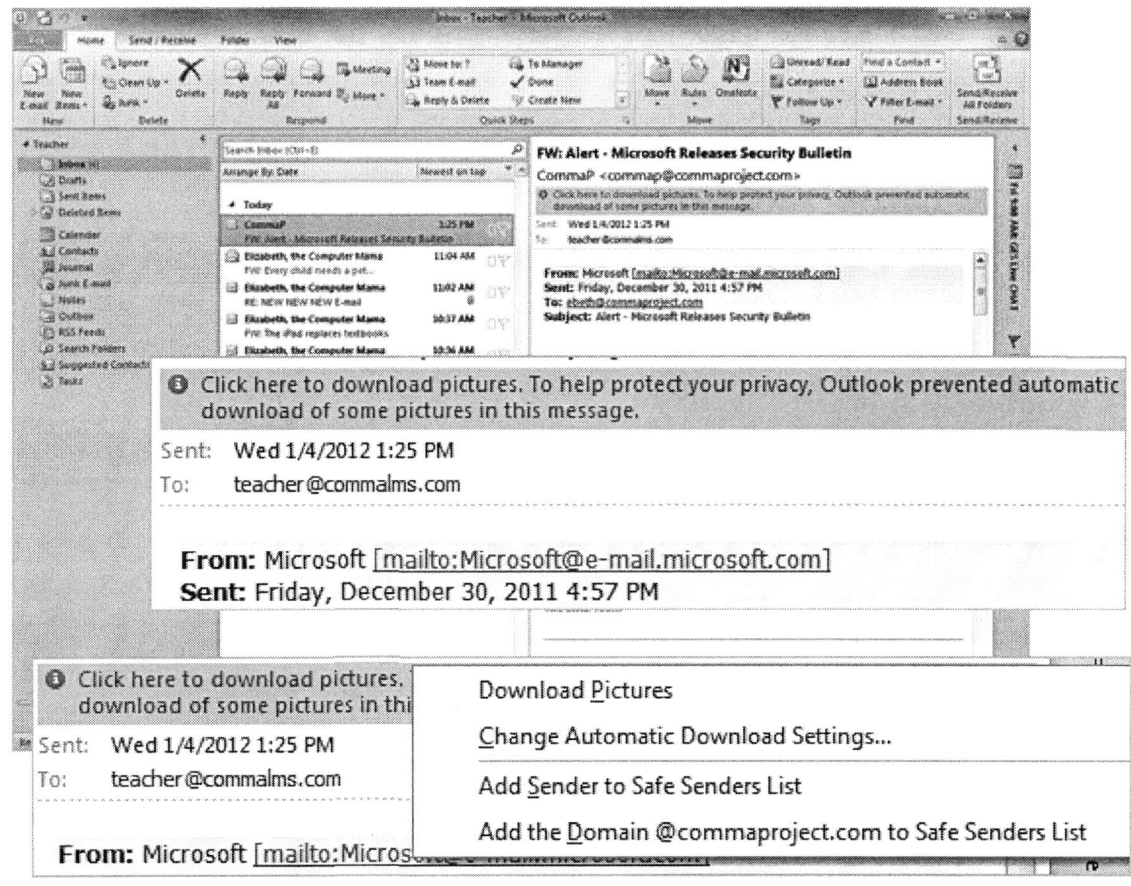

Exam 77-884: Microsoft Outlook 2010
2. Creating and Formatting Item Content
2.5. Attach content to email messages: Privacy and Security

More Concerns

When you open an attachment, Microsoft Outlook will prompt you to consider if the attachment has come from a trusted friend or colleague.

Try it: Open an Attachment
Select the sample Table Talk E-mail.
Double-click the attachment.

What Do You See? The warning box has three options: Open, Save, Cancel.
Click **Open** to see the picture.

Outlook Inbox

Opening Mail Attachment

You should only open attachments from a trustworthy source.

Attachment: Keep It Clean.gif from Inbox - Teacher - Microsoft Outlook

Would you like to open the file or save it to your computer?

Open   Save   Cancel

☑ Always ask before opening this type of file

Exam 77-884: Microsoft Outlook 2010
2. Creating and Formatting Item Content
2.5. Attach content to email messages

Summary

This lesson created an E-mail Blast that has SmartArt as well as pictures. We looked at three different methods for adding pictures to a message: as part of a graphic, inserted into a Table and as an attachment.

Our practice with Attachments introduced the Attachment Tools and options for saving the attachment as well as the E-mail.

Practice is over! An E-mail Blast should have lots and lots of recipients. Grab a couple of cookies and send a message to every customer you know!

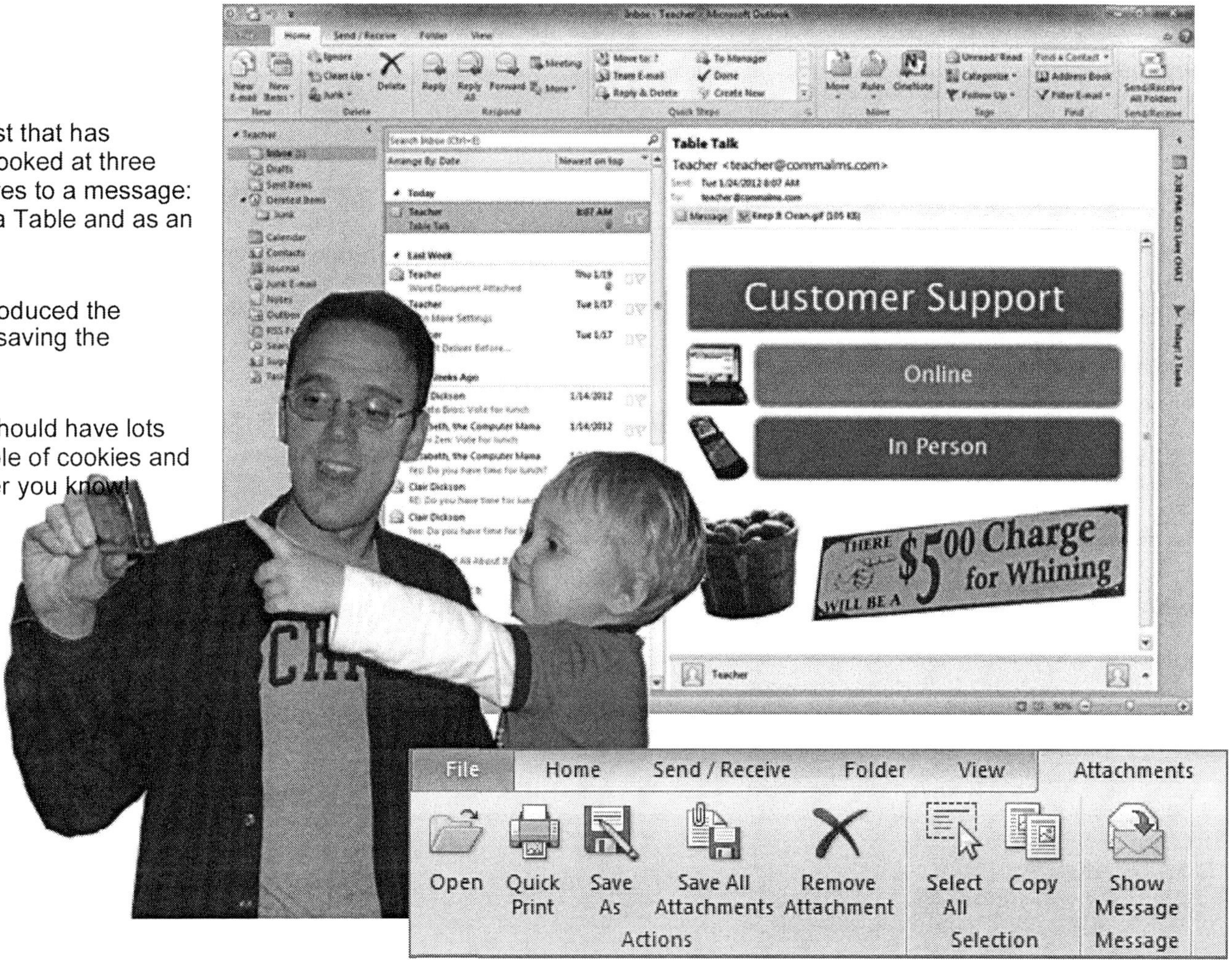

Test Yourself

1. Which of the following can be an attachment? (Give all correct answers.)
A. Word document
B. Excel spreadsheet
C. Presentation
D. Pictures
Tip: Complete Guide to Outlook, page 86

2. Which Ribbon has the command to add an attachment to an E-mail?
A. Options
B. Insert
C. Attachments
D. File
Tip: Complete Guide to Outlook, page 87

3. What does the paper clip icon on an E-mail represent?
A. The e-mail has been forwarded.
B. The e-mail has an attachment.
C. An attachment has been opened.
Tip: Complete Guide to Outlook, page 88

4. Which Ribbon has the command to add a Table?
A. Insert
B. Options
C. Format
D. Table Tools
Tip: Complete Guide to Outlook, page 91

5. Which are the SmartArt Ribbons?
A. Design and Format
B. Design and Layout
C. Options and Format
D. Options and Design
Tip: Complete Guide to Outlook, page 94

6. When applied a Theme also applies to the colors, fonts and effects of Tables and SmartArt
A. True
B. False
Tip: Complete Guide to Outlook, page 96

7. Which Ribbon has the command to add or remove Borders on a Table?
A. Format
B. Table Tools--> Format
C. Table Tools--> Design
D. Design
Tip: Complete Guide to Outlook, page 100

Practice

1. Open a new blank E-mail. Address it to yourself.
2. Add the text: Remaining Stock
3. Insert a Table that's 3 columns by 3 rows.
Add the following data to the columns

Item	Small	Large
Plush bear	10	2
Plush bear with hat	6	14

4. Apply a Table Style of your Choice
Put borders around the outside of the Table, but none between the rows or columns
5. Apply the Theme: Composite
6. Add the picture of a bear to the E-mail
7. Create a new Word document with the text.
Clearance Sale!
Sell the last of the celebration bears!
Save the document as Bear Flyer.
8. Return to Outlook.
Attach the document Bear Flyer to your email.
9. Send the E-mail.
10. Go to the Inbox to confirm.

Application Question: What are the benefits to using a picture with content, such as pictures in an E-mail? What are the benefits of using SmartArt in an E-mail?

Take One

Signed, Sealed and Delivered

Microsoft Outlook Objectives
In this lesson, you will learn how to:

1. Organize the Inbox with folders and move E-mail to those folders

2. Create and modify Rules to automate moving E-mail to the right folders

3. Use Quick Steps to move messages

4. Add custom Rules to the Quick Steps Library

5. Clean up the mailbox

6. Manage Junk Mail

© 2011 Comma Productions, LLC

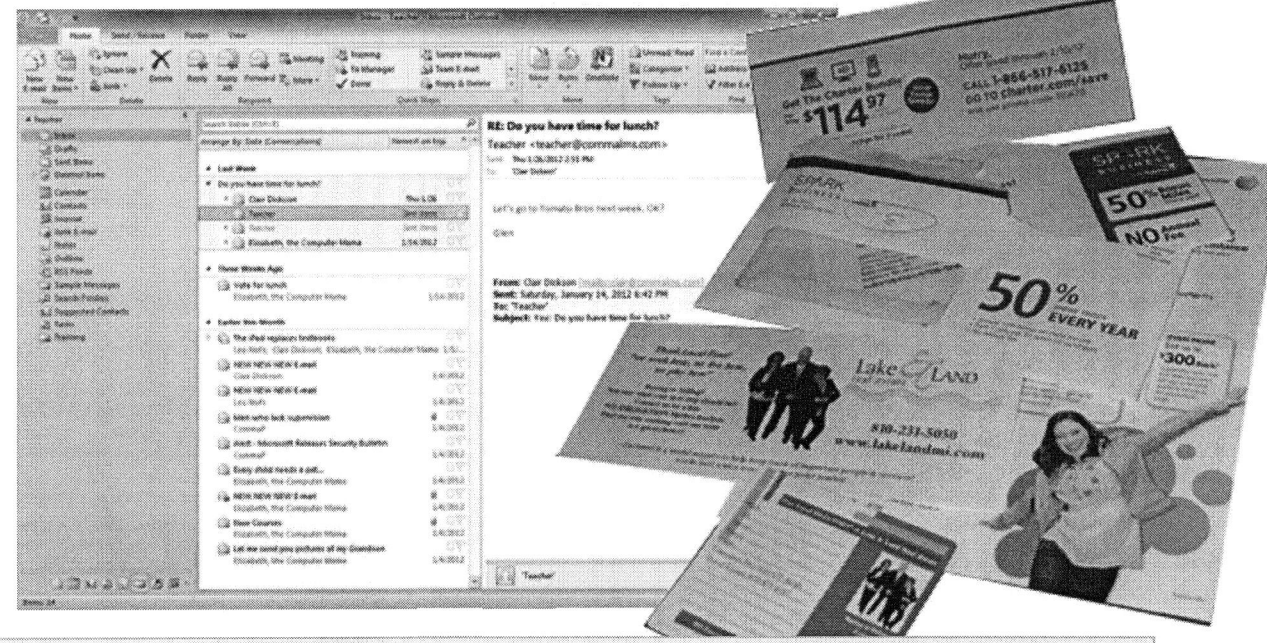

Lesson 5 : Signed, Sealed and Delivered

1. Readings

Read Lesson 5 in the Advanced Excel guide, page 113-147.

Project

Sample E-mails that review the Move and Clean Up options.

Downloads

GlenGlick1.gif,
GlenGlick2.gif,
GlenGlick3.gif
GlenGlick1.gif

2. Practice

Complete the Practice Activity on page 148.

3. Assessment

Review the Test questions on page 148.

Home Ribbon

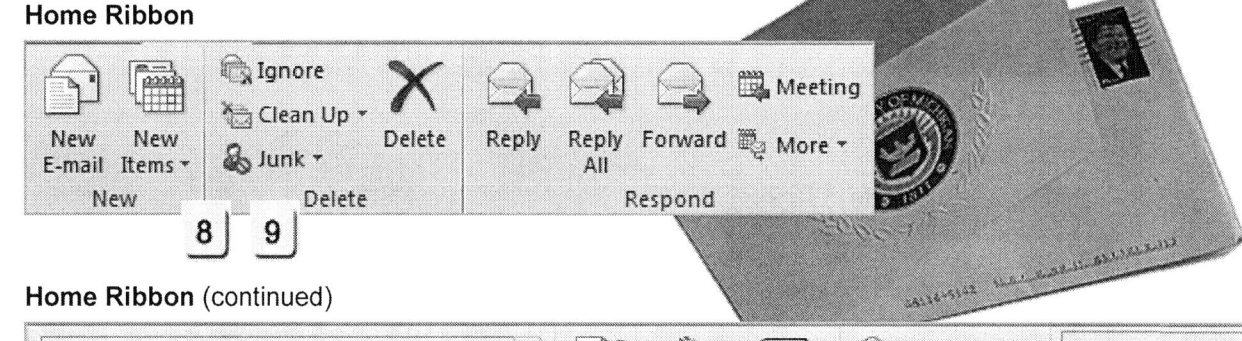

Home Ribbon (continued)

Menu Maps

From the **Home Ribbon**.

1. Home ->Move->Move, page 119
2. Home ->Move->Rules, page 121
3. Home ->Move->Rules->Manage Rules & Alerts, page 124
4. Home ->Move->Rules->Create Rule..., page 126
5. Home ->Quick Steps->Reply and Delete, page 129
6. Home ->Quick Steps->Create New->Options, page 131
7. Home ->Quick Steps->Manage Quick Steps, page 132
8. Home ->Delete->Clean Up, page 138
9. Home ->Delete->Junk, page 141

More Menu Maps

From the **Folder Ribbon**

1. Folder ->New->New Folder, page 117
2. Folder ->Properties, page 137

From the **View Ribbon**

1. View ->Conversations, page 135

Managing the Inbox

The beginning lessons in Microsoft Outlook looked at ways to make rich E-mails and track the responses. Say your E-mail Blast was a success and the Inbox is stuffed with responses. Microsoft Outlook has several options for handling the E-mails. First, we'll process the E-mail by hand, then we'll set up Rules to automate the responses.

Start -> All Programs ->Microsoft Office-> Microsoft Office Outlook 2010

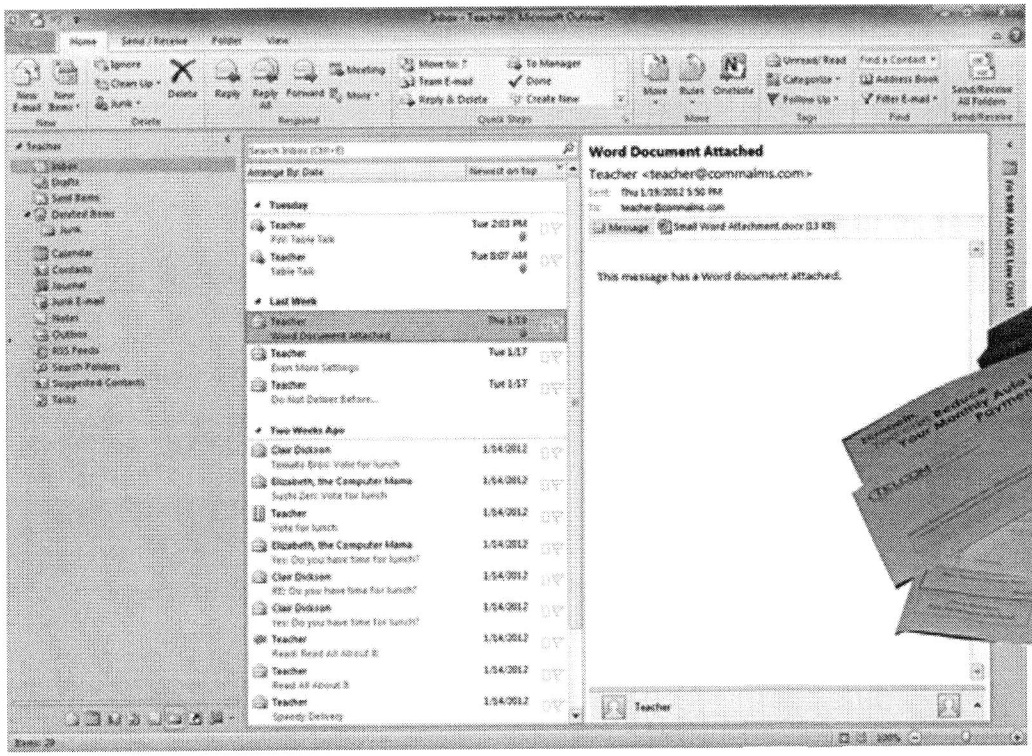

Billions and Billions

By default, all messages arrive at the Inbox. And, by default most users have several thousand messages stuffed in the Inbox: the new ones are sometimes on top.

There is a better way to handle messages. Microsoft Outlook has two new groups on the **Home** Ribbon: Move and Quick Steps.

The **Move** group has Move and Rules. **Quick Steps** simplify E-mail management.

Microsoft Outlook->Inbox

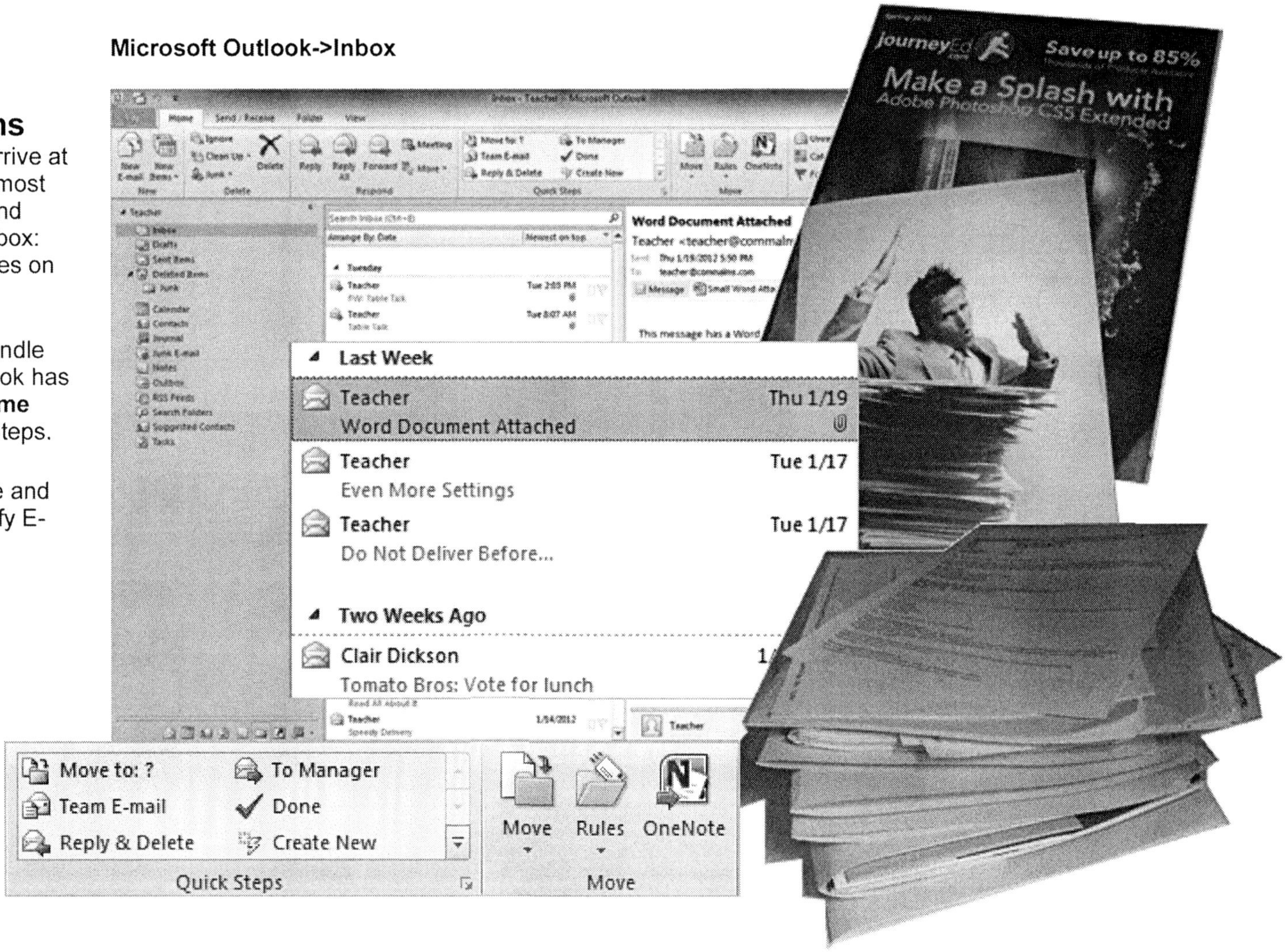

Last Week

| Teacher | Thu 1/19 |
| Word Document Attached | |

| Teacher | Tue 1/17 |
| Even More Settings | |

| Teacher | Tue 1/17 |
| Do Not Deliver Before... | |

Two Weeks Ago

| Clair Dickson | 1 |
| Tomato Bros: Vote for lunch | |

Quick Steps:
- Move to: ?
- Team E-mail
- Reply & Delete
- To Manager
- Done
- Create New

Move   Rules   OneNote

Move

Before You Begin

This lesson begins by creating a new folder to put the messages in. Here are the steps.

1. Try it: Create a Folder
Go to the **Inbox.**
Go to **Folder ->New->New Folder.**

You will be prompted to enter the following:
Name: Sample Messages
Select where to place the folder: Home Folder

Keep going, please...

Memo to Self: The Home Folder is at the top of the list. It has a little house icon. In the example on this page, this Outlook profile belongs to Teacher, so the Home folder says Teacher. Your Home folder may show your name instead.

Folder ->New->New Folder

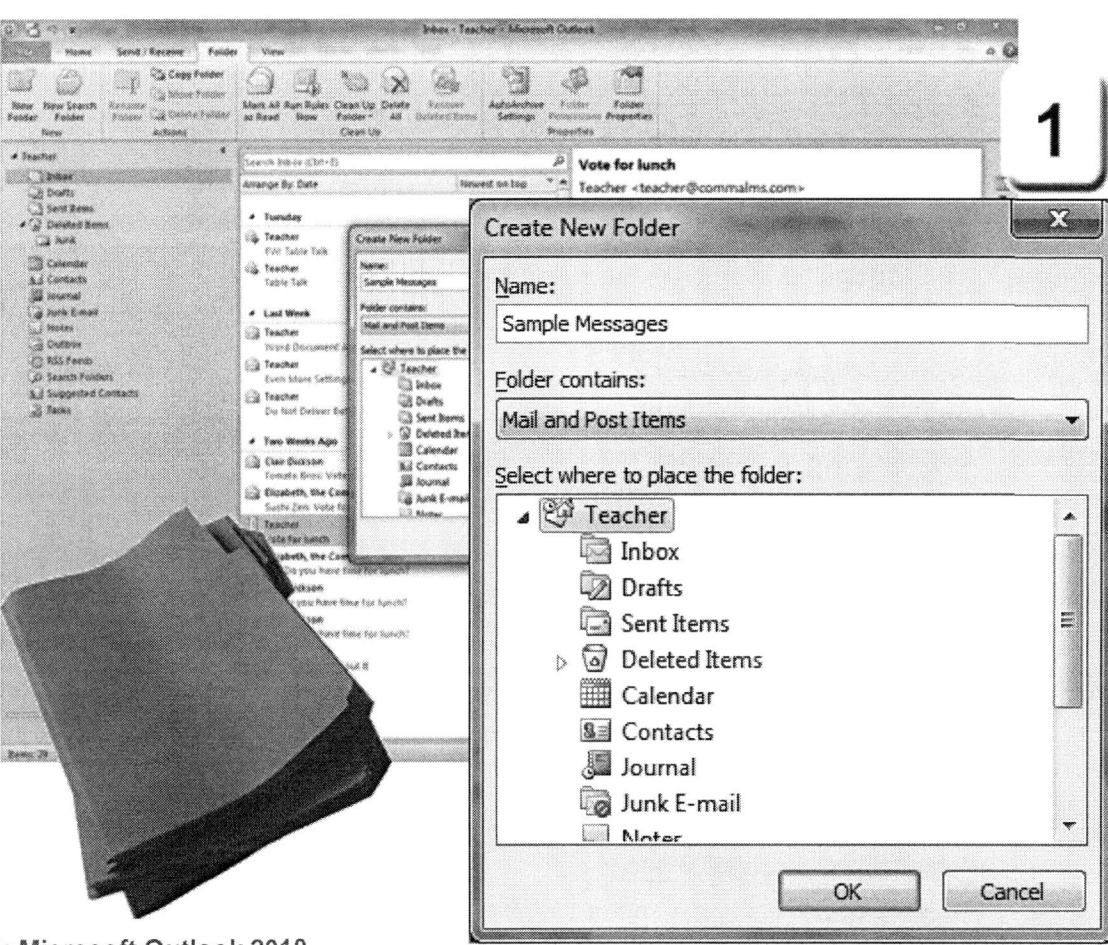

Exam 77-884: Microsoft Outlook 2010
3. Managing Email Messages
3.1. Clean up the mailbox: Create a New Folder

Move the Messages Manually

You can drag and drop any E-mail to the Sample Messages folder, just as you would organize your files with the Windows Explorer.

2. Try it: Drag a Message to Folder

Go to the **Inbox**
Select one of our practice E-mails. Drag the message to the Sample Messages folder.

When you are directly over the folder, the folder will be BOLD. Drop the message.

Keep going...

Microsoft Outlook->Inbox

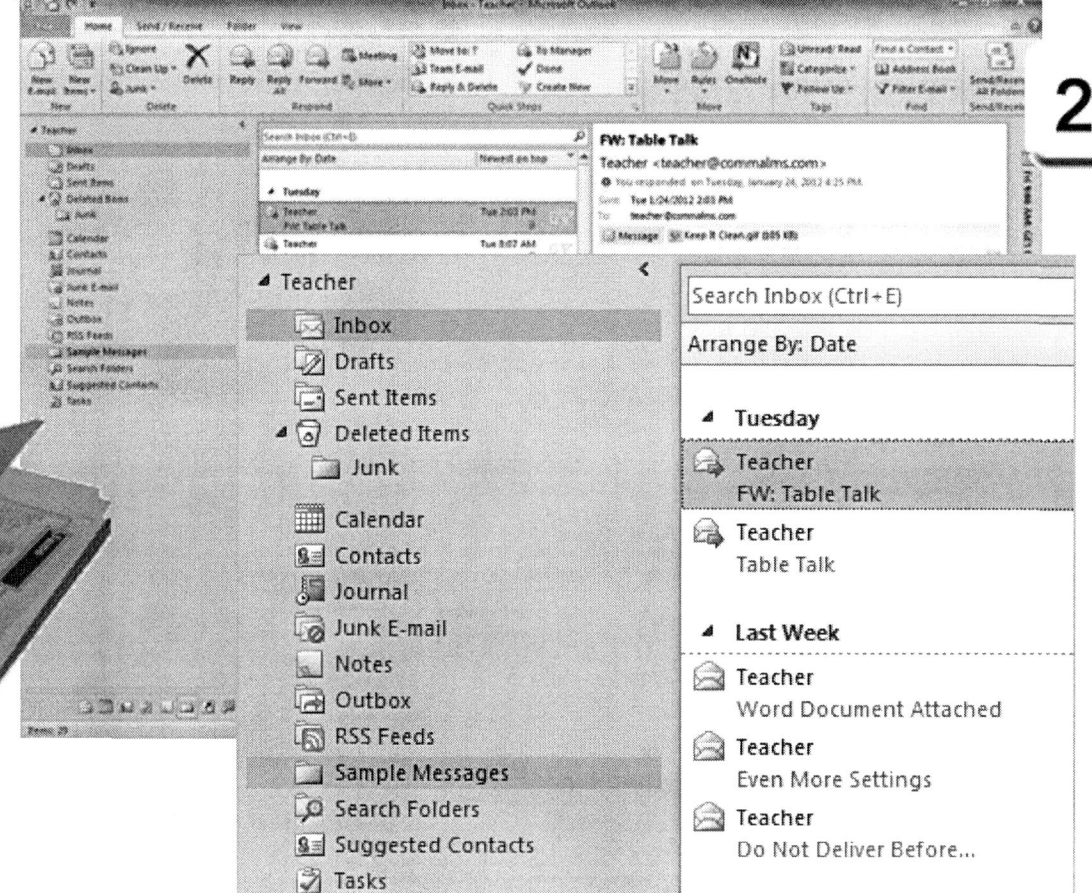

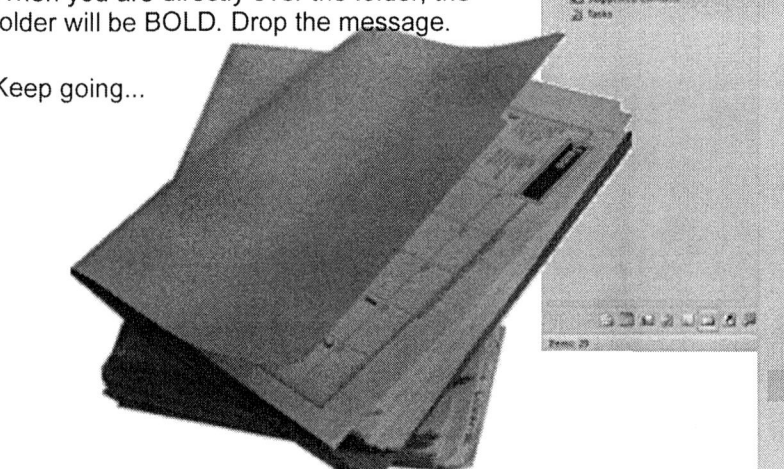

Move Messages Automatically

The **Home** Ribbon has an option to Move your messages. It works rather well.

3. Try it: Move a Message
Select one of the E-mails in the Inbox.
Go to **Home ->Move->Move.**
Please select the Sample Messages folder that we just made.

What Do You See? The other folders are:
Inbox
Deleted Items (trash)
Drafts
etc...

What Else Do You See? You can **Move** a message to another folder. You can also **Copy** a message to a folder.

Keep going, please...

Home ->Move->Move

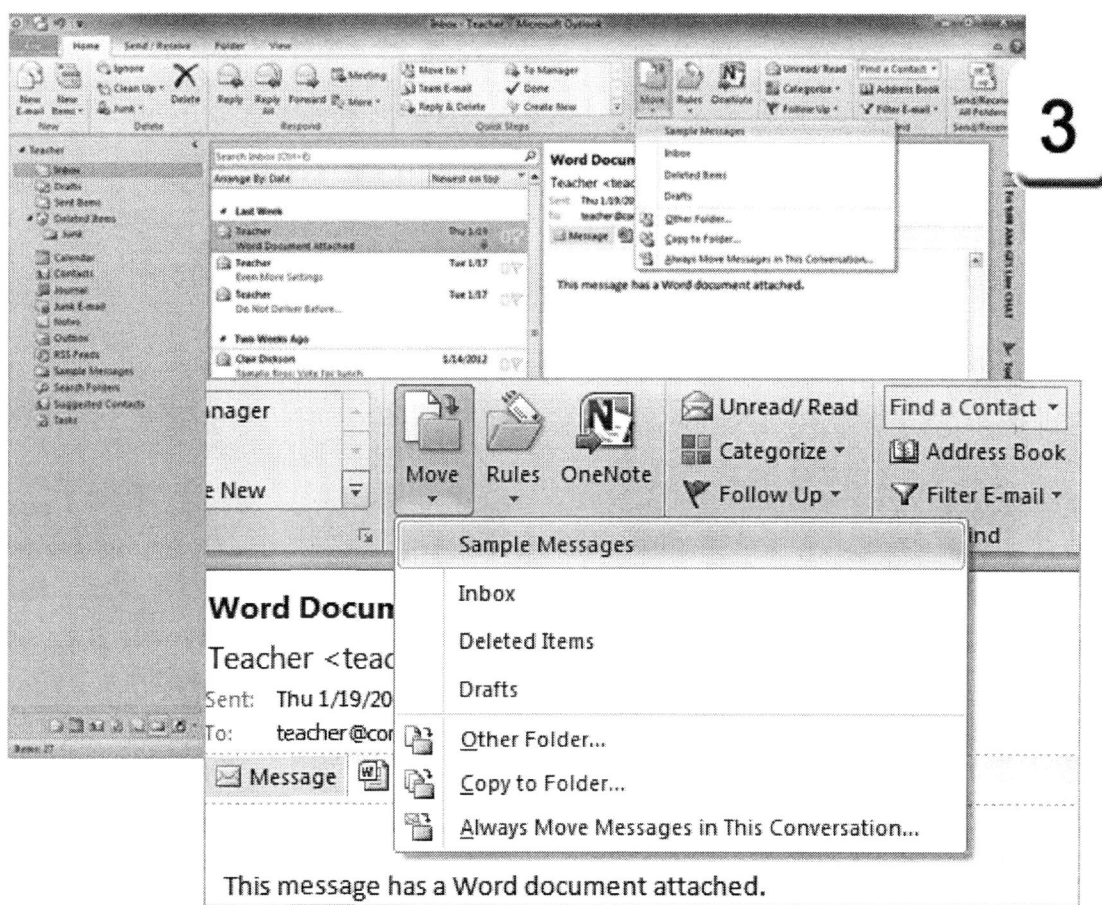

Exam 77-884: Microsoft Outlook 2010
3. Managing Email Messages
3.2. Create and manage rules: Move Messages

HOME

Trust, But Verify

So, did the messages go to the Sample Messages folder? Please confirm.

4. Try it: Find the Moved Messages
Go to **Sample Messages Folder.**

What Do You See? In this screenshot, there are two messages, with their attachments included, that were moved to the Sample Messages folder.

So far, so good.

Outlook ->Sample Messages Folder

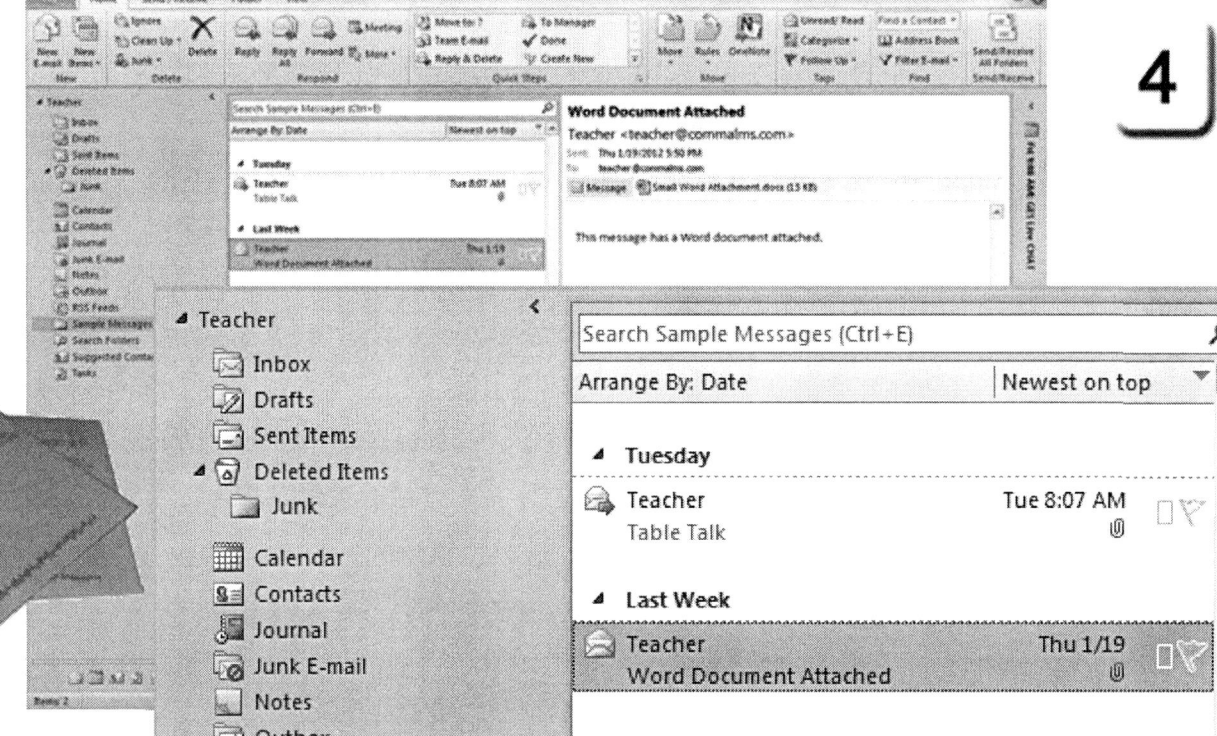

Exam 77-884: Microsoft Outlook 2010
3. Managing Email Messages
3.2. Create and manage rules: Move Messages

Create Business Rules

Business Rules Move Messages based on a criteria. For example, you can move E-mail from someone, say your boss, to a specific folder automatically.

1. Try it: Create a Rule

Please go to the Inbox.
Select one of the practice E-mails that you addressed to yourself.
Go to **Home ->Move->Rules.**
Click on **Always Move Messages From:**

Keep going...

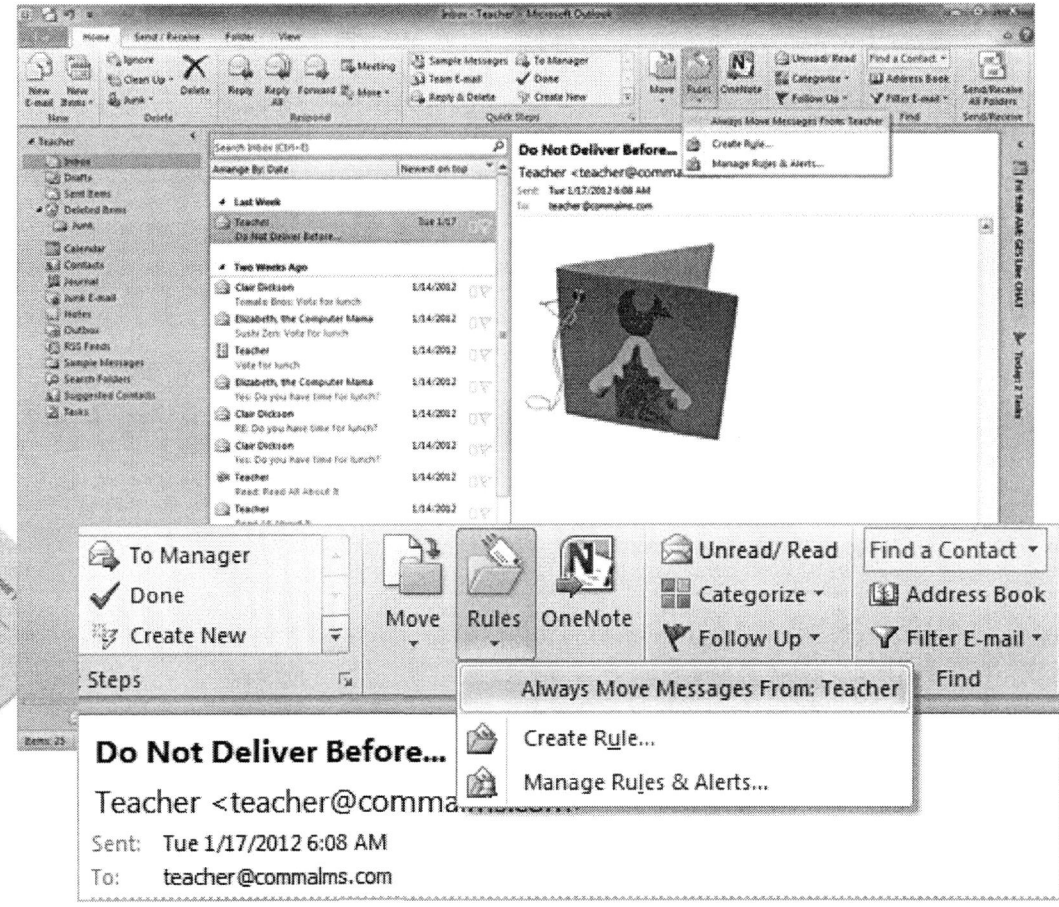

Exam 77-884: Microsoft Outlook 2010
3. Managing Email Messages
3.2. Create and manage rules: Create a Rule

Move Messages to a Folder

What Do You See? You will be prompted to select one of the Outlook folders.

Yes, you can choose the Deleted Items or the Junk E-mail folder if you wish. (It really depends on the person, doesn't it?)

2. Try it: Select a Folder
Choose a Folder: Sample Messages.
Click **OK**. You will return to the Inbox.

What Happens Next? When click OK, Microsoft Outlook will run the rule and move all of the E-mails from this person and place them in the Sample Messages folder.

Home ->Move->Rules->Always Move Message From

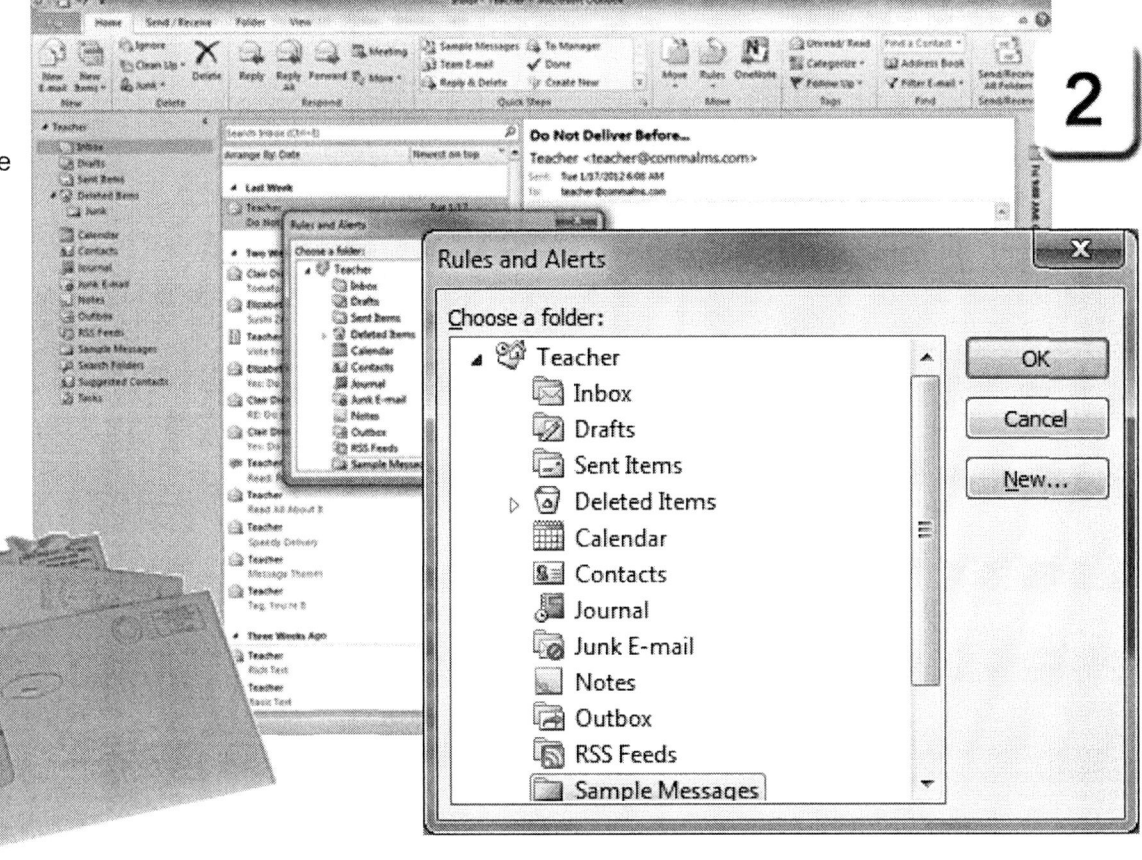

Exam 77-884: Microsoft Outlook 2010
3. Managing Email Messages
3.2. Create and manage rules: Create a Rule

Test the Rules

The little Inbox rules are simple programs that automate message handling. A good programmer always tests the program to see if it works. OK, let's test the rules.

3. Try it: Test the Inbox Rules
Go to **Home-> New-> New E-Mail**.
Enter your E-mail Address.
Enter the Subject: Testing the Rules
Type the message: This message is a test of the Inbox Rules.

Click **Send** to E-mail the message.

What Do You See? The message should come into the Inbox and automatically move to the Sample Messages folder.

Trust But Verify: Please go to the Sample Messages folder and confirm that your E-mail arrived there.

Keep going...

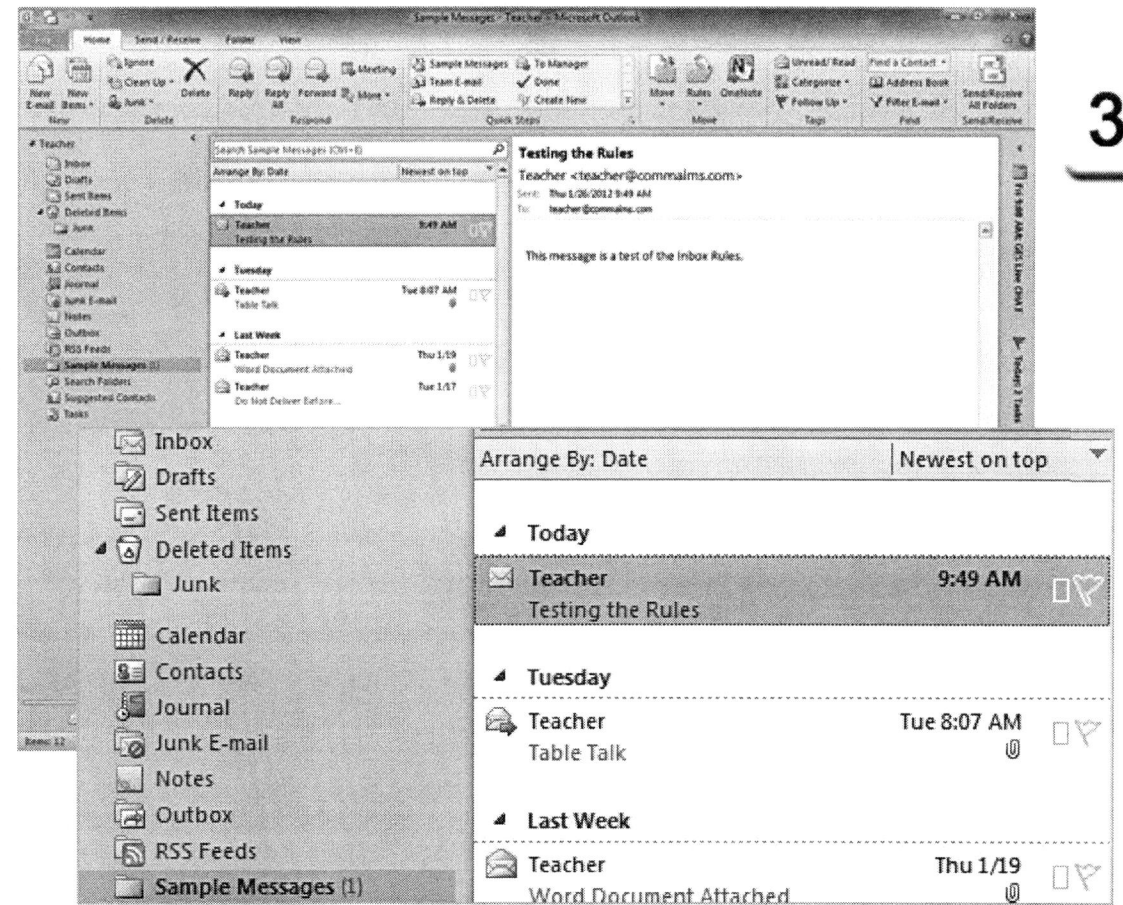

Exam 77-884: Microsoft Outlook 2010
3. Managing Email Messages
3.2. Create and manage rules: Test the Rule

Home ->Move->Rules->Manage Rules & Alerts

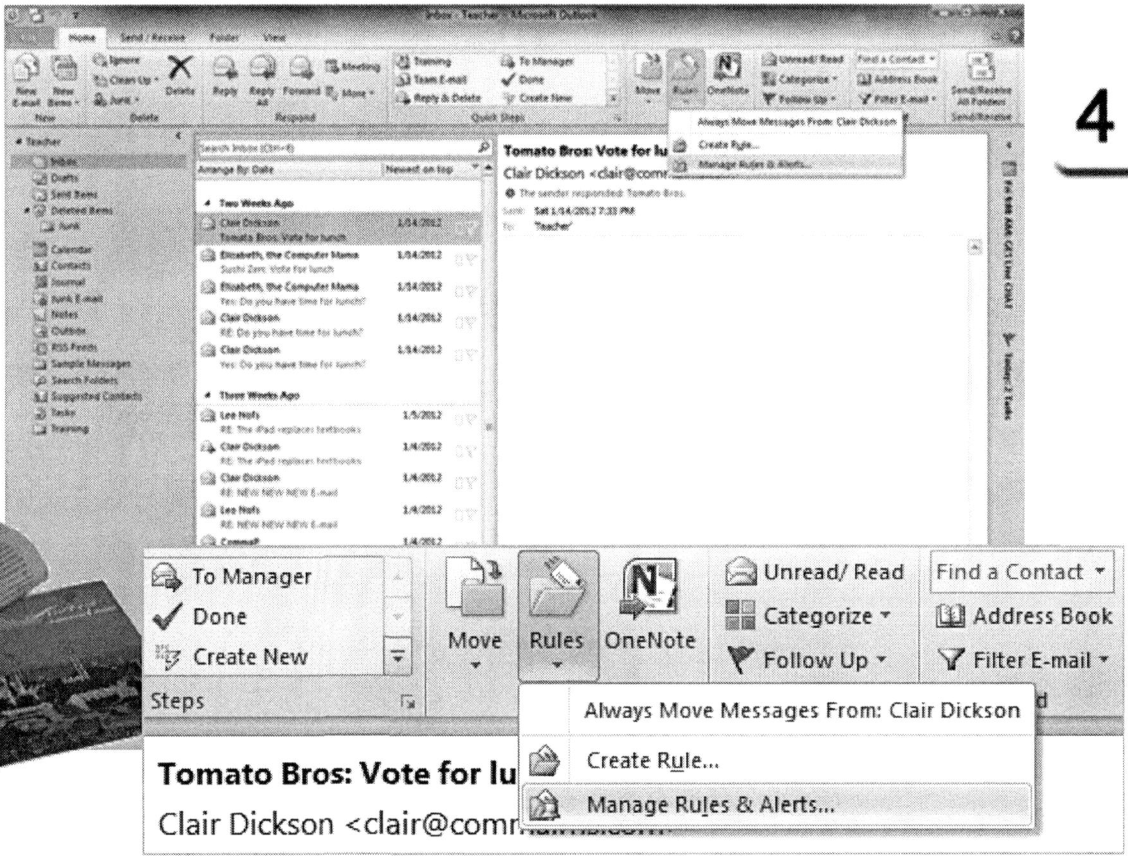

Manage Rules and Alerts

Say you wanted to edit or delete the Rule that you just made. Where does Outlook keep the Rules? Let's find out.

4. Try it: Find the Rules and Alerts
Go to **Home ->Move->Rules**.
Click on **Manage Rules & Alerts**.

Keep going...!

4

To Manager
✓ Done
Create New

Move | Rules | OneNote

Steps

Unread/ Read
Categorize ▾
Follow Up ▾

Find a Contact ▾
Address Book
Filter E-mail ▾

Always Move Messages From: Clair Dickson

Create Rule...

Manage Rules & Alerts...

Tomato Bros: Vote for lu

Clair Dickson <clair@comm

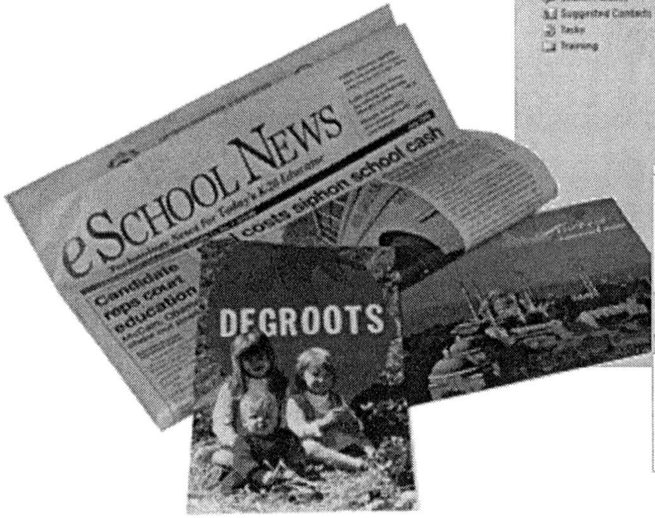

Exam 77-884: Microsoft Outlook 2010
3. Managing Email Messages
3.2. Create and manage rules: Rules and Alerts Management

Rules and Alerts: Options

5. Try it: Review the E-mail Rules

The Email-Rules include options for: New Rule, Change Rule, Copy, and Delete. You can also Run Rules Now.

In the example on this page, there are two Rules: one based on the name Teacher and one that comes with Outlook.

When the Rule for Teacher is selected, the **description** is shown on the bottom. The hyperlinks in the description let you edit the name (Teacher) or the folder (Sample Messages) if you wish.

Try This, Too: Delete a Rule

Select the Rule that you made.
Click on **Delete**.
When asked to confirm, click **Yes**.

Click **Apply** to save your changes.
Click **OK** to return to the Inbox.

Keep going..

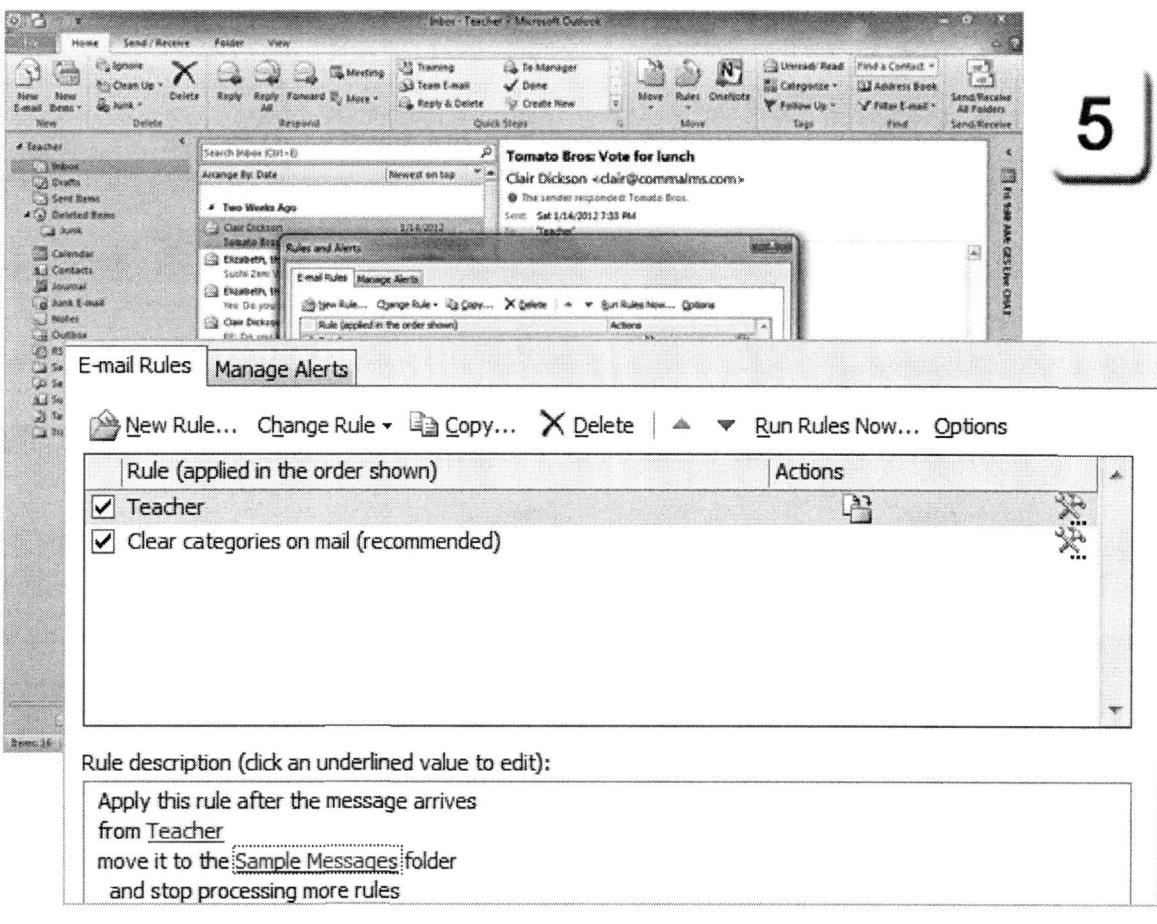

Exam 77-884: Microsoft Outlook 2010
3. Managing Email Messages
3.2. Create and manage rules

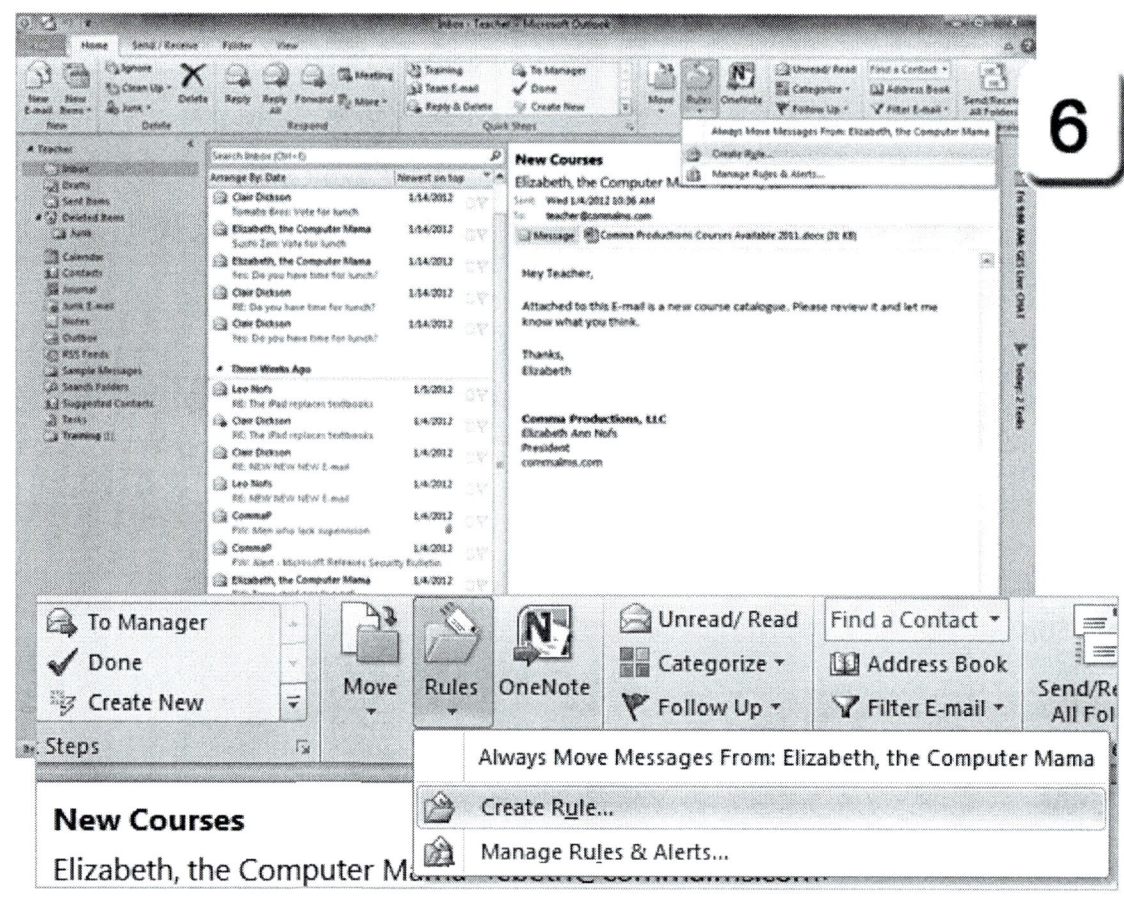

Create a New Rule

Rules can identify messages by several criteria including: Sender, Recipient, Subject, and key words in the message. This example moves a message based on the Subject and places it into a new folder.

Before You Begin: Create Another Folder
Go to the Inbox.
Go to **Folder ->New->New Folder**.

You will be prompted to enter the following:
Name: Training
Select where to place the folder: Home

6. Try it: Create a New Rule
The Inbox is still selected.
Go to **Home ->Move->Rules->Create Rule**...

Keep going...

Home ->Move->Rules->Create Rule...

Exam 77-884: Microsoft Outlook 2010
3. Managing Email Messages
3.2. Create and manage rules: Create a Rule

Create Rule: Options

7. What Do You See? You will be prompted to edit the rule.
First, identify the **conditions**.
Then, program the **response**.

Edit the Conditions:
Subject contains: Outlook Training

Edit the Response: (Do the following)
Display in the New Item Alert Window: yes
Play a selected sound: yes

Move the item to folder: yes.
Click on **Select Folder**. When you are asked, please select the **Training** folder.

Click **OK** to save the Rule. A message will confirm that the Rule has been created and asks if you would like to run this rule on the current folder now.

Click **OK** to this window and keep going...

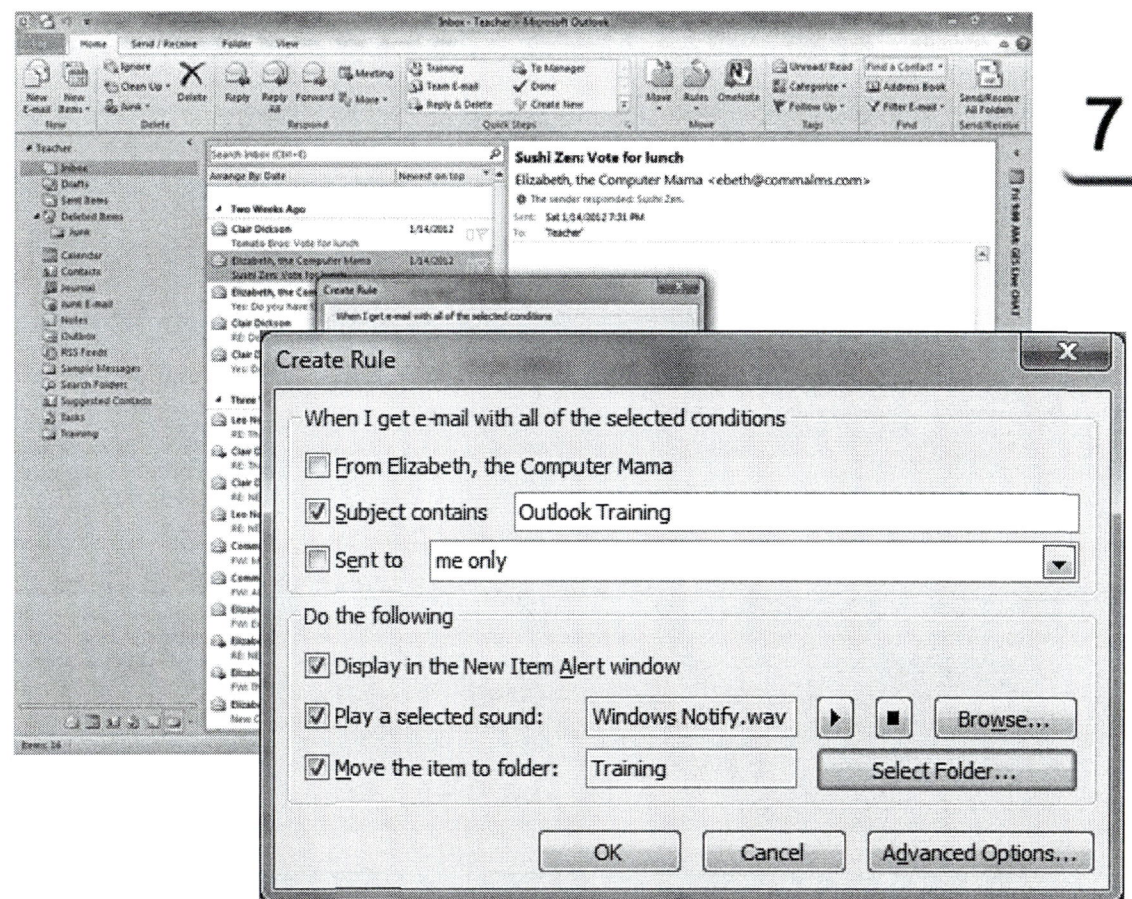

Exam 77-884: Microsoft Outlook 2010
3. Managing Email Messages
3.2. Create and manage rules: Modify a Rule

Test the Rules, Again

This Rule should identify any messages that have Training in the Subject and move the message to the Outlook Training folder. Does it work?

8. Try it: Create a Test E-mail
Go to **Home-> New-> New E-Mail.**
Enter your E-mail Address.
Enter the Subject: New Outlook Training
Type the message: This message is a test of the Training Rule.

Click **Send** to E-mail the message.

What Do You See? The message should automatically go to the Training folder. The **New Mail Alert** should chime.

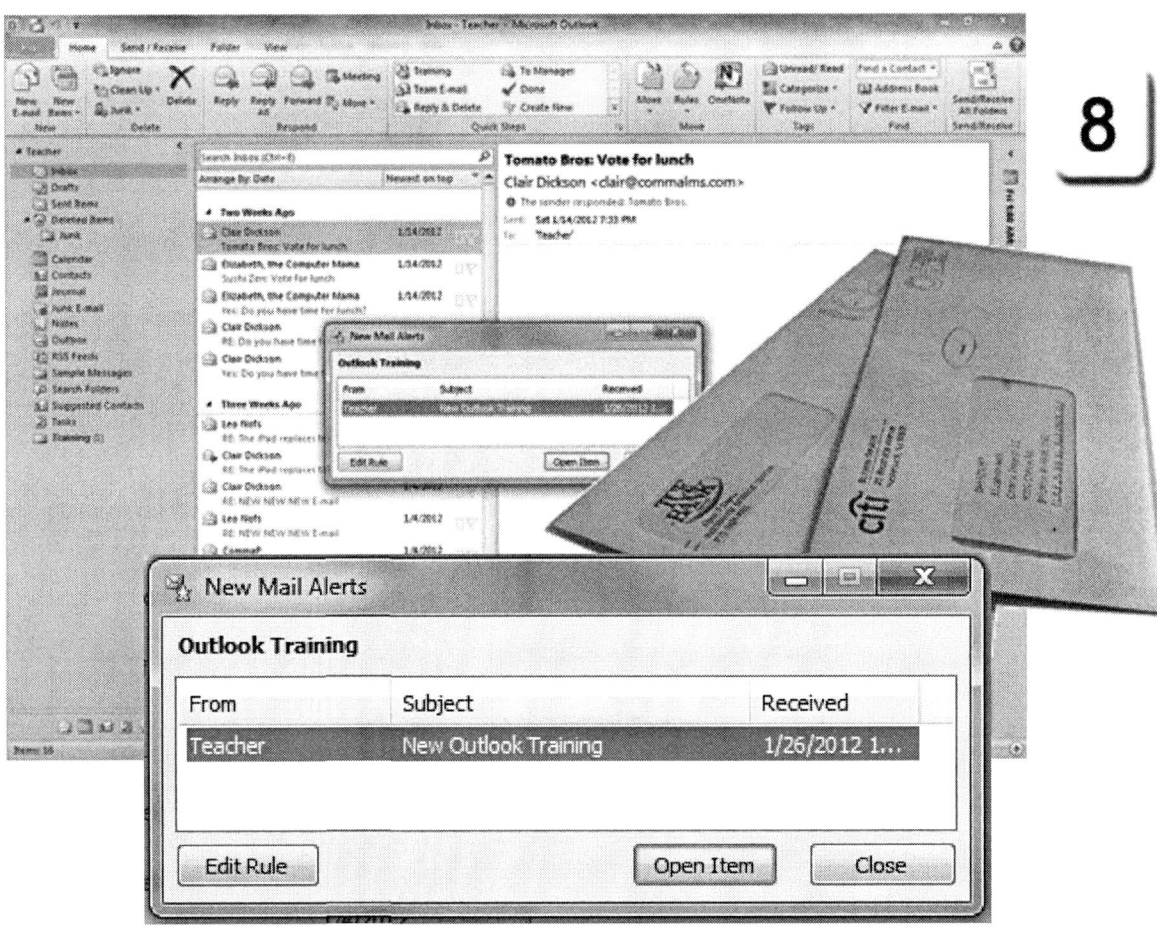

Exam 77-884: Microsoft Outlook 2010
3. Managing Email Messages
3.2. Create and manage rules

Welcome to Quick Steps

Quick Steps give you instant access to the Rules that you use frequently. Outlook comes with a couple of simple Quick Steps. One of the best examples is **Reply and Delete**.

1. Try it: Use Quick Steps
Select one of the practice E-mails.
Go to **Home ->Quick Steps**.
Click on **Reply and Delete.**

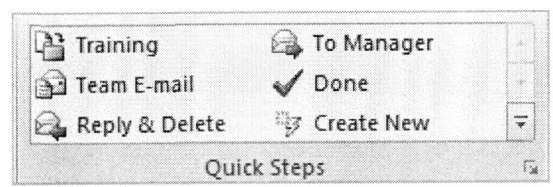

What Do You See? A new message should open in reply to the one you selected. You can edit the reply if you wish. The message you replied to will be sent to the Deleted Items folder.

Keep going...

Home ->Quick Steps->Reply and Delete

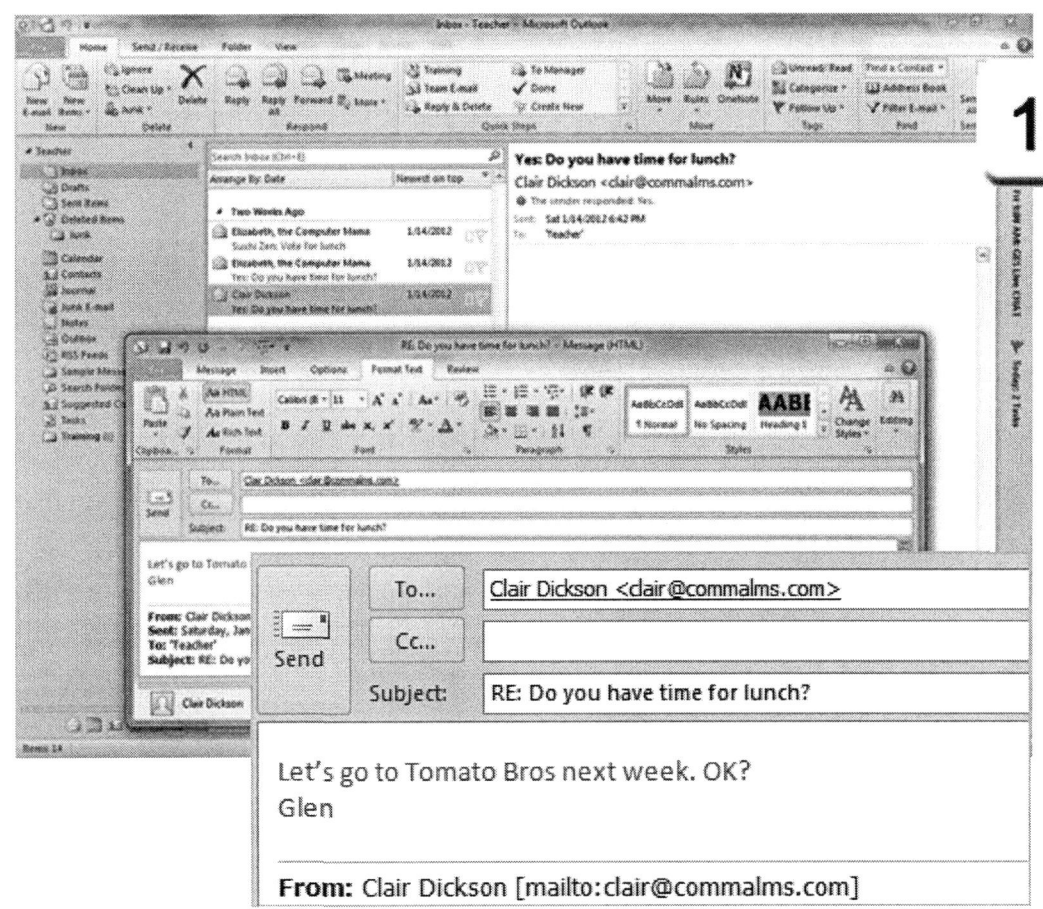

Exam 77-884: Microsoft Outlook 2010
2. Creating and Formatting Item Content
2.2. Create and manage Quick Steps

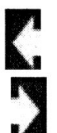

Create Quick Steps

Look again at the Quick Steps. There should be a custom Quick Step for Training. It is a new action button that will move messages to the Training folder we created. Does it work?

2. Try it: Test the Custom Quick Step
Go to **Home ->Quick Steps.**
Click on **Training.**

What Do You See? If this is a First Time Setup, you will be asked to confirm:
Name: Training
Move to Folder: Training
Mark as read

There are more options.
Keep going, please.

Home ->Quick Steps->Reply and Delete

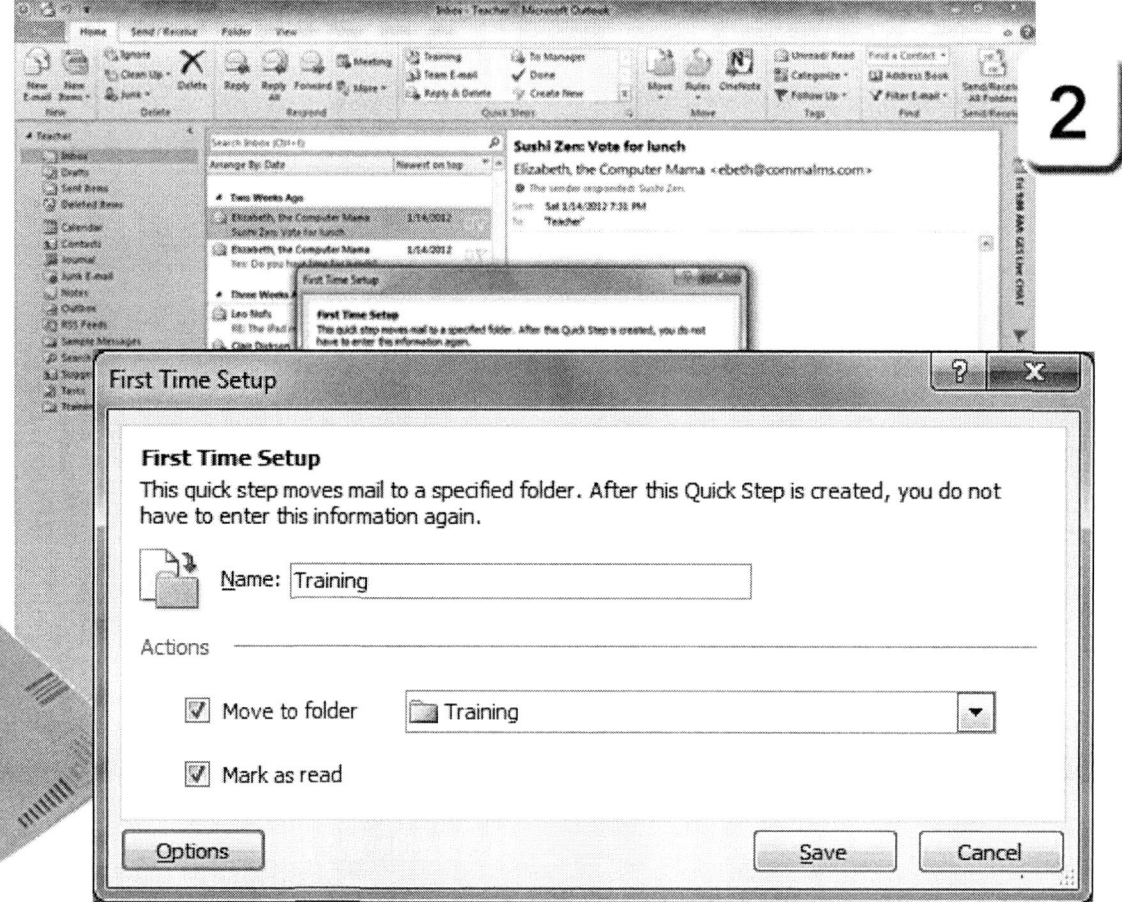

Exam 77-884: Microsoft Outlook 2010
1. Managing the Outlook Environment
1.2. Manipulate item tags: Mark Item as Read or Unread

Edit Quick Steps

Quick Steps, like Macros, can string together several action steps, one after another. In this example the message will be moved to a specific folder, marked as unread and flagged for follow up.

3. Try it: Edit the Quick Steps
Edit the first Action: Move to Folder.
Select the folder: Training.

Edit the second Action: Mark as unread.

Try This, Too: Add Another Action
Click on **Add Action**.
Edit the third Action: Flag Message,
Choose the Follow Up: Tomorrow.

Click **Save** to return to the Inbox.

Trust, but Verify: Select a practice message and try the Training Quick Step. Did it move the practice message, mark it as unread and add a follow up Flag? Keep going...

Memo to Self: You can use the X to the right of any Action to Delete that step.

Home ->Quick Steps->Create New->Options

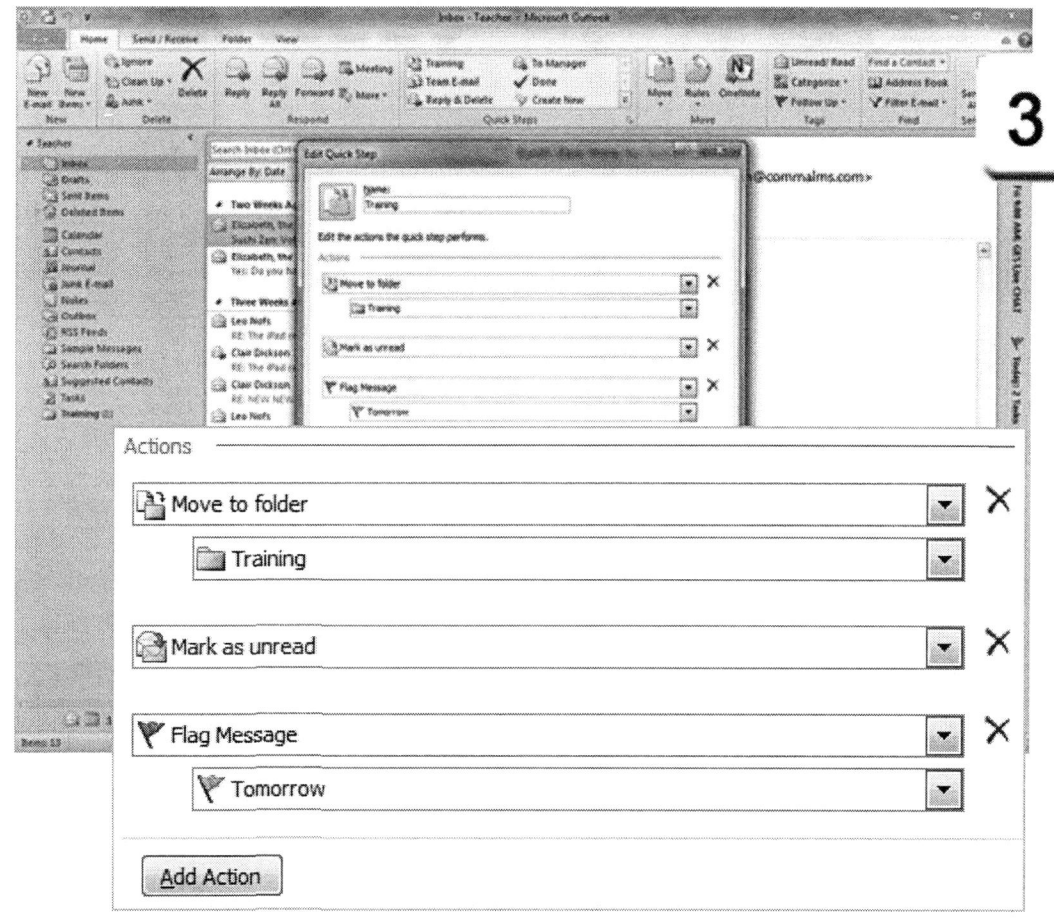

Exam 77-884: Microsoft Outlook 2010
2. Creating and Formatting Item Content
2.2. Create and manage Quick Steps: Edit the Quick Steps

Manage Quick Steps

You can edit the Quick Steps or create your own if you wish. The best place to start is the **Quick Step Manager**.

4. Try it: Manage Quick Steps
Go to **Home ->Quick Steps->More.**
Click on **Manage Quick Steps.**

What Do You See? There are a handful of built-in Actions (Done, Reply & Delete, etc.) as well as the Training Quick Step.

When you select a Quick Step, you will see a Description of the **Actions, Shortcut Key** and **Tooltip**. The Shortcut Key is a combination of key strokes (numbers, letters, or function keys) that will run the Quick Step. The Tooltip is the information that a User sees when a mouse runs over the Quick Steps library.

Manage Quick Steps offers these tools:
Edit, Duplicate, Delete.
Keep going...

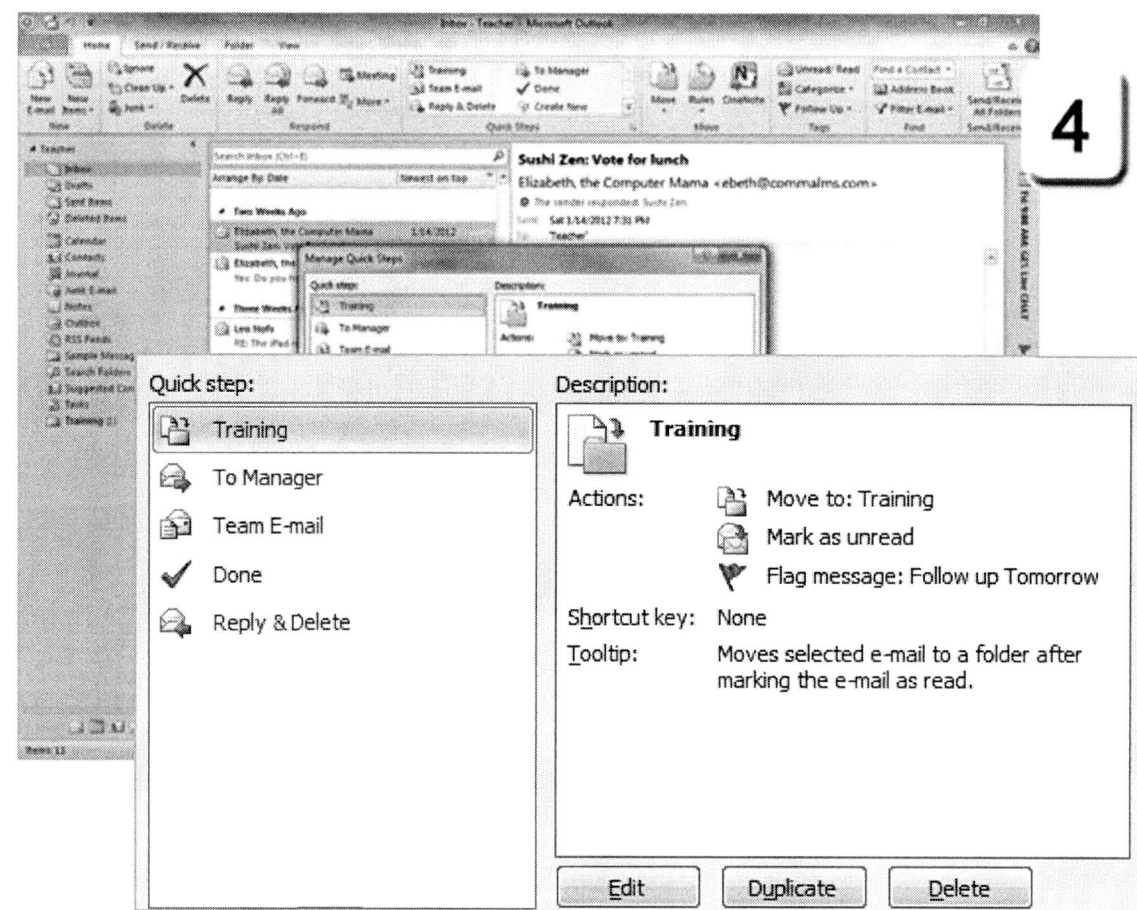

Exam 77-884: Microsoft Outlook 2010
2. Creating and Formatting Item Content
2.2. Create and manage Quick Steps: Manage Quick Steps

Duplicate Quick Steps

5. Try it: Duplicate a Quick Step
Select the Training Quick Step.
Click on **Duplicate**.

What Do You See? You will be prompted to edit a new version of the Quick Step named **Copy of Training.**

Edit the Name: Sample Messages

Edit the Actions
Choose the first Action: Move to folder.
Select: Sample Messages

Choose the second Action: Set Importance
Select the level: High

Delete the third Action: flag message.

Edit the Tooltip text: Move to Sample Messages folder.

Click **Finish**. Keep going.

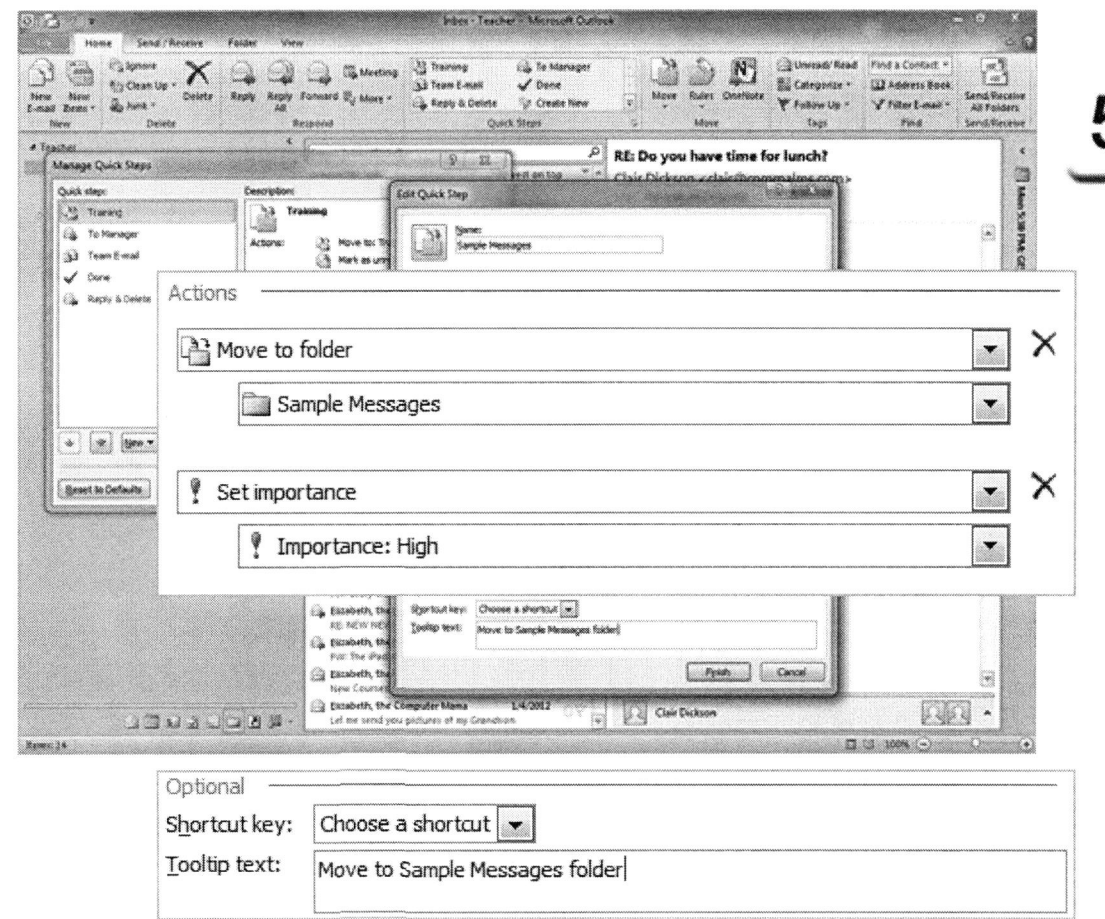

5

Exam 77-884: Microsoft Outlook 2010
3. Managing Email Messages
3.2. Create and manage rules: Duplicate Quick Steps

Home ->Quick Steps->More->Manage Quick Steps->Reset to Default

Review the Quick Steps

6. Try it: Review the Quick Steps
Go to **Home ->Quick Steps.**

What Do You See? The Quick Steps now includes two custom Actions: Training and Sample Messages.

Try This, Too: Delete a Quick Step
Right-click a Quick Step: Team E-mail.
Click on **Delete**.

Made You Look: You can **Restore** the Quick Steps back to the default.

Go to **Home ->Quick Step->More.**
Click on **Manage Quick Steps.**
Click on **Reset to Default.**

That was a quick look at
...Quick Steps!

This is the **ToolTip** that we edited on the previous page.

Exam 77-884: Microsoft Outlook 2010
3. Managing Email Messages
3.2. Create and manage rules: Reset Quick Steps to Default Settings

Working with Lots of Mail

Even with the practice lessons in the class, the Inbox has accumulated dozens of messages. On any given day you may receive more, depending on your work and your social networking.

One of the best new features in Outlook is **Conversations**. Conversations group all of the E-mails that belong to the same topic.

1. Try it: Use the Conversation View
Go to **View ->Conversations**.
Check: **Show as Conversations**.
When you are prompted, choose **This Folder**.

What Do You See? The Inbox has been organized by Date and Conversation. E-mails that belong to the same discussion-even if they are in different folders-are listed together.

Keep going...!

View ->Conversations->Show as Conversations

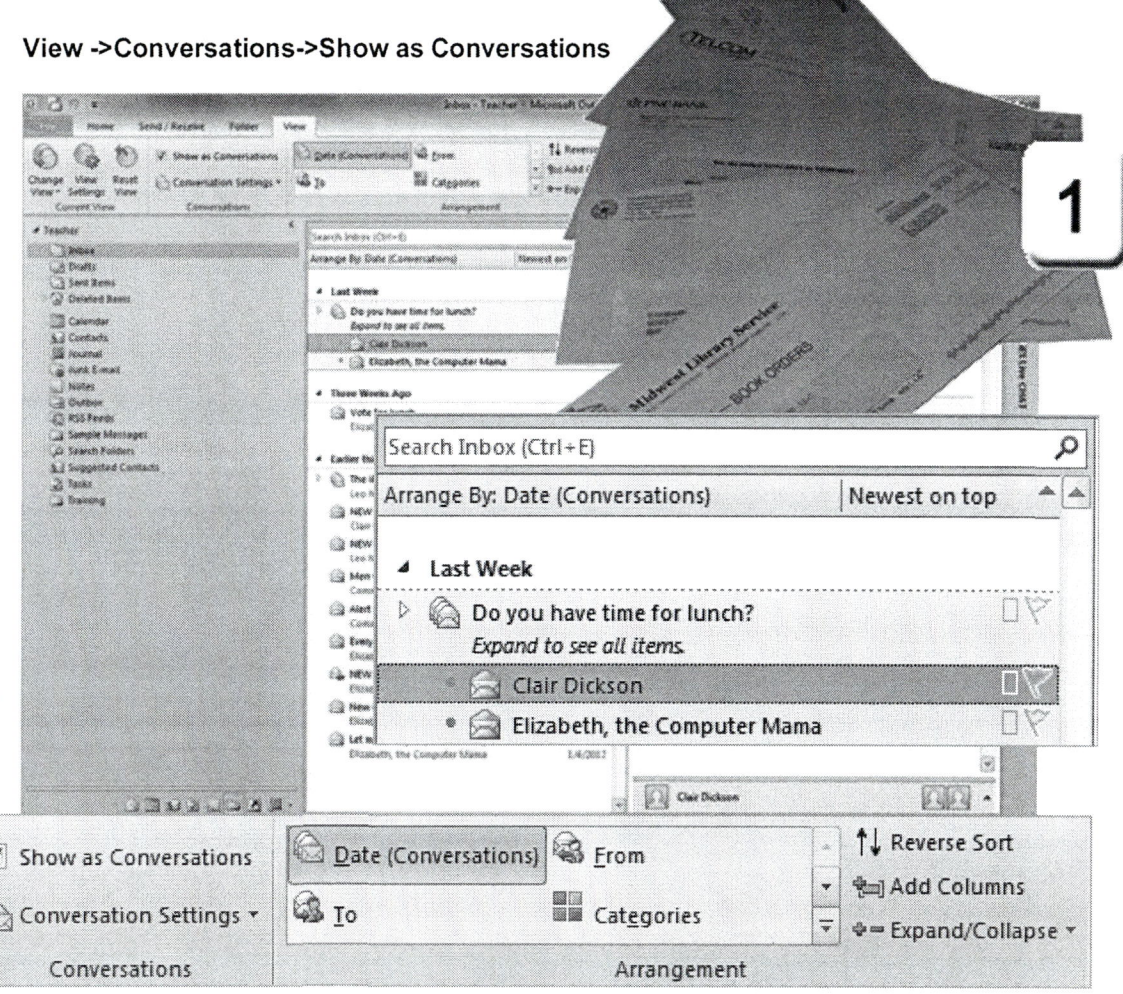

Exam 77-884: Microsoft Outlook 2010
3. Managing Email Messages
3.3. Manage junk mail: Indentify Junk Mail

Change the Conversation

2. Try it: Find the Conversation Settings

Go to **View ->Conversations.**
Click on **Conversation Settings.**

What Do You See? The options include:
Show Messages from Other Folders
Show Senders Above the Subject
Always Expand Conversations
Use Classic Indented View.

What Else Do You See? You can choose a different **Arrangement** if you wish. The default View is Date. The Inbox can be sorted by the Sender (From), the Recipient (To) or other criteria.

Keep going...

View ->Conversations->Conversation Settings

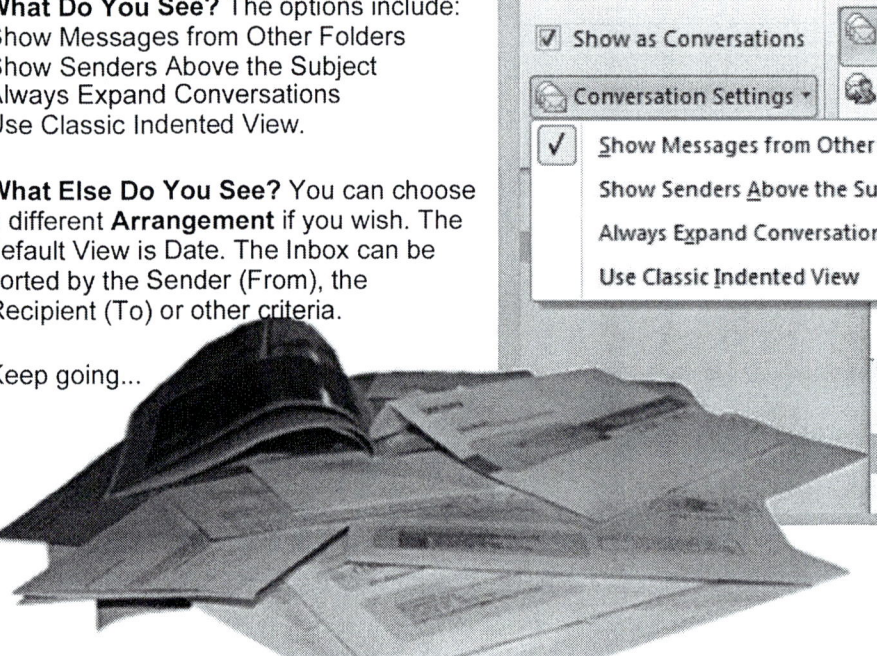

Exam 77-884: Microsoft Outlook 2010
3. Managing Email Messages
3.2. Create and manage rules

View Mailbox Size

How big is the mailbox? Good question: many corporate and government servers have a limit on how much stuff you can keep in Outlook. The data is available in the **Folder Properties**.

Before You Begin: Select the Home folder, the one at the top of the navigation pane. In this example, it is the one called Teacher, the owner of the E-mail account.

3. Try it: View the Mailbox Size
Go to **Folder ->Properties**.
Click on **Folder Properties**.
Go to **General ->Folder Size**.

What Do You See? The Total size is calculated. The size for each subfolder is also shown. For example, the Inbox has 2.5 MB of messages and attachments.

Click **Close** to return to the Properties.
Click **OK** to return to Outlook.

Keep going...

Folder ->Properties->Folder Properties

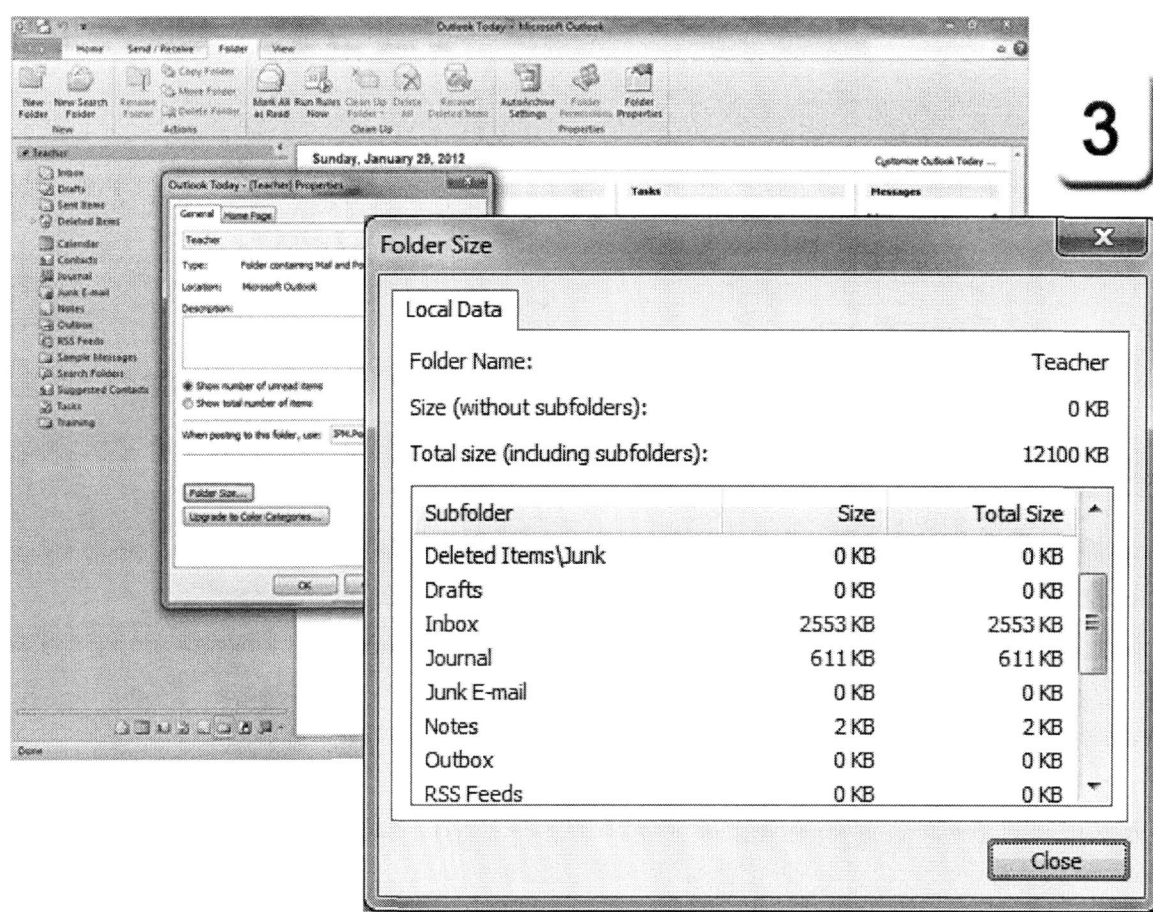

Managing the Mail

Well, there are two kinds of people: those who Reply&Delete, and those who Save everything. The first group has 10 E-mails or less in the Inbox. The second group may have a couple hundred to start. Whatever method you use, some of the messages just beg to be deleted.

4. Try it: View the Delete Group
Select the Inbox.
Go to **Home ->Delete->Clean Up.**

What Do You See? There are three options:
Clean Up Conversation
Clean Up Folder
Clean Up Folder & Subfolders

Click **Clean Up Folder.**
You will be prompted that all redundant messages will be moved to the Deleted Items folder. Why? Click **Settings** and let's see.

Home ->Delete->Clean Up

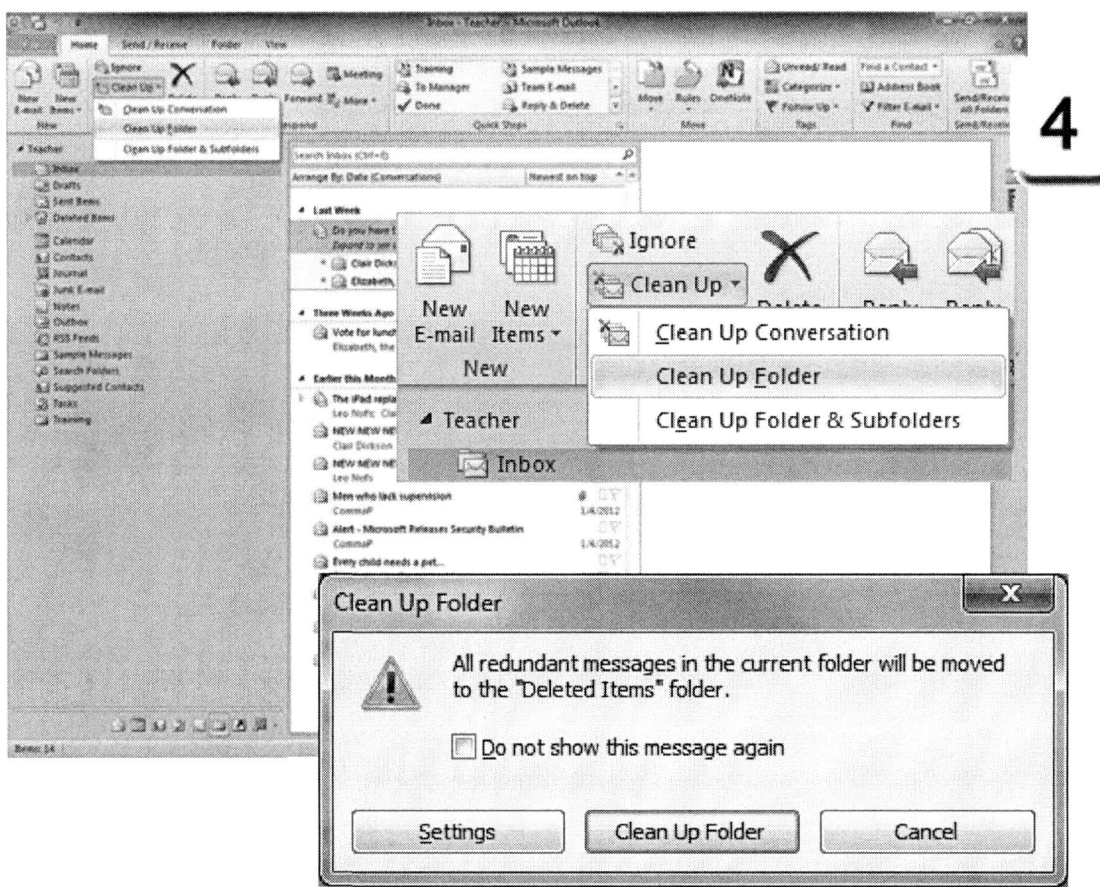

Exam 77-884: Microsoft Outlook 2010
3. Managing Email Messages
3.1. Clean up the mailbox: Use Cleanup Tools

Conversation Clean Up

5. Try it: Review the Clean Up Settings
The Outlook Options list many categories on the left side. The Conversation Clean Up section is in the **Mail** Options, about half way down the page.

What Do You See? You can use the **Browse** button to choose a folder for the Cleaned-up items if you wish.

By default, messages that are unread, categorized, flagged, digitally-signed are not moved to the Deleted Items folder. If someone edits a message in their reply, the original will not be moved, either.

Click **Cancel** to return to the Clean Up. Click **Cancel**, again, to return to the Inbox. Keep going...!

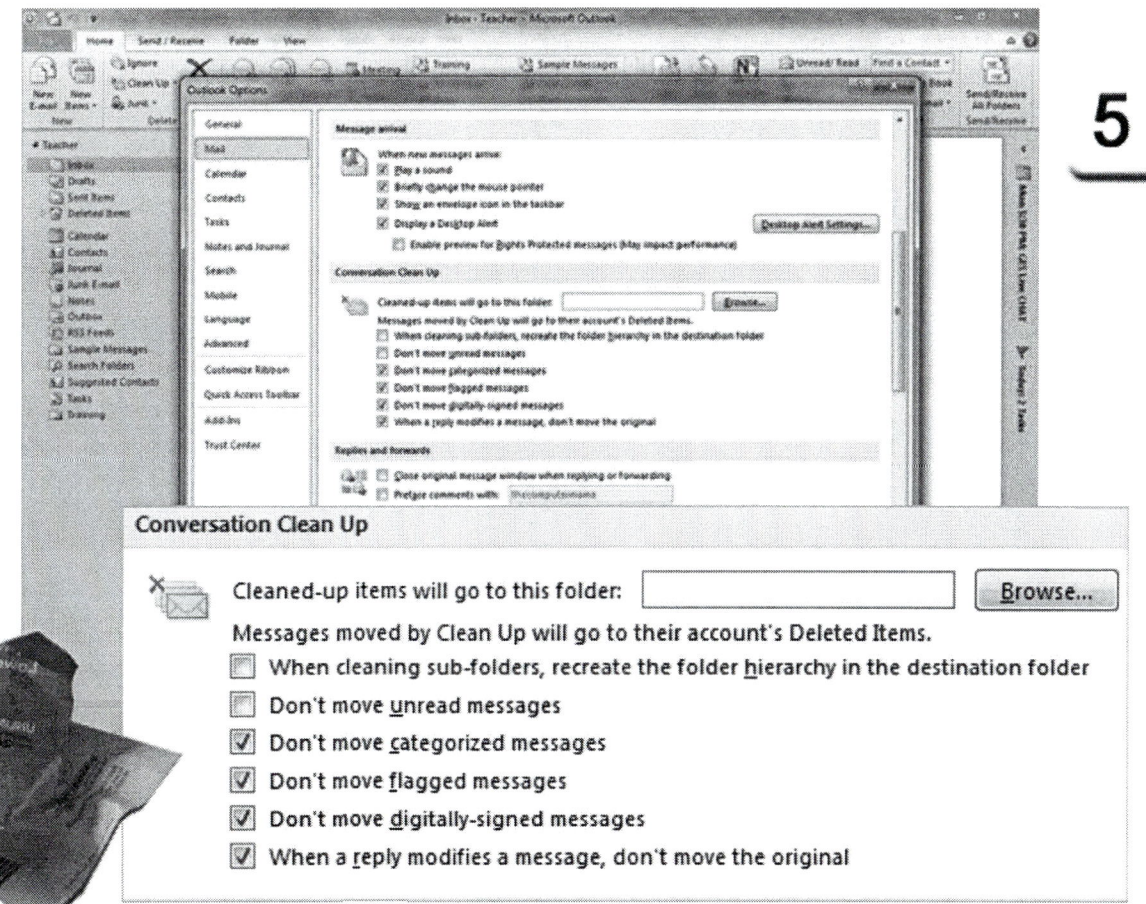

Conversation Clean Up

Cleaned-up items will go to this folder: [   ] Browse...

Messages moved by Clean Up will go to their account's Deleted Items.

☐ When cleaning sub-folders, recreate the folder hierarchy in the destination folder

☐ Don't move unread messages

☑ Don't move categorized messages

☑ Don't move flagged messages

☑ Don't move digitally-signed messages

☑ When a reply modifies a message, don't move the original

Exam 77-884: Microsoft Outlook 2010
3. Managing Email Messages
3.1. Clean up the mailbox: Use Cleanup Tools

Overriding the Programming

Office automation can be very useful. However, with programming, one size does not fit all. There are always exceptions to the Rules.

You can select a conversation and **Ignore** (exclude) it from the Clean Up.

6. Try it: Ignore a Conversation
Go to **Home ->Delete->Ignore**.

You will be prompted twice.
First: This action will apply to all items in the selected conversation.
Click: **OK**

Second: The selected conversation and all future messages will be moved to the Deleted Items folder.

Click: **Ignore Conversation**.

So, when the the Clean Up runs, this Conversation will not be trashed.

Home ->Delete->Ignore

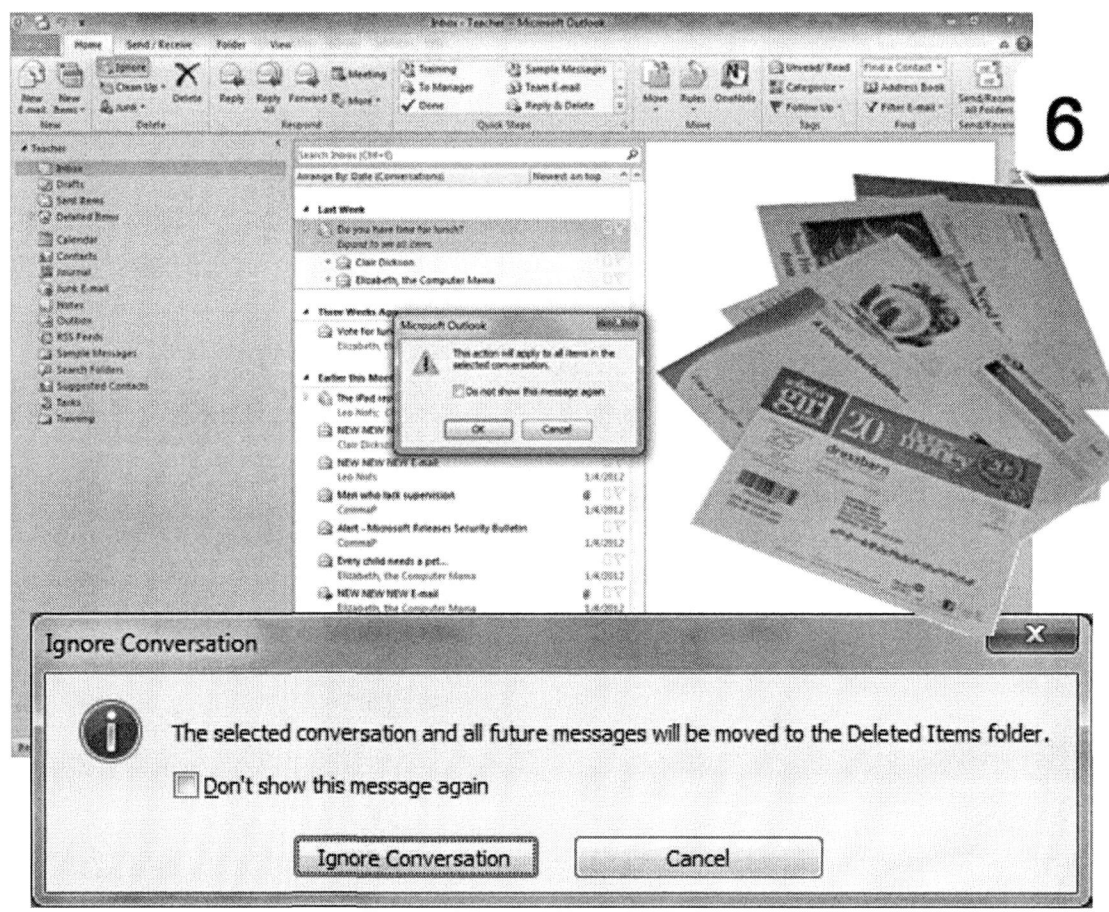

Ignore Conversation

The selected conversation and all future messages will be moved to the Deleted Items folder.

☐ Don't show this message again

[Ignore Conversation]   [Cancel]

Exam 77-884: Microsoft Outlook 2010
3. Managing Email Messages
3.1. Clean up the mailbox: Ignore a Conversation

Handling Junk Mail

If you have an E-mail account you are going to get unsolicited messages that you don't want. Junk mail can be handled with rules as well. Messages can be indentified as junk and moved to the Deleted Items folder (trash) automatically. Spam can be thrown away before it even hits the Inbox. <grin>

There are several ways to filter your E-mail. The basic system is white list/black list. The white list has the names and domains of the "good guys in white hats." These are people or companies that you trust. The black list are ones you cannot trust.

1. Try This: Review the Junk Mail Options
Select a sample E-mail message.
Go to **Home ->Delete->Junk.**

What Do You See? The options include;
Block Sender
Never Block Sender
Never Block Sender's Domain
Never Block This Group or Mailing List

Keep going...

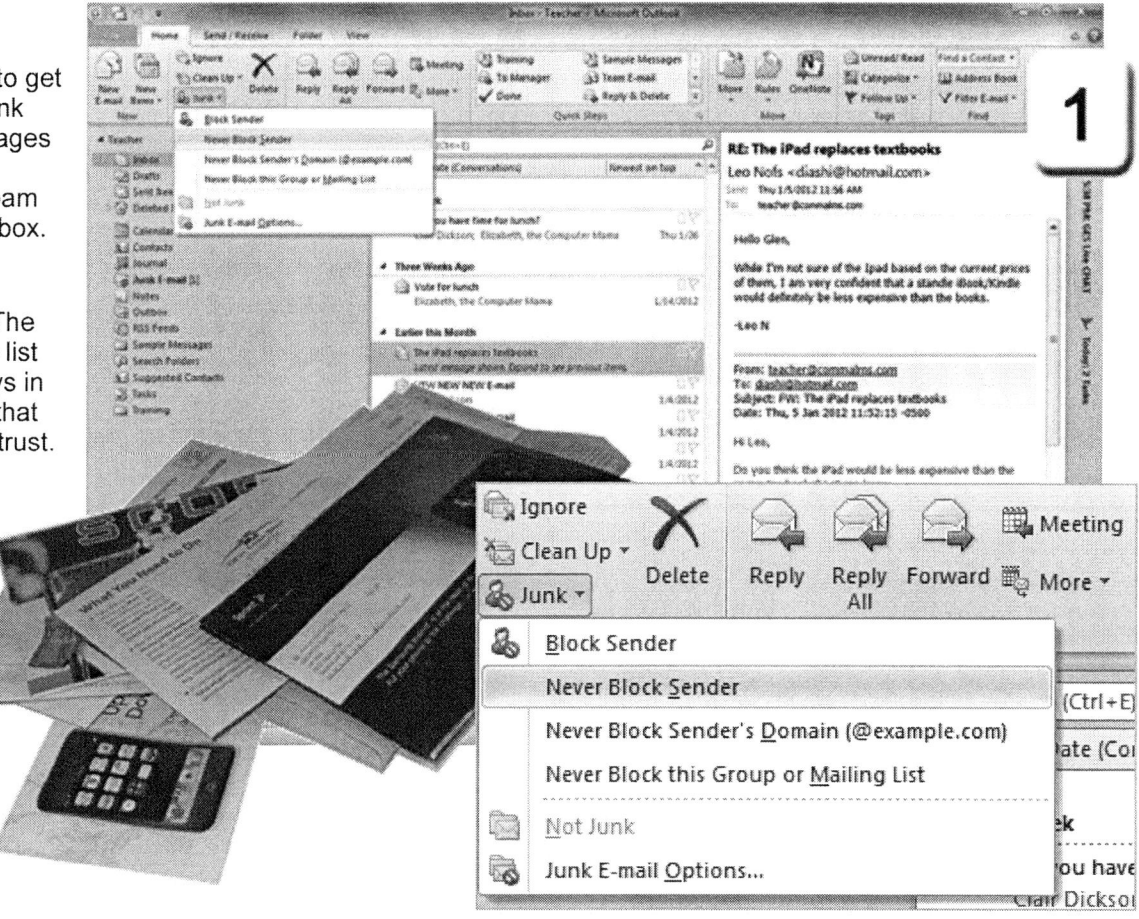

Exam 77-884: Microsoft Outlook 2010
3. Managing Email Messages
3.3. Manage junk mail: Identify Junk Mail

Identify by Person

You can identify the bad people and **Block** their E-mails. When you **Block** a sender, that means your E-mail server won't even send any messages from that sender to your Inbox.

You can also identify good people **(Never Block Sender)** and add them to the Safe Sender List. Here are the steps.

2. Try it: Never Block Sender
Select an E-mail from someone you trust.
Go to **Home ->Junk->Never Block Sender.**

What Do You See? A pop up should confirm that the sender of the selected message has been added to the **Safe Sender List**.

Click **OK**. Keep going...

Memo to Self: You can also use this option for your team if you wish. Select the message that has your team's mailing list and go to **Never Block a Group or Mailing List**.
It works.

Home ->Junk->Never Block Sender

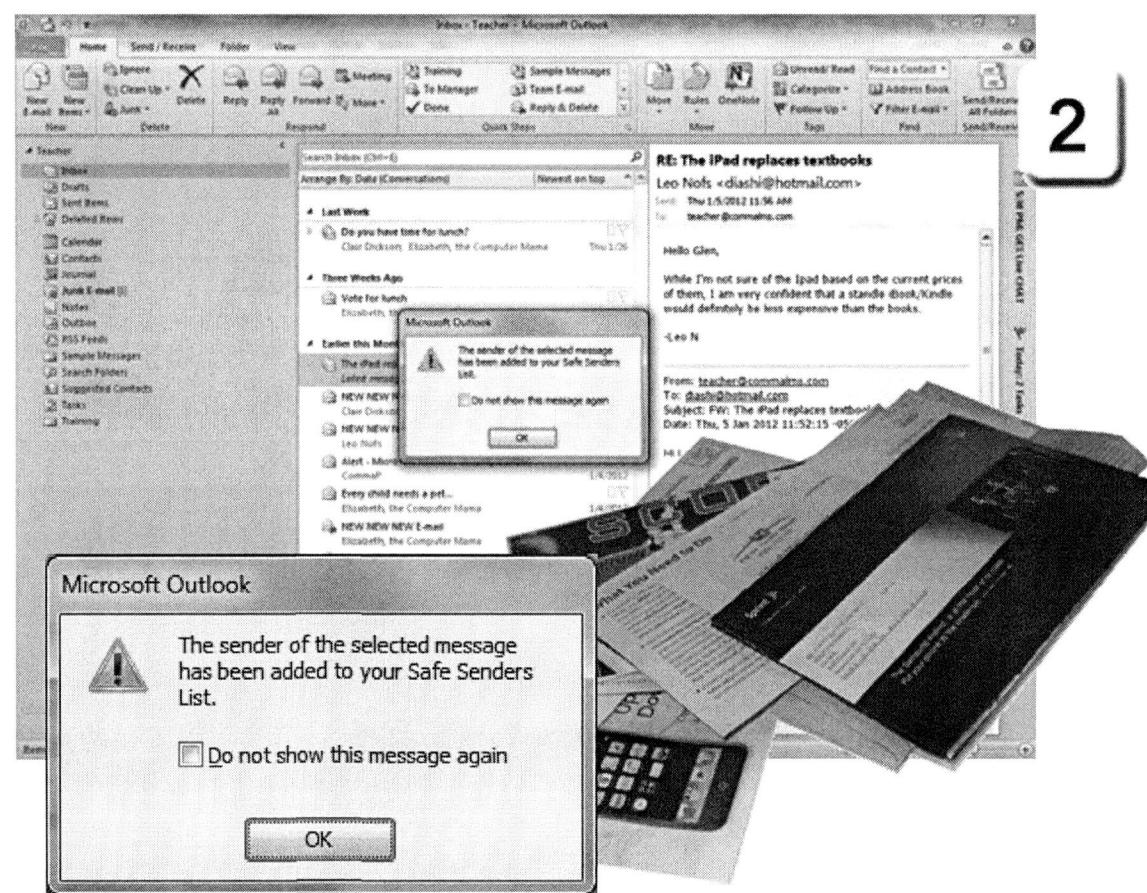

Exam 77-884: Microsoft Outlook 2010
3. Managing Email Messages
3.3. Manage junk mail: Never Block Sender

Identify by Place (Domain)

Every computer has an IP address. A **Domain Name** is how that address is translated into a name, such as www.microsoft.com Domain Naming is hierarchical. The name begins with the function. Commercial domains use .com and educational ones use .edu.

3. Try it: Never Block Sender's Domain

Select a sample E-mail.
In the screenshot on this page, the sample E-mail is from Microsoft.com, a trustworthy firm.

Go to **Home ->Junk.**
Click on **Never Block Sender's Domain.**

What Do You See? A pop up should confirm that the sender of the selected message has been added to the **Safe Sender List**. This option accepts E-mails from anyone from the @microsoft.com domain.

Click **OK**. Keep going...

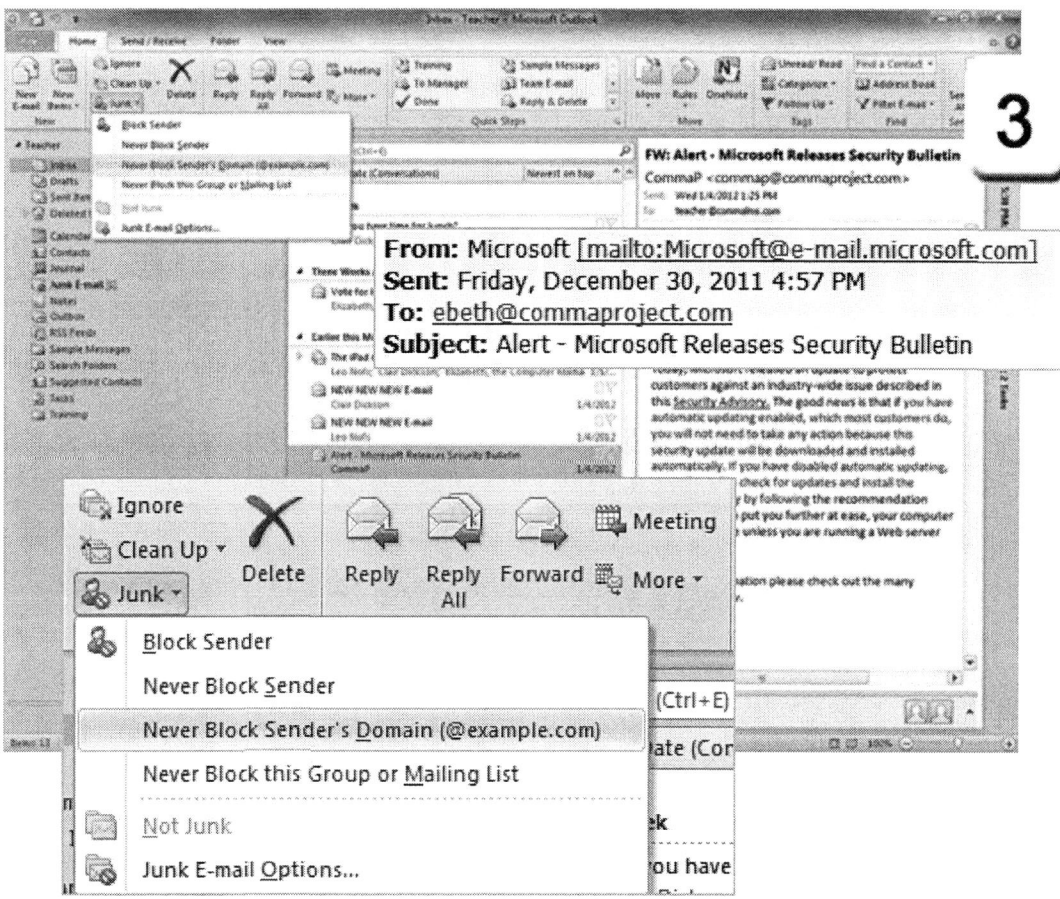

Exam 77-884: Microsoft Outlook 2010
3. Managing Email Messages
3.3. Manage junk mail: Never Block Sender's Domain

Is it Really Junk E-Mail?

By default, junk is moved to the **Junk E-mail** folder. In the example on this page, the Junk E-mail folder has one unread message (1).

Some messages may be misinterpreted as junk. You should check the Junk E-mail folder and check if anything important is in there.

Here are the steps you can take to identify something that should not be marked as junk.

4. Try It: Mark As Not Junk
Go to the Junk E-mail folder.
Select the message you want to identify.
Go to **Home ->Junk->Not Junk.**

What Do You See? A little window will state that the message will be moved back to the Inbox. There may be a check mark to always trust E-mail from this sender.

Home ->Junk->Not Junk

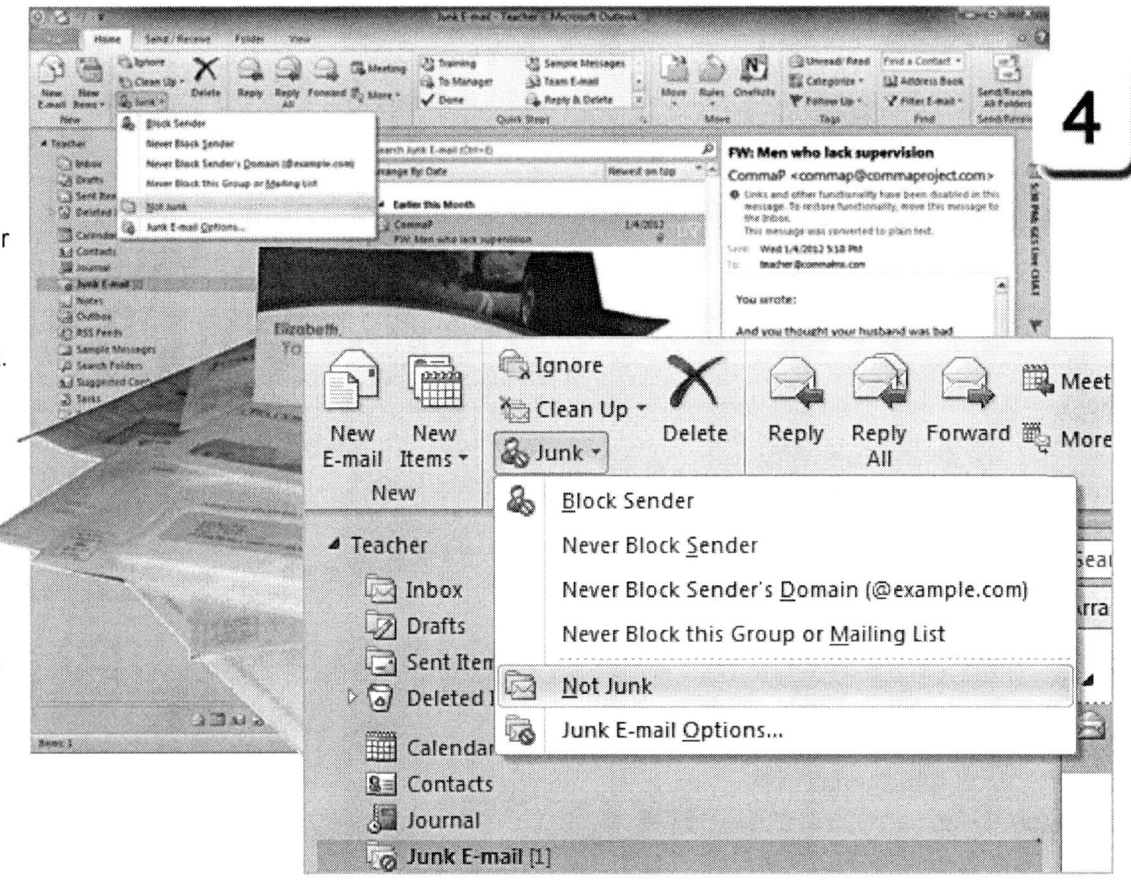

4

Exam 77-884: Microsoft Outlook 2010
3. Managing Email Messages
3.3. Manage junk mail: Allow a Specific Message (Not Junk)

Manage Junk E-Mail

The Safe and Blocked Sender lists are saved in the **Junk E-mail Options**. You can edit the level of Junk E-mail protection you want, too.

5. Try It: Review the Junk Mail Options
Go to **Home ->Junk->Junk E-mail Options.**

What Do You See? The E-mail filter may be set Low-only the most obvious junk is sent to the Junk E-mail folder.

What Else Do You See? By default, you will be warned about suspicious domain names. The links and functions for suspicious E-mail are automatically disabled as well.

Keep going, please...

Memo to Self: You can also **Permanently delete Junk E-mail** instead of moving it to the Junk E-mail folder.

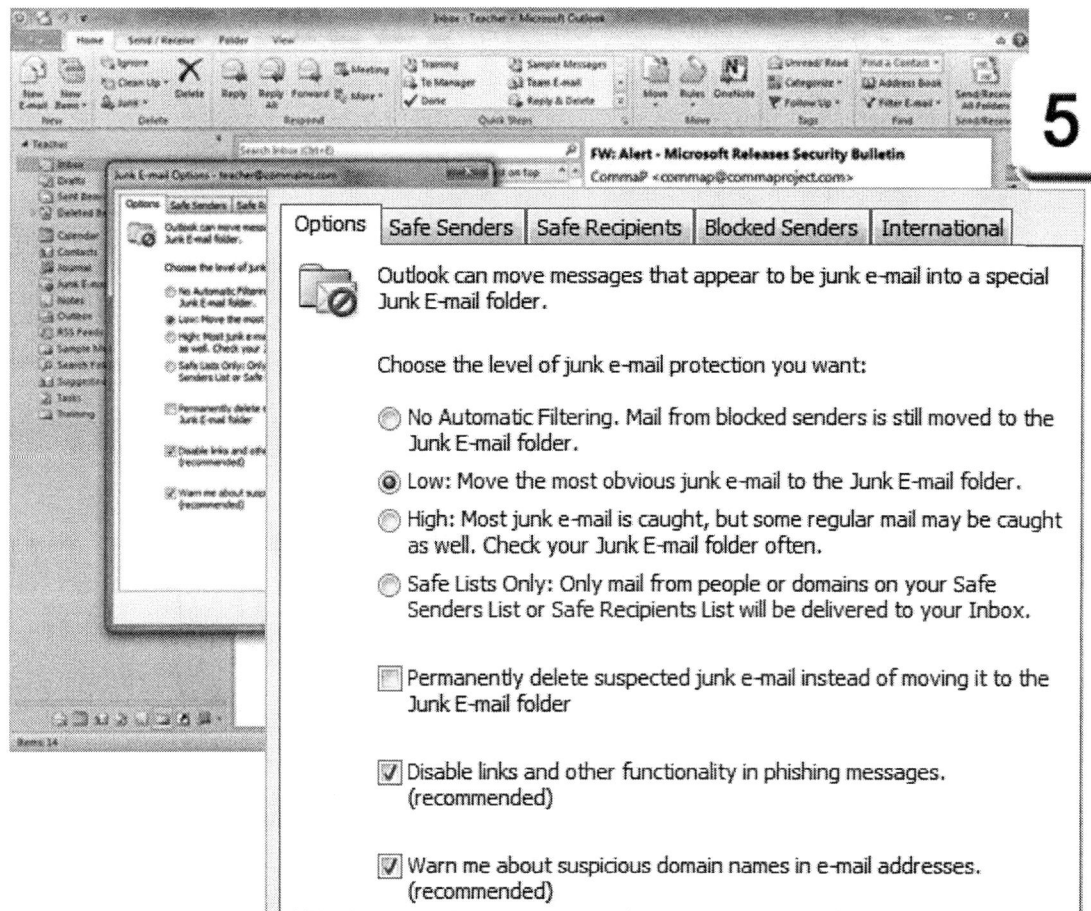

Exam 77-884: Microsoft Outlook 2010
3. Managing Email Messages
3.3. Manage junk mail: Filter Junk Mail

Thoughts to Consider

6. Try it: Review the Safe Senders
The Junk E-mail Options are open.
Go to **Safe Senders**.

What Do You See? The E-mail addresses and domains from people and places you trusted were added here. You can **Add**, **Edit** and **Remove** a Safe Sender.

What Else Do You See? At the bottom of the Safe Senders page are two options:
Also trust e-mail from my Contacts
Automatically add people I e-mail to the Safe Senders List.

Contacts are people's names and addresses that you add to Outlook. They are assumed safe because you chose to include them.

The second option is NOT selected by default. There may be people included on a message that you do not want to add as Safe **automatically**. Something to consider.

Click **OK** to return to the Inbox. Keep going...

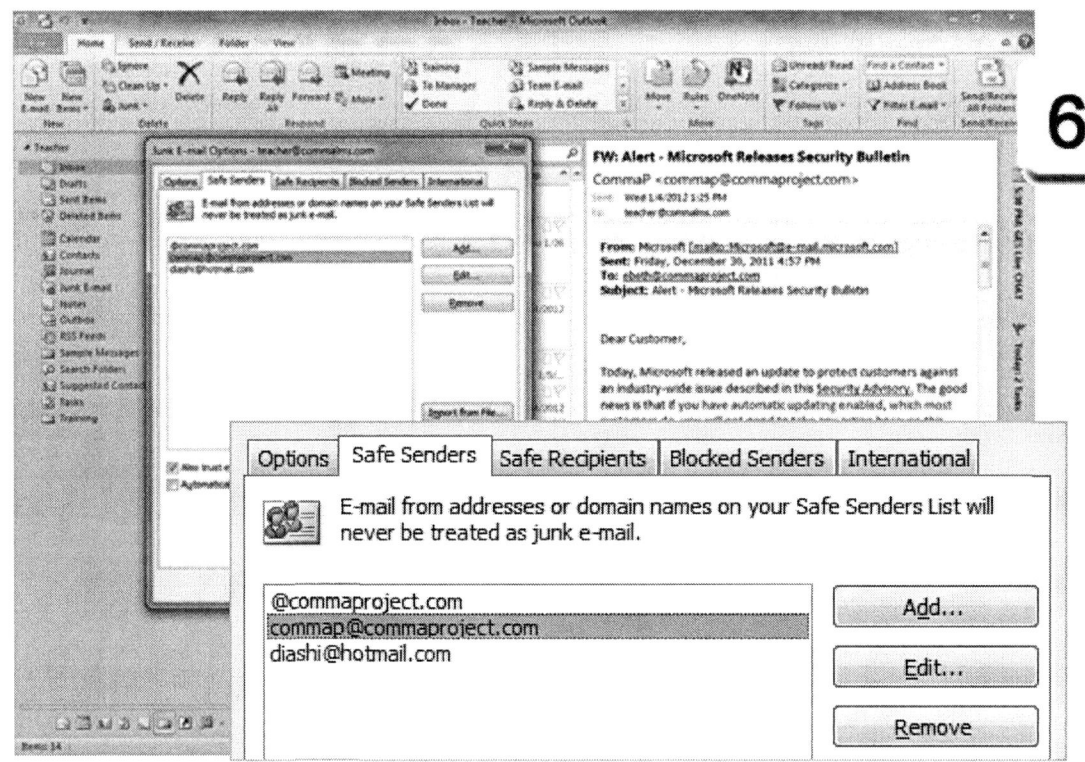

Exam 77-884: Microsoft Outlook 2010
3. Managing Email Messages
3.3. Manage junk mail: Filter Junk Mail

Last, but not Least

When you send an E-mail, a copy is automatically saved in the Sent Folder. You can save it in a different folder. Go to **Options->More-Options**. Select: **Other Folder**.

Summary

This lesson looked at ways to manage the mailbox. Microsoft Outlook has **Rules** that can identify your messages and send them to the right folder. Rules can be placed in the **Quick Steps** library for easy access. **Junk E-mail** can be filtered and managed automatically, as well.

Well, you done good.
You get the cookie!

Exam 77-884: Microsoft Outlook 2010
2. Creating and Formatting Item Content
2.1. Create and send email messages: Specify the Sent Item Folder

Test Yourself

1. Outlook can only have one folder for E-mail, the Inbox.
A. True
B. False
Tip: Complete Guide to Outlook, page 117

2. Which is a method for moving an E-mail message to another folder?
(Give all correct answers.)
A. Drag and Drop
B. Use the command Home->Move-> Move
C. File-> Save As and select the folder
Tip: Complete Guide to Outlook, page 118

3. Which of the following is true about Rules? (Give all correct answers.)
A. The command is Home-> Move-> Rules
B. Rules automate message handling
C. To delete a rule, go to Home-> Move-> Rules-> Manage Rules and Alerts
Tip: Complete Guide to Outlook, page 122

4. Which of the following are criteria that can be used in creating rules?
(Give all correct answers.)
A. Sender
B. Recipient
C. Subject
D. Keywords
Tip: Complete Guide to Outlook, page 126

5. What are the two parts to creating a rule?
(Give all correct answers.)
A. Choose a color
B. Select an e-mail to apply it to
C. Identify the conditions
D. Program the response
Tip: Complete Guide to Outlook, page 127

6. Which are true about Quick Steps?
(Give all correct answers.)
A. Outlook comes with preloaded Quick Steps such as Reply & Delete
B. Custom Quick Steps are not allowed
C. New Quick Steps go through a First Time Setup when first used
D. New rules are added to the Quick Steps group
Tip: Complete Guide to Outlook, page 129

7. How are conversations grouped?
A. Recipient
B. Topic or Subject line
C. Date
D. Keywords
Tip: Complete Guide to Outlook, page 135

Practice

1. Create a new email addressed to yourself with the subject line New Office and send it.

2. Create a new folder: New Office

3. Create a new Rule that moves all E-mails with the subject New Office to the folder named New Office

4. Apply the Rule

5. Create another new E-mail with the subject Update on move to new office and send it

6. Check the New Office folder to verify that both practice emails have been moved based on the Rules

Application Question: What are Rules used for? Give an example of how rules would work in a business setting.

Contacts and Connections

Outlook E-mail Objectives
In this lesson, you will learn how to:

1. Create Contacts in Microsoft Outlook

2. Edit the General and Detail Information about a Contact and include a picture

3. Use the Notes page to document changes

4. Create and manage a Contact Group

5. Forward a Contact Group as an Outlook Contact

6. Install the Microsoft Outlook Social Network connectors for Facebook and LinkedIn

© 2012 Comma Productions, LLC

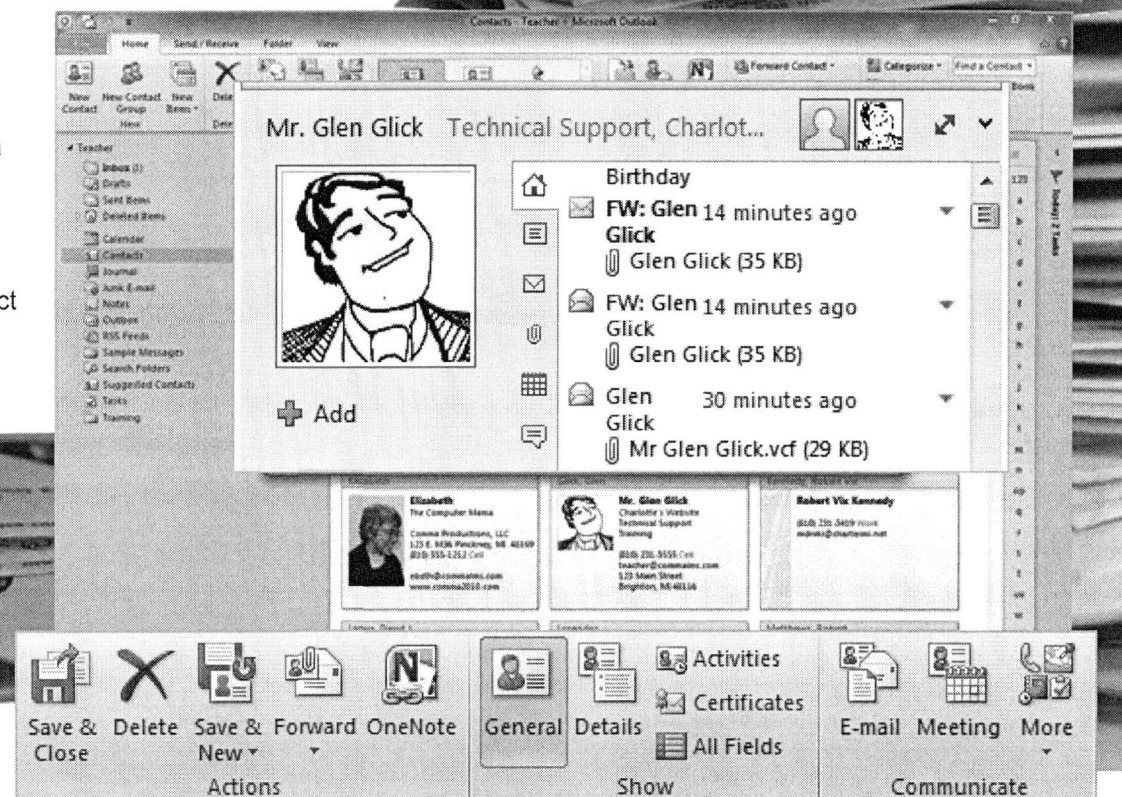

 # Lesson 6 : Contacts and Social Connections

1. Readings
Read Lesson 6 in the Microsoft Outlook guide, page 149-181.

Project
Create Contacts and Contact Groups.

Downloads
GlenGlick1.gif,
GlenGlick2.gif,
GlenGlick3.gif
GlenGlick1.gif

2. Practice
Complete the Practice Activity on page 182.

3. Assessment
Review the Test questions on page 182.

Contacts Ribbon

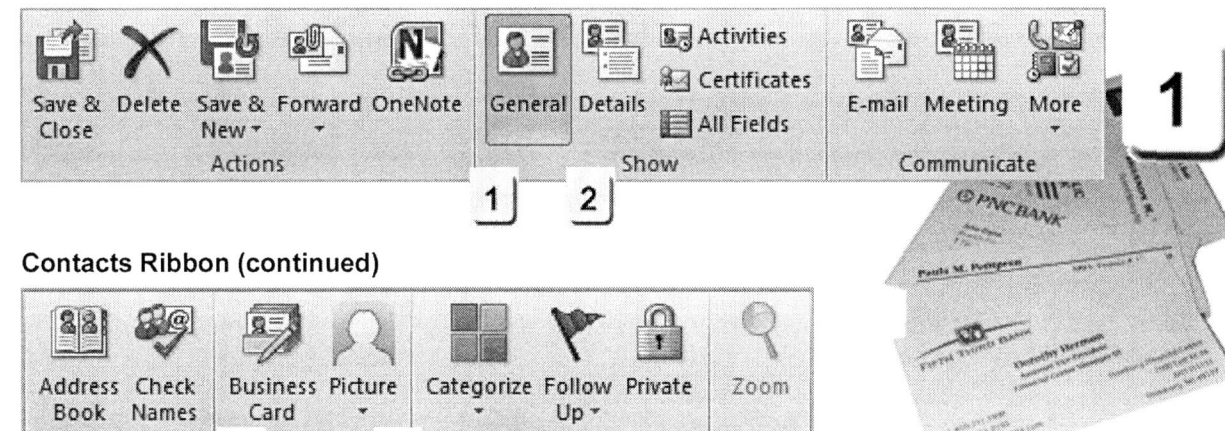

Contacts Ribbon (continued)

Menu Maps

From the Contacts Home Ribbon.
1. Home ->Current View, page 153
2. Home ->New->New Contact, page 154
3. Home ->Share->Forward Contact, page 163
4. Home ->New->New Contact Group, page 166
5. Home->Share->Forward Contact, page 171

From the Outlook View Ribbon
1. View ->People Pane->Account Settings, page 174

More Menu Maps

From the **Contact Ribbon**
1. Contact ->Show->General, page 155
2. Contact ->Show->Details, page 159
3. Contact ->Options->Picture->Add Picture, page 160
4. Contact ->Options->Business Card, page 162

From the **Contact Group Ribbon**
1. Contact Group ->Members-> Add Members, page 167
2. Contact Group->Show->Notes, page 170

Working with Contacts

In the early days of computer hardware, a system would work until you cleaned your desk and moved something. Usually the computer wasn't broken-just not connected right. **Connections, connections, connections**. Nine times out of ten, it's just connections. Social networking and business interactions also need connections. The hardware may be ready, good people, good products, good advertising, but nothing happens until a connection is made. This lesson in Microsoft Outlook looks at **Contacts** and **Social Network Connectors**.

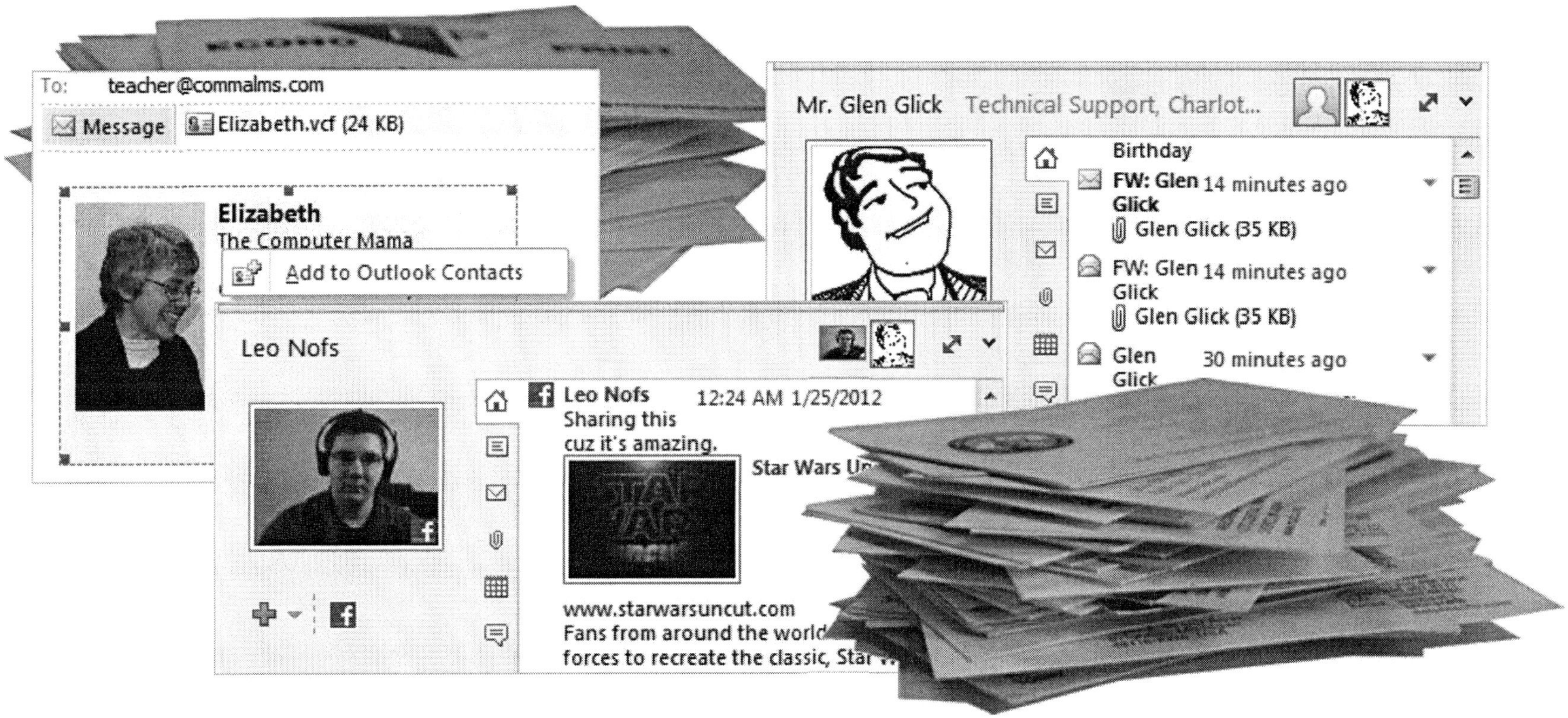

To: teacher@commalms.com

✉ Message 📇 Elizabeth.vcf (24 KB)

Elizabeth
The Computer Mama

Add to Outlook Contacts

Leo Nofs

Mr. Glen Glick Technical Support, Charlot...

Birthday
✉ **FW: Glen** 14 minutes ago
Glick
📎 Glen Glick (35 KB)

✉ FW: Glen 14 minutes ago
Glick
📎 Glen Glick (35 KB)

✉ Glen   30 minutes ago
Glick

🏠 **Leo Nofs** 12:24 AM 1/25/2012
Sharing this
cuz it's amazing.

Star Wars U...

www.starwarsuncut.com
Fans from around the world
forces to recreate the classic, Star...

HOME

Take Two

Before You Begin

By default, Microsoft Outlook opens with the Inbox as the initial view. The **Contacts** can be found by using the Navigation Pane.

Before You Begin: View the Folders
Go to **View->Layout->Navigation Pane**.
Select: **Normal**.

1. Try it: Find the Contacts Folder
Go to the Navigation Pane
Select the **Contacts** Folder.

Keep going...

View->Layout->Navigation Pane->Normal

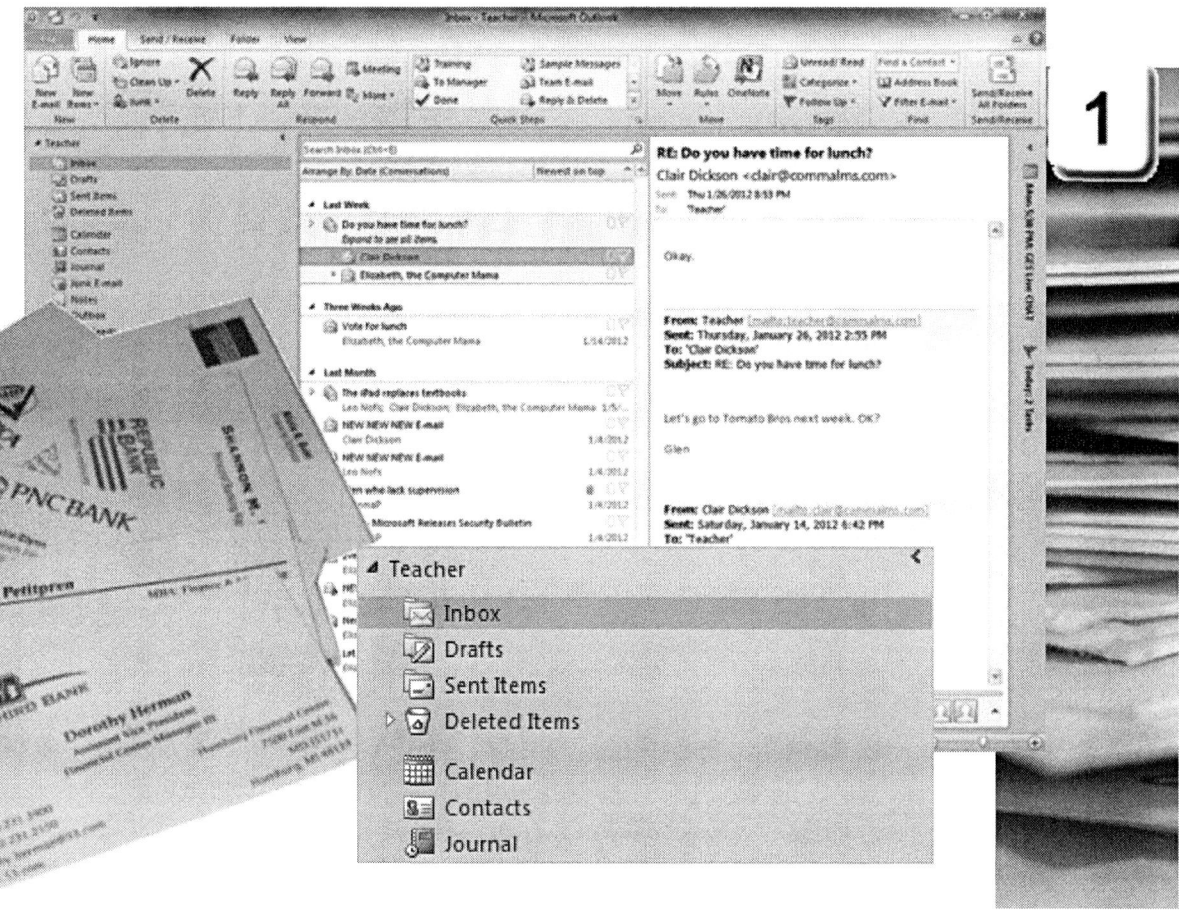

Hello, Contacts!

This screen shot shows a **Contacts Folder** with a dozen Business Cards. The data can be simple--just a name and an email address--or it can include all of the demographics.

The **Home** Ribbon shows options for Contacts, now. These options are different than the ones on the Home Ribbon for the Inbox.

2. Try it: Review the Home Ribbon

The **Home** Ribbon has the following groups:
New
Delete
Communicate
Contact View
Actions
Share
Tags
Find

Keep going...

Memo to Self: If this is the first time, the Contacts Folder will be empty.

Home ->Current View

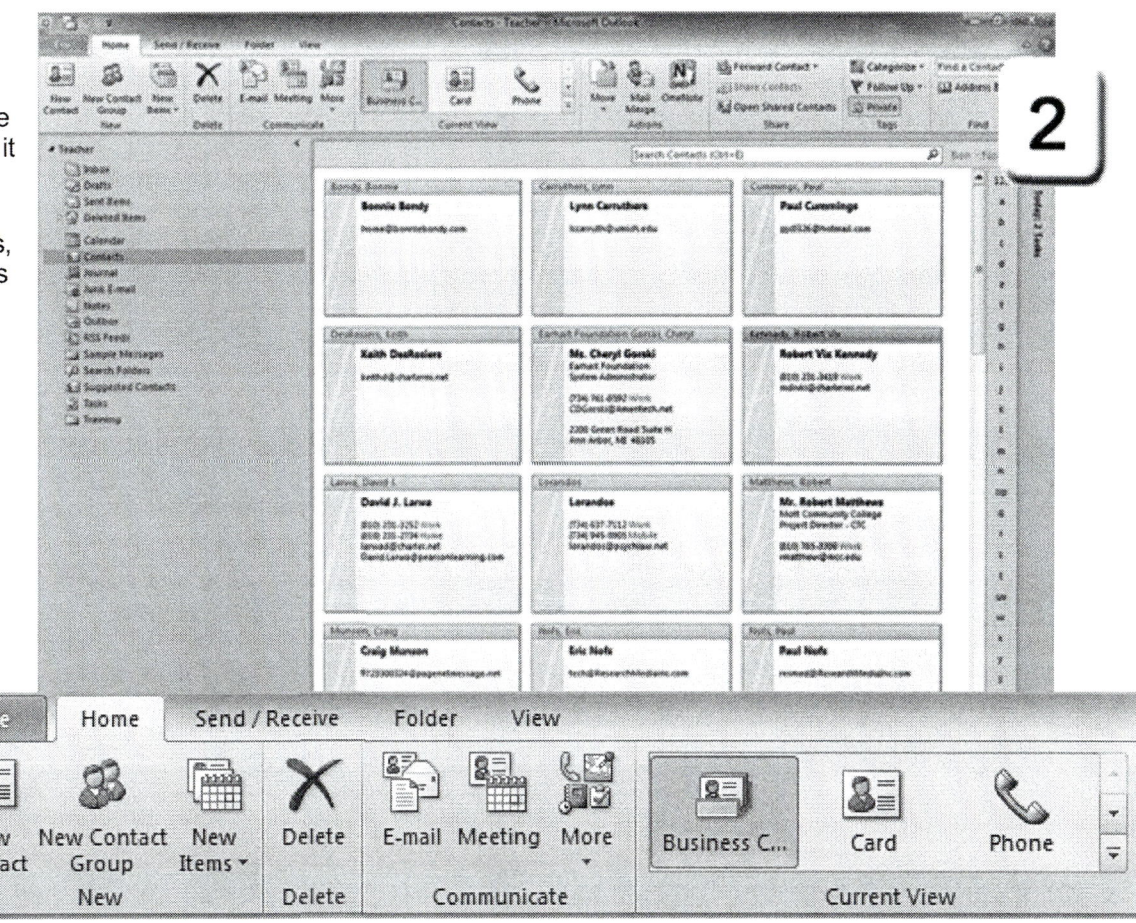

Exam 77-884: Microsoft Outlook 2010
4. Managing Contacts
4.1. Create and manipulate contacts: Change the Current View

Add a New Contact

3. Try it: Add a New Contact
Go to **Home ->New->New Contact.**

What Do You See? A new Contact will open.
There are four Ribbons:
Contact
Insert
Format Text
Review

This lesson will look at the **Contact** Ribbon.
The Insert, Format Text and Review Ribbons
are almost the same as the ones found in a
new E-mail message,

Keep going...

Home ->New->New Contact

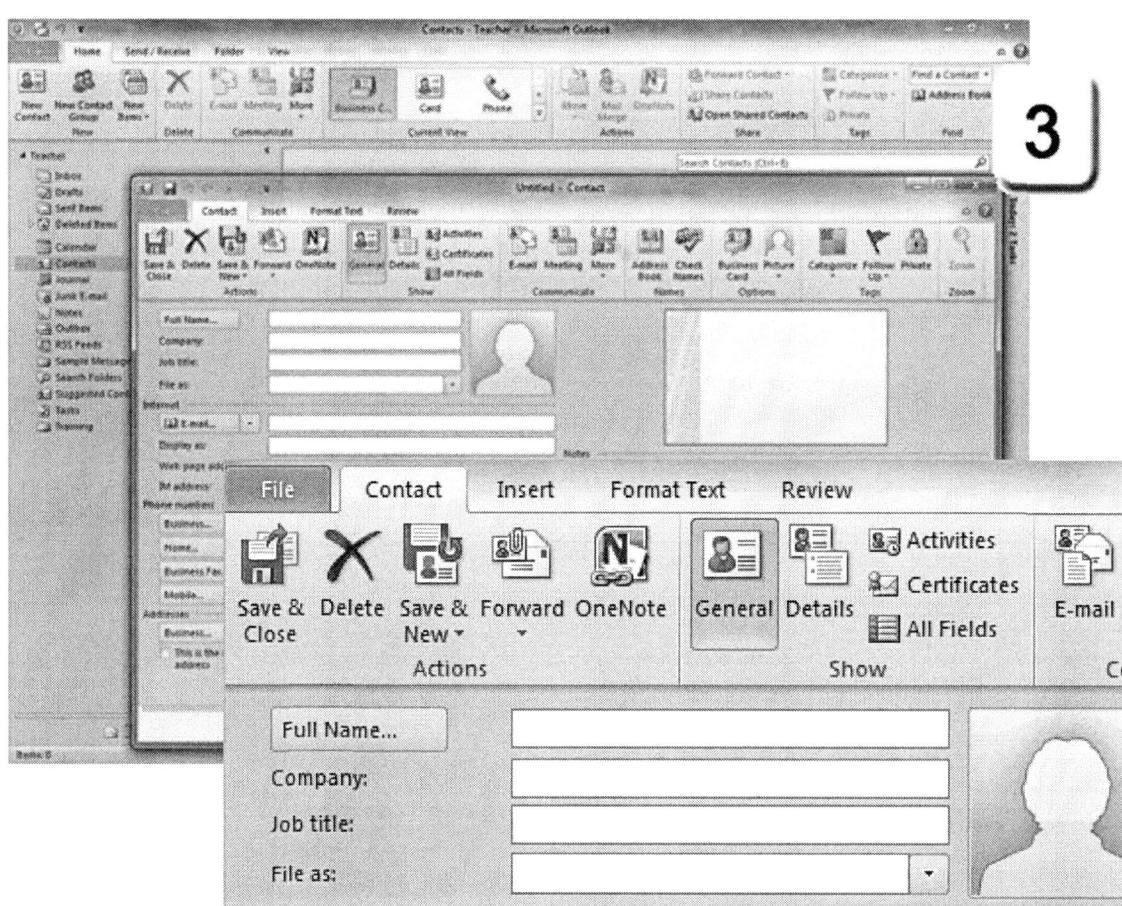

Exam 77-884: Microsoft Outlook 2010
4. Managing Contacts
4.1. Create and manipulate contacts: Edit the Contact

Edit the Contact

4. Try it: Edit the Contact
Enter the following:
Full Name: Glen Glick
Company: Charlotte's Website
Job Title: Technical Support

What Do You See? If you enter data for the Full Name as well as the Company, you can choose how to file this Contact.

The **File As** options include:
Last Name
First Name
Last Name (Company)
Company (Last Name)

Keep going, please...

Memo to Self: This lesson shows a *sample* E-mail address. Students who are studying for the Microsoft Office Specialist certification test are encouraged to create a Contact for a partner who can help them test the options as they send and receive practice messages and appointments.

Contact ->Show->General

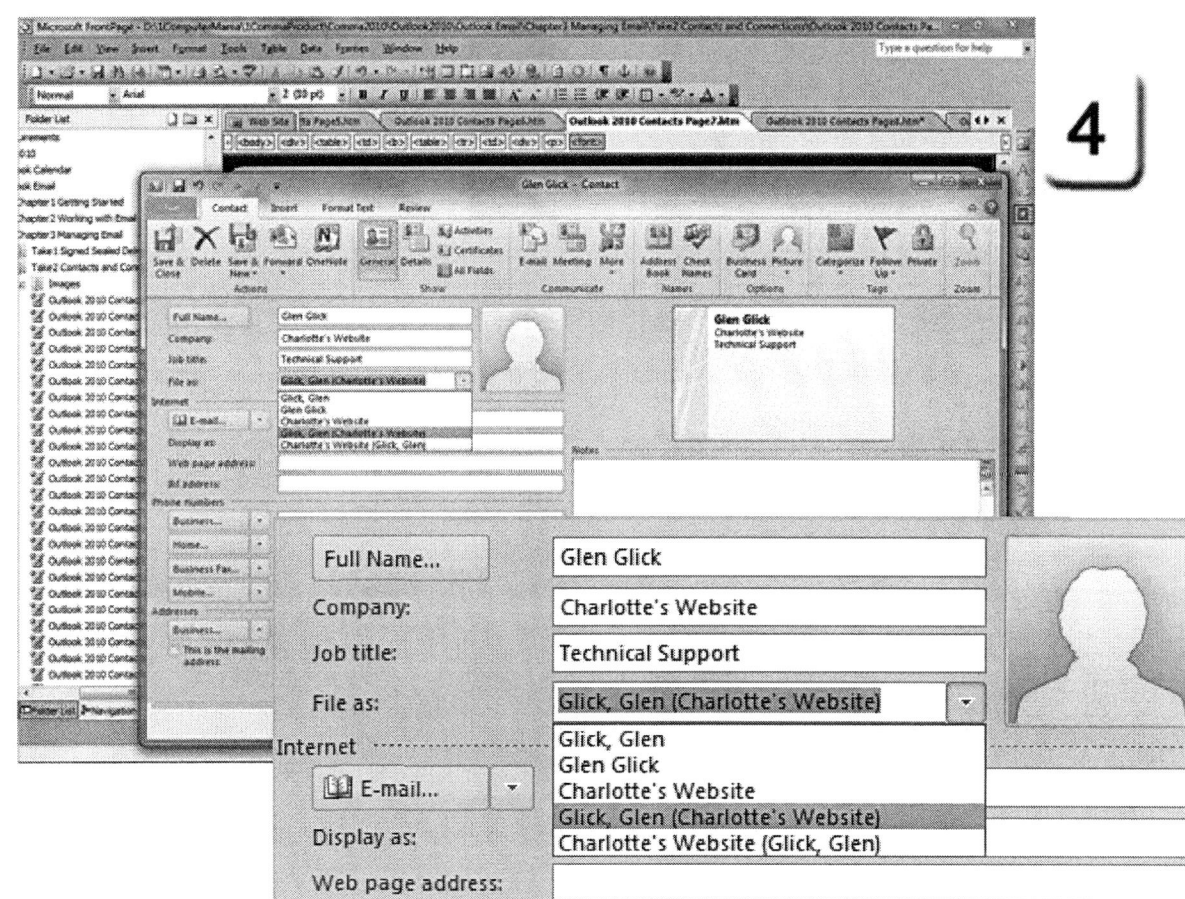

Exam 77-884: Microsoft Outlook 2010
4. Managing Contacts
4.1. Create and manipulate contacts: Edit the General Information

The Data, the Data, the Data

Microsoft Outlook is a database that you can use with a Mail Merge in Word or analyze with a PivotTable Slice in Excel. The Contact folder is a *real* table that collects all of the information entered into the Contact, E-mail, Calendar, Meeting and Task forms.

When you fill in the form fields for a Contact you can check that the details are accurate.

5. Try it: Check Full Name
Go to the Full Name field.
Click on **Full Name**.

What Do You See? You will be prompted to edit the **Name details**. By default, there is a check mark to show this window whenever the data is incomplete or unclear.

Try This, Too: Edit the Name Details
Select a **Title**: Mr.
Click **OK** to return to the Contact form.

Keep going...

Contact ->Show->General->Full Name

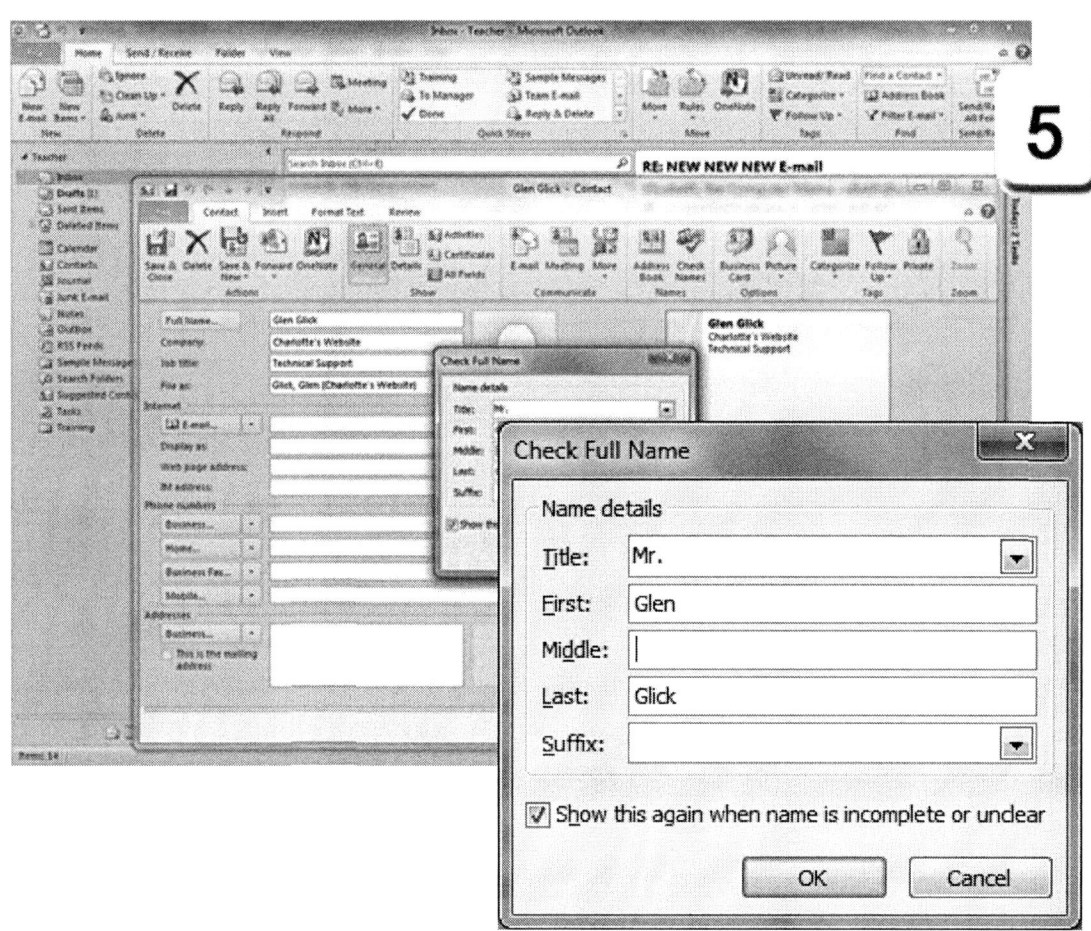

Exam 77-884: Microsoft Outlook 2010
4. Managing Contacts
4.1. Create and manipulate contacts: Edit the General Information

Edit the E-mail and E-mail Display

The Display name does not have to be the same as the E-mail Address. Often, the Contact Name is displayed instead of the E-mail Address.

6. Try it: Edit the E-mail

Enter your E-mail or your partner's in this lesson.
Display as: Glen Glick (Teacher)

Try This, Too: Edit the Phone Numbers

Enter a sample phone: (810) 231-5555

What Do You See? Outlook has places for four phone numbers. You can choose which number you wish to document.

Keep going..

Memo to Self: Some people have several phone numbers including business, fax, home, cell and more. Some have only one.

The Computer Mama sez she maxed out at eight phone numbers. There was a different phone in each pocket. Riiiiiing.

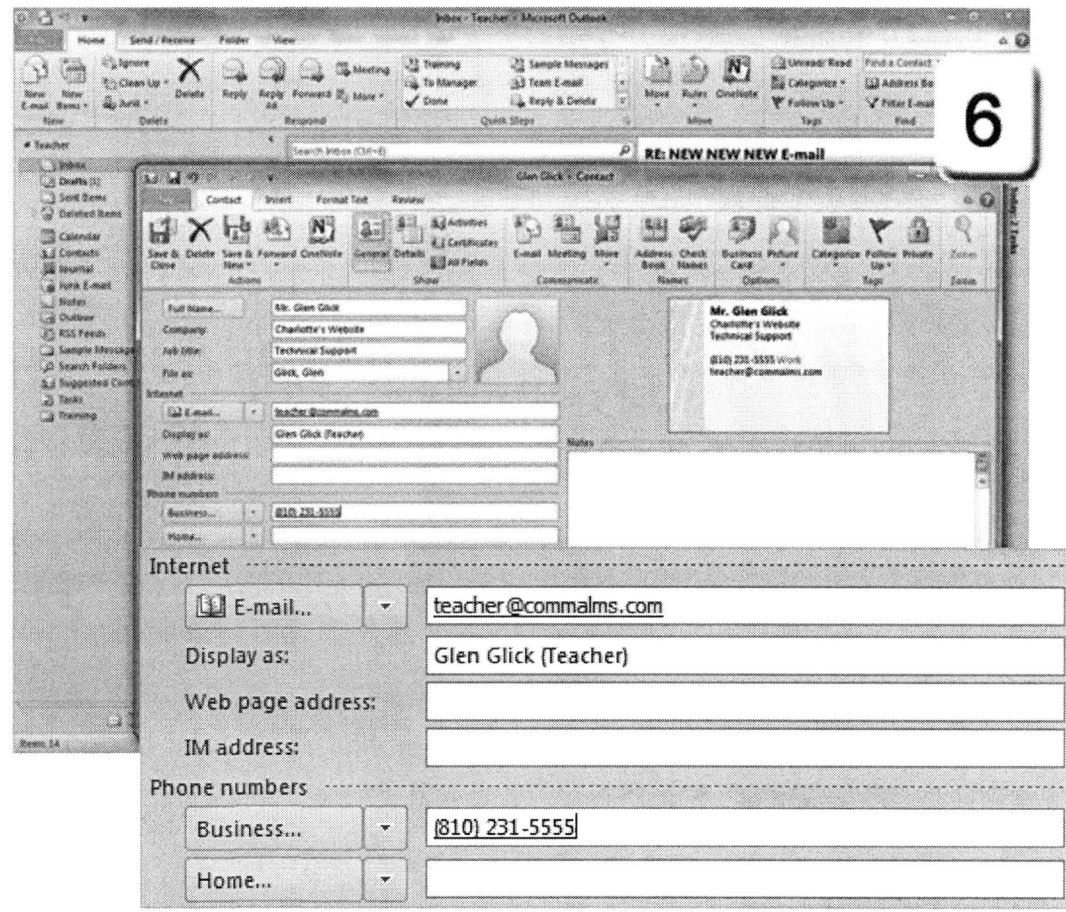

Exam 77-884: Microsoft Outlook 2010
4. Managing Contacts
4.1. Create and manipulate contacts: Edit the General Information

Edit the Address and Map It

One of the new features in Microsoft Outlook 2010 is the **Map It** option. Map it will lookup the Business Address on the Internet. The default Maps website is bing, a Microsoft company.

7. Try it: Enter a Business Address
Enter the Business Address:
123 Main Street
Brighton, MI 48116

You Gotta Try This: Map It
Go to **Map It**
Edit the Map View: Bird's Eye

Close the Internet browser. Keep going...!

Contact ->Show->General->Map It

Exam 77-884: Microsoft Outlook 2010
4. Managing Contacts
4.1. Create and manipulate contacts: Map the Address

Edit the Contact Details

The **Details** view has more fields to record additional information about your Contact.

Before You Begin: Find the Details
Go to **Contacts->Show->Details**.

8. Try it: Edit the Details
Enter the Contact Details:
Department: Training
Office: Brighton
Manager's name: The Computer Mama
Nickname: Teacher
Birthday: Use the Date Picker to select a date.

Go to **Contact ->Show->General.**
Keep going...

Contact ->Show->Details

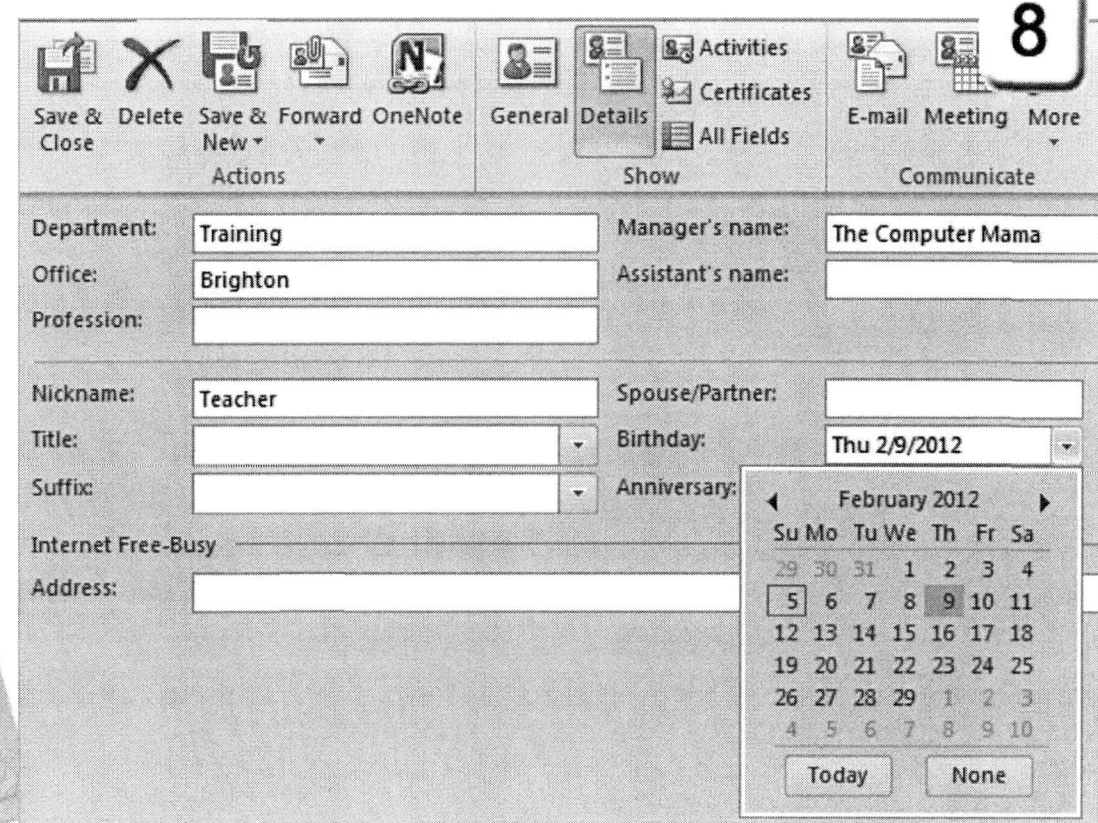

HOME

Add a Picture

Pictures help you match persons, places and projects. Here are the steps.

9. Try it: Sample
Go to **Contact ->Options->Picture**.
Click on **Add Picture.**

Browse to select a picture: GlenGlick2.gif
Click **OK** to return to the Contact form.

Keep going..

Memo to Self: You can download the sample pictures available with this lesson or use your own pictures if you wish.

Contact ->Options->Picture->Add Picture

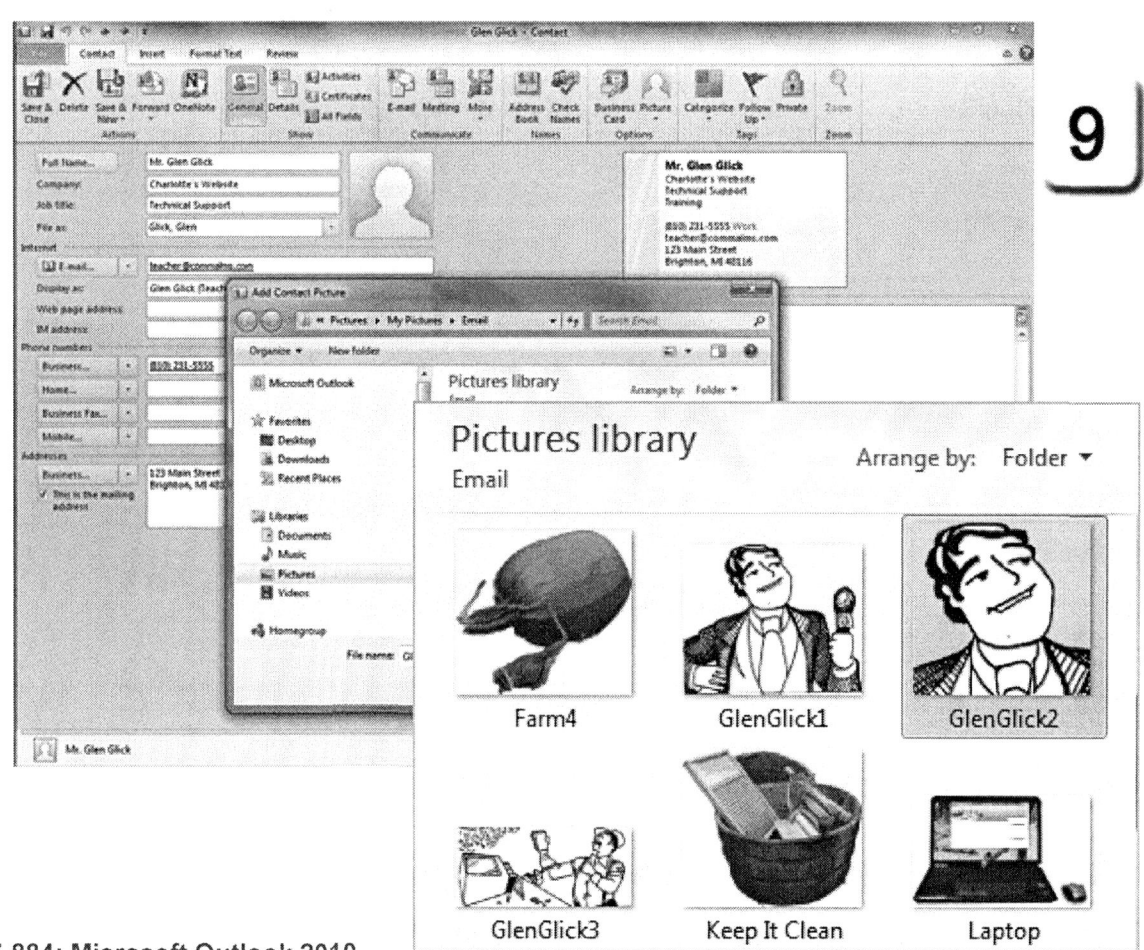

9

Exam 77-884: Microsoft Outlook 2010
4. Managing Contacts
4.1. Create and manipulate contacts: Options-Add Picture

Contact ->Options->Picture->Add Picture

Review the Business Card

What Do You See? The picture that you selected was added to the Contact form.

What Else Did You See? Say, did you notice that the information that you entered into the Contact form fields were added to the little Business Card on the right side?

You can select how much data you would like to publish on your Business Card.

Follow me, please...

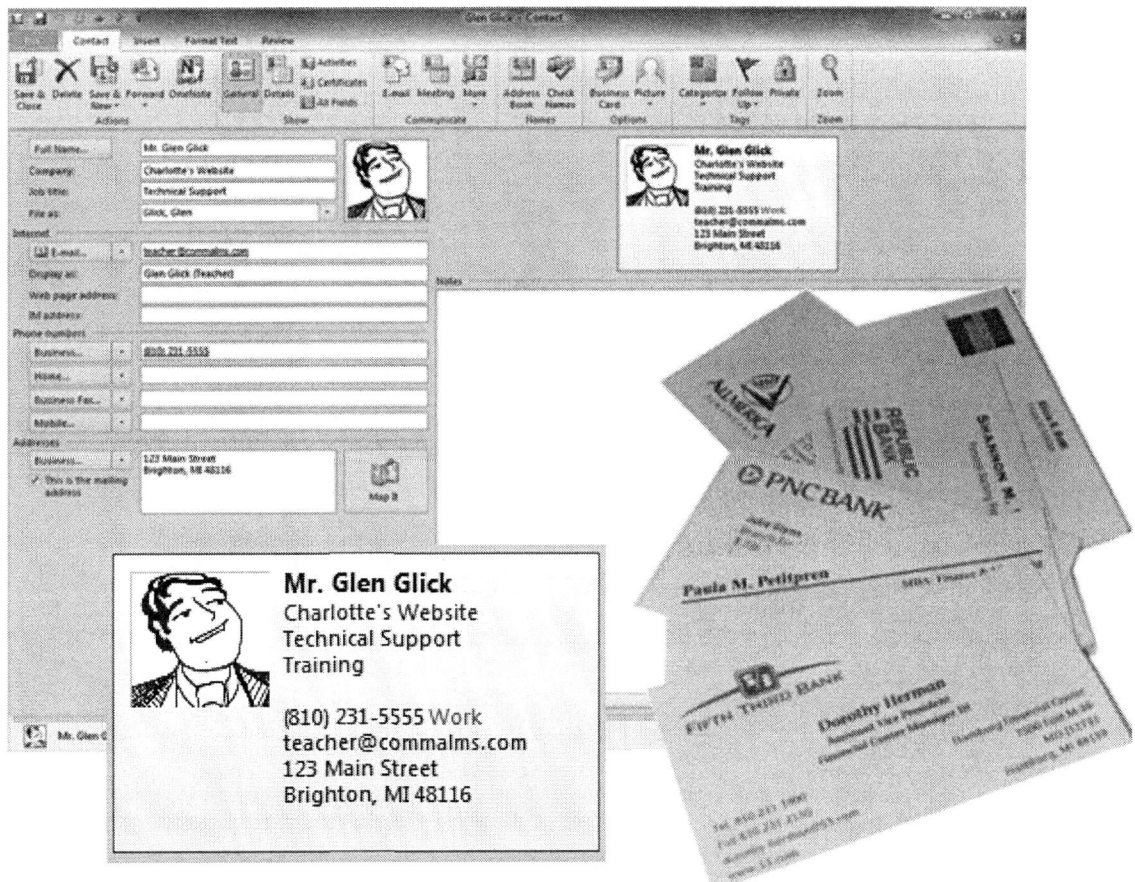

Exam 77-884: Microsoft Outlook 2010
4. Managing Contacts
4.1. Create and manipulate contacts: Options: Business Card

Contact ->Options->Business Card

Edit the Business Card
Try it: Edit the Business Card
Go to **Contact ->Options->Business Card**.
Go to **Card Design->Image Align.**
Select: Top Center.

Try This, Too: Edit the Fields
Select the Business Phone Field.
Edit the Label: Cell

What Do You See? Look at the bottom of the
Field list. You can **Add** or **Remove** any Field
if you wish. The arrows let you move any
Field up or down on the Business Card.

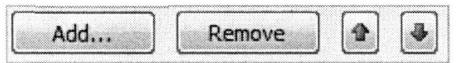

Click **OK** to save these changes.

Do This: Save the Contact
Go to **Contact->Actions->Save & Close.**

You will return to the Contacts Folder. There
should be a new Contact for Glen Glick.

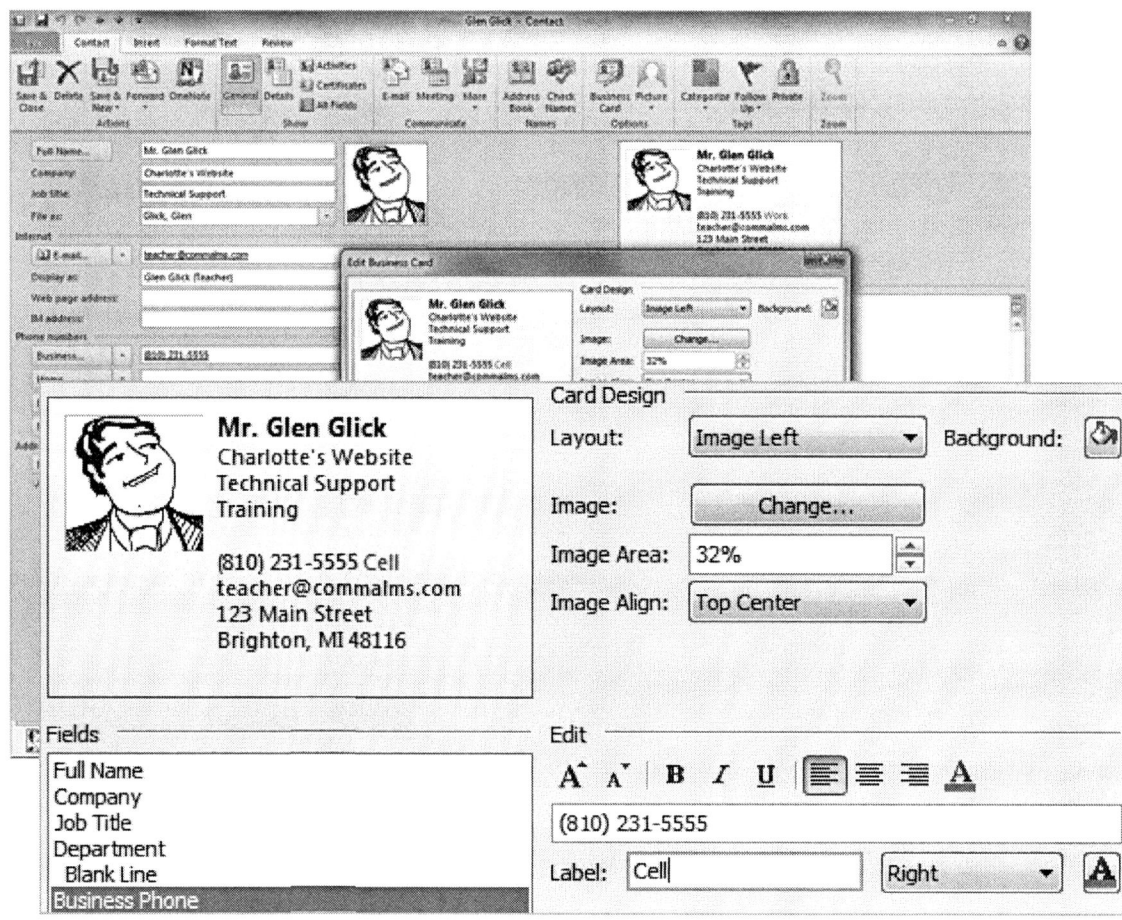

Exam 77-884: Microsoft Outlook 2010
4. Managing Contacts
4.1. Create and manipulate contacts: Edit the Business Card

Hand Out Your Business Card

In Colonial and Ante Bellum times, your card may have been presented on a silver salver. Microsoft Outlook has several methods for sharing your Contact information.

1. Try it: Forward a Contact
Select the sample Business Card.
Go to **Home ->Share->Forward Contact.**

What Do You See? The options include:
As a Business Card
As an Outlook Contact
Forward as a Text Message

Select: **As a Business Card**
Keep going...

Home ->Share->Forward Contact

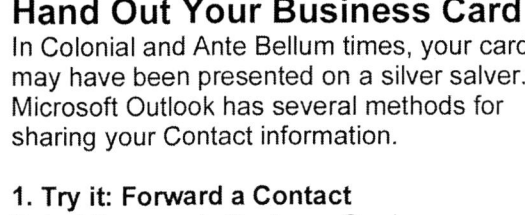

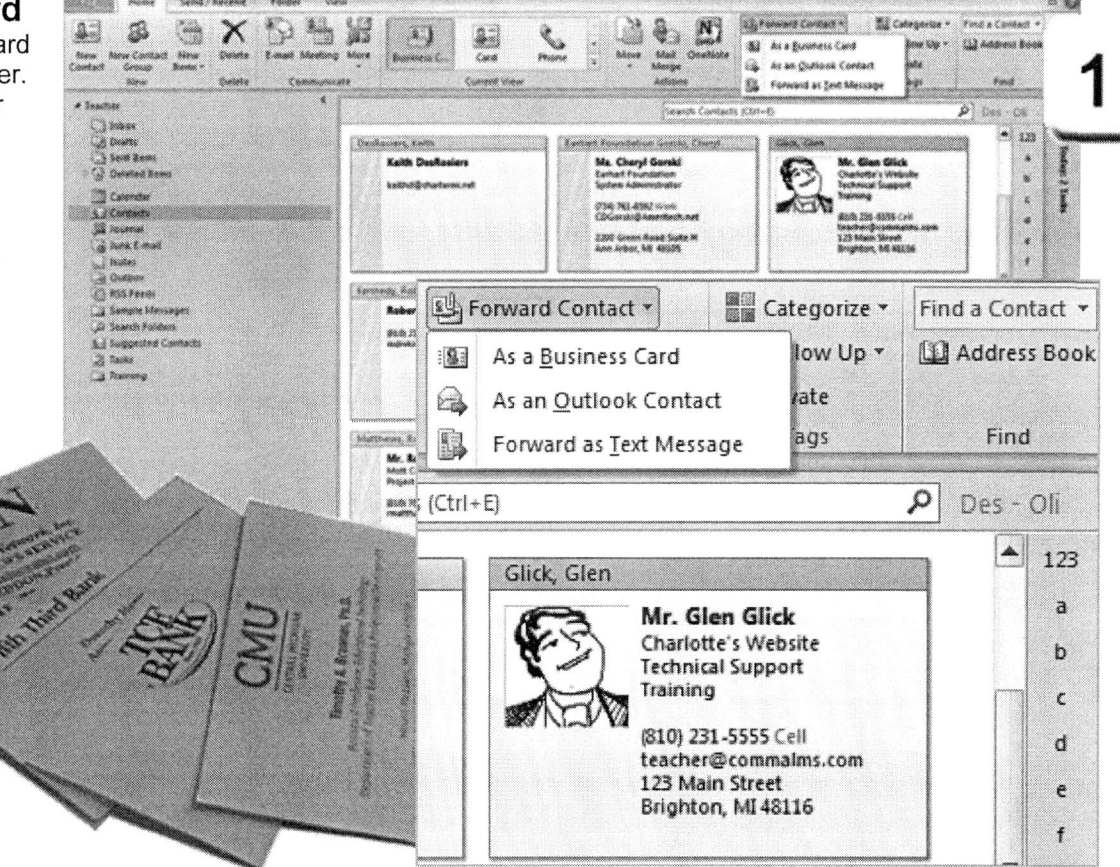

Exam 77-884: Microsoft Outlook 2010
4. Managing Contacts
4.1. Create and manipulate contacts: Forward a Contact

Home ->Share->Forward Contact

Forward as a Business Card

2. What Do You See? When you select **Forward as Business Card** Microsoft Outlook will create a new E-mail that includes the Business Card in the message.

What Else Do You See? The Business Card is attached to this E-mail as a .vcf file.

Do This, Please: Send the Card
Enter your E-mail Address.
Enter the Subject: Glen Glick
Click **Send**.

Keep going...

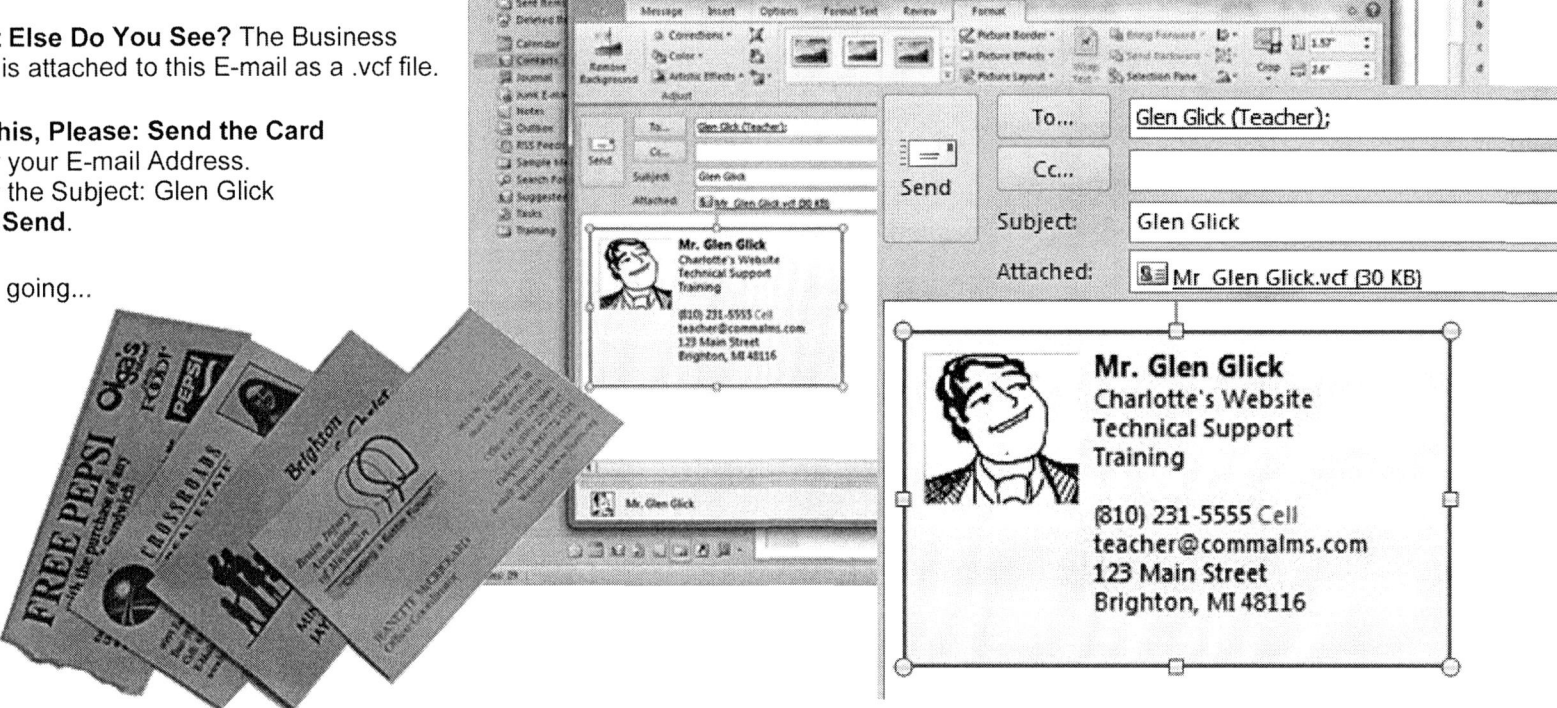

Exam 77-884: Microsoft Outlook 2010
2. Creating and Formatting Item Content
2.5. Attach content to email messages: Attach an Outlook Item

Add to Outlook Contacts

Say someone sent you a Business Card.
How would you add them to your Contacts?

Before You Begin: Find the Attachment
If you wish to practice this step, the E-mail
that was sent from the previous page
should be in the Inbox.

In the example on this page, the E-mail has
a Business Card, Elizabeth.vcf, attached.

3. Try it: Add to Outlook Contacts
Go to the **Inbox.**
Right-Click the Business Card
Click on: **Add to Outlook Contacts**.

So far, so good...

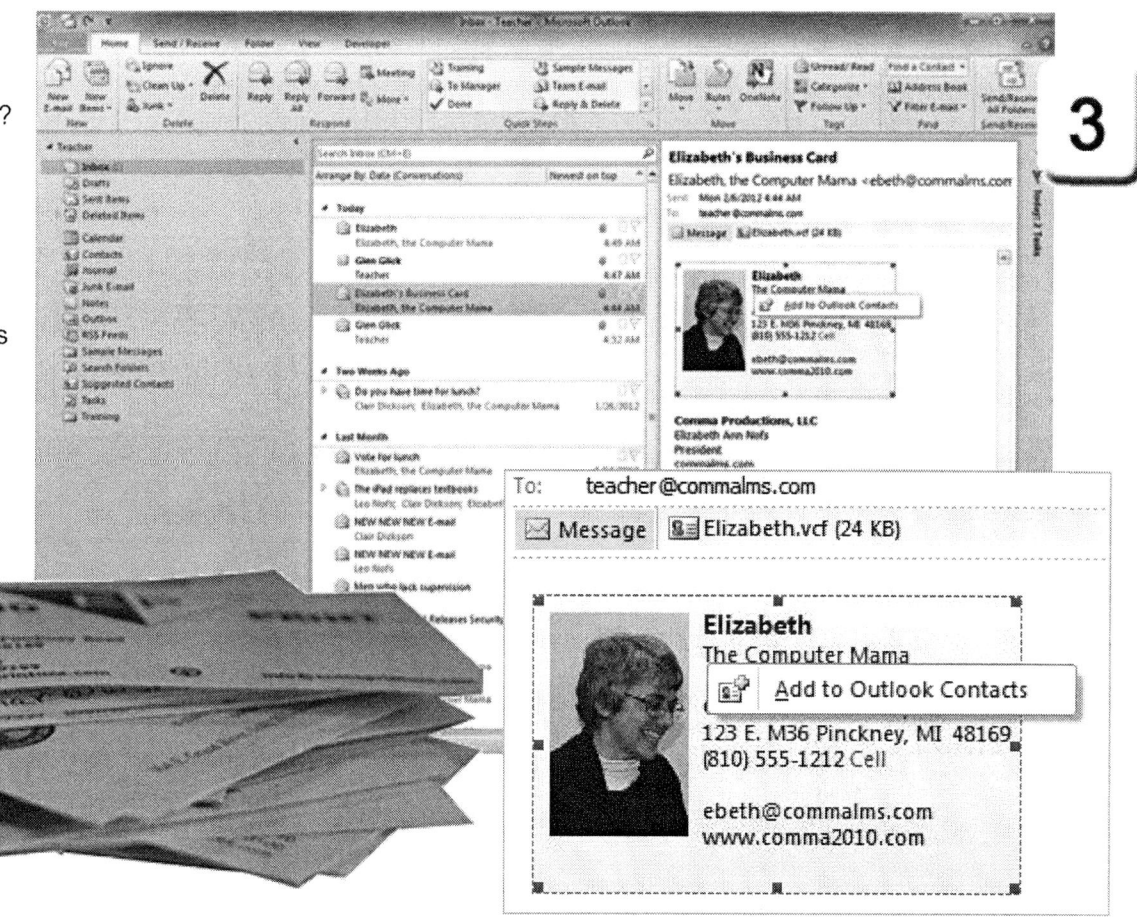

Exam 77-884: Microsoft Outlook 2010
4. Managing Contacts
4.1. Create and manipulate contacts: Add a Business Card to Contacts

Create a Contact Group
Many projects need a team of people to get the job done right. You can create a **Contact Group** to simplify the communications.

1. Try it: Create a Contact Group
The Contacts Folder is selected.
Go to **Home ->New.**
Click on **New Contact Group.**

What Do You See? A New Contact Group Form should open.

The Contact Group Ribbon includes:
Actions
Show
Members
Communicate
Tag
Zoom

Try This, Too: Name the Group
Enter the **Name**: Charlotte's Website.

Keep going, please.

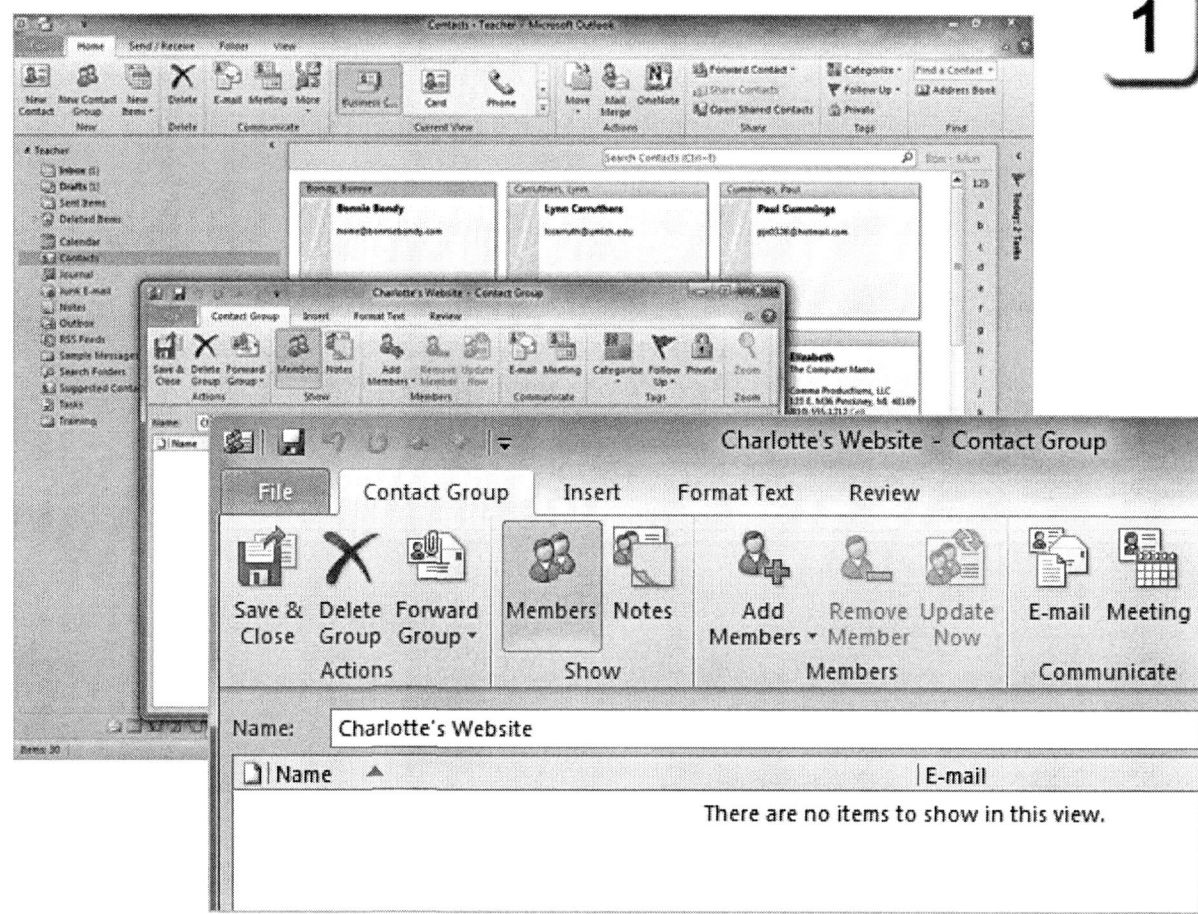

Exam 77-884: Microsoft Outlook 2010
4. Managing Contacts
4.2. Create and manipulate contact groups: Create a Contract Group

Manage Group Membership

Adding or removing **Group Members** is straight forward. Here are the steps.

2. Try it: Manage Group Membership
Go to **Contact Group ->Members.**
Click on **Add Members.**
Select: **From Outlook Contacts.**
Keep going...

Memo to Self: Members can be added from the Outlook Contacts or the Address Book. You can also add a New E-mail Contact if you wish.

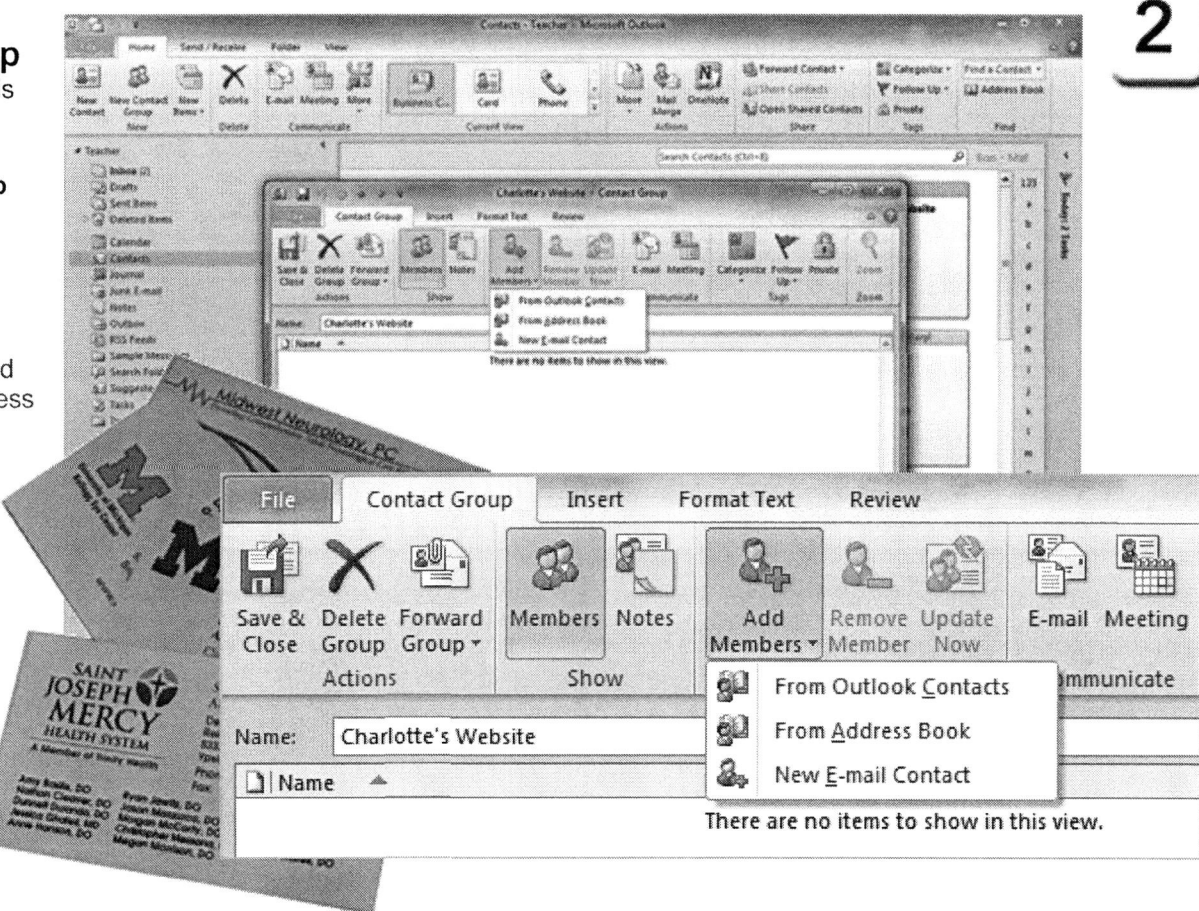

Exam 77-884: Microsoft Outlook 2010
4. Managing Contacts
4.2. Create and manipulate contact groups: Manage Contract Group Membership

Add Members from Contacts

Whether you choose Outlook Contacts or Address Book, the same window will open. The **Address Book** shows the Name, Display Name and the E-mail address for your Contacts. You can use the **Search** options to find someone.

3. Try it: Add a Member from the Contacts

Review the Names in the Address Book. In this example the sample Contact, Glen Glick, is one of the names on the list.

Select a Contact: Glen Glick
Click on **Members**.

Select another Contact: Elizabeth
Click on **Members**.

Both of these names should be listed in the Members field at the bottom of this form.

Click **OK** to close the Address Book and return to the Contact Group. Keep going...

Contact Group ->Members-> Add Members->From Outlook Contacts

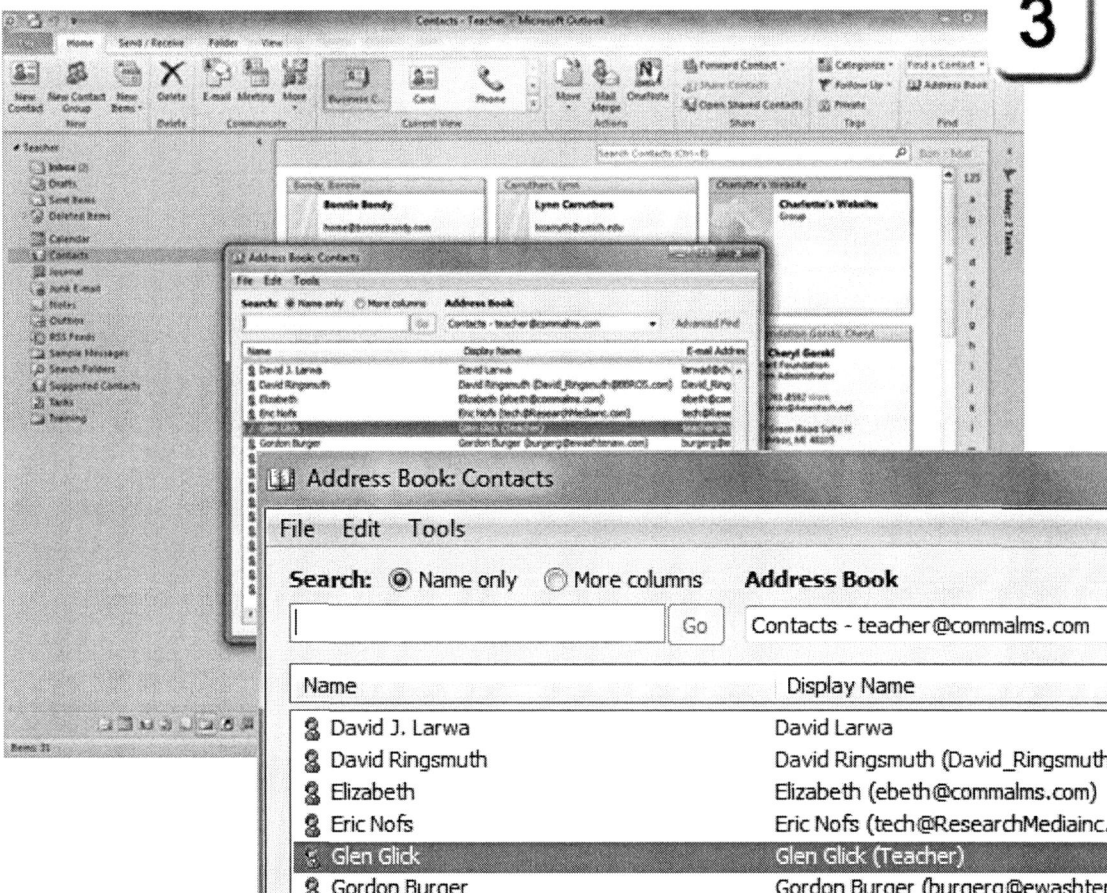

Exam 77-884: Microsoft Outlook 2010
4. Managing Contacts
4.2. Create and manipulate contact groups: Show Contact Group Notes

Contact Group ->Show->Members

Hello, Group Members
4. Try it: Review the Contact Group
There are two new members in the
Contact Group in this example.

You can **Add, Remove** and **Update** the
Members if you wish. **Update Now** will
seek that member and update the data in
all of the Groups that person can be
found.

Keep going...

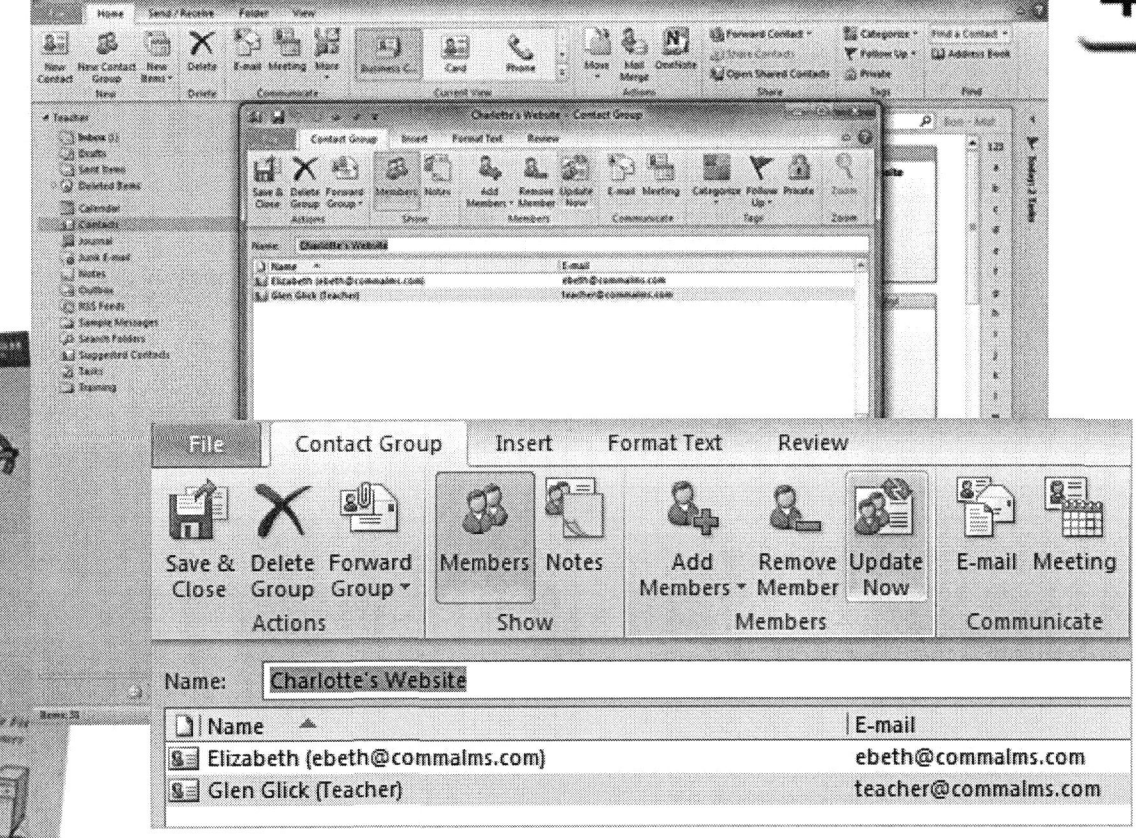

Name ▲	E-mail
Elizabeth (ebeth@commalms.com)	ebeth@commalms.com
Glen Glick (Teacher)	teacher@commalms.com

Exam 77-884: Microsoft Outlook 2010
4. Managing Contacts
4.1. Create and manipulate contacts: Update a Contact in the Address Book

Contact Group->Show->Notes

Show Contact Group Notes

It is a good policy to document changes to a Contact Group or list. Microsoft Outlook has a **Notes** field that you can use.

5. Try it: Show Contact Group Notes
Go to **Contact ->Show->Notes**.
Enter the sample text shown.

Go to **Contact ->Show->Members.**
You should see the Members.

What Else Do You See? The Contact Group **Actions** include:
Save & Close
Delete Group
Forward Group

Save and Delete do exactly as they say.
Click **Save & Close**. Keep going...

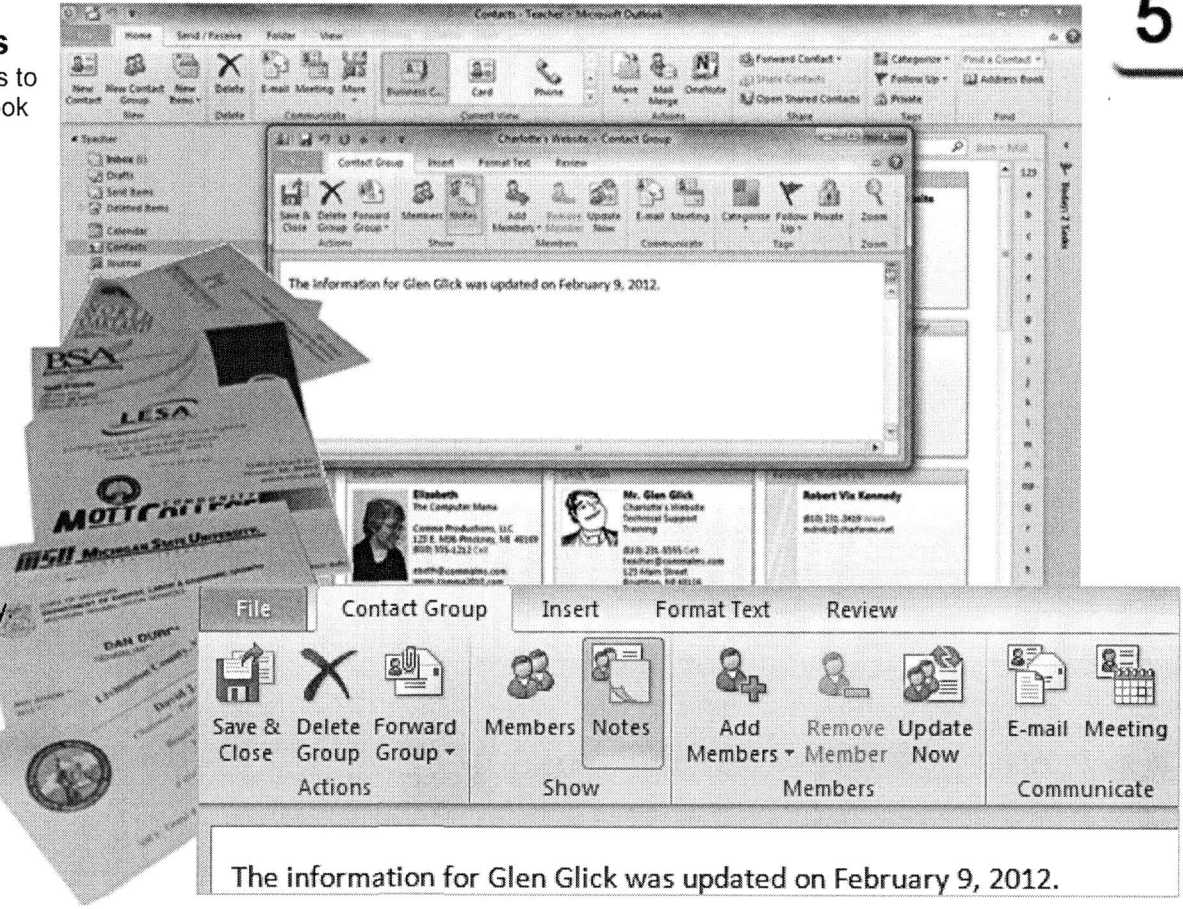

The information for Glen Glick was updated on February 9, 2012.

Exam 77-884: Microsoft Outlook 2010
4. Managing Contacts
4.1. Create and manipulate contacts: Show Contact Group Notes

Forward the Contact Group

You can **Forward** this Contact Group to your team if you wish. Share the wealth...

6. Try it: Share Contacts
Go to the Contacts Folder
Select the Charlotte's Website Contact Group.
Go to **Home->Share.**
Click on **Forward Contact.**

What Do You See? The options are:
As a Business Card (not available for Groups)
As an Outlook Contact
Forward as Text Message

Try This, Too: Forward the Contact Group
Select: **As an Outlook Contact.**
A new message will open.
The Group Contact should be attached.
Enter your E-mail Address.
Enter the sample text: This is an example of a Group Contact.
Click **Send** to E-mail the message.

Keep going...

Home->Share->Forward Contact-> As an Outlook Contact

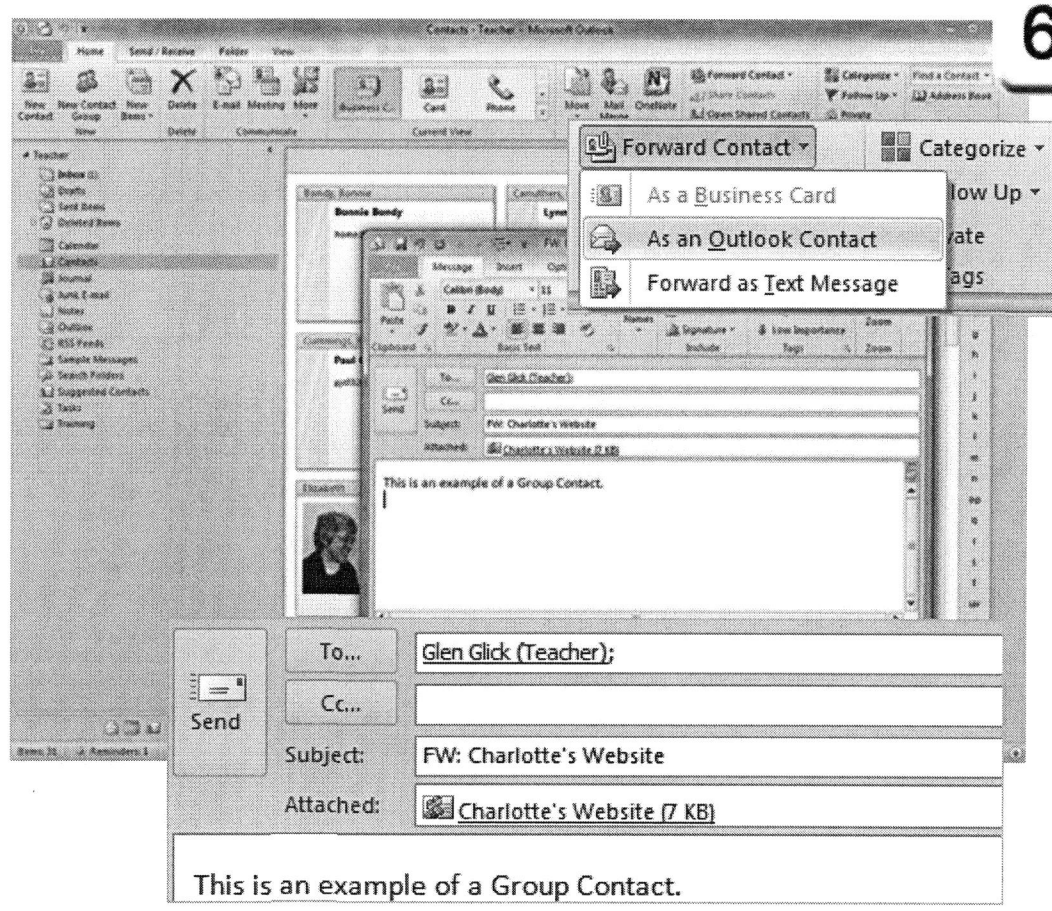

Exam 77-884: Microsoft Outlook 2010
4. Managing Contacts
4.1. Create and manipulate contacts: Forward a Contact Group

Open the Contact Group
Trust But Verify: The message should arrive in the Inbox. Go to the **Inbox** and confirm that your E-mail is there.

7. Try This, Too: Open the Attachment
Select the E-mail with the attachment. Double-click the Contact Group.

What Do You See? The Group Contact should be open. In this example both Contacts are listed and they can be edited.

OK: **Save and Close** the Contact Group. We got 'em.

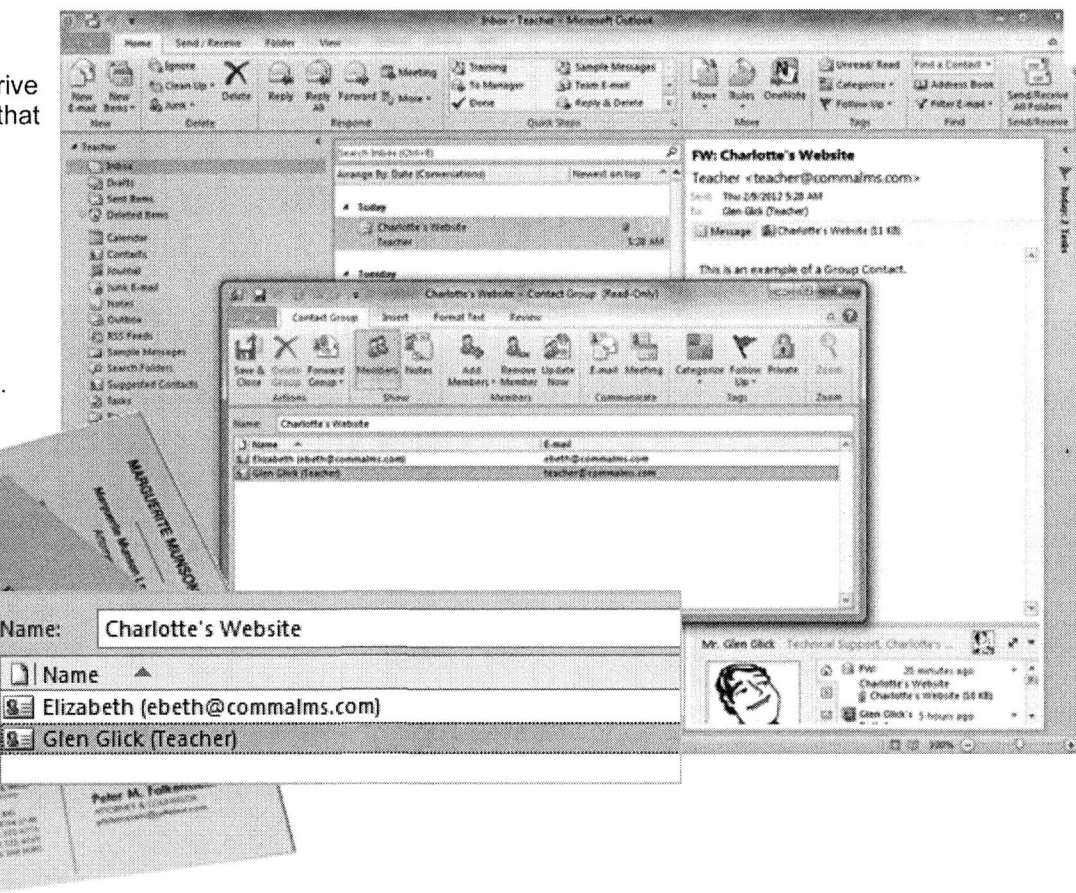

Exam 77-884: Microsoft Outlook 2010
4. Managing Contacts
4.1. Create and manipulate contacts: Forward a Contact Group

Hello, People

Contacts are People. Microsoft Outlook 2010 has a **People Pane** that shows what your Contact has been doing. The People Pane tracks messages, appointments, tasks and activities for everyone in your Contacts folder.

Before You Begin: Select a Message
Go to the **Inbox**.
Go to **View->Reading Pane->Right**.

Select any sample E-mail that you addressed to yourself, please.

1. Try it: View the People Pane
Go to **View ->People Pane->Normal**.

What Do You See? The People Pane has several filters on the left side. The Home view shows all of the activities. The little E-mail filters the list and shows only messages.

Keep going...

View ->People Pane->Normal

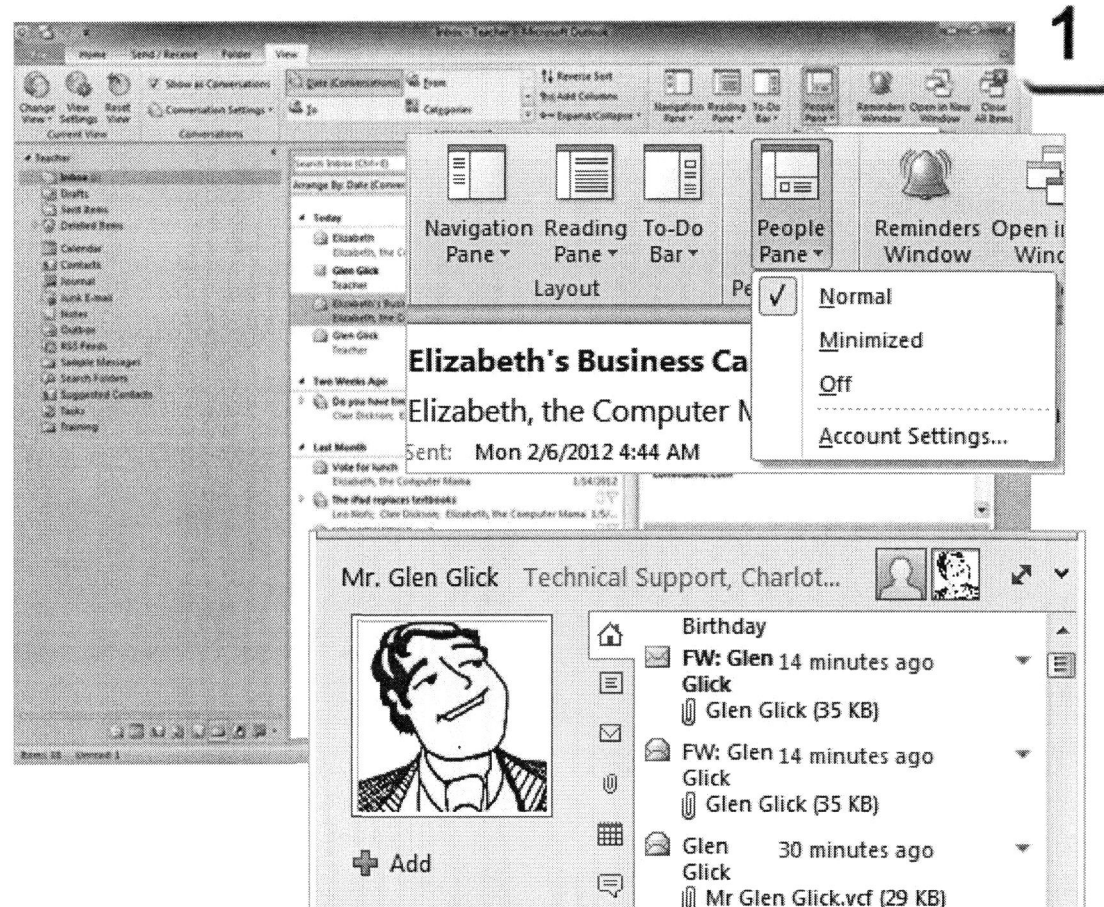

Exam 77-884: Microsoft Outlook 2010
1. Managing the Outlook Environment
1.3. Arrange the Content Pane: Use the People Pane

View ->People Pane->Account Settings

Add a Social Network

One of the best features in Outlook 2010 is the **Social Connectors**. Now, you can link to the popular Social Networks including Facebook and the business website, LinkedIn.

2. Try it: Add a Social Network
Go to **View ->People Pane.**
Click on: **Account Settings**

What Do You See? A Wizard will walk you through the steps to download and install the software.

Each Social Network has a different connection so you will have to got through the steps twice to get both Facebook and LinkedIn, OK?

Keep going...

Memo to Self: You can add the Social Networks in the People Pane as well. Just click on **Add**.

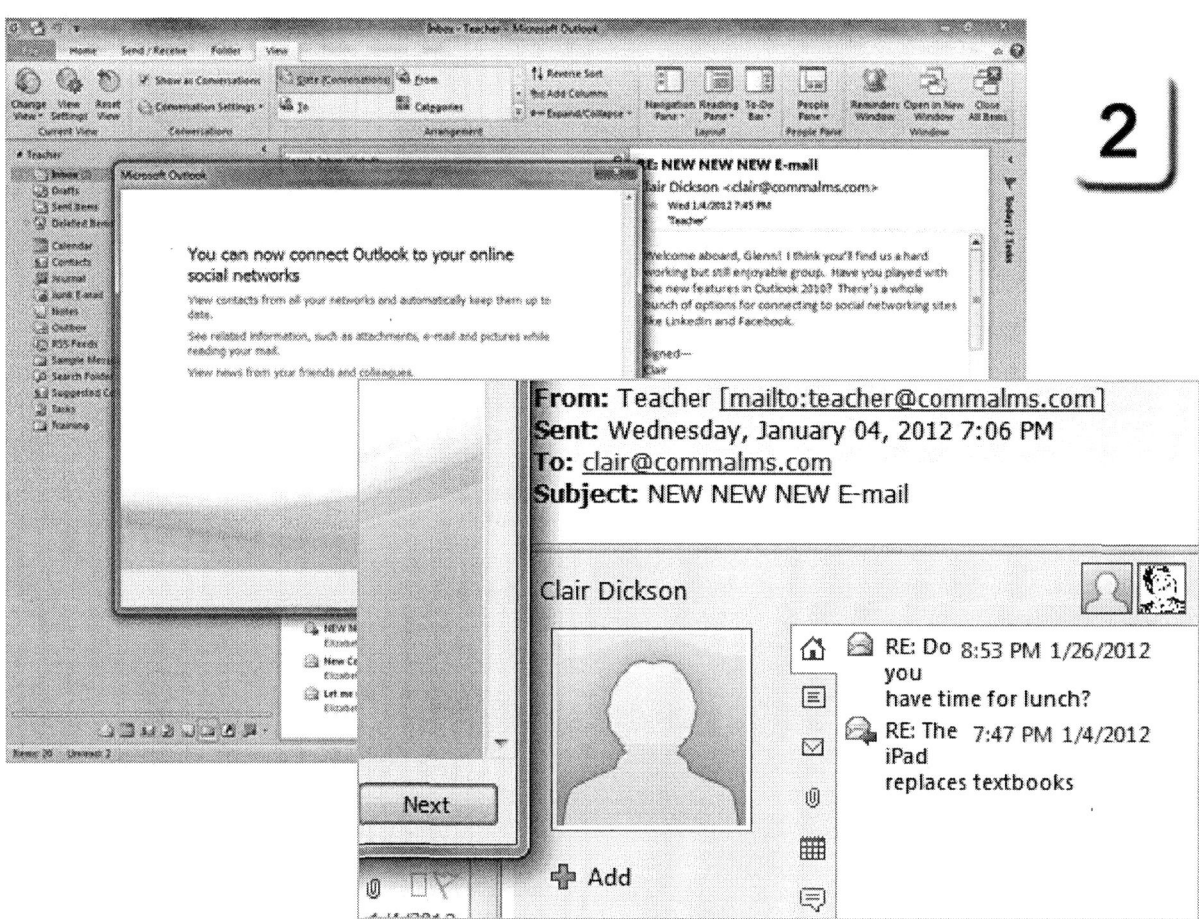

Exam 77-884: Microsoft Outlook 2010
1. Managing the Outlook Environment
1.3. Arrange the Content Pane: Use the People Pane to Add a Social Network

Add a Social Network

Social Network Accounts need to be added to Microsoft Outlook. When you first begin, the Accounts may be blank, with one default icon for My Site.

You need to go online and download the software for Facebook, LinkedIn, Windows Live Messenger and others.

3. Try it: Edit the Account Settings
Go to **View ->People Pane.**
Select: **Account Settings.**
The **Social Network Accounts** window should open.

Click the link to go online: <u>View social network providers available online</u>.

Keep going...

3

Social Network Accounts

Connect Outlook to your online social networks by selecting the networks below and logging in. To connect to additional social networks click the "View social network providers available online" link.

<u>View social network providers available online</u>

☐ 🖽 My Site

Exam 77-884: Microsoft Outlook 2010
1. Managing the Outlook Environment
1.3. Arrange the Content Pane: Use the People Pane to Add a Social Network

Find the Connector Software

When you click the link you will be taken online to a Microsoft Office webpage to select your social networks.

Each Social Network provider offers their own software that enables their website to stream live updates to Microsoft Outlook.

4. Try it: Find Social Network Providers
The Microsoft Office website is open.
Click on LinkedIn.

Keep going...

To get started, click the icons below to download and install social network providers for Outlook.*

Facebook

Linked**in**.

LinkedIn

Windows Live Messenger

viadeo

Exam 77-884: Microsoft Outlook 2010
1. Managing the Outlook Environment
1.3. Arrange the Content Pane: Use the People Pane to Add a Social Network

Download the Connector

5. Try it: Download a Social Connector
When you click on the+ download you will be prompted by your Internet browser to **Run** or **Save** this file.

Click **Run**. You will be asked by the Windows security for your permission to install this software. If you agree, enter your User Name and Password. Click **OK**.

After you install the Connector software, you can repeat these steps for another network, such as Facebook.

You will need to **Restart Outlook** after you install the Social Connectors.

Keep going...

Do you want to run or save **LinkedInOutlookConnector.exe** (1.11 MB)

This type of file could harm your computer.

Exam 77-884: Microsoft Outlook 2010
1. Managing the Outlook Environment
1.3. Arrange the Content Pane: Use the People Pane to Add a Social Network

View ->People Pane->Account Settings

Log Into the Social Network

Before You Begin: Microsoft Outlook has been restarted. The Inbox is selected.

6. Try it: Log Into the Social Network
Go to **View ->People Pane.**
Select: **Account Settings.**
The **Social Network Accounts** window should open. Facebook and LinkedIn are now available.

Try This, Too: Log in to Each Network
Each Social Network has a separate log in.
Select: Facebook.
Enter the User Name and Password.

Select: LinkedIn.
Enter the User Name and Password.

Keep going...

Memo to Self: Outlook does not save the contacts and activities from Facebook. The information is updated when you log in.

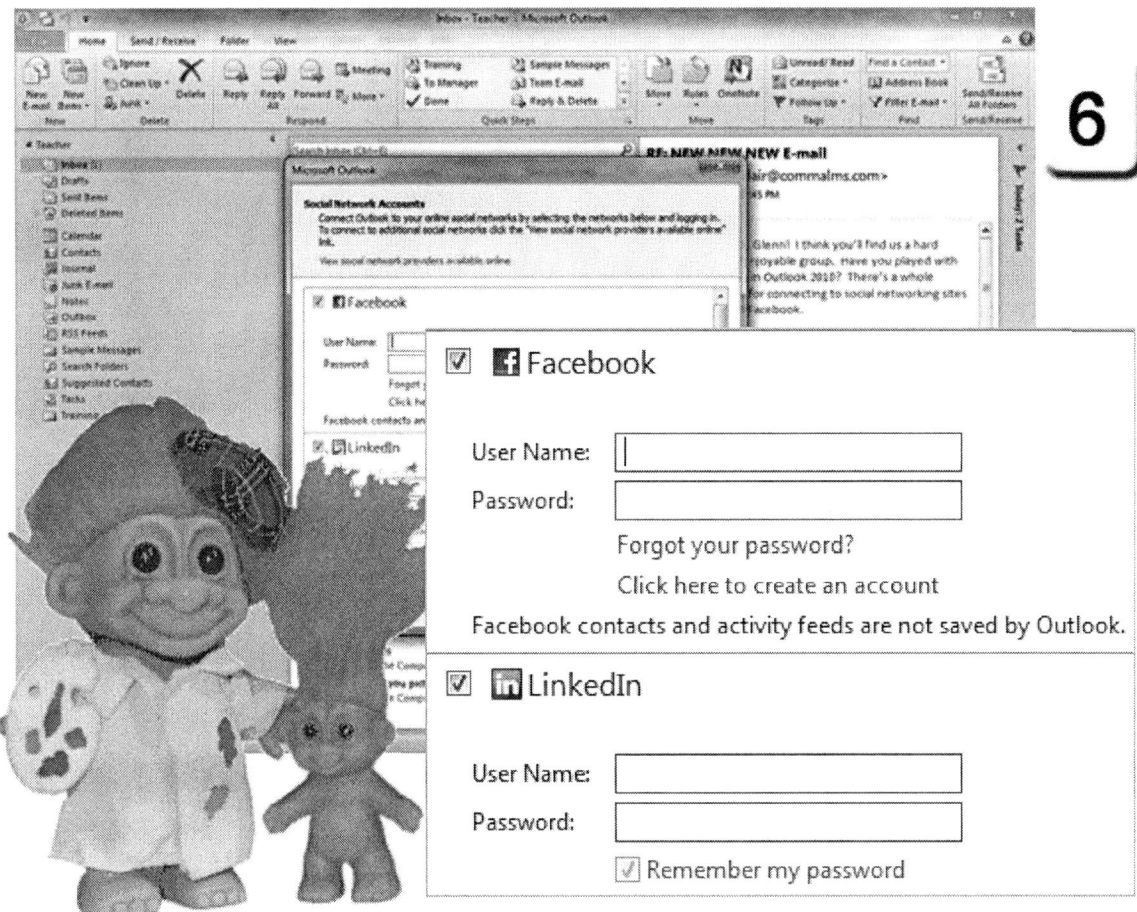

Exam 77-884: Microsoft Outlook 2010
1. Managing the Outlook Environment
1.3. Arrange the Content Pane: Use the People Pane to Add a Social Network

View ->People Pane->Account Settings

Confirm the Connections

7. Try it: Confirm the Connections
Before you can use the connections, you
need to confirm that you are logged in and
connected to the Social Network website.

How Did We Get Here?
Go to **View ->People Pane.**
Click on **Account Settings.**

What Do You See? There should be a
check mark indicating the status: green
means go.

Click **Finish** to close the Account Settings
window and return to Outlook.

Keep going...

Exam 77-884: Microsoft Outlook 2010
1. Managing the Outlook Environment
1.3. Arrange the Content Pane: Use the People Pane to Add a Social Network

Connections, Connections

8. Try it: View the Social Networks
Go to **View ->People Pane.**

There should be an icon for each Social Network. It is interesting to note that the pictures in Facebook are much less formal than the ones in LinkedIn. You may wish to consider: who is your audience?

Keep going...

What If It Doesn't Work? The Social Connectors use an E-mail address to identify people. Your Contact may have a different E-mail Address for Facebook, a social website, than for work.

If your Contact is not already connected to you in Facebook or LinkedIn, you can use the Add option to ask to be linked.

View ->People Pane

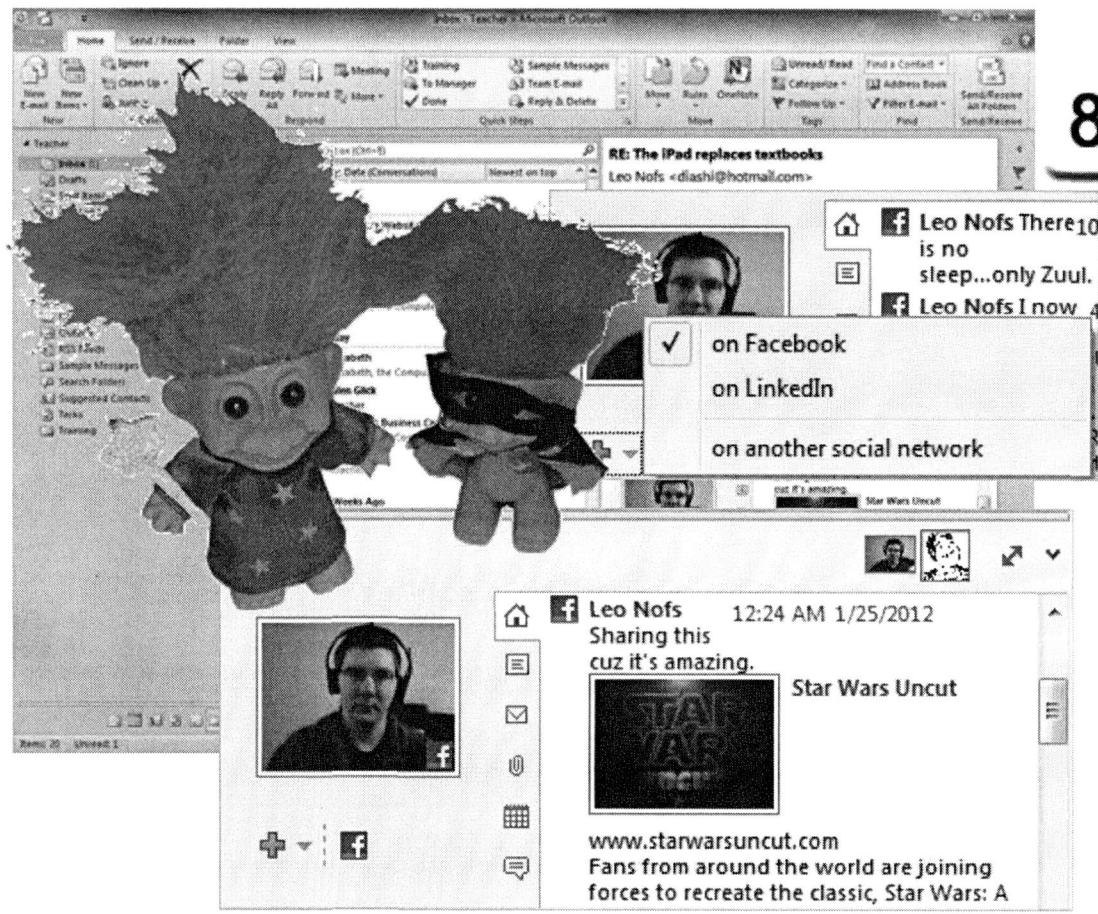

Exam 77-884: Microsoft Outlook 2010
1. Managing the Outlook Environment
1.3. Arrange the Content Pane: Use the People Pane to Add a Social Network

Summary

These pages taught two important options that the Computer Mama uses all of the time: Contacts, and Social Networks.

Microsoft Outlook is the best professional messaging program. And, it's great to collect all of the E-mails in one Inbox.

Well, that was worth two cookies.

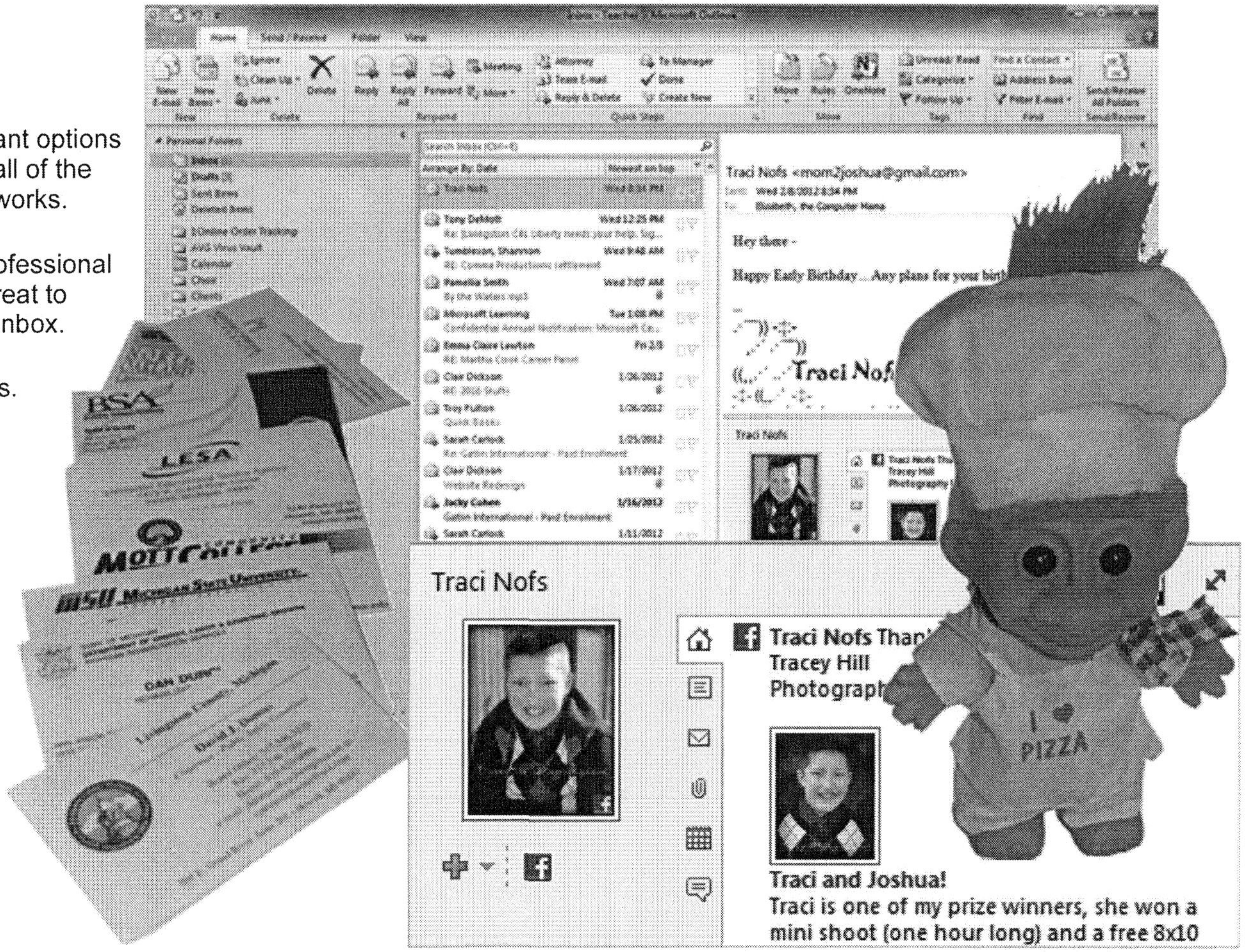

Exam 77-884: Microsoft Outlook 2010
4. Managing Contacts
4.1. Create and manipulate contacts

Test Yourself

1. The options on the Home Ribbon for contacts are different than those on the Home Ribbon for e-mail.
A. True
B. False
Tip: Complete Guide to Outlook, page 153

2. Which are options for filing a Contact?
(Give all correct answers.)
A. First Name
B. Last Name
C. Last Name (Company)
D. Company (Last Name)
Tip: Complete Guide to Outlook, page 155

3. The display name on a Contact is the same as the e-mail address.
A. True
B. False
Tip: Complete Guide to Outlook, page 157

4. Contacts can have a custom picture added to the record.
A. True
B. False
Tip: Complete Guide to Outlook, page 160

5. Which of the following is true about the digital business cards created for Contacts?
(Give all correct answers.)
A. The business card is created using the Contact information entered
B. The business card can be forwarded to another person
C. A business card received via e-mail will be automatically added to the recipients Outlook Contacts
Tip: Complete Guide to Outlook, page 162

6. Which of the following is true about creating Contact Group?
(Give all correct answers.)
A. A Contact Group can be created using current Contacts
B. A Contact Group can be created using the Outlook address book
C. A Contact Group can be created by entering new e-mail addresses
Tip: Complete Guide to Outlook, page 168

7. A Contact Group can be sent as a business card.
A. True
B. False
Tip: Complete Guide to Outlook, page 171

Practice

1. Create a New Contact for Sage Young

2. Enter the Company: Comma Productions

3. File the Contact as Name (Company)

4. Enter your email address as Sage's email address

5. Add the website www.microsoft.com

6. Add the Picture to the Contact

7. View the Business Card and change the image to be on the right side of the Business Card

8. Save and Close the Contact

Application Question: What are two or three advantages to connecting Outlook with social networking sites such as Facebook or LinkedIn?

What are two or three disadvantages to connection Outlook with social networking sites?

Outlook 2010: Working with the Calendar
Eight Days a Week

Microsoft Outlook Objectives
In this lesson, you will learn how to:

1. Select the Calendar and arrange the Calendar View

2. Create Appointments and set the Appointment Options

3. Create a Meeting, invite Attendees and track the responses

4. Update, Propose a new time, and Cancel a Meeting

5. Send a Meeting to a Contact Group

© 2012 Comma Productions, LLC

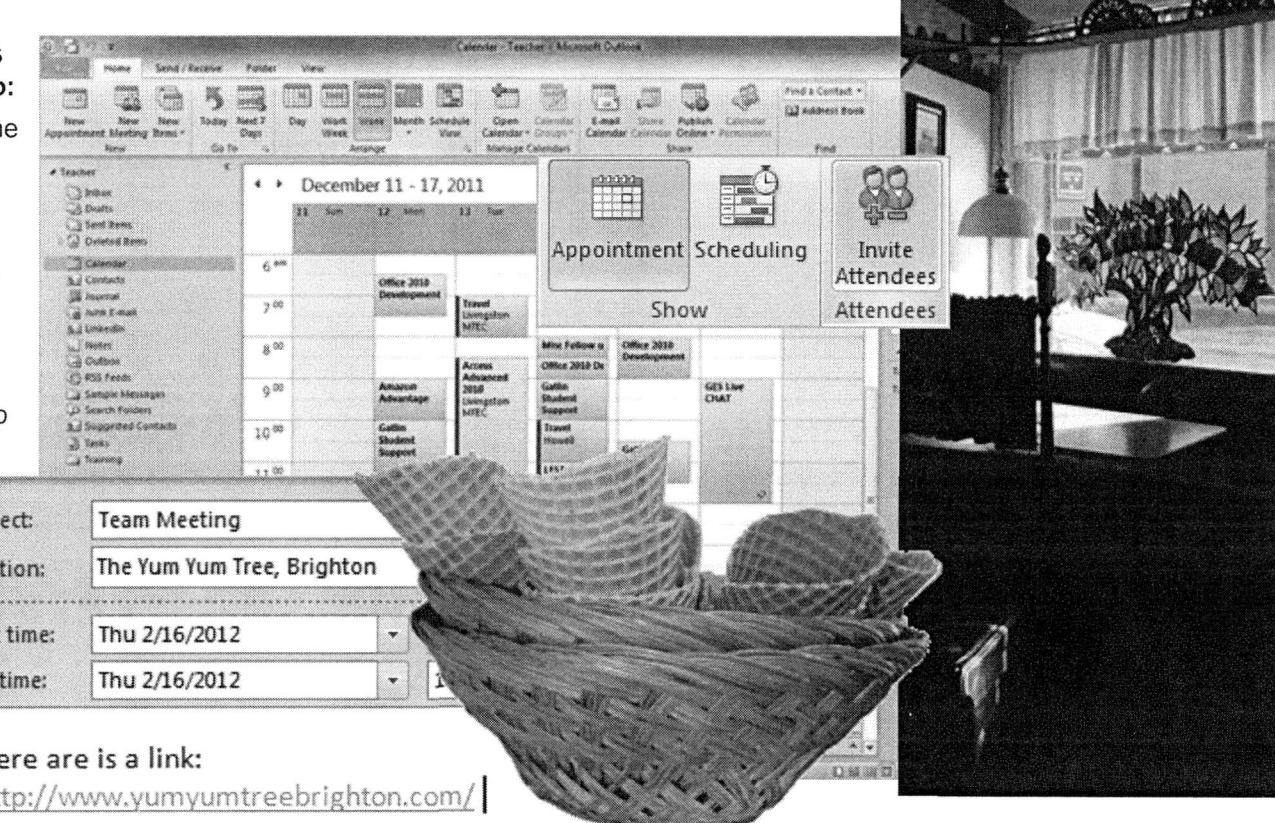

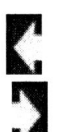

Lesson 7: Eight Days a Week

1. Readings

Read Lesson 7 in the Microsoft Outlook guide, page 183- 215.

Project

Sample Appointments and Meetings that demonstrate the options on the Home and Appointment Ribbons.

Downloads

valentine1.gif, valentine2.gif, valentine3.gif.

2. Practice

Complete the Practice Activity on page 215.

3. Assessment

Review the Test questions on page 216.

Home Ribbon

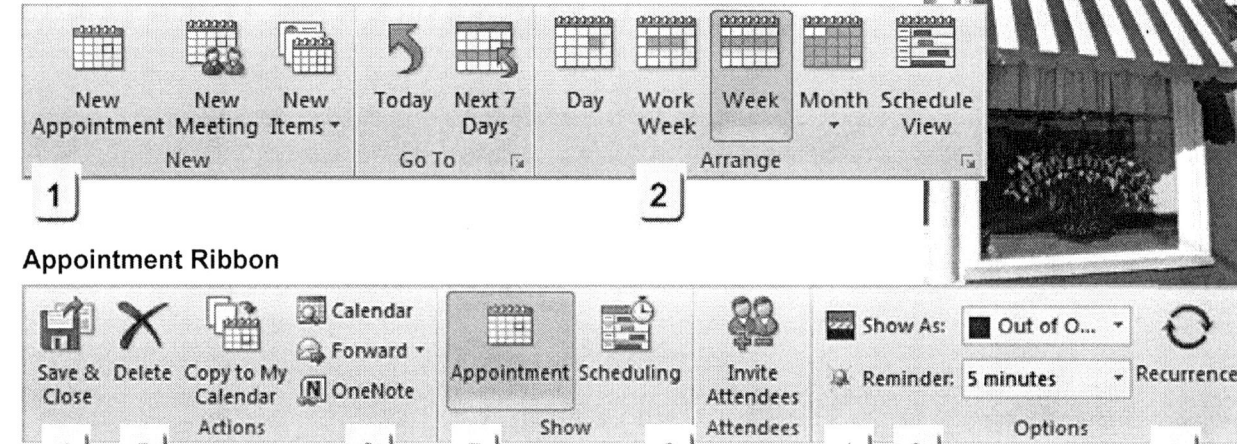

Appointment Ribbon

Menu Maps

From the **Home Ribbon**.
1. Home ->New->New Appointment, page 188
2. Home ->Arrange->Work Week, page 193
3. Home ->Respond->Meeting, page 211 (not shown)

From the **Meeting Ribbon**
1. Meeting ->Attendees->Invite Attendees, page 200
2. Meeting ->Respond->Accept, page 201
3. Meeting ->Show->Tracking, page 204

More Menu Maps

From the **Appointment Ribbon**
1. Appointment ->Options->Show As, page 190
2. Appointment->Options-> Reminder, page 192
3. Appointment ->Options->Recurrence, page 194
4. Appointment ->Actions->Save & Close, page 194
5. Appointment Series->Actions->Delete, page 196
6. Appointment ->Attendees->Invite Attendees, page 200
7. Appointment ->Show->Appointment, page 203
8. Appointment ->Actions->Forward, page 209

Eight Days a Week

There are two compelling reasons to keep a calendar: tracking your promises and managing your commitments. Microsoft Outlook has a robust Calendar that can help you follow up on your Appointments, Tasks and Contacts. This lesson introduces scheduling with the Calendar. Our examples will include Meetings, Tracking Responses and setting the options.

Start -> All Programs ->Microsoft Office-> Microsoft Office Outlook 2010

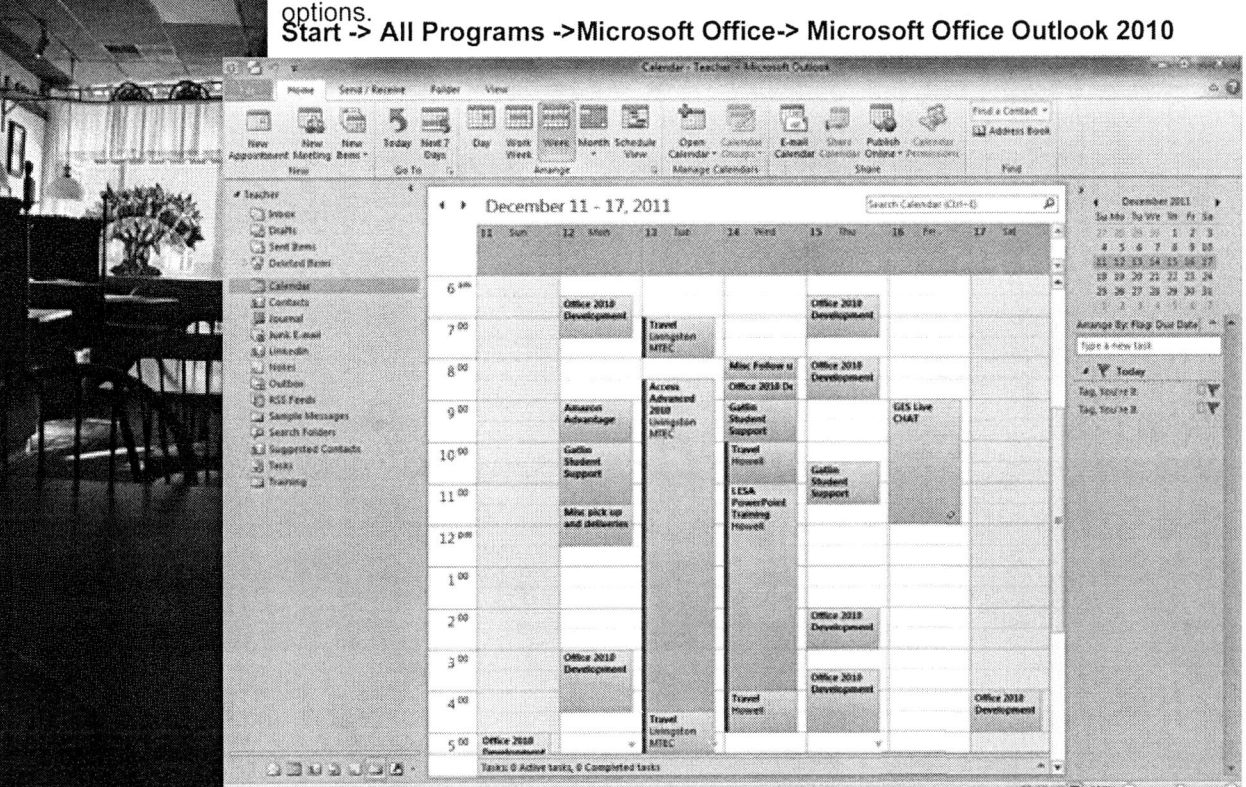

The restaurant shown on these pages is the Yum Yum Tree, Brighton, Michigan. A little HO train circles the room on a track high above the tables and the ice cream counter.

Before You Begin

By default, Microsoft Outlook opens with the **Inbox** as the initial view. The **Calendar** can be found by using the Navigation Pane.

Before You Begin: View the Folders
Go to **View->Layout.**
Click on **Navigation Pane.**
Select: **Normal.**

1. Try it: Find the Calendar Folder
Go to the **Navigation Pane.**
Select the **Calendar** Folder.

Keep going...

Memo to Self: You do not need to MATCH the dates in this book. It is more important that you practice the steps and learn the process.

View->Layout->Navigation Pane->Normal

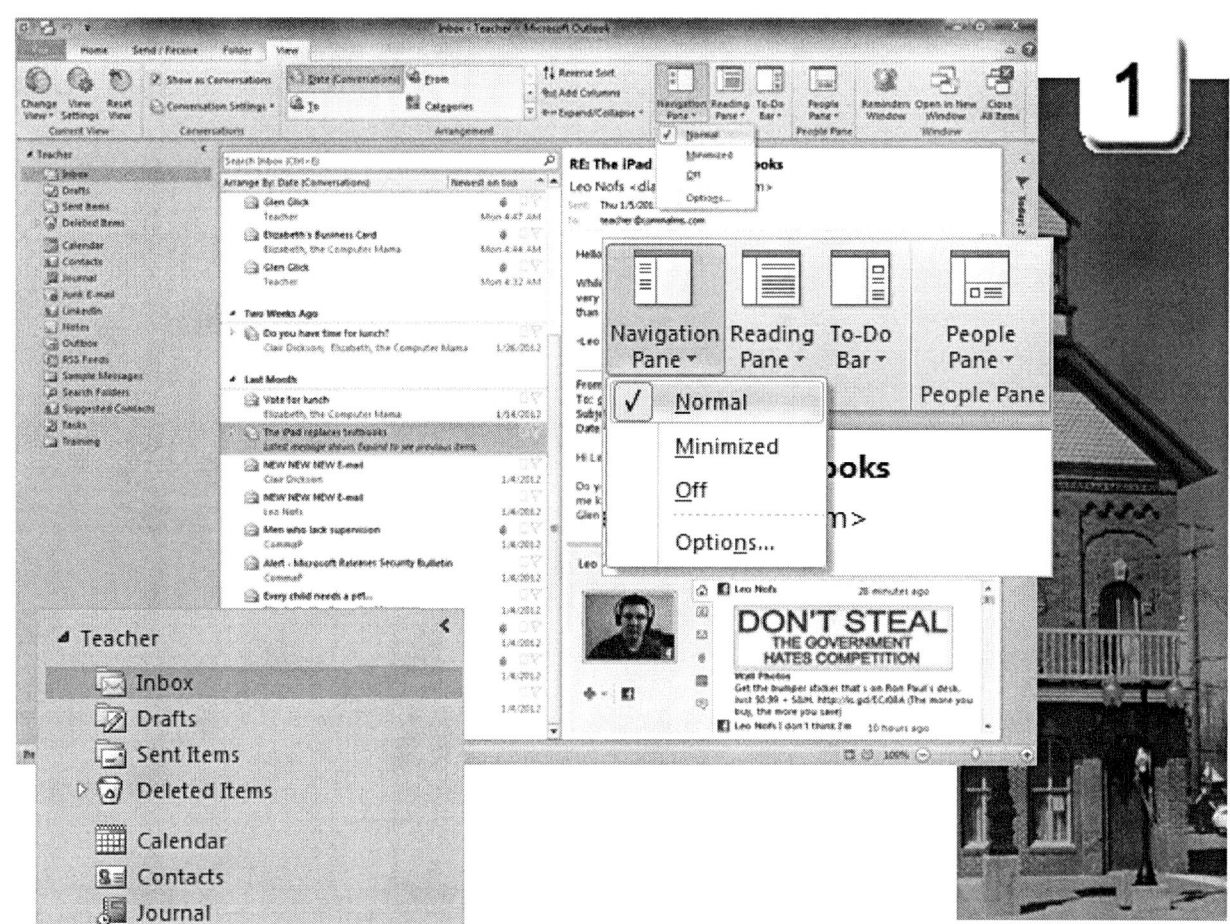

Hello, Calendar

2. Try it: Review the Home Ribbon

The screen shot on this page shows a Calendar with many appointments.

The **Home** Ribbon has these Groups:
New
Go To
Arrange
Manage Calendars
Share
Find

Try This, Too: Arrange the View
Go to **Home->Arrange->Day**.

Keep going, please.

Microsoft Outlook->Calendar

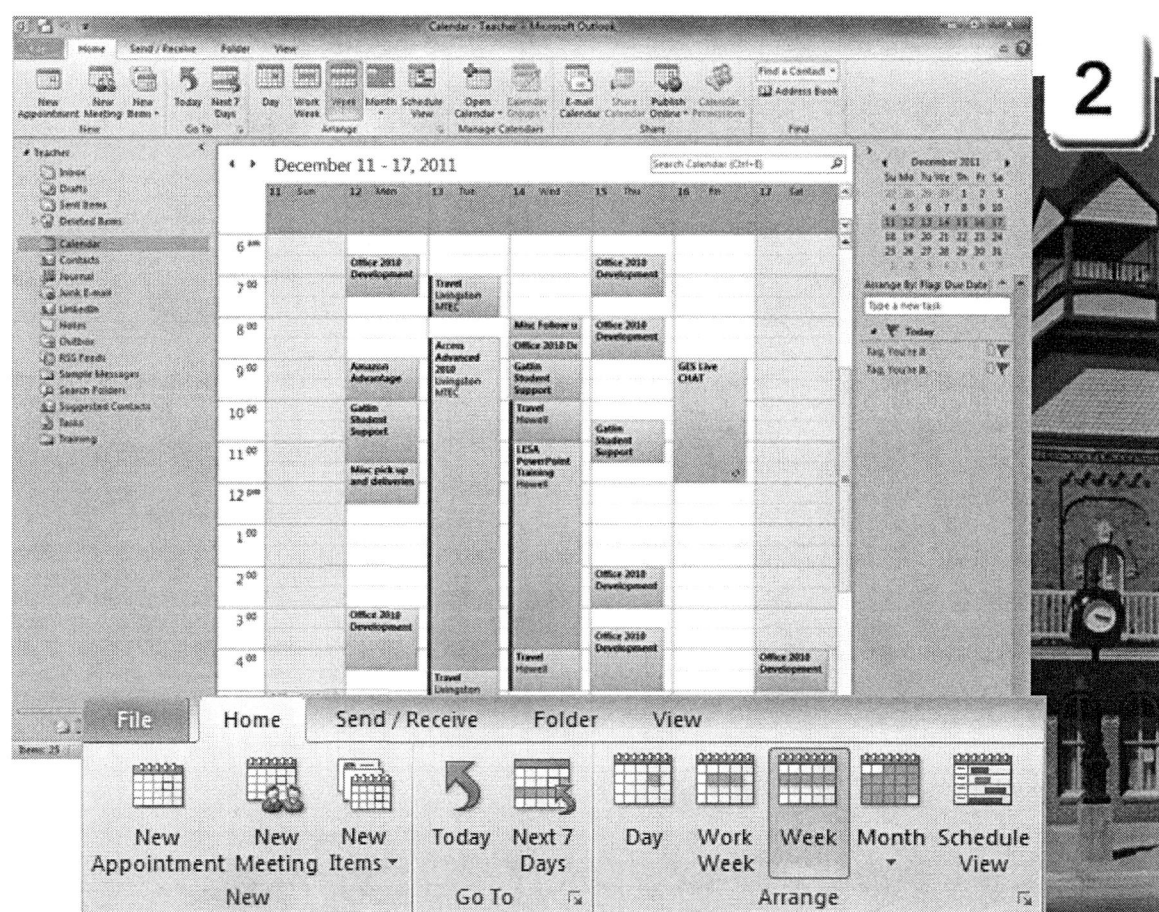

Exam 77-884: Microsoft Outlook 2010
5. Managing Calendar Objects
5.3. Manipulate the Calendar pane: Arrange the Calendar View

Create a New Appointment

There are two schools of thought on how to use a calendar. One way teaches that the calendar should be used only for meetings that you have with other people.

The other method uses the calendar to record time that is spent on projects. Those of us who are consultants call that "Billable Hours."

3. Try it: Create a New Appointment
Go to **Home ->New.**
Click on **New Appointment.**

What Do You See? A new Appointment will open. There are four Ribbons: Appointment, Insert, Format Text and Review.

The Insert and Format Text Ribbons are the same as the ones in a new message. This lesson will focus on the Appointment Ribbon.

Keep going..

Home ->New->New Appointment

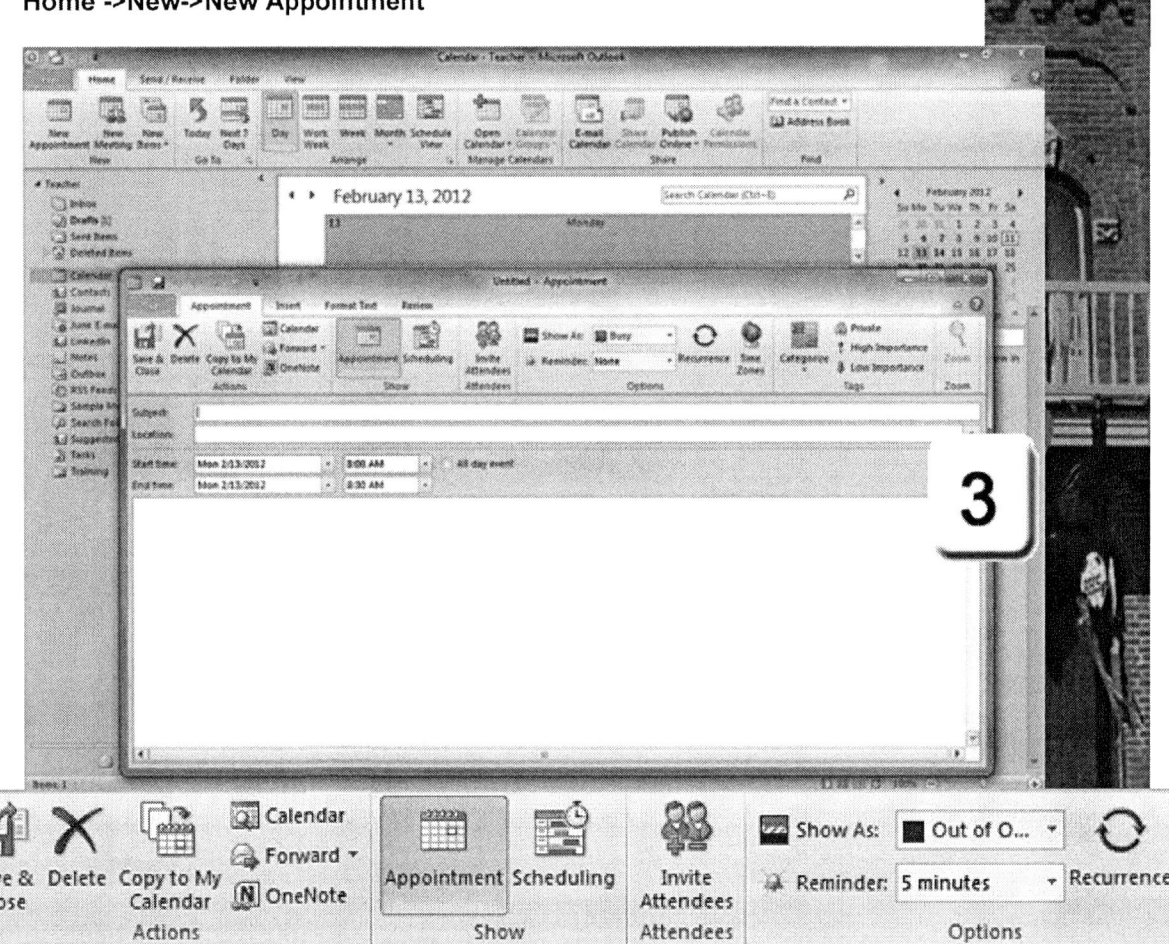

Exam 77-884: Microsoft Outlook 2010
5. Managing Calendar Objects
5.1. Create and manipulate appointments and events: Create an Appointment

Edit the New Appointment

4. Try it: Edit the Appointment
Enter the **Subject**: Outlook Training
Enter the **Location**: Brighton

Select the **Start Time**: 8:30 AM
Select the **End Time**: 4:30 PM

What Do You See? By default, the **Start** and **End times** are set in half hour increments. Please confirm that the Start and End times are on the same day.

Question: What if the class begins at 9:10? You do not have to select one of the times from the list. You can enter another time if you wish. For example, you could type 9:10 AM.

Keep going, please.

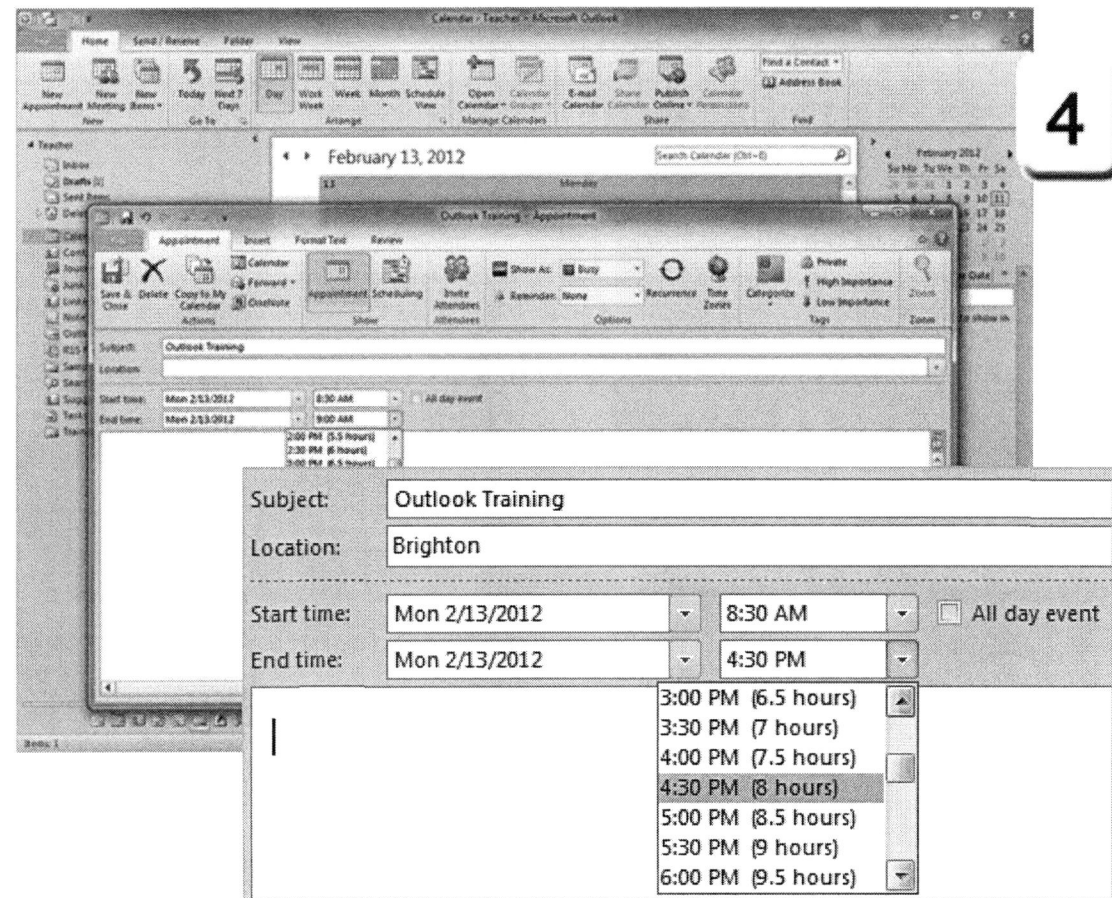

Exam 77-884: Microsoft Outlook 2010
5. Managing Calendar Objects
5.1. Create and manipulate appointments and events: Set Appointment Options

Set the Appointment Options

You can use the **Appointment Options** to document your whereabouts and even remind you when it is time to go.

5. Try it: Set the Appointment Options
Go to **Appointment ->Options->Show As.** Click on **Out of Office**.

What Do You See? The choices are:
Free (White)
Tentative (Blue Pattern)
Busy (Blue)
Out of Office (Purple)

The options and colors are displayed when this Calendar is shared on a network, such as an Exchange Server. They are also visible when the Calendar is published online.

Try This, Too: Set the Reminder
Select: 5 minutes.

Click **Save & Close** to save your appointment and return to the Outlook calendar.
Keep going...

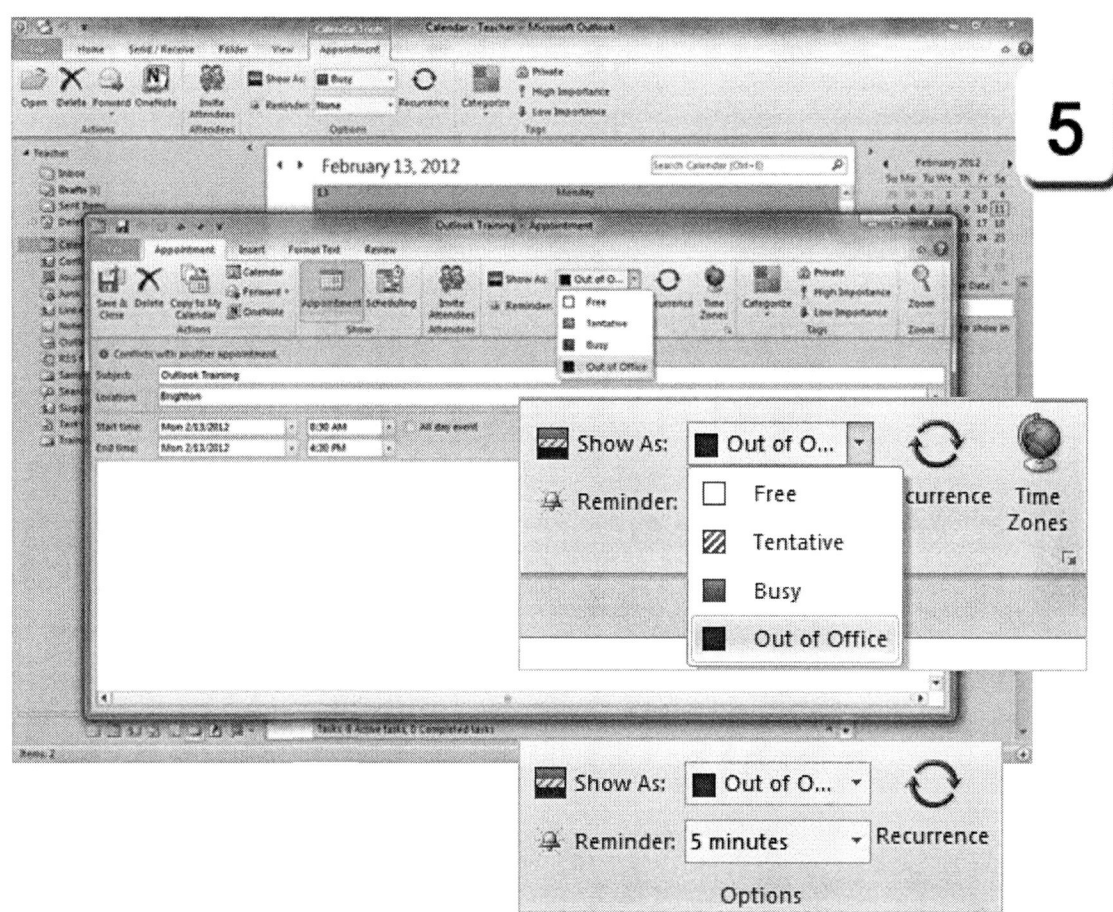

5

Exam 77-884: Microsoft Outlook 2010
5. Managing Calendar Objects
5.1. Create and manipulate appointments and events: Set Appointment Options

Review the Appointment

6: Try This: Review the Appointment
There should be a new appointment in the Calendar. The Subject (Outlook Training) and the Location (Brighton) are displayed.

There is a purple band on the left side which means that this appointment is Out of the Office.

On the right side of the screen is a little calendar called the **Date Navigator**. Each day that has an appointment is BOLD.

The Date Navigator is included on the top of the To-Do list by default. Both options can be turned on or off.

Try This, Too: Find the Date Navigator
Go to **View->Layout->To-Do Bar**.
Select: To-Do Bar and Date Navigator

Keep going, please.

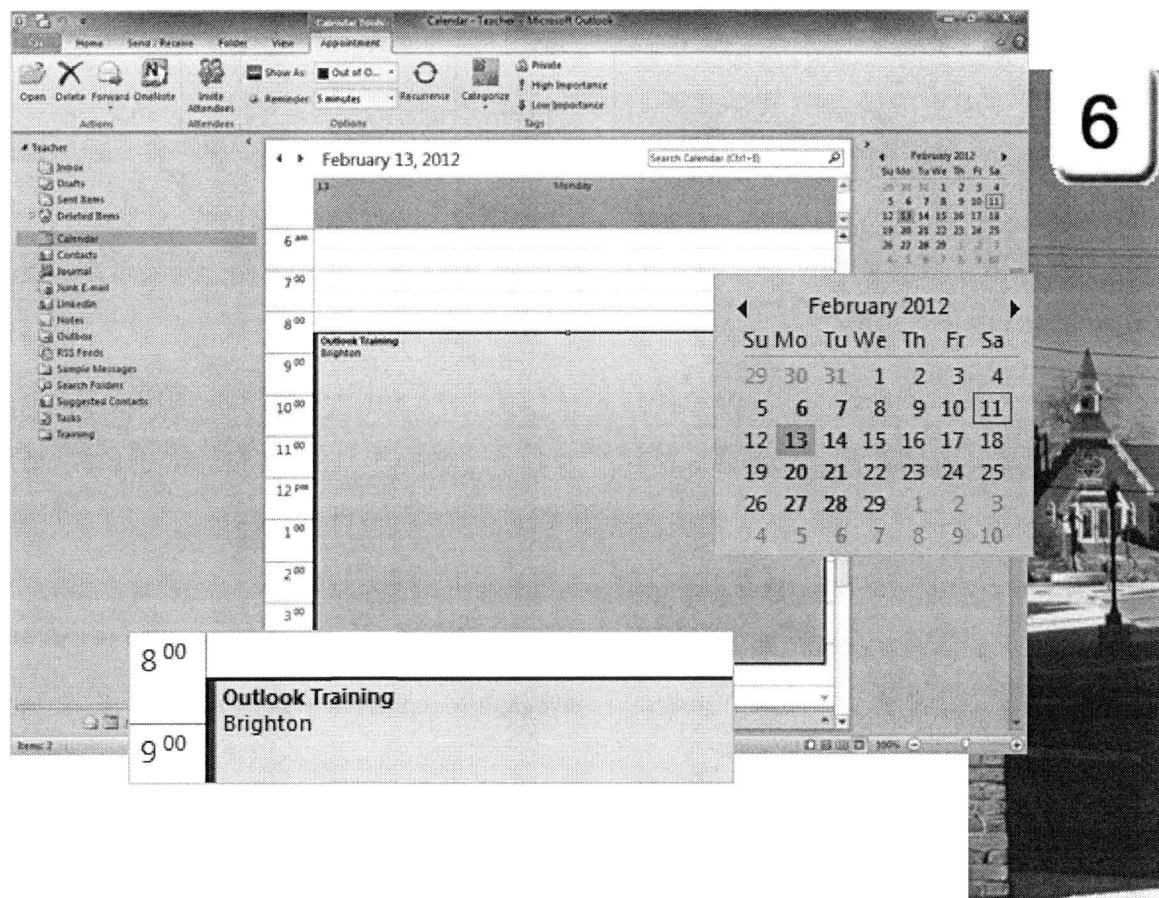

Exam 77-884: Microsoft Outlook 2010
5. Managing Calendar Objects
5.1. Create and manipulate appointments and events: Use the Date Navigator

Snooze, You Loose

If you set the Appointment Reminder, a little alert will pop up and chime when it is time to go.

7. Try it: Set the Snooze
Go to the time and select: 5 minutes.
Click on **Snooze**.

Try This, Too: Dismiss the Reminder
In 5 minutes, the Reminder should chime again. This time, click on **Dismiss All**.

What Do You See, Now? The **Reminder** for this appointment will be set to None.

So far, so good.

Memo to Self: Your appointments and reminder do not need to match the dates and times in these screen shots. It is more important that you review the options.

Calendar Tools ->Appointment->Options-> Reminder

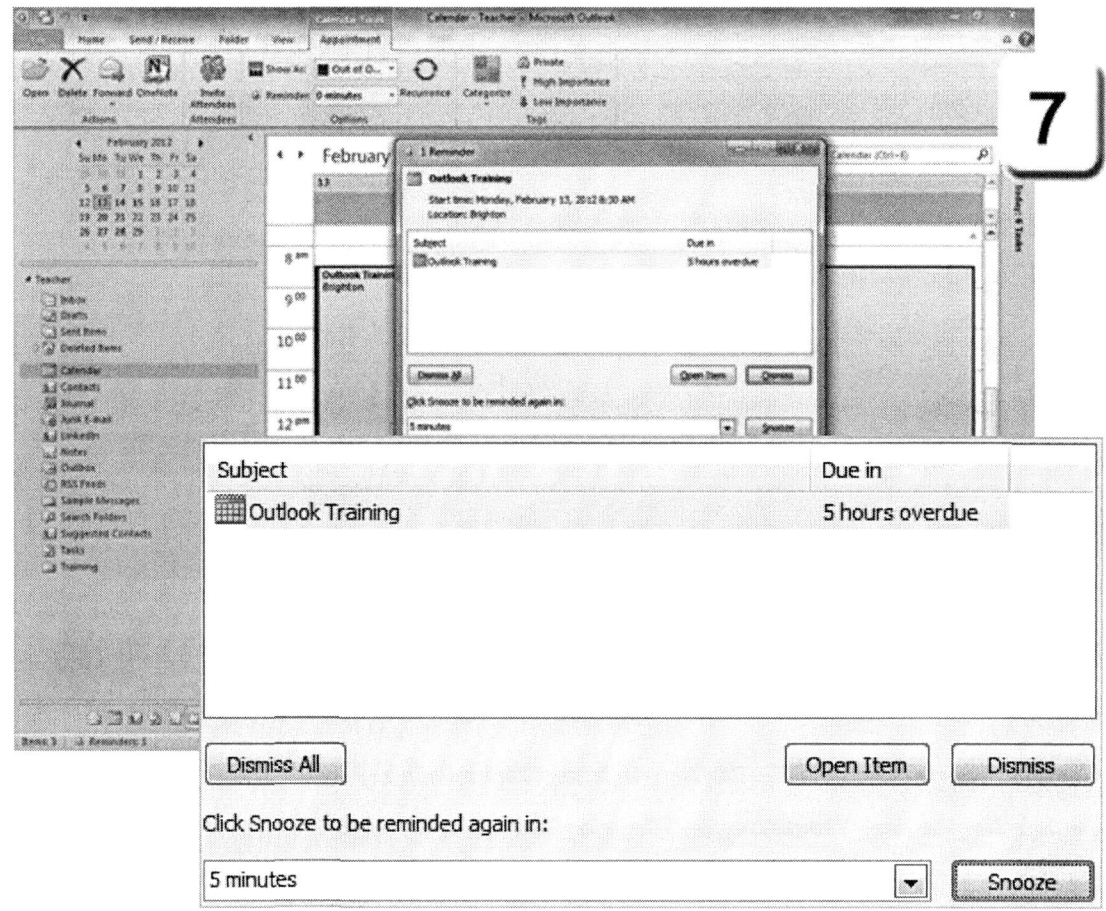

7

Subject	Due in
Outlook Training	5 hours overdue

Dismiss All | Open Item | Dismiss

Click Snooze to be reminded again in:

5 minutes | Snooze

Exam 77-884: Microsoft Outlook 2010
5. Managing Calendar Objects
5.1. Create and manipulate appointments and events: Set the Reminder

Copy and Paste Appointments

Can you copy and paste appointments? Yes, but there are no Ribbon commands to keep it simple. The preferred method is to setup a **Recurring Appointment**. Please make a new appointment to practice the steps.

Before You Begin: Arrange the Calendar
This lesson is easier to see if you arrange the Calendar to show the Week or Work Week.
Go to **Home ->Arrange->Work Week.**

1. Try it: Add Another Appointment
Go to **Home ->New-> New Appointment.**
Enter the Subject: Breakfast Club
Enter the Location: Brighton
Select the Start Time: 7:00 AM
Select the End Time: 7:30 AM

Try This, Too: Copy and Paste
Select the Breakfast Club Appointment.
Type on the keyboard: **CTRL +C**
Click on Wednesday at 7:30 AM.
Type on the keyboard: **CTRL +V**

There are better options. Keep going...

Home ->Arrange->Work Week

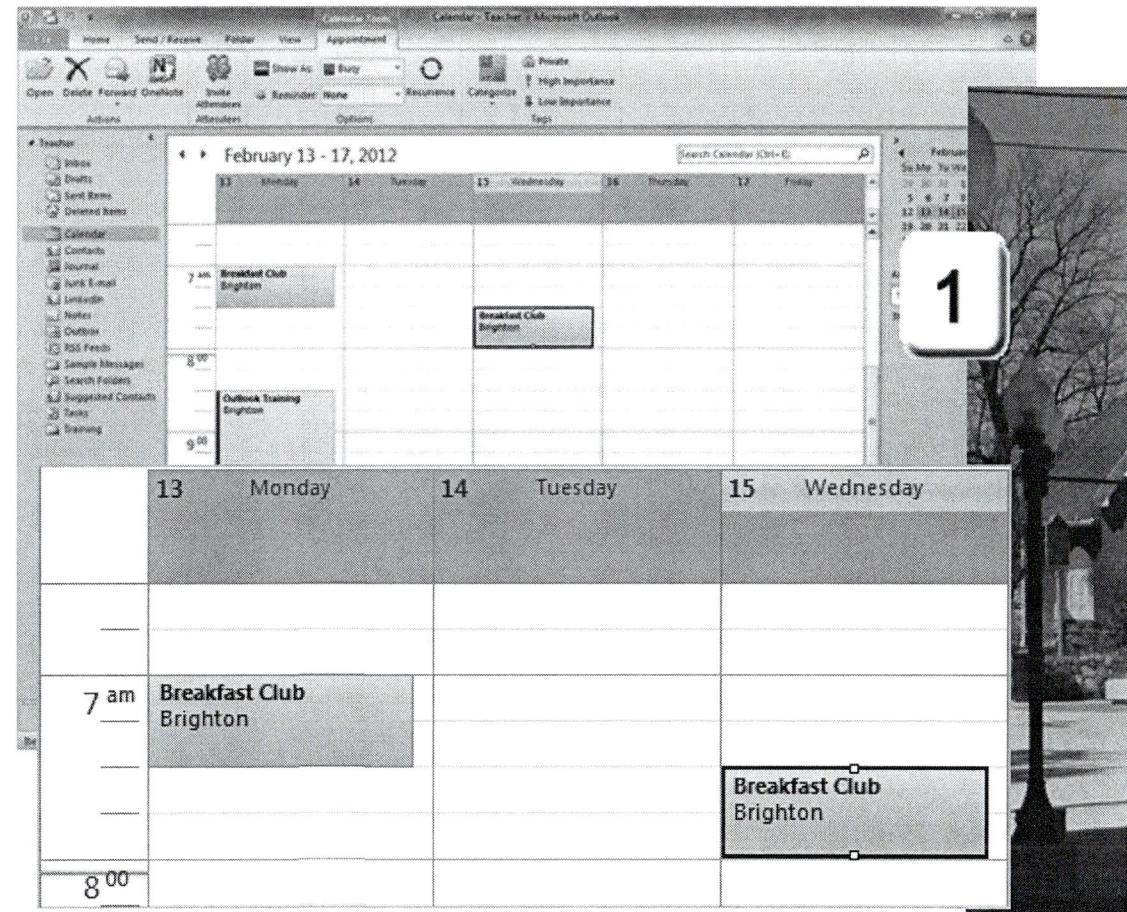

Exam 77-884: Microsoft Outlook 2010
5. Managing Calendar Objects
5.1. Create and manipulate appointments and events: Create Recurring Appointments

Microsoft Outlook 2010   Page 193 of 366

Recurring Appointments

A **Recurring Appointment** can set up many meetings at once. It is a nice bit of programming that saves a lot of time because it is much faster than using Copy/Paste.

2. Try it: Create a Recurring Appointment
Go to Monday at 7:00 AM. Double-click the Breakfast Club appointment to open it, again. The Appointment Ribbon should be available.
Go to **Appointment ->Options.**
Click on **Recurrence**.

Try This, Too: Edit the Recurrence Options
Edit the Recurrence Pattern: Weekly.
Select: Monday, Wednesday, Friday.
Edit the Range: End after 4 occurrences.

Click **OK** to return to the Appointment.
Click **Save & Close** to return to the Calendar.
So, did it work? Let's find out...

Appointment ->Options->Recurrence

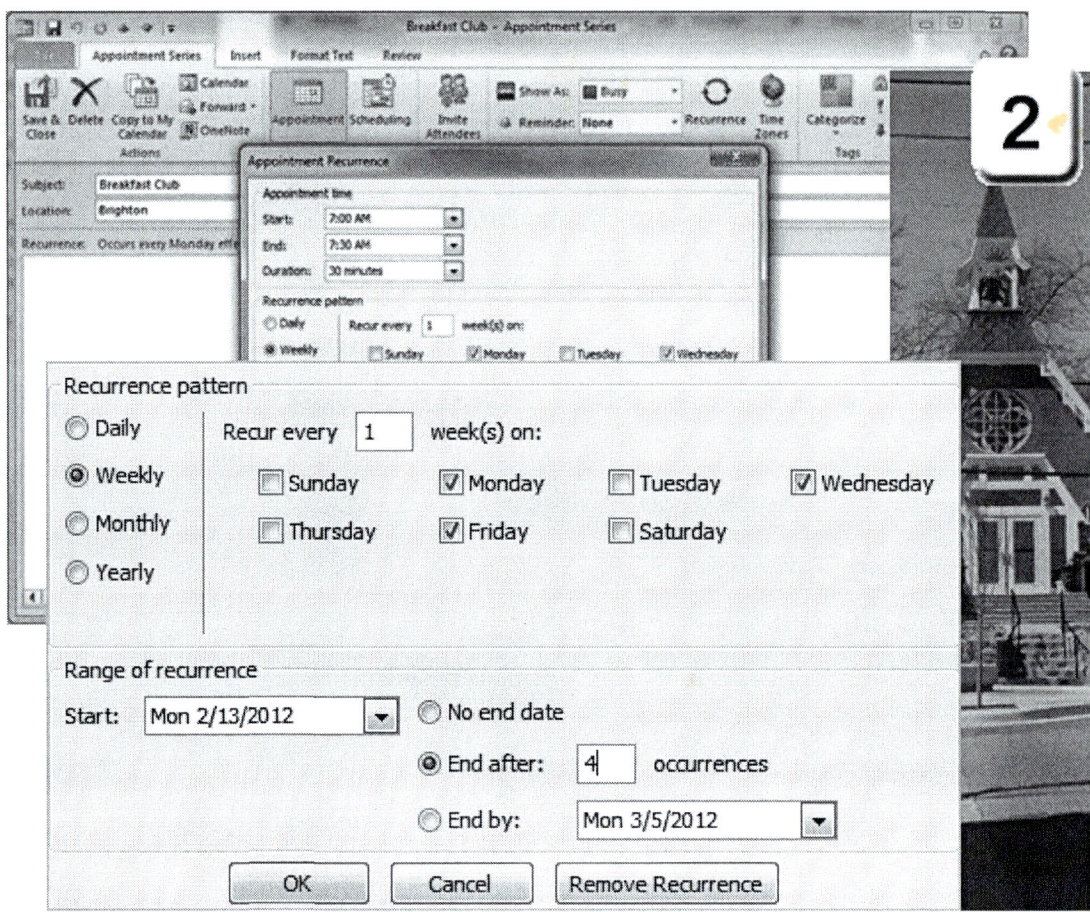

Exam 77-884: Microsoft Outlook 2010
5. Managing Calendar Objects
5.1. Create and manipulate appointments and events: Create Recurring Appointments

Verify the Appointments

3. Try it: Verify the Appointments
Go to **Home ->Arrange->Work Week.**

What Do You See? There are appointments on Monday, Wednesday and Friday.

What Do Else You See? Look on the **Date Navigator** on the right side. Each date that has an appointment is BOLD.

Keep going, please...

Home ->Arrange->Work Week

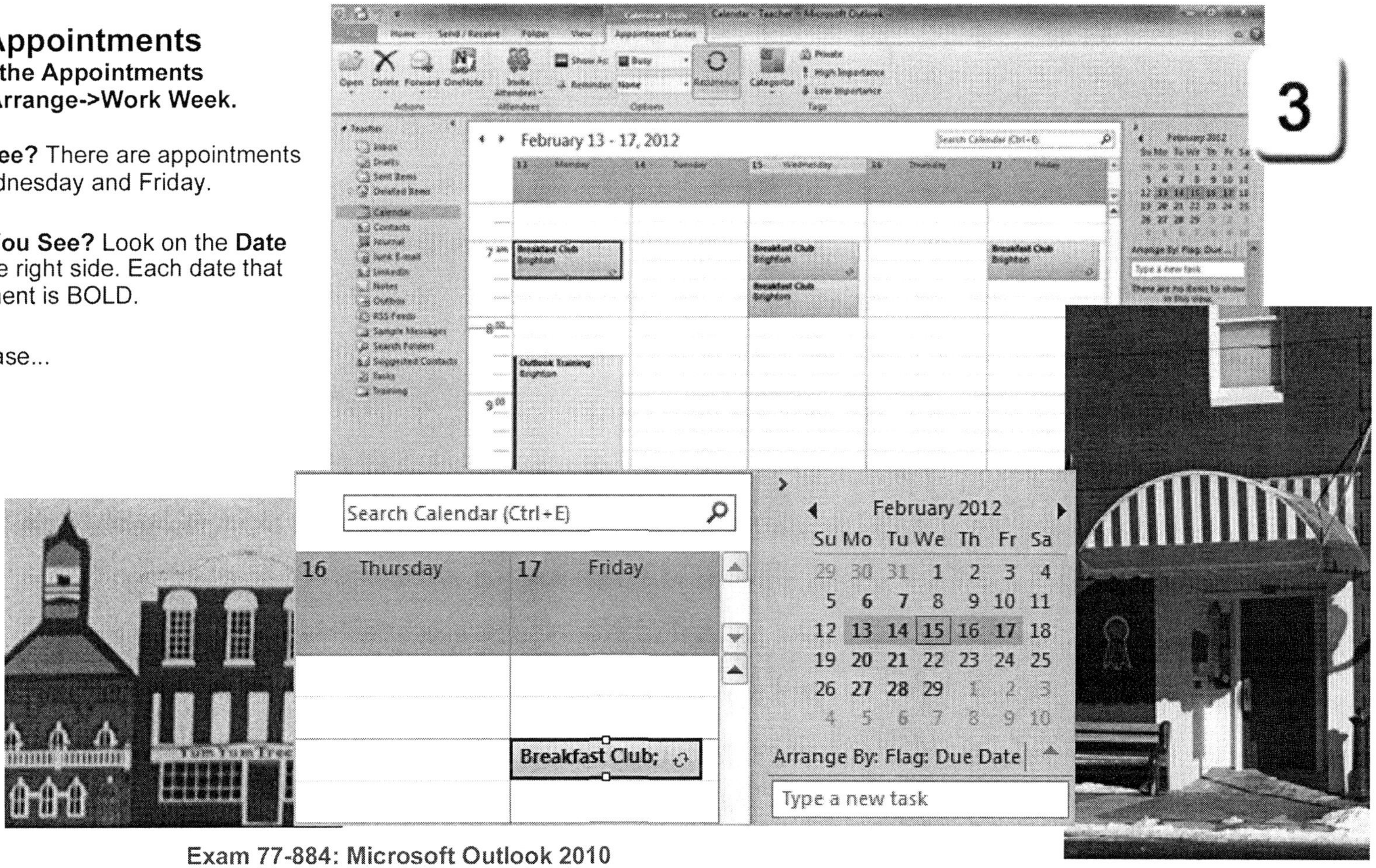

Search Calendar (Ctrl+E)

| 16 | Thursday | 17 | Friday |

Breakfast Club;

February 2012

Su	Mo	Tu	We	Th	Fr	Sa
29	30	31	1	2	3	4
5	6	7	8	9	10	11
12	13	14	15	16	17	18
19	20	21	22	23	24	25
26	27	28	29	1	2	3
4	5	6	7	8	9	10

Arrange By: Flag: Due Date

Type a new task

Exam 77-884: Microsoft Outlook 2010
5. Managing Calendar Objects
5.1. Create and manipulate appointments and events: Create Recurring Appointments

Delete a Recurring Appointment

This lesson created two different appointments on Wednesday. The Recurring Appointment has an icon (a circle with two arrows) in the bottom right. The appointment that was simply copied and pasted does not. What happens if you delete a Recurring Appointment?

4. Try it: Delete an Appointment
Select one of the Recurring Appointments.
The **Calendar Tools** should be available.
Go to: **Calendar Tools ->Appointment Series.**
Go to **Actions->Delete.**
Click on **Delete Occurrence.**

What Do You See? You can choose to Delete this Occurrence or Delete the Series.

Memo to Self: Say you deleted an appointment in a series by using the Delete on your keyboard. Then Outlook would ask you to choose just this occurrence or the whole series.

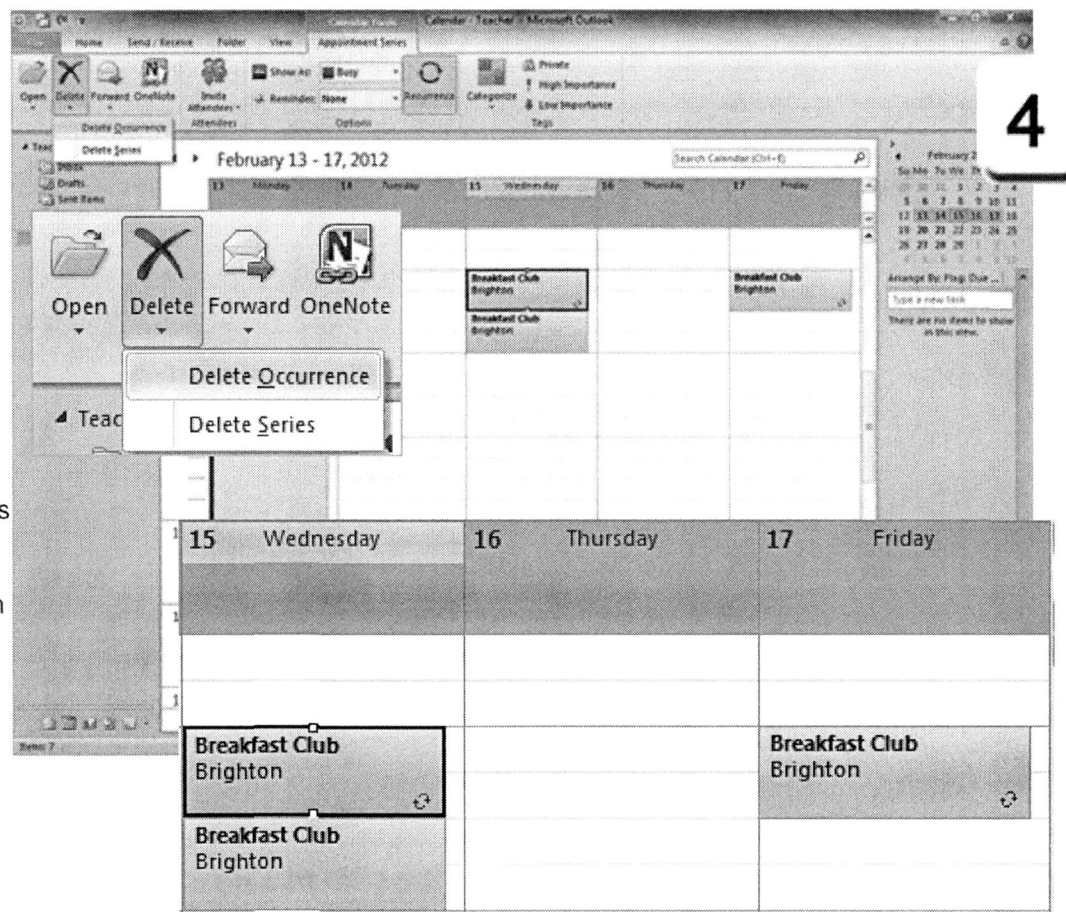

Exam 77-884: Microsoft Outlook 2010
5. Managing Calendar Objects
5.1. Create and manipulate appointments and events: Delete Recurring Appointment

Schedule an Event

An **Event** is displayed a little differently than an Appointment. An Event doesn't have a Start or End Time: It is scheduled as "All day."

Events can be recurring as well. For example, a birthday is an all day Event that brings happy returns each year.

1. Try it: Schedule an Event
Go to **Home ->New-> New Appointment**.
Enter the Subject: Valentine
Select: **All day event**.
Insert->Illustrations->Picture (if you wish).

What Do You See? When you select **All day event**, the Start and End times are disabled. The Ribbon at the top now says Event.

Go to **Event->Actions->Save & Close**.
Keep going, please.

Home ->New-> New Appointment

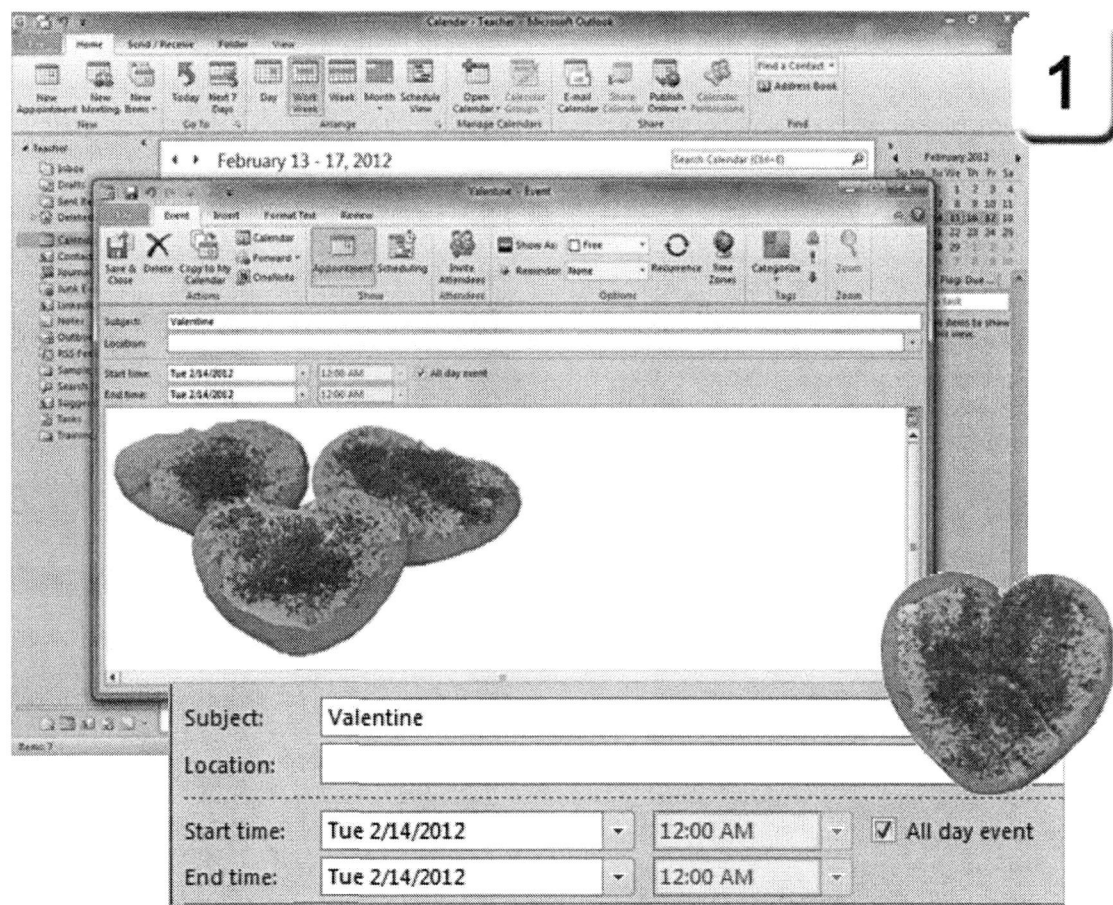

Exam 77-884: Microsoft Outlook 2010
5. Managing Calendar Objects
5.1. Create and manipulate appointments and events: Schedule an Event

Hello, Again, Hello

What does an Event look like in the Calendar?

2. Try it: Review the Event
Go to **Home ->Arrange->Work Week.**

What Do You See? The Event is shown above the hours in the Calendar. In this example, the Valentine Event has an attachment.

Extra for Experts: Make It a Yearly Event
Double click the Event to open it, again.
The Appointment Ribbon should be available.
Go to **Appointment ->Options-> Recurrence.**

Try This, Too: Edit the Recurrence Options
Edit the Recurrence Pattern: Yearly.
Click **OK** to return to the Appointment.
Click **Save & Close** to return to the Calendar.

Home ->Arrange->Work Week

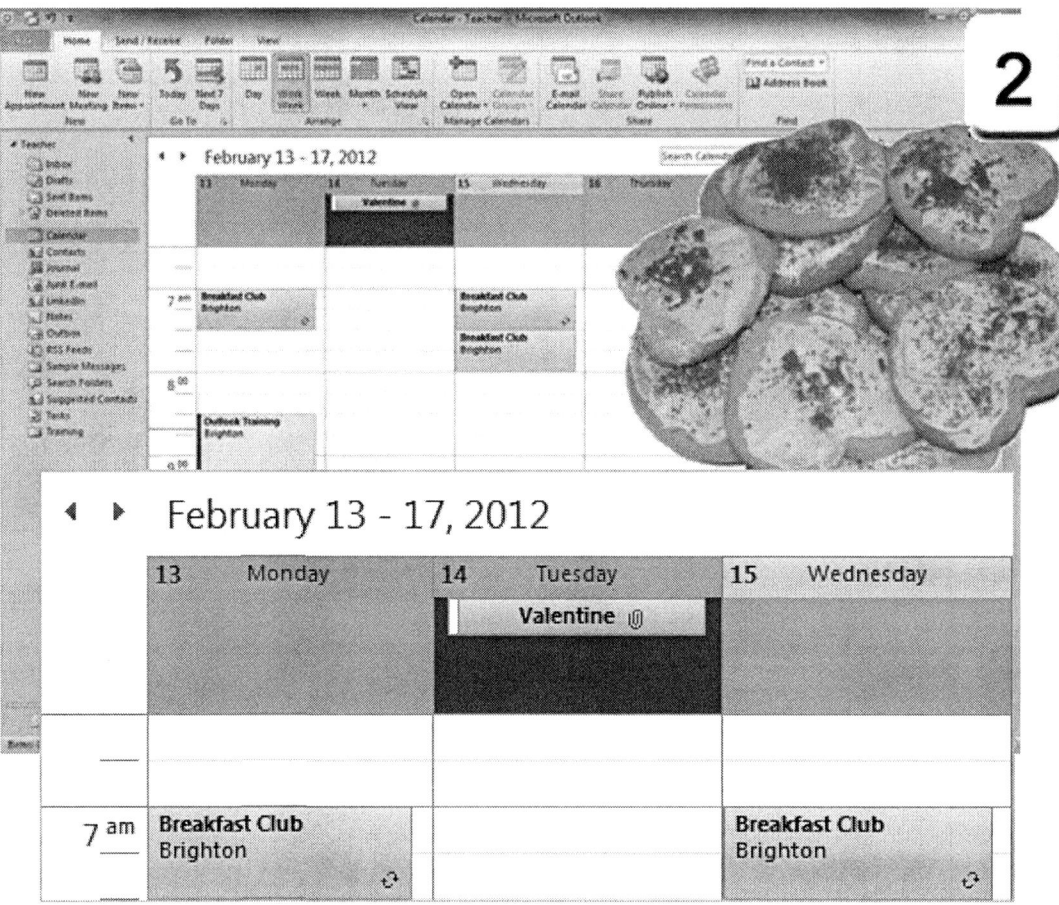

Exam 77-884: Microsoft Outlook 2010
5. Managing Calendar Objects
5.1. Create and manipulate appointments and events: Schedule an Event

Create a Meeting

Meetings and messages go together like donuts and coffee. If you want someone to attend a meeting, then you need to invite them....if that doesn't work, offer donuts.

There are two sides to each example in this lesson: The **Meeting Organizer** (the one who invites everyone to the Meeting) and the **Attendees** (the ones who respond to the Meeting Request and bring donuts.)

1. Try it: Create a New Appointment
Go to **Home ->New-> New Appointment.**
Enter the Subject: Team Meeting
Select the Start Time: 11:00 AM
Select the End Time: 1:00 PM
Type the Location: The Yum Yum Tree, Brighton

Go to **Appointment->Options**.
Show As: **Out of the Office.**

Try This, Too: Add a Hyperlink to the Meeting
Type the following, please.
Here is a link:
http://www.yumyumtreebrighton.com/ .

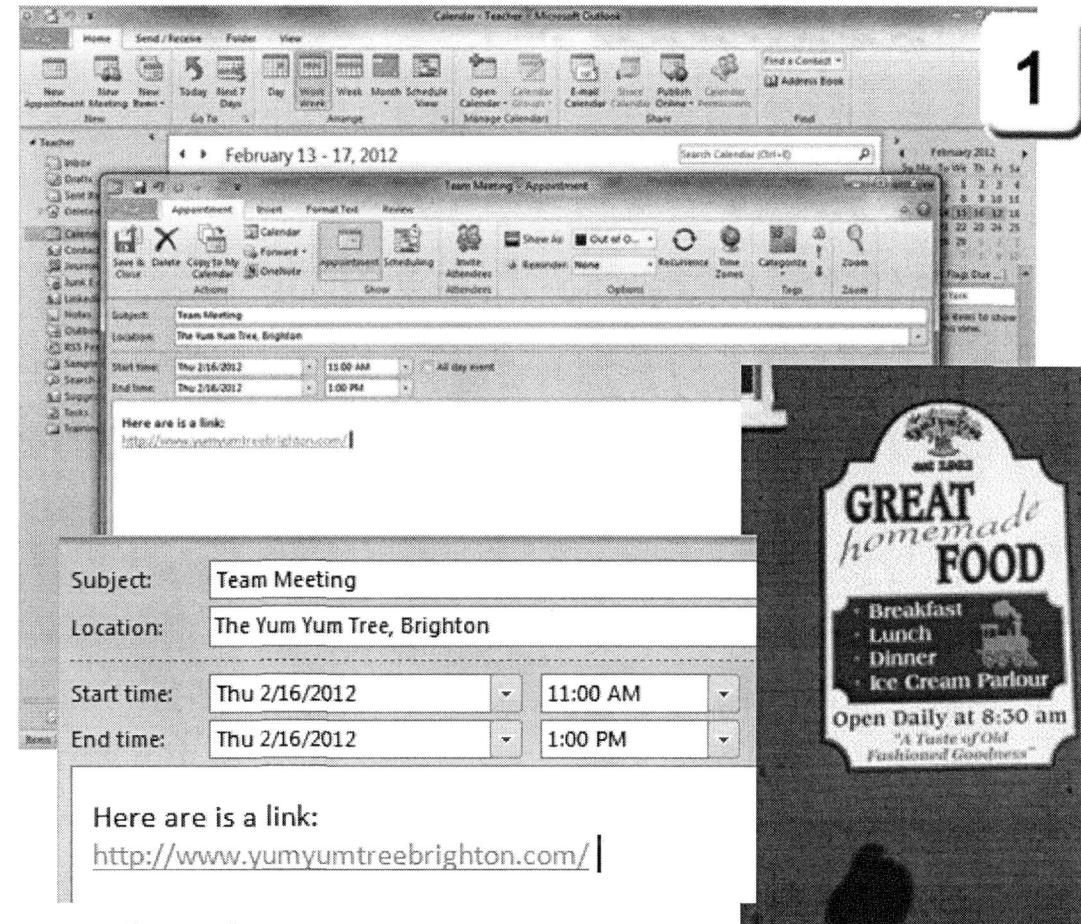

Exam 77-884: Microsoft Outlook 2010
5. Managing Calendar Objects
5.2. Create and manipulate meeting requests: Create a Meeting

Invite Attendees

Attendees are people who can come to your meeting. When you ask someone to attend they will receive an invitation in their E-mail. The recipient can Accept, Decline or Propose a different Time. Let's walk through the steps.

2. Try it: Invite Attendees
The appointment is still open.
Go to **Meeting ->Attendees.**
Click on **Invite Attendees.**

What Do You See? Look above the Subject. The E-mail field is available now.

Enter a partner's E-mail address.
Click **Send** to E-mail the invitation.

Keep going, please.

Request: The Invitation is Addressed and Sent

Meeting ->Attendees->Invite Attendees

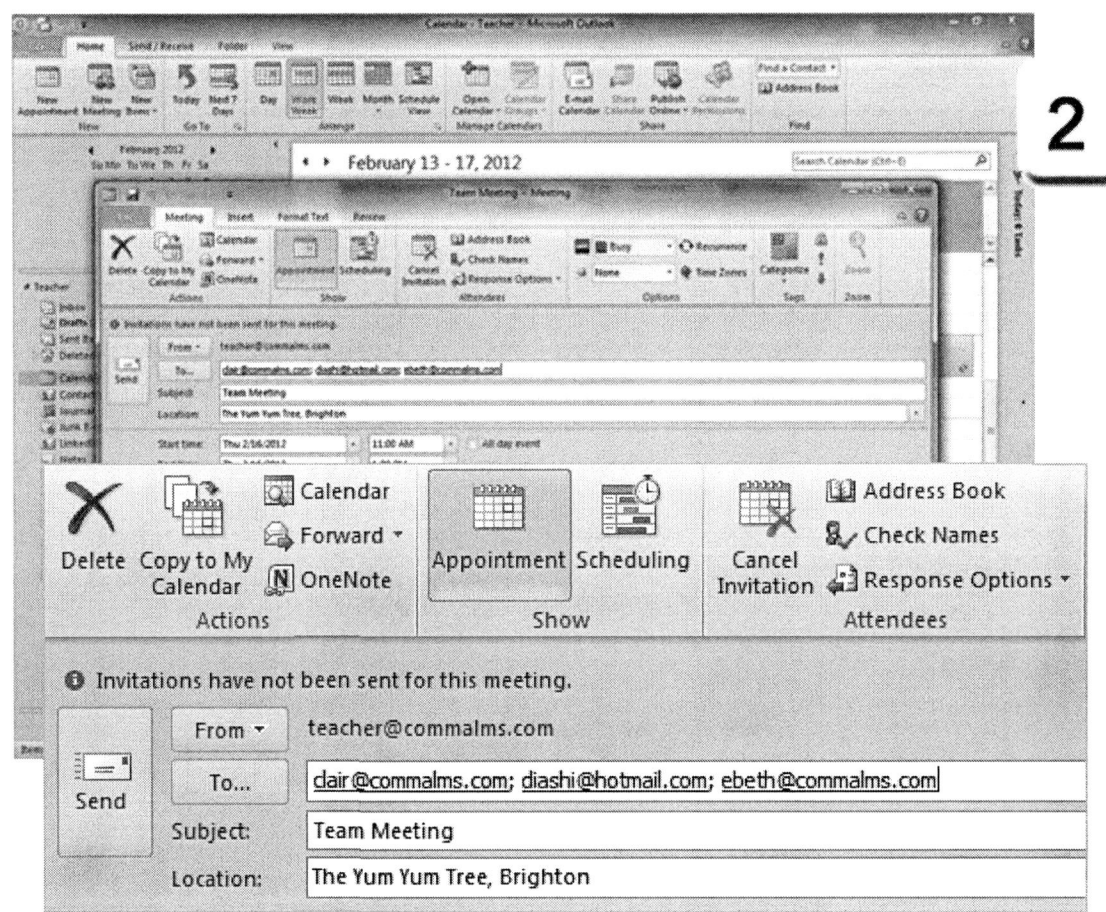

Exam 77-884: Microsoft Outlook 2010
5. Managing Calendar Objects
5.2. Create and manipulate meeting requests: Invite Attendees

Receive an Invitation

An invitation has arrived in the Inbox inviting you to a meeting. How would you respond? Let's look at the options.

The Meeting Ribbon includes:
Accept
Tentative
Decline
Propose New Time
Respond

3. Try it: Respond to a Meeting Request
Go to **Meeting ->Respond->Accept.**

What Do You See? For each Response--Accept, Decline, etc.-- you can choose to:
Edit the Response before Sending
Send the Response Now (don't edit the E-mail)
Do Not Send a Response.

Select: **Send the Response Now.**
An Acceptance E-mail will be sent and the Invitation will be moved to the Deleted Items folder automatically. Keep going, please.

Respond: The Recipient's Inbox

Meeting ->Respond->Accept

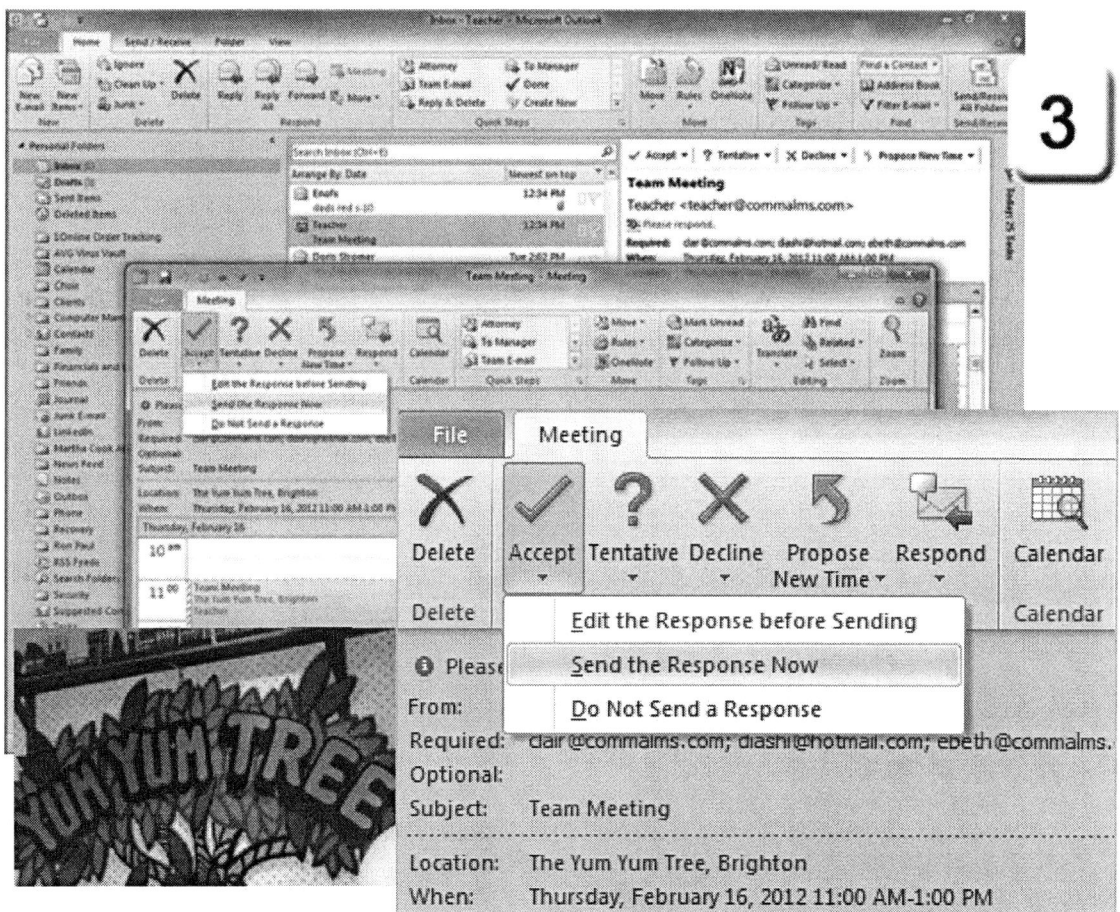

Exam 77-884: Microsoft Outlook 2010
5. Managing Calendar Objects
5.2. Create and manipulate meeting requests: Invite Attendees

Receive the Responses

4. Try it: Review the Responses

If the donuts are good, the Sender's Inbox should fill up with responses. Each response can be tracked in two places: the E-mail and the Appointment.

Keep going, please.

Review: The Sender's Inbox

Outlook ->Inbox

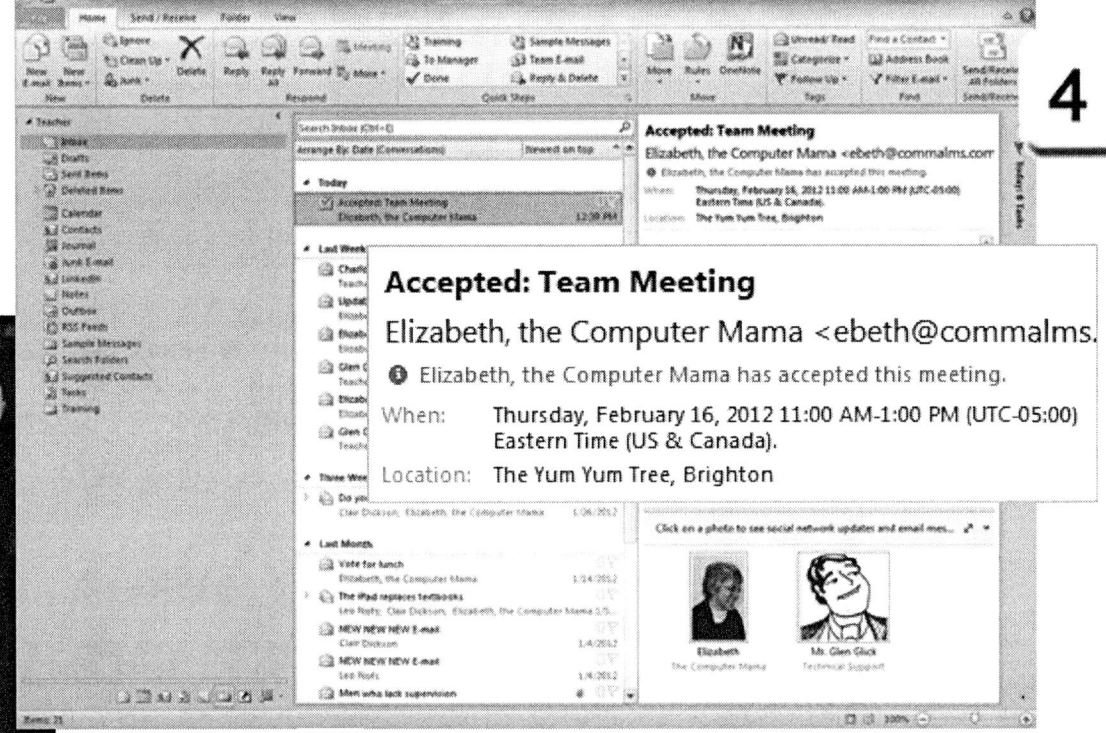

Accepted: Team Meeting

Elizabeth, the Computer Mama <ebeth@commalms.

🔵 Elizabeth, the Computer Mama has accepted this meeting.

When:	Thursday, February 16, 2012 11:00 AM-1:00 PM (UTC-05:00) Eastern Time (US & Canada).
Location:	The Yum Yum Tree, Brighton

Exam 77-884: Microsoft Outlook 2010
5. Managing Calendar Objects
5.2. Create and manipulate meeting requests: Invite Attendees

Review the Attendee Responses

The Reponses are also tallied in the appointment.

5. Try it: Review the Attendee Response
Go to the **Calendar**.
Double click the Team Meeting to open it.

What Do You See? In the example on this page all three attendees accepted the invitation.

What Else Do You See? When you open a meeting, the default view is Appointment. You can show the Tracking as well. Here is how...

Meeting ->Show->Appointment

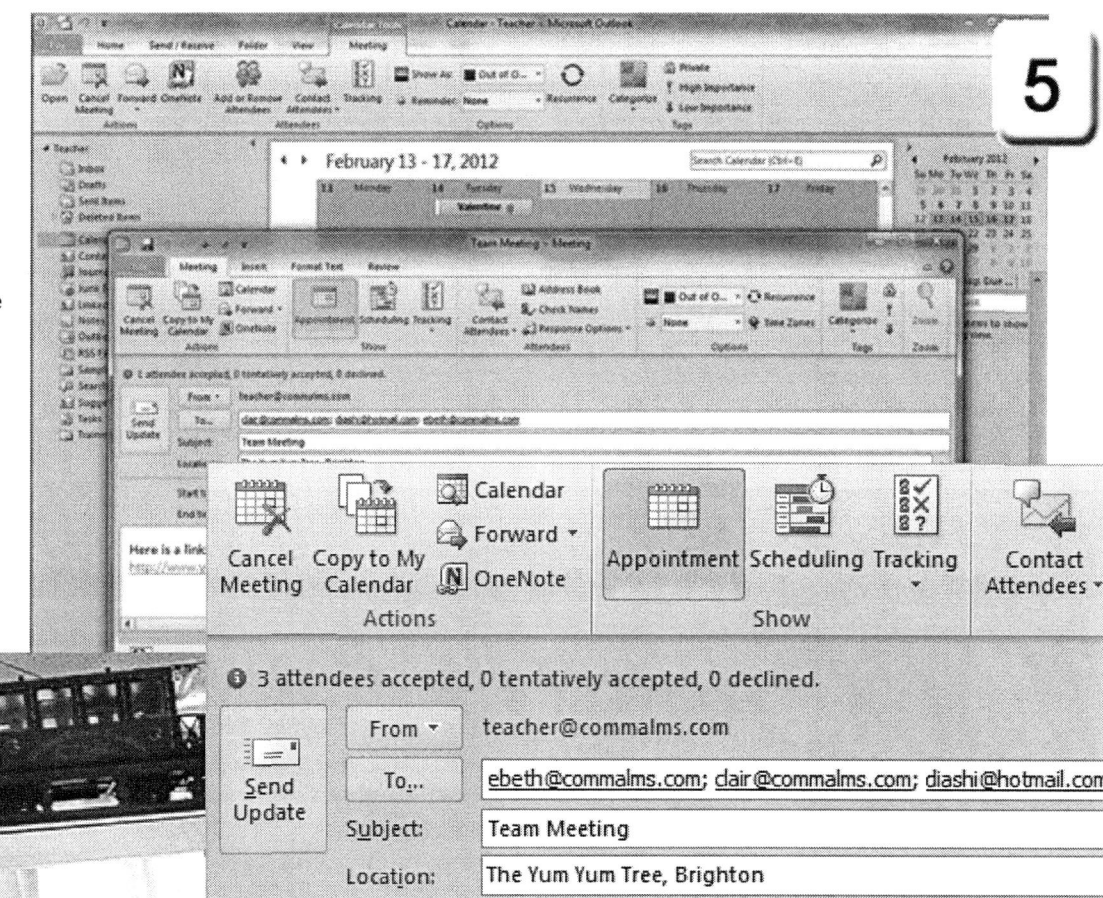

5

Show the Tracking
6. Try it: Show the Tracking
The Team Meeting is open.
Go to **Meeting ->Show->Tracking.**

What Do You See? The responses are listed by name. The person who sent the invitation is the **Meeting Organizer**. The other Attendees responded to the invitation. These responses can be edited if you wish.

Attendance has three options:
Required Attendee
Optional Attendee
Resource (Room or Equipment)

Response has four options:
Accepted
Declined
Tentative
None

Try This, Too: Return to the Appointment
Go to **Meeting ->Show->Appointment.**

Keep going, please.

Meeting ->Show->Tracking

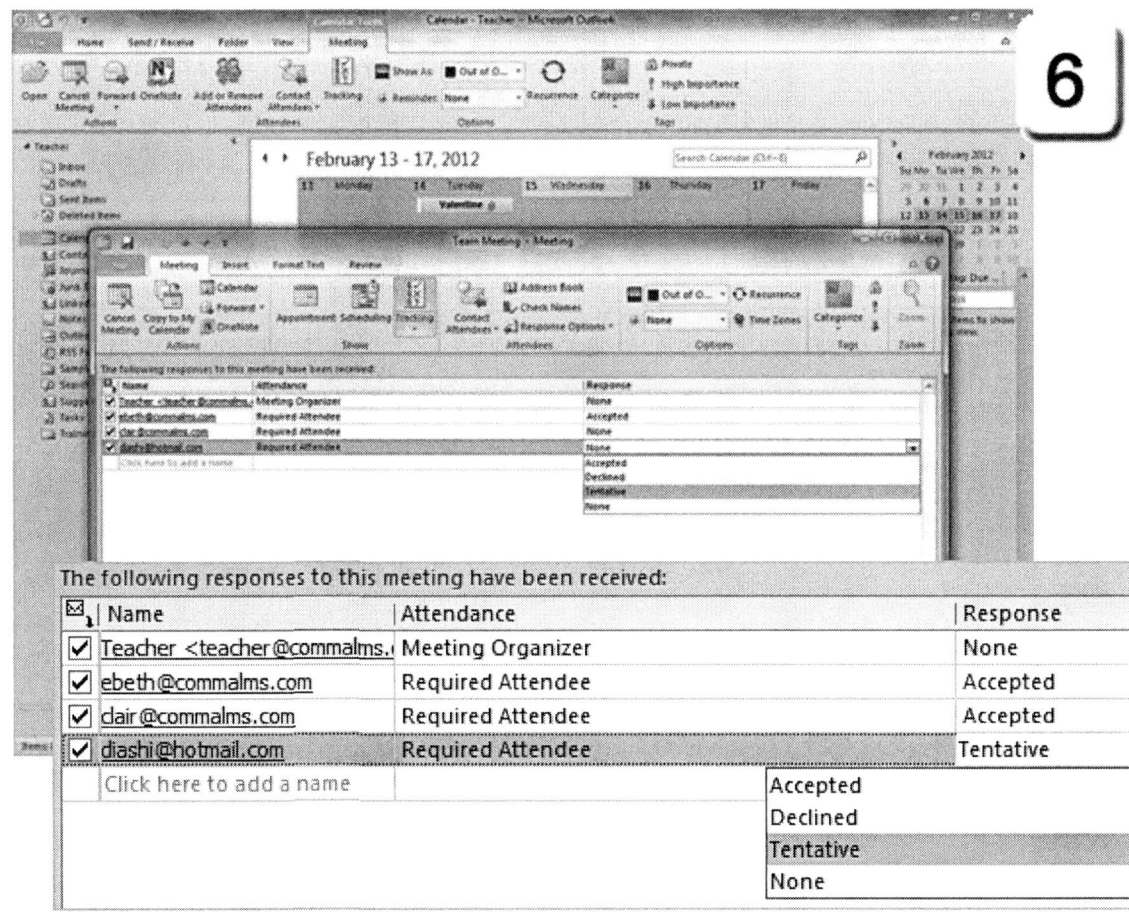

The following responses to this meeting have been received:

✉ Name	Attendance	Response
✓ Teacher <teacher@commalms.	Meeting Organizer	None
✓ ebeth@commalms.com	Required Attendee	Accepted
✓ clair@commalms.com	Required Attendee	Accepted
✓ diashi@hotmail.com	Required Attendee	Tentative
Click here to add a name		Accepted
		Declined
		Tentative
		None

Exam 77-884: Microsoft Outlook 2010
5. Managing Calendar Objects
5.2. Create and manipulate meeting requests: Tracking

Propose a New Time

Say one of your recipients has a scheduling conflict. How would she propose a new time?

1. Try it: Propose a New Time

We are looking at the Attendee's Calendar. When she accepted the invitation, the Team Meeting was added to her Calendar.

The Team Meeting in her Calendar is open.
Go to **Meeting ->Respond.**
Click on **Propose New Time.**
Select: **Tentative and Propose New Time.**

Keep going, please.

Memo to Self: These options may not be available if you made a practice invitation that is addressed to yourself, only.

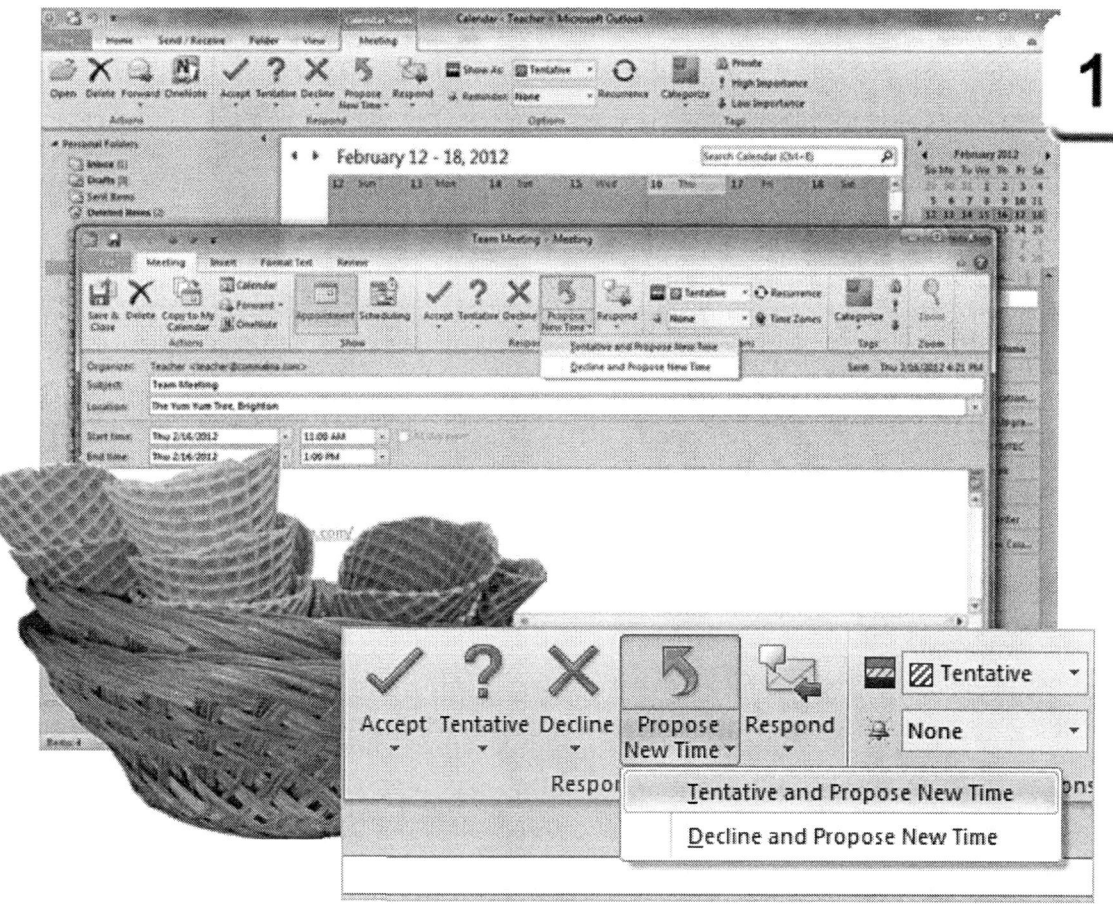

Exam 77-884: Microsoft Outlook 2010
5. Managing Calendar Objects
5.1. Create and manipulate appointments and events: Propose a New Time for a Meeting

Meeting ->Response->Propose New Time

Use the Scheduling Assistant

What Do You See? The **Scheduling Assistant** should open. Each Attendee is listed on the left. The Calendar is on the right. The Current Meeting time is shaded yellow.

The **Proposed New Time** is shown.
The Start Time is the green line at 12:00.
The End Time is the red line at 2:00.

2. Try it: AutoPick Next
Click on **AutoPick Next.**
AutoPick reviews the Calendars and selects the next Start Time that is free for everyone. If there is no data, the Start Time will advance to the next half hour.

If you are following these steps using your own E-mail address, click **Propose Time.** A Meeting Response will open. Click **Send.**

Keep going.

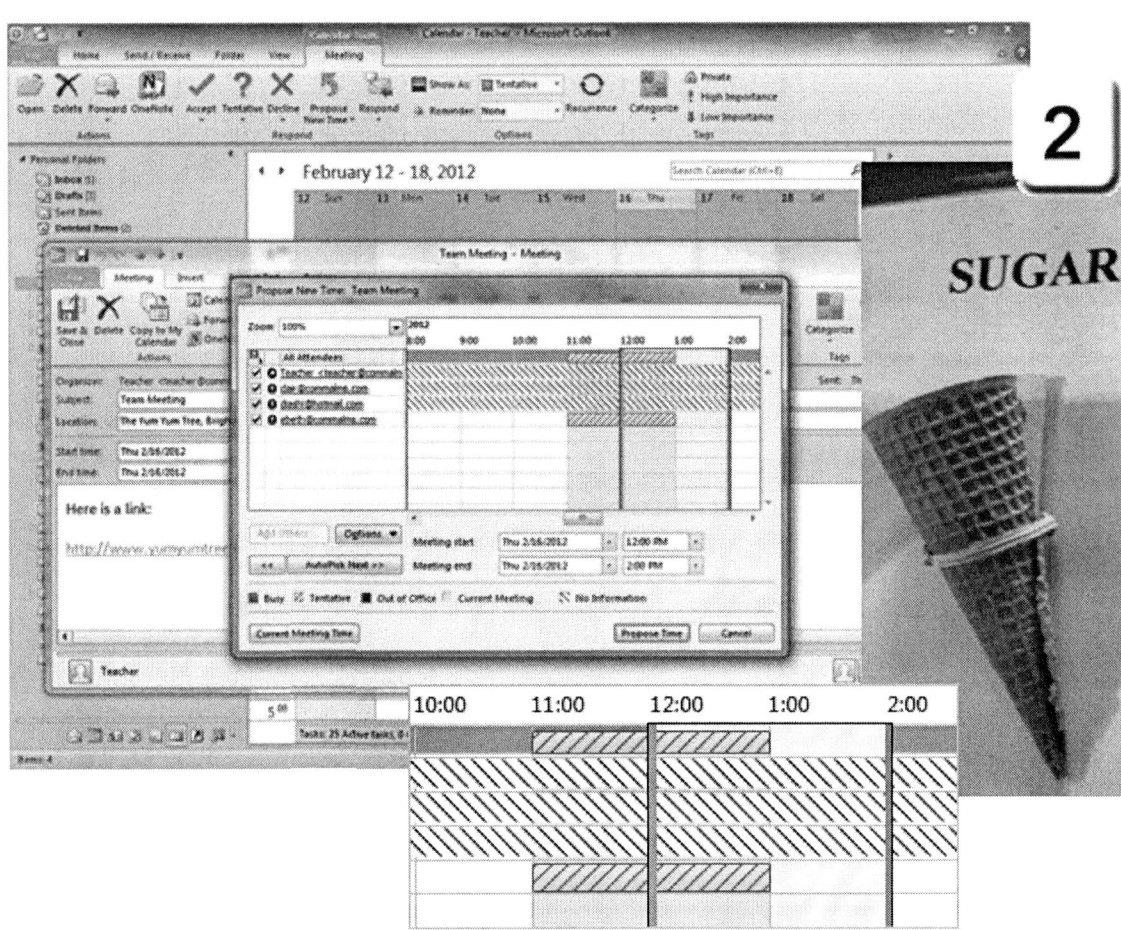

Exam 77-884: Microsoft Outlook 2010
5. Managing Calendar Objects
5.1. Create and manipulate appointments and events: Propose a New Time for a Meeting

View All Proposals

The story continues at the Sender's Inbox.
The response arrives with a Proposal.

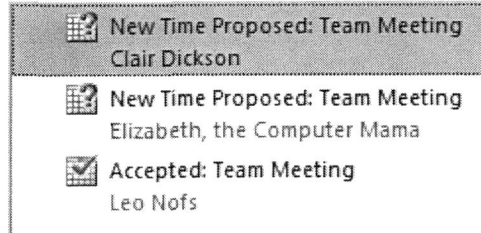

3. Try it: View All Proposals
Select the message with the Subject:
New Time Proposed.

Go to **Meeting Response ->Respond.**
Click on **View All Proposals.**

Keep going, please.

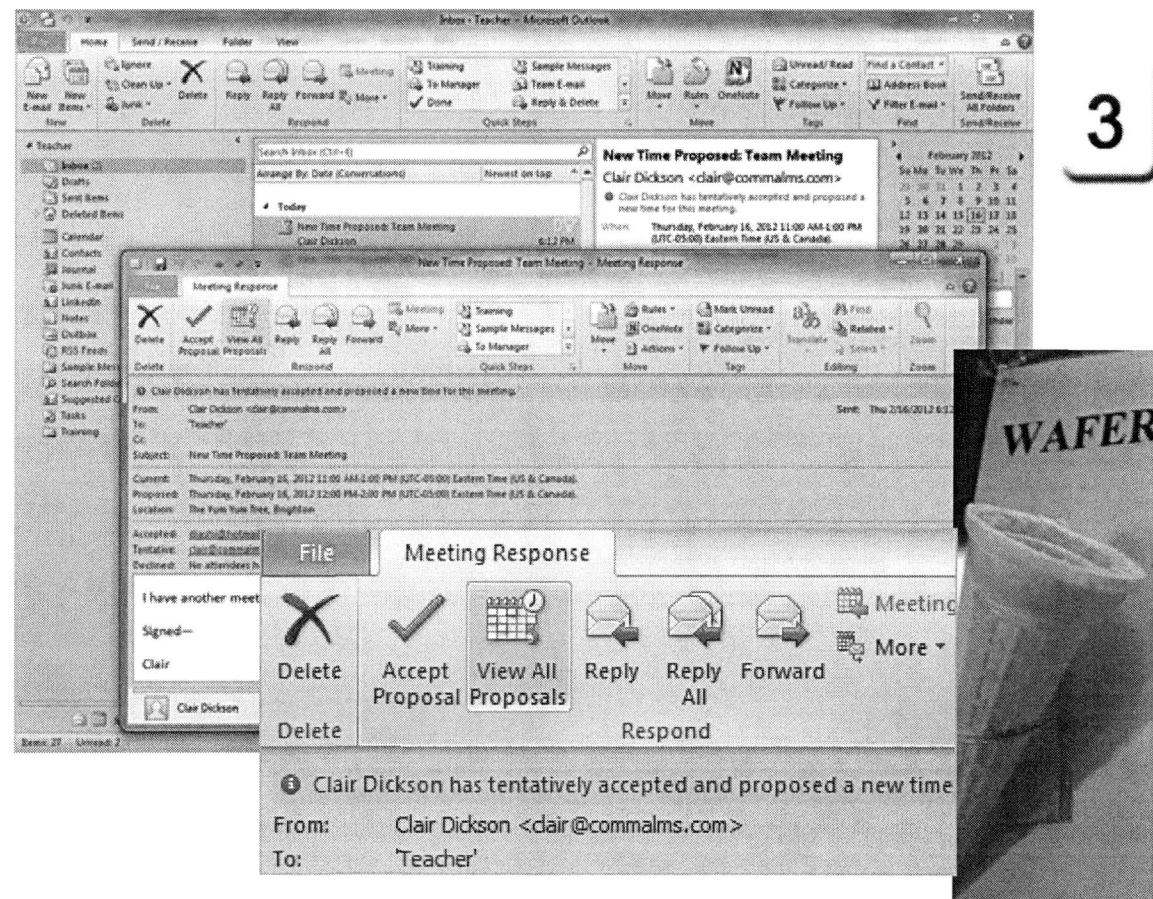

Exam 77-884: Microsoft Outlook 2010
5. Managing Calendar Objects
5.1. Create and manipulate appointments and events: View all Proposals

Meeting: Contact Attendees

What Do You See? When you click View All Proposals, Outlook will show the **Scheduling**.

What Don't You See? These screen shots do not show the **Free/Busy** times for our attendees. The attendees may all use Outlook for their scheduling, however, the Calendars are not yet available online. We will look at the options for publishing a Calendar later in our book.

Update the Meeting Request: If there is no data online, how can you find out more? Ask.

4. Try it: Contact the Attendees
Go to **Meeting ->Attendees.**
Click on **Contact Attendees.**

What Do You See? You can reach out to your attendees with a New E-mail or Reply to All.

What Else Do You See? By default, the Attendees **Response Options** include Request Reponses and Allow New Time Proposals.

Keep going, please.

Meeting ->Attendees->Contact Attendees

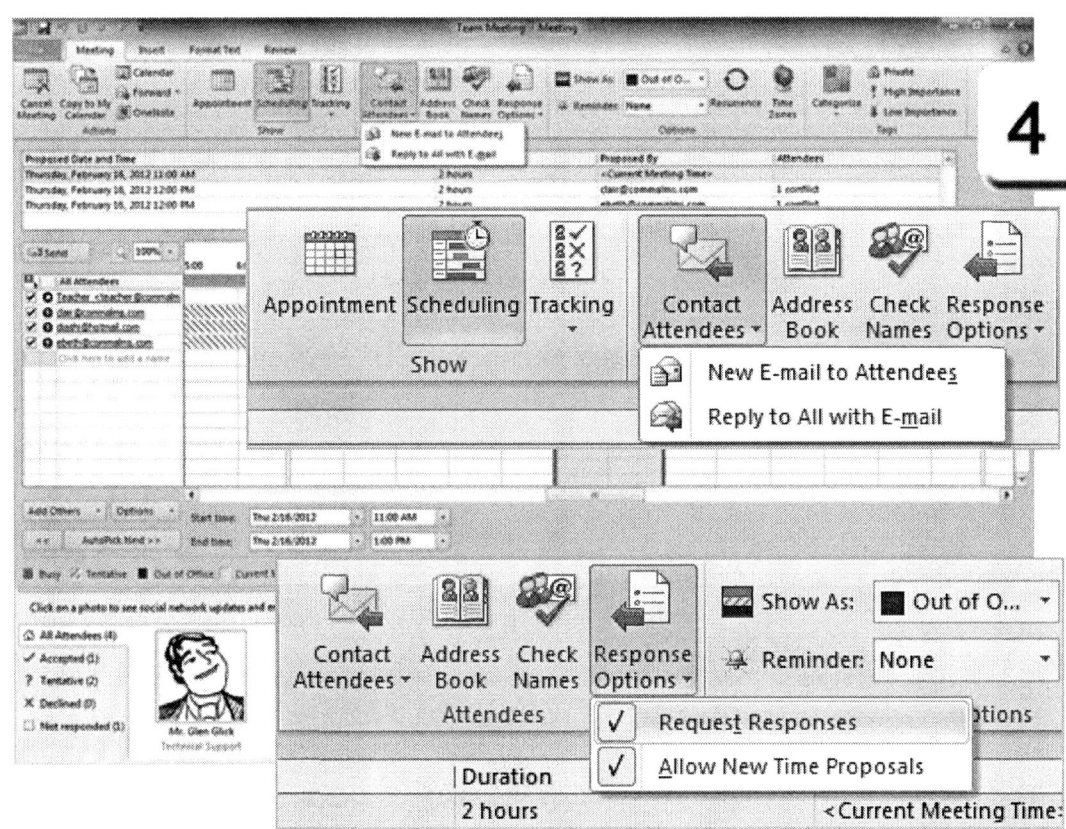

Exam 77-884: Microsoft Outlook 2010
5. Managing Calendar Objects
5.1. Create and manipulate appointments and events: Update a Meeting Request

Forward the Meeting

Let's look at other ways to share a meeting, especially if it is going to be at the Yum Yum Tree. You can **Forward** a meeting to a **Contact Group**. Yep, invite them all.

5. Try it: Forward a Meeting
The Team Meeting is still selected.
The Calendar Tools should be available.
Go to **Calendar Tools ->Actions->Forward.**
Select: Forward as iCalendar.

What Do You See? A new message will open. The iCalendar is an attachment.

Try it, Too: Edit the Forwarded Message
Click **To** and browse the Address Book.
Select the **Contact Group**: Charlotte's Website
Click **Send.**

Keep going: if the Contact Group includes your own E-mail, this message should arrive in your Inbox shortly.

Forward: The Sender's Calendar

Calendar Tools ->Actions->Forward

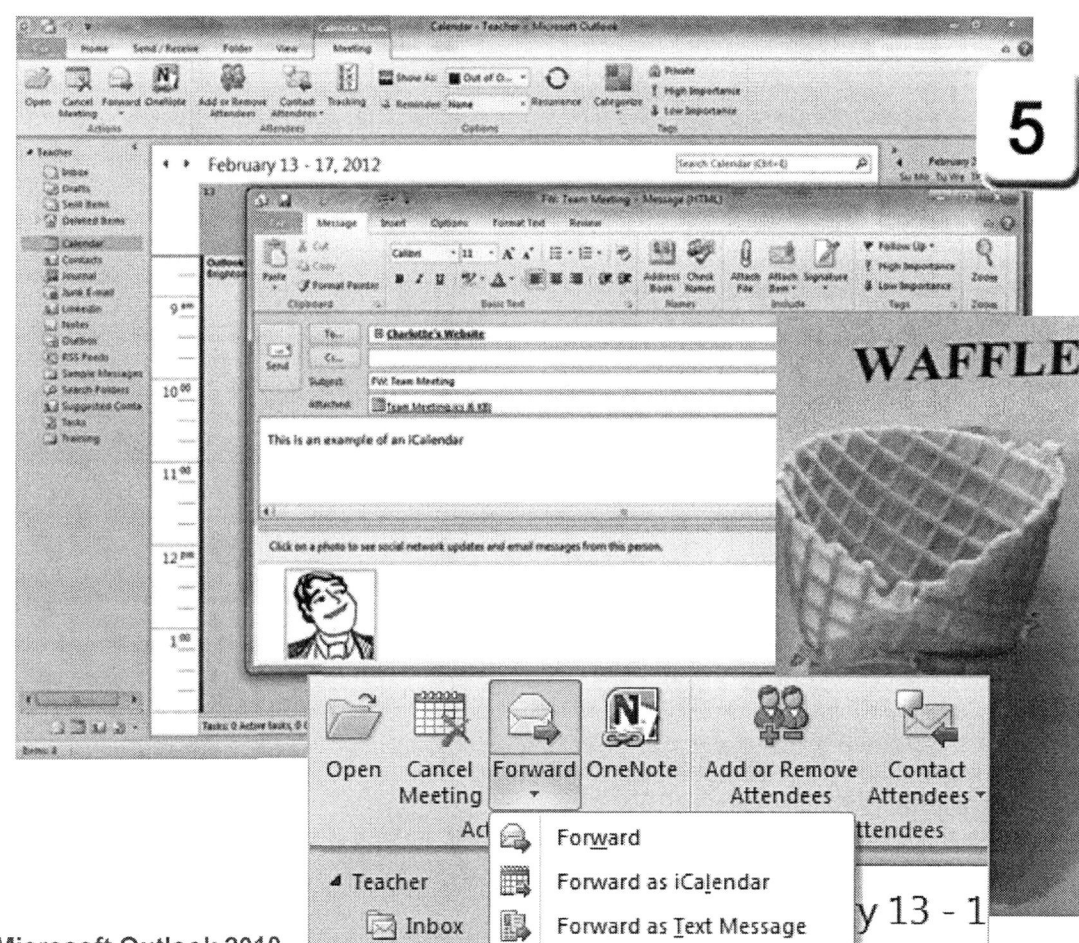

Exam 77-884: Microsoft Outlook 2010
5. Managing Calendar Objects
5.1. Create and manipulate appointments and events: Forward a Meeting to a Contact Group

Open the iCalendar

When you forward a meeting as an iCalendar, the iCalendar arrives as an attachment. This is a form, so it must be opened to see the details. It does not have a preview. Here are the steps.

6. Try it: Open an iCalendar

Double-click the iCalendar attachment.
The Team Meeting should open and the Meeting Ribbon should be available.

The recipients, location and time are listed. The meeting is shown as a Calendar. The link that we typed into the notes is also included.

OK, there are few more ways to work with scheduling. Keep going...

Meeting ->Respond

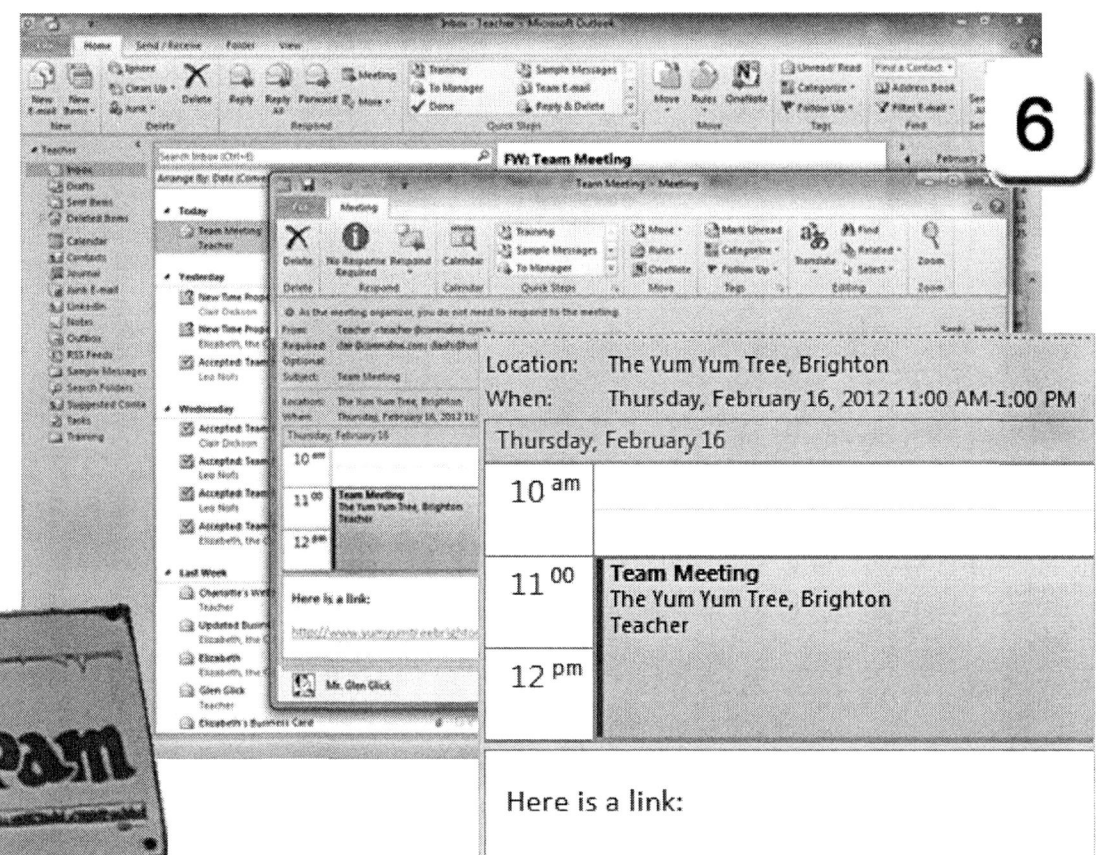

6

| Location: | The Yum Yum Tree, Brighton |
| When: | Thursday, February 16, 2012 11:00 AM-1:00 PM |

Thursday, February 16

10 am	
11 00	**Team Meeting** The Yum Yum Tree, Brighton Teacher
12 pm	

Here is a link:

http://www.yumyumtreebrighton.com/

Exam 77-884: Microsoft Outlook 2010
5. Managing Calendar Objects
5.1. Create and manipulate appointments and events: Forward a Meeting

Respond with a Meeting

Here is a simple step that saves a lot of time. Go to the Inbox and look at the **Home** Ribbon, again. The **Respond** Group has a **Meeting** button. You can invite someone to discuss their E-mail over lunch if you wish.

7. Try it: Respond with a Meeting
Go to the Inbox.
Select a message from one of your Contacts.
Go to **Home ->Respond->Meeting.**

What Do You See? An invitation will open addressed to your Contact. You can edit the location, date and times before you send the invitation. You can also edit the message.

Click **Send**. Keep going, please.

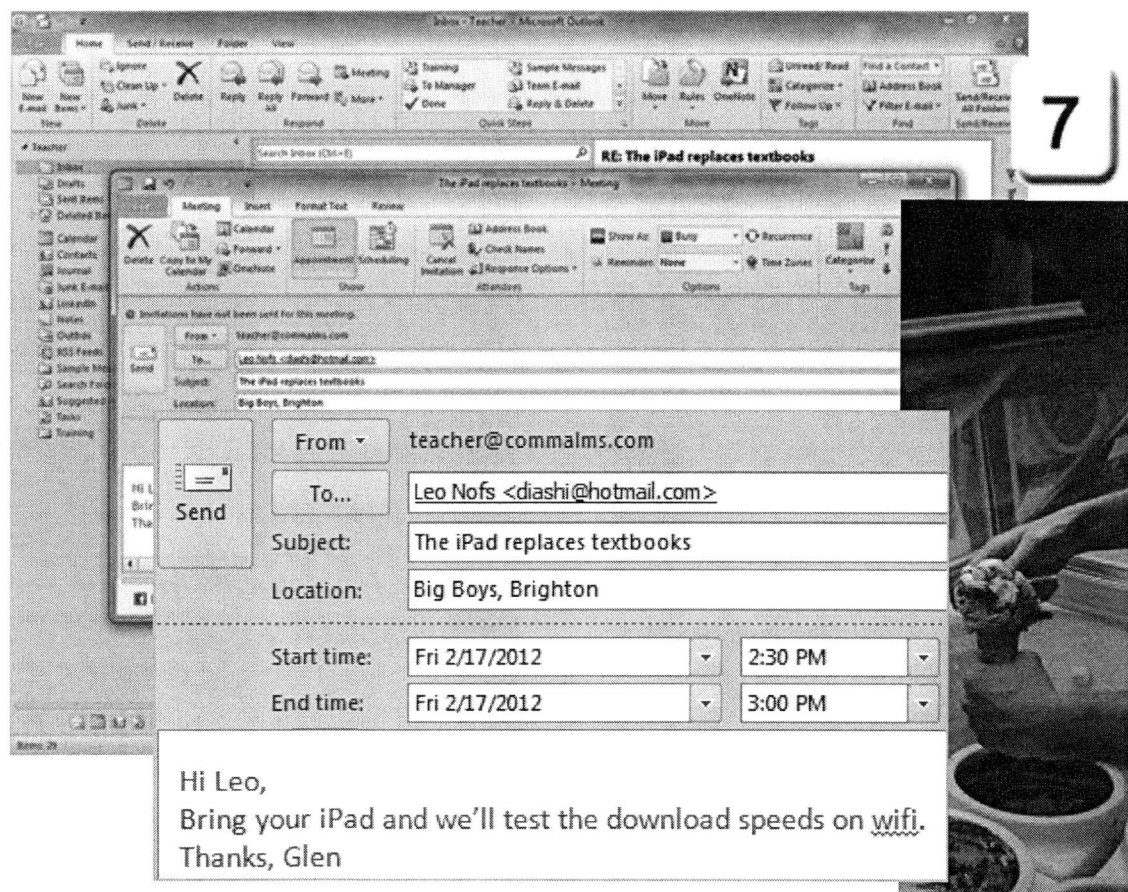

Exam 77-884: Microsoft Outlook 2010
5. Managing Calendar Objects
5.1. Create and manipulate appointments and events: Respond with a Meeting

HOME

Calendar Tools ->Meeting->Respond

Where's the Meeting?
8. Try it: Review the Meeting
Go to the Calendar. The meeting is already placed on your agenda.

When you click on the Meeting, the Calendar Tools will be available.

One more option to review.
Keep going,..

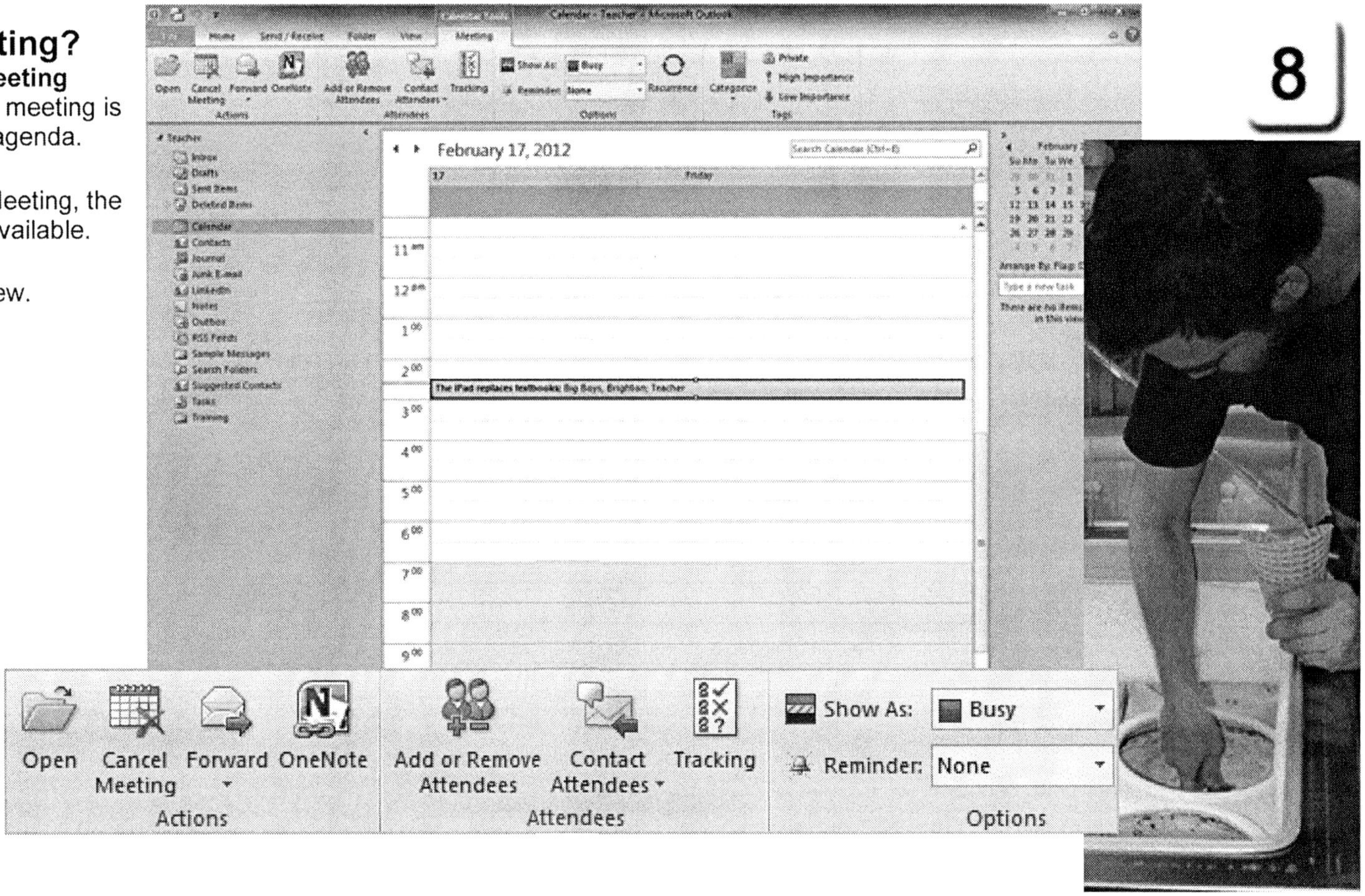

8

Exam 77-884: Microsoft Outlook 2010
5. Managing Calendar Objects
5.1. Create and manipulate appointments and events: Respond with a Meeting

Cancel the Meeting

Some days, the donuts are stale and the meeting invitations aren't accepted.

The **Meeting Organizer** can **Cancel** the Meeting. Outlook will notify all of the Attendees. How does that work?

9. Try it: Cancel the Meeting

Go to the Calendar which is still open. The sample meeting is selected.
Go to **Calendar Tools ->Meeting**.
Click on **Cancel Meeting**.

What Do You See? A new E-mail will open, addressed to the Attendees.

Click **Send Cancellation**. Outlook will E-mail all of your Attendees. No donuts.

Keep going, please.

Calendar Tools ->Meeting->Cancel Meeting

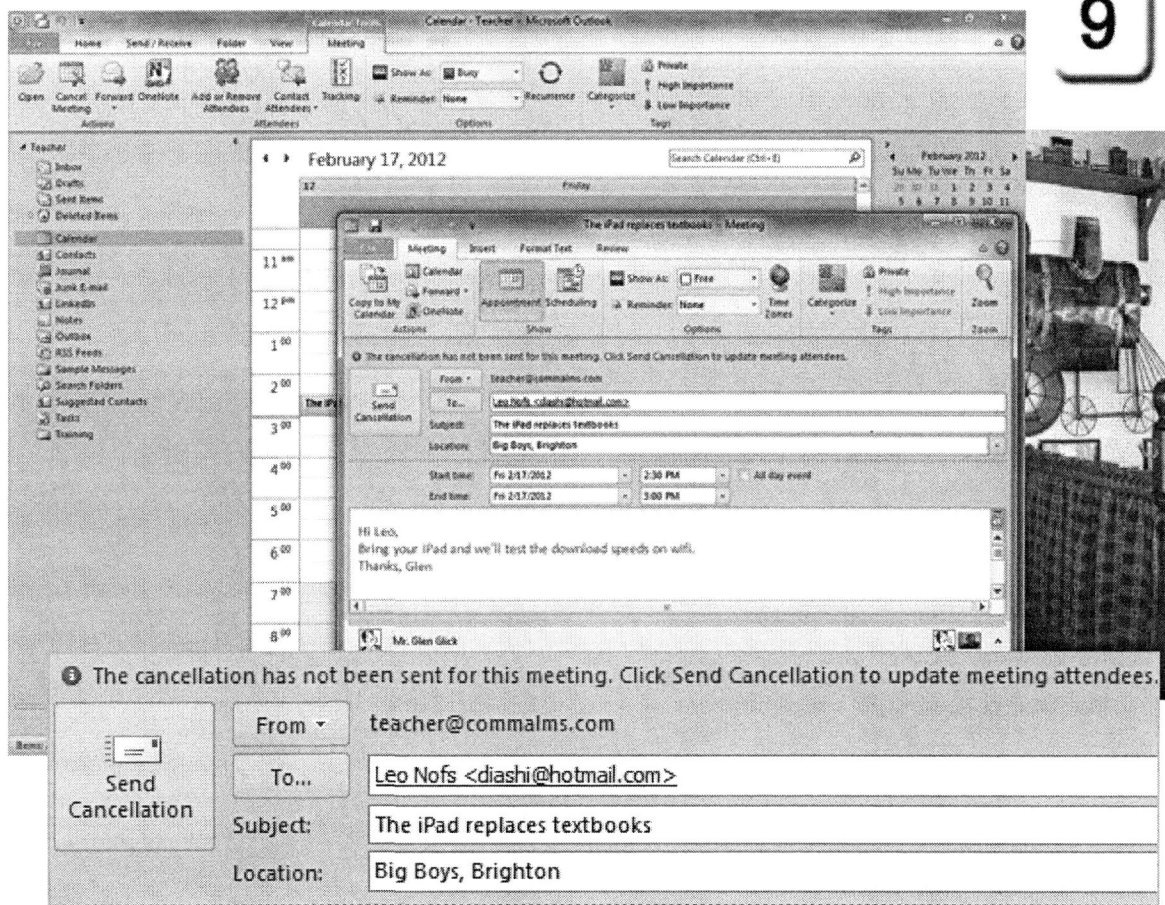

Exam 77-884: Microsoft Outlook 2010
5. Managing Calendar Objects
5.1. Create and manipulate appointments and events: Cancel the Meeting

Regrets

The Cancellation notice arrives in the Attendee's Inbox. There should be an option to Remove the Meeting from the Calendar.

Memo to Self: The Computer Mama was cleaning the office one Friday morning (blue jeans and Beatles) when the phone rings. It is an important Contact, asking if I was coming to Ann Arbor for a meeting that morning....?

After a long pause she asked, "Did I forget to E-mail an invitation?

So, if you do not receive a response from the E-mail invitations, you might consider picking up the phone and calling to confirm, OK?

The Attendee's Inbox

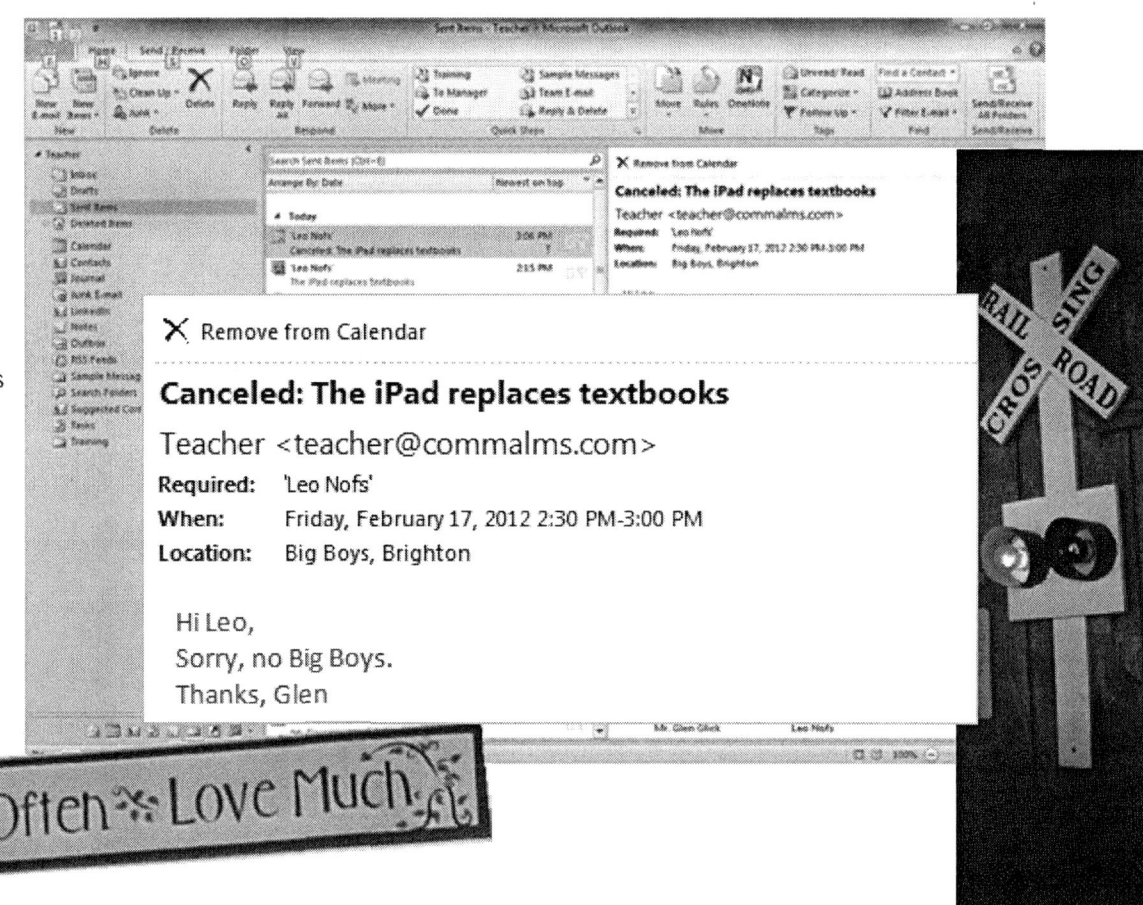

✕ Remove from Calendar

Canceled: The iPad replaces textbooks

Teacher <teacher@commalms.com>

Required: 'Leo Nofs'
When: Friday, February 17, 2012 2:30 PM-3:00 PM
Location: Big Boys, Brighton

Hi Leo,
Sorry, no Big Boys.
Thanks, Glen

Summary

This lesson introduced the Calendar. Our examples reviewed the Calendar Tools as well as the Meeting Ribbon options.

This lesson was interesting because there were two sides to each example: the Meeting Organizer and the Attendees. Many of the pages were titled: request, respond, review.

Well, you done good.
Go ahead, get some ice cream!

Practice Activities

Lesson: Eight Days a Week

Before You Begin: Start Microsoft Outlook 2010. Select the Calendar Folder.

Try This: Do the following steps

1. Create a new Appointment.
2. Name the appointment Test.
3. Set the start time as 10 minutes from your current time.
4. Set the reminder to go off 5 minutes before the Appointment.
5. Create a new Meeting.
6. Invite one or more attendees.
7. Set the Meeting as Out of Office.
8. Arrange the calendar as Work Week.
9. When the Reminder goes off, use the Dismiss option.
10. Cancel the Appointment.

Test Yourself

1. Which of the following are fields for creating an Appointment?
(Give all correct answers.)
A. Subject
B. Location
C. Start Time
D. End Time
Tip: Complete Guide to Outlook, page 189

2. Outlook does not allow custom times, say 8:20am, to be used in Appointments.
A. True
B. False
Tip: Complete Guide to Outlook, page 189

3. How does the calendar date navigator indicate dates with an appointment?
A. Date is in red font
B. Date is in bold font
C. Date blinks
D. Date has no special formatting
Tip: Complete Guide to Outlook, page 191

4. Which of the following are true about Events. (Give all correct answers.)
A. An Event is an all day occurrence, without a start or end time
B. Events can be recurring
Tip: Complete Guide to Outlook, page 197

5. Which of the following is true about repeating an Appointment? (Give all correct answers.)
A. An appointment can be copied and pasted using the keyboard commands Ctrl+C and Ctrl+V
B. An appointment cannot be copied and pasted
C. An appointment can be copied and pasted using the commands on the Home Ribbon
D. An appointment can be set as a recurring appointment
Tip: Complete Guide to Outlook, page 194

6. Which of the following are true about Meeting attendees? (Give all correct answers.)
A. When attendees are added to a meeting, Outlook will e-mail an appointment to the attendees
B. A meeting request e-mail has buttons for attendees to automate responses, such as accept or decline
C. Attendee responses are tracked in both e-mail and the meeting Appointment
Tip: Complete Guide to Outlook, page 200-202

7. Which of the following are Attendee Options in Meeting Tracking? (Give all correct answers.)
A. Required Attendee
B. Tentative Attendee
C. Optional Attendee
D. Resource (Room or Equipment)
E. Other Attendee
Tip: Complete Guide to Outlook, page 204

8. A Meeting can only be forwarded to individuals, not to a Contact Group.
A. True
B. False
Tip: Complete Guide to Outlook, page 209

Application Question: You are scheduling a mandatory training session for several employees. What Appointment and/ or Meeting options would you use?

Tasks and Time Management

Microsoft Outlook Objectives
In this lesson, you will learn how to:

1. Create Tasks to document date, time, location and details for assignments

2. Manage Task Details

3. Assign a Task to another Outlook User

4. Accept or decline a Task assignment

5. Update a Task and send a Status Report

6. Mark a Task complete and move it to a folder

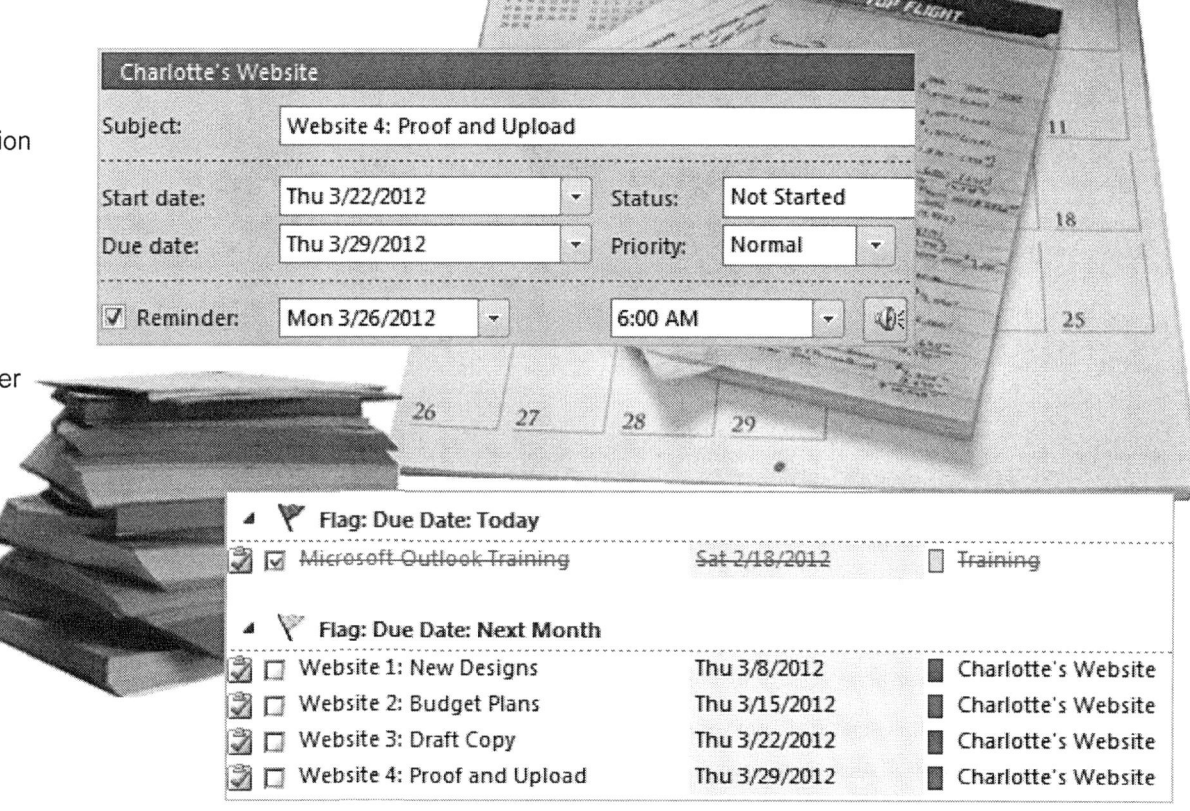

Lesson 8 : Tasks and Time Management

1. Readings

Read Lesson 8 in the Microsoft Outlook guide, page 217-248.

Project

Four Tasks that are tagged for follow up.

Downloads

There are no downloads for this lesson.

2. Practice

Complete the Practice Activity on page 249.

3. Assessment

Review the Test questions on page 250.

Tasks Home Ribbon

Tasks Ribbon

Menu Maps

From the **Tasks Home Ribbon**.
1. Home ->New-> New Task, page 222
2. Home ->Follow Up, page 228
3. Home ->Manage Task->Mark Complete, page 229

More Ribbons (Not Shown)
1. Home ->New-> New Note, page 242
2. Home ->New-> Journal Entry, page 246

More Menu Maps

From the **Tasks Ribbon**.
1. Task->Show->Details, page 224
2. Task->Tags->Follow Up, page 225
3. Task->Tags->Categories, page 226
4. Tasks ->Manage Tasks->Assign a Task, page 233
5. Tasks ->Manage Tasks->Send Status Report, page 235
6. Tasks ->Actions->Move, page 240 (not shown)

Tasks and Time Management

Your work may be part of a larger project that involves other people. Microsoft Outlook uses **Tasks** to document the assignments. Each Task can be tagged for follow up and updates so that everyone on the team can work together to complete the project on time.

Start -> All Programs ->Microsoft Office-> Microsoft Office Outlook 2010

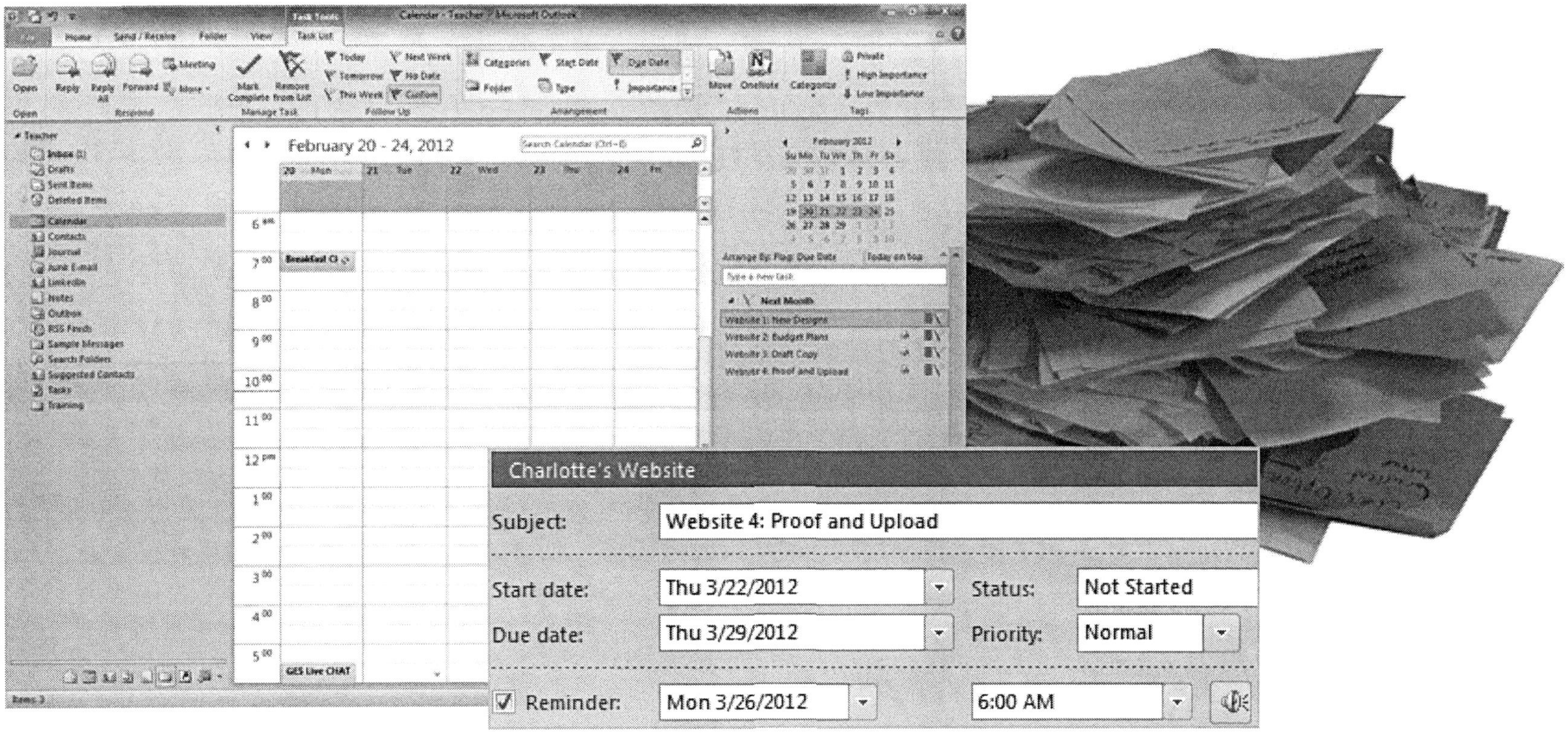

Take Two

View ->Layout->Navigation Pane->Normal

Before You Begin

When you open Microsoft Outlook, you will probably see the Inbox since that is the default for the initial view. The Tasks can be found by using the Navigation Pane, as we did with the Calendar.

Before You Begin: View the Folders
Go to **View->Layout**.
Click on **Navigation Pane**.
Select: **Normal**.

1. Try it: Find the Task Folder
Go to the **Navigation Pane**.
Select the **Tasks Folder**.

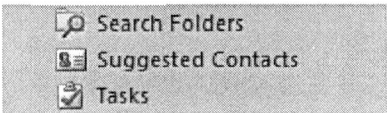

Keep going...

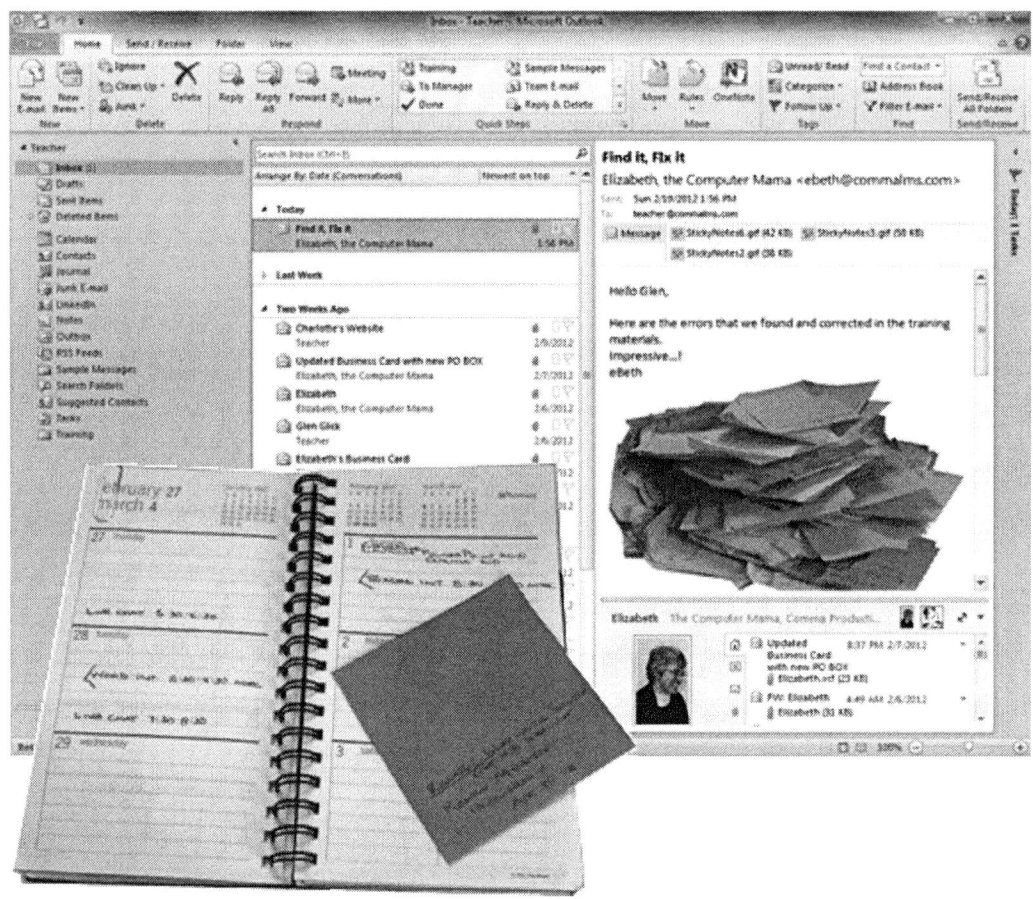

Hello, Tasks

2. Try it: Review the Tasks

This screen shot on this page shows a Task List with many Tasks. The Task includes:
Subject
Status
Due Date
% Complete

You can edit the Status if you wish:
Not Started, In Progress, Completed, Waiting on someone else and Deferred.

The **Home** Ribbon has these Groups:
New
Delete
Respond
Manage Tasks
Follow Up
Current View
Actions
Tags
Find

Keep going...

Microsoft Outlook ->Tasks

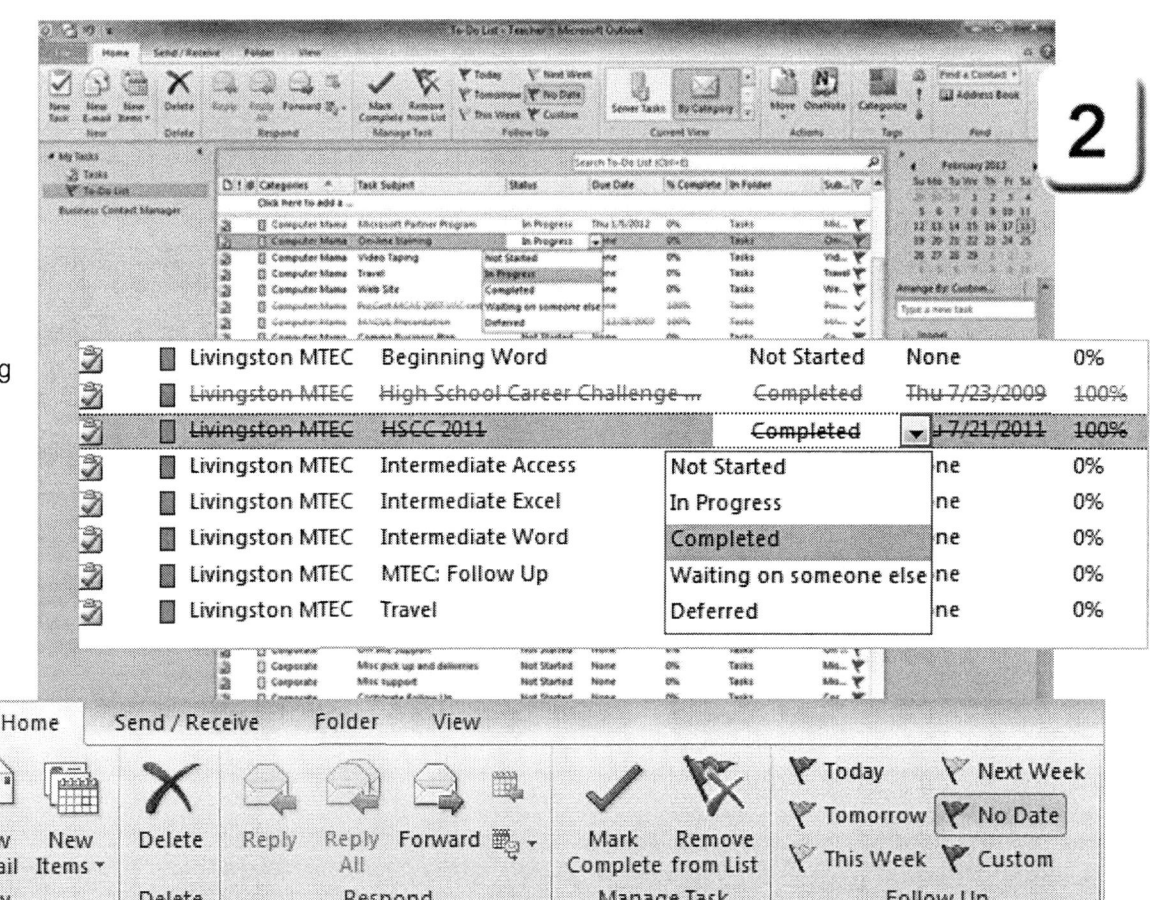

Exam 77-884: Microsoft Outlook 2010
6. Working with Tasks, Notes, and Journal Entries
6.1. Create and manipulate tasks: Use Current View

Create a New Task
A Task is an appointment or meeting that you do again and again. A Task can be Tracked and Assigned to someone else. This first example creates a simple Task as we review the options.

3. Try it: Create a New Task
Go to **Home ->New.**
Click on **New Task.**

What Do You See? A new Task will open. This Task has four Ribbons: Task, Insert, Format Text, Review.

We will look at the tools available on the Task Ribbon to manage, categorize, and follow up the Tasks.

Keep going...

Home ->New-> New Task

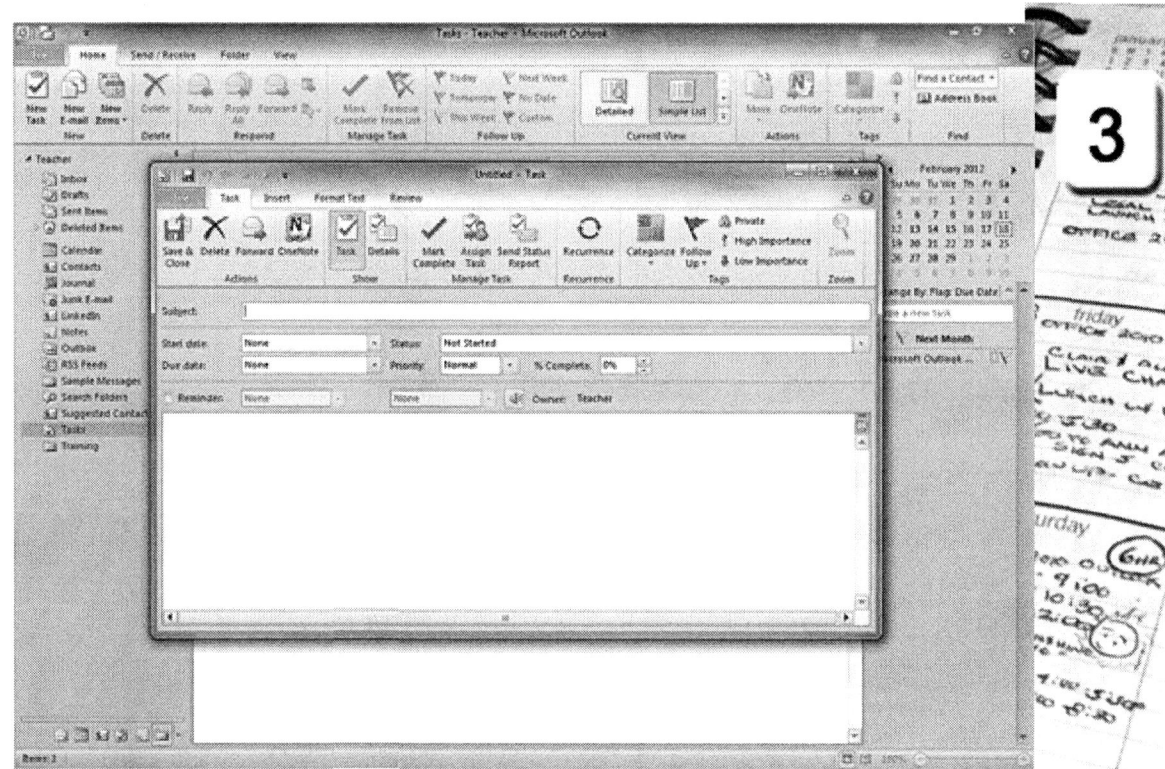

Exam 77-884: Microsoft Outlook 2010
6. Working with Tasks, Notes, and Journal Entries
6.1. Create and manipulate tasks: Create a Task

Edit the New Task

4. Try it: Edit the New Task
Enter the **Subject**: Microsoft Outlook Training

Enter the **Start Date**: Today
Enter the **Due Date**: Pick the first day of next month with the Date Picker.

Select the **Status**: In Progress
Edit the **% Complete**: 25%

Select the **Reminder**. By default, Outlook will enter the Due Date. You can change the Time from 6:00 AM to 9:00 AM if you wish.

Keep going...

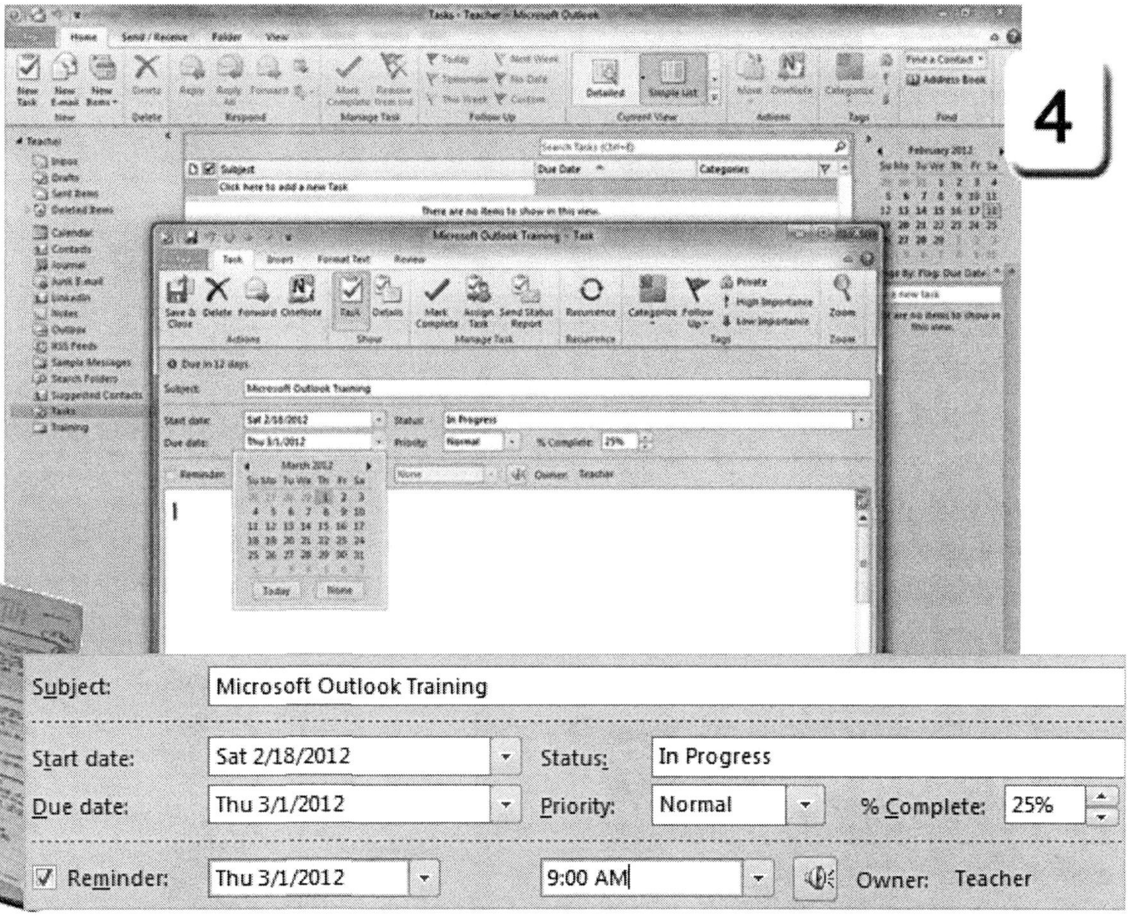

Subject:	Microsoft Outlook Training			
Start date:	Sat 2/18/2012	Status:	In Progress	
Due date:	Thu 3/1/2012	Priority:	Normal	% Complete: 25%
☑ Reminder:	Thu 3/1/2012	9:00 AM	Owner: Teacher	

Exam 77-884: Microsoft Outlook 2010
6. Working with Tasks, Notes, and Journal Entries
6.1. Create and manipulate tasks: Create a Task

Edit the Task Details

A Task may include travel, mileage and the work (in hours or days). You can use the **Task Details** to document this information.

The **Total work** shows the hours that this Task should take to complete. The **Actual work** is how many hours it really took. In this example, the Actual work is still zero because this Task hasn't started yet. The **Mileage** and **Billing** fields are useful for tracking your travel costs.

Before You Begin: Find the Details
Go to **Task->Show->Details**.

5. Try it: Edit the Task Details
Date completed: none
Total work: 1 day
Actual Work: 0 hours
Mileage: 15 Miles
Billing Information: Training Grant
Company: Charlotte's Website

Try This, Too: Return to the Task View
Go to **Task->Show->Task.** Keep going...

Task->Show->Details

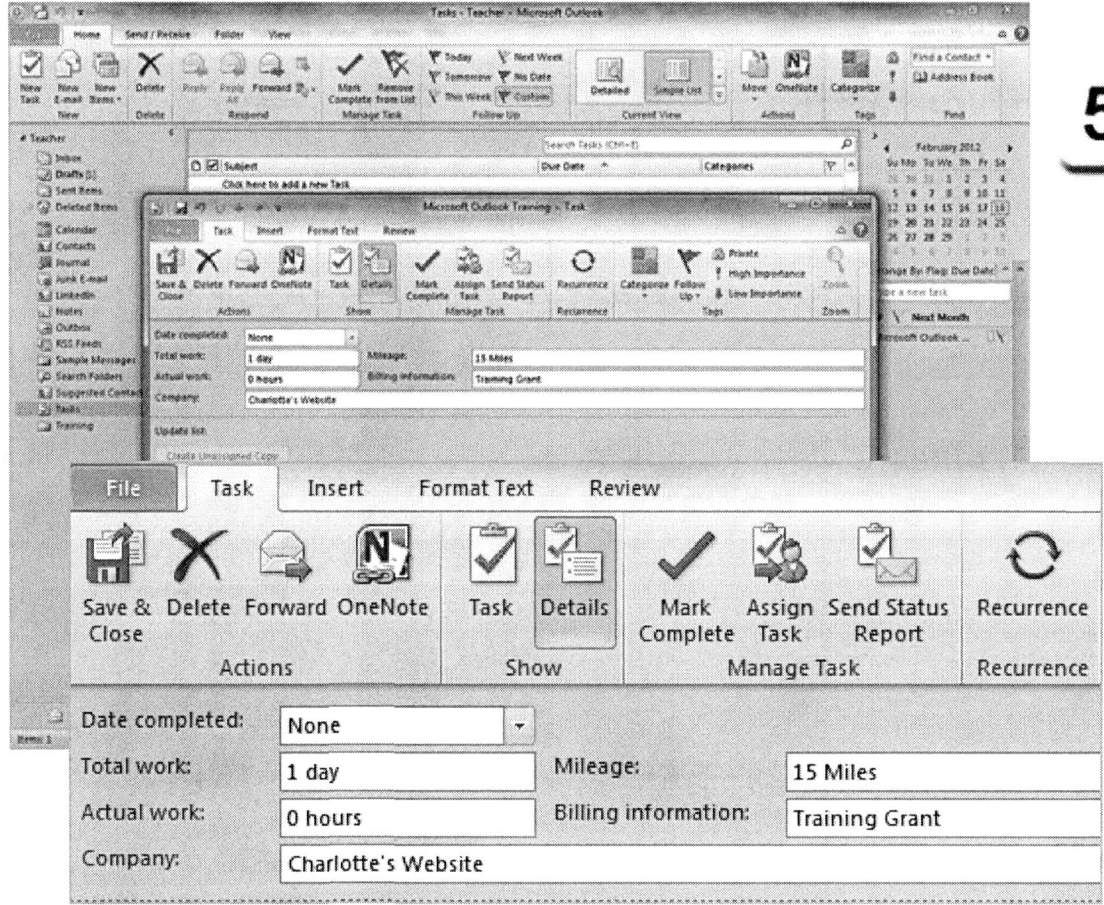

Exam 77-884: Microsoft Outlook 2010
6. Working with Tasks, Notes, and Journal Entries
6.1. Create and manipulate tasks: Edit the Contact Details

Tag the Task for Follow Up

The purpose of using Tasks is to manage your time and commitments. Tasks, like Messages and Meetings, can be programmed to get your attention...so that you remember to complete your work on time.

6. Try it: Set the Task Options
The Task is still open.
Go to **Task->Tags->Follow Up**
Select: Today

What Do You See? You can select a flag from the list: Today, Tomorrow, or Next Week. You can also select No Date.

What Else Do You See? You can tag this Task as **Private** and set the **Importance** as High or Low.

Keep going...

Task->Tags->Follow Up

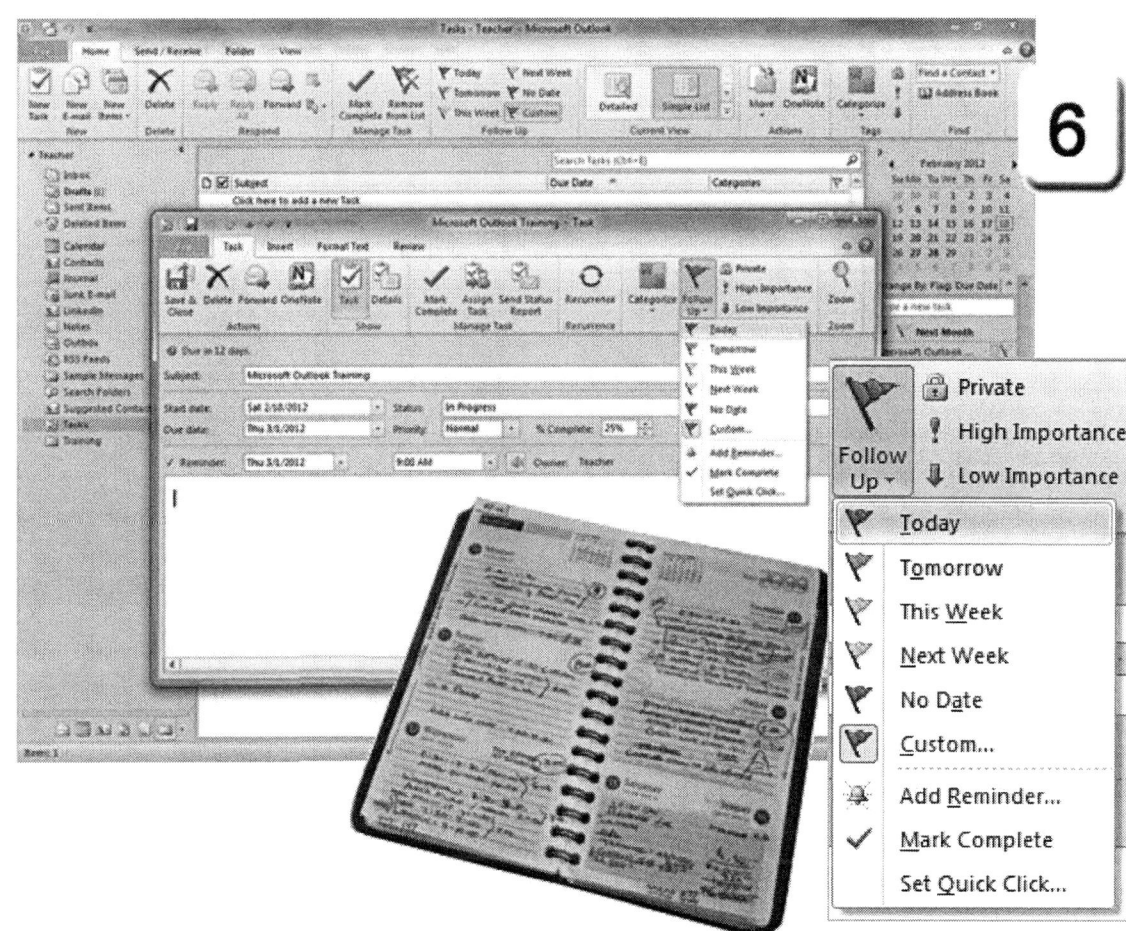

Exam 77-884: Microsoft Outlook 2010
6. Working with Tasks, Notes, and Journal Entries
6.1. Create and manipulate tasks: Set the Task Options

Use Categories

Categories organize Microsoft Outlook items by name and color. This lesson applies Categories to the Tasks, but you can tag Messages, Meetings and Contacts with Categories as well.

7. Try it: Review the Categories
Go to **Task->Tags->Categories**.

What Do You See? The default Categories are primary colors: Red, Blue, Green, Orange, etc. You can create your own Categories that might be more meaningful.

Follow me, please...

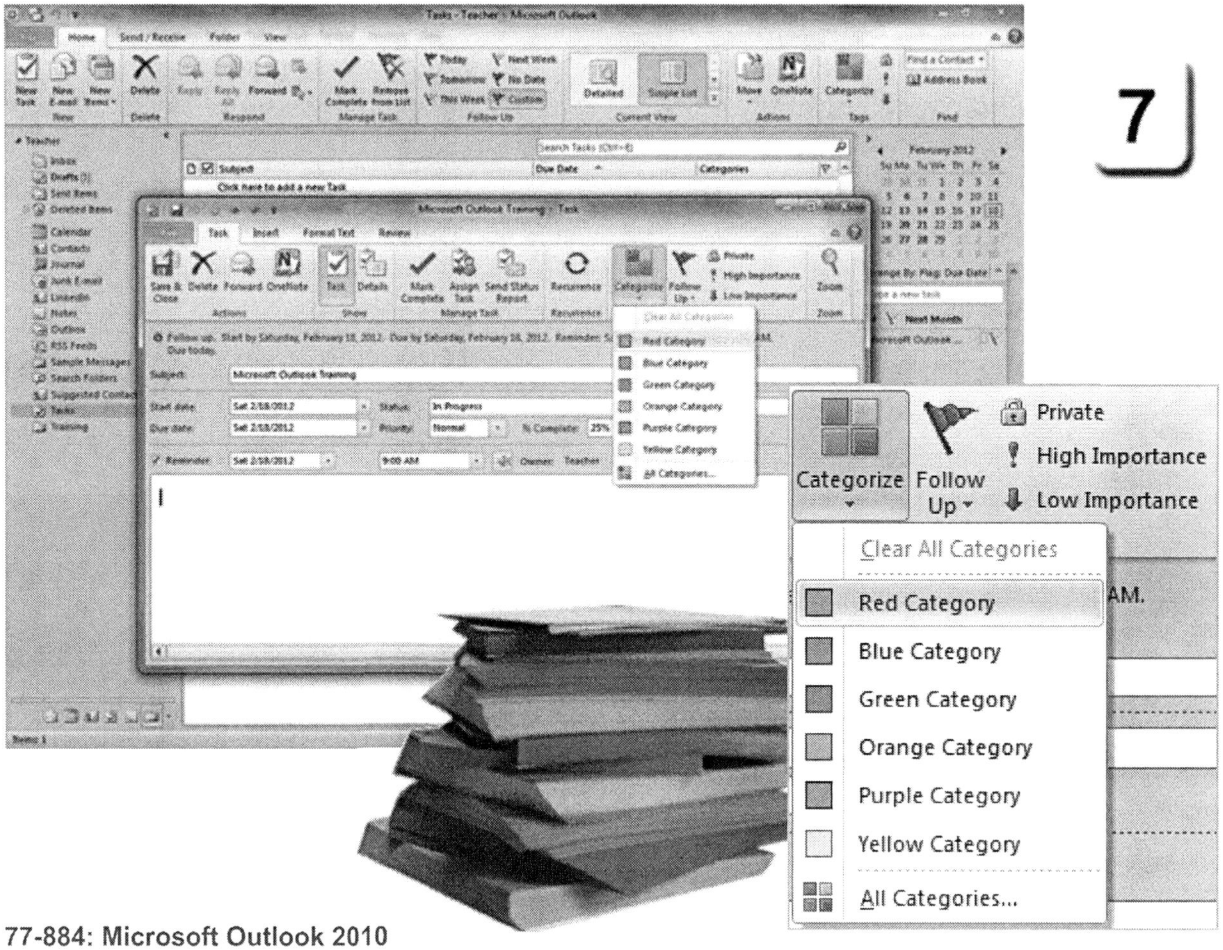

Exam 77-884: Microsoft Outlook 2010
1. Managing the Outlook Environment1.
2. Manipulate item tags: Categorize Items

Custom Categories

8. Try it: Create Your Own Category
Go to **Task->Tags->Categories**.
Select: **All Categories**.

What Do You See? The default Categories (Blue, Green, etc) are listed. You can Rename a Category if you wish.

Try This, Too: Create Two New Categories
Click **New**...
Enter the Name: Training
Select a Color: Peach.
Click **OK**.

Click **New**...
Enter the Name: Charlotte's Website
Select a Color: Dark Green.
Click **OK**.

Look Again: Both of the new Categories have a check mark. Please unselect Charlotte's Website. This Outlook Training Task will be tagged with the Training Category, only.

Click **OK**. Then **Save & Close**. Keep going...

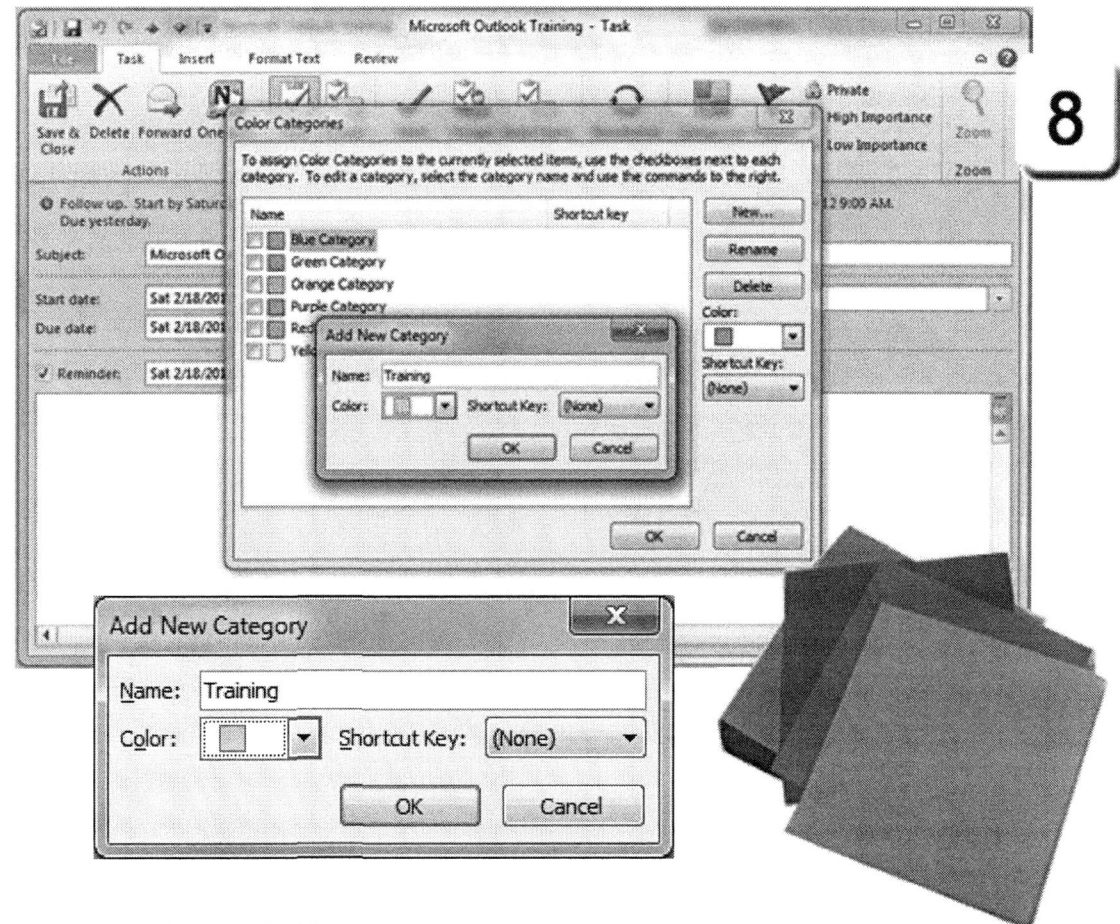

Exam 77-884: Microsoft Outlook 2010
1. Managing the Outlook Environment1.
2. Manipulate item tags: Categorize Items

Use the Clues

What Do You See? The Task list shows the Subject, Categories and Due Date. There is also a column for Follow Up. This training Task has two tags: a Follow Up Reminder and a Category.

What Else Do You See? The Date Navigator on the right side of the Calendar also shows the Tasks. By default, they are sorted by Due Date.

What Are the Clues? The Microsoft Outlook Training is red, indicating that it is overdue. The **Reminder Window** may also chime in. The purpose of these little hints is to help you remember what comes next: managing promises and tracking commitments. Keep going...

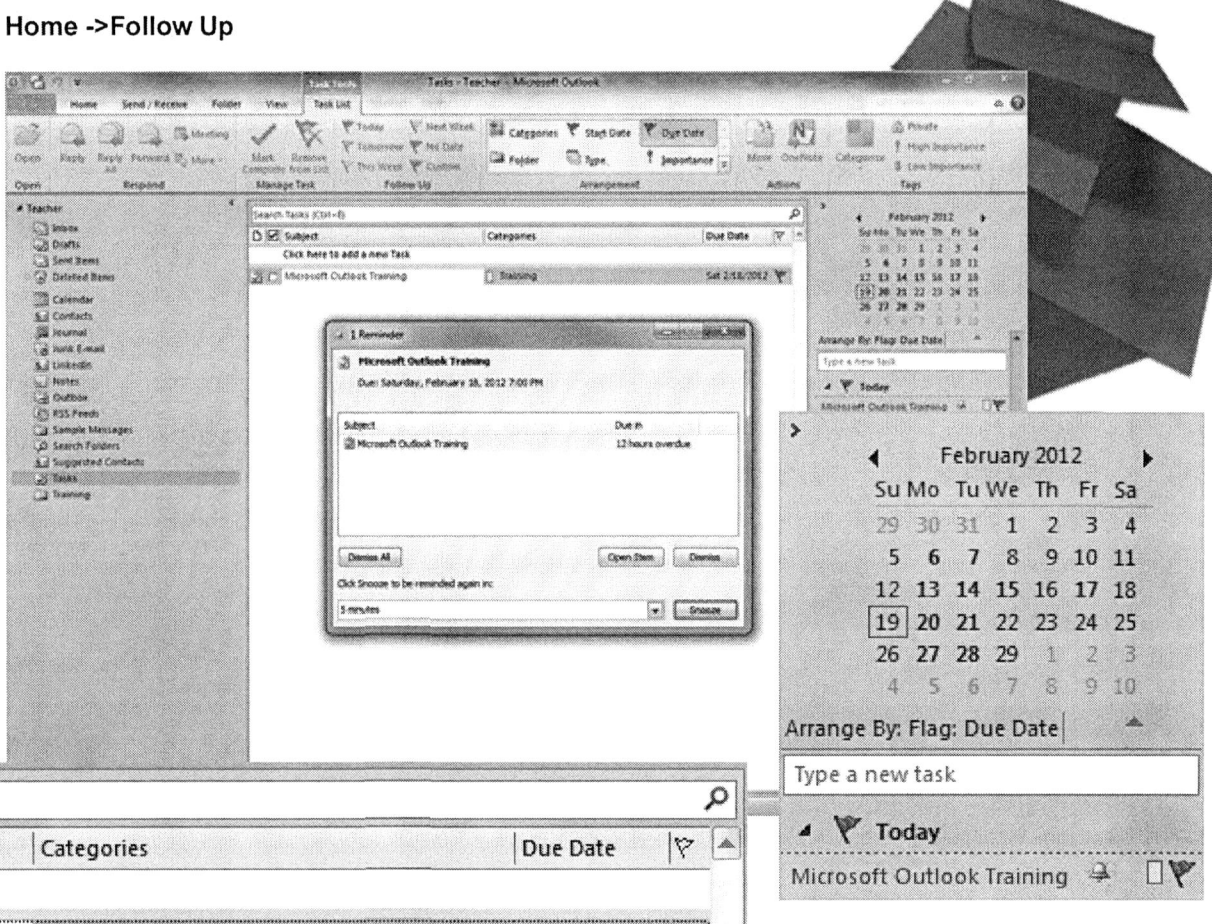

◄			February 2012			►
Su	Mo	Tu We	Th	Fr	Sa
29	30	31	1	2	3	4
5	6	7	8	9	10	11
12	13	14	15	16	17	18
19	20	21	22	23	24	25
26	27	28	29	1	2	3
4	5	6	7	8	9	10

Arrange By: Flag: Due Date

Type a new task

◢ ▼ Today

Microsoft Outlook Training

Search Tasks (Ctrl+E)

🗋	✔	Subject	Categories	Due Date	▼
		Click here to add a new Task			
✔	🗌	Microsoft Outlook Training	🗌 Training	Sat 2/18/2012	▼

Exam 77-884: Microsoft Outlook 2010
1. Managing the Outlook Environment
1.3. Arrange the Content Pane: Use the Reminders Window

Mark a Task Complete

When you mark a Task **Complete**, the Status and progress (% Complete) will be updated. When you look in the Task List, the Task will be crossed out.

9. Try it: Mark a Task Complete
Go to **Home ->Manage Task**.
Click on **Mark Complete.**

What Do You See? After you mark a Task complete, you can also select it and **Remove From List**.

Keep going...!

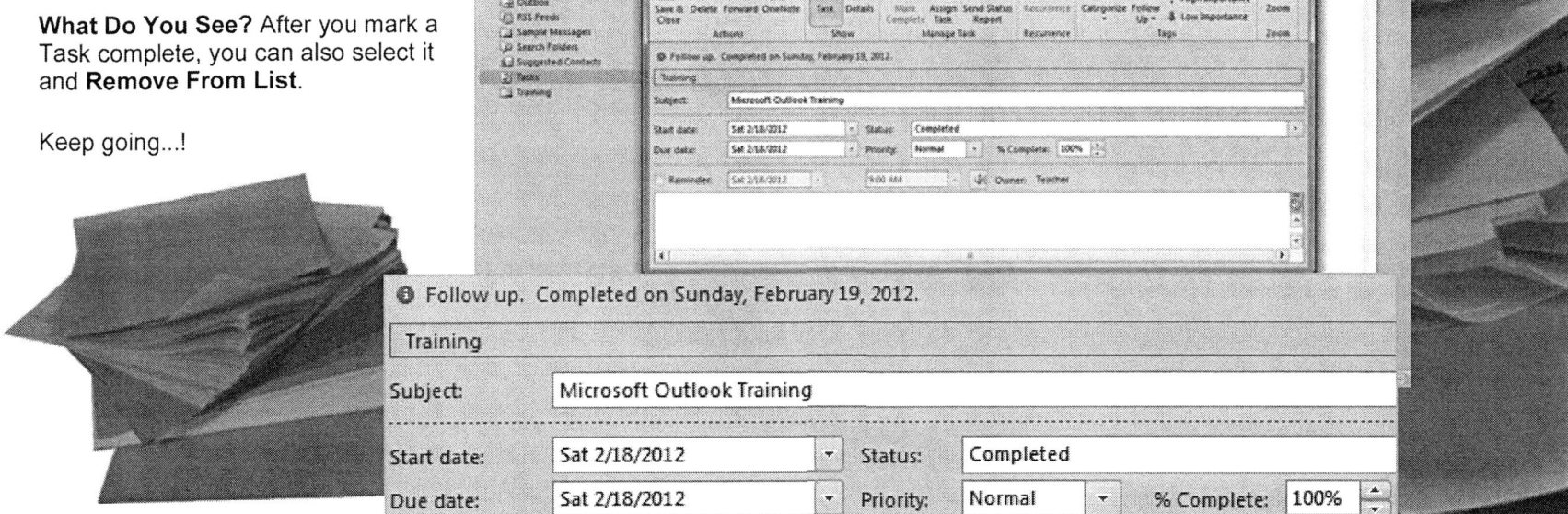

❶ Follow up. Completed on Sunday, February 19, 2012.

Training					
Subject:	Microsoft Outlook Training				
Start date:	Sat 2/18/2012	▼	Status:	Completed	
Due date:	Sat 2/18/2012	▼	Priority:	Normal ▼	% Complete: 100% ⬍

Exam 77-884: Microsoft Outlook 2010
6. Working with Tasks, Notes, and Journal Entries
6.1. Create and manipulate tasks: Mark a Task Complete

Assigning Tasks

Microsoft Outlook has several robust tools for collaborating. We will create four new Tasks that are steps in a bigger project. The Tasks will be tagged with a Category as well as dates for follow up. The dates in these lessons happen to be the first of March. Each Task begins one week (7 days) after the previous Task.

These Tasks will be assigned and tracked.
This example works best if you have a partner who also uses Microsoft Outlook so that you can send and receive the assignments.

1. Try it: Add a New Task
Go to **Home ->New->New Task**.
Enter the Subject: Website 1: New Designs
Enter the Start date: Thu 3/1/2012
Enter the Due date: Thu 3/8/2012
Check the Reminder: Mon 3/5/2012
Go to **Task->Tags-> Category**.
Select a Category: Charlotte's Website
Go to **Task->Actions->Save & Close**.

That was one. We need some more...

Home ->New->New Task

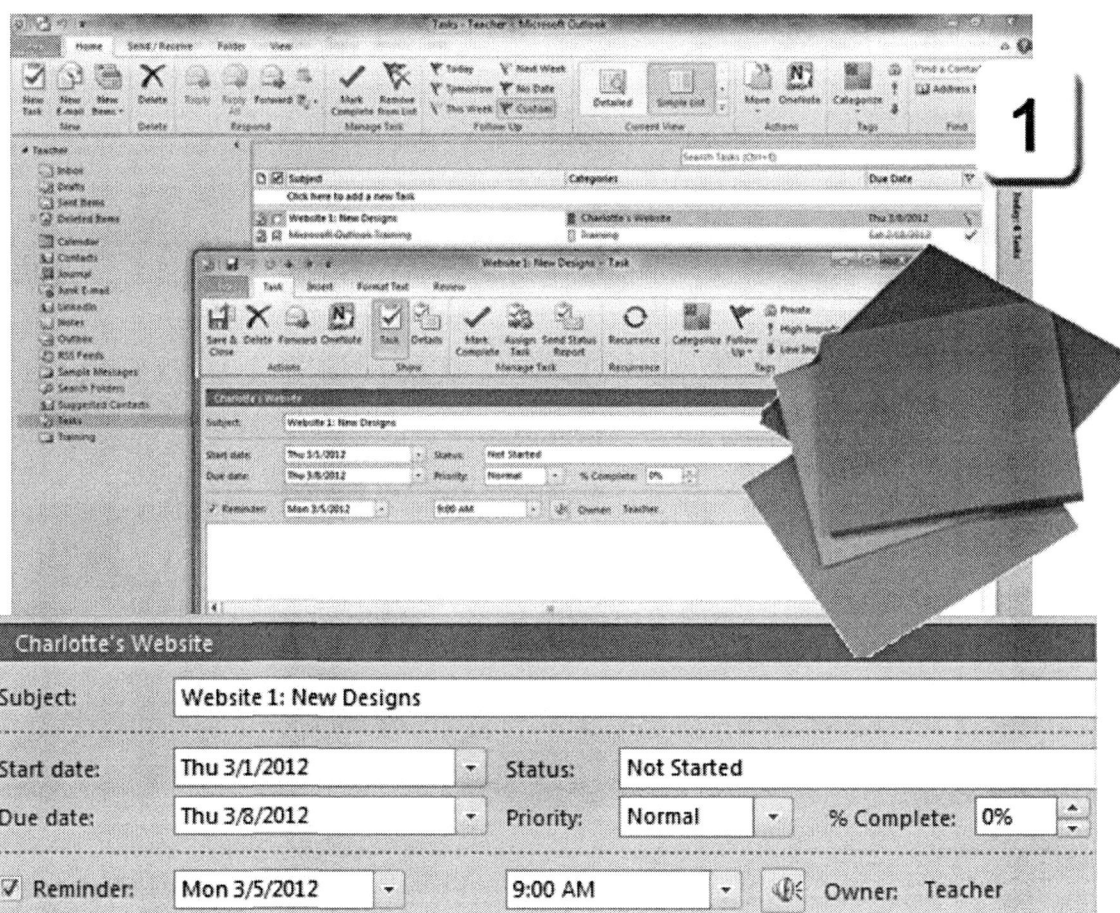

Charlotte's Website				
Subject:	Website 1: New Designs			
Start date:	Thu 3/1/2012	Status:	Not Started	
Due date:	Thu 3/8/2012	Priority:	Normal	% Complete: 0%
✓ Reminder:	Mon 3/5/2012	9:00 AM	Owner: Teacher	

Exam 77-884: Microsoft Outlook 2010
6. Working with Tasks, Notes, and Journal Entries
6.1. Create and manipulate tasks: Create a Task

Add Some More Tasks

2. Try it: Add More New Tasks
Go to Home ->New->New Task.
Enter the Subject: Website 2: Budget Plans
Enter the Start date: Thu 3/8/2012
Enter the Due date: Thu 3/15/2012
Check the Reminder: Mon 3/12/2012
Select a Category: Charlotte's Website.
Go to **Task->Actions->Save & Close.**

Go to Home ->New->New Task.
Enter the Subject: Website 3: Draft Copy
Enter the Start date: Thu 3/15/2012
Enter the Due date: Thu 3/22/2012
Check the Reminder: Mon 3/19/2012
Select a Category: Charlotte's Website.
Go to **Task->Actions->Save & Close.**

Go to Home ->New->New Task.
Enter the Subject: Website 4: Proof and Upload
Enter the Start date: Thu 3/22/2012
Enter the Due date: Thu 329/2012
Check the Reminder: Mon 3/26/2012
Select a Category: Charlotte's Website.
Go to **Task->Actions->Save & Close.**

Home ->New->New Task

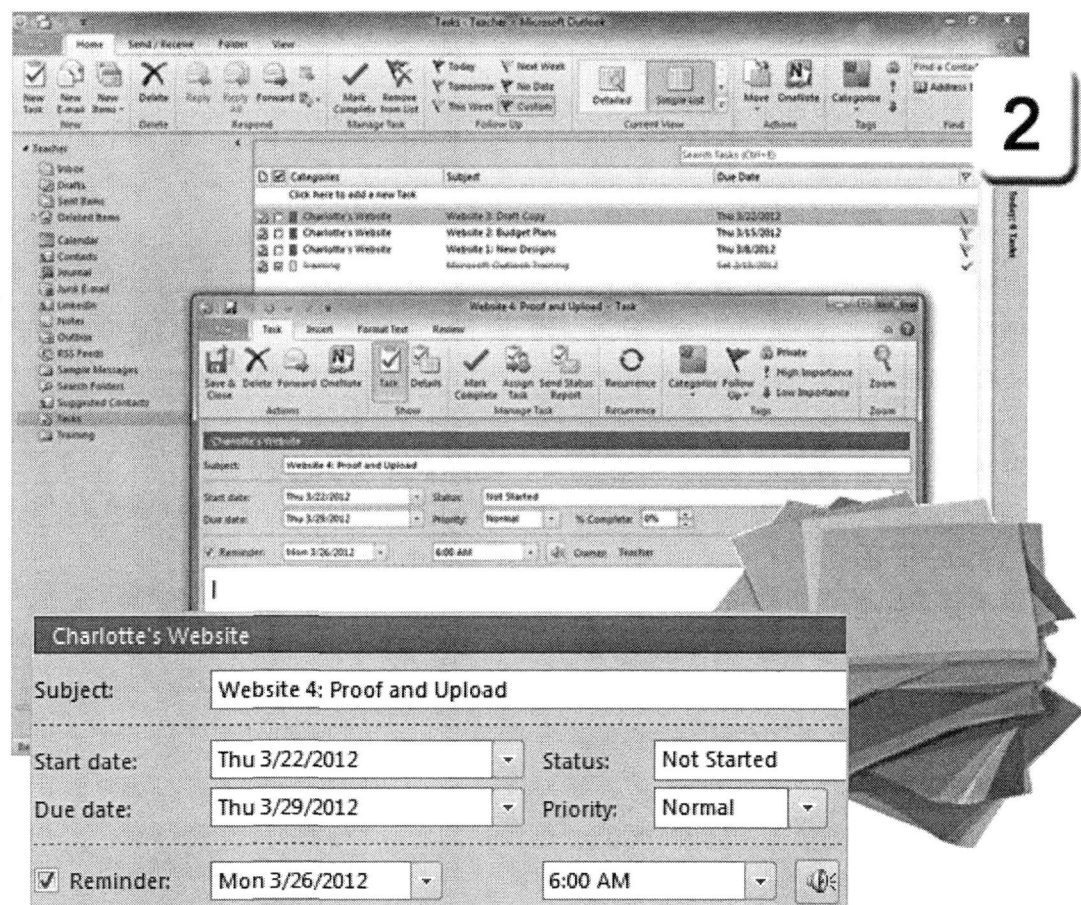

Exam 77-884: Microsoft Outlook 2010
6. Working with Tasks, Notes, and Journal Entries
6.1. Create and manipulate tasks: Create a Task

Take Two

Review the Task List
3. Try it: Group by Category
Go to **View ->Arrangement.**
Select: **Due Date.**

Go to **View ->Arrangement.**
Select: **Show in Groups.**

What Do You See? Now, the Task List is organized by Category and sorted by the Due Date. So far, so good.

Who has time to do all of these tasks? Keep going...

View ->Arrangement->Due Date

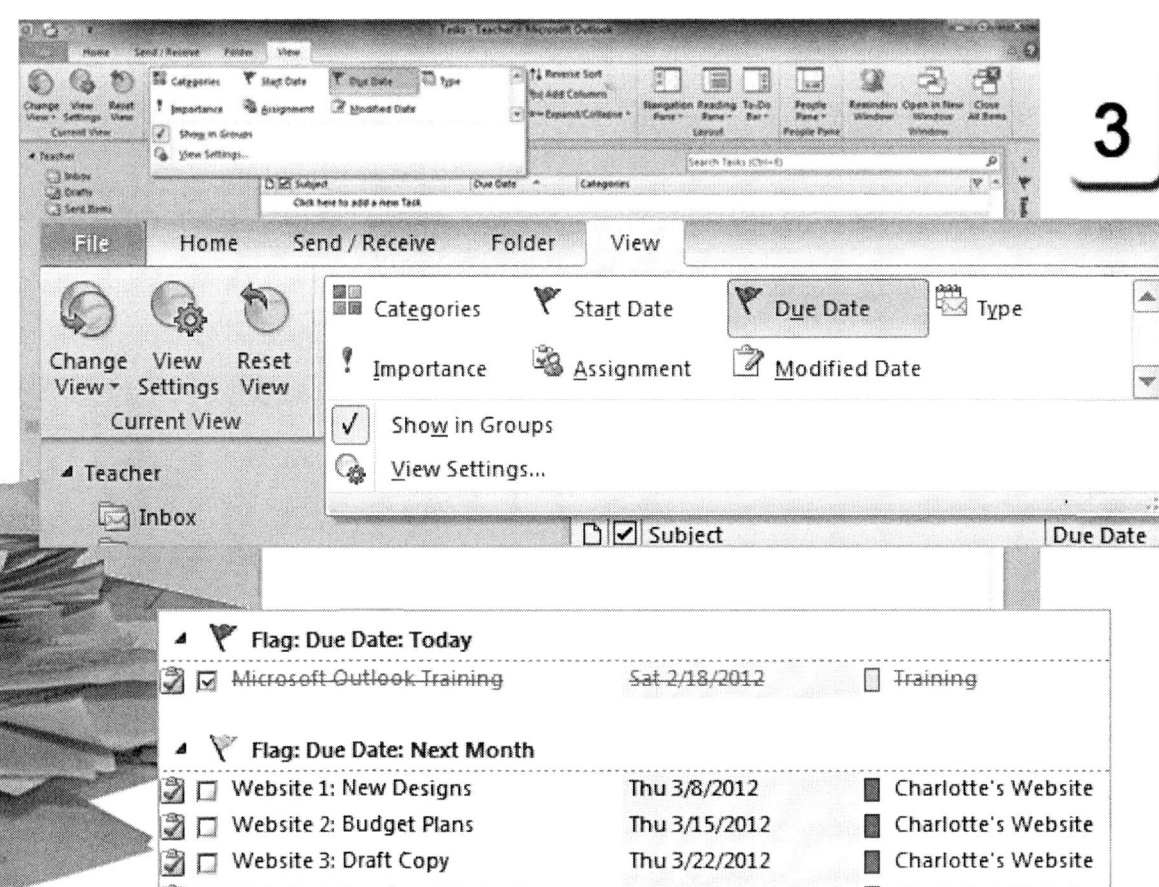

3

Exam 77-884: Microsoft Outlook 2010
6. Working with Tasks, Notes, and Journal Entries
6.1. Create and manipulate tasks

Assign a Task

A big project may have many, many process steps. If you work with a good team, you can **Assign** a Task to the best one(s) who can complete the assignment.

4. Try it: Assign a Task
Open a Task: Website 1: New Designs.
Go to **Tasks ->Manage Tasks.**
Click on **Assign a Task.**

What Do You See? The E-Mail field is available. You can assign a Task to a person or a Contact Group if you wish.

Try This ,Too: Send the Task Request
Enter a **E-Mail** from your Contact.
Click **Send**. The Task Request will be sent to the Contact. Keep going...

Memo to Self: The Task List keeps an updated copy of the Task in your Task List and sends a status report automatically when the Task is marked complete.

Assign a Task: The Sender's Task List

Tasks ->Manage Tasks->Assign a Task

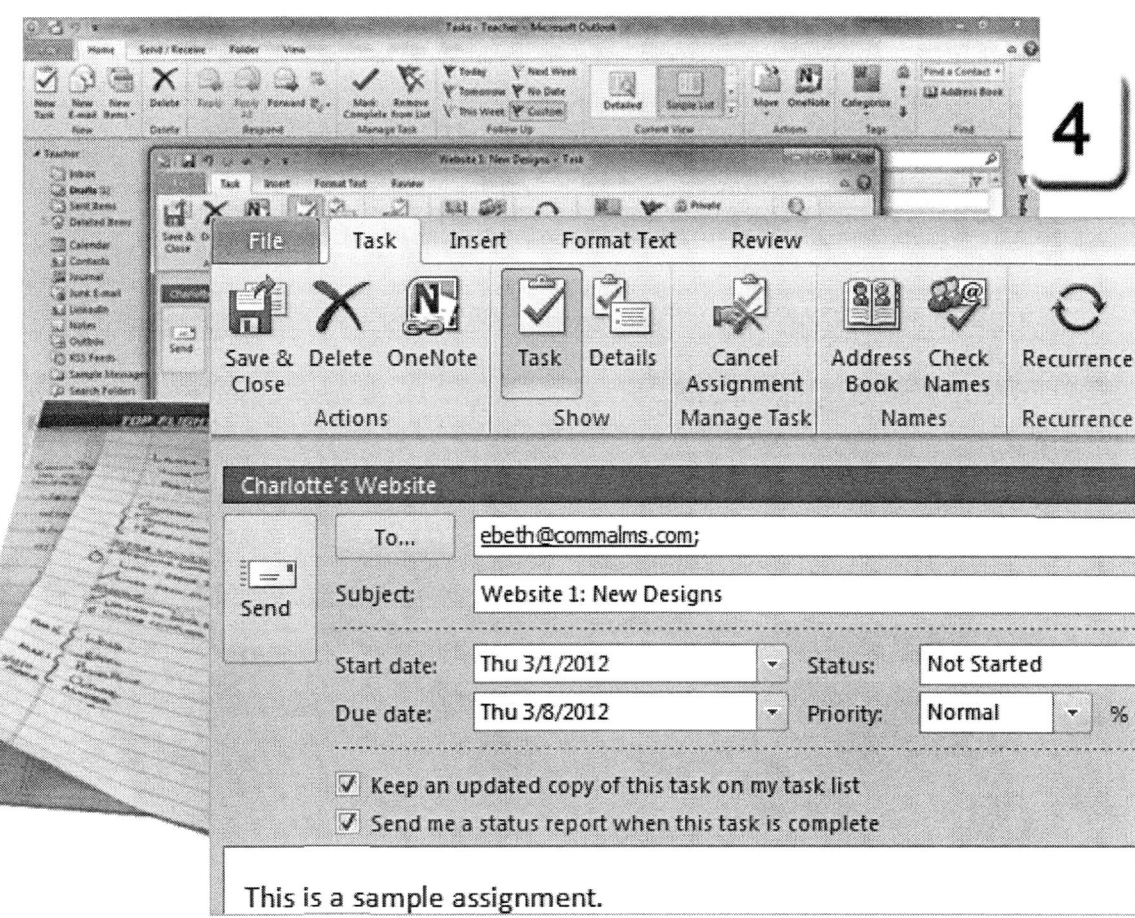

Exam 77-884: Microsoft Outlook 2010
6. Working with Tasks, Notes, and Journal Entries
6.1. Create and manipulate tasks: Assign a Task

Microsoft Outlook 2010   Page 233 of 366

Take Two

Accept a Task Assignment

The Task Request has been sent and it arrives in the Recipient's Inbox. The E-mail prompts her to to Accept or Decline. Here are the steps she needs to take.

5. Try it: Accept a Task Assignment
Click on **Accept**.
Click **OK** to Send the response now.

What Happens Next? The Task Request will be moved to the Deleted Items folder and a new Task will be added to the Recipient's Task List.

Keep going...

Accept a Task: The Recipient's Inbox

Microsoft Outlook ->Inbox

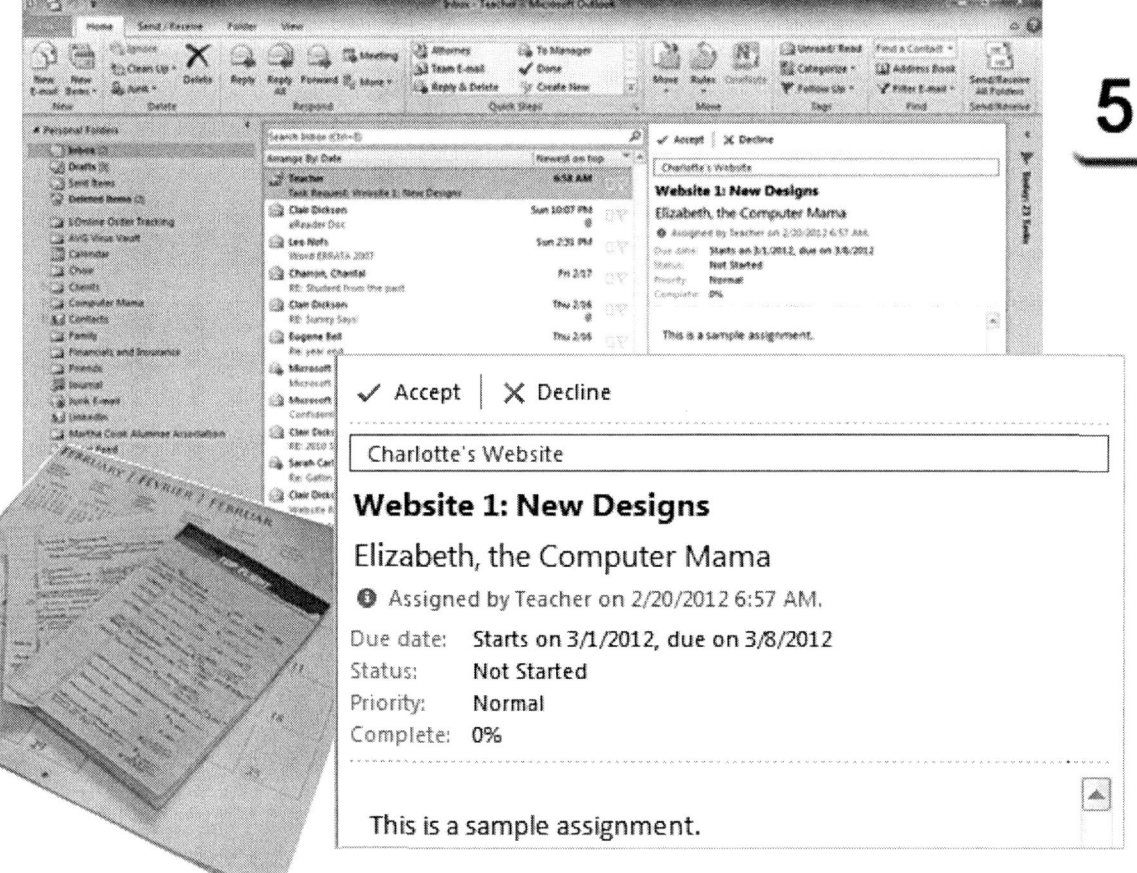

✓ Accept | ✕ Decline

Charlotte's Website

Website 1: New Designs
Elizabeth, the Computer Mama

ⓘ Assigned by Teacher on 2/20/2012 6:57 AM.

Due date: Starts on 3/1/2012, due on 3/8/2012
Status: Not Started
Priority: Normal
Complete: 0%

This is a sample assignment.

Exam 77-884: Microsoft Outlook 2010
6. Working with Tasks, Notes, and Journal Entries
6.1. Create and manipulate tasks: Accept or Decline a Task

Update an Assigned Task

Say your colleague worked hard on the Task. Here are the options she can take to update the status and document the progress.

6. Try it: Update an Assigned Task

Open a Task: Website 1: New Designs.
Go to **Tasks ->Manage Tasks**.
Edit the Status: In Progress.
Edit the % Complete: 50%
Edit the message with sample text and a picture if you wish.

Try This, Too: Send a Status Report.
Go to **Tasks ->Manage Tasks.**
Click on: **Send Status Report.**

The Status Report will be E-mailed to the one who assigned this Task.
Keep going, please. There's more...

Update a Task: The Recipient's Inbox

Tasks ->Manage Tasks->Send Status Report

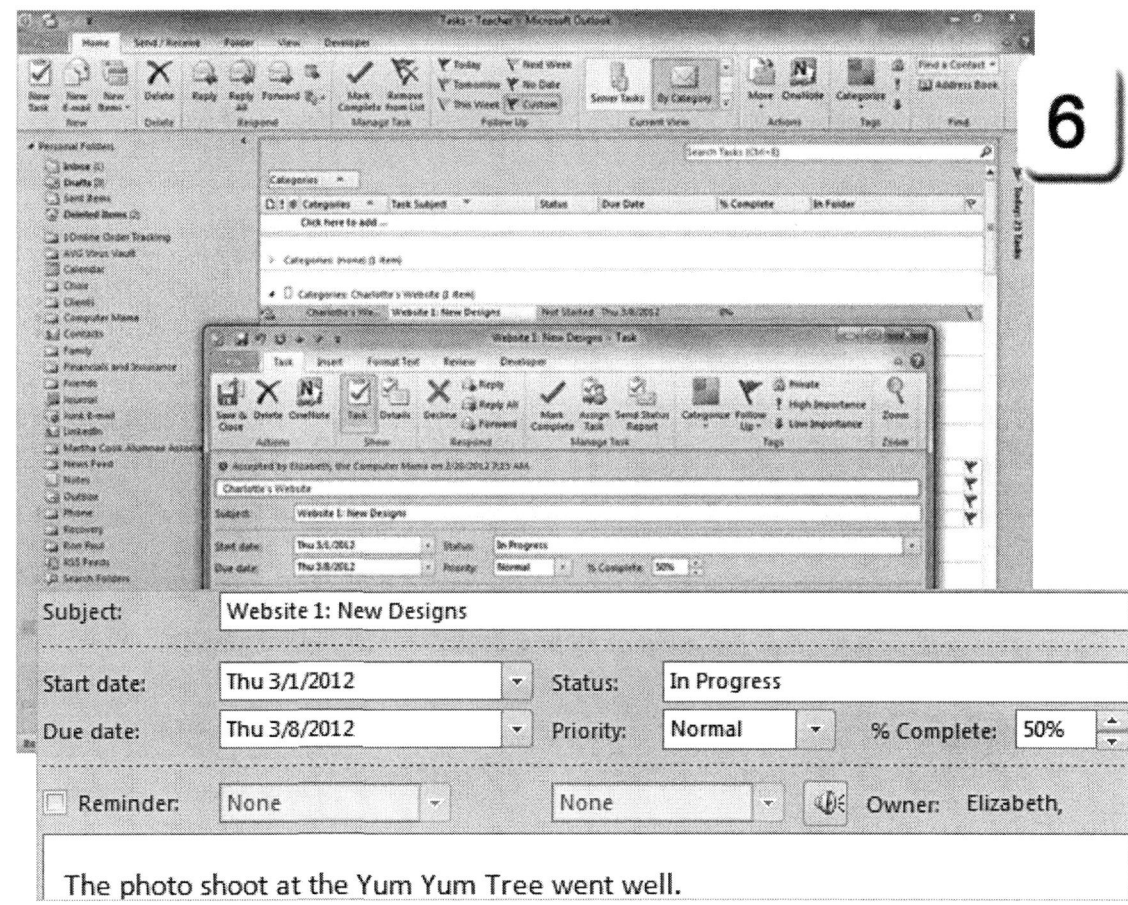

6

Subject:	Website 1: New Designs				
Start date:	Thu 3/1/2012	Status:	In Progress		
Due date:	Thu 3/8/2012	Priority:	Normal	% Complete:	50%
☐ Reminder:	None	None		🔊 Owner:	Elizabeth,

The photo shoot at the Yum Yum Tree went well.

Exam 77-884: Microsoft Outlook 2010
6. Working with Tasks, Notes, and Journal Entries
6.1. Create and manipulate tasks: Update an Assigned Task

Manage the Tasks: The Sender's Inbox

Microsoft Outlook ->Inbox

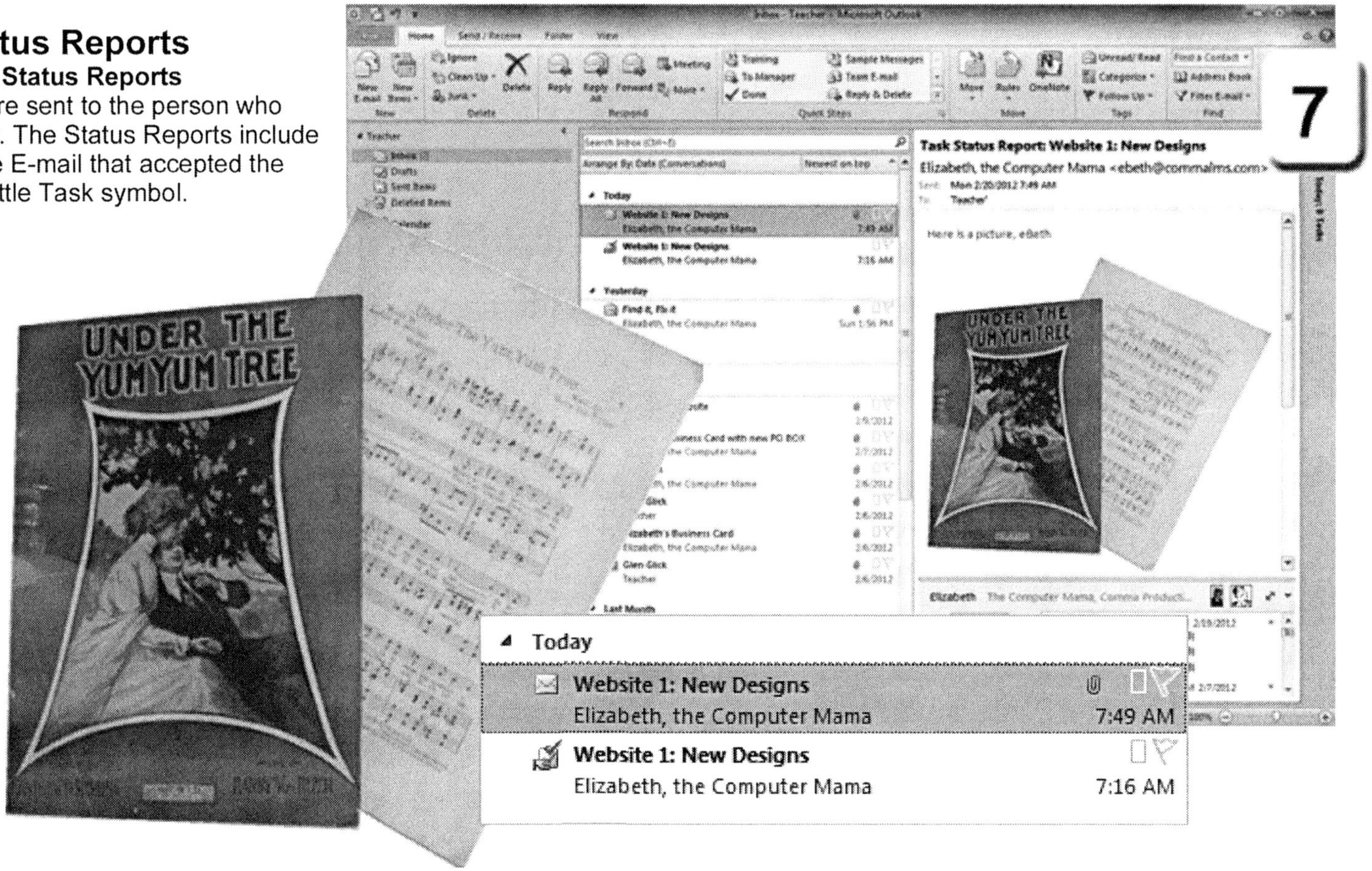

Review the Status Reports

7. Try it: Review the Status Reports

The Status Reports are sent to the person who made the assignment. The Status Reports include the Task Subject. The E-mail that accepted the Website Task has a little Task symbol.

Keep going...

▲ Today

✉	**Website 1: New Designs**	📎		
	Elizabeth, the Computer Mama			7:49 AM
📋	**Website 1: New Designs**			
	Elizabeth, the Computer Mama			7:16 AM

Exam 77-884: Microsoft Outlook 2010
6. Working with Tasks, Notes, and Journal Entries
6.1. Create and manipulate tasks: Update an Assigned Task

Review the Task Updates

Try This, Too: Review the Updates
Go to the **Tasks** folder.
Open the Assigned Task.

What Do You See? The date and time of the last update are shown. In the example on this page, the Status and % Complete were amended. The notes regarding the Photo shoot were added as well.

Keep going...

Manage the Tasks: The Sender's Task List

Tasks ->Show-> Task

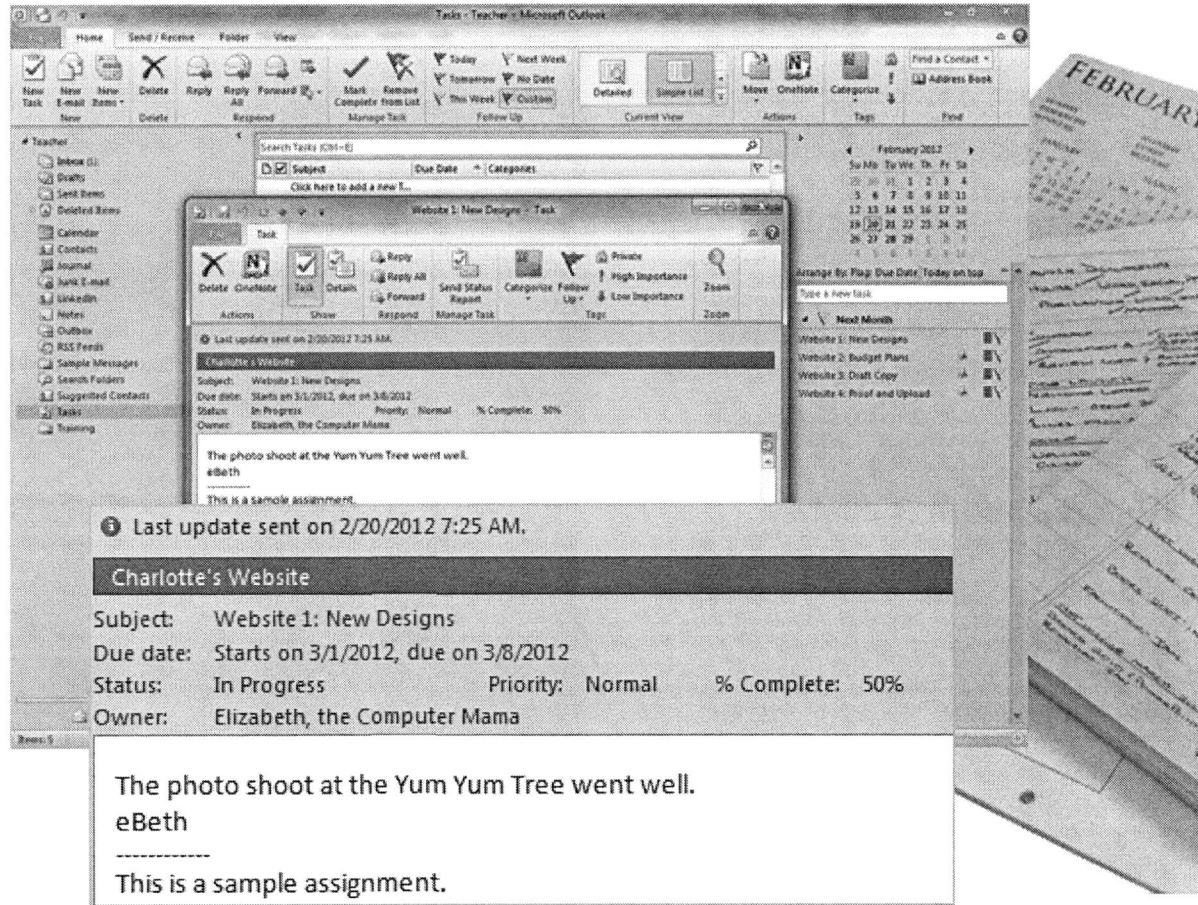

ⓘ Last update sent on 2/20/2012 7:25 AM.

Charlotte's Website

Subject: Website 1: New Designs
Due date: Starts on 3/1/2012, due on 3/8/2012
Status: In Progress   Priority: Normal   % Complete: 50%
Owner: Elizabeth, the Computer Mama

The photo shoot at the Yum Yum Tree went well.
eBeth

This is a sample assignment.

Exam 77-884: Microsoft Outlook 2010
6. Working with Tasks, Notes, and Journal Entries
6.1. Create and manipulate tasks: Update an Assigned Task

Respond to a Task: The Sender's Calendar

Task Tools->Task List-> Respond-> Meeting

Respond to a Task with a Meeting
The Calendar keeps an updated list of Tasks and Meetings. The Tasks are listed under the little calendar on the right side of the screen.

Before You Begin: Find the Task List
Go to the **Calendar.**
Go to **View->Layout-> To-do Bar-> Normal**.

8. Try it: Respond to a Task with a Meeting
Select a Task. The Task Tools should be available.
Go to **Task Tools->Task List-> Respond.**
Click on **Meeting.**

Keep going...

Memo to Self: The Task list includes Tasks that you have assigned as well as ones you have not. The Meeting option is available for the Tasks that have been assigned to someone else.

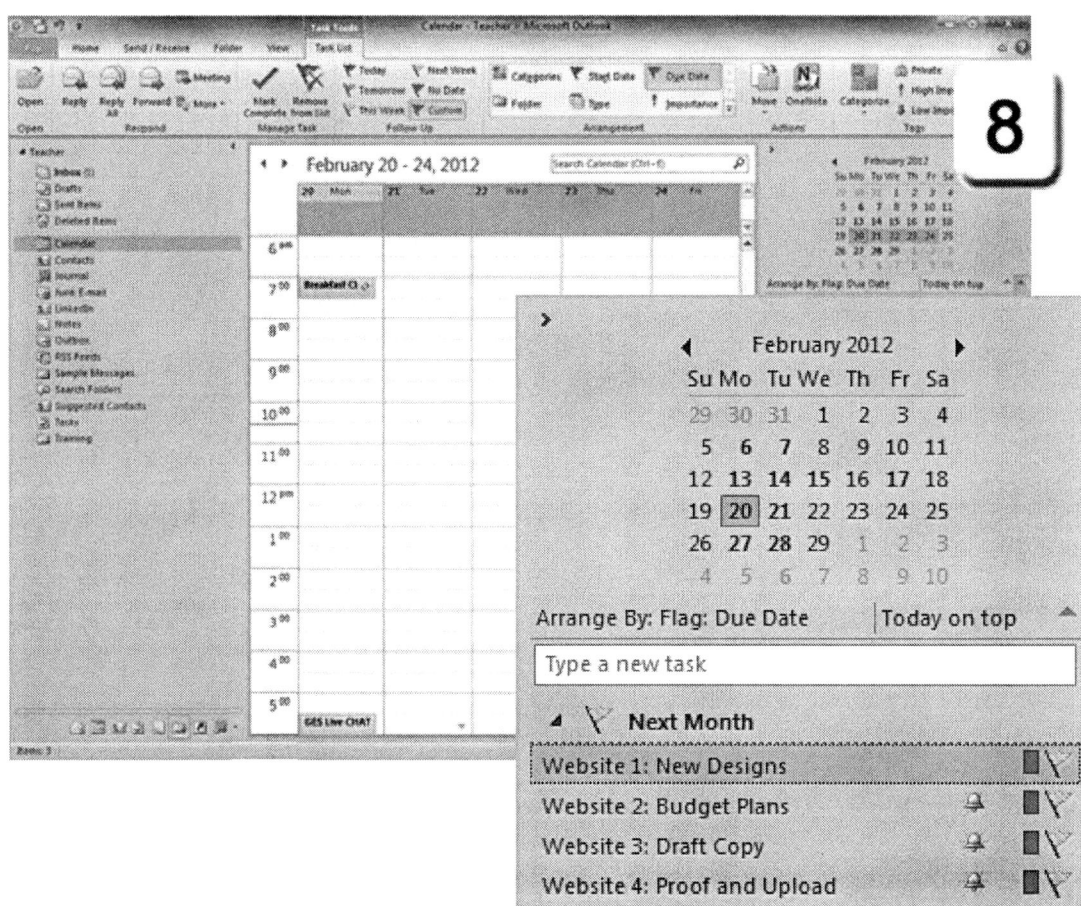

Exam 77-884: Microsoft Outlook 2010
6. Working with Tasks, Notes, and Journal Entries
6.1. Create and manipulate tasks: Respond to a Task

Edit the Meeting Request

9. Try This, Too: Edit the Meeting Request
By Default, the Meeting Request is addressed to the person who was assigned this Task. You can invite more Attendees if you wish. The Subject was also filled in.

Edit the Location: The Yum Yum Tree, Brighton
Click Send to E-mail the Meeting Request.

Trust But Verify: Find the Meeting
Go to the Calendar and confirm that a new Meeting has been scheduled. When you select the Meeting, the **Calendar Tools** should be available: Actions, Attendees and Options.

One more little lesson on Tasks...

Respond to a Task: The Sender's Calendar

Calendar Tools ->Attendees->Tracking

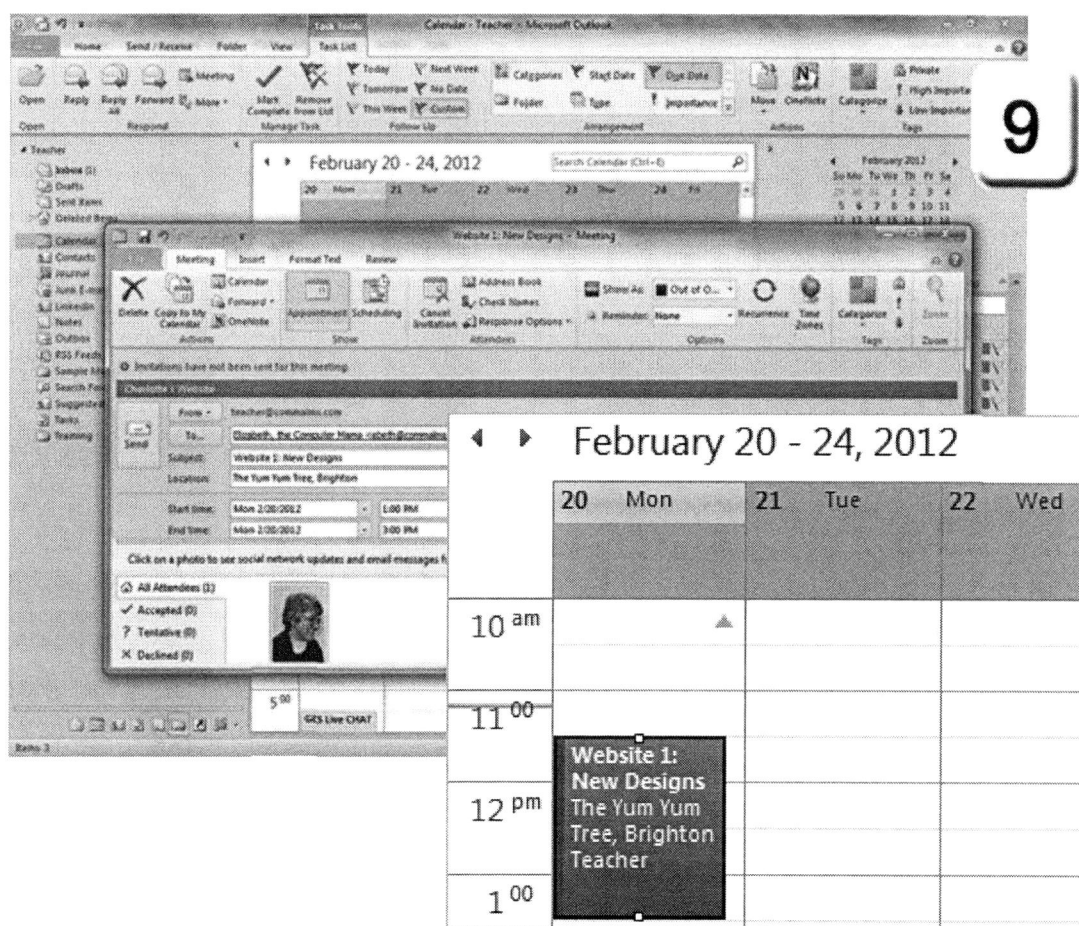

Exam 77-884: Microsoft Outlook 2010
6. Working with Tasks, Notes, and Journal Entries
6.1. Create and manipulate tasks: Respond to a Task

Move a Task to a Folder

Earlier in our Microsoft Outlook lessons we created a custom Action Button that Moves messages from the Inbox to a Training Folder. (Outlook, page 119). The same Action button can Move the Tasks as well.

Try This: Move the Task to a Folder
Go to the **Tasks** Folder.
Select the Outlook Training Task.
Go to **Home ->Actions->Move**
Click on the Training folder.

Trust But Verify: Find the Tasks
Go to the Training Folder and confirm that the Tasks are there.

OK, that will do for Tasks.

Home ->Actions->Move

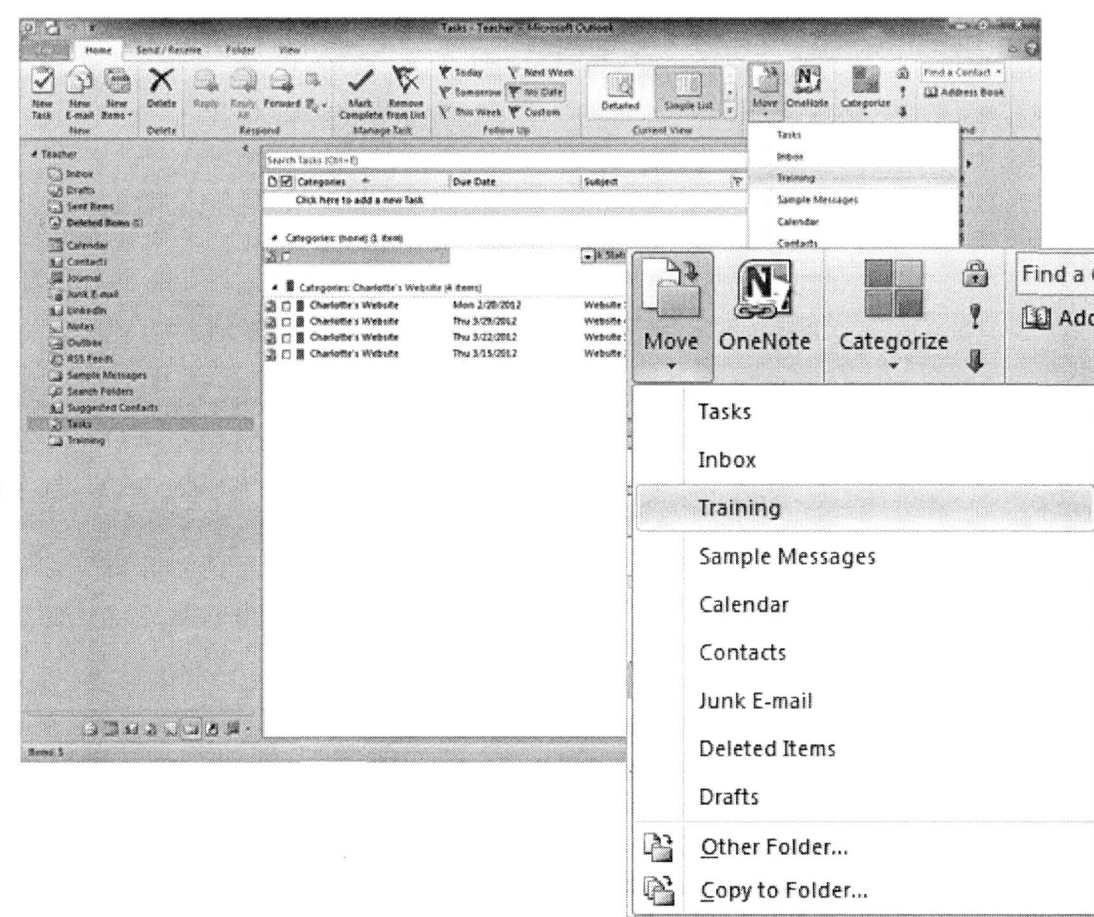

Exam 77-884: Microsoft Outlook 2010
6. Working with Tasks, Notes, and Journal Entries
6.1. Create and manipulate tasks: Move the Tasks to a Folder

Using the Notes
Microsoft Outlook has **Notes** that you can use to write down important information. The Notes can be organized, tagged for follow up and even merged with Word.

The Notes can be found by using the Navigation Pane, as we did with the Calendar and the Tasks.

Before You Begin: View the Folders
Go to **View->Layout**.
Click on **Navigation Pane**.
Select: **Normal**.

1. Try it: Find the Notes Folder
Go to the **Navigation Pane**.
Select the **Notes Folder**.

Keep going...

View ->Layout->Navigation Pane->Normal

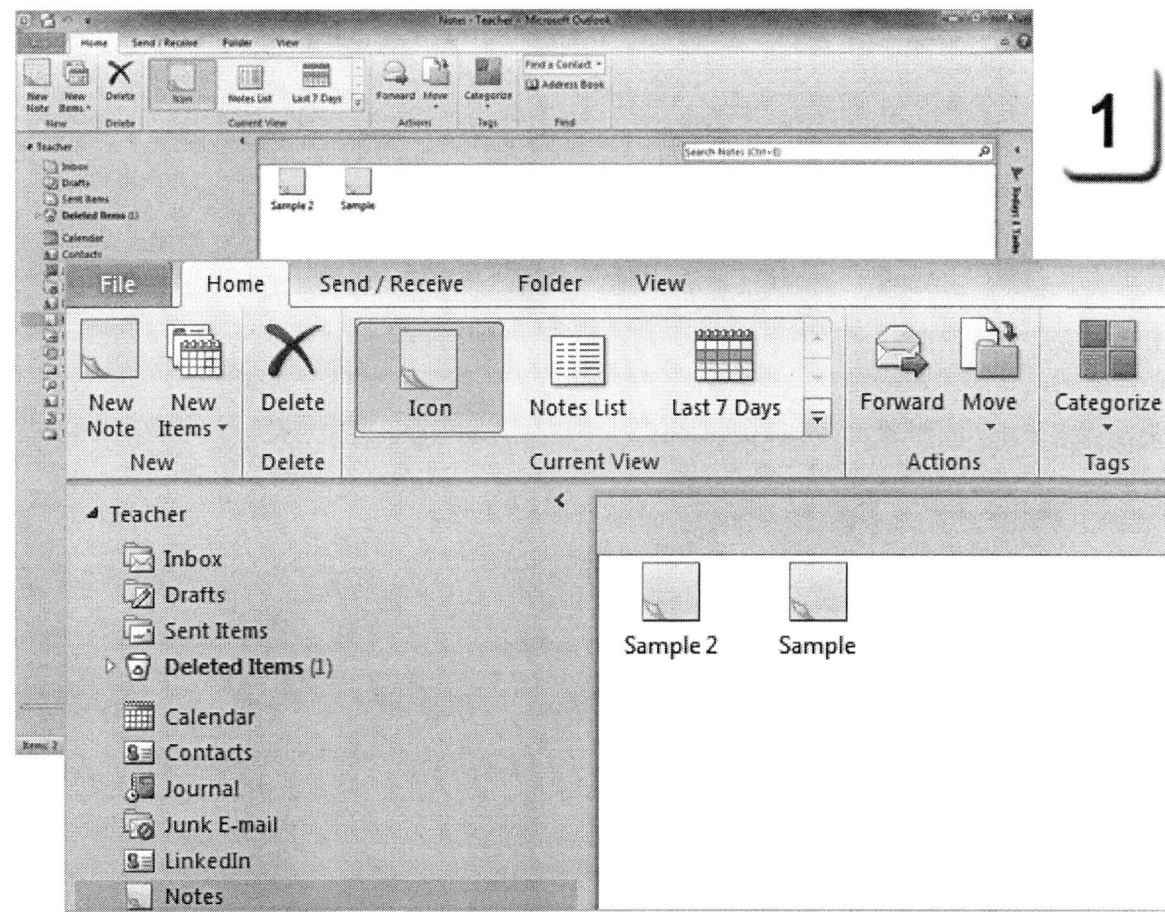

Exam 77-884: Microsoft Outlook 2010
6. Working with Tasks, Notes, and Journal Entries
6.2. Create and manipulate notes: Create a Note

Take Two

Hello, Notes

2. Try it: Create a New Note
Go to **Home ->New-> New Note.**
Type the following sample text:
Charlotte's Website Ideas:
New Logo
Add Facebook and LinkedIn sample

What Do You See? You can move and resize the Note if you wish.

Keep going...!

Home ->New-> New Note

Charlotte's Website Ideas:
New Logo
Add Facebook and LinkedIn

2/20/2012 12:03 PM

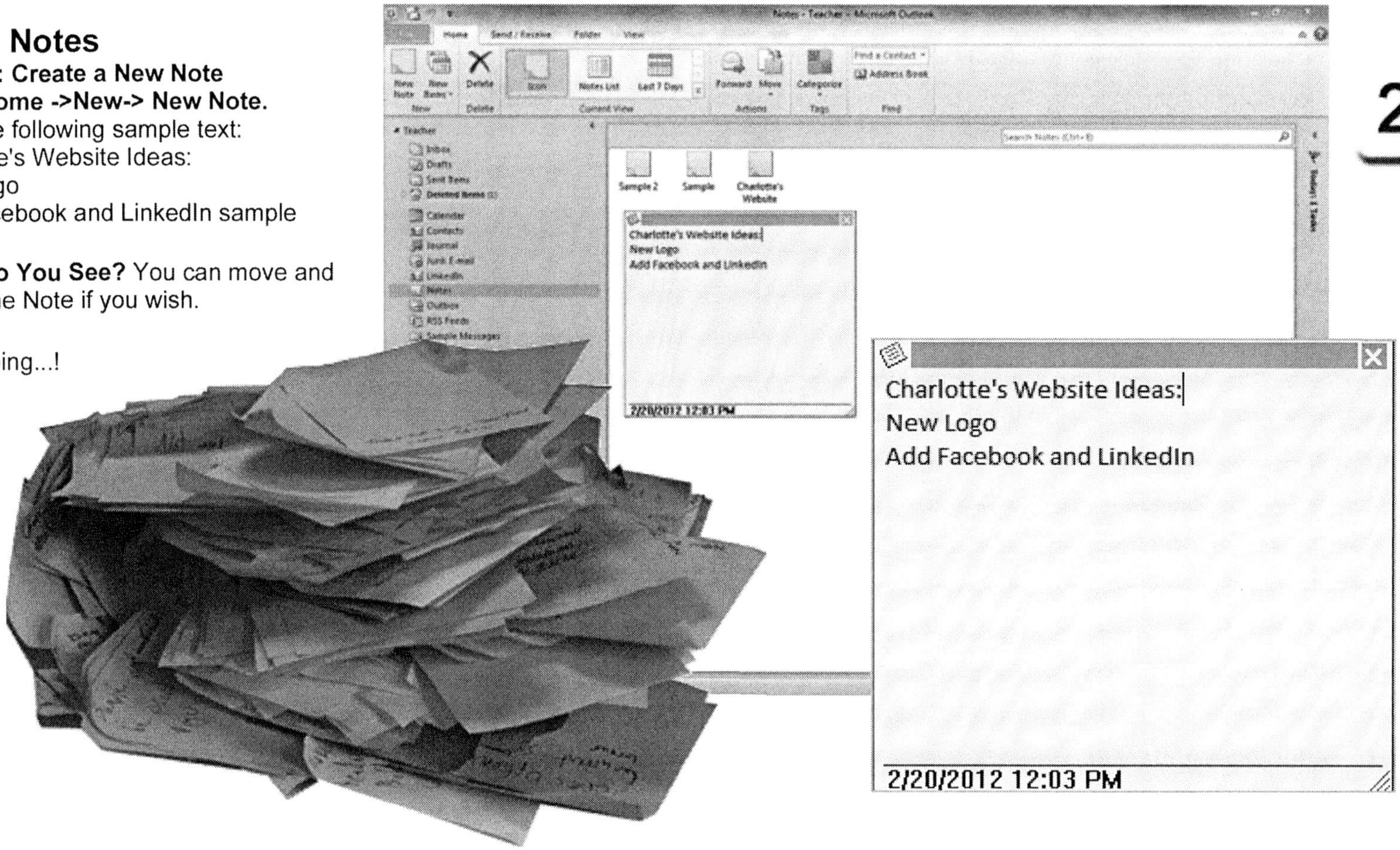

Exam 77-884: Microsoft Outlook 2010
6. Working with Tasks, Notes, and Journal Entries
6.2. Create and manipulate notes: Create a Note

Pick a Color, Any Color

Categories can be added to Notes, too.

3. Try it: Tag a Note with a Category
Select the sample Note.
Go to **Home ->Tag-> Categorize**.
Select a Category: Red Category.

What Do You See? In this screen shot, the sample Note is tagged with the Red Category. The Notes related to Training have the Training Category.

Keep going.

Home ->Tag-> Categorize

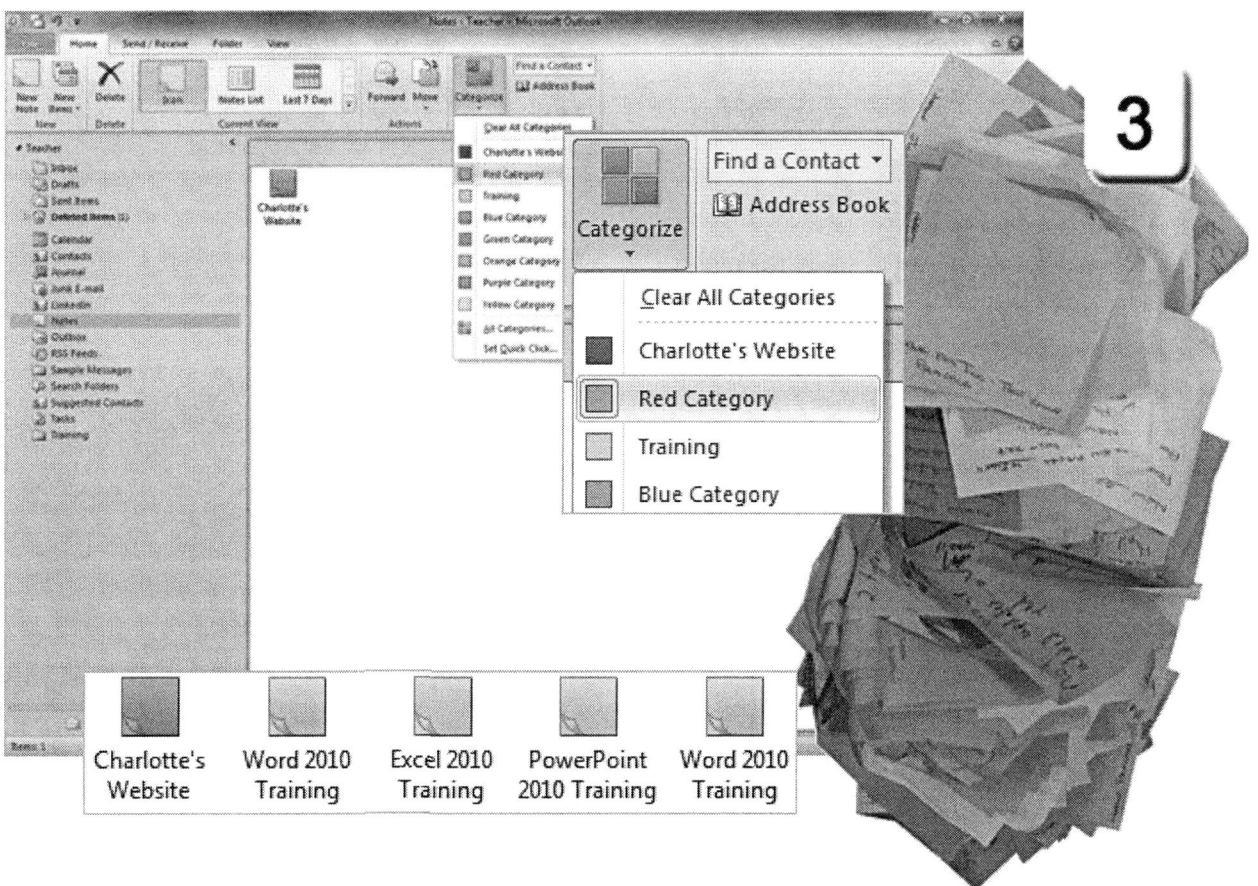

Exam 77-884: Microsoft Outlook 2010
6. Working with Tasks, Notes, and Journal Entries
6.2. Create and manipulate notes: Categorize the Notes

Make it Work for You

By default, Microsoft Outlook displays the Notes as little icons. Here is a different View that you may find more productive.

4. Try it: Change the Current View
Go to **Home ->Current View-> Notes List**.

Try This, Too: Add the Reading Pane
Go to **View->Layout->Reading Pane**.
Select: **Bottom**.

What Do You See, Now? The Notes are grouped by Categories. The Reading Pane lets you see the information at a glance.

Enough about Notes...(small pun)

Home ->Current View-> Notes List

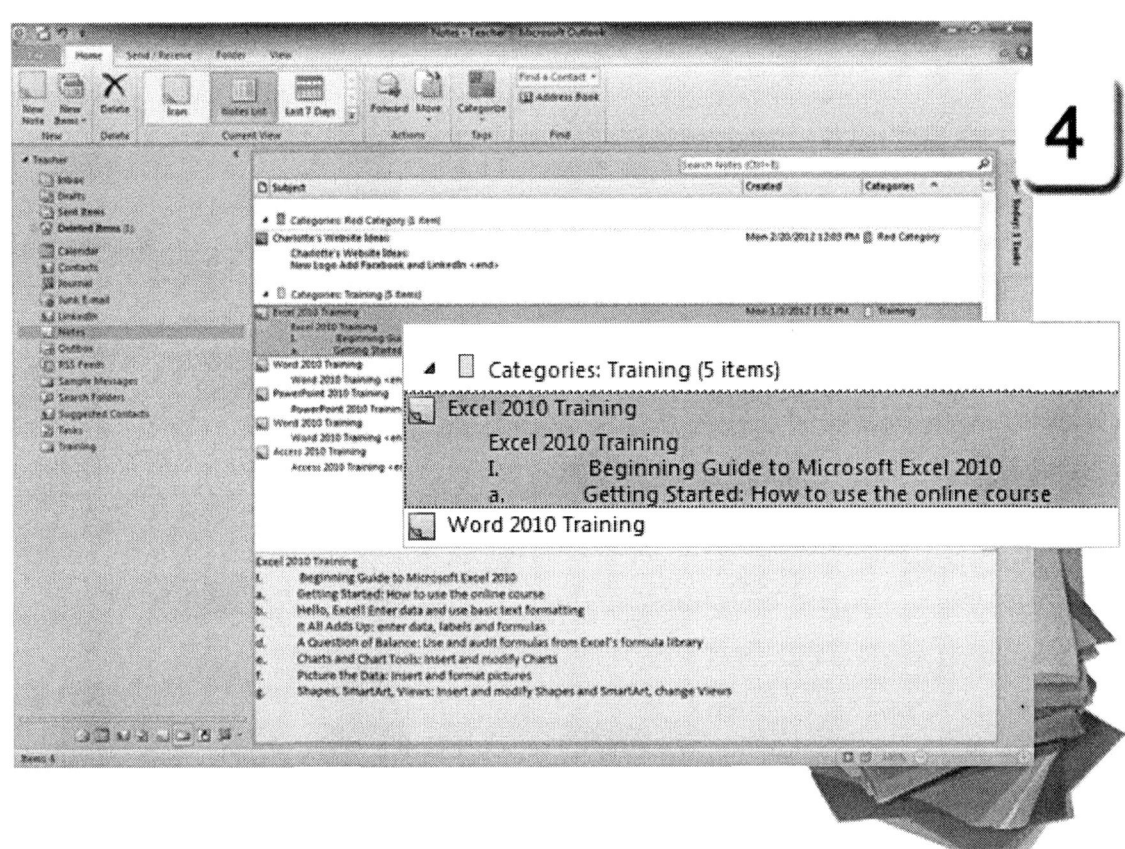

Exam 77-884: Microsoft Outlook 2010
6. Working with Tasks, Notes, and Journal Entries
6.2. Create and manipulate notes: Change the Current View

Use the Journal to Record

You can automatically track your Outlook activity (messages, tasks, etc.) with the Journal. You can also use the Journal to track the time that you work on a document or spreadsheet.

The Journal can be found by using the Navigation Pane, as we did with the Calendar, Tasks and Notes.

1. Try it: Find the Journal
Go to the **Navigation Pane**.
Select the **Journal**.

What Do You See? The screenshot on this page shows a Journal with several entries for Excel and Word.

What Else Do You See? The Journal's **Home Ribbon** include: New, Delete, Arrangement, Current View, Actions, Tags and Find. These options are similar to the ones for the Calendar.

Keep going...

View ->Layout->Navigation Pane->Normal

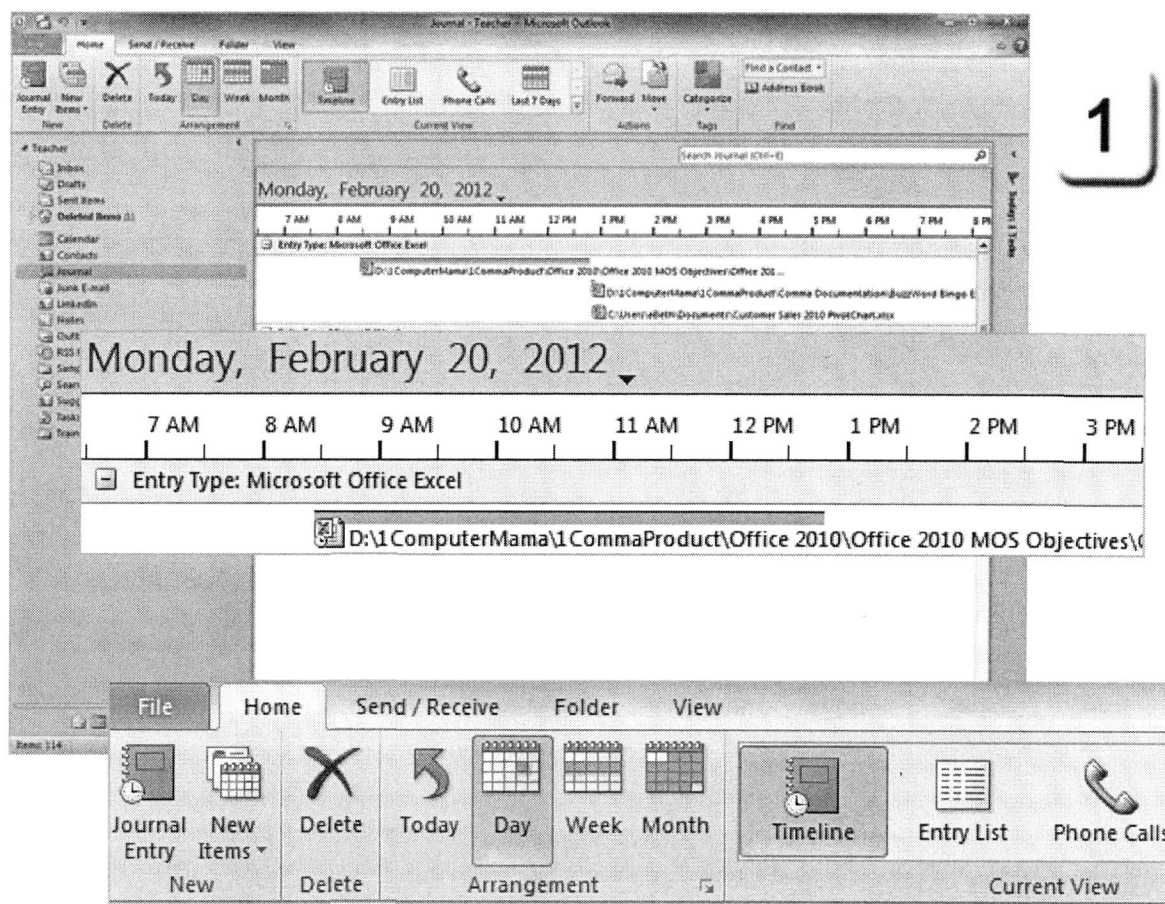

Exam 77-884: Microsoft Outlook 2010
6. Working with Tasks, Notes, and Journal Entries
6.3. Create and manipulate Journal entries

Create a New Journal Entry

2. Try it: Create a New Journal Entry
Go to **Home ->New-> Journal Entry**.
A new Journal Entry will open.

Enter the Subject: Website Consultation
Select the Entry Type: Phone call
Select the Start time and Duration.

Try This, Too: Edit the Duration
You can use the **Timer** to record the minutes (or hours!) that you are on the phone. If you take a break, click on Pause Timer and then Resume when you return.

Do This: Save Your Journal Entry
Go to **Journal Entry->Actions**.
Click on **Save & Close**.

Keep going...

Home ->New-> Journal Entry

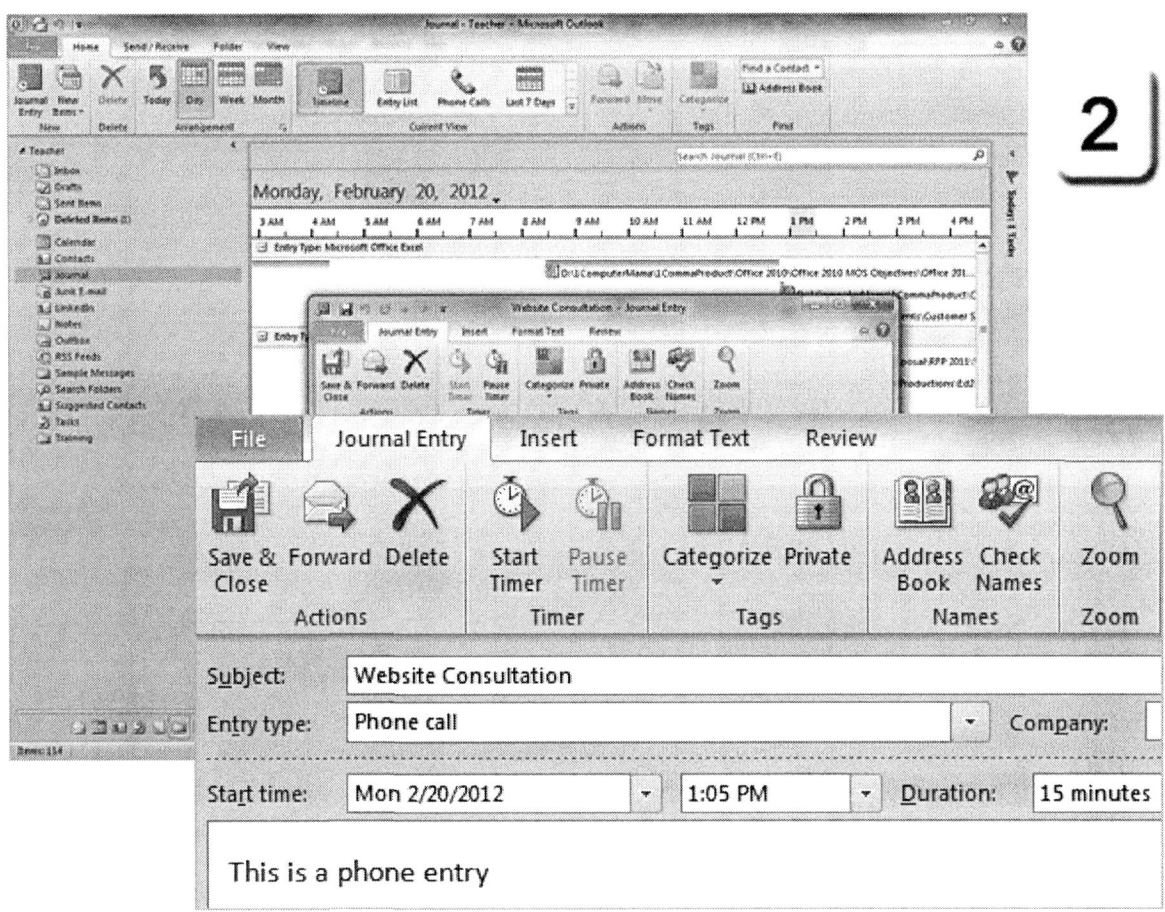

Exam 77-884: Microsoft Outlook 2010
6. Working with Tasks, Notes, and Journal Entries
6.3. Create and manipulate Journal entries: Edit a Journal Entry

Journal Options

The Journal may not record the Outlook items automatically. Please go to the Backstage to find the **Journal Options**.

3. Try it: Find the Journal Options
Go to **File ->Options.**
Select: **Notes and Journal.**
Click on Journal Options.

What Do You See? You can record the Outlook items for all Contacts or only the ones you select. You can also record the time spent on your Office files: Access, Excel, PowerPoint, Visio and Word.

Select all of the Outlook and Microsoft Office items.

Click **OK** to return to the Backstage.
Click **OK**, again, to return to the Journal.

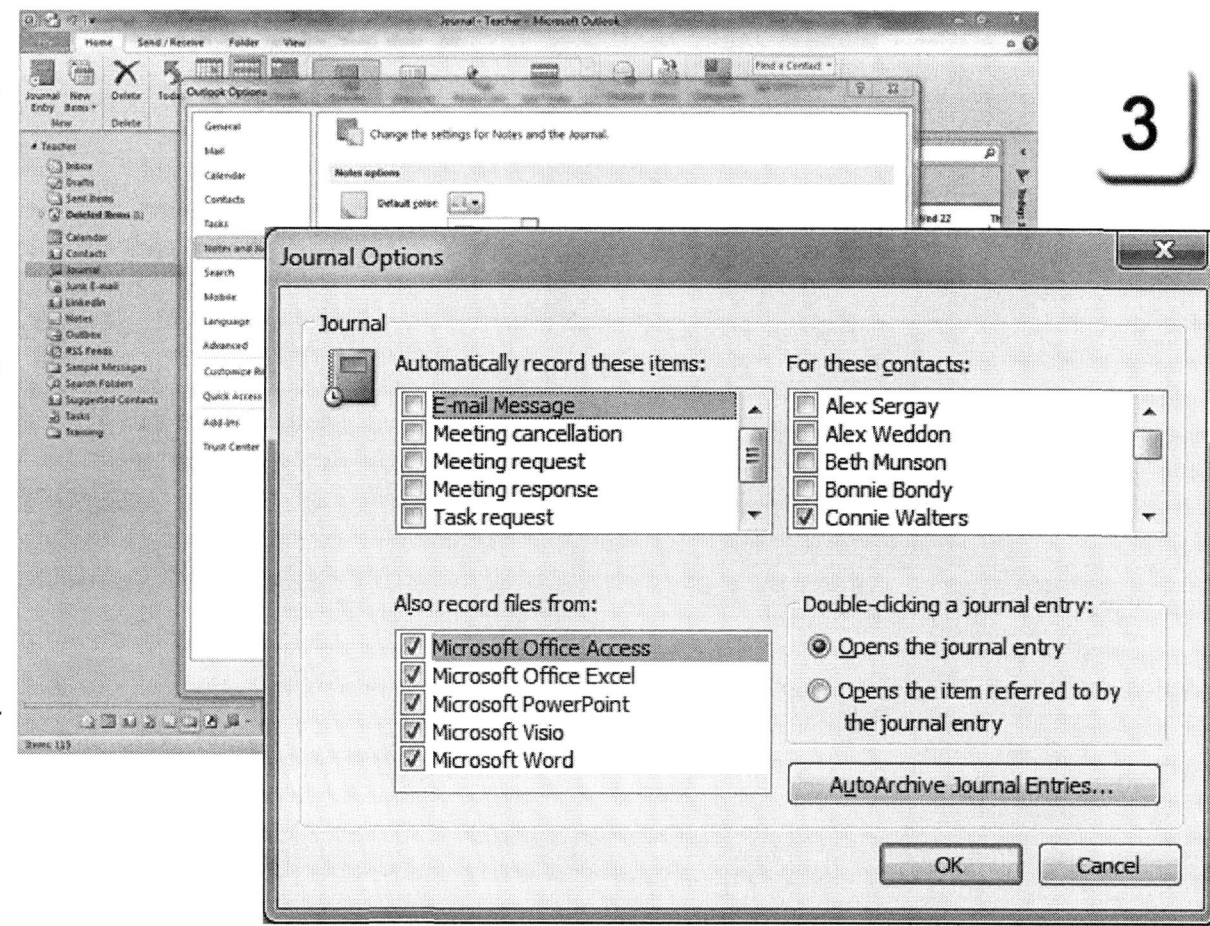

Exam 77-884: Microsoft Outlook 2010
6. Working with Tasks, Notes, and Journal Entries
6.3. Create and manipulate Journal entries: Automatically Record Outlook Items

Summary

This discussion introduced **Tasks** as a way to document assignments.

We also looked at **Notes** and **Journal Entries**.

Allez, Allez in Free.
You done real good.
You get two cookies.

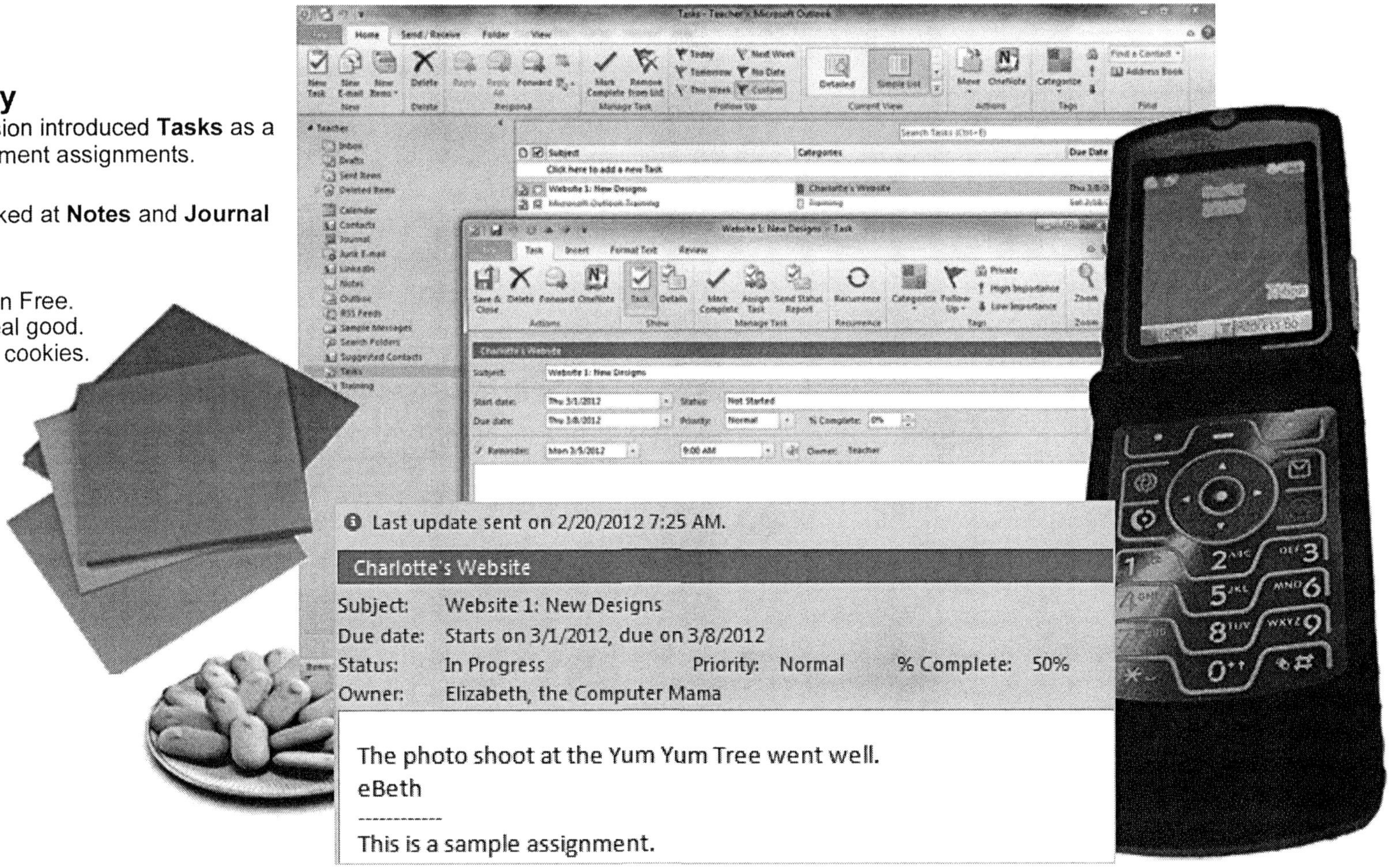

ⓘ Last update sent on 2/20/2012 7:25 AM.

Charlotte's Website

Subject:	Website 1: New Designs
Due date:	Starts on 3/1/2012, due on 3/8/2012
Status:	In Progress Priority: Normal % Complete: 50%
Owner:	Elizabeth, the Computer Mama

The photo shoot at the Yum Yum Tree went well.
eBeth

This is a sample assignment.

Practice Activities

Lesson 8: Tasks and Time Management
Try This: Do the following steps

1. Create a new Task called Computer Training

2. Apply the Blue Category

3. Rename the Blue Category as Training

4. Send (assign) the task to someone else

5. Send a meeting request about the Task

6. Create another new task called Staff Meeting

7. Apply the Red Category to Staff Meeting

8. Mark the Staff Meeting Task Complete

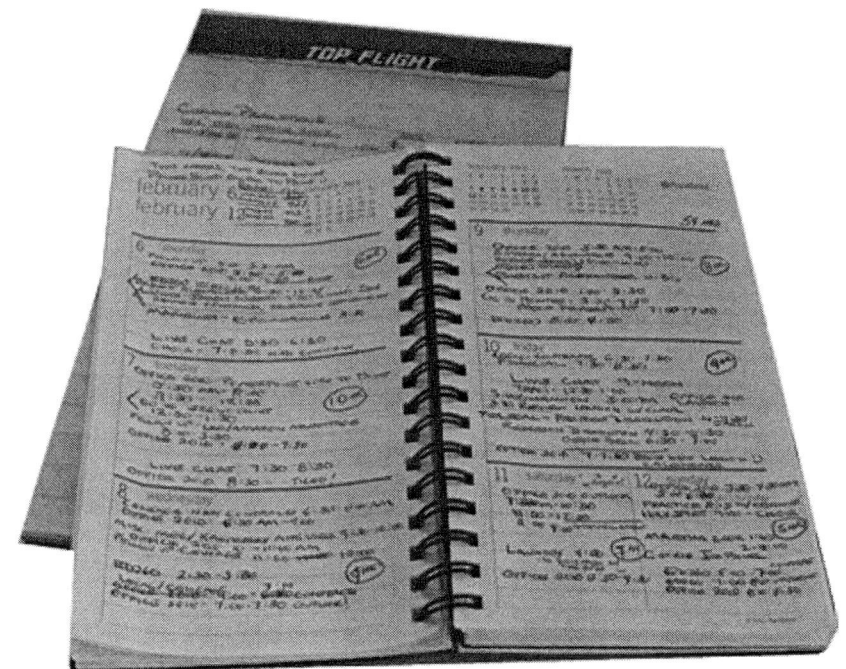

Test Yourself

1. Which of the following are Status Options available for Tasks?
(Give all correct answers.)
A. Not Started
B. In Progress
C. Completed
D. Waiting on someone else
E. Deferred
Tip: Complete Guide to Outlook, page 221

2. A Task in Outlook has its own set of dedicated Ribbons.
A. True
B. False
Tip: Complete Guide to Outlook, page 222

3. Which of the following can have Categories? (Give all correct answers.)
A. Tasks
B. Messages
C. Meetings
D. Contacts
E. E-mails
Tip: Complete Guide to Outlook, page 226

4. You can change the name of Red Category to a name of your choice.
A. True
B. False
Tip: Complete Guide to Outlook, page 227

5. By default, Tasks are sorted by name.
A. True
B. False
Tip: Complete Guide to Outlook, page 228

6. A task can be assigned to which of the following? (Give all correct answers.)
A. A person
B. A Contact Group
Tip: Complete Guide to Outlook, page 233

7. When sending a meeting request in response to a Task, which of the following are true? (Give all correct answers.)
A. By default, the meeting request is addressed to the person who was assigned the Task
B. By default, the meeting request is addressed to the person who assigned the Task
C. Other attendees cannot be added
D. Other attendees can be added
E. The meeting request response is not addressed to anyone by default
Tip: Complete Guide to Outlook, page 239

8. Which parts of Outlook are found in the Navigation Pane?
(Give all correct answers.)
A. Calendar
B. Notes
C. Tasks
Tip: Complete Guide to Outlook, page 241

9. What does the Journal tool track?
(Give all correct answers.)
A. Outlook Activity
B. Time spent on task in a document or spreadsheet
Tip: Complete Guide to Outlook, page 245

10. Which of the following is true about Tasks?
(Give all correct answers.)
A. A Task is an appointment or meeting that you can do again and again
B. A Task can be Tracked
C. A Task can be assigned to someone else
D. To create a new Task, go to Home->New-> New Task
Tip: Complete Guide to Outlook, page 222

Application Question: How are Tasks different from Appointments? Give at least three things.
Give an example of a Task.

Outlook: Online

Microsoft Outlook Objectives
In this lesson, you will learn how to:

1. Use the Backstage Ribbon to create E-mail Signatures and Stationery

2. Select a Theme for HTML messages

3. Specify options for Reply and Forward

4. Review the General options for Outlook

5. Set the Mail, Calendar, Tasks, Notes and Journal and Language options in the Backstage

6. Publish a Calendar online and invite someone to subscribe to that Calendar

© 2012 Comma Productions, LLC

 # Lesson 9 : Outlook Online

File->Options

1. Readings
Read Lesson 9 in the Microsoft Outlook guide, page 251-288.

Project
Create automated E-mail messages that include a signature and a Theme.

Downloads
There are no downloads in this lesson.

2. Practice
Do the Practice Activity on page 289.

3. Assessment
Review the Test questions on page 290.

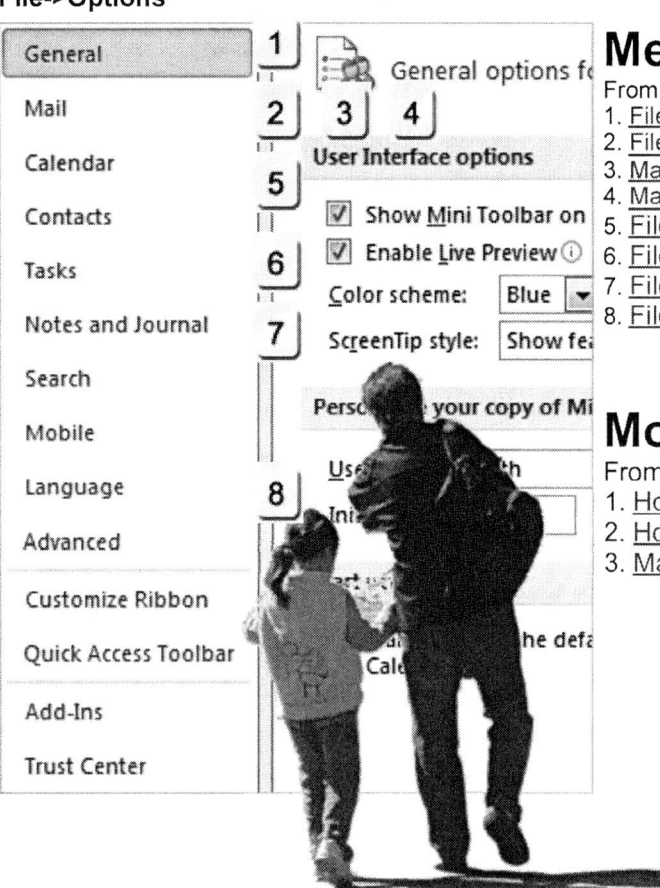

Menu Maps
From the **Backstage**
1. File ->Options ->General, pg 256
2. File ->Options ->Mail, pg 257
3. Mail ->Compose Messages ->Signatures, pg 260
4. Mail ->Compose Messages ->Personal Stationery, pg 262
5. File ->Options ->Calendar, page 271
6. File ->Options ->Tasks, page 274
7. File ->Options ->Notes and Journal, page 275
8. File ->Options ->Language, page 277

More Menu Maps
From the **Home Ribbon**
1. Home ->Manage Calendars, page 278
2. Home ->Share ->Publish Online, page 281
3. Manage Calendars ->Calendar Groups, page 287

Microsoft Outlook: Online

The **Outlook Options** lets you manage how you want to present yourself online. You can use the Options to create a simple signature that includes your Social Connections to LinkedIn or Facebook. You can also use the Options to publish your Calendar online. This lesson looks at the Options, first. In the next lesson we will see how it all **prints**.

Start -> All Programs ->Microsoft Office-> Microsoft Office Outlook 2010

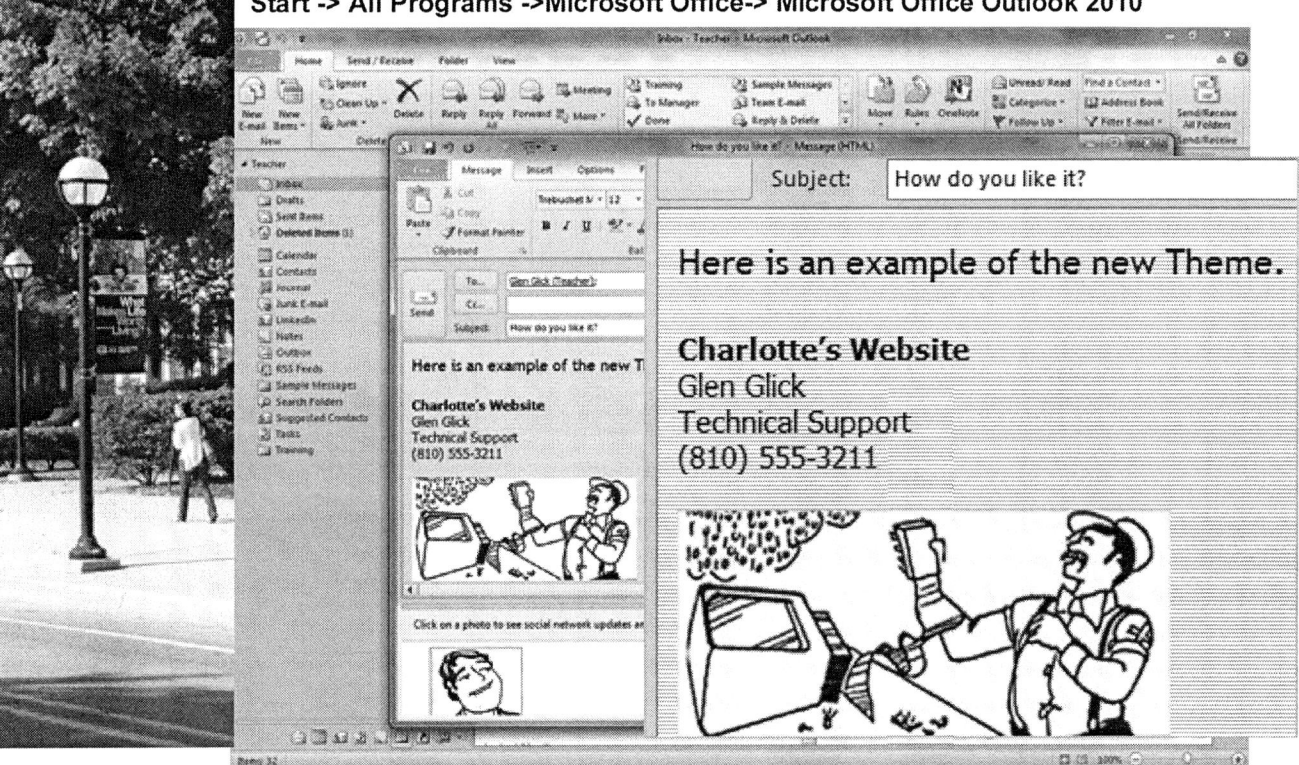

The Theme is "Etched in Stone."

So much of our lives are digital it is interesting to look up and see the statue of Portia, the smartest woman in literature, (shown on the cover of this lesson) or a gargoyle wearing glasses.

The stone faces were found in Ann Arbor, Michigan. The buildings in metal, brick and wood can be found in the little towns north of the city.

Before You Begin

Microsoft Office 2010 has **Options** that you can use to make the software work best for you and your business.

You can modify almost everything in Word, Excel, Access, PowerPoint and even Outlook if you wish.

Let's find the Options.

By default, Microsoft Outlook opens with the **Inbox** as the initial view. The Options can be found by going to the Backstage.

Keep going...!

Microsoft Outlook ->Inbox

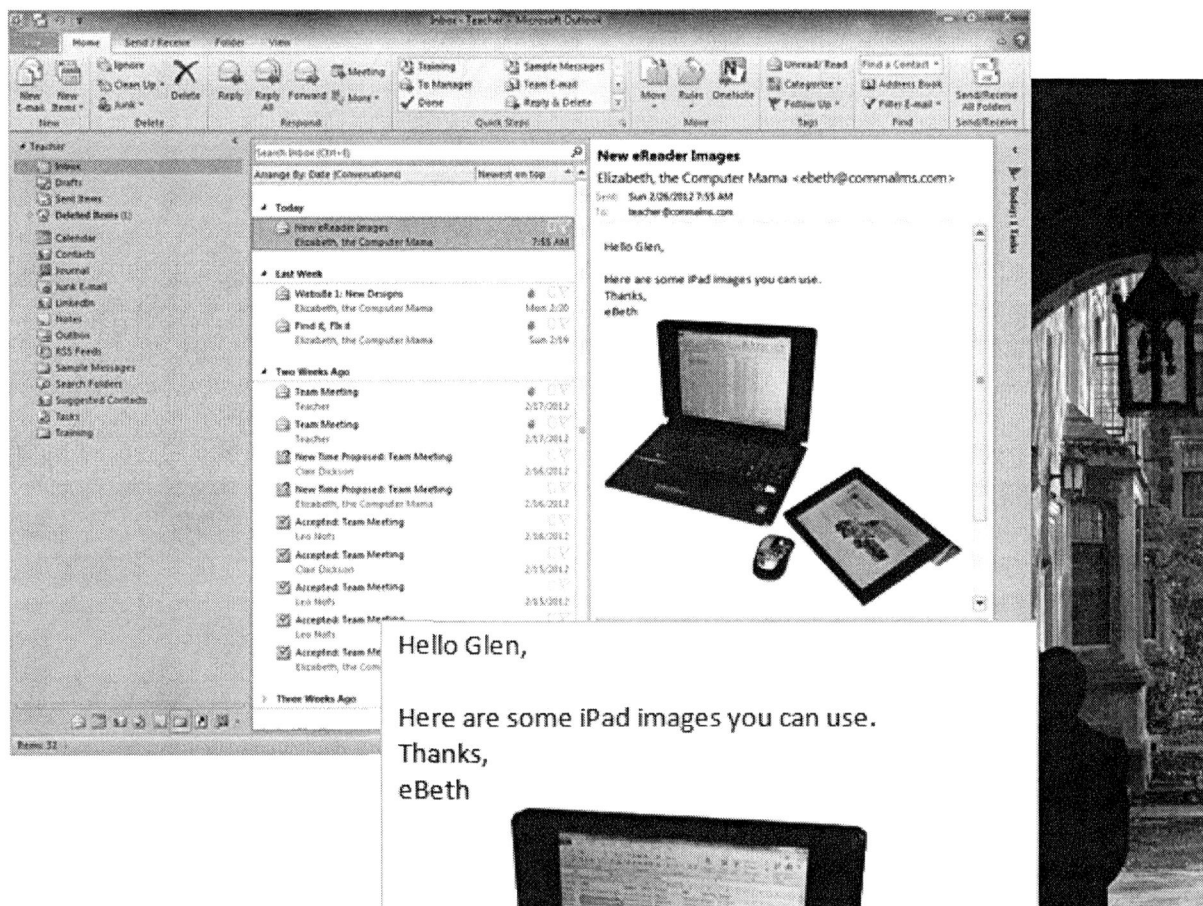

Hello Glen,

Here are some iPad images you can use.
Thanks,
eBeth

Find the Options
1. Try it: Find the Options
Go to **File ->Options**.

What Do You See? The Outlook
Options are divided into groups:
General
Mail
Calendar
Tasks
Notes and Journal
Search
Mobile
Language
Advanced

The Advanced Option Groups include:
Customize Ribbon
Quick Access Toolbar
Add-Ins
Trust Center

Keep going, please.

File ->Options

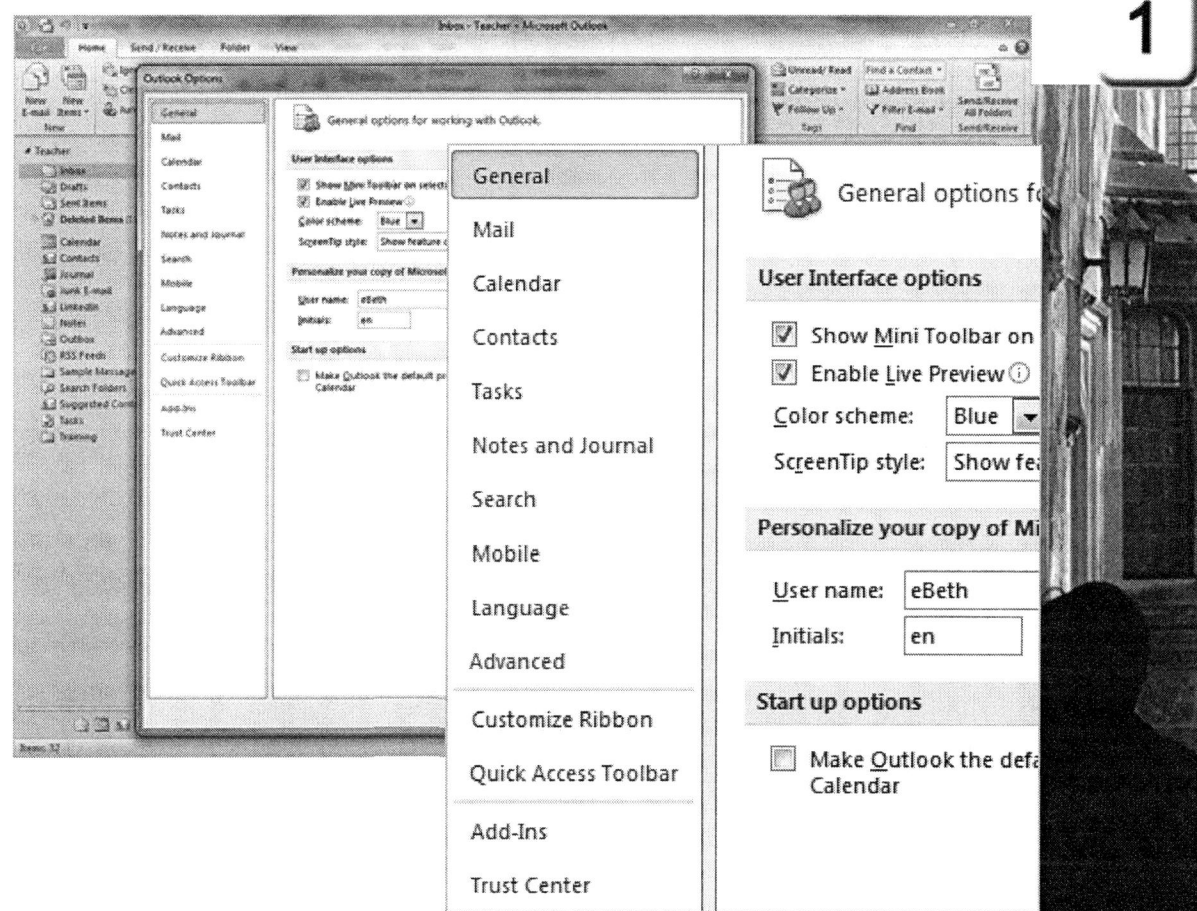

Exam 77-884: Microsoft Outlook 2010
1. Managing the Outlook Environment
1.1. Apply and manipulate Outlook program options: Set General Options

Take One

File ->Options ->General

General Options for Outlook

2. Try it: Review the General Options
Go to **File ->Options->General.**

What Do You See? The General Options are divided into three groups:

User Interface options: You can choose to Show the Mini Toolbar and the Live Preview. You can also choose a Color Scheme.

Personalize: You can edit your User Name and Initials.

Start up options: You can make Outlook your default program for E-mail, Contacts and Calendar.

Keep going...

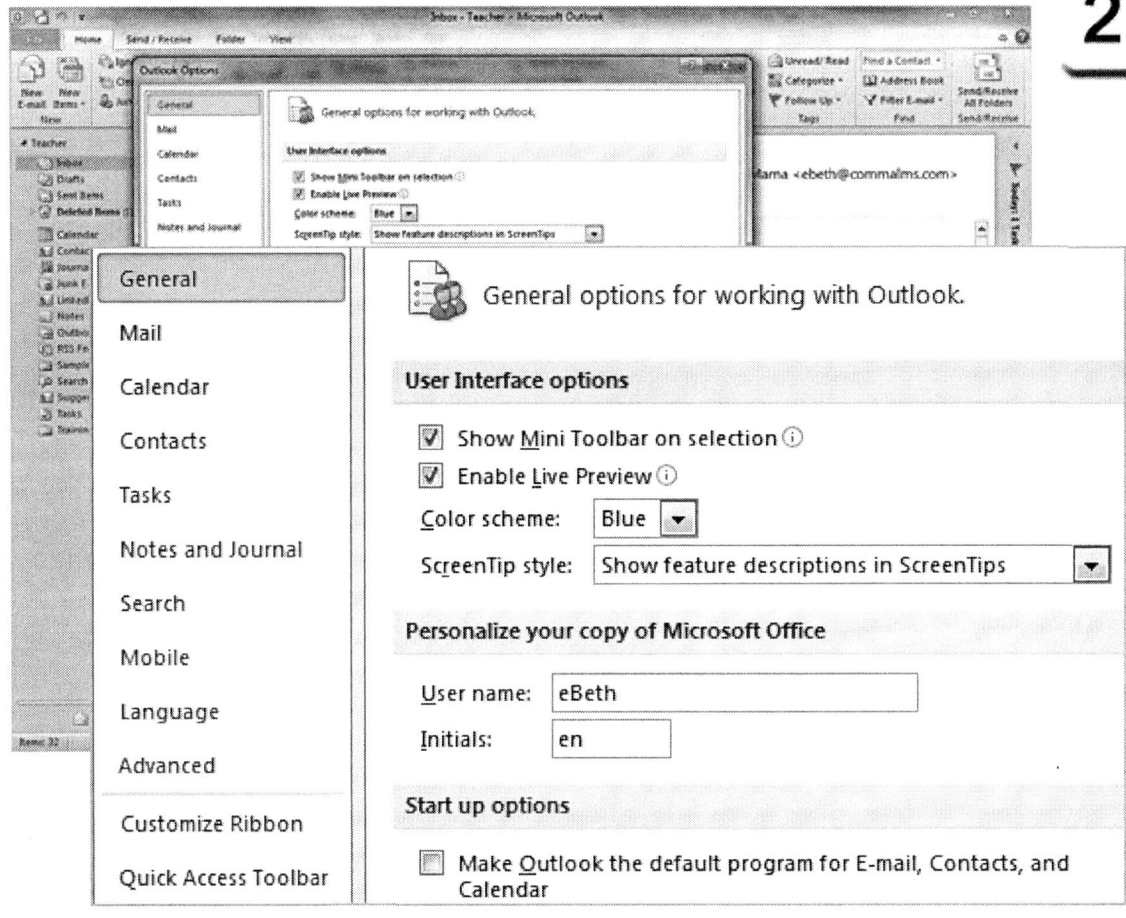

Exam 77-884: Microsoft Outlook 2010
1. Managing the Outlook Environment
1.1. Apply and manipulate Outlook program options: Set General Options

Outlook Options: Mail

You can change how Outlook composes new E-mail messages. You can also add a signature and specify a default stationery if you wish. These options can be found in the Mail category.

3. Try it: Review the Mail Options
The Outlook Options are open.
Select a Category: Mail

What Do You See? The Mail Options are divided into 10 groups:
Compose messages
Outlook panes
Message arrival
Conversation Clean Up
Replies and forwards
Save messages
Send messages
Tracking
Other

Keep going...

File ->Options ->Mail

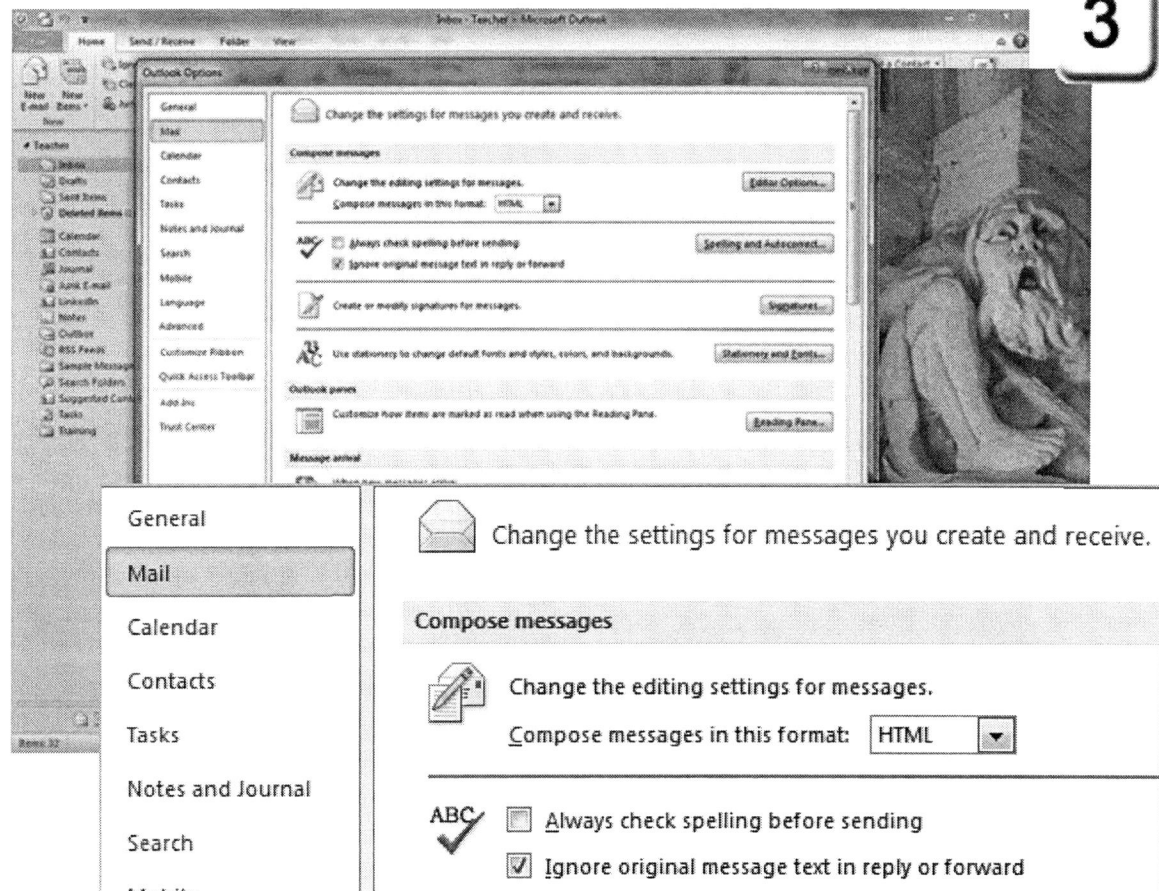

Exam 77-884: Microsoft Outlook 2010
1. Managing the Outlook Environment
1.1. Apply and manipulate Outlook program options: Set Mail Options

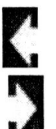

Mail Options: Compose

By default, Microsoft Outlook composes rich E-mail messages in the **HTML** format.

HTML means **Hyper Text Markup Language**. It is the design language for the Internet. So, the E-mail messages can be formatted like web pages, as we did with an E-mail Blast in a previous lesson.

4. Try it: Review the Message Format
The Outlook Options are open.
The Mail Category is selected.
Go to **Compose Messages**.
Select a format: HTML

What Do You See? E-mail messages can also be formatted with **Rich Text** (all of the Font and Paragraph formatting available in Word) or **Plain Text**.

Keep going...

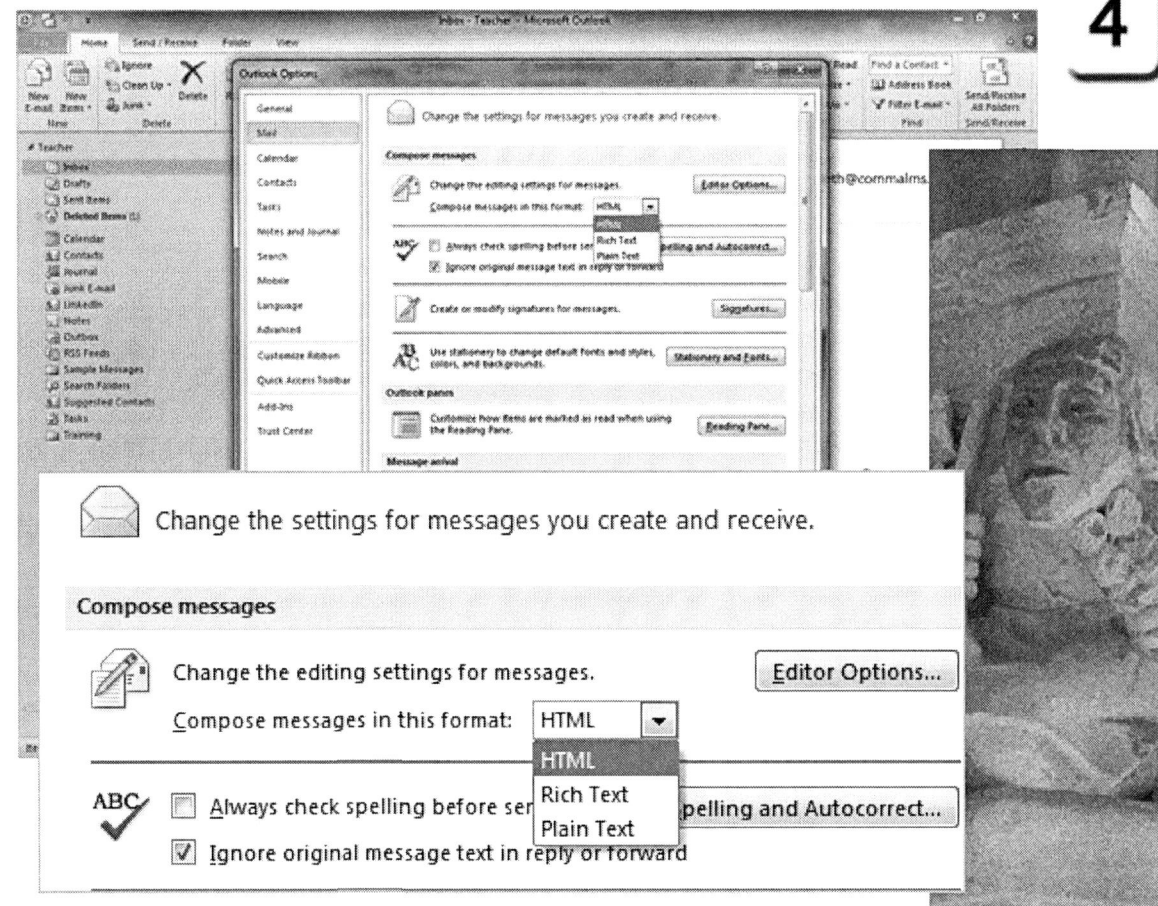

Exam 77-884: Microsoft Outlook 2010
3. Managing Email Messages
3.4. Manage automatic message content: HTML or Plain Text Messages

Compose: Check Spelling

The **Review Ribbon** in a Microsoft Outlook Message has all of the robust tools found in Word including Spelling & Grammar, Research and Thesaurus. However, the Spell Checker may not be turned on. You can use the Outlook Options to configure the Spelling and Autocorrect settings.

5. Try it: Enable the Spell Checking
The Outlook Options are open.
The Mail Category is selected.
Go to **Compose Messages**.
Select: Always check spelling before sending

What Do You See? By default, Outlook does not check the spelling in the original message when you reply or forward it.

Keep going...

File ->Options ->Mail ->Compose Messages-> Spelling

5

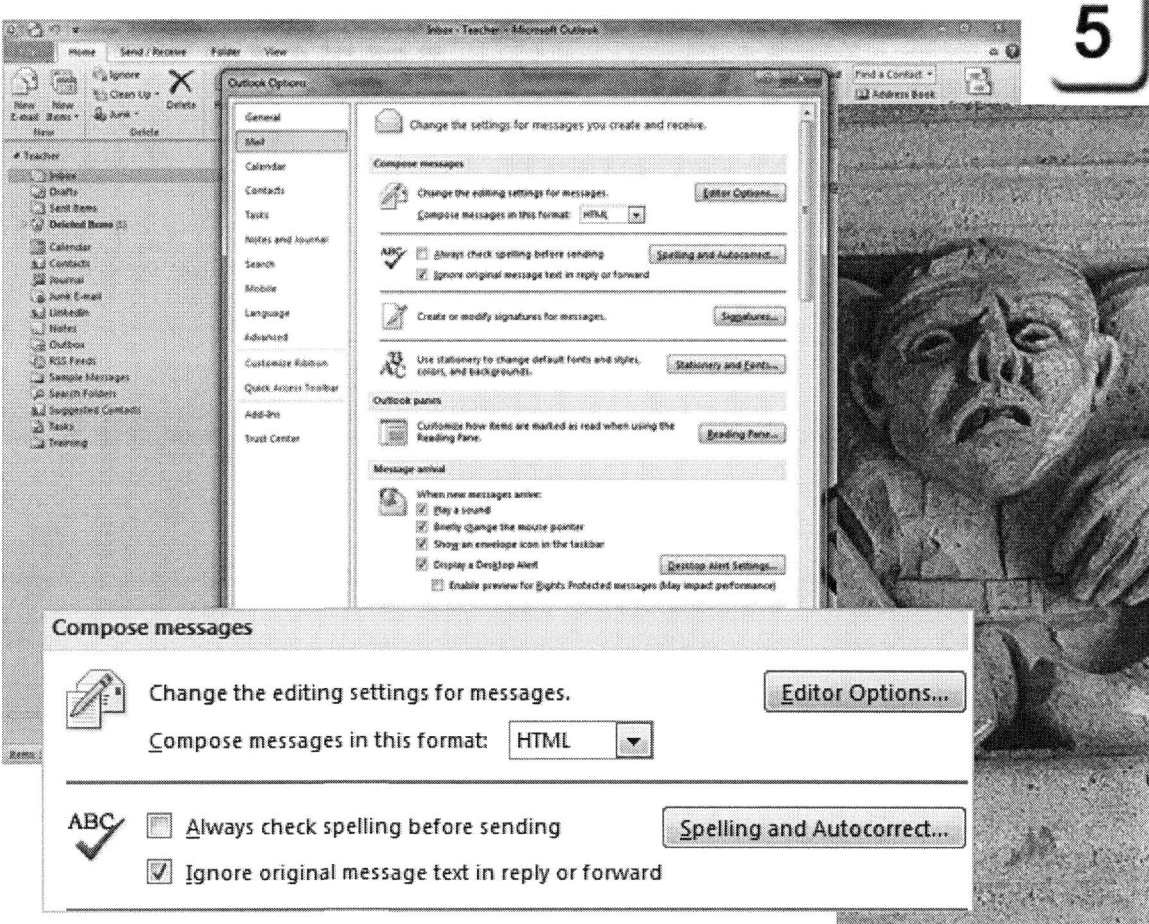

File ->Options ->Mail ->Compose Messages ->Signatures

Compose: Signatures

You can add more **E-mail Signatures** if you wish. For example, the Signature for all new messages can be formal and complete. It may include your name, business, and contact information. You can have a different, simple signature for any messages that you reply or forward.

6. Try it: Create an E-mail Signature
The Outlook Options are still open and the Mail Category is selected.
Go to **Compose Messages->Signatures**.
Enter a name: Glen Glick.

Keep going...

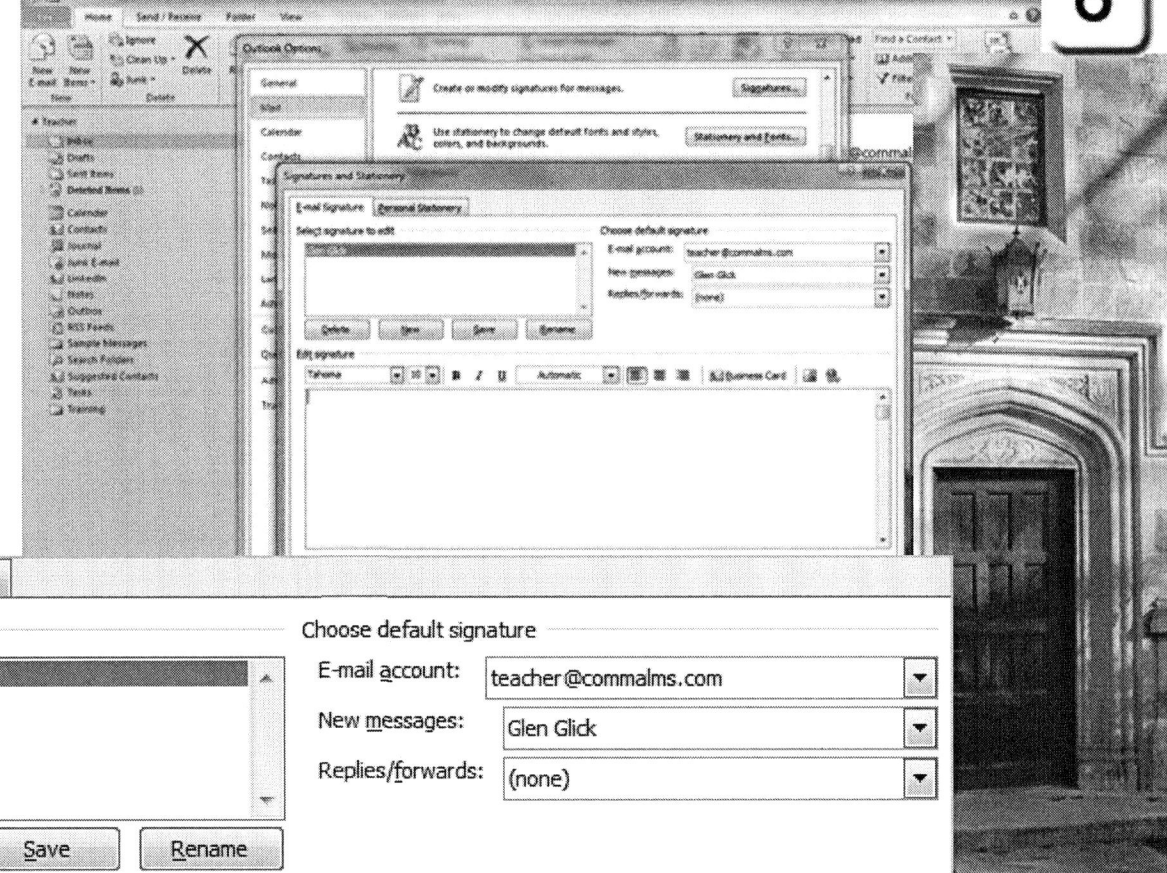

Exam 77-884: Microsoft Outlook 2010
3. Managing Email Messages
3.4. Manage automatic message content: Manage Signatures

Edit the Signature

7. Try it: Edit the Signature
Enter the following sample text:
Charlotte's Website
Glen Glick
Technical Support
(810) 555-3211

Select all of the type.
Format the Font: Tahoma
Select the Size: 10 pt

Select: Charlotte's Website.
Format the Text: **Bold**.

What Do You See? You can add a Business Card, picture or website.

Do This, Too: Select a Signature
Choose a default signature for all New messages: Glen Glick.

Click **Save**. Do not close this window, yet. Keep going.

File ->Options ->Mail ->Compose Messages ->Signatures

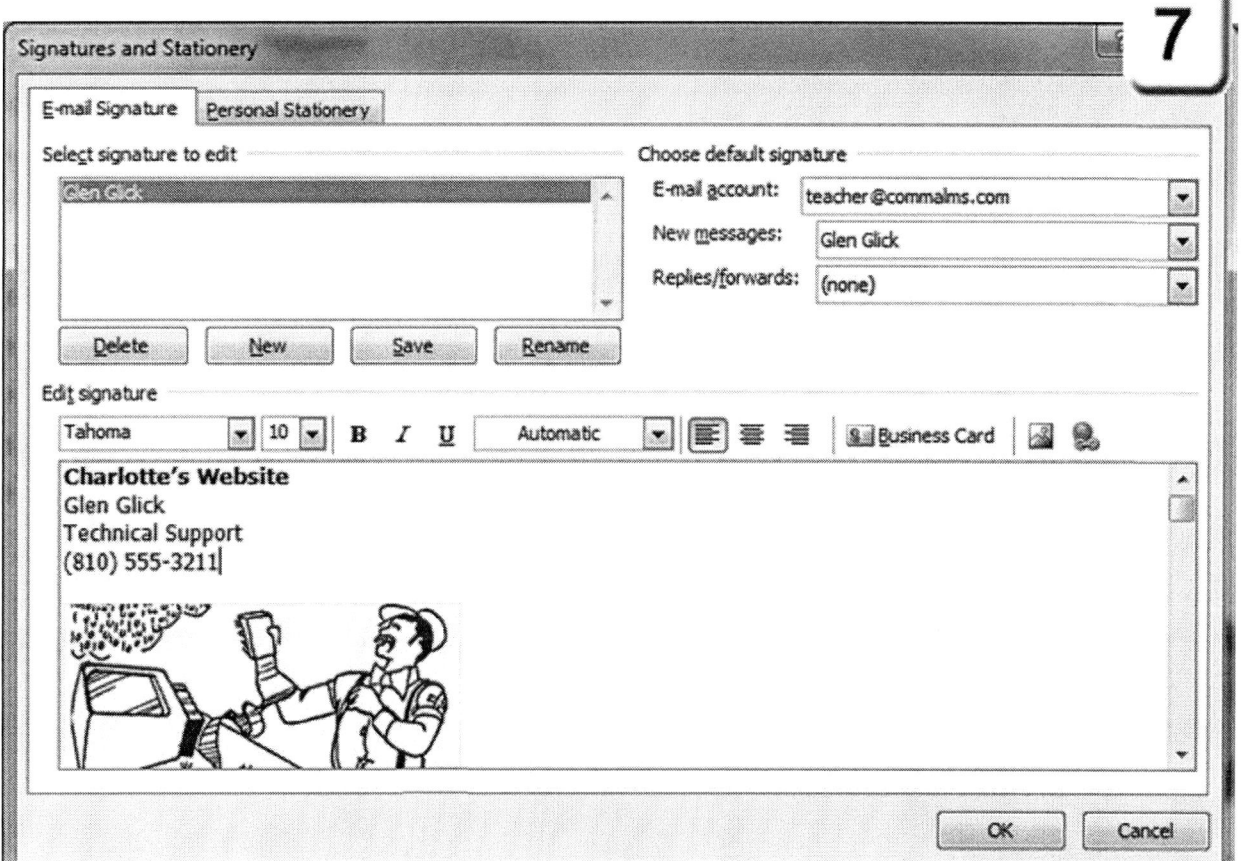

Exam 77-884: Microsoft Outlook 2010
3. Managing Email Messages
3.4. Manage automatic message content: Manage Signatures

Edit the Personal Stationery

You can design your E-mail messages so that each new message uses a Theme. The Personal Stationery can be found on the tab next to the Signatures.

8. Try it: Edit the Personal Stationery
The Outlook Options are still open and the Mail Category is selected.
Go to **Compose Messages.**
Click on Personal Stationery.

What Do You See? You can select a **Theme** that would be applied to all new HTML messages. You can also edit the **Font** (type, size, color) for new E-mails as well as messages you Forward or Reply.

What Else Do You See? You can **Mark your Comment**s with your name. You can also pick a new color when you Reply or Forward a message.

Click on **Theme**, please.

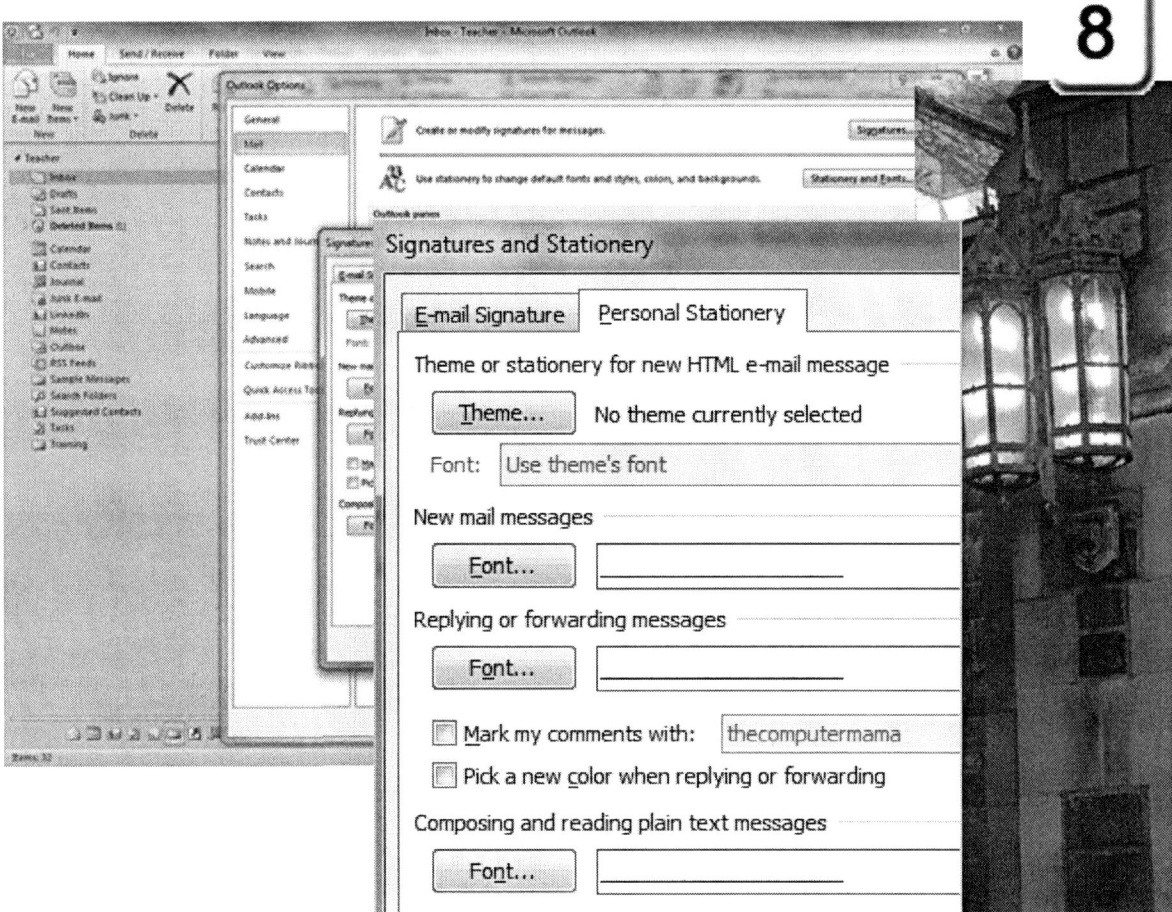

Exam 77-884: Microsoft Outlook 2010
3. Managing Email Messages
3.4. Manage automatic message content: Edit the Personal Stationery

Personal Stationery: Theme

9. Try it: Select a Theme

Select a Theme: Profile.

What Do You See? There are **Themes** and there are some templates labeled **Stationery**. The Themes have options for Vivid Colors, Active Backgrounds as well as a Background Image. When you select a Stationery, these options are grayed out.

Click **OK** to return to Signatures and Personal Stationery. Keep going...!

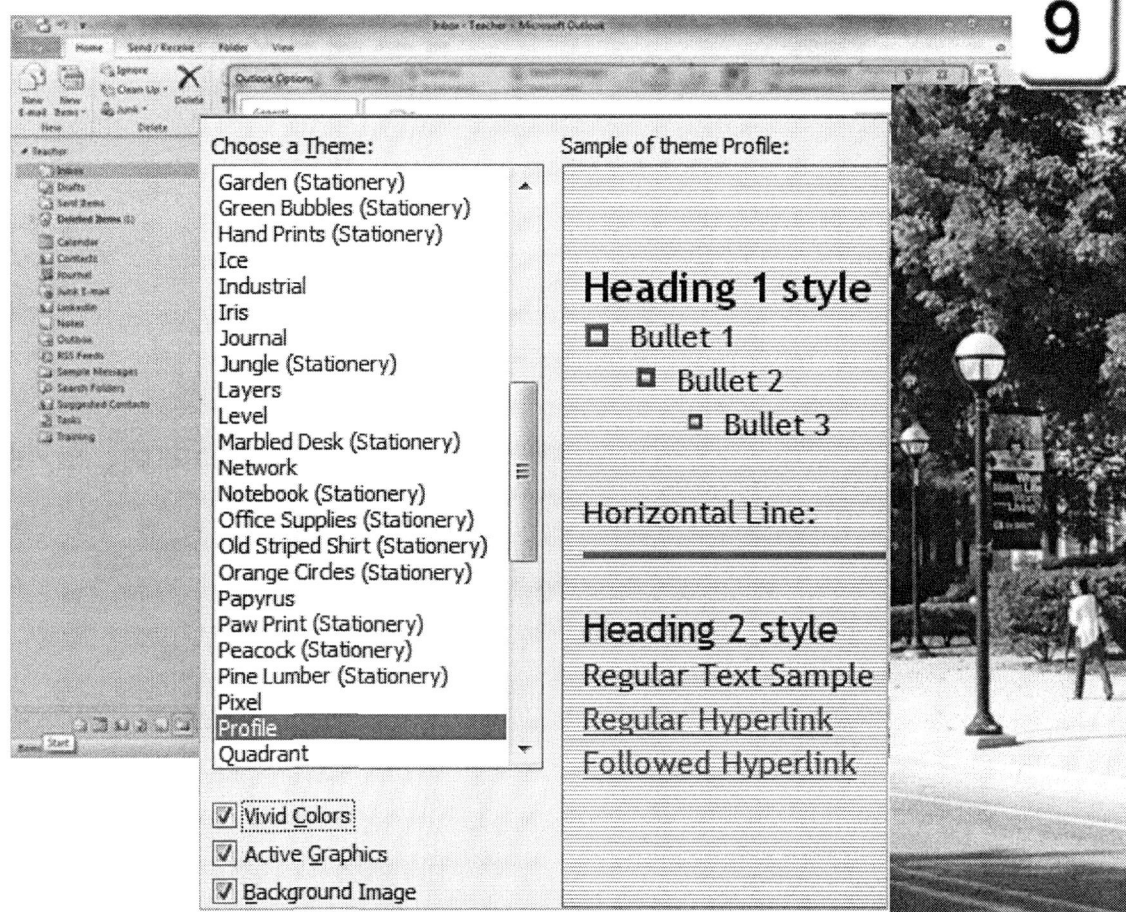

Exam 77-884: Microsoft Outlook 2010
3. Managing Email Messages
3.4. Manage automatic message content: Set a default Theme for all HTML messages

HOME

Take One

File ->Options ->Mail ->Compose Messages ->Personal Stationery->Font

Personal Stationery: Font

Say you selected a Theme. By default, Outlook will use the Theme Font for new HTML E-mail messages. There are a few more options you can consider.

Try This, Too: Review the Font Options
Signatures and Stationery window is open. The Personal Stationery is selected.
Go to **Font**.
Select: **Use theme's font.**

What Do You See? You can use the Theme Fonts or Fonts you selected for Reply and Forward. You can also decide to Always use your fonts.

Sooo what would a new E-mail look like? Click **OK** to return to the Outlook Options. Click **OK** to return to the Inbox.

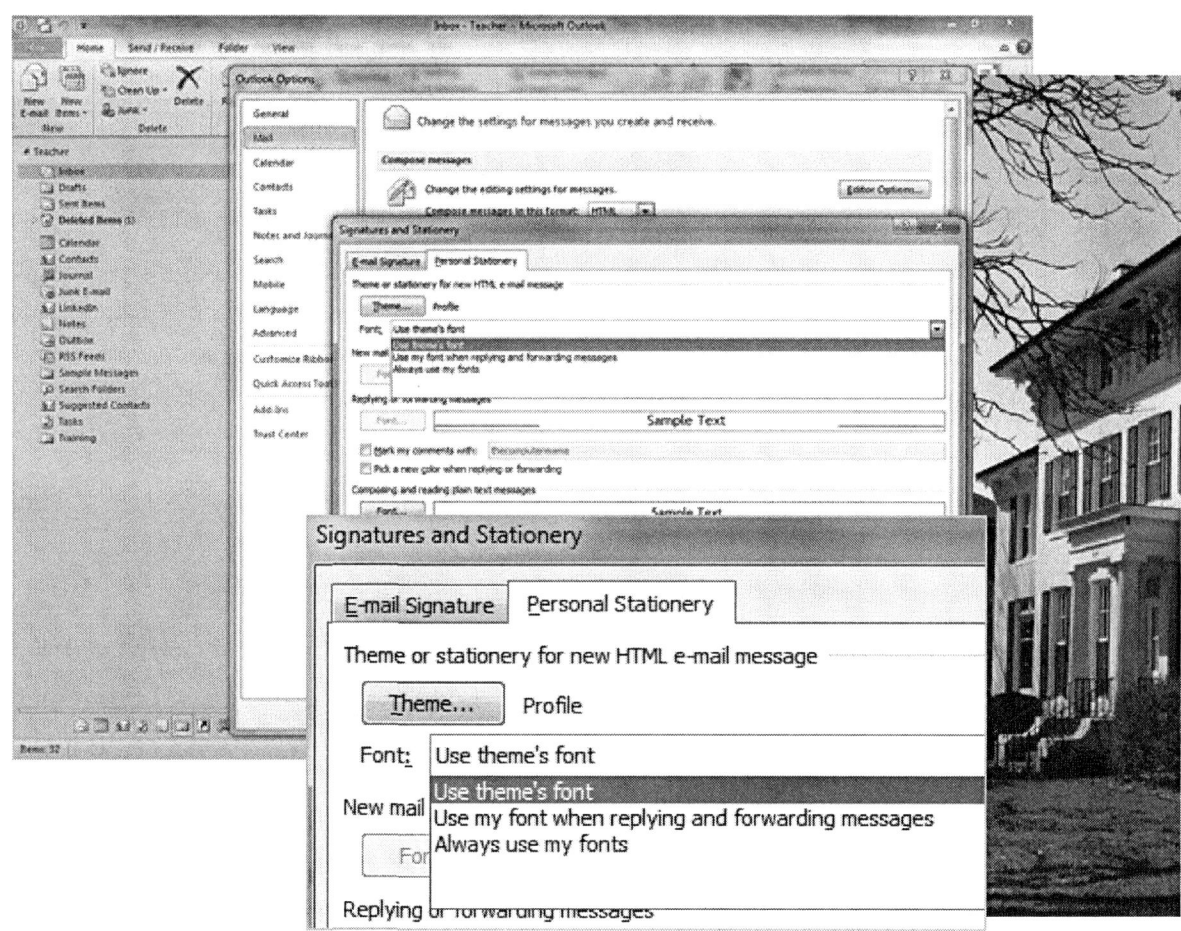

Exam 77-884: Microsoft Outlook 2010
3. Managing Email Messages
3.4. Manage automatic message content: Set a default Font for all HTML messages

Create a New E-mail

Try it: Create a New E-Mail
Go to **Home-> New-> New E-Mail.**
Enter your E-mail Address.
Enter the Subject: How do you like it?
Type the message text:
Here is an example of the new Theme.

What Do You See? The new HTML
message includes a **Signature** that
has a cartoon. The message uses the
Theme Font. There is a background
image as well.

Go ahead and click **Send**. In a few
minutes a new message should arrive
in your Inbox, formatted with Theme.

Very good.

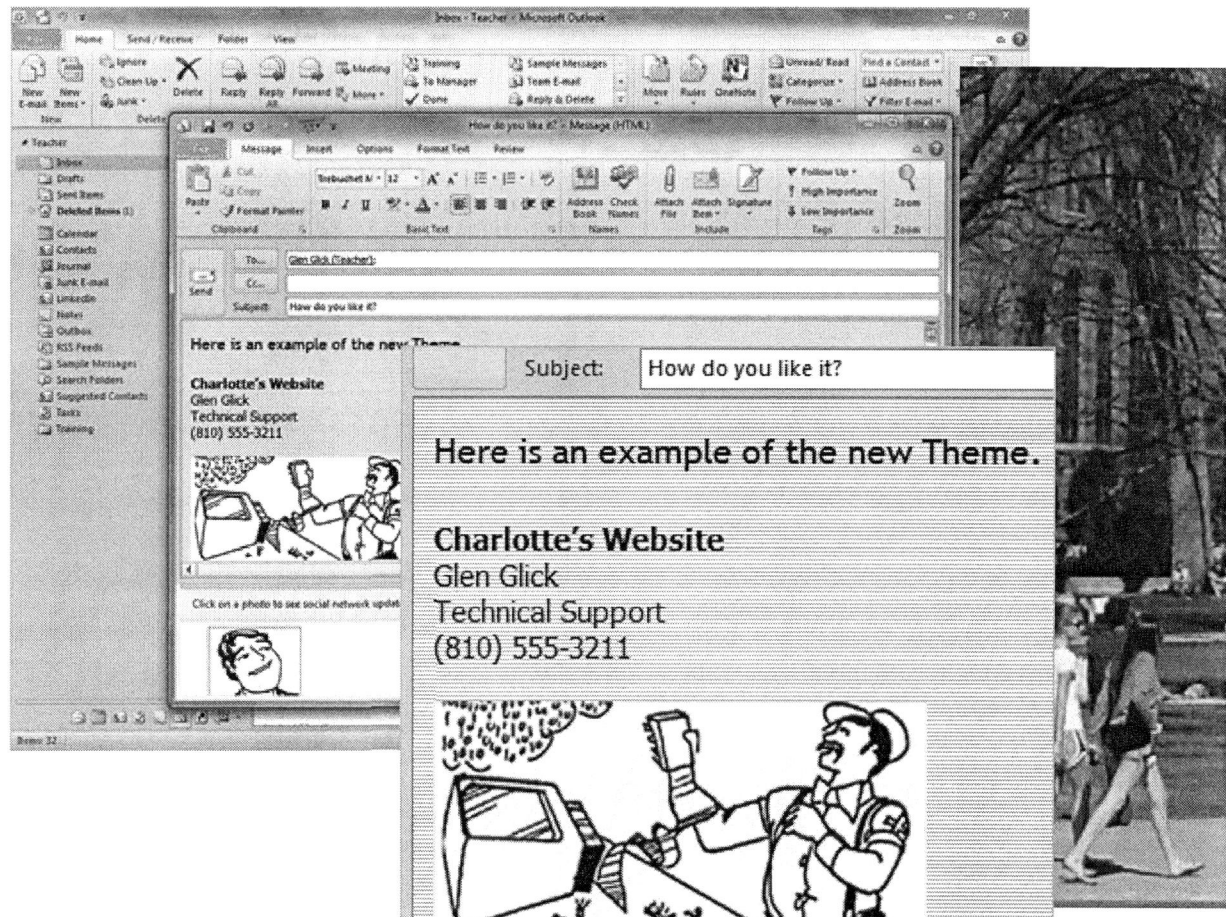

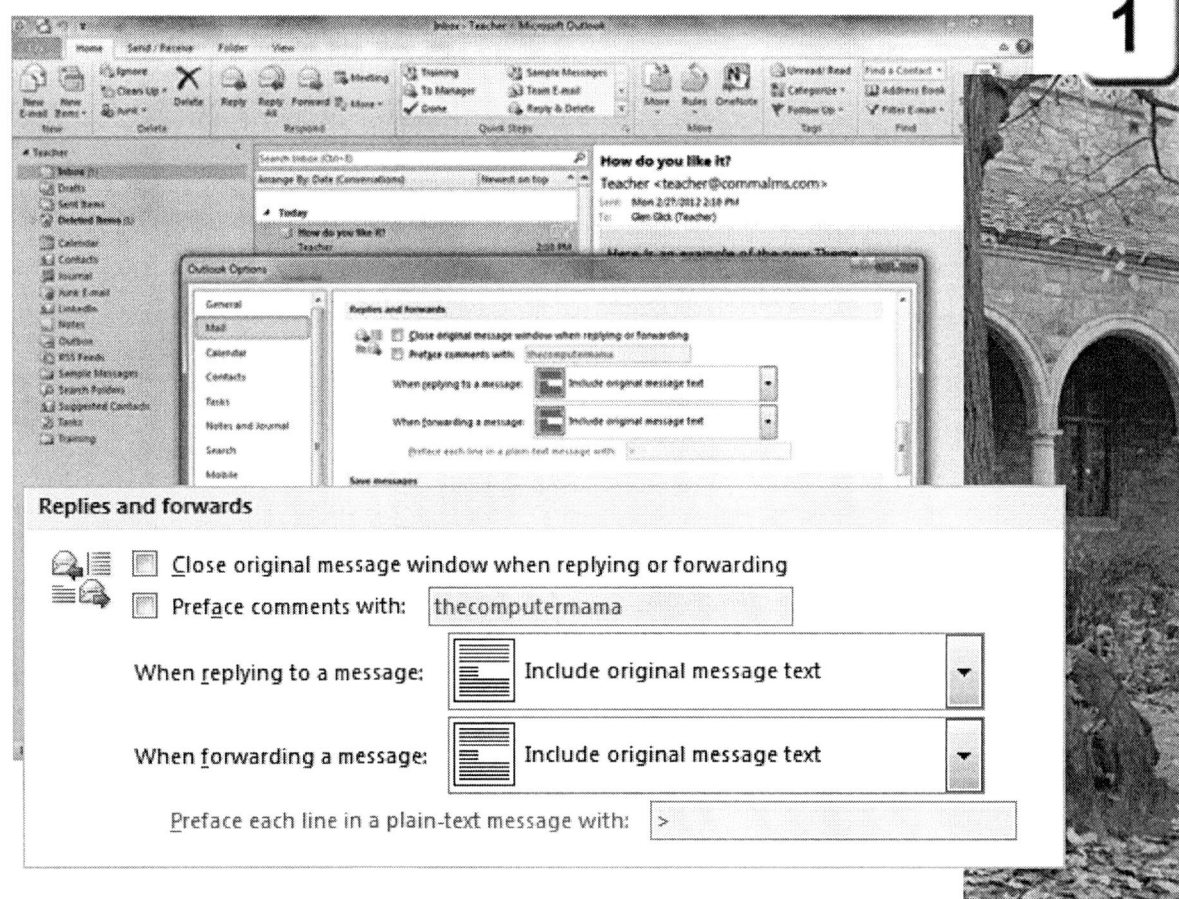

More Mail Options

There are a few more Mail Options that you should review and consider. Please return to the Outlook Options.

1. Try it: Replies and Forwards
Go to **File ->Options ->Mail**.
Go to **Replies and Forwards.**

What Do You See? You can choose to **Close original message** when replying or forwarding or **Preface comments** with your name or nym.

What Else Do You See? By default, the original message text is included when you reply or forward an E-mail.

The other options include:
Do not include original (for Reply, only)
Attached original text
Include original text
Include and indent original text
Include and prefix each line of the original

Keep going...

Exam 77-884: Microsoft Outlook 2010
3. Managing Email Messages
3.4. Manage automatic message content: Reply and Forward Options

Options: Save
2. Try it: Review the Save Options
The Outlook Options are still open and the Mail Category is selected.
Go to **Save Messages**.

What Do You See? Microsoft Outlook automatically saves items that have not been sent in 3 minutes in the Drafts folder. You can edit the time or select another folder with the controls.

What Else? The messages that you send, including ones you forwarded, are saved in the **Sent Items** folder.

Keep going...

File ->Options ->Mail-> Save Messages

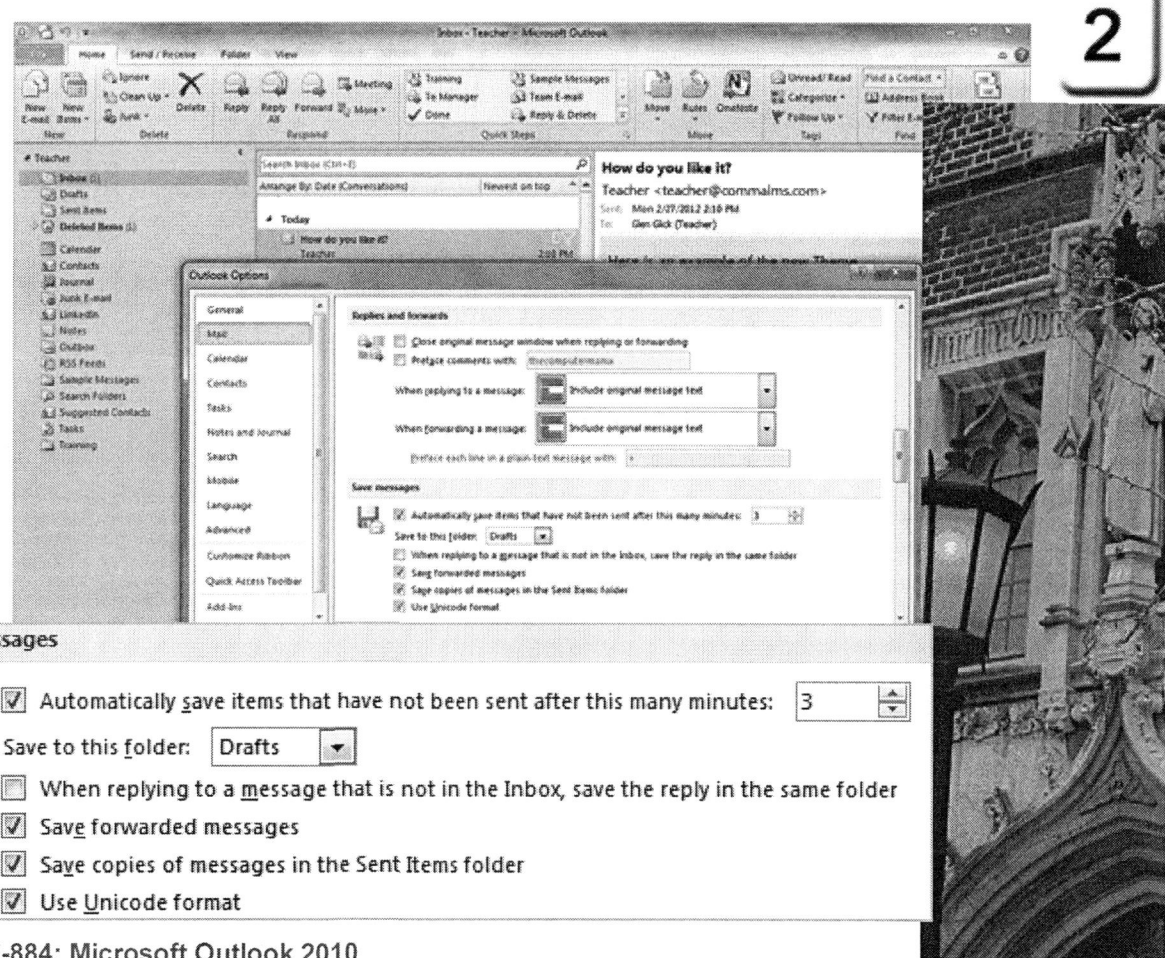

Save messages

- [✓] Automatically save items that have not been sent after this many minutes: [3] [▲▼]
- Save to this folder: [Drafts ▼]
- [ ] When replying to a message that is not in the Inbox, save the reply in the same folder
- [✓] Save forwarded messages
- [✓] Save copies of messages in the Sent Items folder
- [✓] Use Unicode format

Exam 77-884: Microsoft Outlook 2010
3. Managing Email Messages
3.4. Manage automatic message content: Options for Saving Messages

Take One

Options: Send Messages
3. Try it: Options for Send Messages
Go to **Send Messages.**

What Do You See? You can edit the default **Importance** and **Sensitivity** levels.

You can also automatically do the following before you send a message:

Mark messages as expired...
Separate recipient names with commas
Automatic name checking

Delete meeting requests from the Inbox after responding (nice, saves some steps)

Enable the keyboard command, CTRL+ENTER to send a message

Use Auto-Complete List

Keep going...!

File ->Options ->Mail-> Send Messages

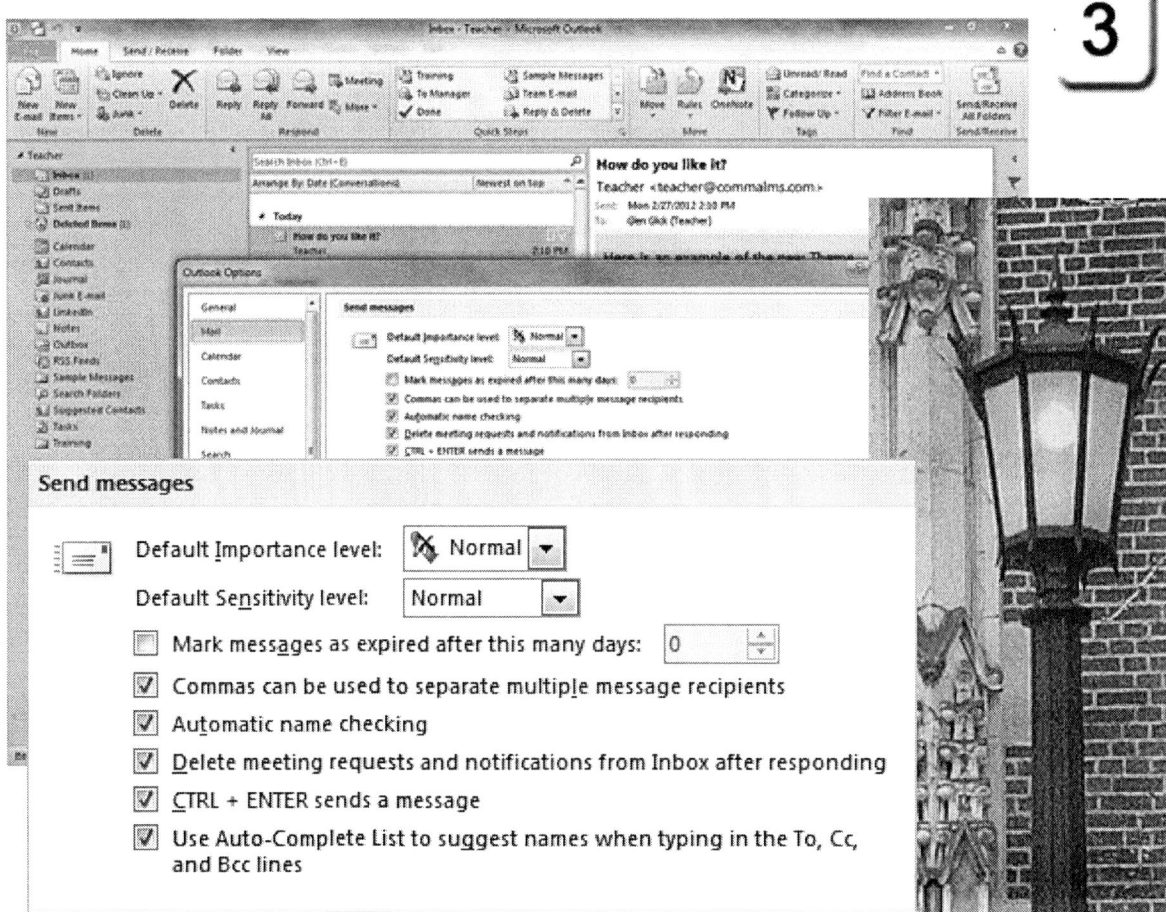

Exam 77-884: Microsoft Outlook 2010
3. Managing Email Messages
3.4. Manage automatic message content: Send Messages

Options: Tracking
4. Try it: Configure the Tracking Options
Go to **Tracking.**

What Do You See? There are options for
the recipients, messages and tracking.

Send a Tracking Request: For each
message that you create and send, you can
choose to always request Delivery and
Read receipts.

Receive a Tracking Request: For each
message that you receive that asks you for
a read recipient, you can select to Always
send, Never Send, or Ask.

These options manage the Tracking:
Automatically process meeting requests
Automatically update the original item sent

Update the tracking and delete responses
Update the tracking and move receipts

Keep going...

File ->Options ->Mail->Tracking

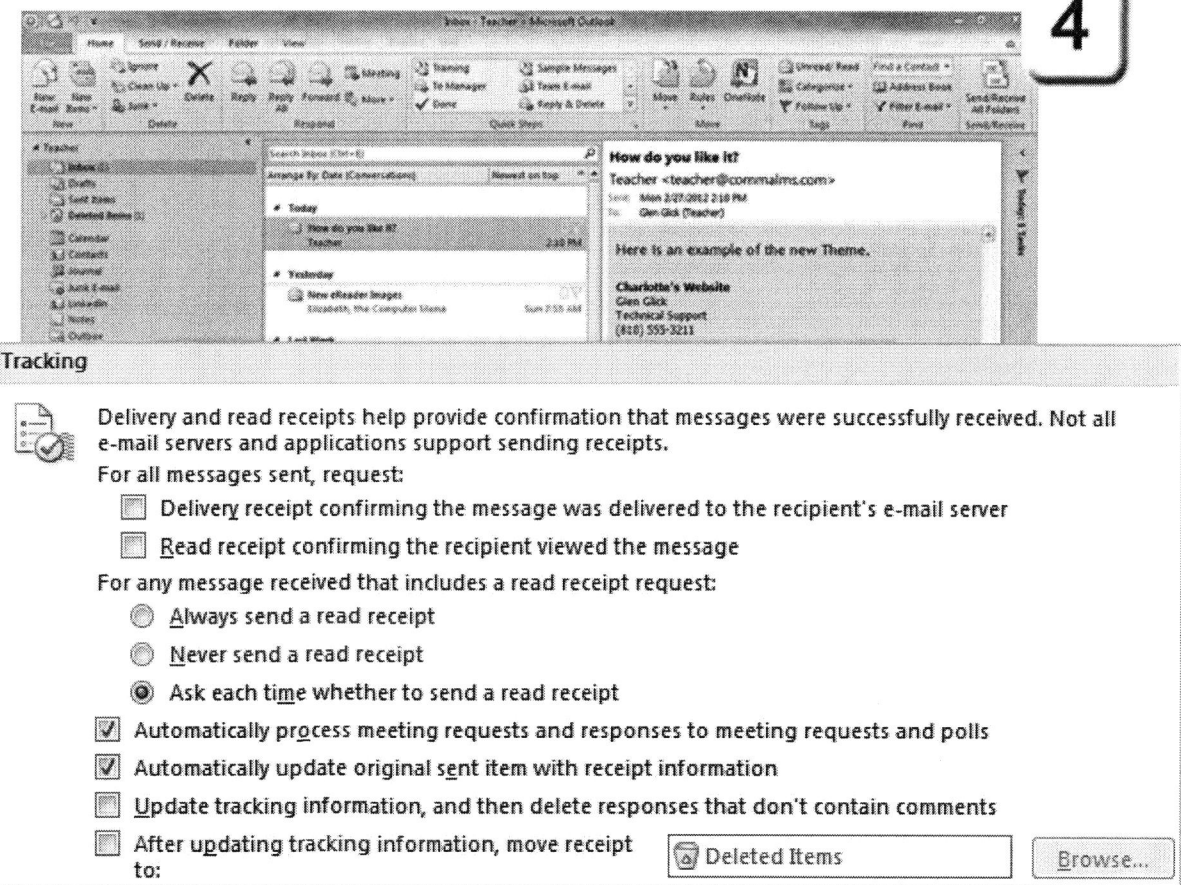

Exam 77-884: Microsoft Outlook 2010
2. Creating and Formatting Item Content
2.1. Create and send email messages: Configure Tracking Options

Options: Message Format

5. Try it: Review the Message Format
Go to **Message Format**.

What Do You See? The E-mail messages use Cascading Style Sheets (CSS) for the Themes and formatting.

By default, Outlook will reduce message size by stripping off the formatting when you are sending a message to a format that cannot see or use that formatting, say a plain-text phone.

What Else Do You See? The **Other** category has options for showing the Paste button, Microsoft InfoPath E-mail Forms, Message Headers and Conversations.

That should cover all of the Mail Options. Let's look at the ones for the Calendar.

File ->Options ->Mail-> Message Format

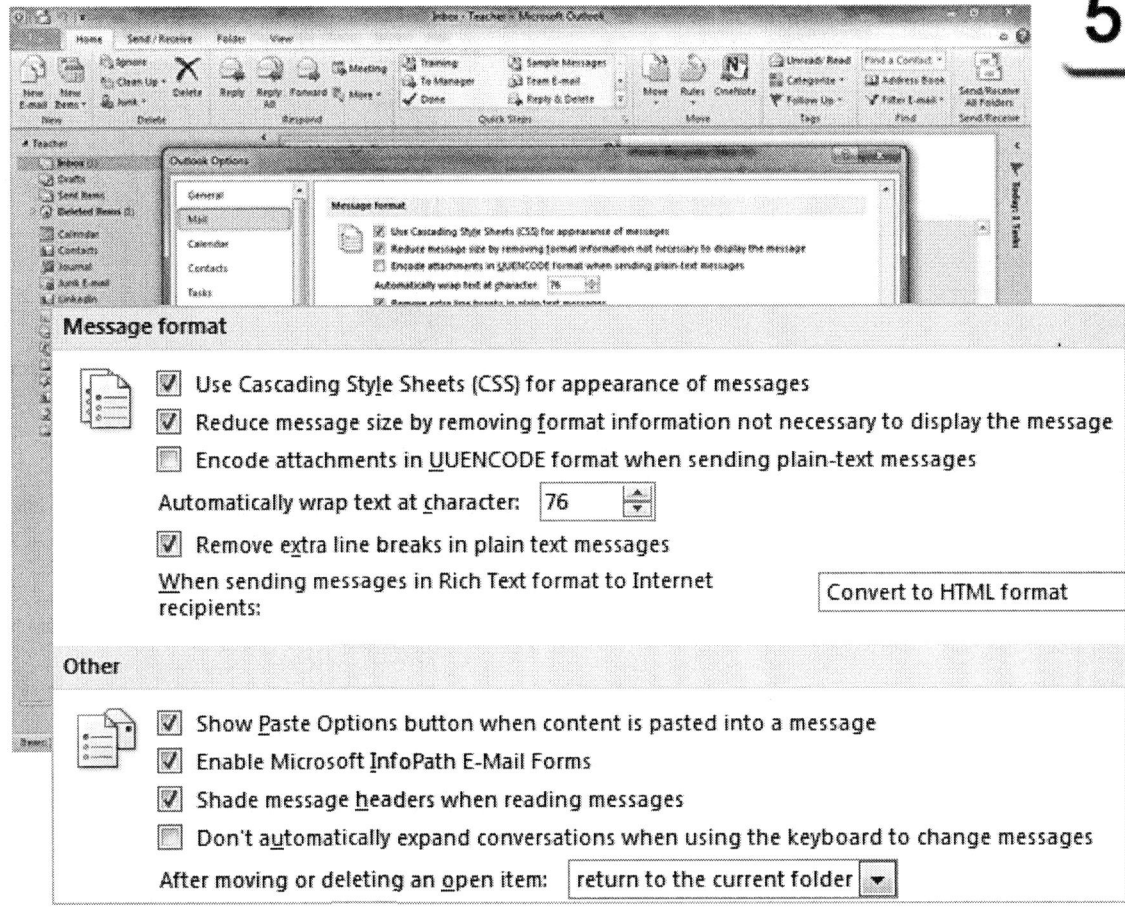

Message format

☑ Use Cascading Style Sheets (CSS) for appearance of messages

☑ Reduce message size by removing format information not necessary to display the message

☐ Encode attachments in UUENCODE format when sending plain-text messages

Automatically wrap text at character: 76

☑ Remove extra line breaks in plain text messages

When sending messages in Rich Text format to Internet recipients: Convert to HTML format

Other

☑ Show Paste Options button when content is pasted into a message

☑ Enable Microsoft InfoPath E-Mail Forms

☑ Shade message headers when reading messages

☐ Don't automatically expand conversations when using the keyboard to change messages

After moving or deleting an open item: return to the current folder ▼

Exam 77-884: Microsoft Outlook 2010
3. Managing Email Messages
3.4. Manage automatic message content

Review the Calendar Options

Each profession may have a different work week. A fire fighter's schedule will be different from a doctor or plant manager. You can use the Calendar options to edit the **Work Time**.

1. Try it: Edit the Work Time

The Outlook Options are still open and the **Calendar** Category is selected.
Go to **Work Time**.

What Do You See? The default Work hours start at 6:00 AM and End at 7:00 PM. The Work week is Monday through Friday, You can select different days if you wish.

Keep going...

File ->Options ->Calendar->Work Time

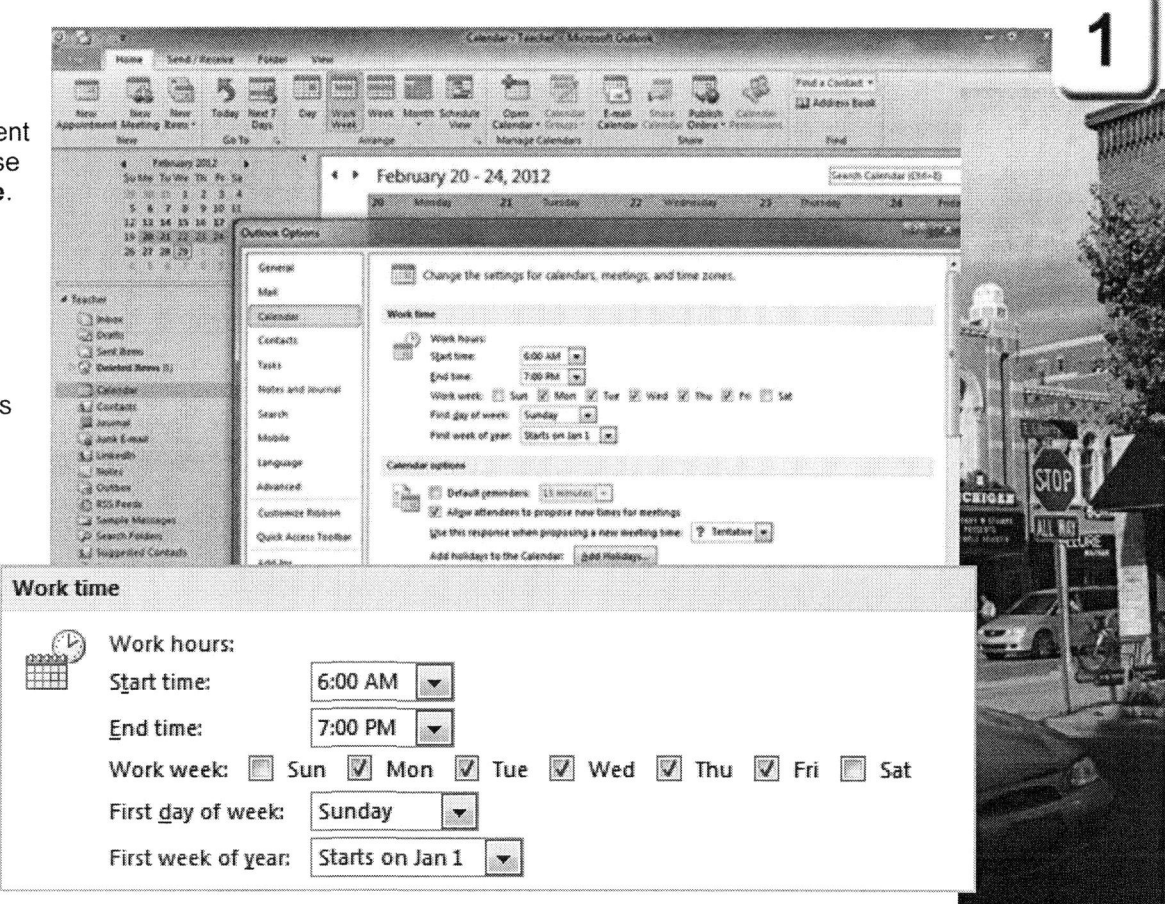

Exam 77-884: Microsoft Outlook 2010
1. Managing the Outlook Environment
1.1. Apply and manipulate Outlook program options: Set Calendar Options

Calendar Options

2. Try it: Review the Calendar Options
Go to the **Calendar Options.**

What Do You See? There are options for reminders, meetings, and holidays.

As we saw earlier, attendees can propose a new meeting time. You can choose a default response when proposing a new meeting time (Tentative, Accept or Decline) if you wish.

When you click **Add Holidays**, you will be prompted to choose which ones you want to add by selecting a country from the list.

You can also edit the **Free/Busy Options**. By default, Microsoft Outlook publishes 2 months of **Free/Busy time** to the Server. The Free/Busy information is updated every 15 minutes.

Keep going, please.

File ->Options ->Calendar-> Calendar Options

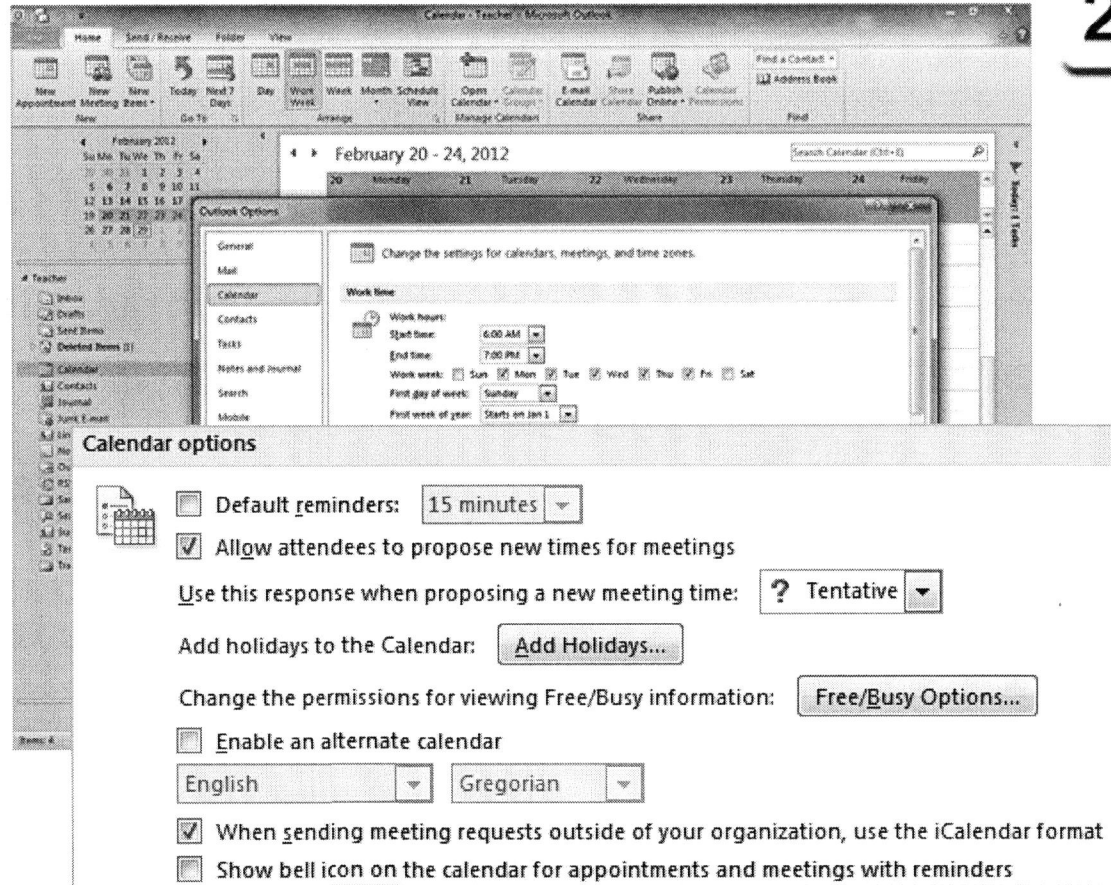

Exam 77-884: Microsoft Outlook 2010
1. Managing the Outlook Environment
1.1. Apply and manipulate Outlook program options: Set Calendar Options

Calendar: Display Options

3. Try it: Review the Display Options
The Calendar Options are still selected.
Go to the **Display Options.**

What Do You See, Now? The options are:
Default calendar color
Date Navigator font

You can also select the following:
Show Click to Add prompts in calendar
Show the week numbers
Show free appointments in Schedule View

Automatically switch from vertical layout to schedule view when there are many calendars

Automatically switch from schedule view to layout view when there is only one calendar.

Keep going...

File ->Options ->Calendar->Display Options

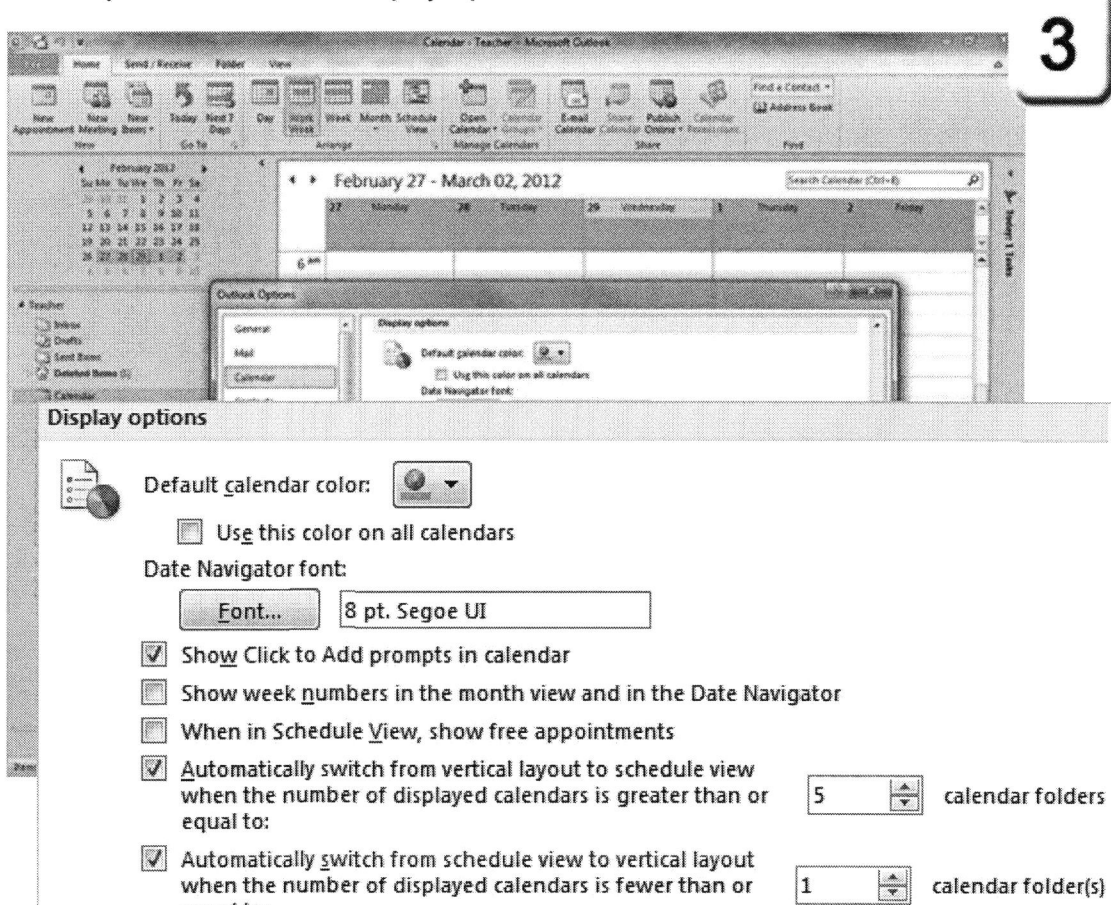

Exam 77-884: Microsoft Outlook 2010
5. Managing Calendar Objects
5.3. Manipulate the Calendar pane: Change the Calendar Color

Review the Task Options

4. Try it: Review the Task Options
Select the **Tasks** category.

What Do You See? The **Task Options**
format Reminders and Work hours.

Outlook will update the Task List when the
assigned Tasks are changed.

Outlook will also send s Status Report when
you complete an assigned Task.

What Else Do You See? You can edit the
color for Overdue and Completed Tasks.

Keep going...

File ->Options ->Tasks

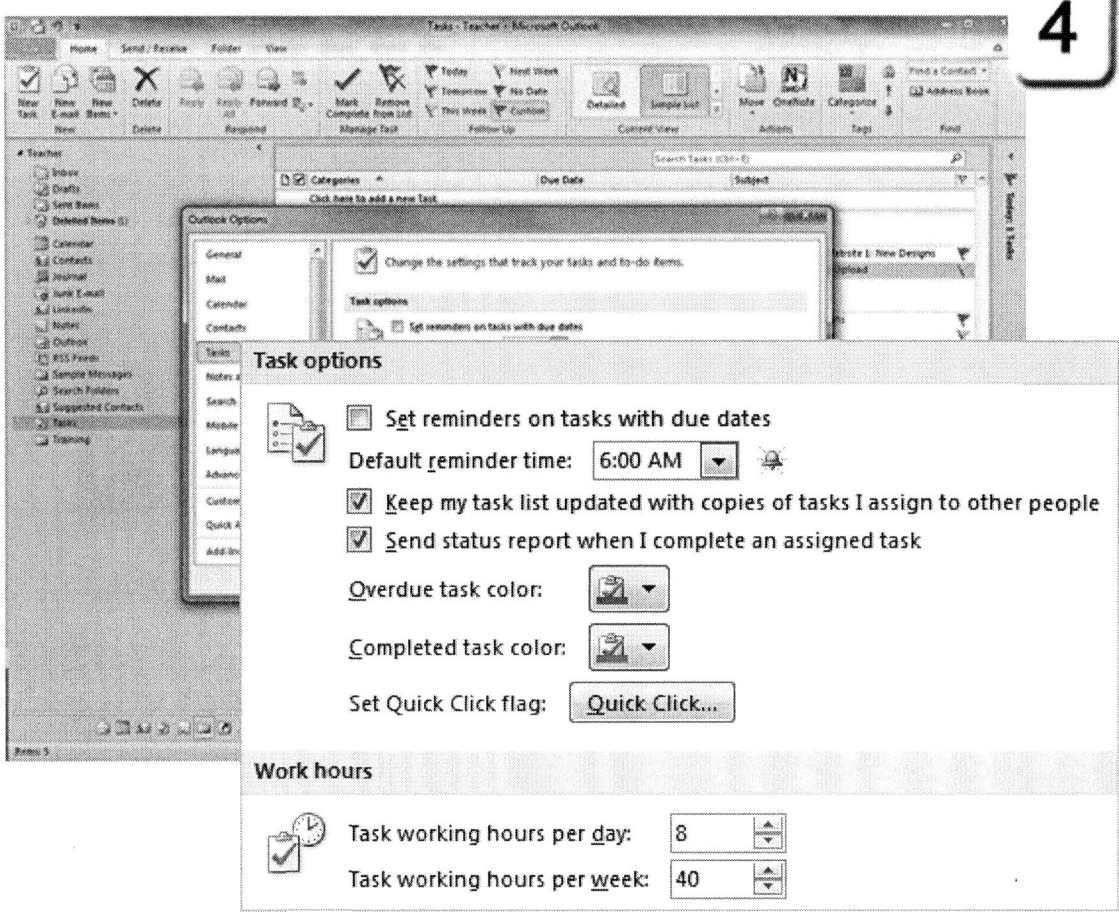

Exam 77-884: Microsoft Outlook 2010
1. Managing the Outlook Environment
1.1. Apply and manipulate Outlook program options: Set Task Options

Review the Notes Options
5. Try it: Review the Notes Options
The Outlook Options are still open.
Select **Notes and Journal.**

What Do You See? The **Notes**
options are very simple: color, size
and font.

By default, the Note shows the date
and time that the Note was changed.

Keep going...

File ->Options ->Notes and Journal

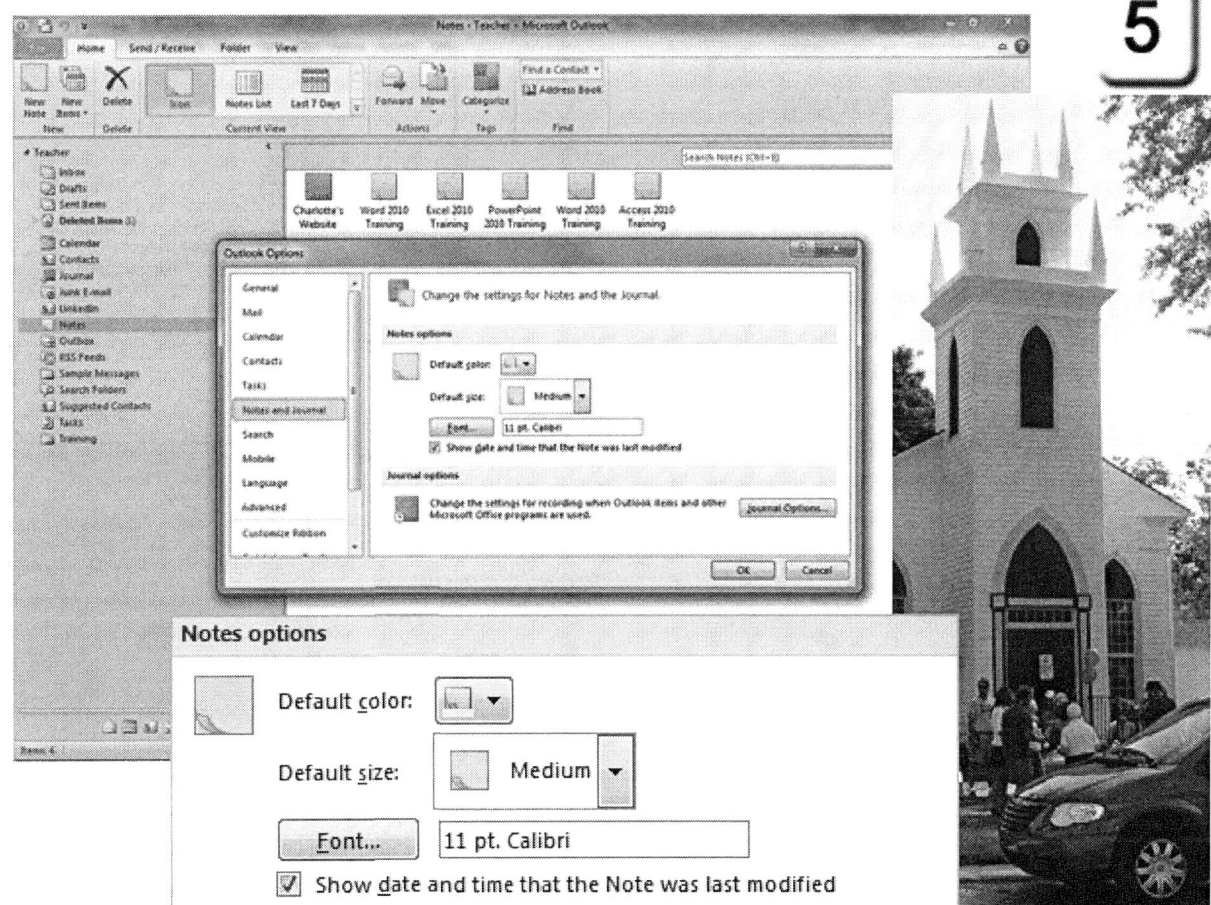

Notes options

Default color: [▼]

Default size: [Medium ▼]

[Font...] [11 pt. Calibri]

☑ Show date and time that the Note was last modified

Exam 77-884: Microsoft Outlook 2010
1. Managing the Outlook Environment
1.1. Apply and manipulate Outlook program options: Set Notes and Journal Options

Review the Journal Options

6. Try it: Review the Journal Options
The Outlook Options are still open.
The **Notes and Journal** are selected.
Click on **Journal Options**.

What Do You See? We found the Journal Options in the previous lesson. You can set the Journal to automatically record messages, meetings, tasks and time spent on Microsoft Office files.

Keep going...one more Outlook Option.

File ->Options ->Notes and Journal

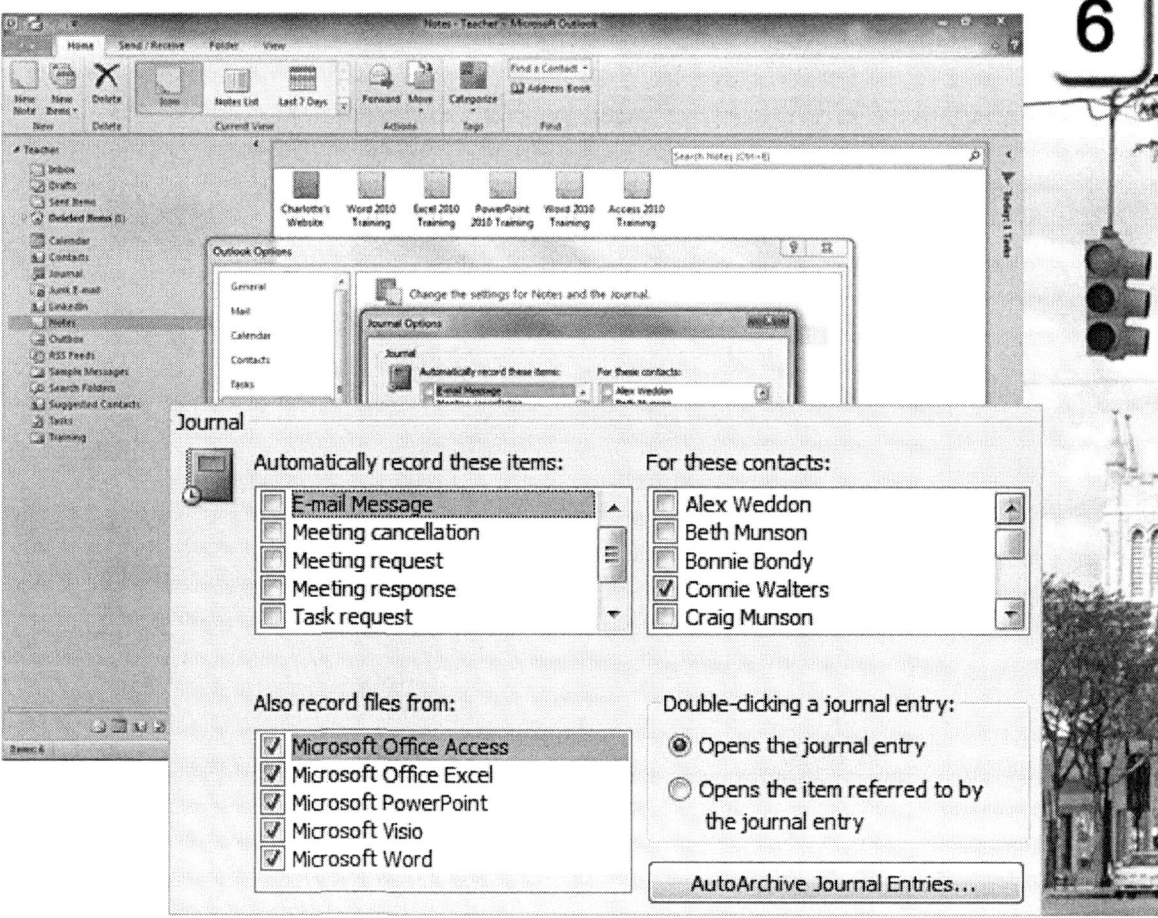

Exam 77-884: Microsoft Outlook 2010
1. Managing the Outlook Environment
1.1. Apply and manipulate Outlook program options: Set Notes and Journal Options

Review Language Options

Microsoft Outlook can have more than one **Language** for editing, dictionaries, grammar check and sorting.

7. Try it: Review the Language Options
The Outlook Options are still open.
Go to the **Language** Options.

What Do You See? You can **Add additional editing languages.** You can also choose which language is your primary editing language for the buttons, tabs and Help.

OK, that completes this review of the Outlook Options. Let's work with the Calendars.

File ->Options ->Language

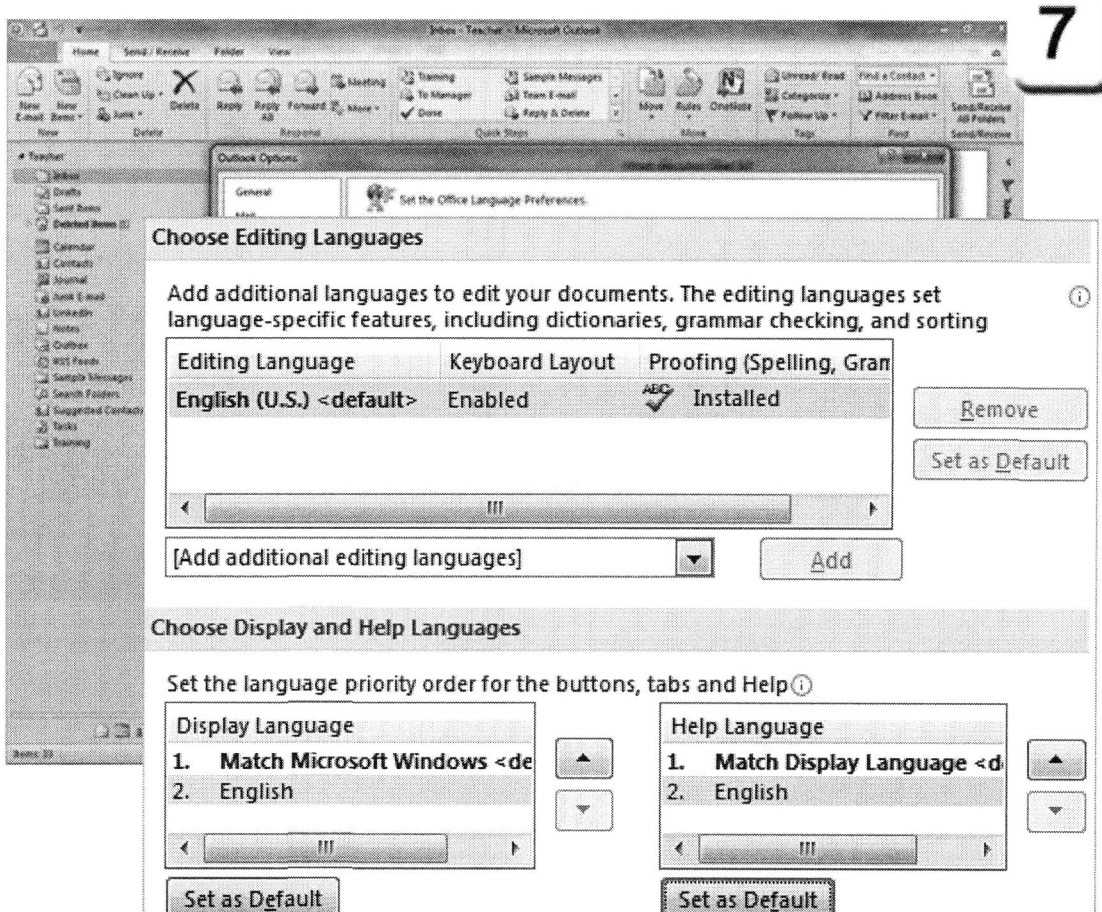

Exam 77-884: Microsoft Outlook 2010
1. Managing the Outlook Environment
1.1. Apply and manipulate Outlook program options: Set Language Options

Create Another Calendar

Microsoft Outlook can have more than one **Calendar** for recording your activities and meetings. For example, each room or resource in the office can have a Calendar.

1. Try it: Create Another Calendar
The Outlook Calendar is selected.
Go to **Home ->Manage Calendars**
Click on **Open Calendar**.
Select: **Create New Blank Calendar**.

Keep going...

Home ->Manage Calendars->Open Calendar ->Create New Blank Calendar

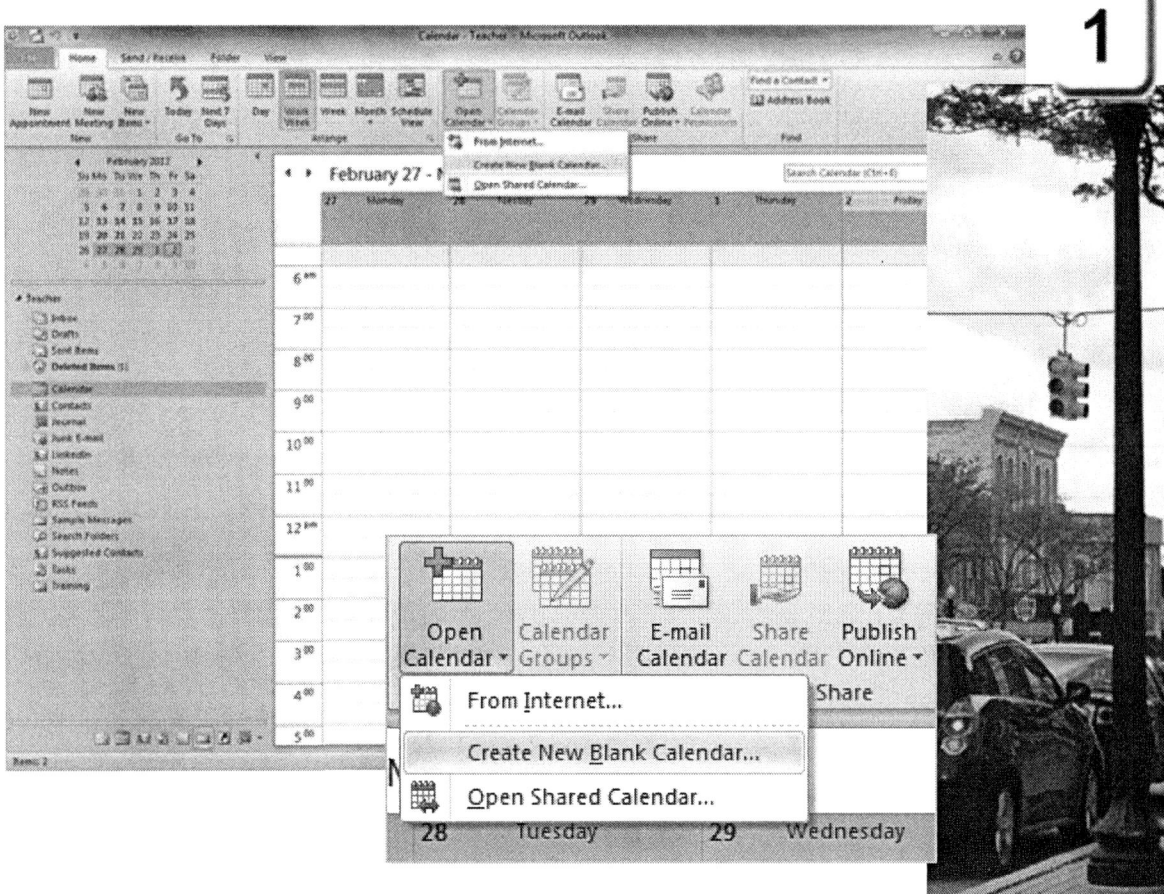

Exam 77-884: Microsoft Outlook 2010
5. Managing Calendar Objects
5.3. Manipulate the Calendar pane: Create a New Calendar

Create a New Folder

2. Try it: Select a Place for the Calendar
The new Calendar is a folder. You will be prompted to choose where you would like to place your new Calendar Folder.

Enter a Name: Conference Room
Select a Place: The Calendar Folder.
Click **OK**.

Keep going...

Create New Folder

Name:

Conference Room

Folder contains:

Calendar Items

Select where to place the folder:

- ⬙ Teacher
  - Inbox
  - Drafts
  - Sent Items
  - ▷ **Deleted Items** (1)
  - Calendar
  - Contacts
  - Journal
  - Junk E-mail
  - LinkedIn

OK   Cancel

Exam 77-884: Microsoft Outlook 2010
5. Managing Calendar Objects
5.3. Manipulate the Calendar pane: Create a New Calendar

Take One

Find The New Calendar
3. What Do You See? The new **Conference Room** Calendar will be placed under the primary **Calendar**.

In the example on this page, the Conference Room Calendar is a different color than the default blue of the Outlook Calendar.

Keep going...

Microsoft Outlook->Calendar

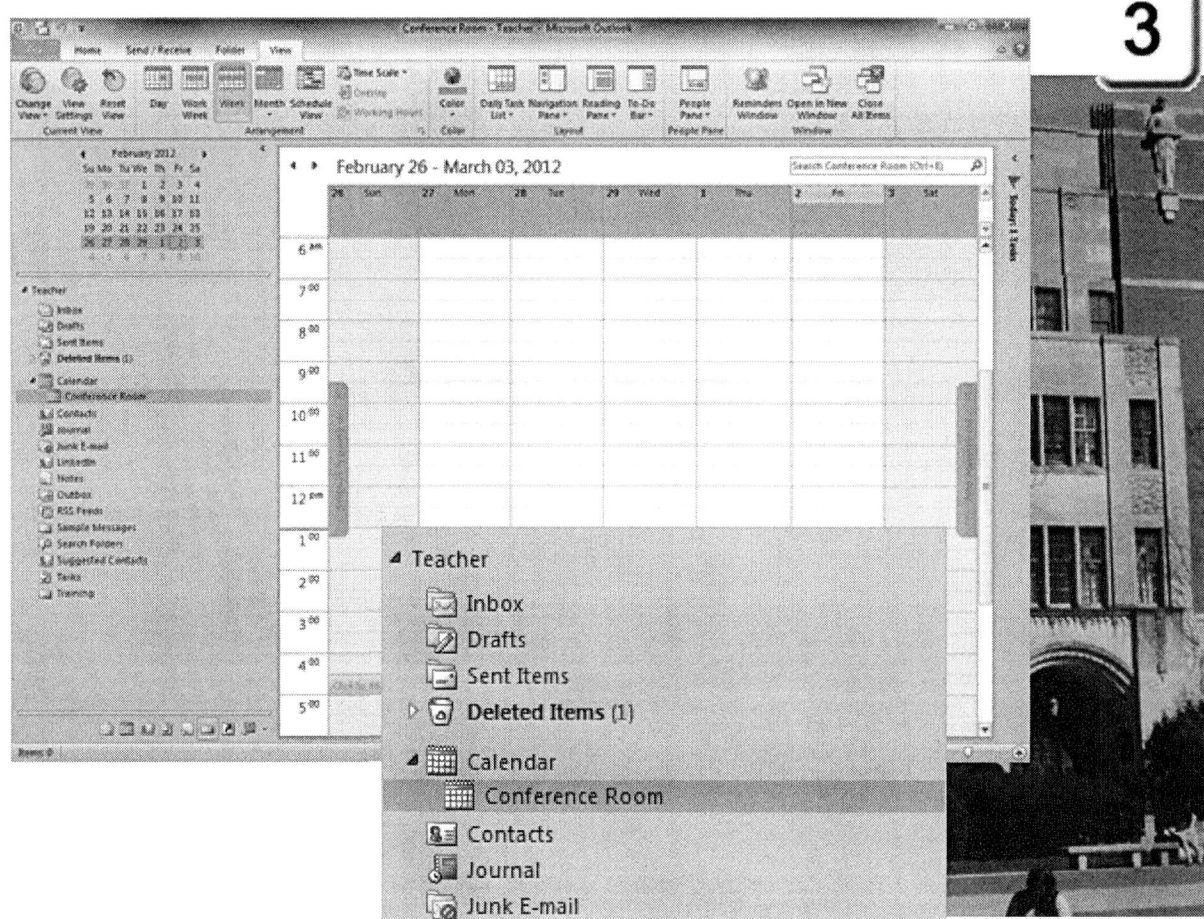

Exam 77-884: Microsoft Outlook 2010
5. Managing Calendar Objects
5.3. Manipulate the Calendar pane: Create a New Calendar

Publish a Calendar Online

In a big company you can Share your Calendar with the other people on your Microsoft Exchange or SharePoint Server.

In a little company, you can use **Publish Online** to share a Calendar if you do not have a Exchange or SharePoint Server.

1. Try it: Publish a Calendar Online
The Outlook Calendar is still open.
Go to **Home ->Share ->Publish Online**.
Select: **Publish to Office.com...**

Keep going...

Home ->Share ->Publish Online

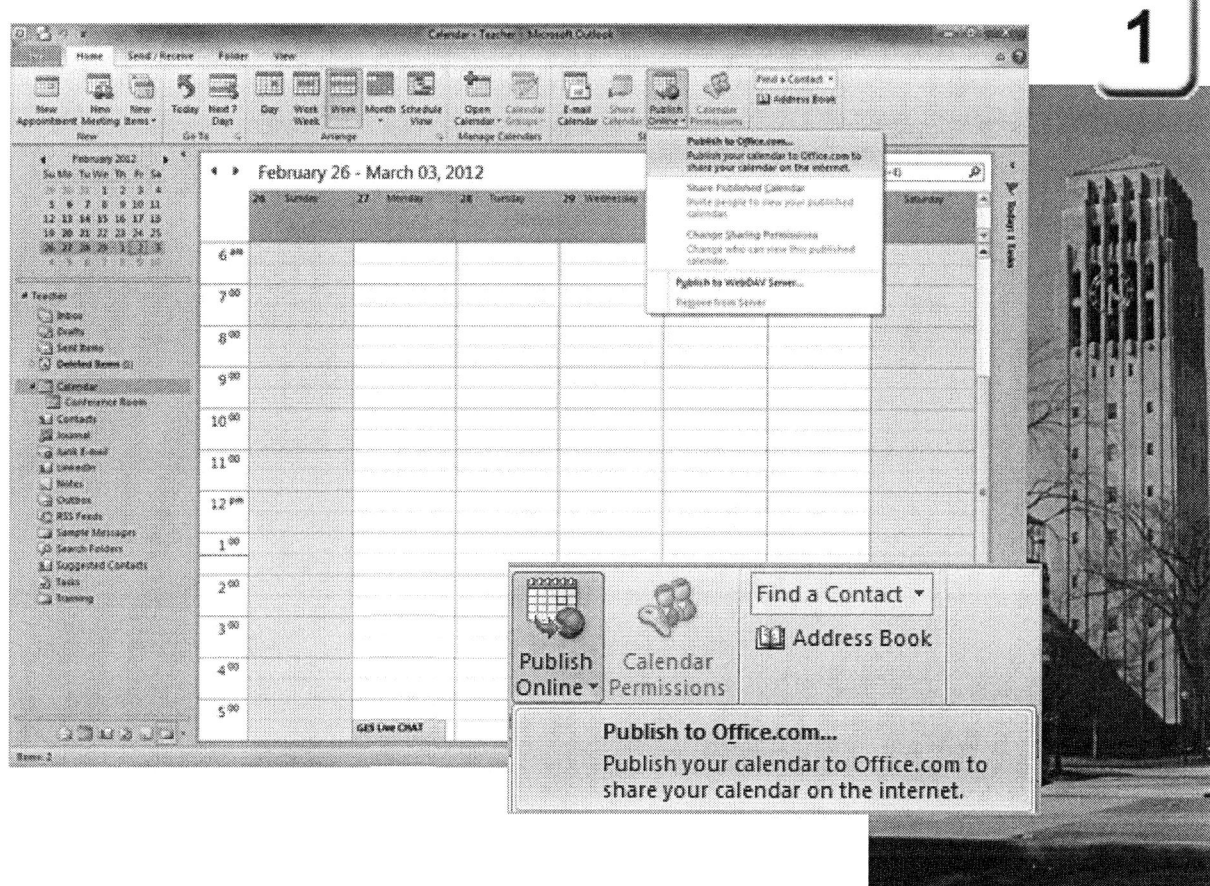

Exam 77-884: Microsoft Outlook 2010
5. Managing Calendar Objects
5.3. Manipulate the Calendar pane: Publish a Calendar Online

Identify Yourself: Log In with a Windows Live ID

2. Try it: Login with a Windows Live ID
You need to identify yourself when you publish a Calendar online. Microsoft Office.com prefers that you log in with a Windows Live passport.

What Do You See? You can create a new Windows Live passport if you wish. This account is free and only takes a few minutes to setup.

Keep going...

Home ->Share ->Publish Online

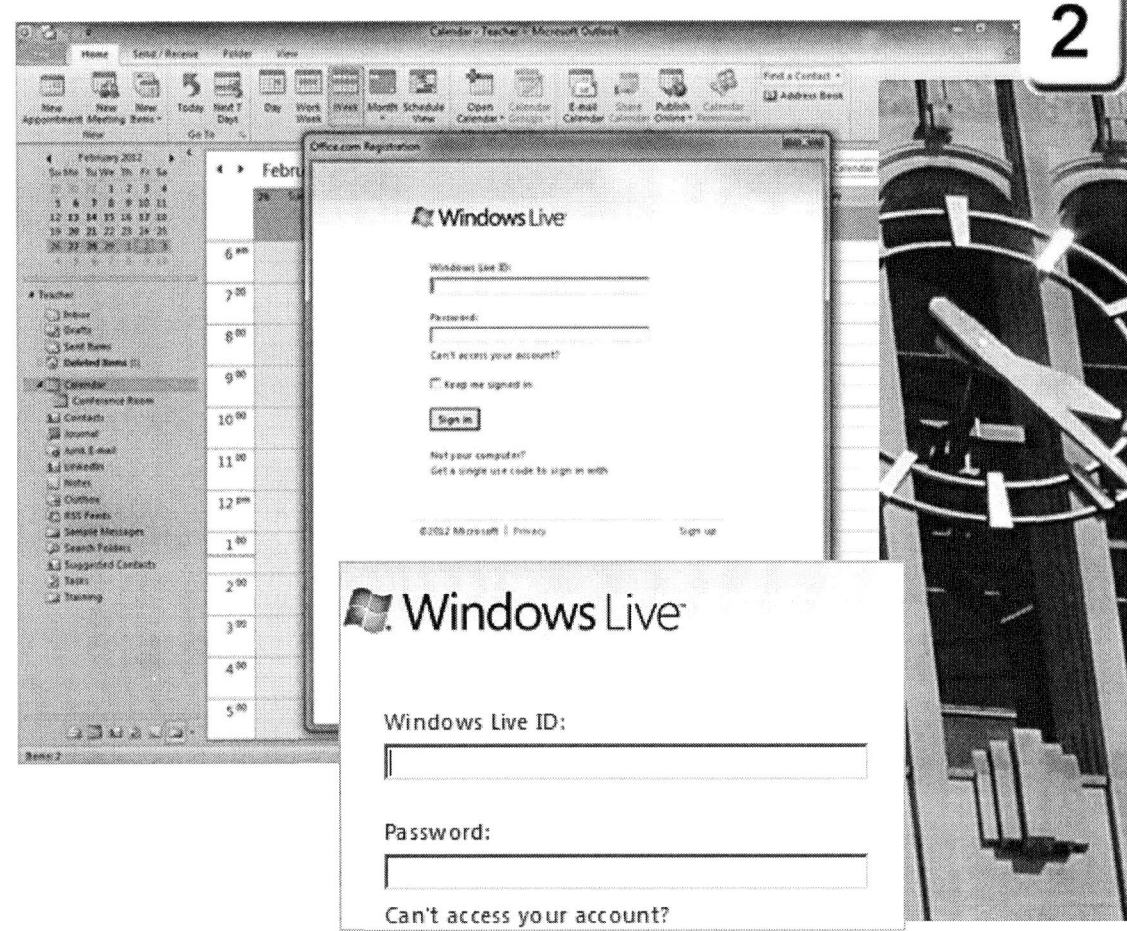

Exam 77-884: Microsoft Outlook 2010
5. Managing Calendar Objects
5.3. Manipulate the Calendar pane: Publish a Calendar Online

Edit the Publication Options

3. Try it: Edit the Publication Options
You can edit the Time Span, Detail and Permissions if you wish.

The Detail options are:
Availability Only (Free, Busy, Out of Office)
Limited Details (Availability and Subject)
Full Details (Availability and all of the data)

The Permissions are:
Only invited users can subscribe
Anyone can subscribe

Click **OK**. Keep going...

Home ->Share ->Publish Online

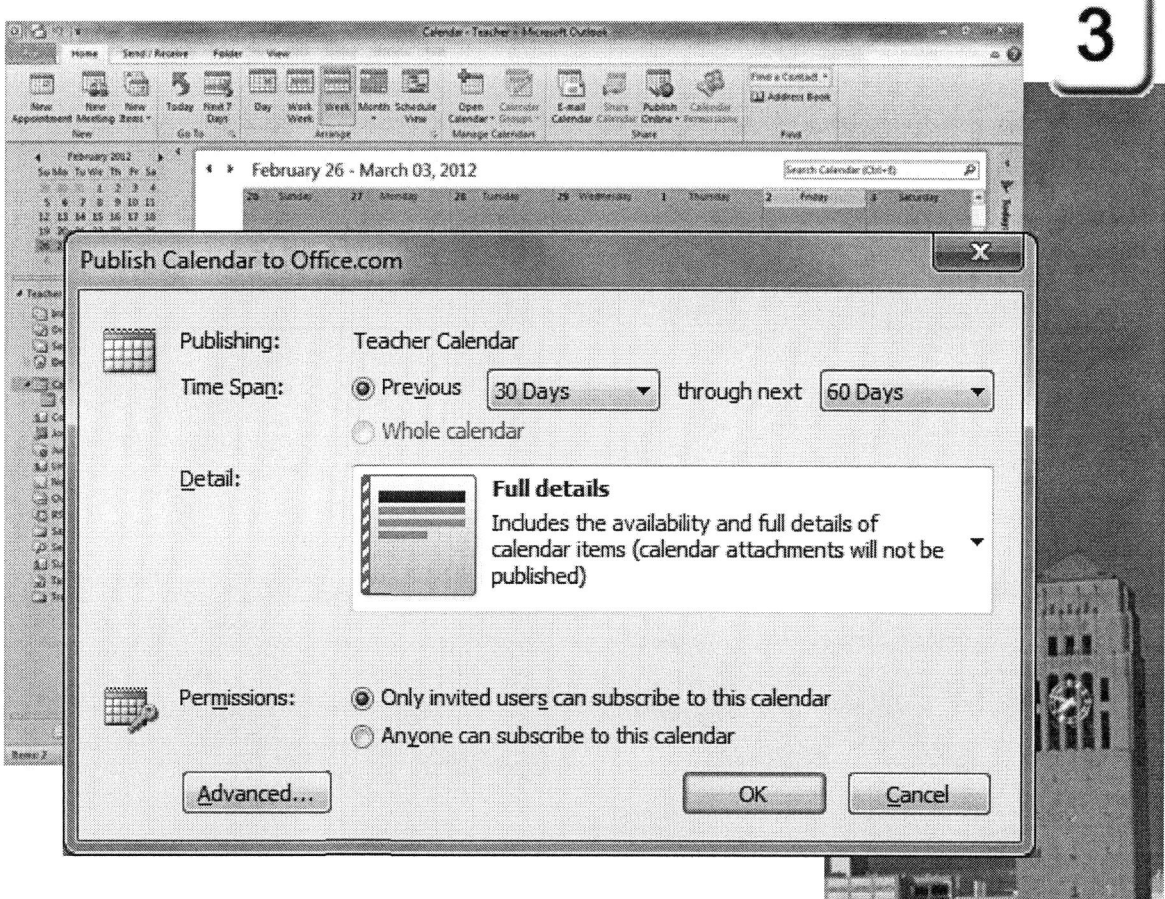

Exam 77-884: Microsoft Outlook 2010
5. Managing Calendar Objects
5.3. Manipulate the Calendar pane: Publish a Calendar Online

Share an Internet Calendar
4. Try it: Share an Internet Calendar
When you publish your Calendar to the Internet, you will be prompted to Share it.

Select "Yes", a new E-mail message will open with the Subject Line: Internet Calendar.

Enter a Recipient: Choose an E-mail address for one of your Contacts.

Click **Send**. Keep going...

Home ->Share ->Publish Online

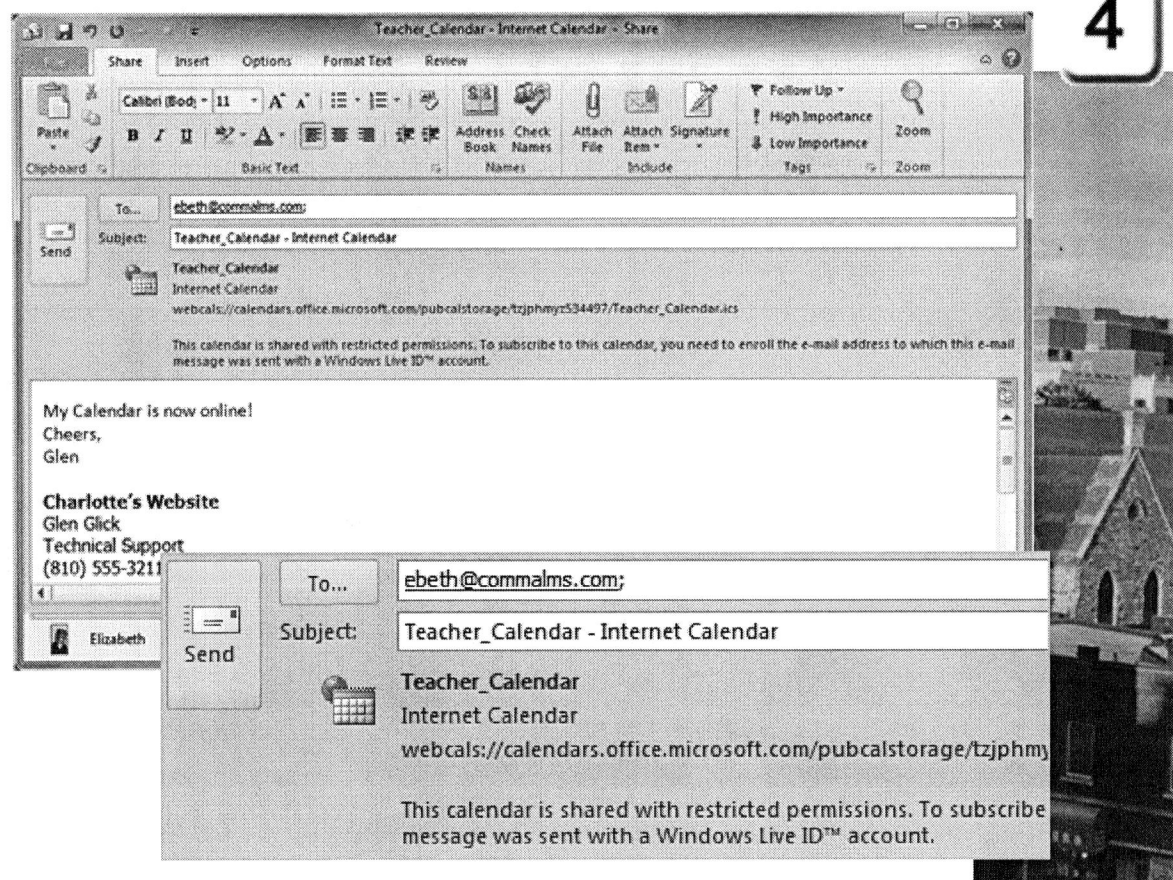

Exam 77-884: Microsoft Outlook 2010
5. Managing Calendar Objects
5.3. Manipulate the Calendar pane: Share an Internet Calendar

Add an Internet Calendar and Subscribe to Updates

5. Try it: Add an Internet Calendar
Say you are invited to share an Internet Calendar. You should receive an E-mail asking you to **Subscribe to this Calendar**.

This connection, like E-mail, requires Internet Access. When you click **Yes**, Outlook will go online and subscribe to the Calendar link in this invitation.

Keep going...

Memo to Self: Calendars are private. calendars.office.microsoft.com is a public web site. The Computer Mama strongly recommends that you mark your personal appointments **Private**!

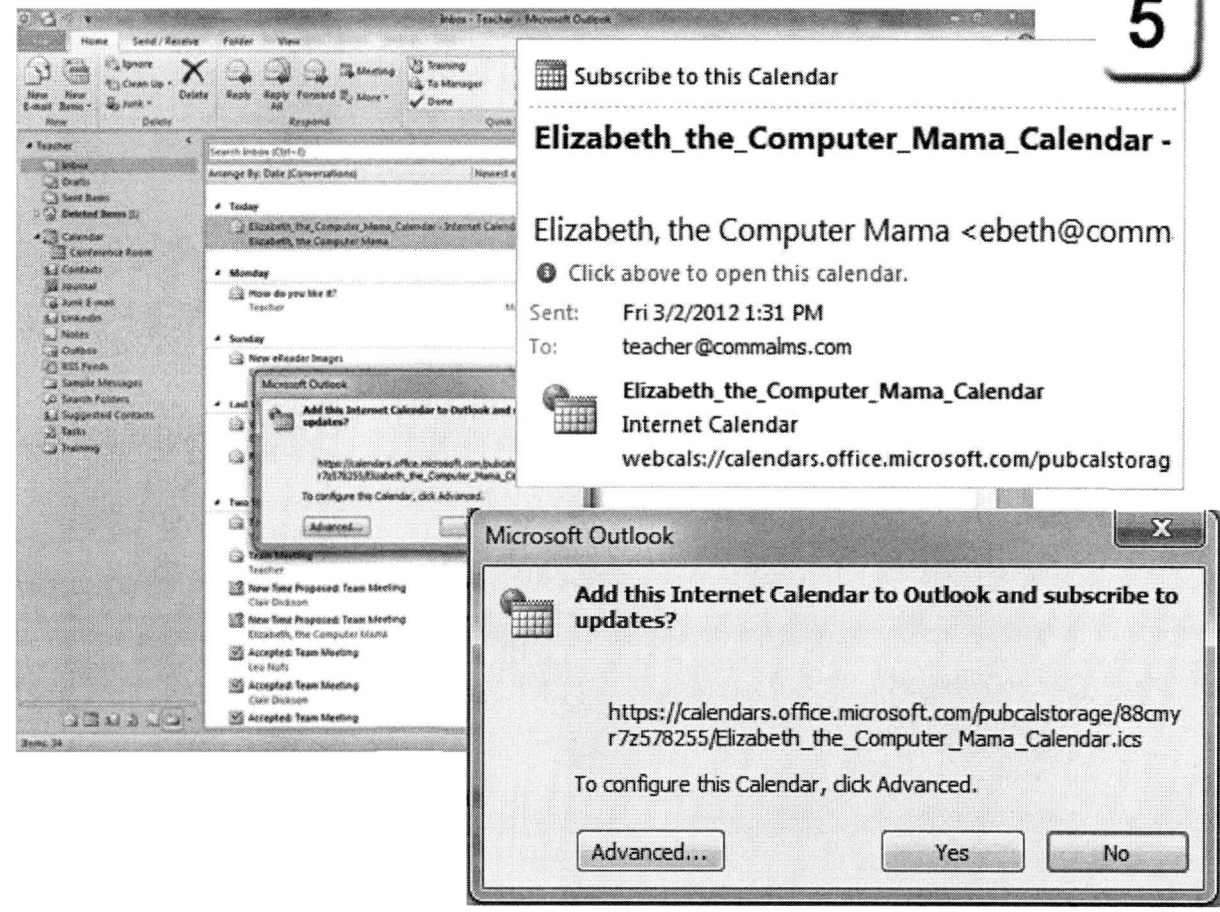

Exam 77-884: Microsoft Outlook 2010
5. Managing Calendar Objects
5.3. Manipulate the Calendar pane: Add an Internet Calendar

View->Layout->Navigation Pane->Normal

Show a Calendar Group

6. Try it: Show or Hide Calendars
Three Calendars are open In the example on this page: My Calendar, the Conference Room and the Shared Calendar. Each Calendar has a different color. The Calendars can be arranged differently as well: Day, Week, or Month view.

Try This, Too: Use the Navigation Pane
Go to **View->Layout->Navigation Pane.**
Click on **Normal.**
The Navigation Pane should open on the left side.

What Do You See? Each Calendar is listed. My Calendars are the folders in my Outlook file. The Shared Calendar is online. It is the one we just subscribed.

You can **Show or Hide** the Calendars with the check mark if you wish.

Keep going...

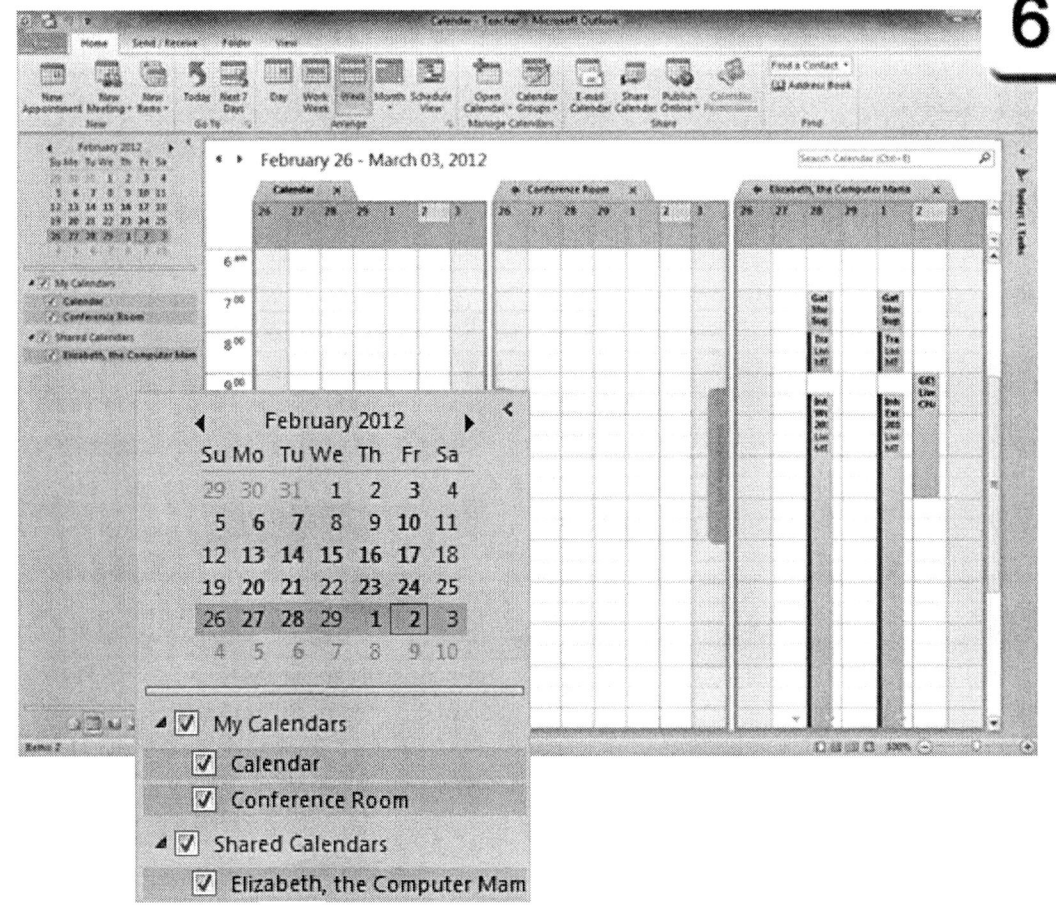

Exam 77-884: Microsoft Outlook 2010
5. Managing Calendar Objects
5.3. Manipulate the Calendar pane: Show or Hide Calendars

Create a Calendar Group

Say you work with several Calendars all of the time. You can create a **Calendar Group** that saves your layout.

7. Try it: Create a Calendar Group
Three Calendars are open.
Go to **Home ->Manage Calendars.**
Click on: **Calendar Groups**.

What Do You See? You can **Create a New Calendar Group.** You can also Save the current Calendars as a Calendar Group.

Select: **Save as New Calendar Group.**
You will be prompted to name the Group.
Type: My Calendar Group.
Click **OK**.
Keep going...

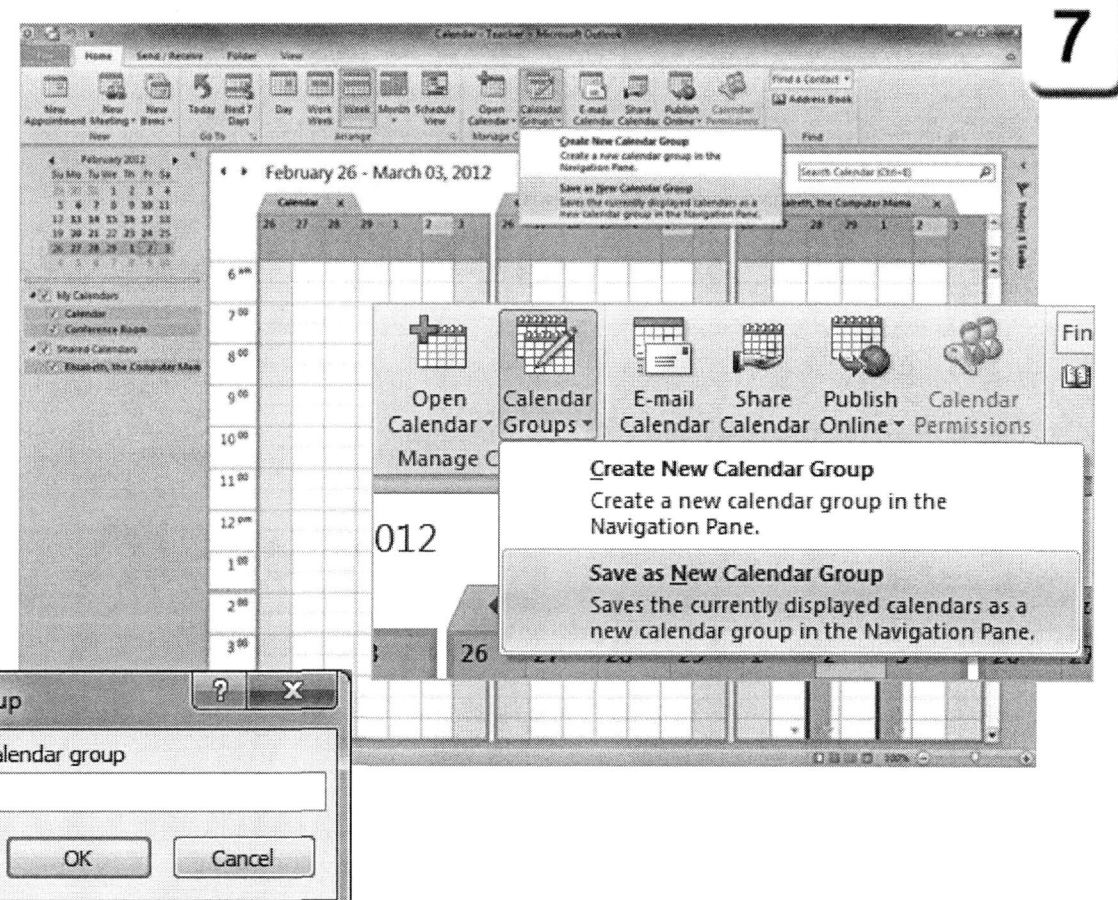

Exam 77-884: Microsoft Outlook 2010
5. Managing Calendar Objects
5.3. Manipulate the Calendar pane: Create a Calendar Group

Summary

This lesson provided a look behind the scenes in Outlook. We reviewed the General options for Outlook as well as options for Mail, Calendars, Tasks, Notes, the Journal and Language.

The lesson also demonstrated how to customize E-mail with Themes and Signatures. We used the Backstage to automatically respond to E-mails.

You done real good.
You get the cookies.

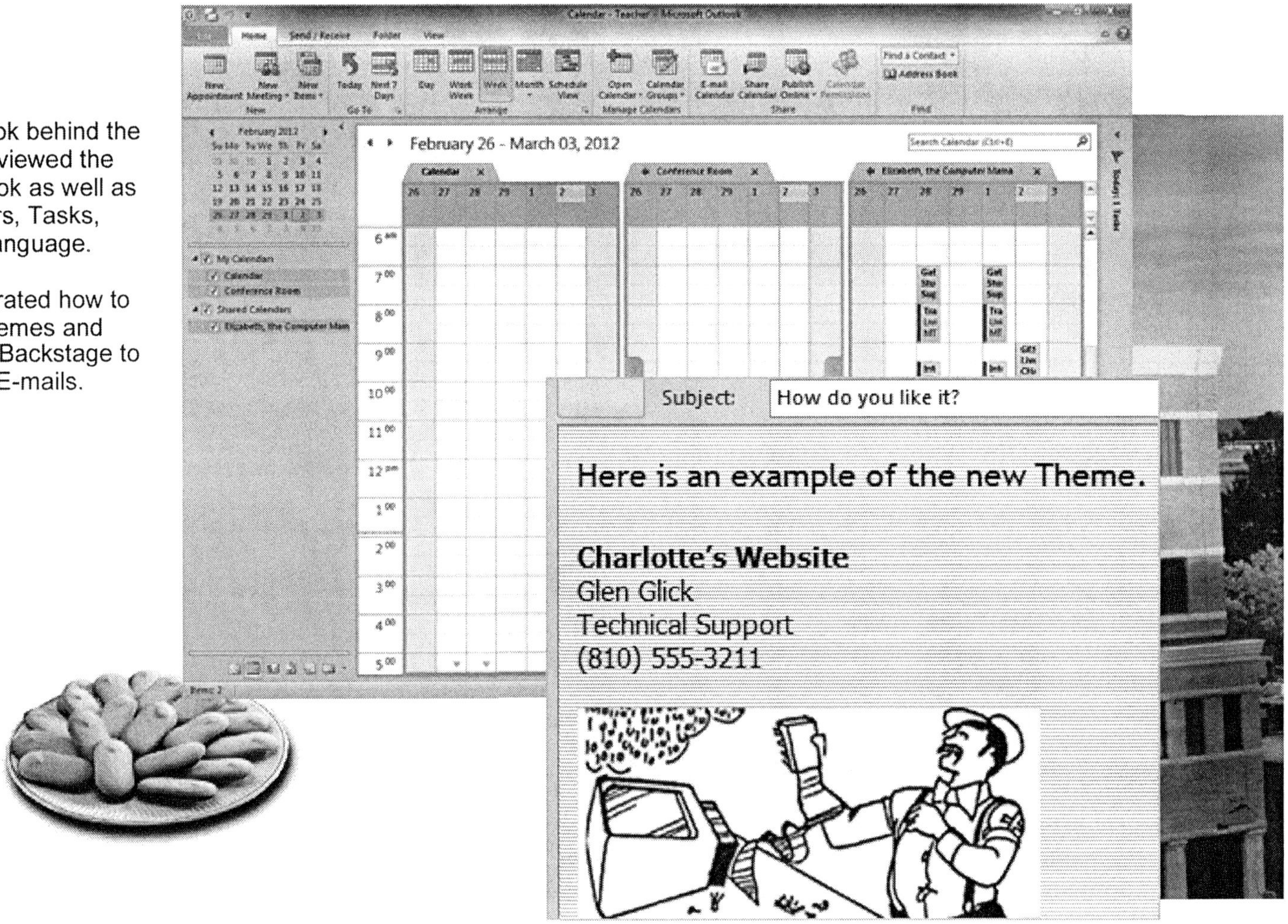

Test Yourself

1. Options are found in the File Menu.
a. True
b. False
Tip: Complete Guide to Outlook, page 255

2. Which of the following are defaults available for the format of E-mail?
(Give all correct answers.)
a. HTML
b. Rich Text
c. Plain Text
d. Word document
Tip: Complete Guide to Outlook, page 258

3. Which is true about Spell Checking?
(Give all correct answers.)
a. By default, Outlook checks spelling in an E-mail
b. Outlook does not check spelling of an original message when forwarded
Tip: Complete Guide to Outlook, page 259

4. Which can be included in an e-mail signature?
(Give all correct answers.)
a. Bold text
b. An Outlook Business Card
c. A picture
d. A website
Tip: Complete Guide to Outlook, page 260-261

5. Which are options when replying to or forwarding an e-mail? (Give all correct answers.)
a. Include original text
b. Include and indent original text
c. Do not include original text (reply only)
Tip: Complete Guide to Outlook, page 266

6. Outlook automatically saves unsent e-mails in the Drafts folder after 15 minutes.
a. True
b. False
Tip: Complete Guide to Outlook, page 267

7. Which is true about Work Time? (Give all correct answers.)
a. The default hours are from 9 am to 5 pm
b. The default work week is Monday through Friday
c. The Work Time is editable in the Outlook Calendar Options
Tip: Complete Guide to Outlook, page 271

Test Yourself

8. What are the Notes options? (Give all correct answers.)
a. Color
b. Size
c. Font
Tip: Complete Guide to Outlook, page 275

9. You can have more than one Outlook Calendar.
a. True
b. False
Tip: Complete Guide to Outlook, page 278

10. Which is an option for publishing a Calendar? (Give all correct answers.)
a. Microsoft Exchange Server
b. SharePoint Server
c. Office.com
Tip: Complete Guide to Outlook, page 281

Application Question: Which of the options discussed do you think you would be most likely to customize? Explain.

Look on top of the truck. While everyone is busy setting up the booths... someone is just watching!

PowerPoint 2010: Sharing and Collaboration

Outlook: In Print

Microsoft Outlook Objectives
In this lesson, you will learn how to:

1. Print Messages and Attachments

2. Print Multiple Messages at the same time

3. Print Calendars in different layouts and sizes

4. Use the Print Options to edit the Page Setup for the Calendar print outs

5. Print Tasks and Task Lists;

6. Print Contacts and Contact Lists

7. Print Notes in Table and Memo Styles

© 2012 Comma Productions, LLC

Print

Specify how you want the item to be printed and then click Print.

Print style

Weekly Agenda Sty
Weekly Calendar S
Monthly Style

Page Setup...

Define Styles..

Page range

◉ All
○ Pages:

Type page numbers and/or page ranges separated by commas counting from the start of the item. For example, type 1, 3 or 5-12.

Print range

Start: Mon 3/5/2012

End: Fri 3/9/2012

☐ Hide details of private appointments

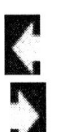

 # Lesson 10: Outlook in Print

1. Readings
Read Lesson 10 in the Microsoft Outlook guide, page 295-314.

Project
Practice and review the Print options.

Downloads
There are no downloads for this lesson.

2. Practice
There is Practice Activity for this lesson

3. Assessment
Review the Test questions on page 315.

Menu Maps
From the **Backstage: File->Print**
1. Print E-mail Messages, page 295
2. E-Mail Print Settings: Table Style, page 296
3. Print Attachments, page 298
4. Print Calendars, page 300
5. Calendar Print Settings , page 301
6. Edit the Calendar Page Setup, page 303
7. Print Appointment Details, page 307
8. Print Tasks, page 308
9. Print Contact Records, page 310
10. Print Notes, page 312

Outlook: In Print

When computers were invented people thought that computers would reduce the amount of paper that it takes to run a business. Everyone talked about the "paperless office," so...are we there, yet? Maybe, maybe not. There are still many things that are easier to proof and review in hard copy. This lesson looks at the **Print Options** for Microsoft Outlook. Each object- Messages, Calendar, Tasks, Notes and Contacts.

Start -> All Programs ->Microsoft Office-> Microsoft Office Outlook 2010

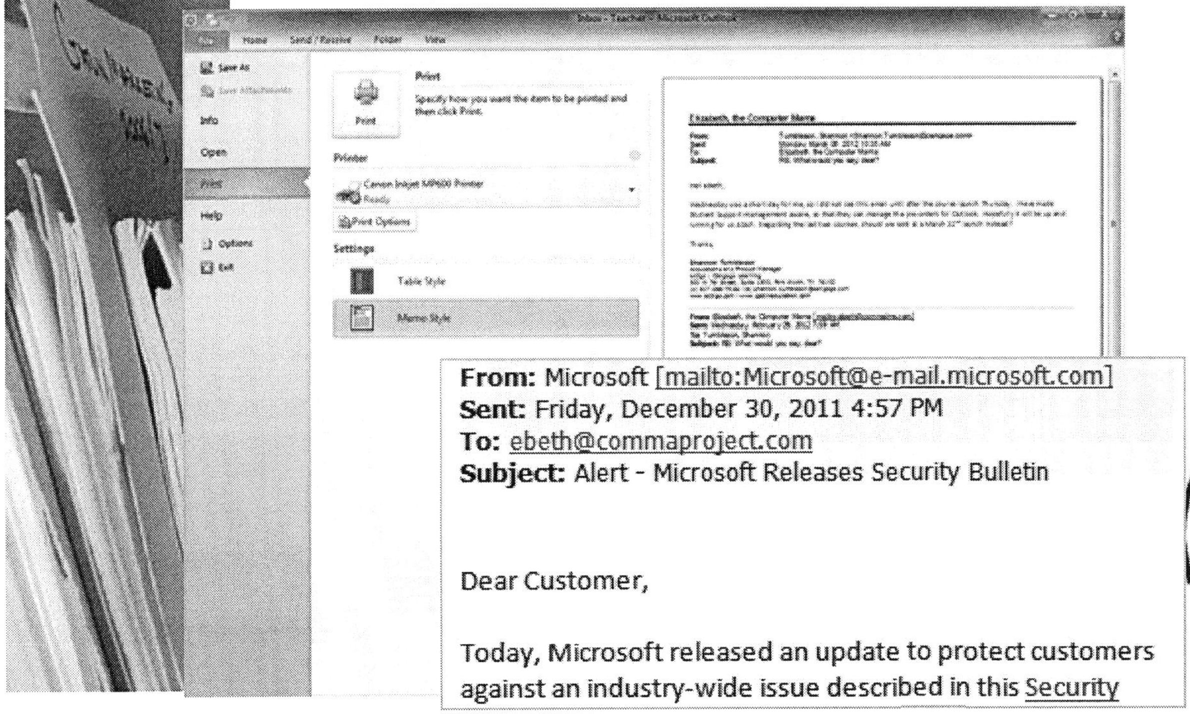

From: Microsoft [mailto:Microsoft@e-mail.microsoft.com]
Sent: Friday, December 30, 2011 4:57 PM
To: ebeth@commaproject.com
Subject: Alert - Microsoft Releases Security Bulletin

Dear Customer,

Today, Microsoft released an update to protect customers against an industry-wide issue described in this Security

Before You Begin

This lesson demonstrates how to print Messages, Calendars, Tasks, Contacts, Notes and Journal Entries. Therefore, you need an example of each Outlook item if you wish to practice the steps.

Memo to Self: You may notice that each printer has its own set of features and benefits. It is not necessary that your printer MATCH the ones in this book.

Microsoft Outlook Inbox

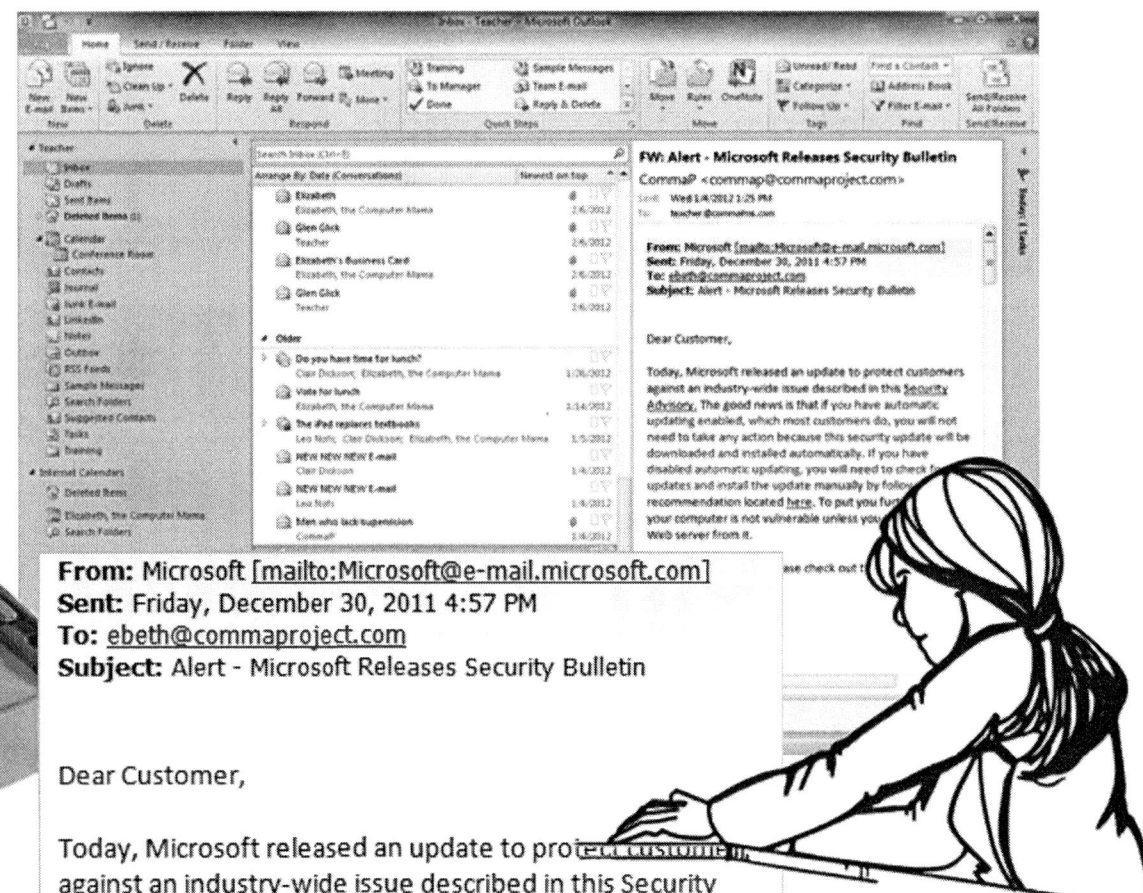

From: Microsoft [mailto:Microsoft@e-mail.microsoft.com]
Sent: Friday, December 30, 2011 4:57 PM
To: ebeth@commaproject.com
Subject: Alert - Microsoft Releases Security Bulletin

Dear Customer,

Today, Microsoft released an update to protect customers against an industry-wide issue described in this Security

Exam 77-884: Microsoft Outlook 2010
3. Managing Email Messages
3.4. Manage automatic message content

File ->Print

Print E-mail Messages

Let's begin with how to print a message.
These lessons will focus on the options
that are available in Microsoft Outlook.

1. Try it: Print a message
Select any message in the Inbox.
Go to **File->Print**.

What Do You See? Outlook will **preview**
the message on the right side.

There are two **Print Settings**:
Table Style
Memo Style.
The example on this page is Memo Style.
Keep going...

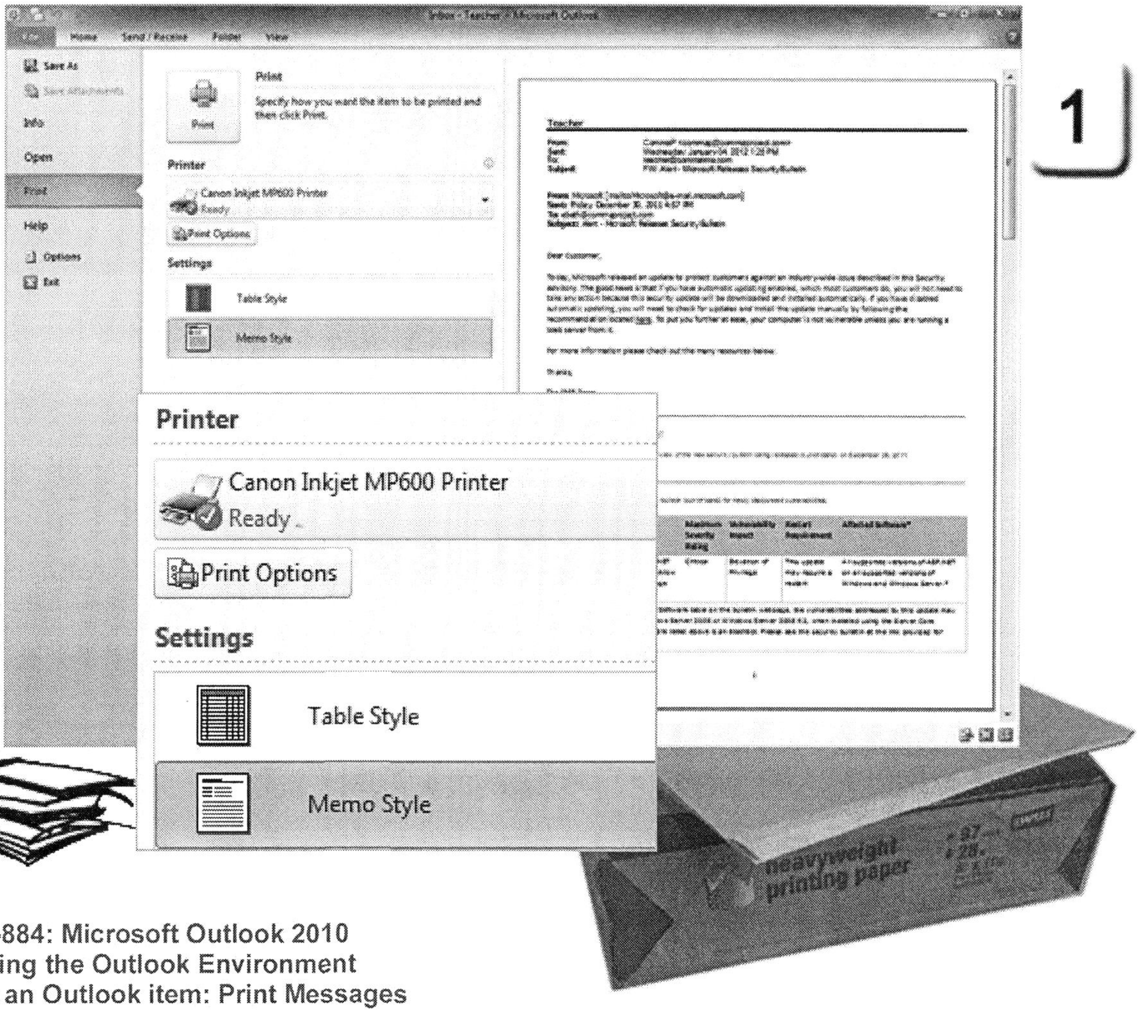

Exam 77-884: Microsoft Outlook 2010
1. Managing the Outlook Environment
1.5. Print an Outlook item: Print Messages

Print Settings: Table Style

2. Try it: Review the Print Options
The Inbox is selected.
Go to **File ->Print-> Settings**
Select a Setting: **Table Style.**

What Do You See? The Table Style
prints a list of the messages. The
messages are sorted and grouped as they
appear in the Outlook Inbox.

If you click **Print**, the Table Style will be
sent to your printer. Keep going...

File ->Print-> Print Settings-> Table Style

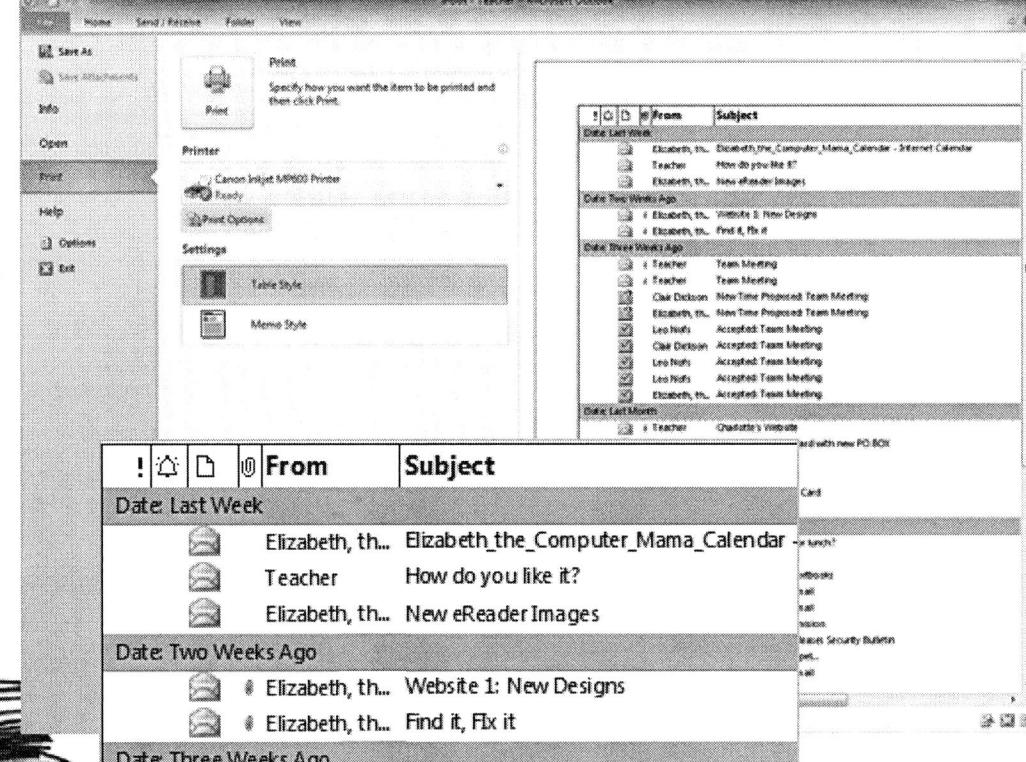

Exam 77-884: Microsoft Outlook 2010
1. Managing the Outlook Environment
1.5. Print an Outlook item: Print Messages

Review the Print Options

3. Try it: Review the Print Options
Go to **File ->Print-> Print Options.**

What Do You See? The Print Dialog window will open. Your printer should be named at the top. Look below the name, the **Print style** lets you edit the **Page Setup** and **Define Styles.**

You can edit the **Copies** as well:
Number of Pages
Number of Copies

What Else Do You See? There is a little Print Option in the bottom left corner. You can check to **Print attached files** if you wish.

If you click **Print**, the message and the attachments will print.

Keep going...

Memo to Self: The attachments will print to the default printer, only.

File ->Print-> Print Options-> Print Attached Files

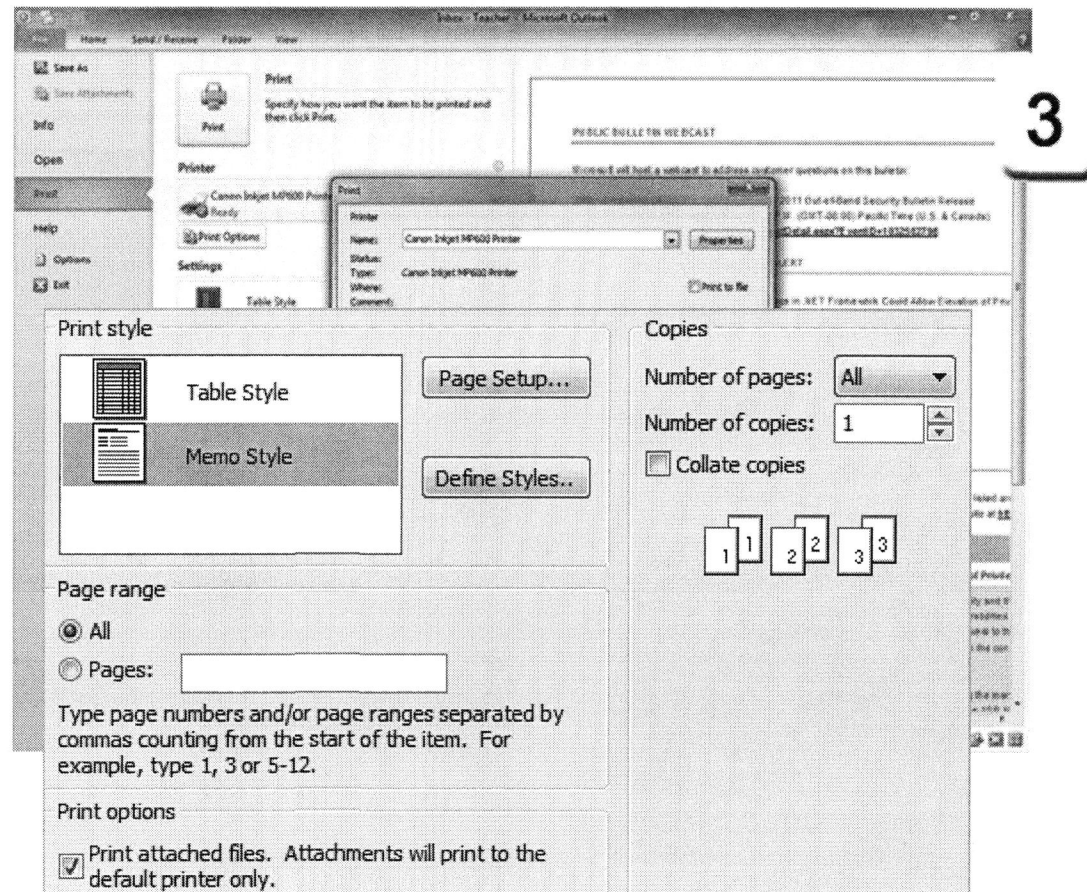

Exam 77-884: Microsoft Outlook 2010
1. Managing the Outlook Environment
1.5. Print an Outlook item: Print Attachments

Attachment Tools ->Attachment->Actions-> Quick Print

Print: Attachments
There is another way to print attachments.
Here are the steps.

4. Try it: Print an Attachment
Go to the Inbox.
Select any message with an attachment.
Click on the attachment. **The Attachment Tools** should be available.

Go to **Attachment Tools ->Attachment.**
Go to **Actions->Quick Print.**
The attachment will be printed.

Keep going...!

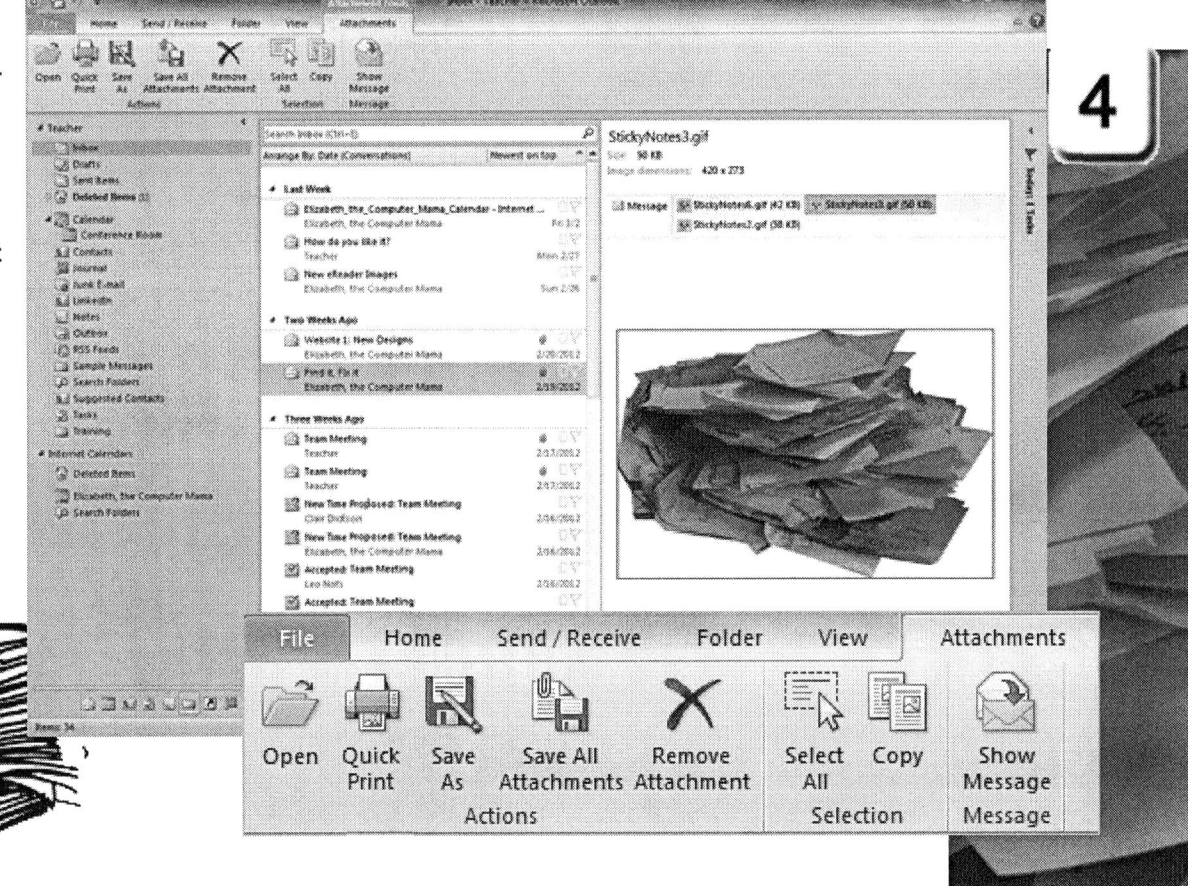

Exam 77-884: Microsoft Outlook 2010
1. Managing the Outlook Environment
1.5. Print an Outlook item: Print Attachments

Print: Lots of Messages

Say you needed to print a lot of E-mail messages at once. You can select multiple messages and print them at the same time.

5. Try it: Print Multiple Messages
Go to the Inbox.
Select one message.
Hold the Control key (Ctrl) on your keyboard as you select a second, third and fourth message. The messages do not have be consecutive.

Go to **File ->Print.**

What Do You See? Each message that you selected will be displayed in the Print Preview. The messages will print one after the other.

Keep going...

File ->Print

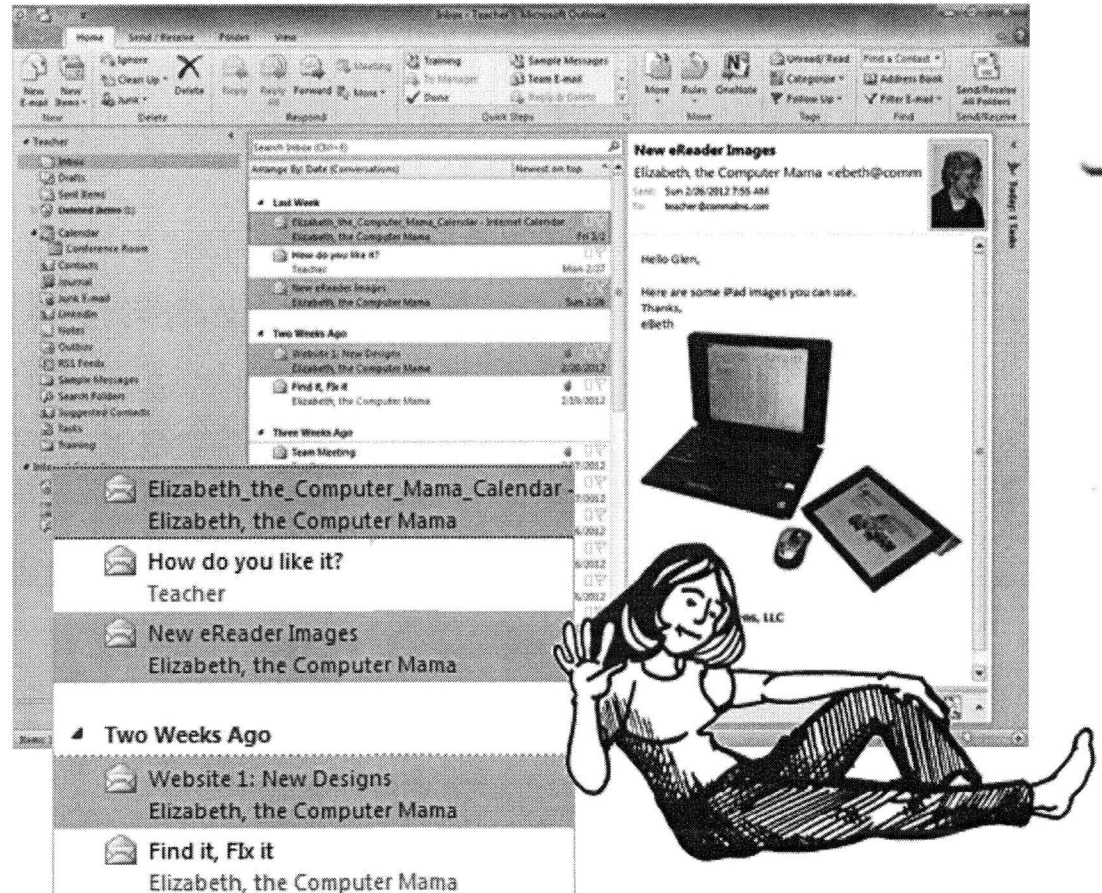

5

Exam 77-884: Microsoft Outlook 2010
1. Managing the Outlook Environment
1.5. Print an Outlook item: Print Multiple Messages

Print Calendars

A Calendar can be simple or decorated with details. When you look at a Calendar on screen you can choose to show or hide the details, such as the Daily Task List or the To-Do Bar. You can customize the print out the same way.

1. Try it: Change the Calendar View
Select the Calendar.
The Calendar Tools should be available.

Go to **Calendar Tools ->View-> Layout.**
To-Do Bar: Normal
Include the Date Navigator and Task List.

OK. That's one way to view your Calendar when you are working with it. How do you want it to look when you print it out?

Keep going...

Calendar Tools ->View-> Layout

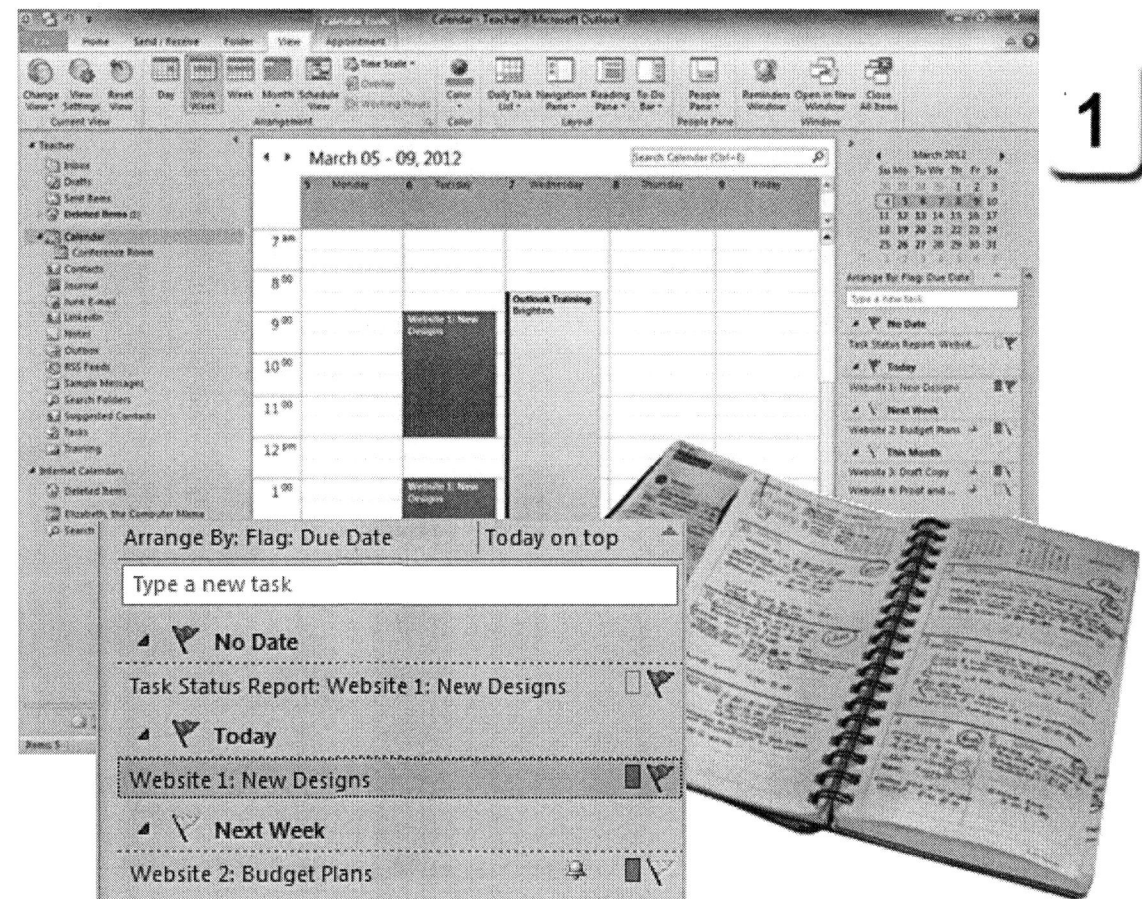

Exam 77-884: Microsoft Outlook 2010
1. Managing the Outlook Environment
1.5. Print an Outlook item: Print Calendars

Calendar Print Settings

One of the best features about Outlook is the print options. Your Calendar can be printed to fit the professional planner sizes. For example, many executives use a Cambridge Planner to organize their commitments and agendas. Another popular print out is the tri-fold size.

2. Try it: Review the Print Settings
The Calendar is selected.
Go to **File ->Print->Settings.**

What Do You See? The Styles include:
Daily Style
Weekly Agenda Style
Weekly Calendar Style
Monthly Style
Tri-fold Style
Calendar Details Style
Memo Style

Keep going...

File ->Print->Settings

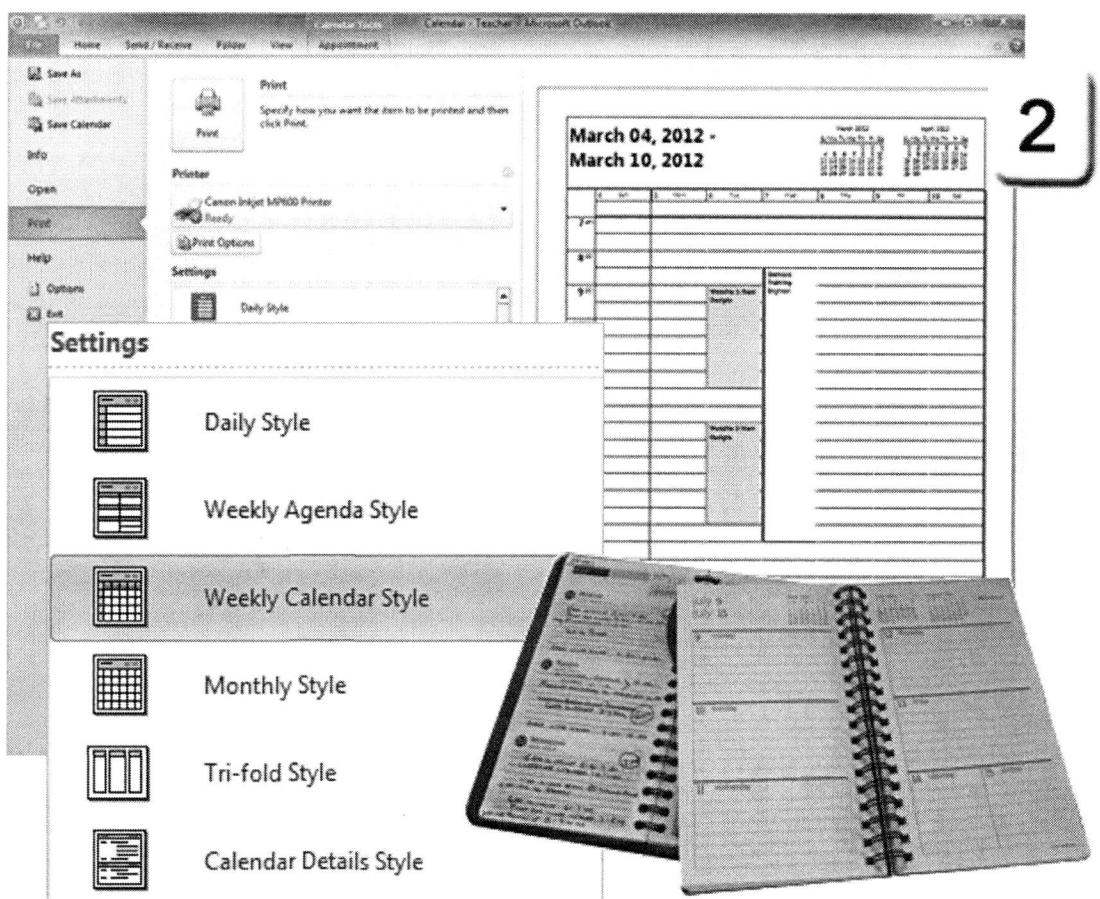

Exam 77-884: Microsoft Outlook 2010
1. Managing the Outlook Environment
1.5. Print an Outlook item: Print Calendars

Review the Print Options

3. Try it: Review the Print Options
Go to **File ->Print-> Print Options.**

What Do You See? The Print Dialog window will open. Your printer should be named at the top. Look below the name, the **Print style** lets you edit the **Page Setup** and **Define Styles**.

You can edit the **Copies** as well:

What Else Do You See? The Print Range sets the **Start and End dates** for your Calendar. The example on this page shows one 5 day work week, that starts with the day that was selected. You can select other dates if you wish.

Keep going...

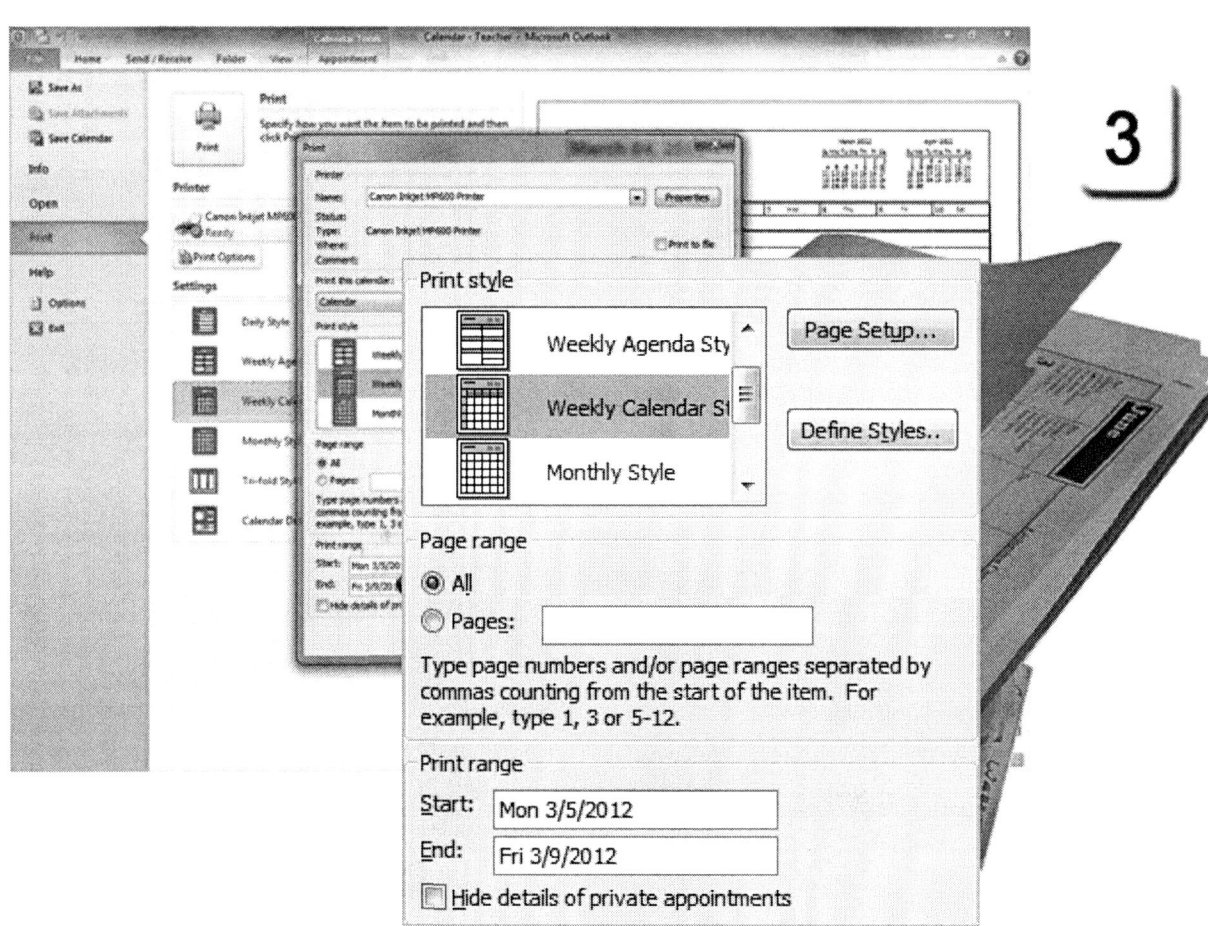

Exam 77-884: Microsoft Outlook 2010
1. Managing the Outlook Environment
1.5. Print an Outlook item: Print Calendars

Edit the Page Setup

To the right of the **Print Style** you should see the button for **Page Setup**. This is the place to select what you would like to see on the Calendar print out.

4. Try it: Edit the Page Setup
The Calendar is still selected.
Go to **File ->Print->Print Options**.
The Print Dialog window will open.
Click on **Page Setup**.

What Do You See? There are three tabs of Page Setup Options:
Format
Paper
Header/Footer

Keep going...

File ->Print->Print Options->Page Setup

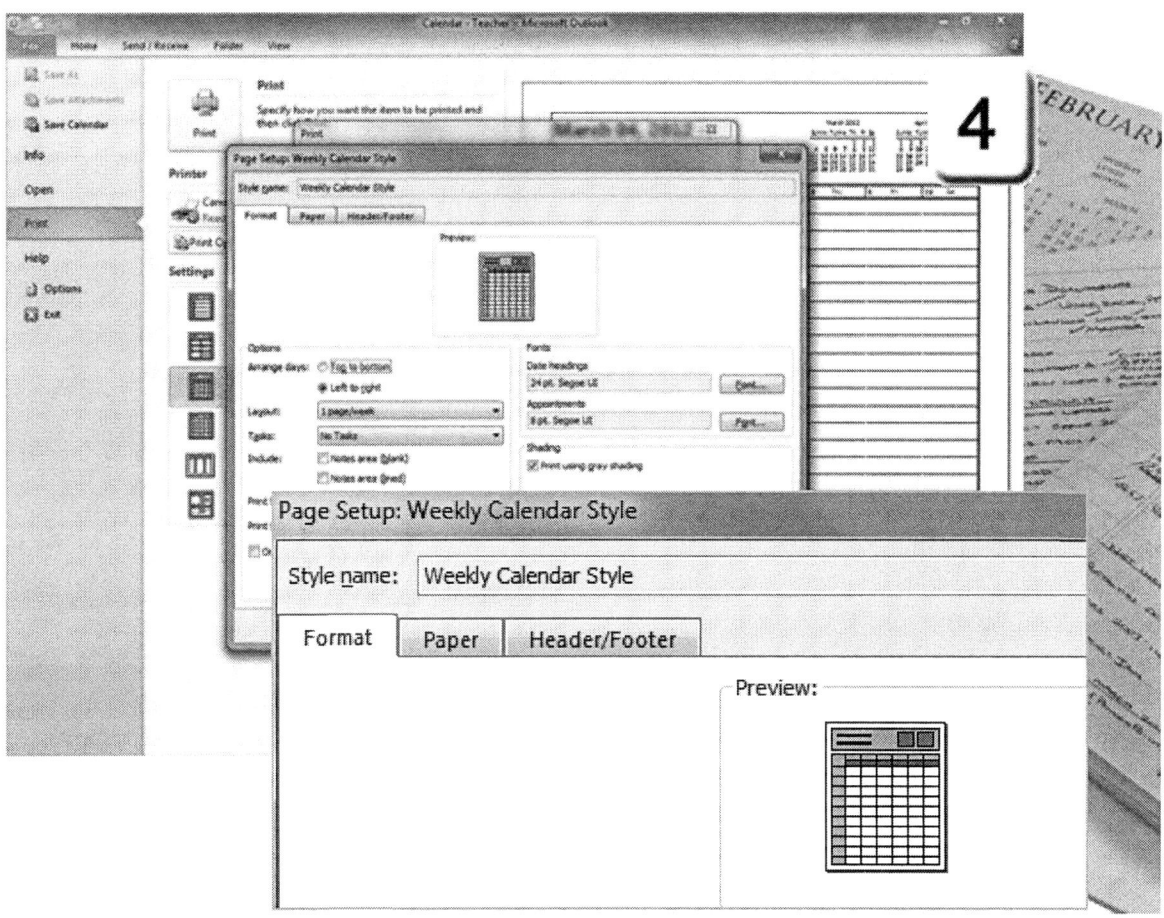

Exam 77-884: Microsoft Outlook 2010
1. Managing the Outlook Environment
1.5. Print an Outlook item: Print Calendars

HOME

Page Setup: Format

5. Try it: Edit the Page Format
Go to the **Format** tab.

What Do You See? The Options are:
Arrange Days: Left to right
Layout: 1 page/week
Tasks: No Tasks.
Include: Notes area (blank or lined)
Print from: Start time each day
Print to: End time for each day

What Else Do You See? There is an option to **Only Print Workdays**.

Look Again: You can also edit the Fonts for the Date headings and Appointments.

Keep going...

File ->Print->Print Options->Page Setup->Format

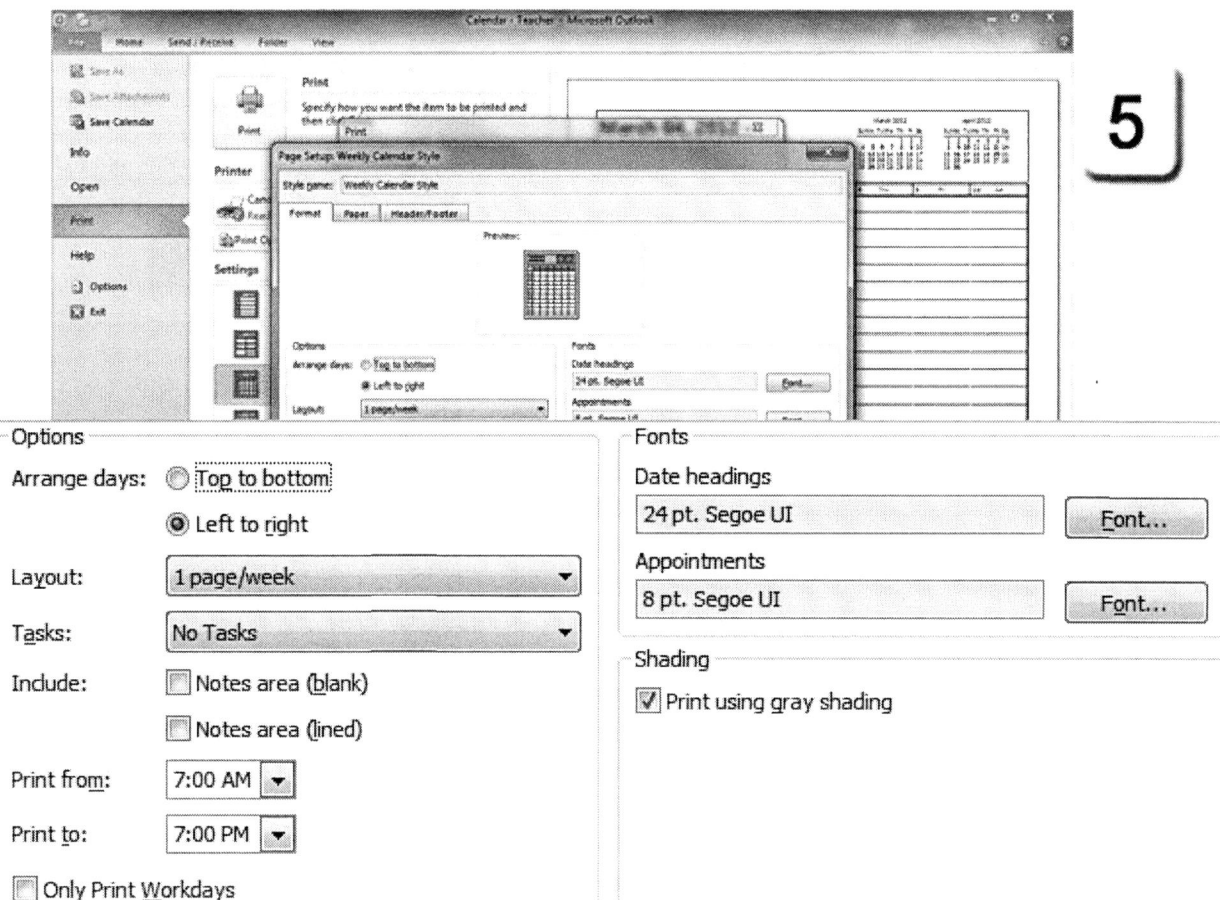

Exam 77-884: Microsoft Outlook 2010
1. Managing the Outlook Environment
1.5. Print an Outlook item: Print Calendars

Page Setup: Paper

6. Try it: Edit the Paper Setup
Go to the **Paper** tab.

What Do You See? There are two groups of Options: **Paper** and **Page**.

The Paper options include:
Type
Dimensions
Paper Source
Margins

The Page options include:
Size
Dimensions
Orientation

What Else Do You See? You can choose a Paper and Page that matches your Day-Timer or Franklin Planner.

Keep going...

File ->Print->Print Options->Page Setup->Paper

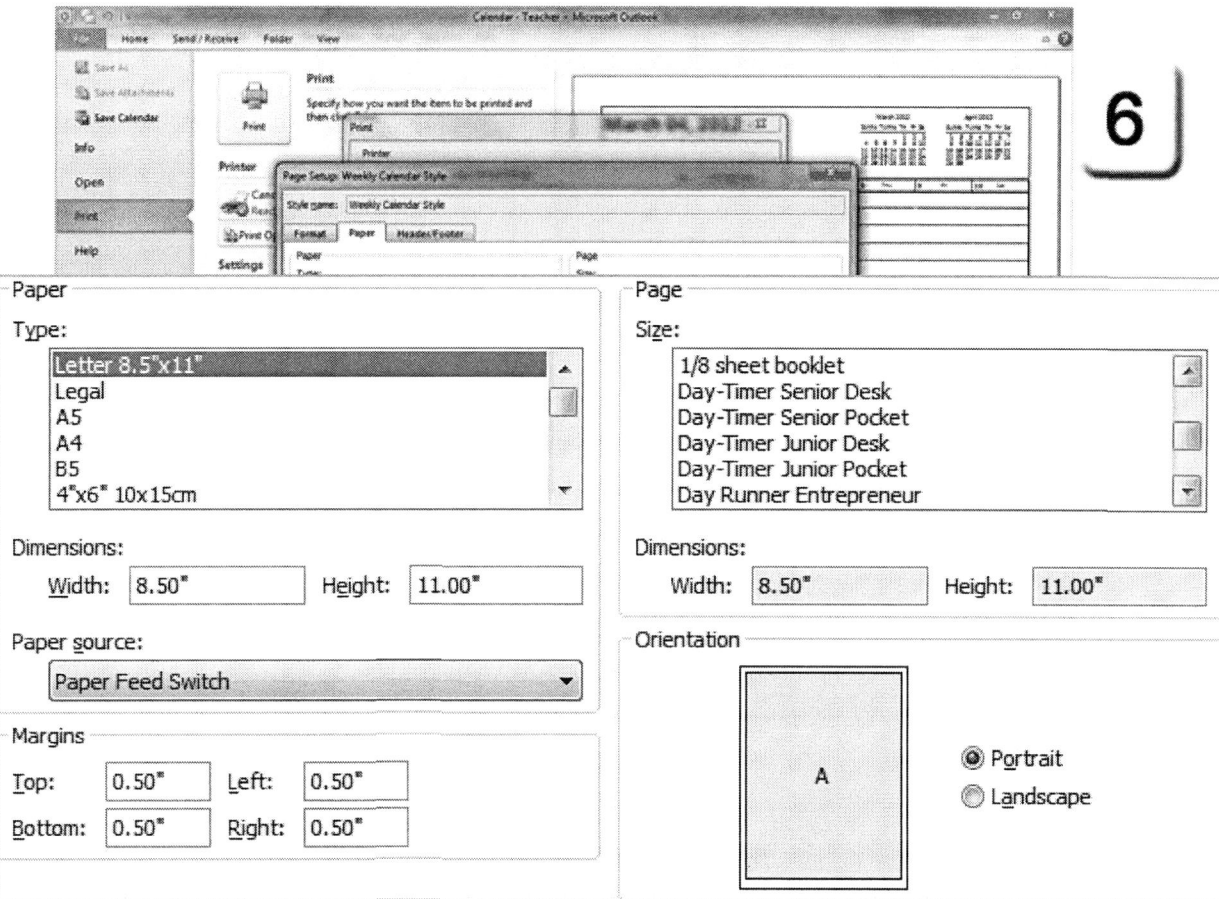

Exam 77-884: Microsoft Outlook 2010
1. Managing the Outlook Environment
1.5. Print an Outlook item: Print Calendars

Page Setup: Header/Footer

7. Try it: Edit the Header/Footer
Go to the **Header/Footer** tab.

What Do You See? The Header and Footer have the same options. There are three Text Boxes placed left, center and right on the page.

By default, the **Footer** has User Name, Page number and the Date Printed. You can edit the User Name and add the name of your business or department.

What Else Do You See? There is a check box you can select to **Reverse** the layout on even pages.

Click **OK** to close the **Page Setup**.
If you click **Print**, the Calendar will print.

File ->Print->Print Options->Page Setup-> Header/Footer

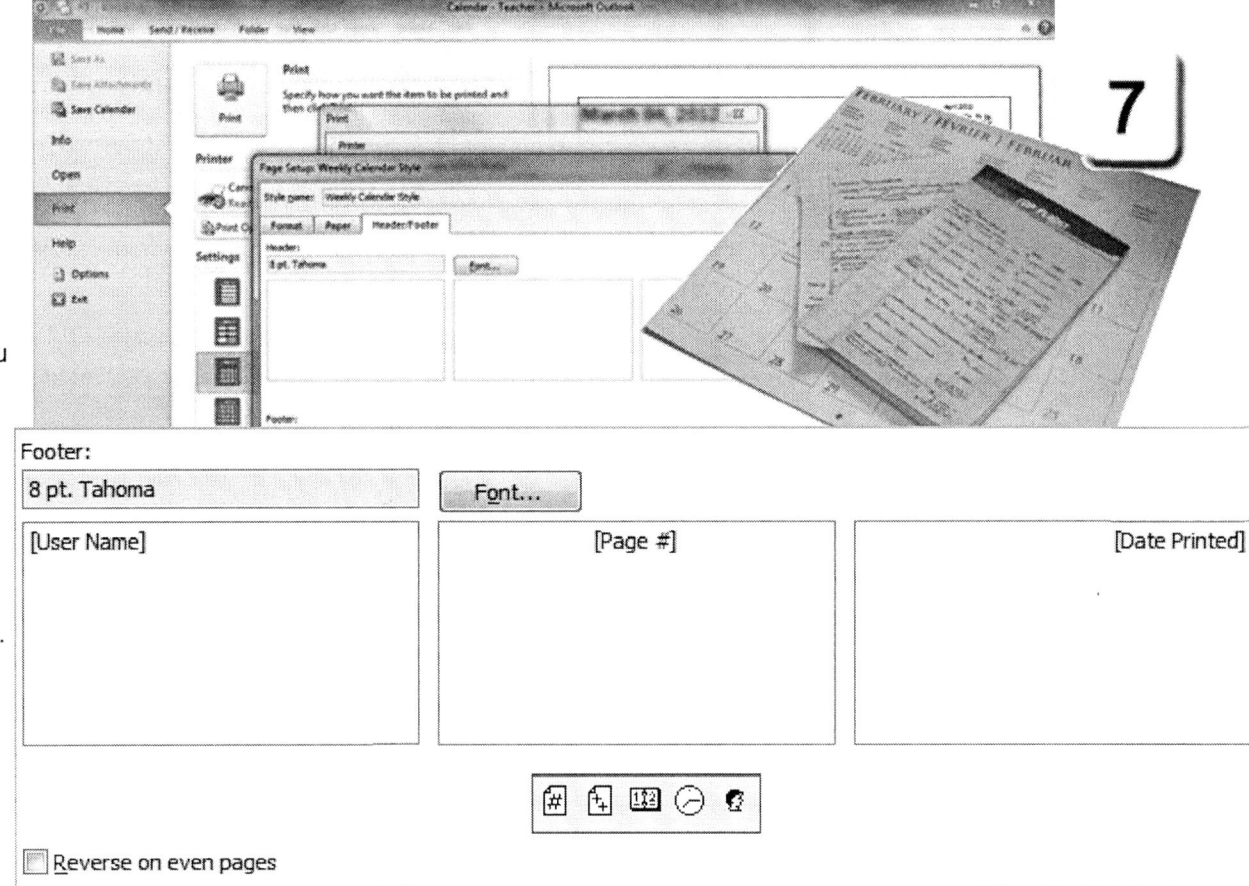

Footer:

| 8 pt. Tahoma | | Font... |

| [User Name] | [Page #] | [Date Printed] |

☐ Reverse on even pages

Exam 77-884: Microsoft Outlook 2010
1. Managing the Outlook Environment
1.5. Print an Outlook item: Print Calendars

Print Appointment Details

The preceding print layouts were visual: the Calendar is represented as days and weeks. For people who work well with lists, the **Calendar Details Style** can be useful.

8. Try it: Print Appointment Details
The Calendar is selected.
Go to **File ->Print->Settings.**
Select a Setting: **Calendar Details Style.**

What Do You See? The **Calendar Details** will be shown in the Preview on the right side.

The meetings and tasks are grouped by date. The Calendar Details includes the Subject, Start Date and Due Date, Status, Percent Complete, Total and Actual Work as well as the Owner and the Category.

If you click **Print**, Outlook will print the appointment details. Done and Done.

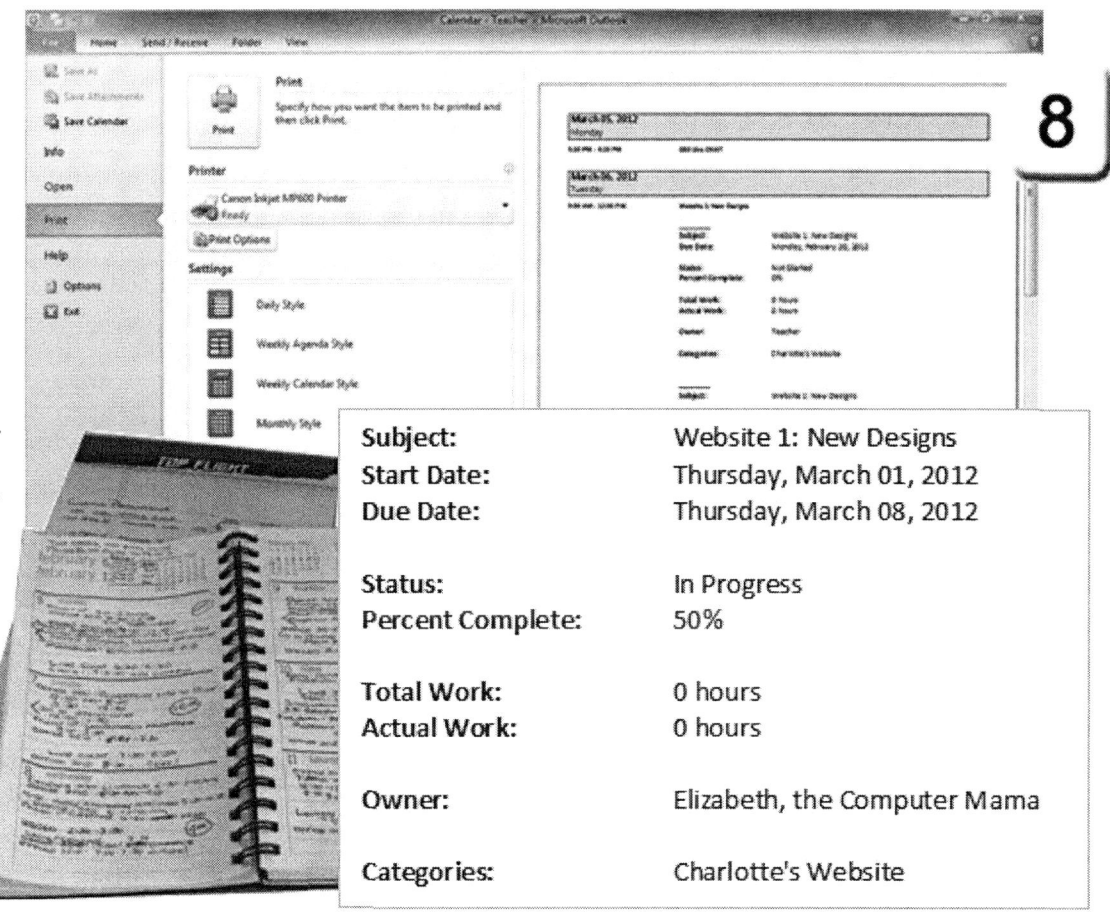

Subject:	Website 1: New Designs
Start Date:	Thursday, March 01, 2012
Due Date:	Thursday, March 08, 2012
Status:	In Progress
Percent Complete:	50%
Total Work:	0 hours
Actual Work:	0 hours
Owner:	Elizabeth, the Computer Mama
Categories:	Charlotte's Website

Exam 77-884: Microsoft Outlook 2010
5. Managing Calendar Objects
5.1. Create and manipulate appointments and events: Print Appointment Details

Print Tasks

Tasks, like appointments and messages have two print options: the Task (Form View) and the Task List.

1. Try it: Change the Task View
Select the **Tasks**.
The **Home** Ribbon should have the options for managing Tasks.

Go to **Home ->Current View.**
Select: **Simple List.**

What Do You See? In the example on this page the Tasks are grouped by Category and sorted by Date.

Keep going...

Home ->Current View-> Simple List

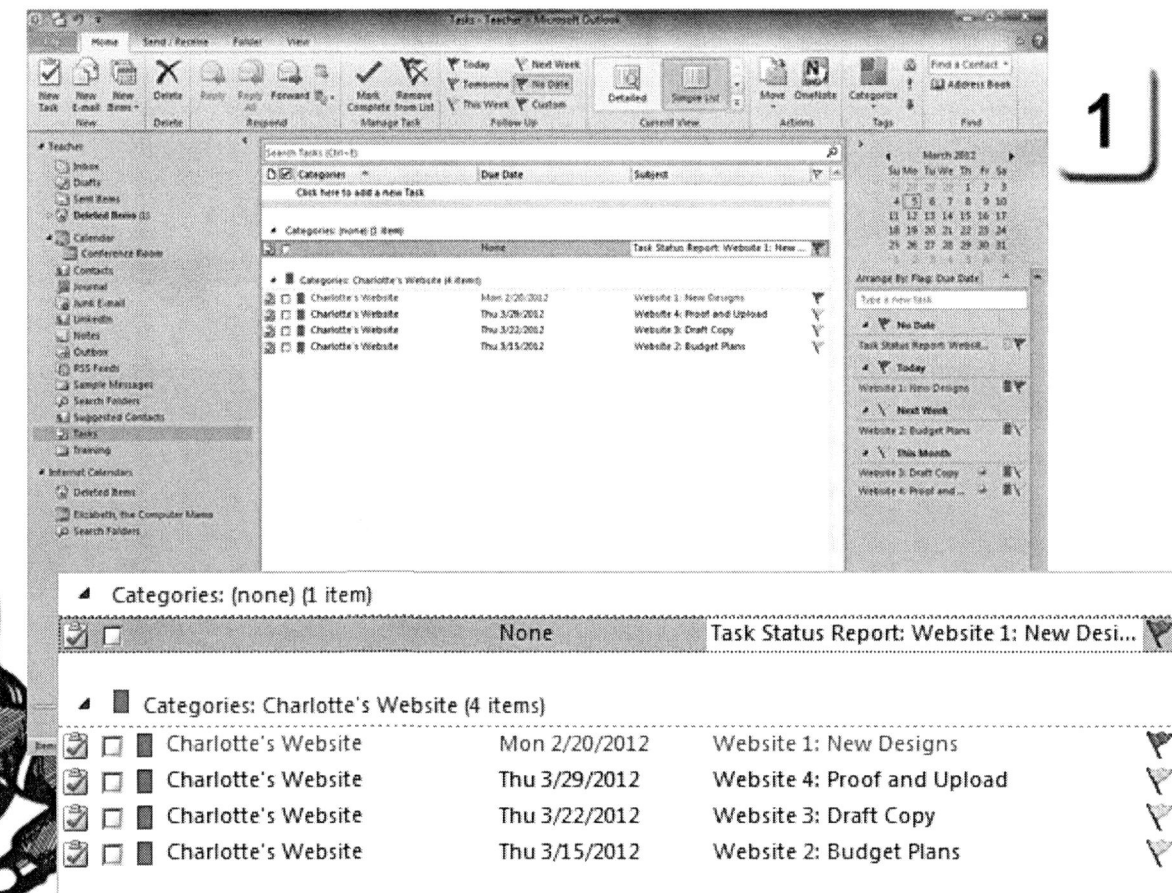

Exam 77-884: Microsoft Outlook 2010
1. Managing the Outlook Environment
1.3. Arrange the Content Pane: Show or Hide Fields in a List View

Print the Task List

2. Try it: Print the Tasks
The Tasks are still selected.
Go to **File ->Print->Settings.**

What Do You See? There are two settings.

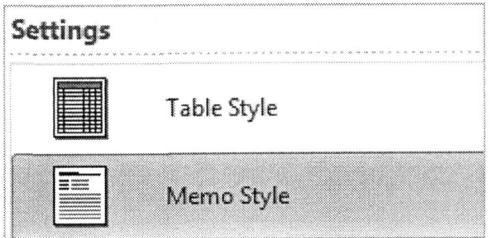

Settings

▦	Table Style
▤	Memo Style

The **Table Style** prints the Task list as it looks in Outlook including the color Categories.

The **Memo Style** prints each Task with all of the details including Subject, Priority, Dates, Status and Work. The name of the person who requested this Task is also listed.

If you click **Print**, Outlook will print the Task List.

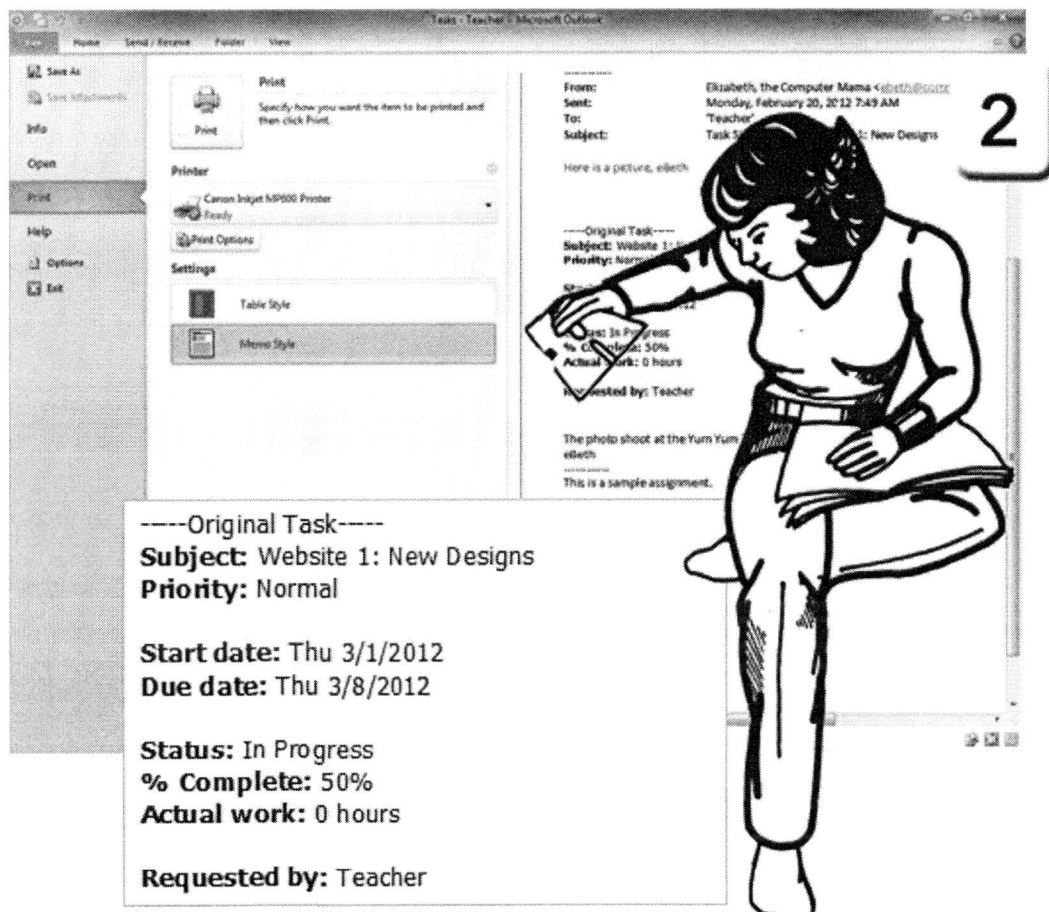

-----Original Task-----
Subject: Website 1: New Designs
Priority: Normal

Start date: Thu 3/1/2012
Due date: Thu 3/8/2012

Status: In Progress
% Complete: 50%
Actual work: 0 hours

Requested by: Teacher

Exam 77-884: Microsoft Outlook 2010
1. Managing the Outlook Environment
1.5. Print an Outlook item: Print Tasks

HOME

Print a Contact Record

There are the same options for Contacts. You can print a Memo Style or a List View.

1. Try it: Change the Contacts View
Select the **Contacts.**
The **Home** Ribbon should have the options for managing Contacts.

Go to **Home ->Current View.**
Select: **Business Card.**

What Do You See? This View shows the Contact name, title, company, address, phone and E-mail.

Keep going...

Home ->Current View-> Business Card

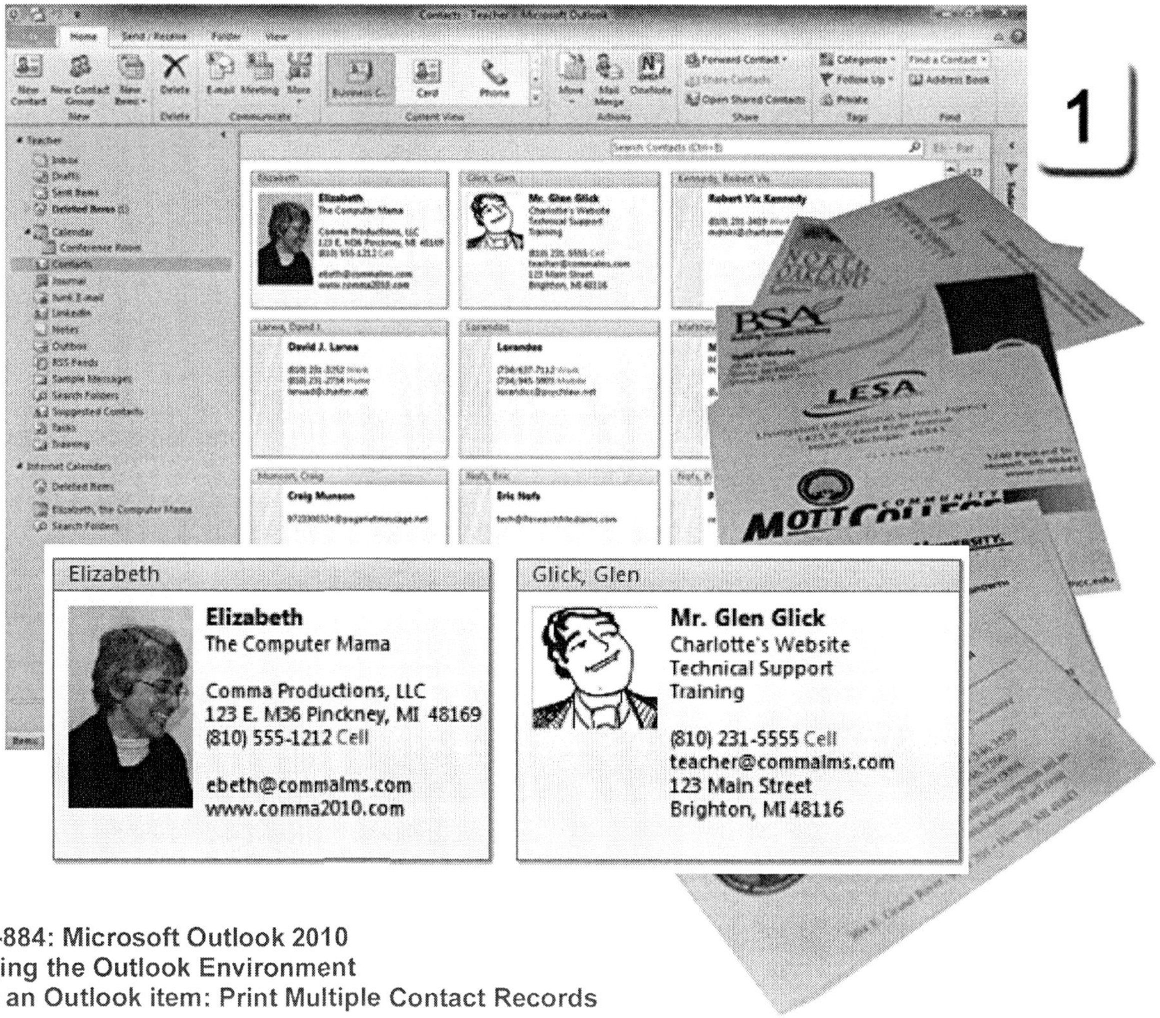

1

Elizabeth
Elizabeth
The Computer Mama

Comma Productions, LLC
123 E. M36 Pinckney, MI 48169
(810) 555-1212 Cell

ebeth@commalms.com
www.comma2010.com

Glick, Glen
Mr. Glen Glick
Charlotte's Website
Technical Support
Training

(810) 231-5555 Cell
teacher@commalms.com
123 Main Street
Brighton, MI 48116

Exam 77-884: Microsoft Outlook 2010
1. Managing the Outlook Environment
1.5. Print an Outlook item: Print Multiple Contact Records

Print Lots of Contacts

There are some Settings that make it easy to print your multiple Contacts as a small booklet or phone directory.

2. Try it: Print Multiple Contact Records
The Contact folder is still selected.
Go to **File ->Print-> Settings.**

What Do You See? The Settings are:
Card Style (prints in two columns)
Small Booklet Style (prints on half page)
Medium Booklet Style
Memo Style
Phone Directory Style.

Memo to Self: None of these Settings included the Contact's picture or logo.

File ->Print-> Settings

Exam 77-884: Microsoft Outlook 2010
1. Managing the Outlook Environment
1.5. Print an Outlook item: Print Multiple Contact Records

Print Notes

1. Try it: Change the Note View
Select the **Notes**.
The **Home** Ribbon has the options for Notes.

Go to **Home ->Current View-> Notes List.**

Try This, Too: Add the Reading Pane
Go to **View ->Layout-> Reading Pane.**
Select: **Right.**

What Do You See? This View displays the Notes List arranged by Date. The Reading Pane should be available on the right side.

So, does it print?
Keep going...

Home ->Current View-> Notes List

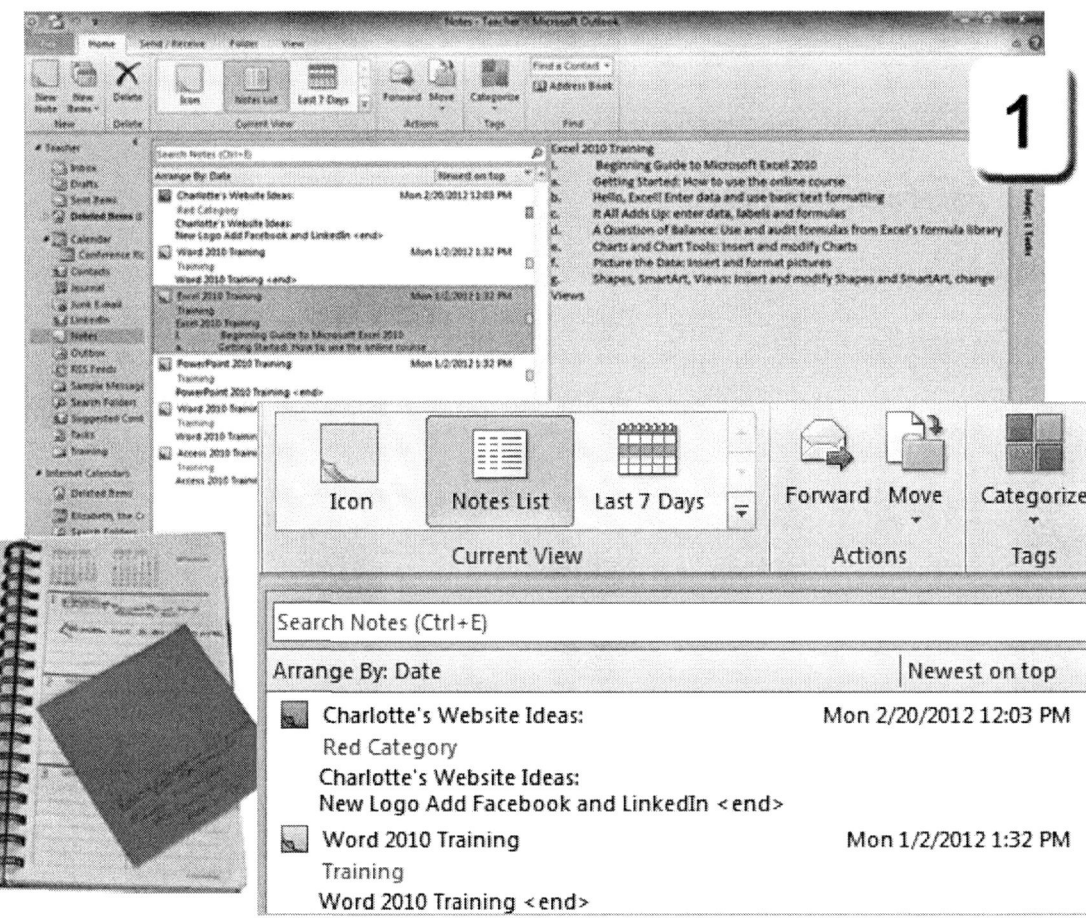

Exam 77-884: Microsoft Outlook 2010
1. Managing the Outlook Environment
1.5. Print an Outlook item: Print Notes

Print Lots of Notes

2. Try it: Print Notes
The Notes folder is selected.
Go to **File ->Print**.

What Do You See? There are two Settings:
Table Style (Notes List)
Memo Style (The Note that is selected)

Very good. Outlook can print Notes.

File ->Print

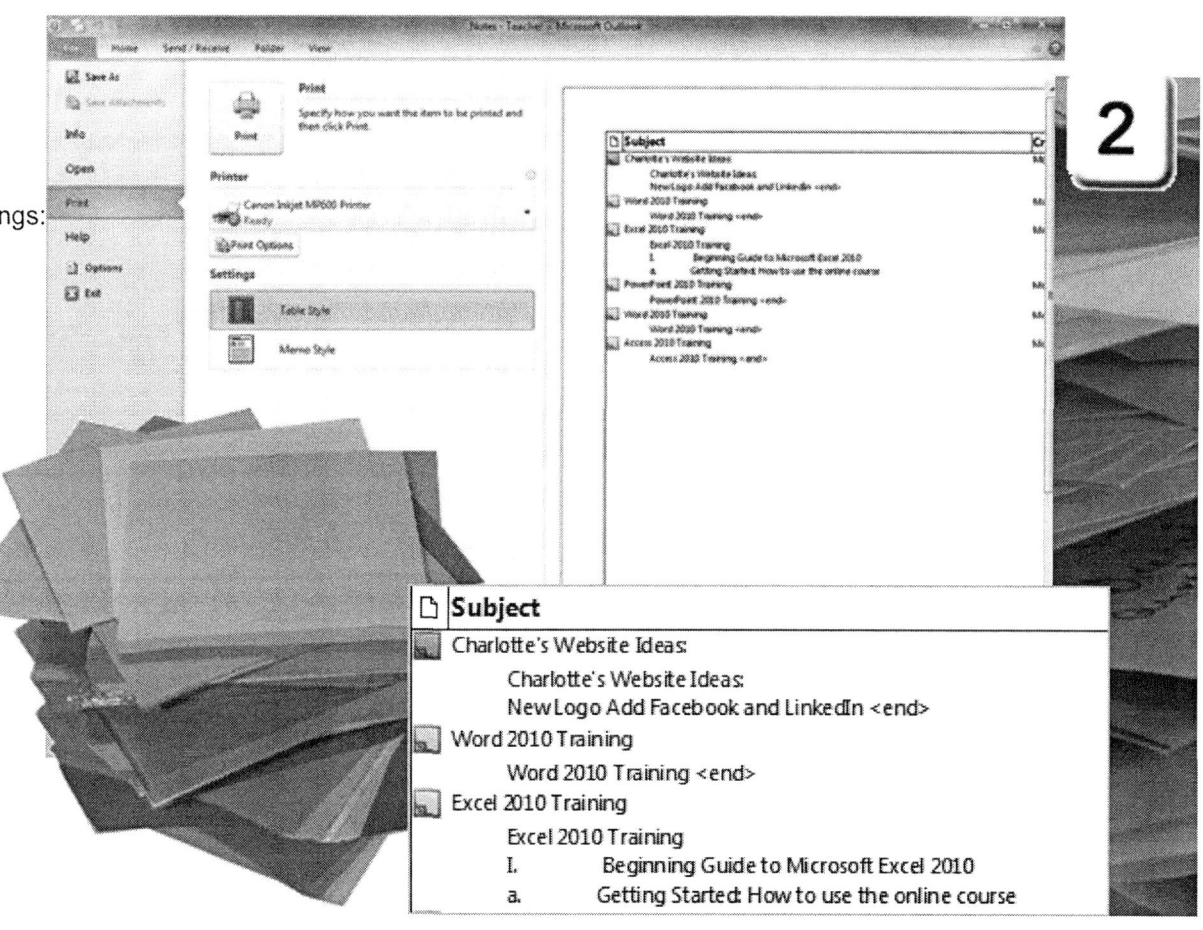

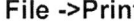

Exam 77-884: Microsoft Outlook 2010
1. Managing the Outlook Environment
1.5. Print an Outlook item: Print Notes

Summary

So, you may not have a paperless office, today. Microsoft Outlook, and in particular the new Print Options in the Backstage, makes it simple to print what you want.

This lesson looked at the Print Settings and Print Options for E-mail, Calendars, Tasks, Contacts and Notes.

You done good.
You can get two cookies.

Test Yourself

1. Which of the following are print settings? (Give all correct answers.)
a. Table Style
b. Memo Style
c. E-mail Style
d. List Style
Tip: Complete Guide to Outlook, page 295

2. E-mails can only be printed one at a time.
a. True
b. False
Tip: Complete Guide to Outlook, page 299

3. Which of the following are calendar printing options? (Give all correct answers.)
a. Daily Style
b. Weekly Agenda Style
c. Weekly Calendar Style
d. Monthly Style
Tip: Complete Guide to Outlook, page 301

4. Outlook includes page sizes that correspond with popular brands of calendars and planners, such as Day-Timer and Franklin Planner.
a. True
b. False
Tip: Complete Guide to Outlook, page 305

5. Which are things that Outlook can print? (Give all correct answers.)
a. Calendar
b. E-mail
c. List of e-mail messages
d. Tasks
e. Contacts
f. Notes
Tip: Complete Guide to Outlook, page 296, 301, 308, 310, 312

Application Question: What would be the advantage of having Outlook print pages that correspond with popular brands of calendars and planners, such as the Day-Timer or Franklin Planner?

Outlook 2010: Managing Microsoft Outlook
Advanced Options

Microsoft Outlook Objectives
In this lesson, you will learn how to:

1. Use the Search box to find Inbox and Calendar data by keyword

2. Expand the Scope of a Search from the Current Folder to All Outlook Items

3. Refine the Search by using Filters for Attachments or Categories

4. Use the Advanced Options to Export data from Outlook into Excel

© 2012 Comma Productions, LLC

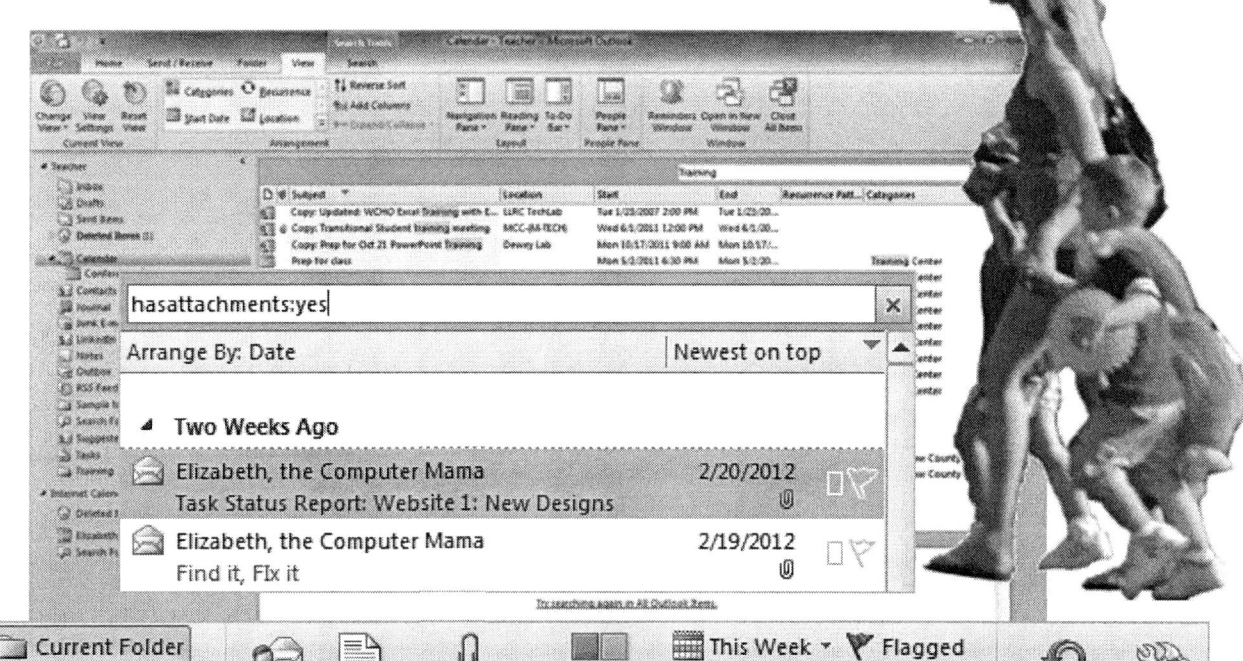

 Take One

Lesson 11 : Advanced Options

1. Readings

Read Lesson 11 in the Microsoft Outlook guide, page 317-339.

Project

This lesson exports sample Calendar items into an Excel spreadsheet.

Downloads

Export from Outlook March 2012.xls

2. Practice

There is no Practice Activity for this lesson.

3. Assessment

Review the Test questions on page 340.

Search Ribbon

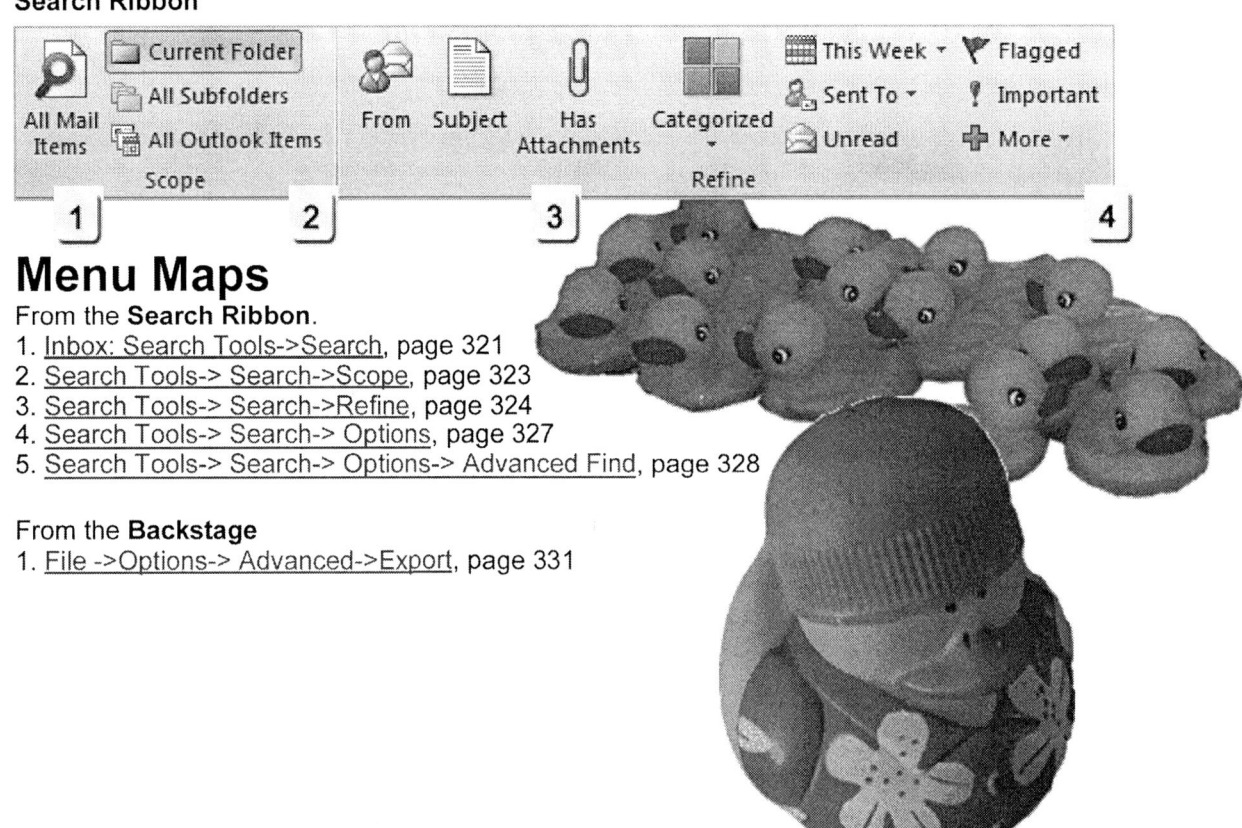

Menu Maps

From the **Search Ribbon**.
1. Inbox: Search Tools->Search, page 321
2. Search Tools-> Search->Scope, page 323
3. Search Tools-> Search->Refine, page 324
4. Search Tools-> Search-> Options, page 327
5. Search Tools-> Search-> Options-> Advanced Find, page 328

From the **Backstage**
1. File ->Options-> Advanced->Export, page 331

Working with Data

Microsoft Outlook is a **database.** The previous lessons demonstrated how to create E-mails, Meeting Requests, Contacts, and Tasks. Each folder--the Inbox, Calendar, Contacts, Tasks and Notes--is a separate Table. These records of time and talent can be used to manage projects and coordinate departments. For example, the time our County Sheriffs spend assisting the local townships is tracked in Outlook. This information is then exported to Microsoft Excel and used to prepare budgets and grants.

So, the last lesson in our Complete Guide to Outlook looks at ways to Search the folders and export the data into Microsoft Excel.

Start -> All Programs ->Microsoft Office-> Microsoft Office Outlook 2010

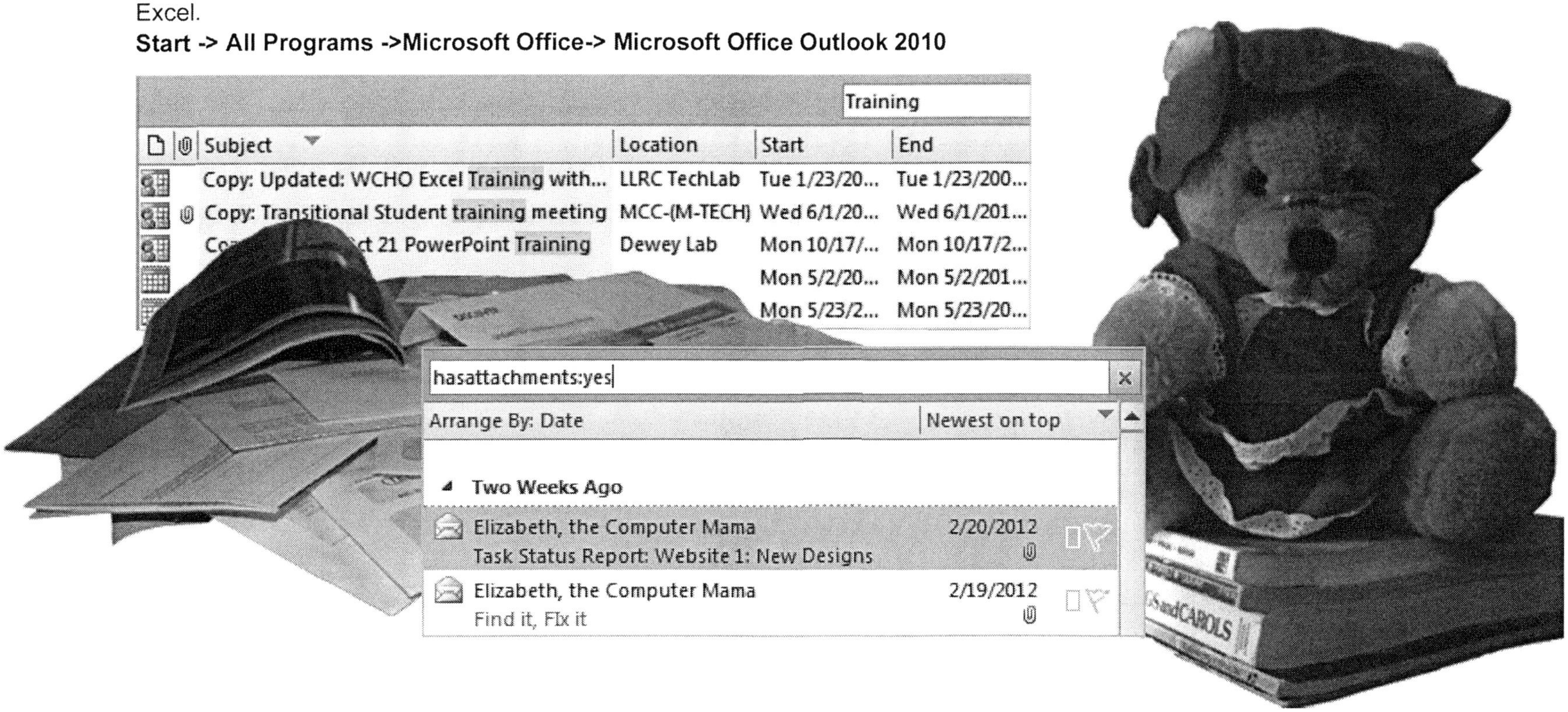

		Training			
🗅	🔘 Subject ▼		Location	Start	End
	Copy: Updated: WCHO Excel Training with...		LLRC TechLab	Tue 1/23/20...	Tue 1/23/200...
	🔘 Copy: Transitional Student training meeting		MCC-(M-TECH)	Wed 6/1/20...	Wed 6/1/201...
	Co... ...ct 21 PowerPoint Training		Dewey Lab	Mon 10/17/...	Mon 10/17/2...
				Mon 5/2/20...	Mon 5/2/201...
				Mon 5/23/2...	Mon 5/23/20...

hasattachments:yes	✕
Arrange By: Date	Newest on top ▼ ▲

◢ **Two Weeks Ago**

✉	Elizabeth, the Computer Mama	2/20/2012
	Task Status Report: Website 1: New Designs	🔘
✉	Elizabeth, the Computer Mama	2/19/2012
	Find it, Fix it	🔘

Before You Begin

1. Try it: Find the Search Box
The **Search Box** sits on top of the Inbox.
Click on the **Search box.**

What Do You See? The Search Box will be outlined with a bright orange border.

Keep going...

Memo to Self: The following pages use the sample Messages, Appointments, Tasks and Contacts that were designed through the various lessons. It is not necessary to MATCH the steps. Rather, it is more important that you can find the tools and see the options.

Microsoft Outlook Inbox

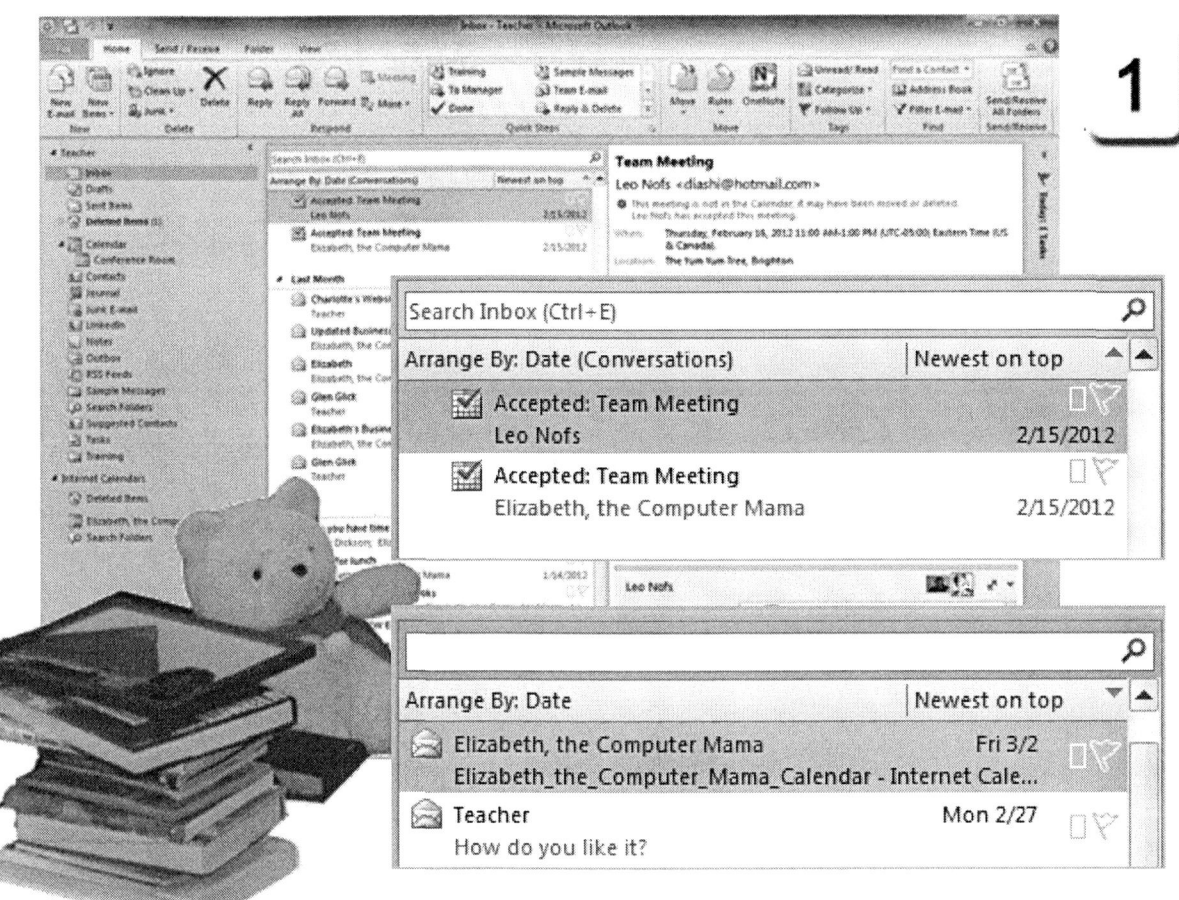

Exam 77-884: Microsoft Outlook 2010
1. Managing the Outlook Environment
1.4. Apply search and filter tools: Search the Inbox

Hello, Search Tools

2. Try it: Review the Search Tools

When you click on the Search box, the **Search Tools** should become available.

The **Search** Ribbon has four groups:
Scope
Refine
Options
Close

The **Scope** defines which Folders will be included in this Search. In this example on this page, the **Current Folder** is the Inbox.

You can expand the Scope to include **All Subfolders** or **All Outlook Items** (E-mail, Calendar, Tasks, and Contacts).

Keep going, please.

Search Tools

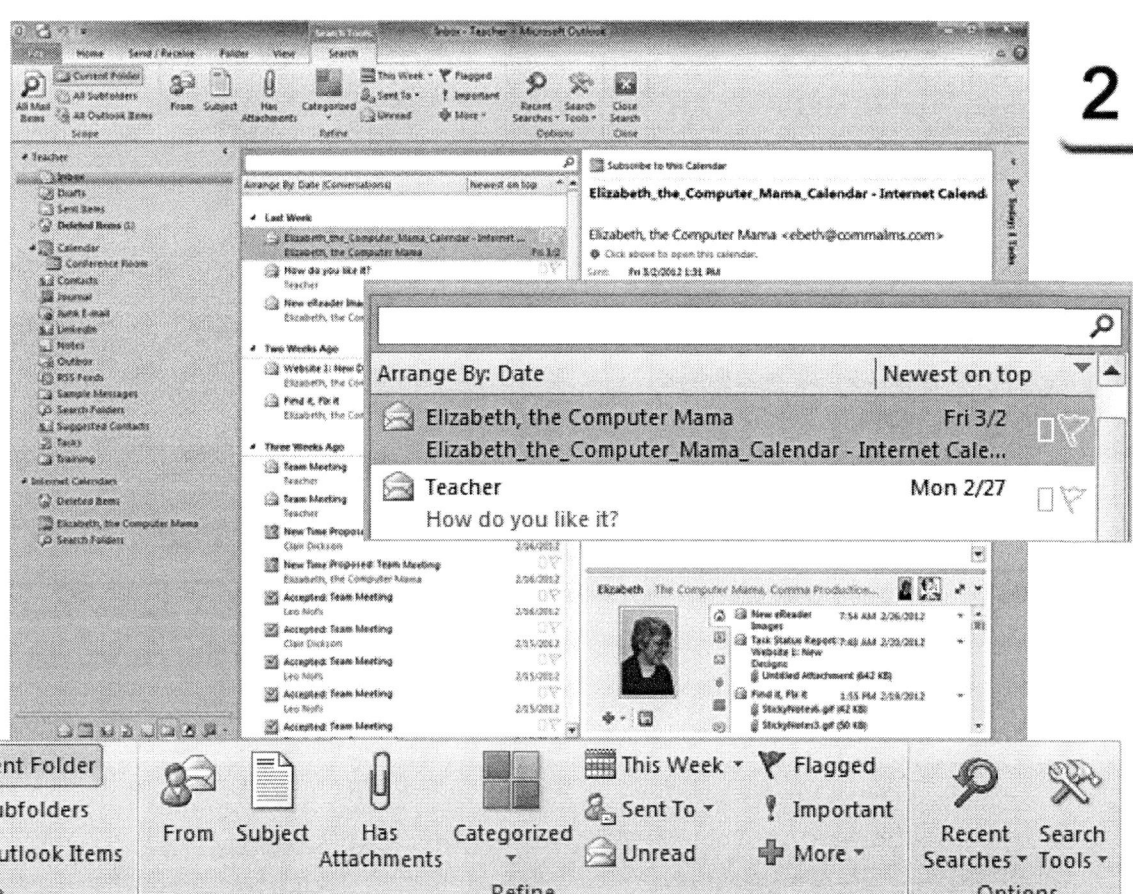

Exam 77-884: Microsoft Outlook 2010
1. Managing the Outlook Environment
1.4. Apply search and filter tools: Search the Inbox

Microsoft Outlook 2010   Page 321 of 366

Take One

Review the Search Results

3. Try it: Search by Keyword
Go to the Search Box.
Type: iPad

What Do You See? All of the E-mails that mention iPads in the Subject, Text or Attachment fields are listed. The results are arranged by Date. Each instance of the keyword, iPad, is highlighted.

What Else Do You See? Microsoft Outlook searched the current folder, the Inbox. So, the search only found E-mails that say something about the keyword.

You can expand your search and include all Outlook Items if you wish.

Keep going...

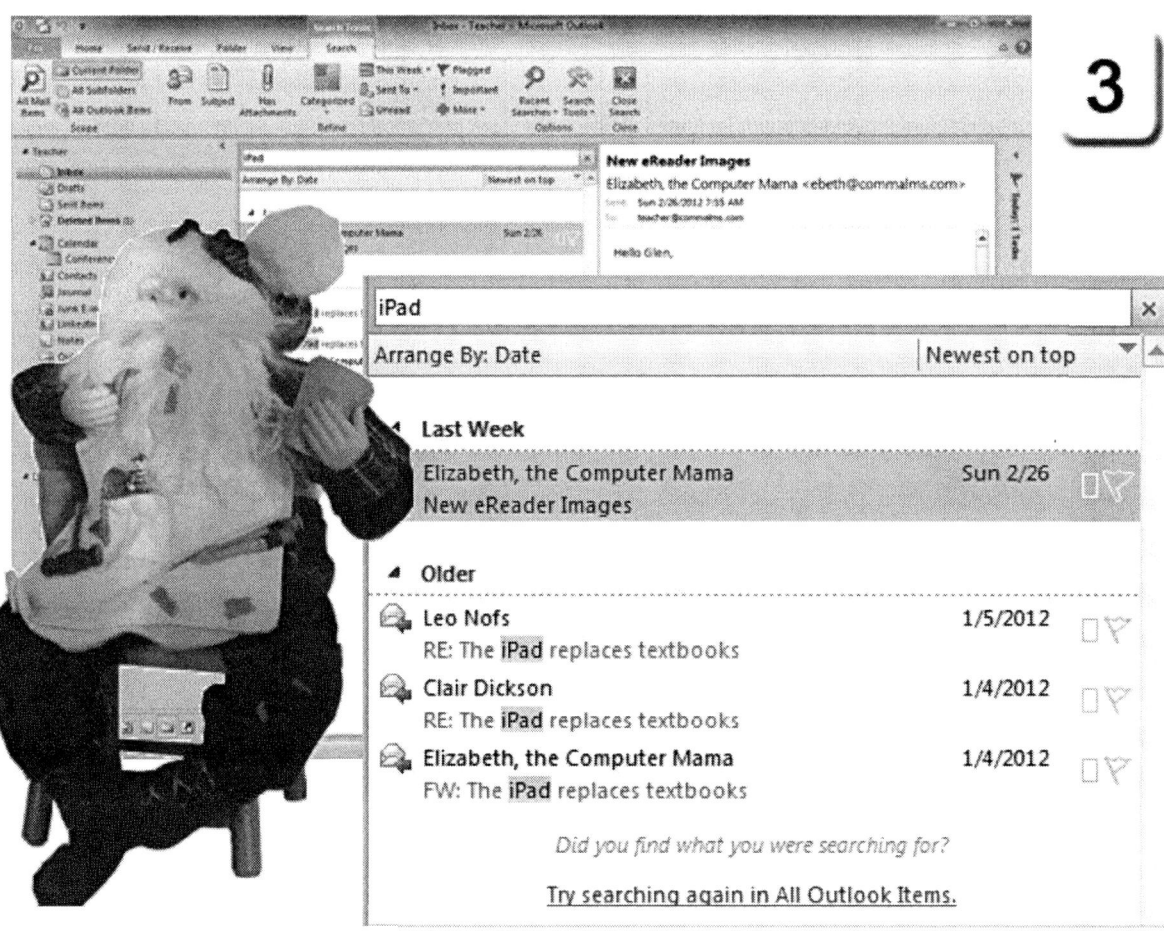

Exam 77-884: Microsoft Outlook 2010
1. Managing the Outlook Environment
1.4. Apply search and filter tools: Search the Inbox

Expand the Scope of the Search

4. Try it: Expand the Scope of the Search
The Inbox is still selected.
The Search Tools are available as well.

Go to **Search Tools-> Search->Scope.**
Click on **All Outlook Items**

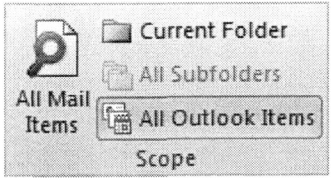

What Do You See, Now? Microsoft Outlook looked in all folders, including the Sent Items. The Search Results included the Meeting Invitation as well as the notice that the meeting was canceled.

This is a simple search.
Let's try another.

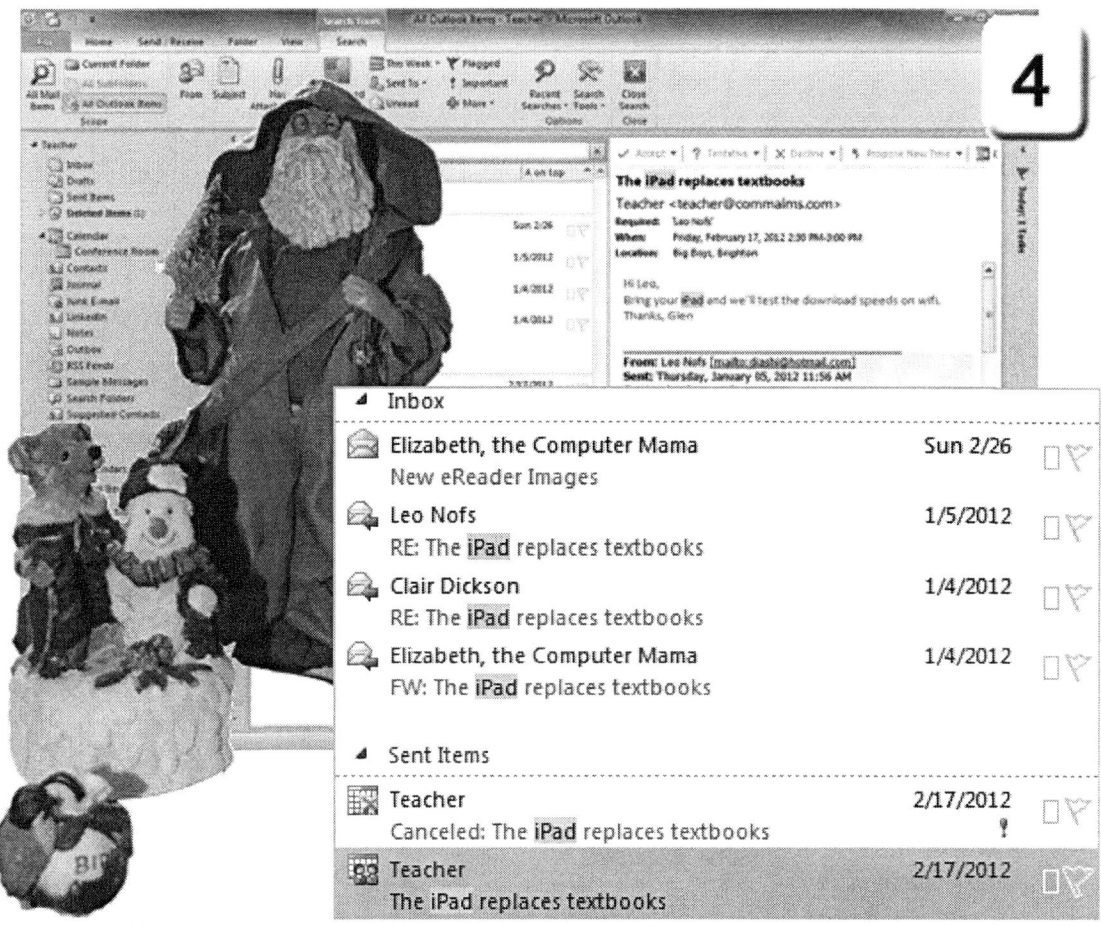

Exam 77-884: Microsoft Outlook 2010
1. Managing the Outlook Environment
1.4. Apply search and filter tools: Search the Inbox

HOME

Take One

Search Tools-> Search->Refine->Has Attachments

Refine the Search with Filters

5. Try it: Refine the Search
Go to the Inbox and click on the Search box.
The Search Tools will be available.

Go to **Search Tools-> Search->Refine.**
Click on **Has Attachments.**

What Do You See? The Search box says:
hasattachements:yes.

The results list all of the E-mail messages in
the current folder, the Inbox, that have
Attachments. The results are sorted by date.

What Else Do You See? You can search by
any method that you used to organize your
information in Outlook: From, Subject,
Category and Follow up Flags.

Keep going...

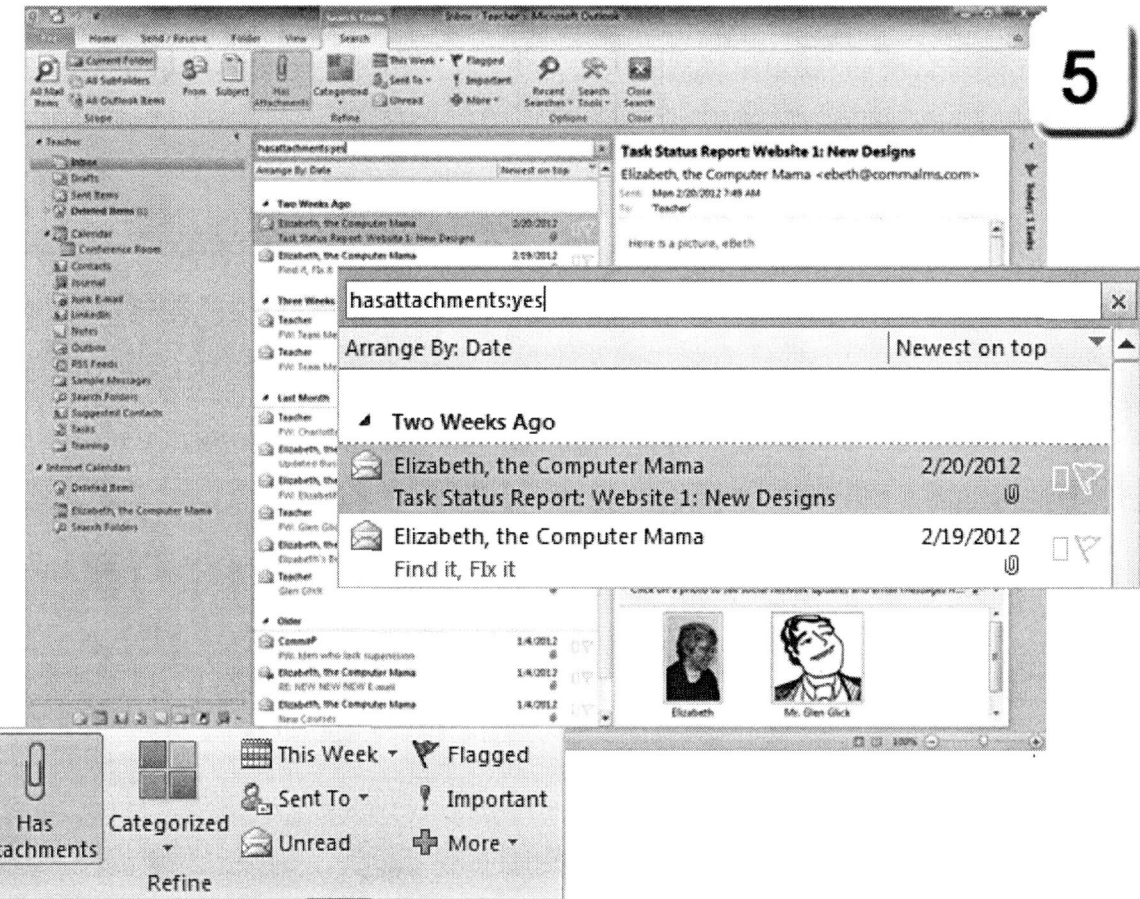

Exam 77-884: Microsoft Outlook 2010
1. Managing the Outlook Environment
1.4. Apply search and filter tools: Search the Inbox

Search the Calendar

Microsoft Outlook is a **database** that can be searched for answers. Each Meeting and Task is a record that can be analyzed in Microsoft Excel or Access. You can search the Calendar and use that data to calculate the hours and mileage on a Task.

6. Try it: Find the Search Box
The Search Box is in the upper right corner of the Calendar. Click on the Search box.

What Do You See? The Search Box will be outlined with a bright orange border.

Keep going...

Microsoft Outlook Calendar

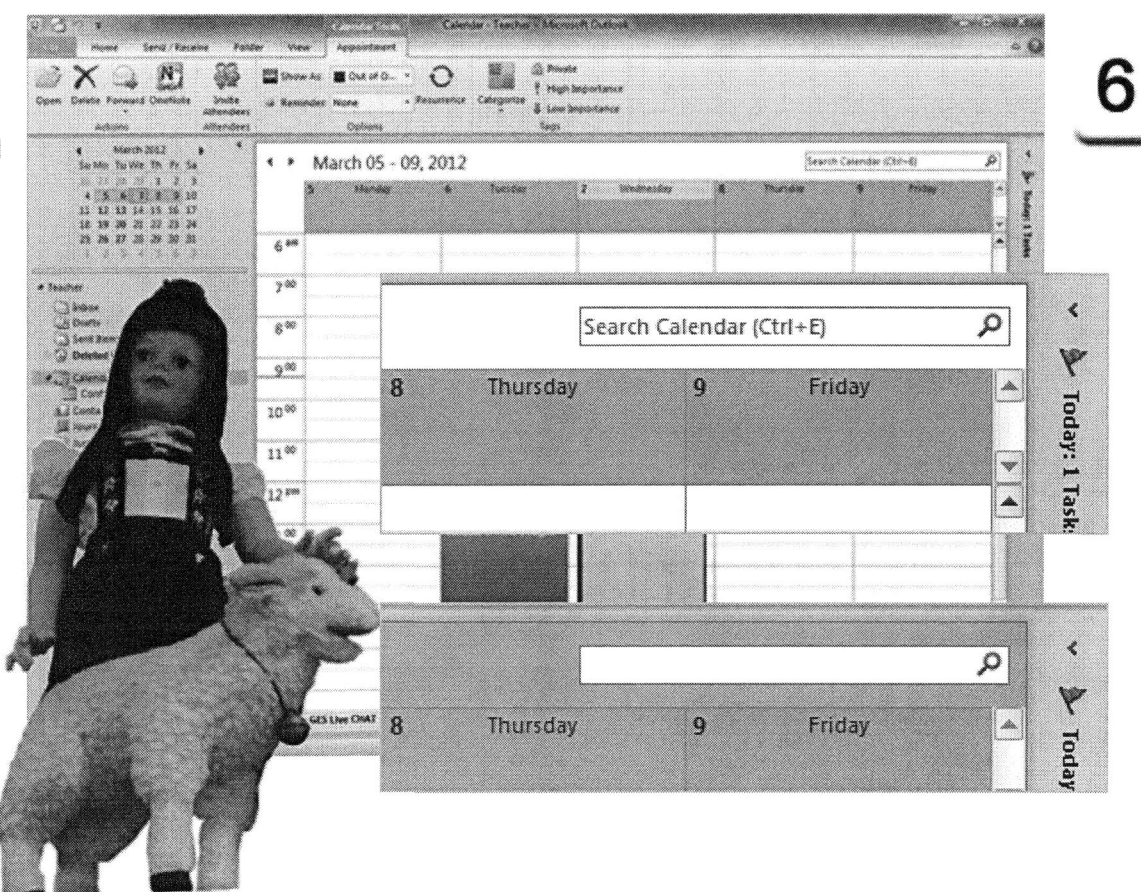

Exam 77-884: Microsoft Outlook 2010
1. Managing the Outlook Environment
1.4. Apply search and filter tools: Search the Calendar

Take One

Search Tools-> Search

Review the Search Results
7. Try it: Search by Keyword
Go to the Search box.
Type: Training

What Do You See? Microsoft Outlook searched the current folder, the Calendar. So, the search only found Meetings that include the keyword in the Subject, Organizer or Meeting.

Keep going...

7

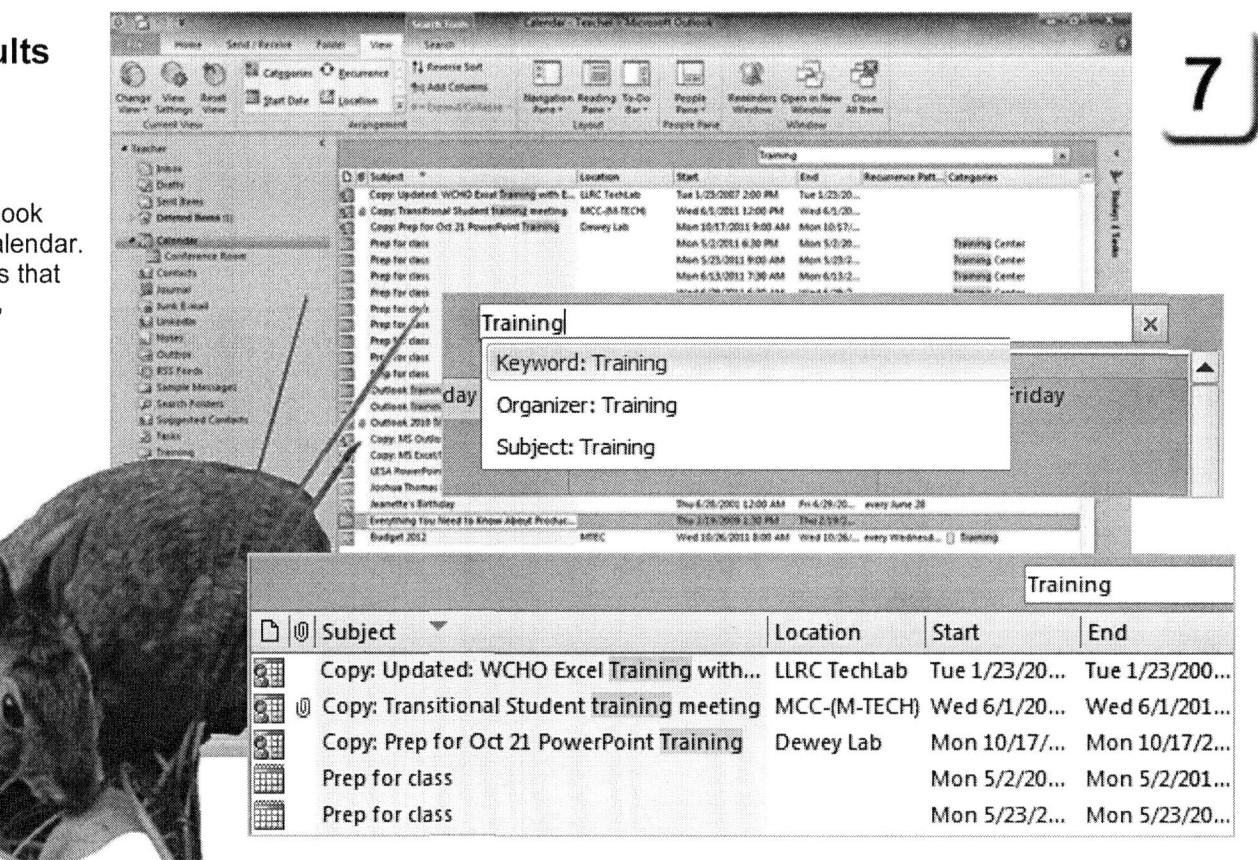

Exam 77-884: Microsoft Outlook 2010
1. Managing the Outlook Environment
1.4. Apply search and filter tools: Search the Calendar

Use the Search Options

There are two additional **Search Options** that are worth considering: **Recent Searches** and **Search Tools**.

8. Try it: Use the Search Options
The Calendar is still selected.
The Search Results are listed and the Search Tools should be available.

Go to **Search Tools-> Search-> Options**.

What Do You See? The **Recent Searches** shows the Search by the keyword (Training) that we just did.

The **Search Tools** has four choices:
Indexing Status
Locations to Search
Advanced Find
Search Options

In this example, there are two locations to search: the local Calendar (for Teacher) and the Internet Calendars. Keep going...

Search Tools-> Search-> Options

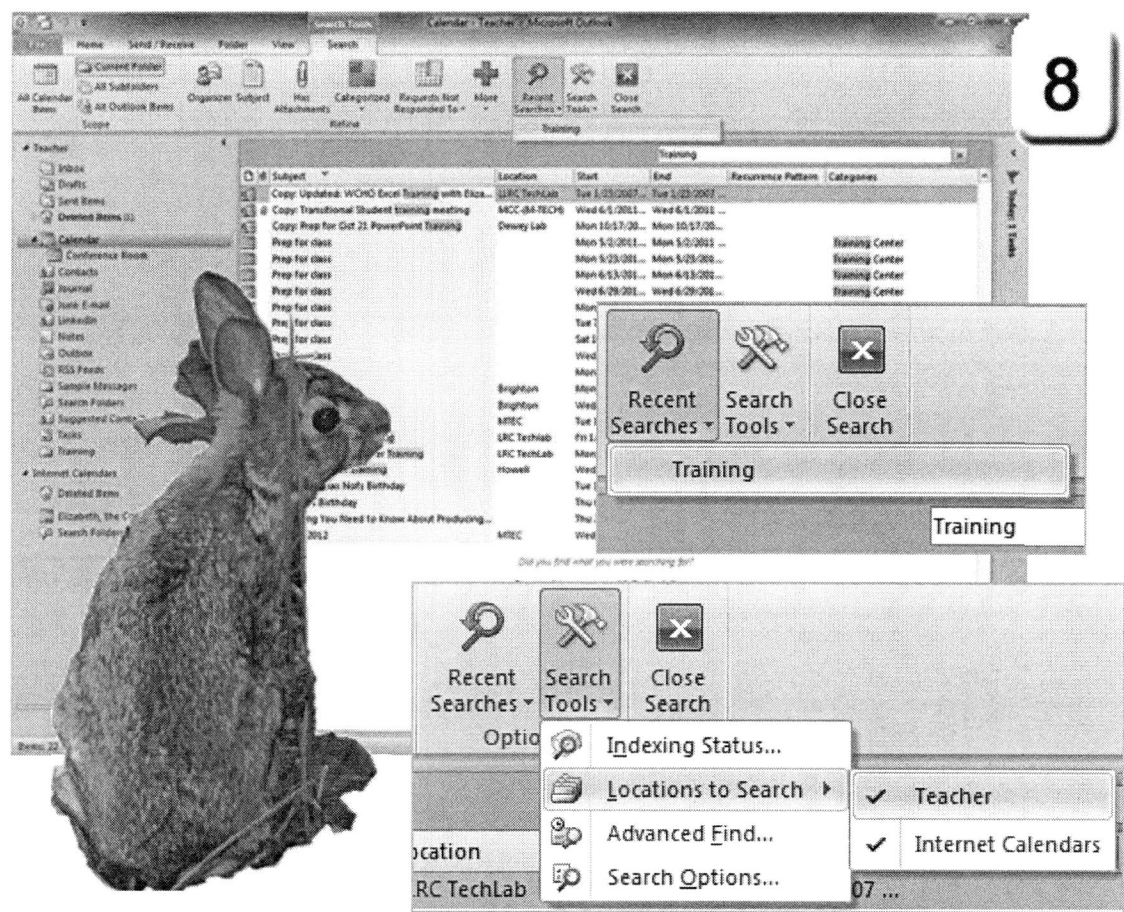

8

Exam 77-884: Microsoft Outlook 2010
1. Managing the Outlook Environment
1.4. Apply search and filter tools: Use Built-in Search Folders

Search Tools-> Search-> Options-> Search Tools-> Advanced Find

Use Advanced Find

Advanced Find has three methods for finding information in the Calendar:
Appointments and Meetings
More Choices
Advanced

Appointments and Meetings lets you search by keyword. Look at More Choices.

1. Try it: Use Advanced Find

Select the Search Box in the Calendar. The Search Tools should be available.

Go to **Search Tools-> Search-> Options.**
Go to **Search Tools-> Advanced Find.**
Select: **More Choices**.

There are options for:
Status (Read, Unread)
Attachments (One or more, No)
Importance (Normal, High, Low)
Tags (Follow up flags, Marked Complete)

By default, all of these search options are not checked. Keep going.

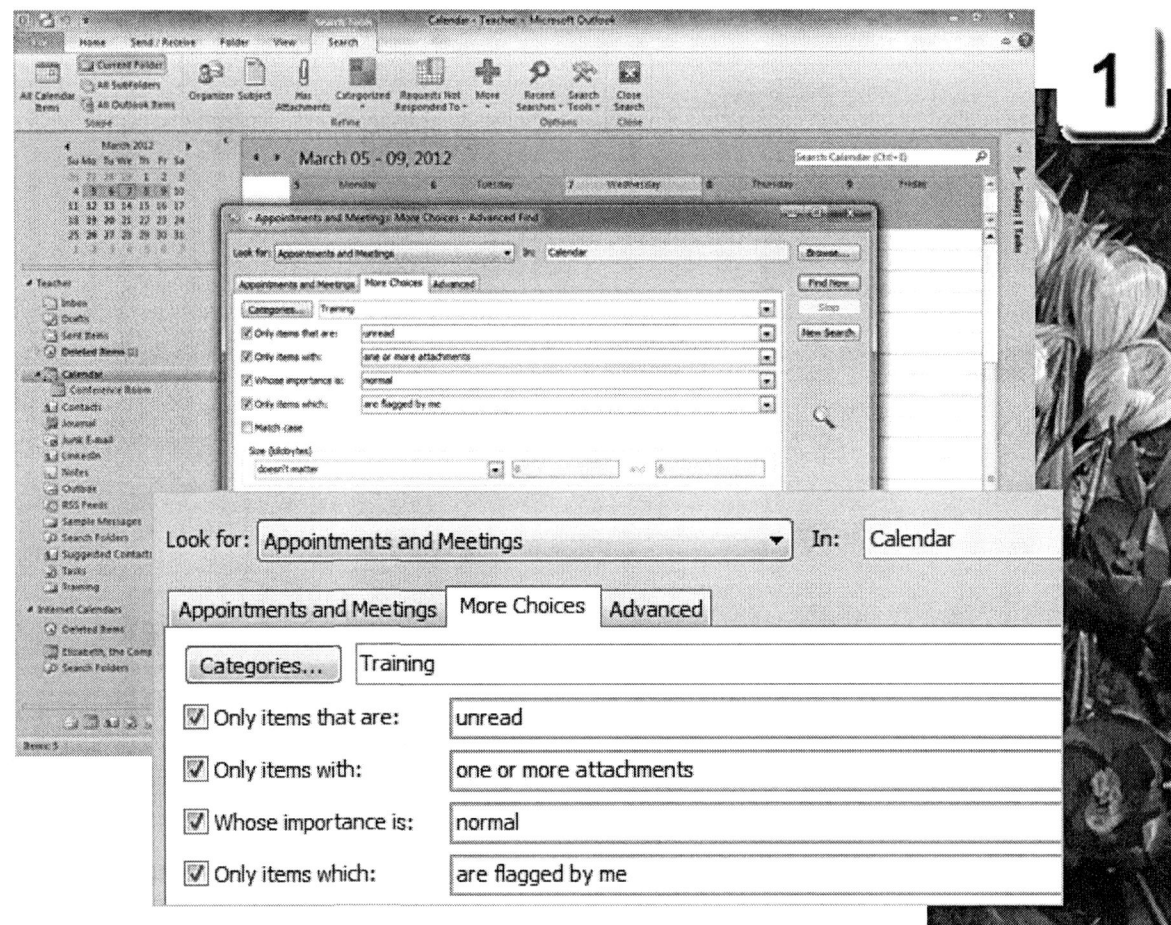

Exam 77-884: Microsoft Outlook 2010
1. Managing the Outlook Environment
1.4. Apply search and filter tools: Advanced Find

Advanced Find Options

The **Search** settings can be found in the Backstage. You can change the **Sources** and the **Results**.

Indexing a small collection of files makes the searches very fast. You can choose which folders and drives you would like to include in the index. Adding ALL of the folders on your drive defeats the definition of a "small collection." By default, the program files are excluded from the index: there's no data there.

2. Try it: Review the Search Options
Go to **File ->Options ->Search.**

What Do You See? The Results options are:
Include results only from: Current folder
Display results as query is typed
Improve speed by limited number of results shown
Highlight search terms
Highlight color.
Notify when results might be limited because search indexing is not complete.

File ->Options ->Search

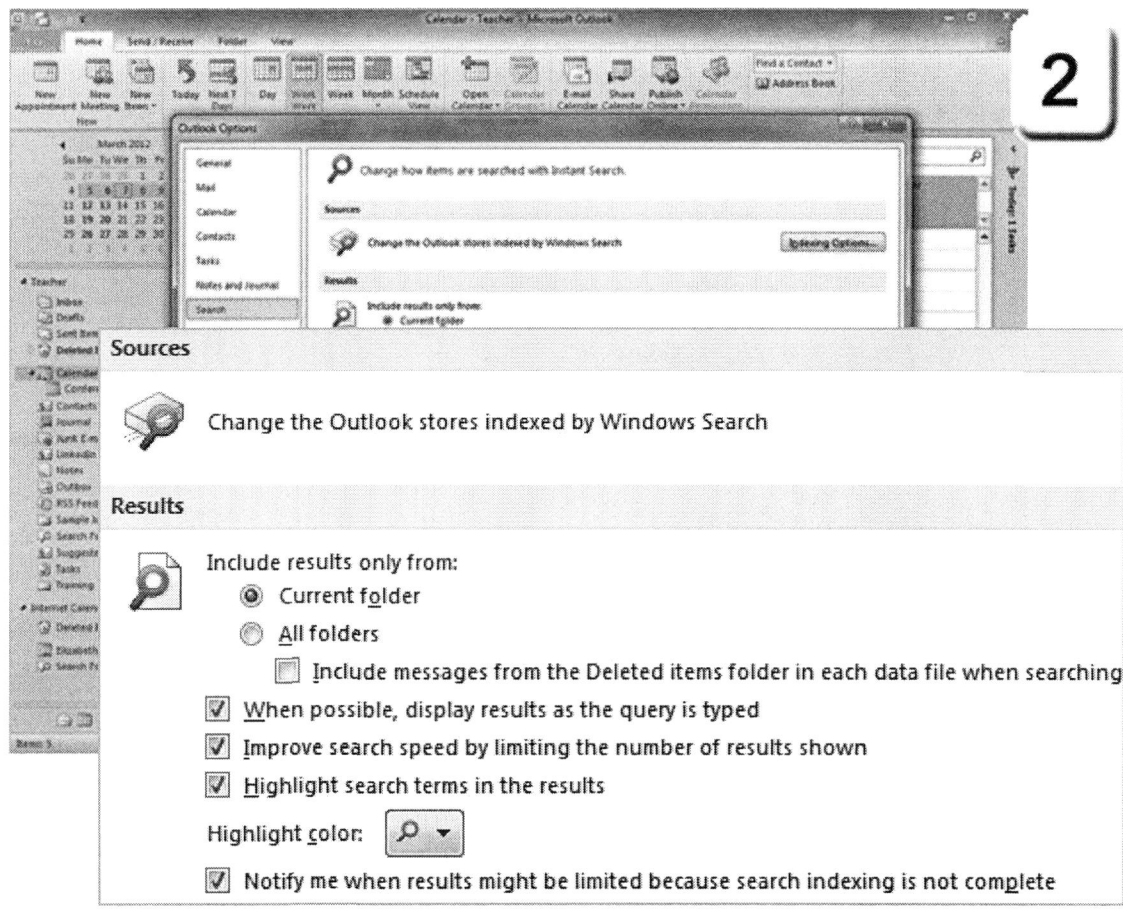

Exam 77-884: Microsoft Outlook 2010
1. Managing the Outlook Environment
1.1. Apply and manipulate Outlook program options: Set Advanced Options

Export Outlook Information

Microsoft Excel and Access both have good tools to query and organize data into reports. How do you get the information out of Outlook and into Excel?

3. Try it: Find the Export Options
Go to **File ->Options-> Advanced**.
Go to the **Export** category.
Click on **Export**.

Keep going...

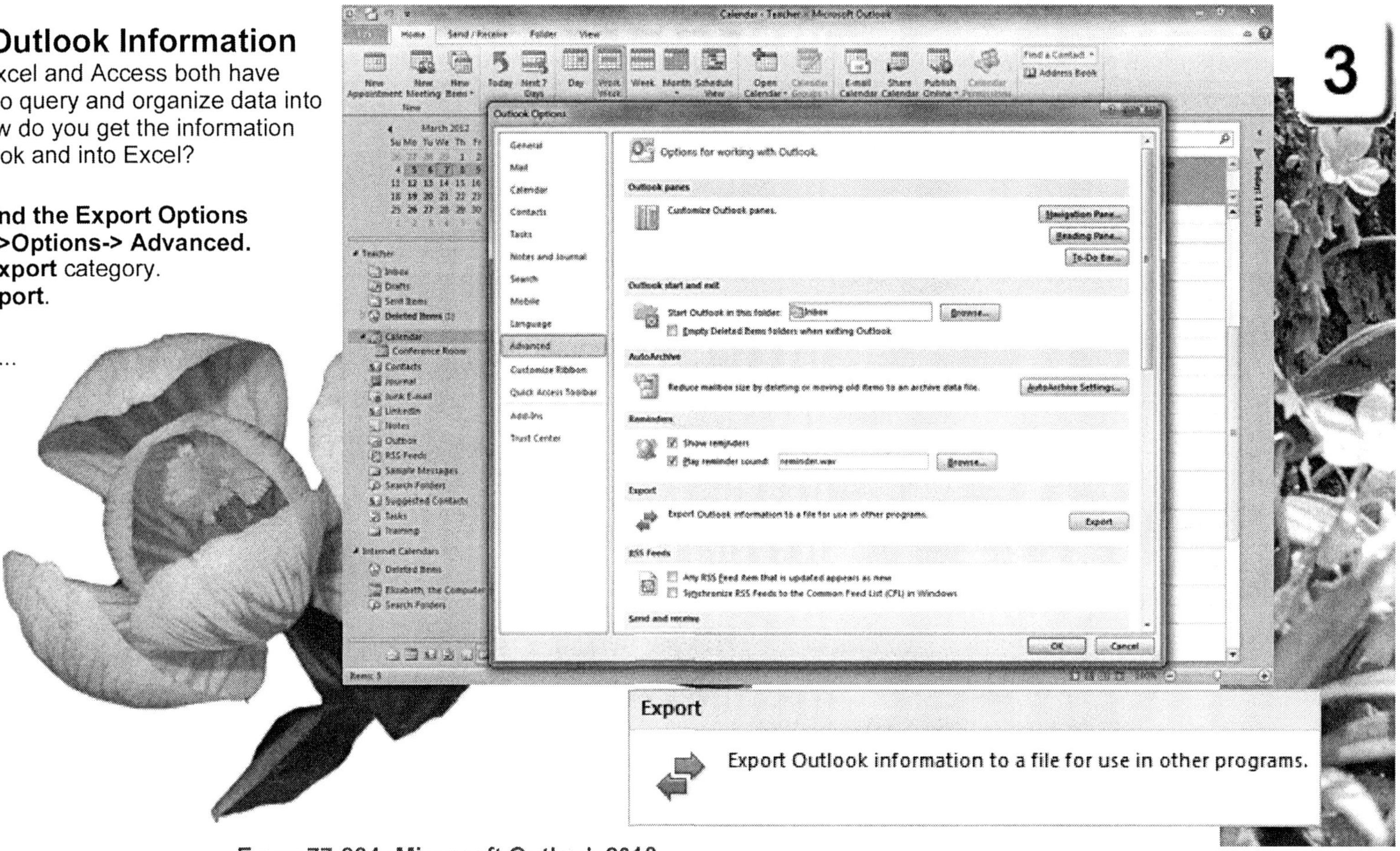

3

Export

Export Outlook information to a file for use in other programs.

Exam 77-884: Microsoft Outlook 2010
1. Managing the Outlook Environment
1.1. Apply and manipulate Outlook program options: Export a File

Advanced Find Results
4. Try it: Review the Advanced Find Results
The **Advance Find** window is open.
The page for **More Choices** is selected.

Enter a Category: Training
None of the Search Criteria are selected.
Click **Find Now**.

What Do You See? The Results are listed
under the Search criteria. Each of the field
headers (Subject, Location, Start, End) can be
used to sort the data.

So, how do you get the data out of Outlook and
into another program such as Excel?

Please turn to page to find out...

Please turn to page to find out...

Search Tools-> Search-> Options-> Search Tools->Advanced Find

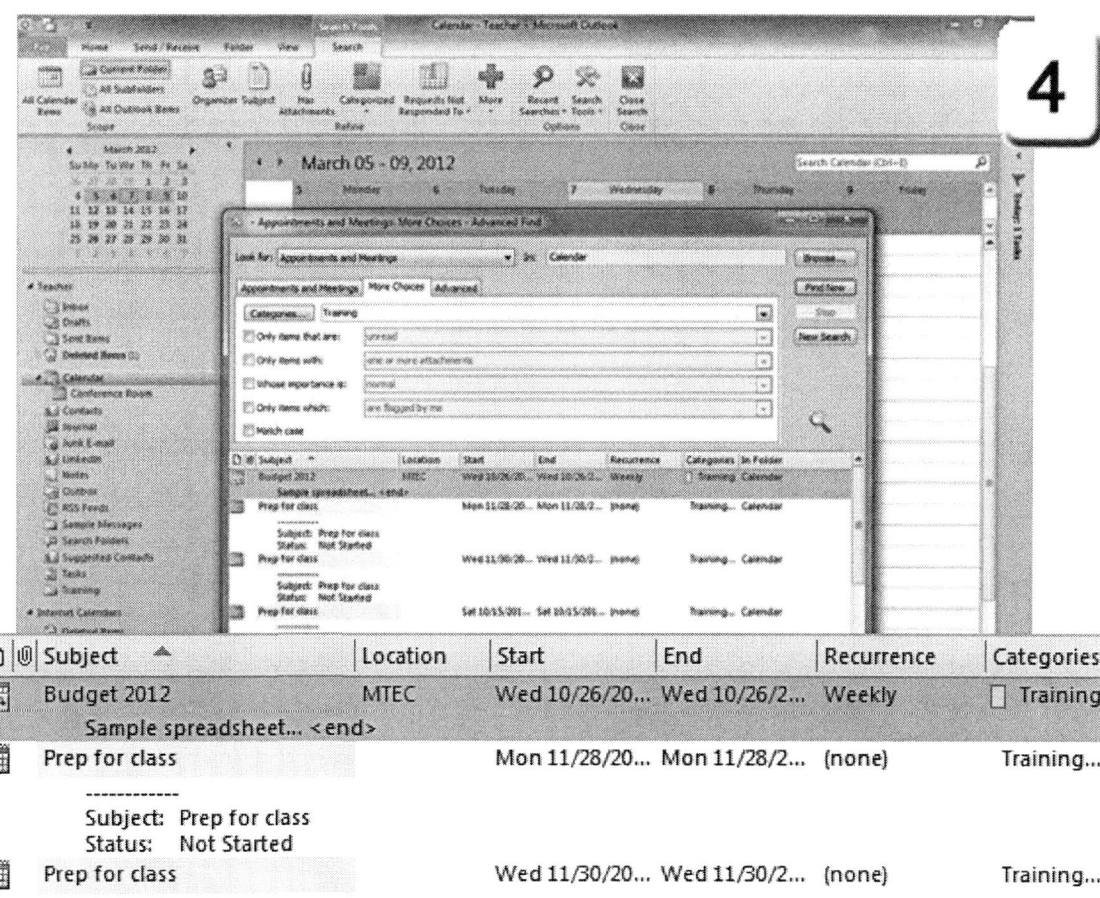

D	ⓤ	Subject ▲	Location	Start	End	Recurrence	Categories
📇		Budget 2012	MTEC	Wed 10/26/20...	Wed 10/26/2...	Weekly	☐ Training
		Sample spreadsheet... <end>					
▦		Prep for class		Mon 11/28/20...	Mon 11/28/2...	(none)	Training...

		Subject: Prep for class					
		Status: Not Started					
▦		Prep for class		Wed 11/30/20...	Wed 11/30/2...	(none)	Training...

Exam 77-884: Microsoft Outlook 2010
1. Managing the Outlook Environment
1.4. Apply search and filter tools: Advanced Find

Take One

Import and Export Wizard

The **Import and Export Wizard** will walk you through the process. There are two export choices and a half dozen file that can be imported into Outlook.

5. Try it: Export to a File
The Import and Export Wizard is open.
Select: **Export to a file**.
Click **Next**.

Keep going...

File ->Options-> Advanced->Export

5

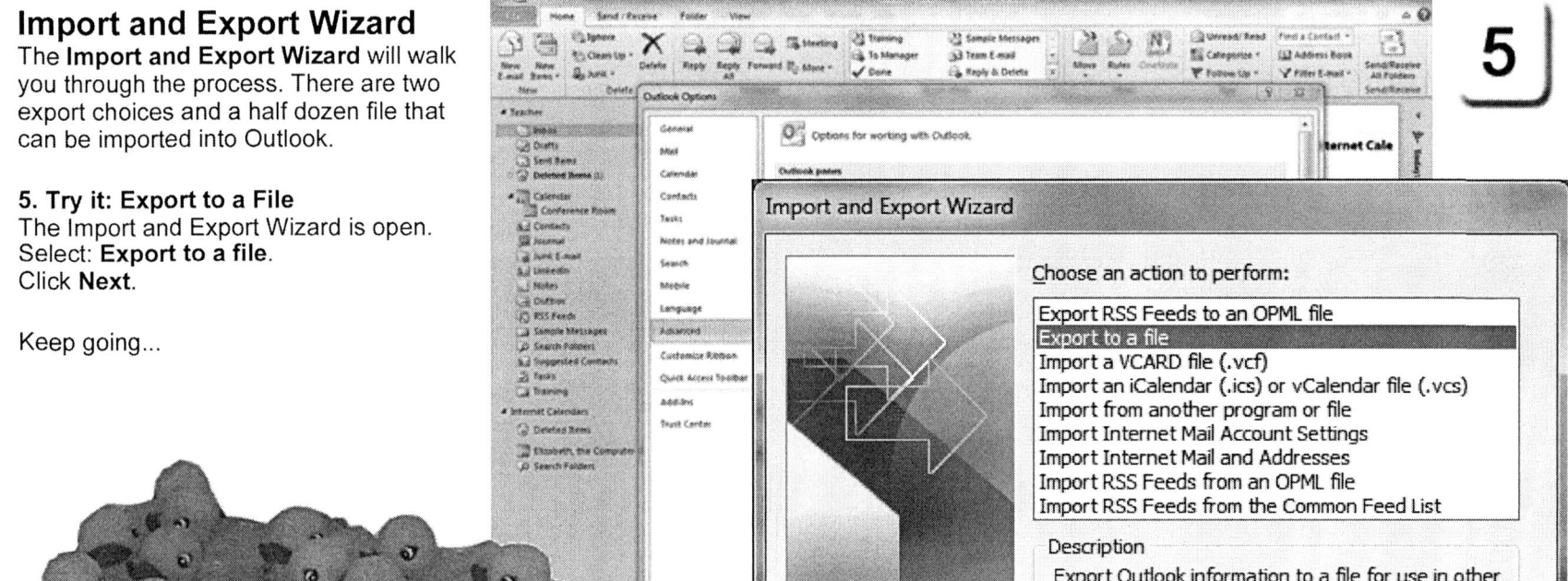

Exam 77-884: Microsoft Outlook 2010
1. Managing the Outlook Environment
1.1. Apply and manipulate Outlook program options: Export a File

Export: Select a File Type

6. Try it: Select a File Type to Export
There are seven file types that you can choose for your export. You can create a legacy file format such as Comma Separated Values for DOS or for Windows as well as an Access database or an Excel spreadsheet.

Select: **Microsoft Excel 97-2003**.
Click **Next**.

Keep going...

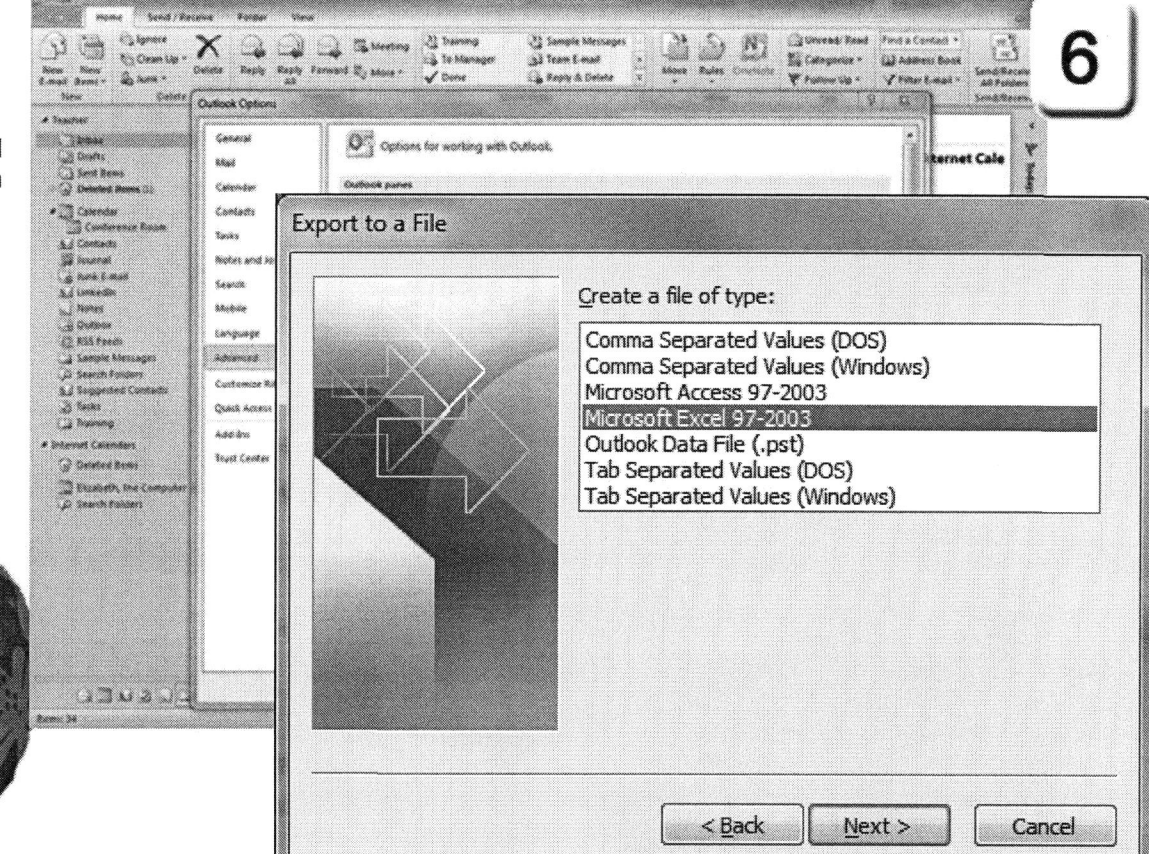

Exam 77-884: Microsoft Outlook 2010
1. Managing the Outlook Environment
1.1. Apply and manipulate Outlook program options: Export a File

Select a Folder to Export

This step asks you to select which folder you would like to Export. You can select any folder (and all of its subfolders).

You can also select the entire database by choosing the Home folder. In the example on this page, the owner is Teacher, which is the name of the Home folder at the top of the directory.

7. Try it: Select a Folder to Export
Select folder to export from: Calendar.
Click **Next**.

Keep going...

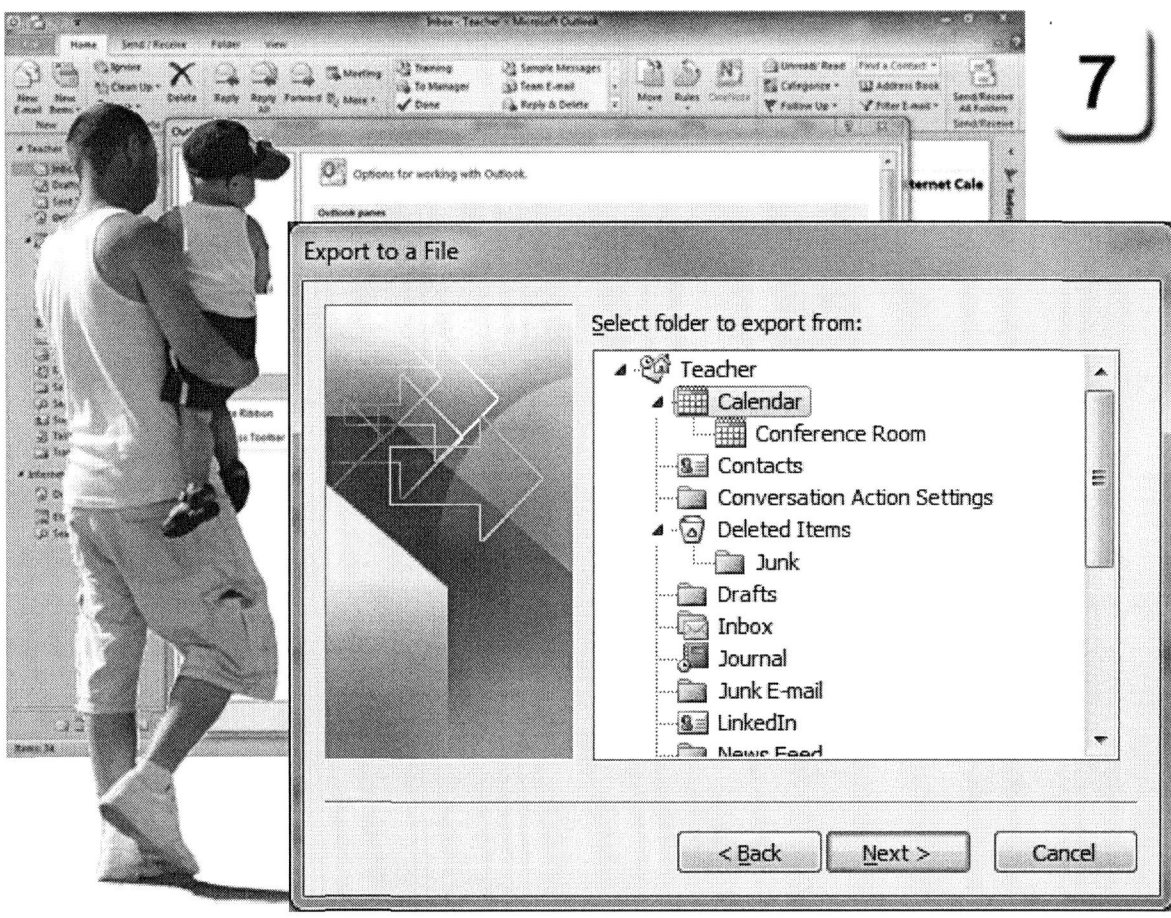

7

Exam 77-884: Microsoft Outlook 2010
1. Managing the Outlook Environment
1.1. Apply and manipulate Outlook program options: Export a File

Save the Exported File

The Wizard will prompt you to name the file and Browse for a place to save it.

8. Try it: Save Exported File As
Type a name: Export from Outlook (date)
Browse to the Documents folder.
Click **Next**.

Keep going...

File ->Options-> Advanced->Export

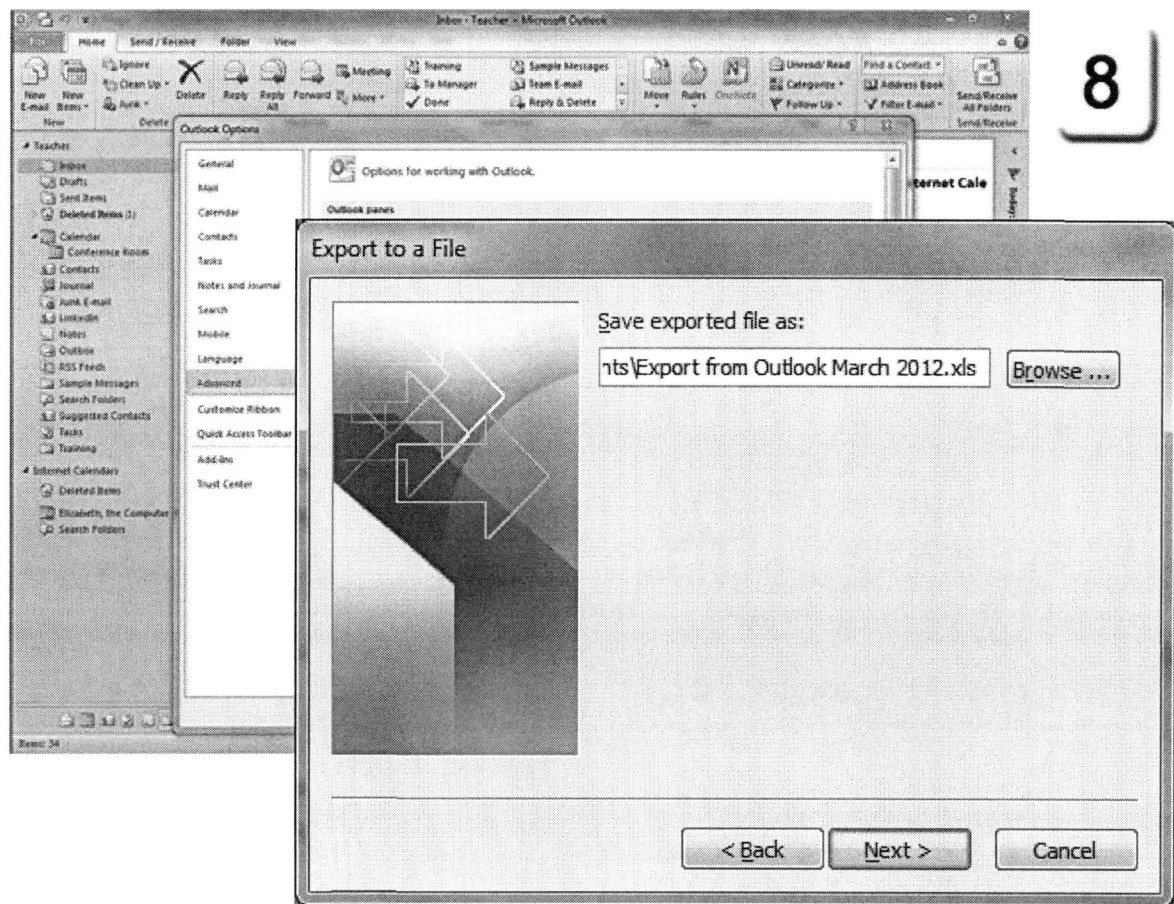

Exam 77-884: Microsoft Outlook 2010
1. Managing the Outlook Environment
1.1. Apply and manipulate Outlook program options: Export a File

File ->Options-> Advanced->Export

Map Custom Fields

Microsoft Outlook assigns names to the data fields: Last Name, First Name, Business, City, State, Postal Code, etc. These field names may not be identical to the ones in your spreadsheets.

Say your data uses the name Zip Code instead of Postal Code. You can use this step to Map Custom Field... and match the different names.

9. Try it: Review the Custom Mapping
Click on **Map Custom Fields**.
Review the field names in the list.
Click **OK** to return to the Export Wizard.

Click **Finish.** If this a calendar, you will be prompted to enter the start and end dates.

What Happens Next? A new spreadsheet will be saved to the Documents folder.

So,....what kind of data was exported?

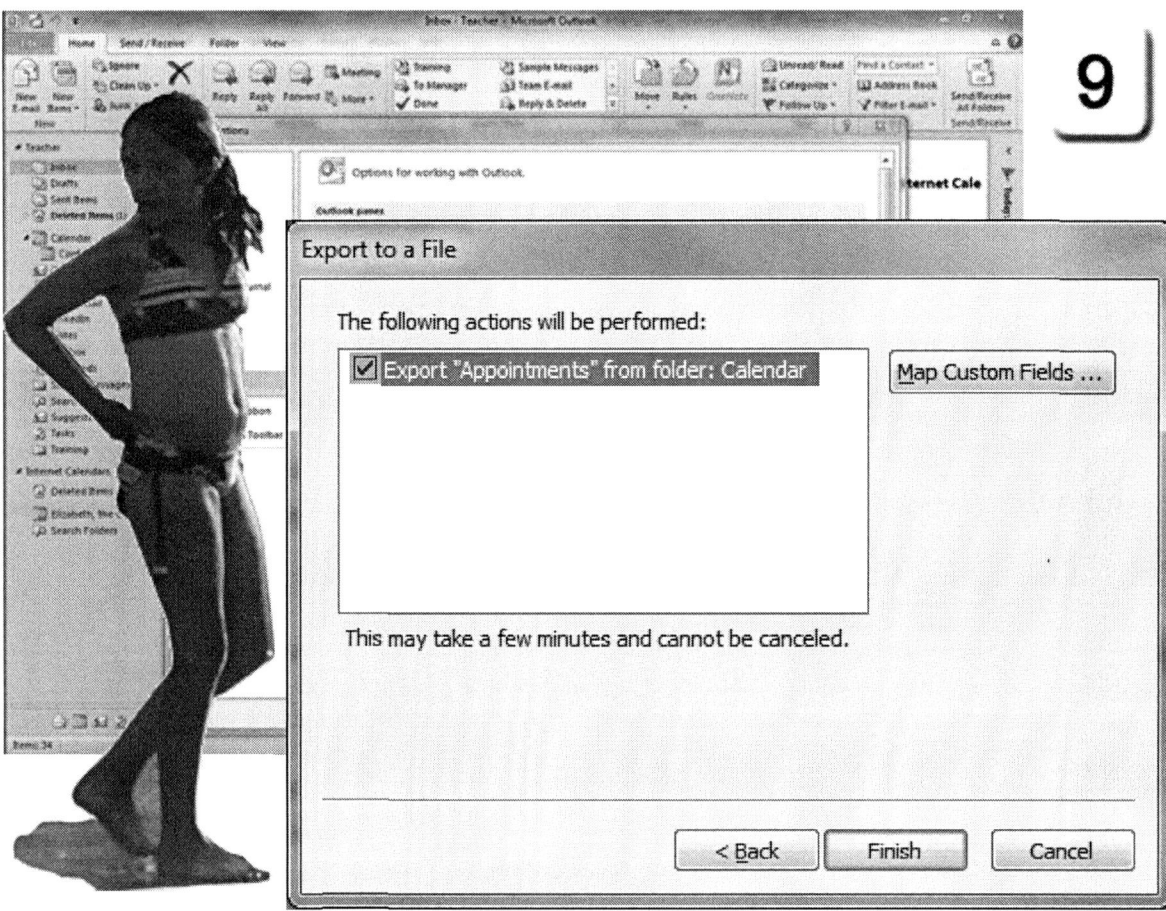

9

Export to a File

The following actions will be performed:

☑ Export "Appointments" from folder: Calendar   Map Custom Fields ...

This may take a few minutes and cannot be canceled.

< Back   Finish   Cancel

Exam 77-884: Microsoft Outlook 2010
1. Managing the Outlook Environment
1.1. Apply and manipulate Outlook program options: Export a File

Review the Export File

Here are the steps to open the Export File that was saved to the Documents folder.

Try it: Open the Export Spreadsheet
Browse to the Documents folder.
Find the file: **Export from Outlook. xls**
Double click that file to open it.
The spreadsheet should open in Excel.

What Do You See? The field names are listed in Row 1. The Calendar data can be sorted, grouped and analyzed.

OK, this works. We know how to handle data in a spreadsheet.

Microsoft Excel

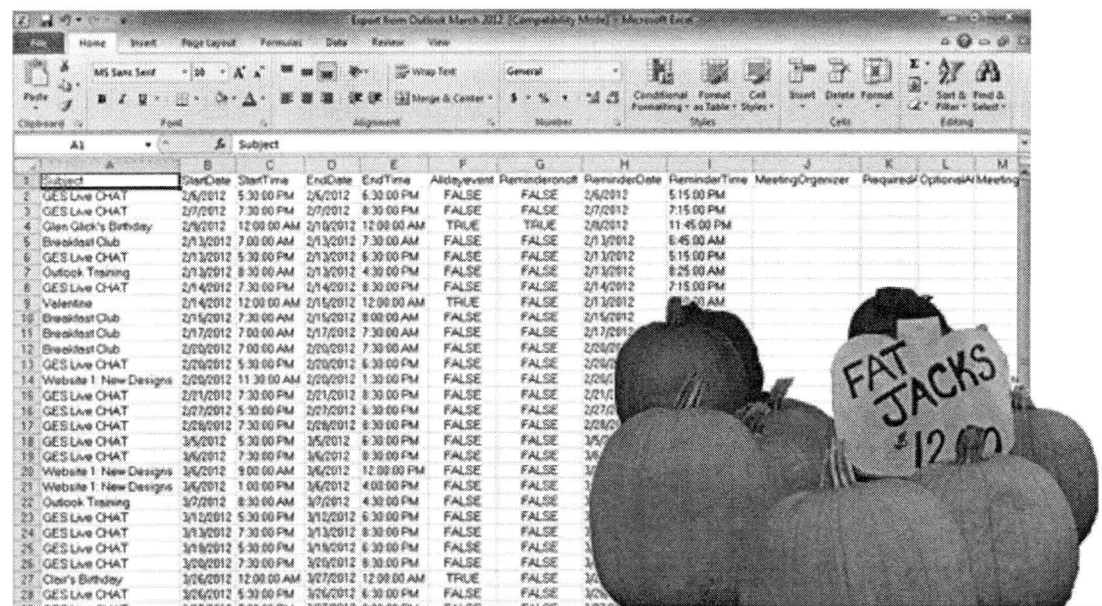

	A	B	C	D	E	F	G
1	Subject	StartDate	StartTime	EndDate	EndTime	Alldayevent	Reminderonoff
2	GES Live CHAT	2/6/2012	5:30:00 PM	2/6/2012	6:30:00 PM	FALSE	FALSE
3	GES Live CHAT	2/7/2012	7:30:00 PM	2/7/2012	8:30:00 PM	FALSE	FALSE
4	Glen Glick's Birthday	2/9/2012	12:00:00 AM	2/10/2012	12:00:00 AM	TRUE	TRUE
5	Breakfast Club	2/13/2012	7:00:00 AM	2/13/2012	7:30:00 AM	FALSE	FALSE
6	GES Live CHAT	2/13/2012	5:30:00 PM	2/13/2012	6:30:00 PM	FALSE	FALSE

Extra for Experts

There are a couple more Advanced options that you can change if you wish.

1. Try it: Review the Advanced Options
Microsoft Outlook is open.
Go to **File ->Options-> Advanced.**

What Do You See? The options include:

Reminders: The default options are Show the reminders and Play the reminder sound. (Yes, you can Browse for your own sound!)

RSS Feeds: RSS means Really Simple Syndication. These options update and synchronize your newsgroup feeds.

Keep going...

File ->Options-> Advanced

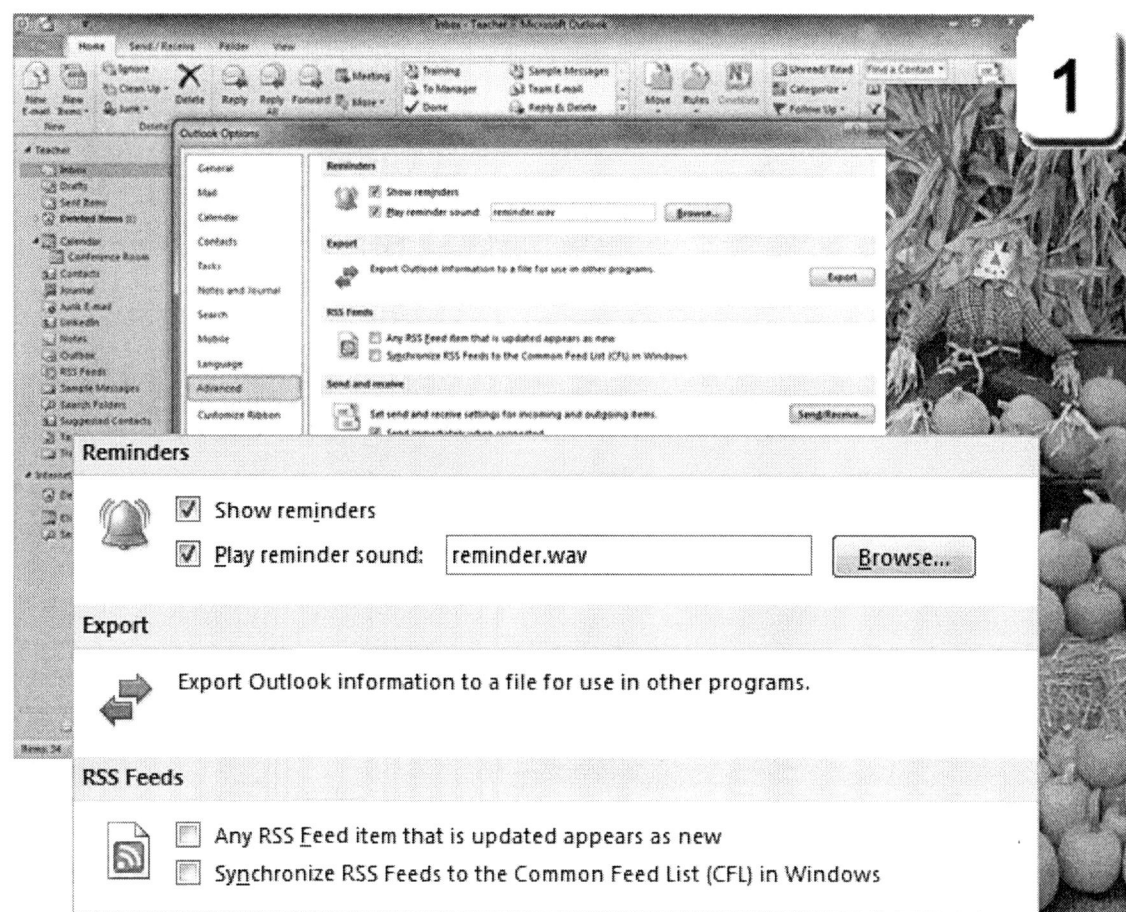

Exam 77-884: Microsoft Outlook 2010
1. Managing the Outlook Environment
1.1. Apply and manipulate Outlook program options: Set Advanced Options

More Advanced Options

2. Try it: Review More Options

Send and receive: Microsoft Outlook sends your E-mail as soon as you are connected to the Internet.

Developers: You can design your own Outlook forms if you wish. This option is used by Developers for troubleshooting user interface errors.

Dial-Up Connections: For folks in rural areas who still do not have high-speed Internet access, this option manages the Dial-Up phone connection.

That will do. You can close the Outlook Options and call it a day.

Allez. Allez in free!
You can get the cookie!

File ->Options-> Advanced

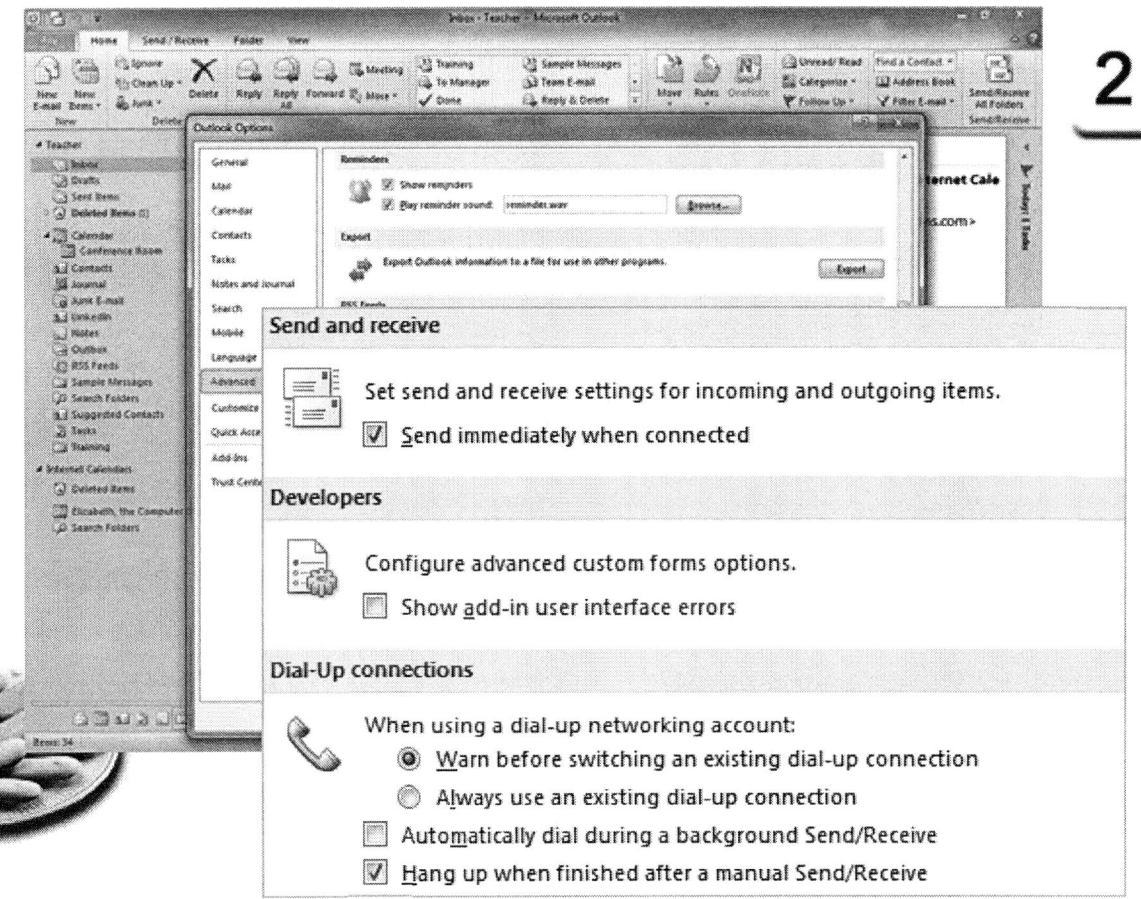

Exam 77-884: Microsoft Outlook 2010
1. Managing the Outlook Environment
1.1. Apply and manipulate Outlook program options: Set Advanced Options

Test Yourself

1. How is the Search Tools Ribbon Accessed?
a. Go to View-> Search Tools
b. Click the Search box
c. Go to File-> Options-> Ribbons-> View Search tools
Tip: Complete Guide to Outlook, page 321

2. Which are options for the scope of a search? (Give all correct answers.)
a. Current Folder
b. All Subfolders
c. All Outlook Items
Tip: Complete Guide to Outlook, page 321

3. Which is an option for searching? (Give all correct answers.)
a. From
b. Subject
c. Category
d. Follow Up Flags
e. Has Attachment
Tip: Complete Guide to Outlook, page 324

4. Outlook is a database.
a. True
b. False
Tip: Complete Guide to Outlook, page 325

5. Which of the following Outlook items are searchable? (Give all correct answers.)
a. E-mail
b. Calendar
Tip: Complete Guide to Outlook, page 320, 325

6. Which are options for exporting from Outlook? (Give all correct answers.)
a. Comma Separate Value (CSV)
b. Excel Spreadsheet
c. Access Database
Tip: Complete Guide to Outlook, page 333

7. You can change the sound played for Reminders.
a. True
b. False
Tip: Complete Guide to Outlook, page 338

8. Which is true about Indexing? (Give all correct answers.)
a. Makes the search faster
b. Should only be used on select folders
c. Does not include program files by default
Tip: Complete Guide to Outlook, page 330

Application Question: You know that you received an E-mail from a former co-worker, whose last name you forgot about an exciting seminar in your field. Give two ways to search for the E-mail.

Outlook 2010: Managing Outlook

E-mail Accounts

Advanced Outlook Objectives

In this lesson, you will learn how to:

1. Add a new E-mail Account to Outlook
2. Test the Account Settings and troubleshoot errors
3. Find and backup the Outlook Data File
4. Use the Advanced options to set up AutoArchive
5. Review and manage the Send/Receive Groups

© 2012 Comma Productions, LLC

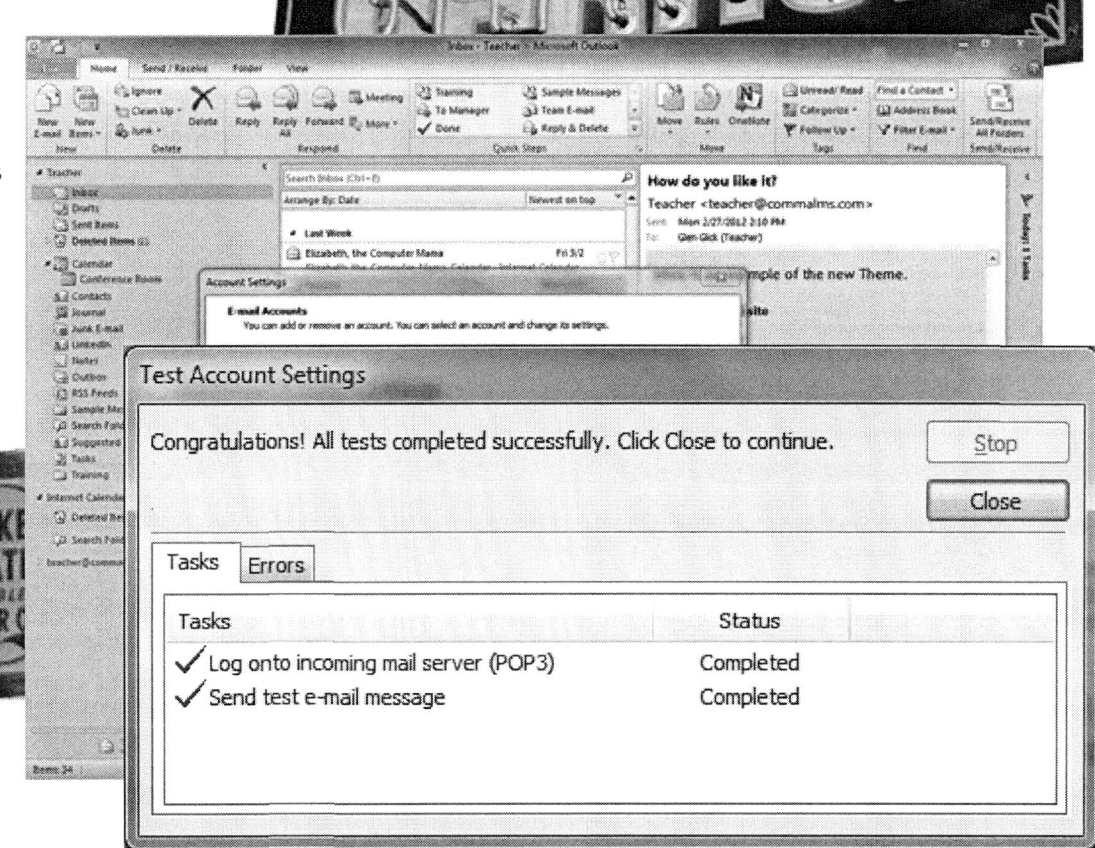

 # Lesson 12: E-mail Accounts

Send/Receive Ribbon

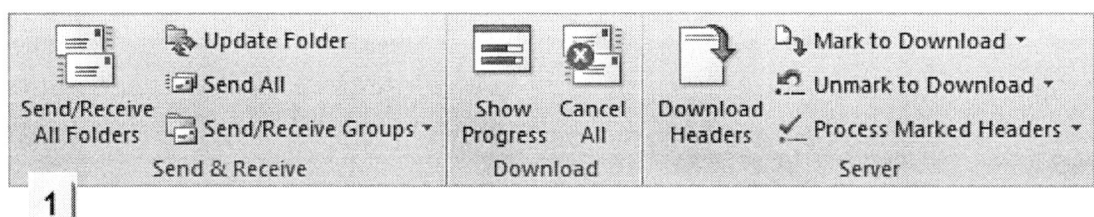

1. Readings
Read Lesson 12 in the Microsoft Outlook guide, page 341-360.

Project
Step-by-step demonstration of how to set up an E-mail account in Microsoft Outlook

Downloads
There are no downloads for this lesson.

2. Practice
There is no Practice Activity for this lesson.

3. Assessment
Review the Test questions on page 361.

Menu Maps
From the **File Ribbon**.
1. File ->Info->Add Account, page 344
2. File ->Info->Account Settings-> E-mail, page 351
3. File ->Info->Account Settings->Data Files, page 352
4. File ->Options-> Advanced->AutoArchive Settings, page 355

From the **Send/Receive Ribbon**
1. Send/Receive->Send & Receive, page 357

Setting up the E-mail Accounts

Without an E-mail account, the Inbox is just a Dead Letter Box. Microsoft Outlook needs to connect to the Internet and access an E-mail server to download your messages. There are two parts to this process: gathering information about your E-mail Account and entering that information into Outlook. Not all E-mail Accounts work with Outlook.

The following pages show, in general, how to set up an E-mail Account and test the settings. Some accounts may need to be addressed by your E-mail provider. That said, let's get started.

Start -> All Programs ->Microsoft Office-> Microsoft Office Outlook 2010

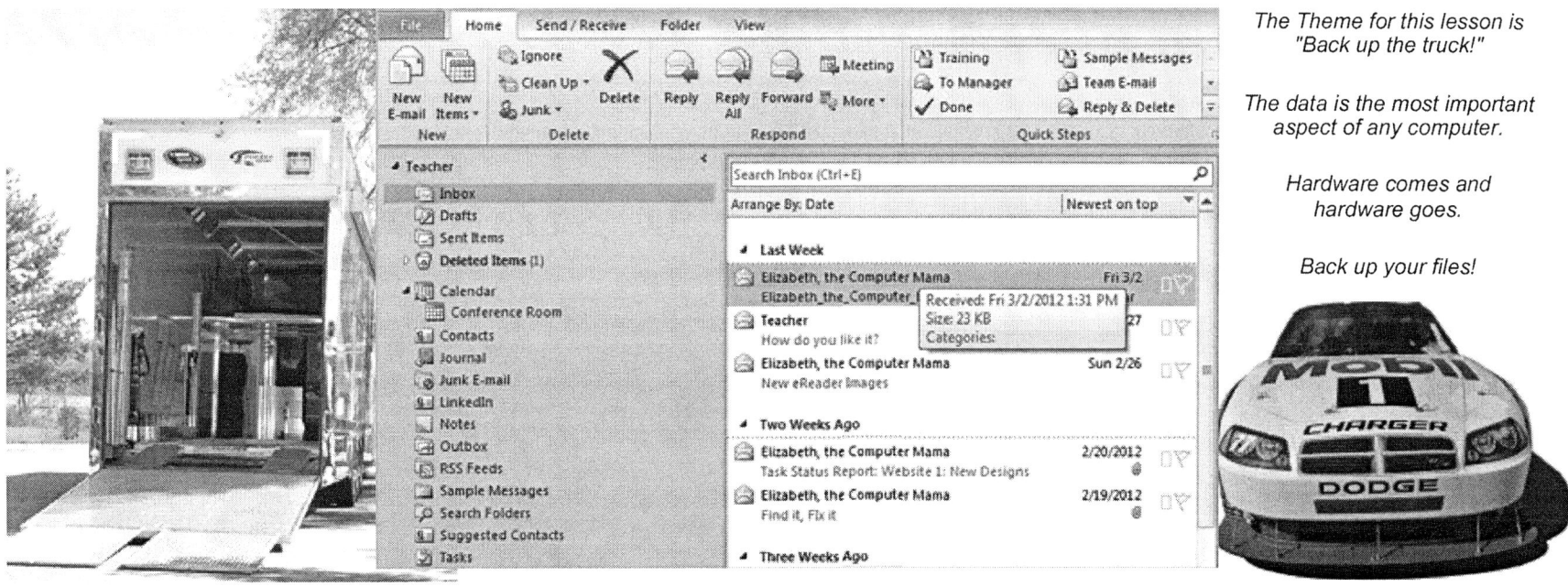

The Theme for this lesson is "Back up the truck!"

The data is the most important aspect of any computer.

Hardware comes and hardware goes.

Back up your files!

Before You Begin

The **Account Information** and **Account Settings** can be found in the Microsoft Outlook **Backstage**.

1. Try it: Find the Account Information
Go to **File->Info**.

What Do You See? If Outlook is set up to send and receive E-mail, the Account Information will be listed. In the example on this page, the Account is for teacher@commalms.com

What Else Do You See? There is a bright green button to **Add Account**.

Try This, Too: Add an Account
Go to **File ->Info**.
Click on **Add Account**.

Keep going...

Memo to Self: teacher@commalms.com is a SAMPLE E-mail address. Please use your own E-mail address to setup Outlook.

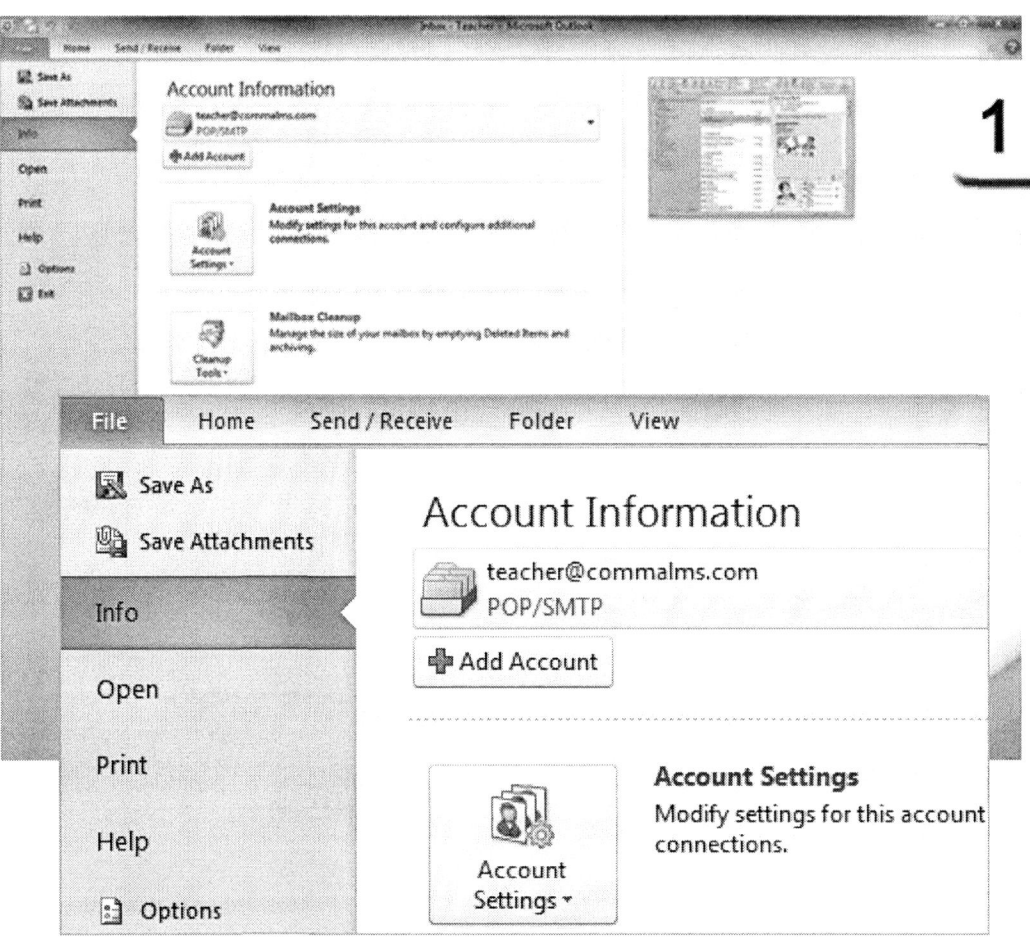

Add an Account

2. Try it: Add an E-mail Account

When you create a new E-mail account, you will be prompted to identify yourself: Name, E-mail Address and Password.

If you click Next, Microsoft Outlook will try to locate your E-mail server. This may or may not be successful. Instead, please consider doing your own homework and entering the data yourself. Homework is defined by looking up the information about your E-mail provider.

Say you get your E-mail from AOL, MSN, Charter, etc. You can go to that company's website to find the Outlook Account Settings.

Go to **Manually configure serve settings**. Click **Next**. Keep going...

File ->Info->Add Account

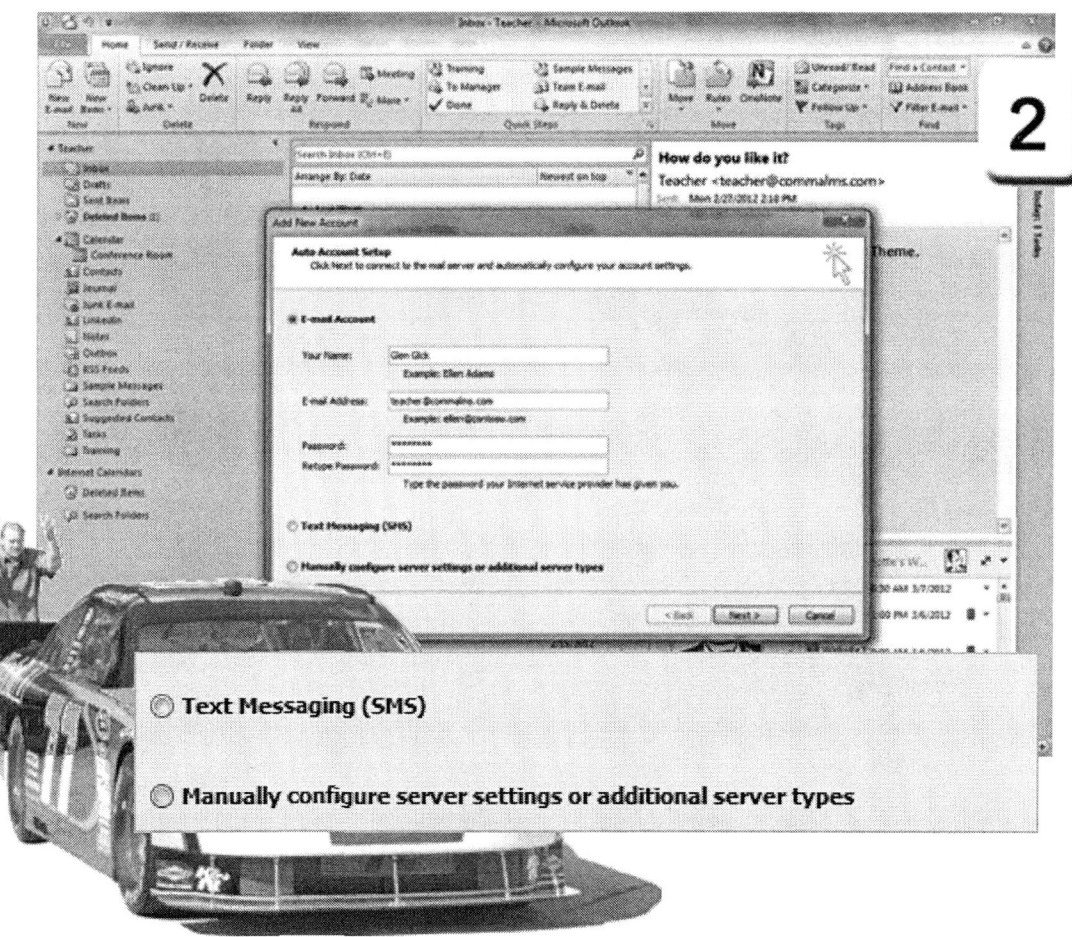

Take Two

Choose a Service

3. Try it: Choose a Service
When you choose to manually configure a new E-mail account, Microsoft Outlook walks you through the steps with a little wizard.

The first question asks how you will connect to your E-mail. The choices for Service are:

Internet E-mail (POP3 server)
Microsoft Exchange Server (a corporate server)
Text Messaging (SMS)
Other (such as a Fax server)

Choose a Service: Internet E-mail.
Click **Next**. Keep going...

File ->Info->Add Account

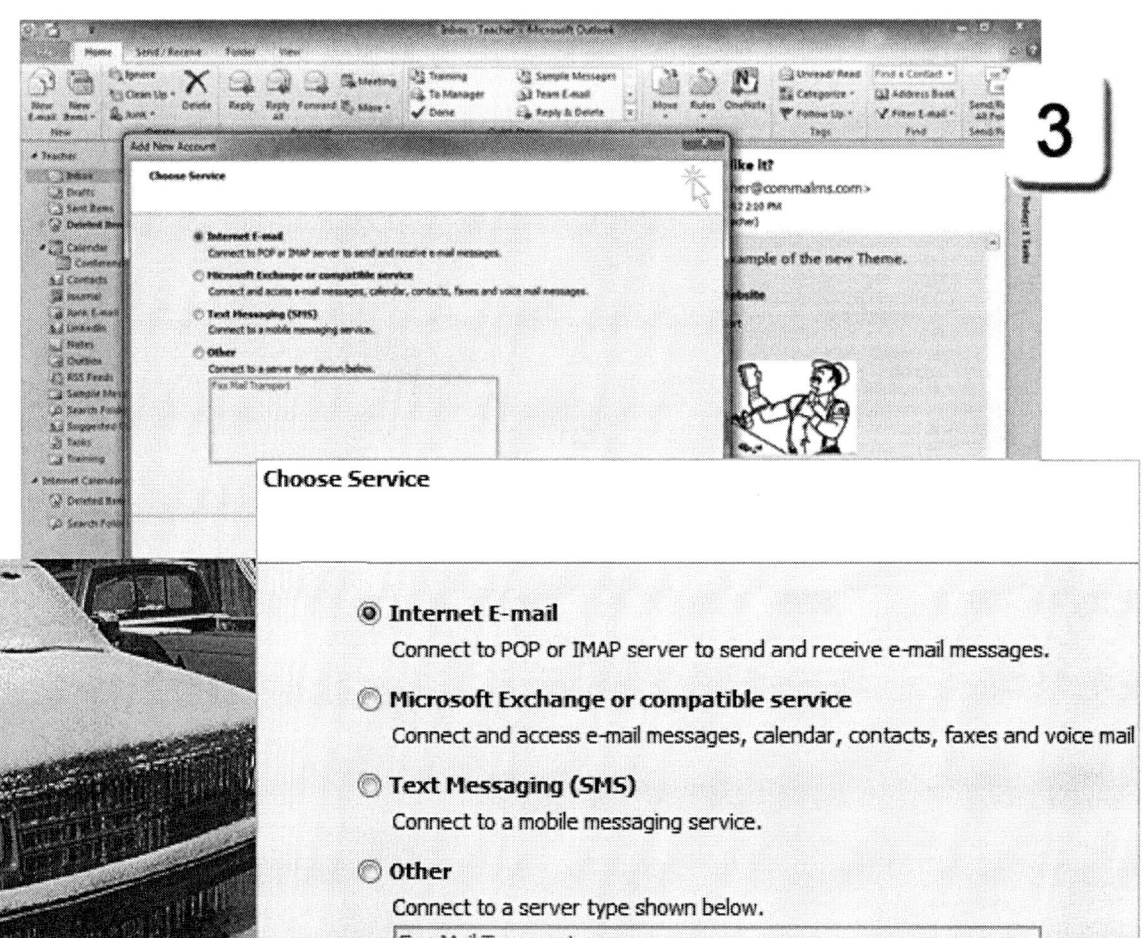

Choose Service

◉ **Internet E-mail**
   Connect to POP or IMAP server to send and receive e-mail messages.

◉ **Microsoft Exchange or compatible service**
   Connect and access e-mail messages, calendar, contacts, faxes and voice mail

◉ **Text Messaging (SMS)**
   Connect to a mobile messaging service.

◉ **Other**
   Connect to a server type shown below.
   Fax Mail Transport

Internet E-mail Settings

These settings are required to connect to your Server, identify yourself, and download your messages. The Server information comes from whomever is your E-mail provider.

4. Try it: Edit the Internet E-mail Settings

The User Information
Your Name: This is how your name is displayed at the top of each E-mail.
E-mail Address: Please enter your address.

The Server Information
Account Type: POP3
POP3 is a standard format so it is the default.

Incoming mail server and Outgoing mail servers may or may not be the same. The Incoming server may host your E-mail, while the Outgoing server may be your Internet Provider.

The Logon Information
For many E-mail Servers, your User Name may be your E-mail address. There is a check mark to remember your password so that you do not have to enter it every time Outlook sends and receives.

File ->Info->Add Account

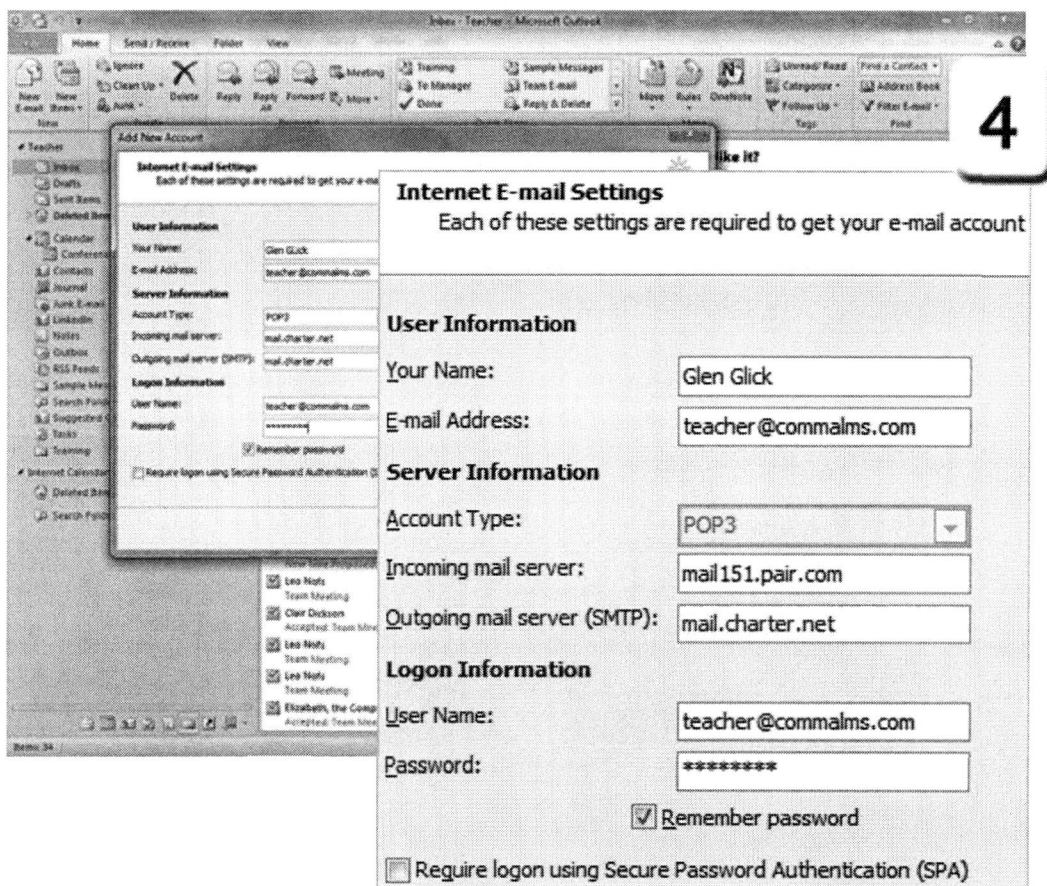

Internet E-mail Settings
Each of these settings are required to get your e-mail account

User Information

Your Name: | Glen Glick

E-mail Address: | teacher@commalms.com

Server Information

Account Type: | POP3

Incoming mail server: | mail151.pair.com

Outgoing mail server (SMTP): | mail.charter.net

Logon Information

User Name: | teacher@commalms.com

Password: | ********

☑ Remember password

☐ Require logon using Secure Password Authentication (SPA)

HOME

Take Two

Test the Account Settings
Test, test, test. Confirm that these
Internet E-mail Settings work for you.

5. Try it: Test the Account Settings
Click on **Test Account Settings.**
Keep going...

Memo to Self: If this is the first time you
have worked with Outlook, go to **Deliver
new messages to** and create a **New
Outlook Data File**.

If you are adding another E-mail
Account to Outlook, you can deliver
messages to an **Existing Outlook Data
File**.

File ->Info->Add Account

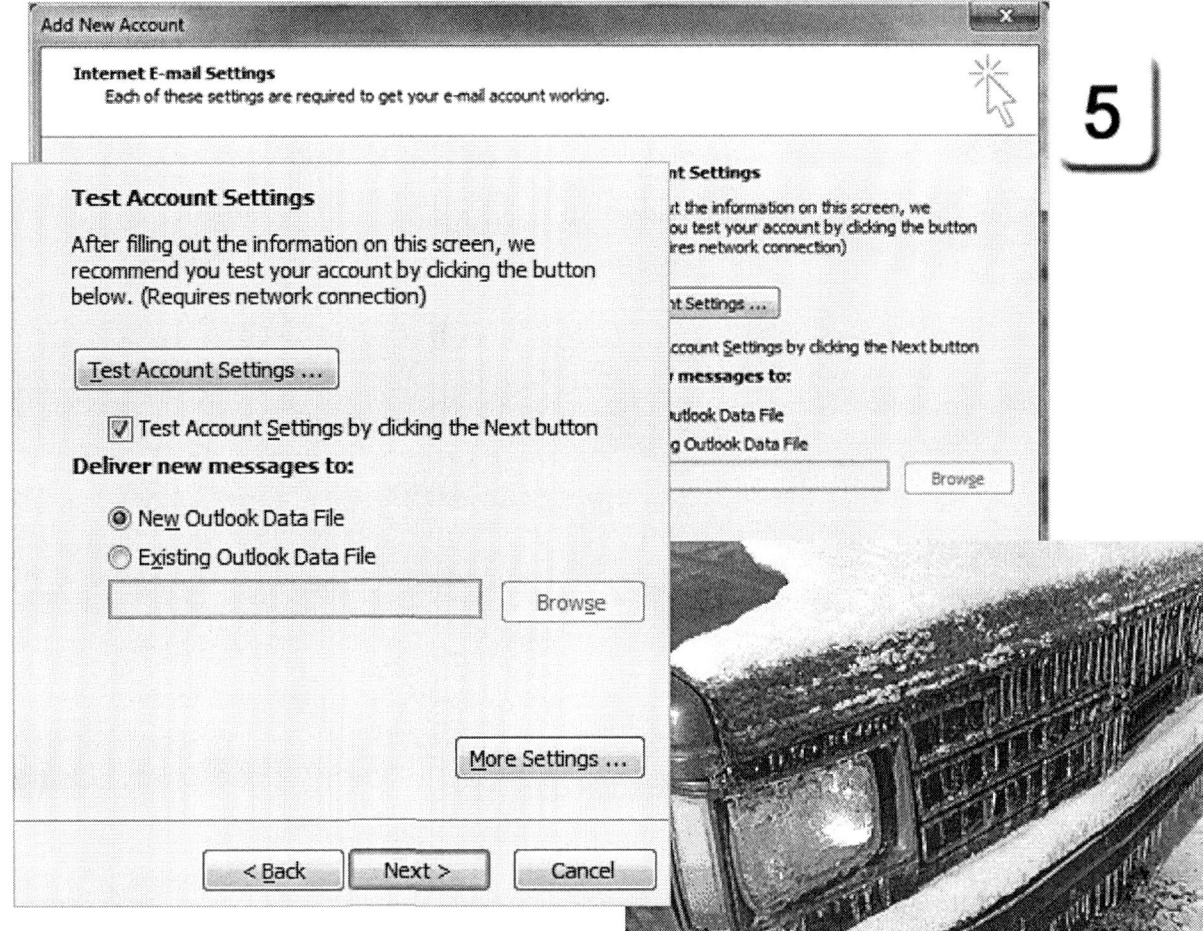

Success!

6. Try it: Confirm the Test

If you test the Account Settings Outlook logs into the incoming POP3 mail server and sends a test E-mail message.

When both Tasks are completed you will see a little confirmation notice.

Click **Close** to finish the Test and return to the Account Settings.

Keep going...

File ->Info->Add Account

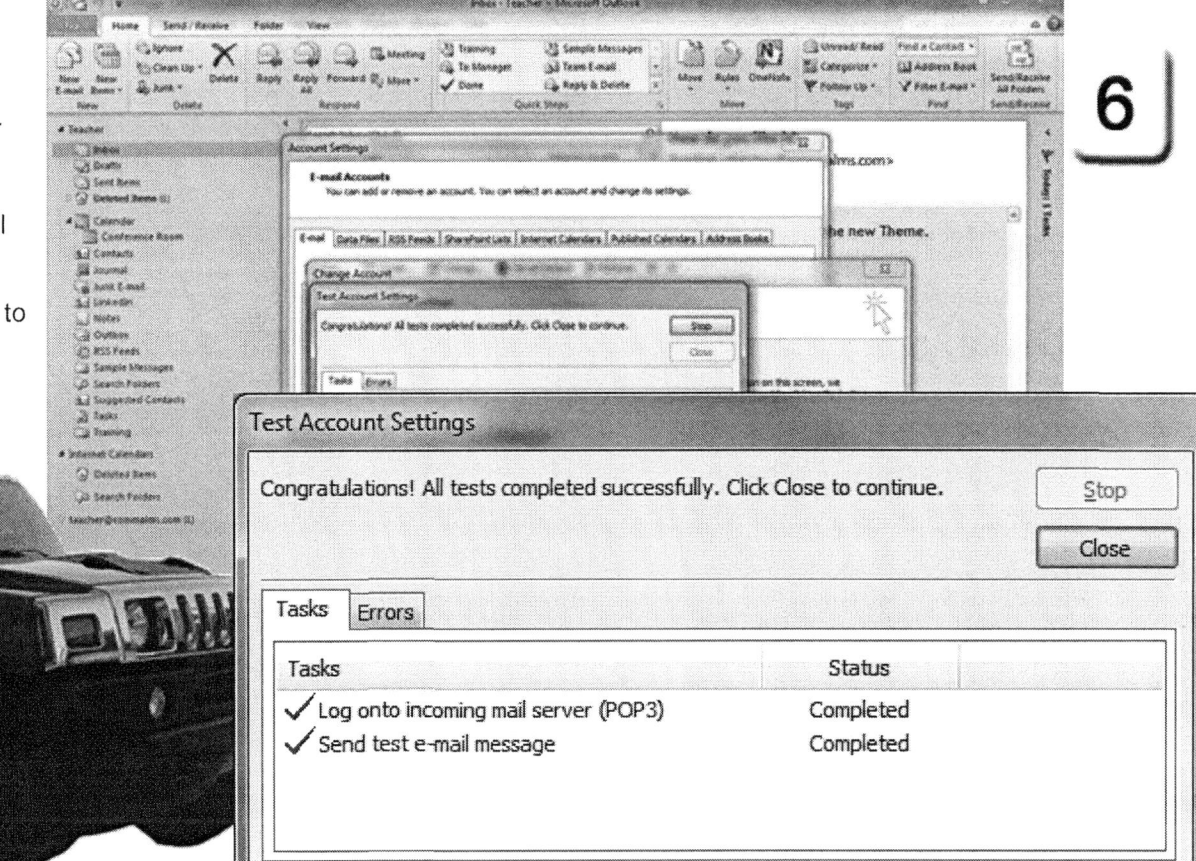

HOME

What If It Doesn't Work?

7. What If It Doesn't Work?

The test will indicate if the Task failed. Look for the clues. In the example on this page, the Log into the server failed.

So, how would you find the error and fix it?

Click **Close** to go back to the Account Settings and check:

The spelling of the User Name

The spelling of the Password

The spelling of the incoming mail server

Then click on **Test Account Settings** again to confirm that it works, now.

So far, so good...

File ->Info->Add Account

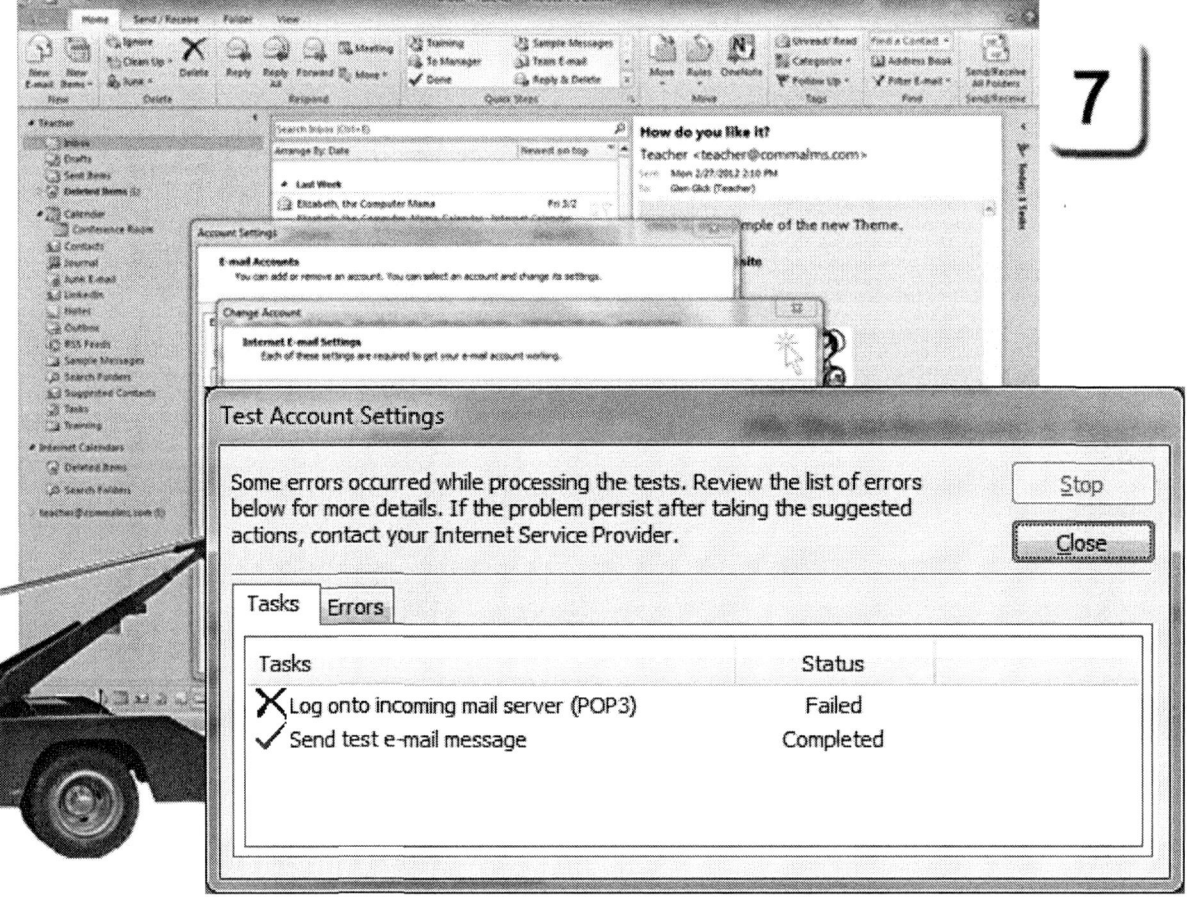

Test Account Settings

Some errors occurred while processing the tests. Review the list of errors below for more details. If the problem persist after taking the suggested actions, contact your Internet Service Provider.

Stop

Close

Tasks	Status
✕ Log onto incoming mail server (POP3)	Failed
✓ Send test e-mail message	Completed

Review the Account Settings

You can edit your E-mail Account if you wish. You can also add or remove additional E-mail Accounts. Here is the pathway back to the Account Settings.

1. Try it: Review the Account Settings
Go to **File ->Info->Account Settings**.

What Do You See? The E-mail Accounts are listed by Name and Type. The options include:
New
Repair
Change
Set as Default (if you have more that one)
Remove

Keep going...

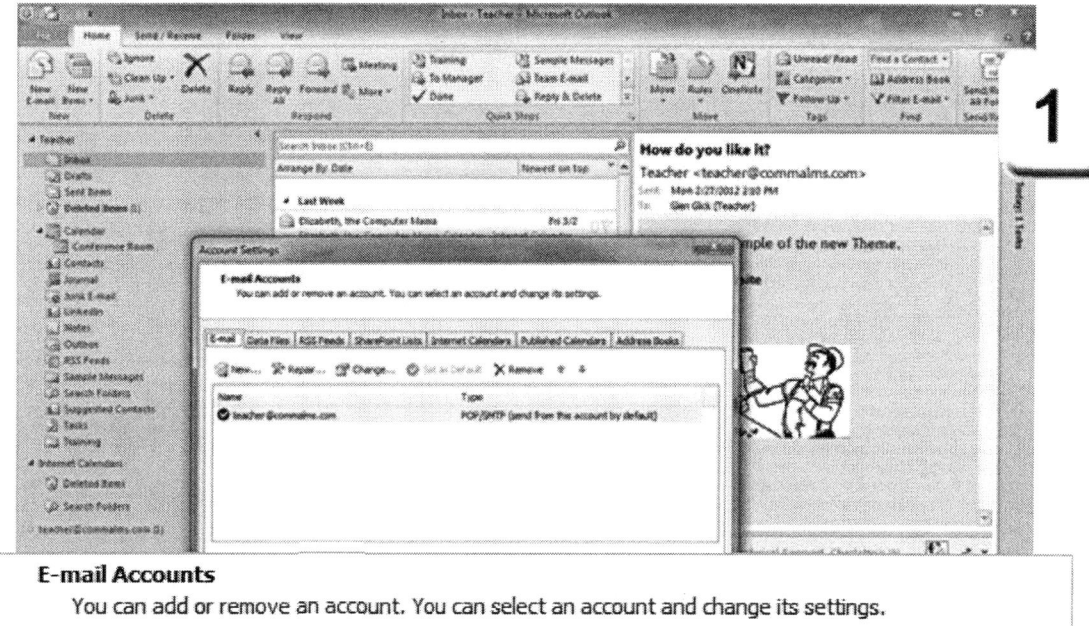

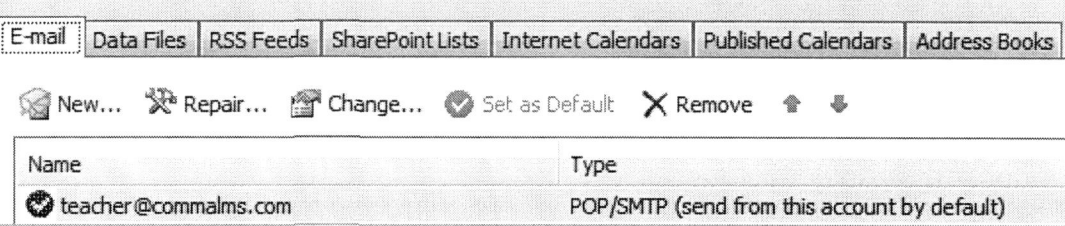

Exam 77-884: Microsoft Outlook 2010
3. Managing Email Messages
3.4. Manage automatic message content

File ->Info->Account Settings->Data Files

Find the Data File

Microsoft Outlook is a **database**.
So, where is the data file?

2. Try it: Review the Data File Options
Go to the **Data Files** tab, please.

What Do You See? The options are
similar to the ones on the E-mail tab:
Add
Settings
Set as Default (if you have more that one)
Remove
Open File Location

Keep going...

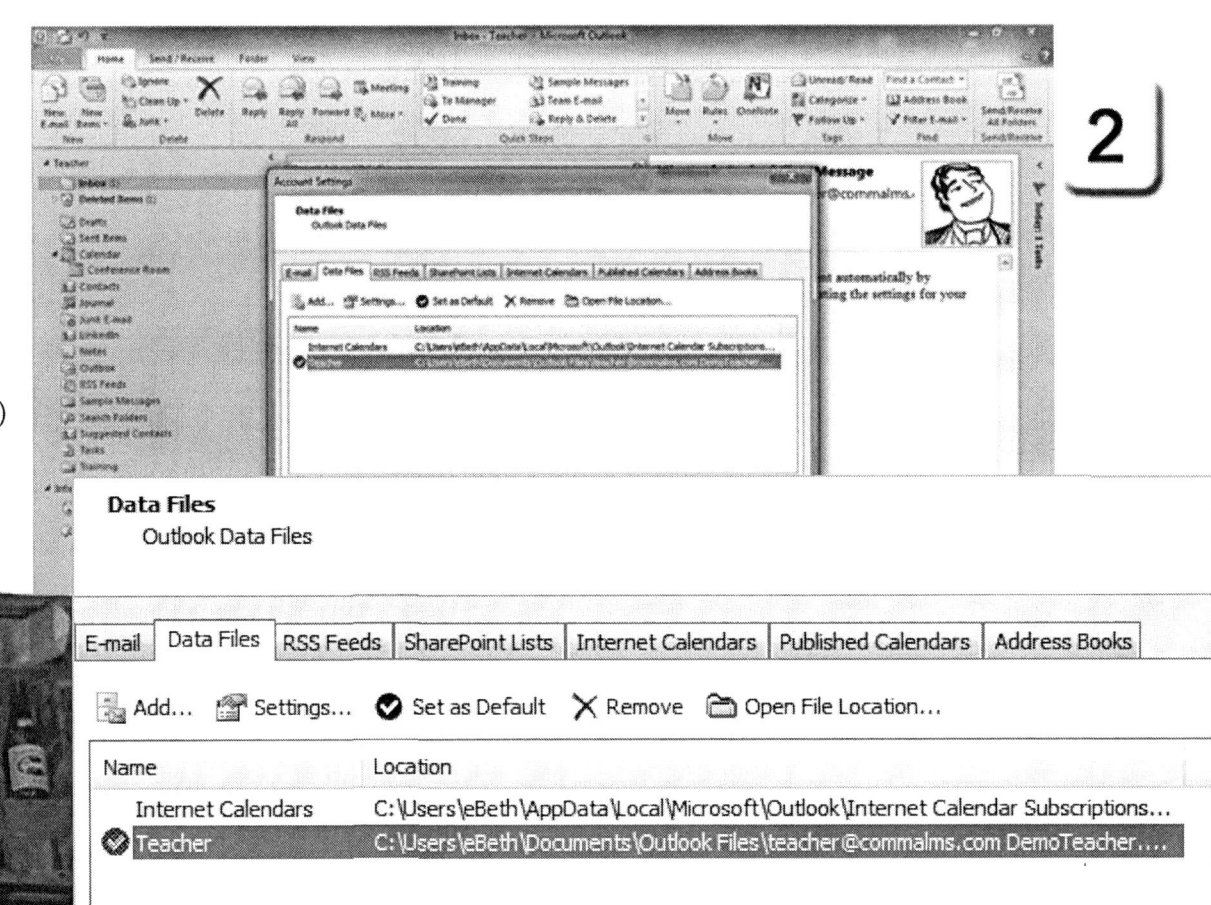

Data Files
   Outlook Data Files

| E-mail | Data Files | RSS Feeds | SharePoint Lists | Internet Calendars | Published Calendars | Address Books |

🖉 Add...   📷 Settings...   ✅ Set as Default   ✕ Remove   📁 Open File Location...

Name	Location
Internet Calendars	C:\Users\eBeth\AppData\Local\Microsoft\Outlook\Internet Calendar Subscriptions...
✅ Teacher	C:\Users\eBeth\Documents\Outlook Files\teacher@commalms.com DemoTeacher....

Open File Location
3. Try it: Find the Data File
The Account Settings are open.
The Data File tab is selected.
Click on **Open File Location.**

What Do You See? The Outlook Data file
is a *.pst file. You can confirm that it is the
real database by looking at the file
properties. The **Date modified** should be
recent (perhaps today) and the **File size**
may get rather large if you save pictures
and attachments.

Do This: Copy the Data File
This is the actual database...
and this is the file you want to backup.

Please write down the location so you can
copy and paste this file to your backup
drive or memory stick.

Close the folder with your Outlook files.
The Account Settings should be open.

Keep going...

File ->Info->Account Settings->Data Files

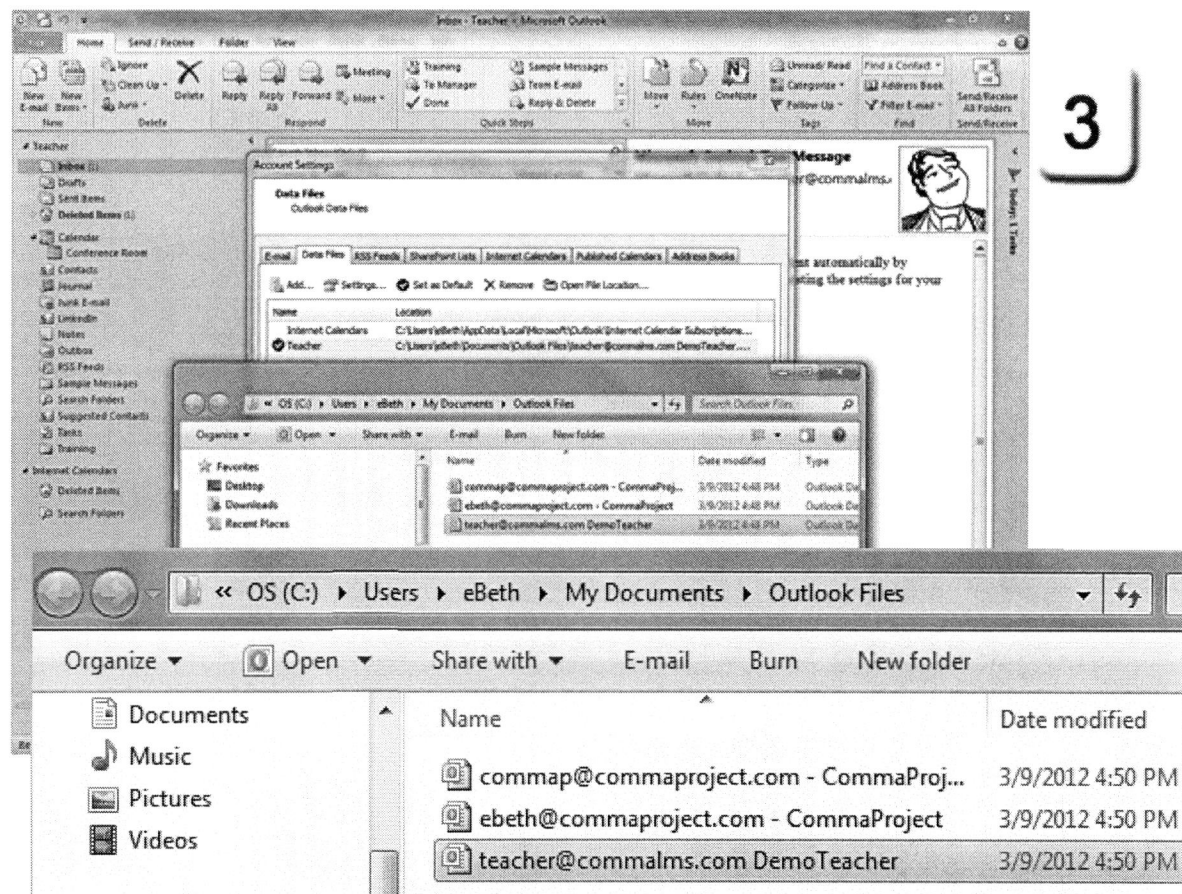

Data File Settings

All databases need to be maintained and compacted. When you **Compact** a database you reduce the size and make it run faster.

4. Try it: Compact the Data File
The Account Settings are open.
The Data File tab is selected.
Click on **Settings**.

What Do You See? You can edit the following:
Name
Filename:
Format

What Else Do You See? The options include:
Change Password
Compact Now

Click **Compact Now**.
Click **OK** to close this window when it is done.

File ->Info->Account Settings->Data Files

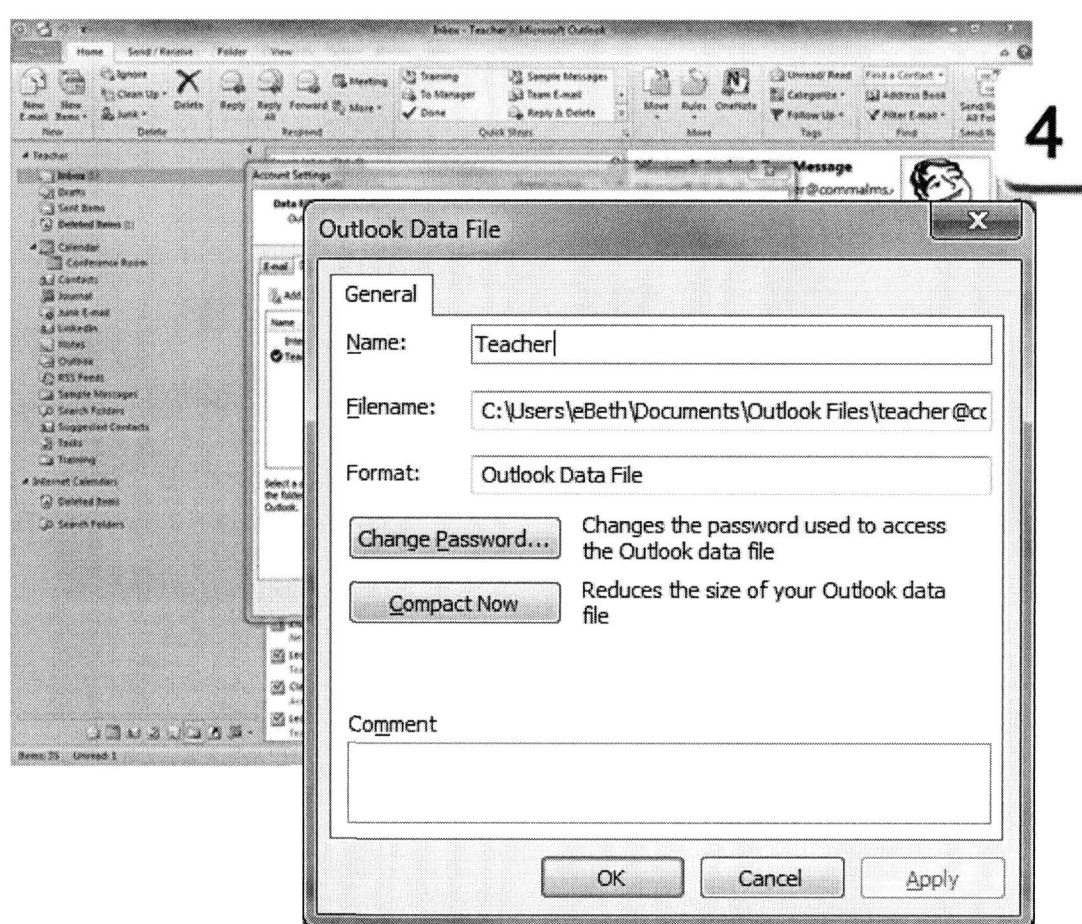

AutoArchive

There is another data management task we should discuss: archiving. You can program Microsoft Outlook to **archive** old items from the database.

The archived items can be saved to a different data file, archive.pst, or deleted .

1. Try it: Find the AutoArchive Settings
Go to **File ->Options-> Advanced.**
Click on **AutoArchive Settings**.

Keep going...

File ->Options-> Advanced->AutoArchive Settings

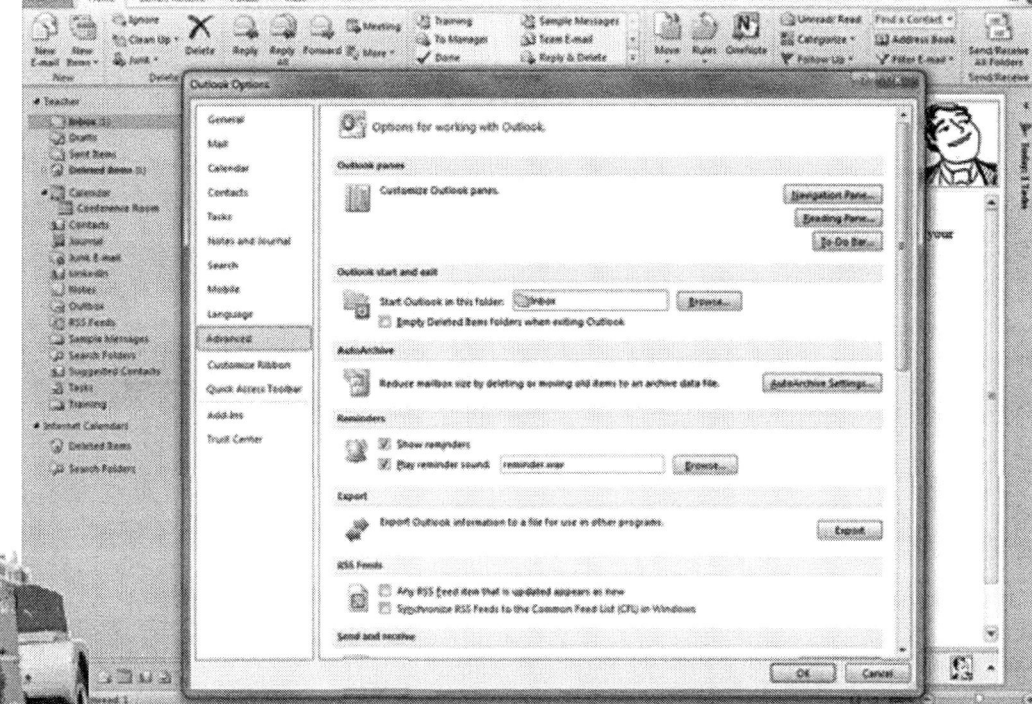

AutoArchive

Reduce mailbox size by deleting or moving old items to an archive data file.

Exam 77-884: Microsoft Outlook 2010
1. Managing the Outlook Environment
1.1. Apply and manipulate Outlook program options: Set Advanced Options

File ->Options-> Advanced-> AutoArchive Settings

Edit the AutoArchive Settings
2. Try it: Edit the AutoArchive Settings
Click on **Run AutoArchive every...**
All of the options will become available.

The AutoArchive will run every 14 days. You can change the timing if you wish. You will be prompted before the AutoArchive runs.

The AutoArchive can do the following:
Delete expired E-mails
Show the Archive Folder

You can choose how to handle the old items:
Move them to an archive.pst folder
Permanently Delete.

You do not need to run the AutoArchive now.
Uncheck **Run AutoArchive every...**

Click **Cancel** to return to the Outlook Options. Close the Options window and go to the Inbox.

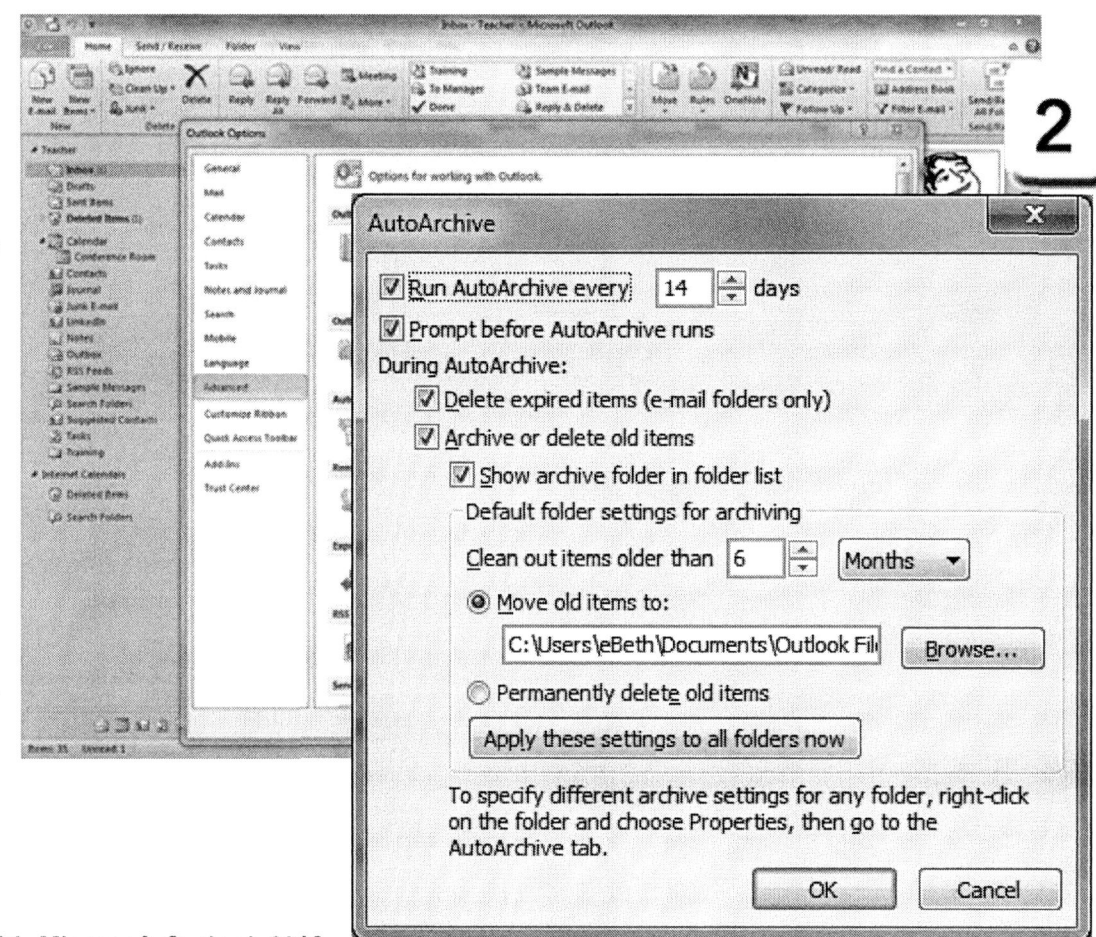

Exam 77-884: Microsoft Outlook 2010
1. Managing the Outlook Environment
1.1. Apply and manipulate Outlook program options: Set Advanced Options

The Send/Receive Group

Outlook uses Send & Receive to manage when the E-mail, Social Connections and Newsgroup postings are updated.

1. Try it: Review the Send/Receive Ribbon
Go to **Send/Receive.**

What Do You See? The **Send/Receive**
Ribbon has the following:
Send & Receive
Download
Server
Preferences

Keep going...

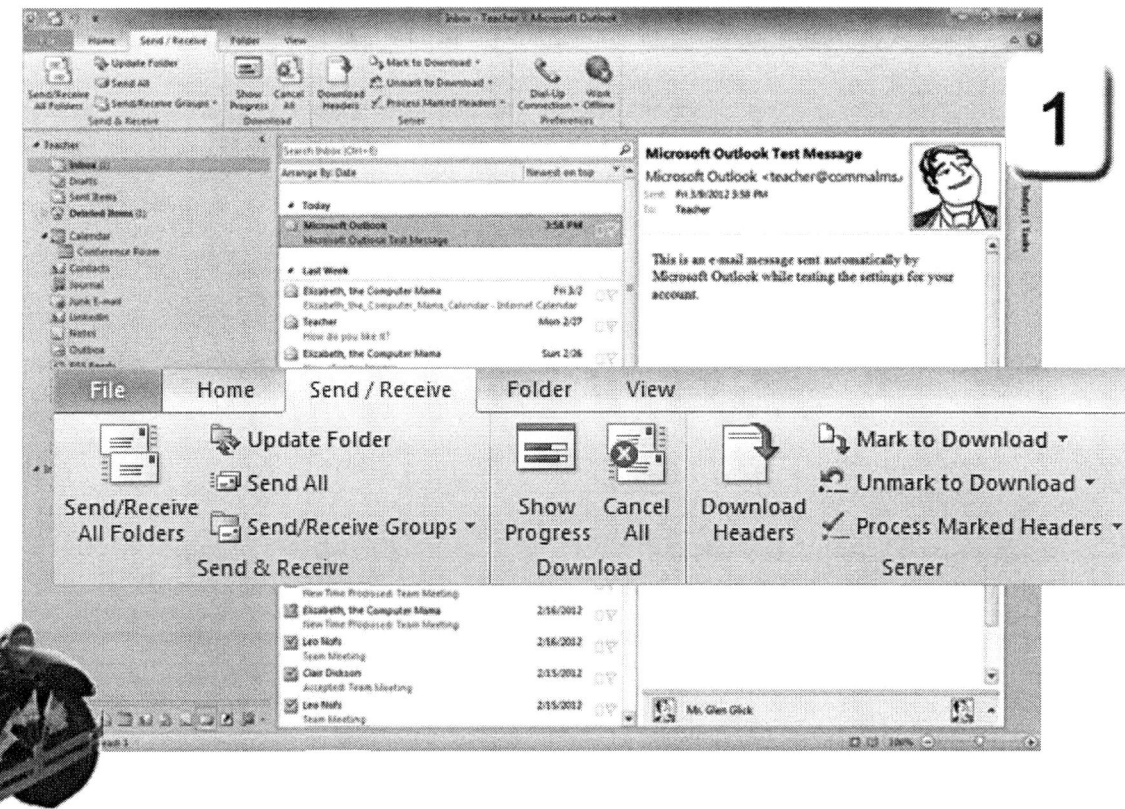

Exam 77-884: Microsoft Outlook 2010
1. Managing the Outlook Environment
1.1. Apply and manipulate Outlook program options: Set Advanced Options

Send/Receive->Send & Receive-> Send/Receive Groups->Define Send/Receive Groups

Send/Receive Groups
By default, Outlook has a Send/Receive Group named All Accounts.

2. Try it: Find the Send/Receive Groups
Go to **Send/Receive->Send & Receive.**
Click on **Send/Receive Groups.**
Select: **Define Send/Receive Groups.**

What Do You See? The default Group is scheduled to send/receive **automatically** every 30 minutes. You can change the time interval if you wish.

The options include: New, Edit, Copy, Remove and Rename.

Try This, Too: Edit the Group
Select the Group: All Accounts.
Click **Edit.**
Keep going...

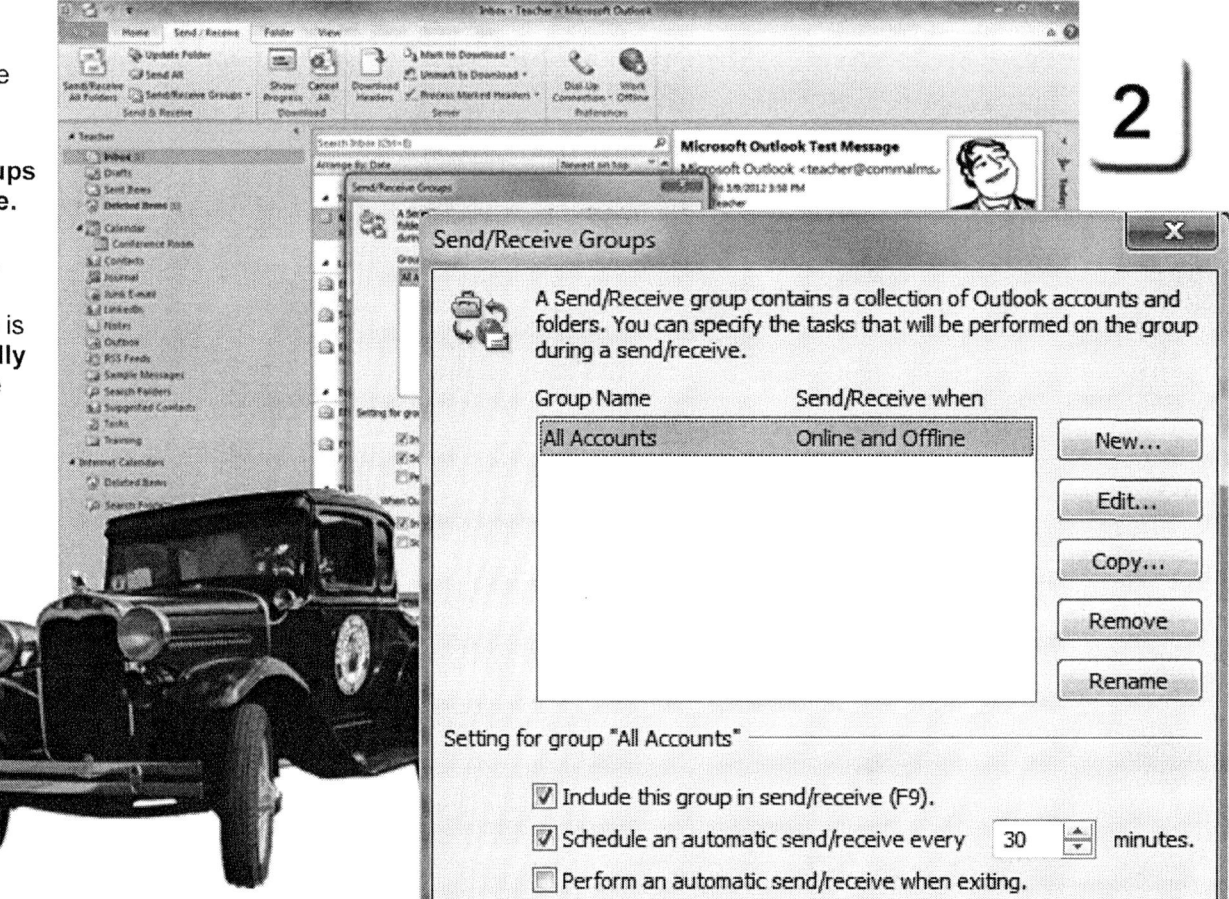

Exam 77-884: Microsoft Outlook 2010
3. Managing Email Messages
3.4. Manage automatic message content

Send/Receive->Send & Receive-> Send/Receive Groups->Define Send/Receive Groups

Edit the Accounts

3. Try it: Review the Accounts

There are two Send/Receive Settings:
Account Options and Folder Options

Account Options let you select which Account(s) are part of the Send/Receive Group. The Account can be an E-mail address or a Published Calendar.

You can also check if this Account should:
Send Mail Items
Receive Mail Items

Folder Options manage Downloads. The default location is the Inbox, although you can chose a different folder.

The Folder Options are:
Download headers only
Download complete items including attachments
Download only headers for items larger than 50 KB.

Click **OK** to close the window.

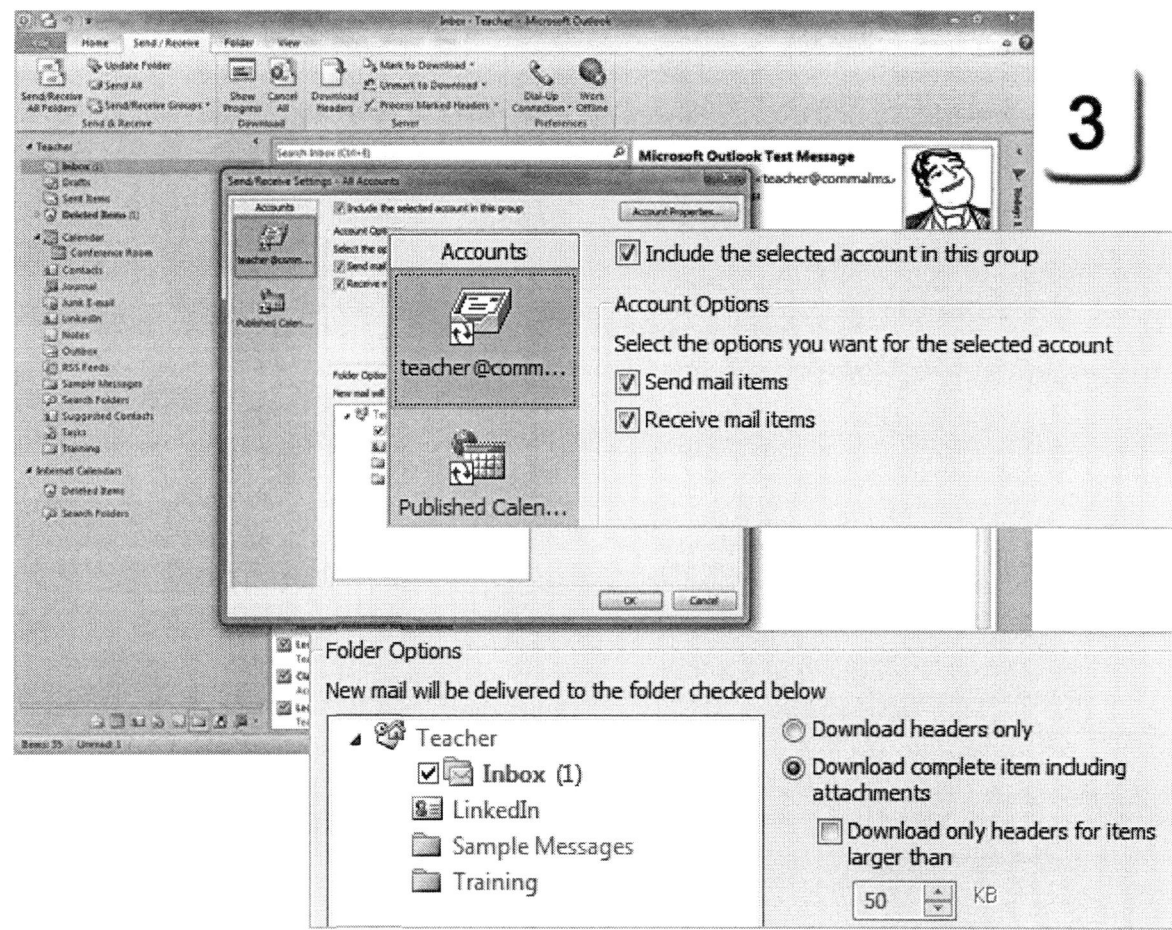

Exam 77-884: Microsoft Outlook 2010
2. Creating and Formatting Item Content
2.1. Create and send email messages: Specify the Sending Account

Summary

This concludes the Complete Guide to Microsoft Outlook 20102.This lesson demonstrated how to add an Account and troubleshoot the Account Settings.

We've looked at just about every Ribbon and option there is.

You done good.

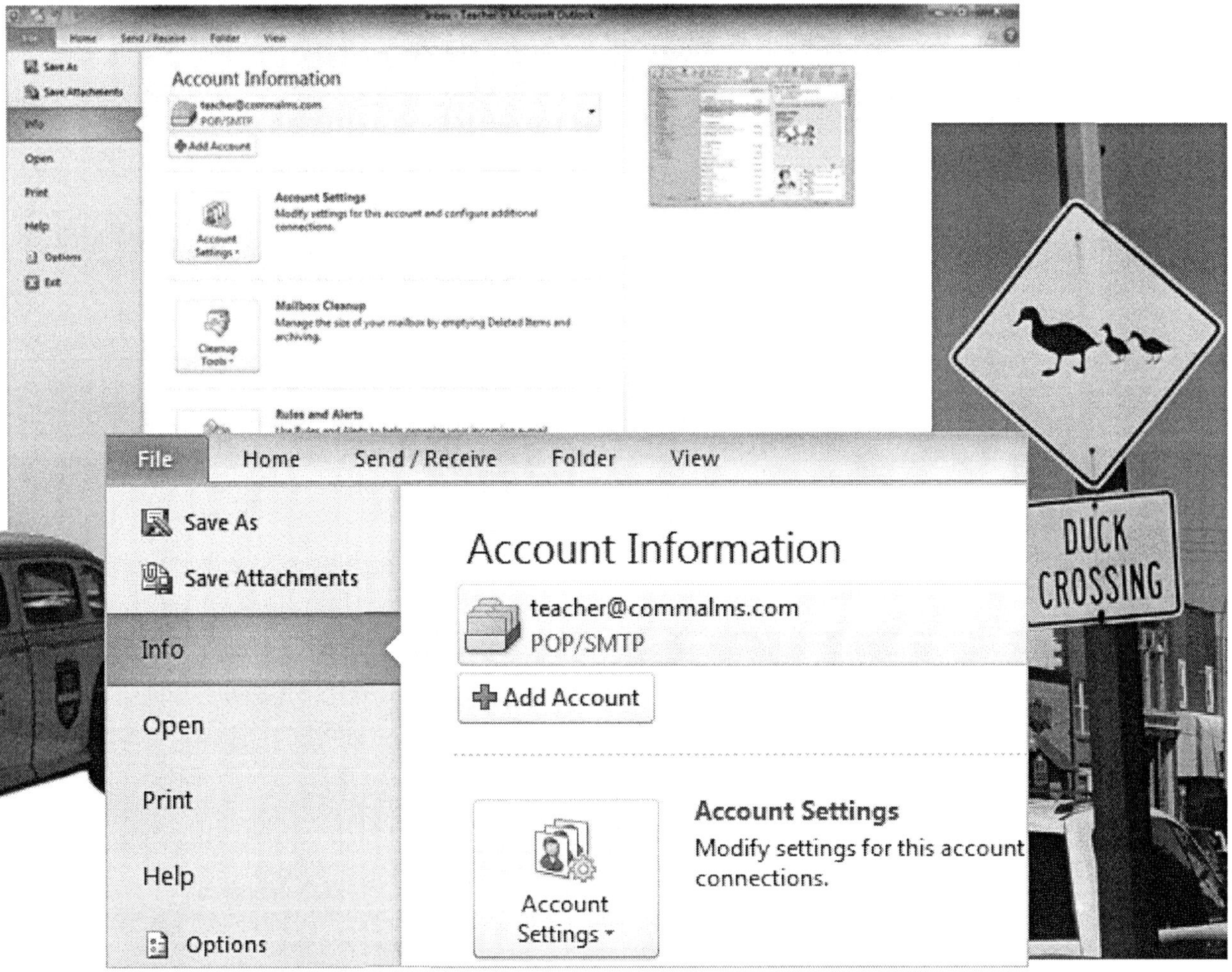

Test Yourself

1. Where are the settings to set-up an E-mail account?
a. Go to File-> Backstage
b. Access the Backstage by going Home-> Settings
c. Go to View-> Account Settings
d. Access the Backstage by going File-> Info
Tip: Complete Guide to Outlook, page 344

2. Where would a user get the E-mail account settings from?
a. Microsoft
b. Their E-mail provider
c. Their computer teacher
d. Make them up
Tip: Complete Guide to Outlook, page 347

3. Which are options for reducing the size of the Outlook data file? (Select all correct answers.)
a. Compress pictures
b. Compact
c. Archive
Tip: Complete Guide to Outlook, page 354-355

4. In the Account Settings dialogue box, which of the following are available options for E-mail accounts? (Give all correct answers.)
a. New
b. Add
c. Repair
d. Set as Default
e. Remove
f. Delete
Tip: Complete Guide to Outlook, page 351

5. By default, how often does Outlook Send/Receive?
a. 5 minutes
b. 30 minutes
c. 15 minutes
d. 60 minutes
e. Only when the Send/ Receive button is clicked
Tip: Complete Guide to Outlook, page 358

Beginning Microsoft Outlook 2010: Glossary

Microsoft Office Specialist (MOS): Exam 77-884 for Outlook 2010

Appointment: arrangement to meet another at a specific time and place; record of such arrangement in an Outlook calendar, pg. 188

Attachment: a picture, document, or other file that is sent with an E-mail, pg.36

BCC: means Blind Carbon Copy; a copy of the E-mail is sent to all recipients, but recipients cannot see the E-mail addresses in the BCC field, pg. 64

Business card: virtual card created using contact information in Outlook; can be E-mailed to others, pg. 162

CC: means Carbon Copy; a copy of the E-mail is sent to all recipients with E-mail addresses visible, pg. 64

Clean Up: Outlook command that removes redundant E-mail messages, pg. 138

Contacts: list of E-mail addresses and other contact information stored in Outlook, pg.152

Conversations (E-mail): E-mail sorting feature that groups E-mails by topic or subject line, pg. 135

Delivery Receipt: E-mail confirmation that the sent E-mail was received; does not track if the E-mail was opened, pg. 67

E-mail Blast: marketing message sent to a mailing list, pg. 90

E-mail header: includes information about who sent the E-mail, when, and the size of any attachments, pg. 102

Event: Outlook appointment that is marked as occurring all day, such as a birthday, anniversary, or other all day appointment, pg. 197

Forward (an E-mail): send an E-mail to another party, not the original recipient(s), pg. 37

HTML: Hyper Text Mark-Up Language; the coding that is use to create web pages; files saved in HTML format generally open in a web browser by default, pg. 90

Inbox: an electronic folder in Outlook and other E-mail programs that contains incoming E-mail messages, pg. 30

Journal: Outlook command for tracking, including Outlook activity as well as time working on a document or spreadsheet, pg. 245

Junk mail: unsolicited, undesired mail, including spam, that is sorted based on pre-set and user defined settings into a special folder to reduce inbox clutter, pg. 141

Navigation Pane: lets you choose the folder you wish to view, such as Inbox, Journal, Calendar, etc, pg. 32

Outbox: an electronic folder in Outlook an other E-mail programs that contains E-mail waiting to be sent, pg. 77

People Pane: shows activity related to the sender of an E-mail, pg. 173

Personal stationery: Outlook options to modify Theme, Styles, colors and fonts of an E-mail and apply to all new messages by default, pg. 262

Quick Steps: Outlook feature that applies multiple-step tasks in one click, pg. 129

Read Receipt: E-mail confirmation that requests the recipient to confirm if they have read the E-mail, pg. 68

Reading Pane: displays the contents of an E-mail message without opening a separate window, pg. 33

Recurring Appointment: Outlook appointment that repeats at regular intervals, pg. 194

Rules (E-mail) sort and move messages based on user identified criteria, pg. 121

Beginning Microsoft Outlook 2010: Glossary
Microsoft Office Specialist (MOS): Exam 77-884 for Outlook 2010

Scheduling Assistant: helper application that displays meeting attendees calendars in one place to facilitate finding a time that all attendees are available to meet, pg. 206

Signature (E-mail): text added at the bottom or end of an E-mail that usually includes the sender's name, address, website, or other content, pg. 260

SmartArt: editable graphics, charts and diagrams, pg. 93

Social Network: online communities such as Facebook, LinkedIn, and MySpace that allow users to be connected and interact, pg. 174

Styles: collection of preset formatting to be applied to text or objects, pg. 42

Task: an Outlook record of work to be completed, pg. 219

Theme: when applied, formats text, paragraph, layout and color palette, pg. 59

To-Do Bar: list of appointments and tasks that is located on the right side of the Outlook window, pg. 34

Voting buttons: buttons added to an E-mail that track the users responses to a question; can be customized, pg. 70

Beginning Microsoft Outlook 2010: Index

Microsoft Office Specialist (MOS): Exam 77-884 for Outlook 2010

Appointment: Cancel Meeting Request, 213
Appointment: Propose New Time, 205
Appointments: Forward, 209
Appointments: Options, 190
Appointments: Meeting with Sender, 211
Appointments: Set Response Options, 208
Appointments: Update a Meeting Request, 207

Attach: External Files, 88
Attach: Outlook Item (Business Card), 164

Automatic: Message Options, 297
Automatic: Signatures, 260
Automatic: Specify Default Theme, 263
Automatic: Specify Fonts, 261
Automatic: Specify Fonts, 264
Automatic: Specify Forward Options, 266
Automatic: Specify HTML Format, 258
Automatic: Specify Plain Text Format, 258
Automatic: Specify Reply Options, 266
Automatic: Specify Stationery, 262

Backstage: Advanced Options, 355
Backstage: Calendar Options, 271
Backstage: General Options, 256
Backstage: Language Options, 277
Backstage: Mail Options, 257
Backstage: Notes and Journal Options, 275
Backstage: Task Options, 274

Calendar: Arrange Calendar View, 187
Calendar: Calendar Groups, 287
Calendar: Change Calendar Color, 273
Calendar: Hide or Display Calendars, 286

Clean Up Mailbox: Cleanup Tools, 138
Clean Up Mailbox: Conversations, 140
Clean Up Mailbox: View Mailbox Size, 137

Contacts: Contact Group Membership, 167
Contacts: Contact Groups, 166
Contacts: Delete Contact Group, 170
Contacts: Forward a Contact, 164
Contacts: Forward Contact Group, 171
Contacts: Modify Business Card, 162
Contacts: Meeting to a Contact Group, 209
Contacts: Show Notes, 170
Contacts: Update Business Card, 169

Content: Reading Views, 33
Content: Reminders Window, 12
Content: Show or Hide Fields in a List , 308
Content: View People Pane, 173

E-Mail: Contact Groups, 209
E-Mail: Delivery Options, 76
E-mail: Reminder for Recipient, 66
E-Mail: Show Cc and Bcc fields, 64
E-Mail: Specify Sending Account, 359
E-Mail: Specify Sent Item Folder, 147
E-Mail: Tracking Options, 67
E-Mail: Voting Options, 70

Format Content, 41
Format Graphics, 94
Format: Paste Special, 50
Format: Theme, 59

Graphics, 61

Hyperlinks, 199

Journal: Edit Journal Entry, 246
Journal: Record Office Items, 247
Journal: Record Outlook Items, 245

Beginning Microsoft Outlook 2010: Index
Microsoft Office Specialist (MOS): Exam 77-884 for Outlook 2010

Junk Mail: Allow a Message, 144
Junk Mail: Block Sender, 141
Junk Mail: Block Sender's Domain, 143
Junk Mail: Filter Junk Mail, 145
Junk Mail: Never Block Group or List, 141
Junk Mail: Never Block Sender, 142

Message Format, 49
Message Format: HTML (web), 258
Message Format: Plain Text, 35
Message Format: Rich Text, 40

Note: View, 221
Notes: Arrange View, 244
Notes: Create, 242
Notes: Use Categories, 243

Print Appointment Details, 307
Print Attachments, 298
Print Contact Records, 310
Print Multiple Messages, 299
Print Notes, 312
Print Tasks, 308
Print: Calendars, 300

Quick Steps, 129
Quick Steps: Create Steps, 130
Quick Steps: Delete Steps, 132
Quick Steps: Duplicate, 133
Quick Steps: Edit Steps, 131
Quick Steps: Reset Back to Default, 134

Rules: Create Rules, 121
Rules: Delete Rules, 125
Rules: Modify Rules, 127

Save Attachment, 104
Save Message, 107

Search and Filter, 321

Styles: Apply Styles, 42
Styles: Create Styles, 48

Tag Items: Categories, 226
Tag Items: Mark as Read/Unread, 130
Tag Items: Sensitivity Level, 80
Tag Items: Set Flags, 65
Tag Items: View Message Properties, 80

Tasks: Accept or Decline Tasks, 234
Tasks: Assign Tasks, 233
Tasks: Create Tasks, 222
Tasks: Manage Task Details, 224
Tasks: Mark Task Complete, 229
Tasks: Move Tasks, 240
Tasks: Send Status Report, 235
Tasks: Update Assigned Tasks, 235